North America's
GREATEST
Fishing
Lodges

North America's
GREATEST
Fishing
Lodges

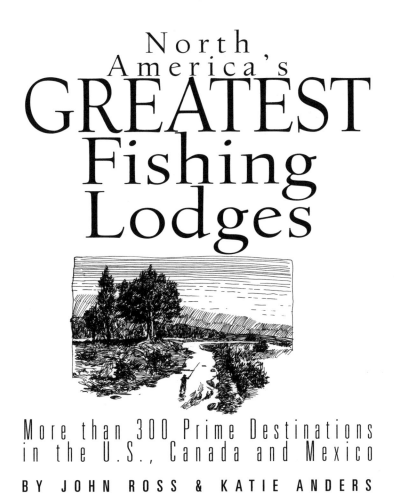

More than 300 Prime Destinations
in the U.S., Canada and Mexico

BY JOHN ROSS & KATIE ANDERS

Printed in the United States of America

Designed by Gretter Designs
Maps and Illustrations by R. L. Gretter
Cover Photograph by Val Atkinson

Library of Congress Cataloging-in-Publication Data

Ross, John, 1946-
     North America's greatest fishing lodges : more than 250 destinations in the United States, Canada & Central America / by John Ross.--
[New rev. ed.].
          p. cm. -- (Willow Creek guides)
     ISBN 1-57223-297-8
     1. Fishing lodges--North America--Guidebooks. 2. North America--Guidebooks. I. Title. II. Series.

SH462.R685 2000
799.1'0257--dc21   00-026389

Published by
WILLOW CREEK PRESS
PO Box 147
Minocqua, WI 54548

Acknowledgements

A LOT OF HATCHES have come off my stream since the first edition of this book hit the shelves in 1997. Katie and I have done more than our share of traveling, and without exception, wherever we were, we met anglers eager to share what they know (although not always their secret spots—something you never tell an angling writer).

Andrea Donner, editor at Willow Creek, repaired my grammar, a task much like picking out the strands of an impossible backlash. Gary Gretter, one of the Sports Afield expats, worked his magic in design. Thanks to them, and the photographers who contributed art, we have a book.

Coverage of Canada has expanded, thanks to the efforts of Frank LaFleche of the Canadian Embassy in Washington, and his able and efficient colleagues in the provinces. Siegfried Gagnon, of Tourism Quebec, was also especially helpful.

Our deepest appreciation goes to the many readers of this book. They used this book as a guide and told lodge owners so. And on those rare occasions when they were disappointed, they wrote to tell us. To those few, we are deeply grateful. Based on their comments, we dropped some lodges that did not measure up, and added others.

And I must tell you that without Katie, this book would not have happened. She allowed me to postpone numerous domestic responsibilities while I finished the manuscript. Her love and confidence nourish me, and her critical comments — delivered with good grace that I could never muster — have made this a much better book.

C o n t

e n t s

C o n t

e n t s

Contents

The Bulkely River, which joins the Skeena and races to the Pacific through British Columbia's Coast Range, is known for its steelhead and drift fishing trips by Frontiers Farwest.

Introduction

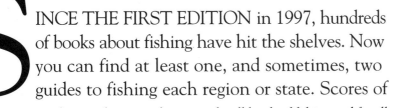

SINCE THE FIRST EDITION in 1997, hundreds of books about fishing have hit the shelves. Now you can find at least one, and sometimes, two guides to fishing each region or state. Scores of new volumes provide savvy how-to information for all kinds of fishing and for all kinds of fish. And for those nights by the fire, or reading in bed before turning out the lights, there are a plethora of little books of delightful essays that feed the souls of anglers and give them rest. This book, though, remains the only book that brings the fishing together with information about where to stay when you do it.

Over the last five years, we've logged thousands of miles visiting angling lodges. And we've interviewed hundreds of friends and colleagues who travel and fish. We've learned of some new great places, particularly in the East and South, but also in the West and Canada, where excellent angling and exquisite accommodations go hand-in-hand. You'll find more than 300 of those places in this book.

What makes a lodge great? It's a matter of taste and priorities. In the first edition, we related our story of our first trip to Alaska, when I told Katie we would be staying in "upscale" wilderness lodges. To me, "upscale" meant private bath. To Katie, former senior editor of *Country Inns*, it meant down comforters with matching duvets. For me, the fishing comes first. Are the fish healthy and in ample supply? Is the locale the kind of natural place that makes my heart sing? Is the angling technique one which I enjoy? I go for the fishing, but I always ask: "Is there more to the place — native cultures, history, literature, art — than just the fishing?" Fill these needs of mine, and I'm happy as a brown sipping caddis. If the fishing is good, I'm content to bundle up in a sleeping bag on an air mattress in virtually any shelter that's dry, reasonably warm, and relatively free of vermin. Don't get me wrong. I'm not opposed to spending a night reposed in a four-poster featherbed, knowing that the staff will deliver freshly squeezed juice and good black coffee with my wake-up call in the morning. The Ross and Anders approach to angling accommodations remains unchanged. In the main, I still think that rooms are for sleeping when it's too dark to fish. Yet, Katie believes that a room should soothe travel-worn guests, and on that perspective, you'll not get much argument from me.

We've focused on the fishing because that's what's most important to anglers. North America is known for its excellent angling, and you'll find a range of accommodations. Some are those grand Adirondack-style lodges of deep-toned log and river rock; others are charming bed-and-breakfasts of the Victorian era.

You'll find tents on platforms of plywood and two-by-fours where light comes from a gas lantern and running water is gravity fed from a spring. These are often on the banks of rivers you can only reach if you ride one of DeHavilland's Beavers or similar Clydesdale of the bush. At times, a great fishing lodge may be a motel with a restaurant where anglers hole-up when not fishing, or it could be a stuccoed villa beneath the palms on a Caribbean isle, off which bonefish swim. Here you'll find lodges that fit every pocketbook, from $6,000 a week to $150 a week. There's fun to be had at all.

As in the first edition, we have made no attempt to rate these lodges. Tastes and needs are personal, and the true measure of the greatness of a lodge is how well it suits you, not us. This is a guide to a variety of places — but by no means all — where angling and accommodations are highly regarded. We hope this book leads you to your own greatest fishing lodge.

—John Ross and Katie Anders
Upperville, Virginia, 2000

The big radial engine of a DeHavilland Beaver sits quietly
at Alaska's Crystal Creek Lodge, waiting for guests
it will fly to isolated rivers where rainbows and salmon swim.

How to
Pick A Lodge

WHAT FIRES YOUR FISHING FANCY? Bonefish ripping you down to backing on that first run, fast as greased lightning? That heart-stopping leap of a silver-sided steelhead where you learn he could go 40-inches if you ever get him to net? Little native brook trout so bright with rich color that each must have been hand-painted? A smallmouth that somersaults across the river under the sycamores? It's all out there.

Let your imagination run the way you would a big fish. You can go anywhere and do anything that time and money allow. Dream those dreams during the dreary months of winter, but act before spring. Often, slots at lodges are booked well in advance, at least six months, and often a year or more. Plan early and make plans to change plans — that is, think of alternatives — if unforeseen circumstances arise.

Information abounds on fishing lodges. With this book as your guide, you can begin your search. You'll fish the Internet for websites that teem with information about fishing here or there. At sports shows, you'll meet hundreds of operators of fishing lodges, each eager to sign you up. Magazines are filled with articles about going there and doing that, and in the back is page after page of ads. Television, too, carries dozens of fishing programs, many of which are videoed on location at a camp or lodge.

From all of this hype and hustle, you'll be tempted to believe that at fishing lodges, every other cast connects with a fish nudging a state record; it may get cloudy, but it never rains; the camp cook is on loan from your favorite restaurant; and the bed is as comfortable as yours at home. Too many angling vacations fall, somehow, short of the mark. The bray of promotional videos, quick summaries in books and magazines, glib recommendations from friends, and, unfortunately, professional advice, all heighten expectations, sometimes, unrealistically.

To keep expectations and reality in harmony, remember:

If it's pounds of fish you want, visit a fish market. Nobody can guarantee that you'll catch any fish, or lots of fish, or lots of big fish. Credible lodge operators, and the guides who work for them, do their best to put you on fish. But the variables in the equation — weather and angler skills, primarily — are too great to ensure success. Lodge operators stack the odds in your favor but, after all, it's still called "fishing."

Plan thoroughly. Determine what you, and those going with you, want to gain from a vacation (or business meeting) at an angling lodge. Write down your objectives and priorities. Do as much of your own research as you can. The more you know about a place before you get there, the better the trip will be.

Be reasonable. Most of us have become accustomed to basic amenities when we travel: a room with private bath, TV, maid service, room service, laundry service, telephone, data ports, and extensive menus. You'll find these at some lodges, but not at most. What might be considered fairly primitive for business travel in the U.S. can seem utterly palatial if it's located 300 air miles from the nearest highway. My old canvas tent by the Tree River had a wooden floor and screening that kept most, but not all, of the mosquitoes out. After a day of catching char, however, I wouldn't have cared where I slept as long as it was close to that river.

Planning the perfect trip

What's the secret to the perfect trip? Planning, planning, planning. Start a notebook. In vinyl pocket pages, you can store brochures and other information from lodges and the states or provinces where they're found. On lined paper, write the answers to the following questions, and keep notes from meetings with the pals who'll be going with you.

Who will be going? Make a list. The makeup of your group will determine the kind of fishing experience you will have. Is your spouse or significant other joining you? What about your boss or best client? Kids? Your lifelong fishing buddy? Or is it just you? Your needs are very different when you travel solo than when you travel with someone else. Most anglers who travel do so with a friend or a spouse (and in some delightful happenstance, they're the same person), or a group of three or four. Everybody who's going should take an active role in trip planning.

It's a really important idea at this point to think about the makeup of the group. Everybody has a great time when everything's going according to schedule. But what if you're rain-delayed in some godforsaken hamlet for three days, waiting for the ceiling to lift so the bush plane can fly? Is this a group of guys and gals who'll find a way to have fun no matter what? Are these folks people who you can share a tent with for a week or more? The more remote the destination, the greater the chance of unexpected events, and the more adaptable a group needs to be. Make a list of members of the group and invite them over to your house (or office if this is a business deal) to tackle the next questions. If you can't get everyone together, try conference calls.

What kind of fishing experience do you want? Variables include species, geography, terrain, climate, type of fishing, kind of accommodations and level of service. The possibilities are endless — casting for monster pike, trolling for lakers, spinning for smallmouths, fishing dries for savvy browns. Lakes, rivers, streams, saltwater flats, blue water — all hold fish. Do you prefer to wade, fish from a drift boat or troll under power? Does choppering into an isolated rapid whet your imagination? Would you prefer to fish, one-on-one, with a personal guide, or would you rather explore new water on your own? Do it your way; all the options are out there.

But think about physical limitations. An angler who has trouble walking (even though he may not admit it) isn't going to be completely happy wading among slippery boulders. On the other hand, drift and other boat trips can provide a good range of fishing possibilities for a group of anglers of varying physical condition. Consider also the travel. How much of your trip do you want to devote to sitting on airliners or in terminals? There may be a great locale a half-day's drive from where you live, or you may really get turned on by fishing as far from home as you can.

What accommodations do you expect? In a similar vein, does a room with fireplace, whirlpool bath, queen-size bed, balcony with a river view and fine dinners of veal chop, accompanied by the likes of Chateau Beaucastel du Pape '95, slake your thirst for total comfort? Or are you more comfortable in a tent camp on barren tundra with an air mattress and sleeping bag, and meals eaten around a fire? How important are private rooms (or tents), private baths, daily maid service, and collateral activities such as horseback riding, tennis or golf? Is it necessary to be near a town with restaurants and shopping?

How much time and money do you have to spend? Time is harder to find than money. You'll need one or two days to travel to most fly-in or remote lodges, and an equal amount of time to return. The final legs of most flights into lodges depart from hub airports early in the morning. That invariably means an overnight stay en route. And while flights out from lodges depart in the mornings, they frequently fail to connect with anything other than red-eye returns. It is a law of nature. And then, of course, there is the weather. The more remote the locale, the more fickle the weather and the more iffy the travel.

Many lodges offer two- or three-day packages. There's some attraction to these. If you haven't been to a lodge or region before, it may make sense to opt for a shorter stay rather than a full week. That way you can check out the lodge and the fishing, and see if they are really offering what you want. If you decide to go this route, keep in mind that much depends on the weather. Heavy rains and high water during the three days of your stay may knock fishing into a cocked hat. If you can extend the trip, the water may go down and the fishing may improve. Some anglers and booking agents line up itineraries where you'll spend two days

at each of several lodges. That's a great way to get a look at a number of different places. But don't count on much serious fishing. You'll no sooner arrive than it'll be time to go, and that famed hatch of blue-winged olives may not come-off as planned because the afternoon sun made an unscheduled appearance.

Despite the vagaries of weather, fishing is better at some times during a season than it is in others. Most fish behave in reasonably consistent annual cycles. Most anglers want to time trips to coincide with the best fishing. Those dates fill up early. On the other hand, most Americans vacation in the summer, so the weeks from mid-July through the end of August are extremely popular. Often spring (before June) and fall (after August) fishing is spectacular, and lodges may offer discounts for these periods. In the Caribbean, better fishing is frequently found not in January, but in October and November, or March and April. To secure prime weeks, you'll need to book early, sometimes as far as a year in advance.

A week at a truly first-class lodge in the Rockies can cost $6,000 or more with travel. For similar accommodations and fishing in Alaska, the tab will nudge $7,000. The same is true of the Caribbean. But for $3,000 or so, including travel, you can find many full-service lodges where the fishing is superb, meals hearty, and rooms comfortable. If you're willing to do your own cooking, a week in Canada or Maine can cost less than $1,000. Plush surroundings, daily flyouts, full-time guides and gourmet cuisine all add to the cost. But they can make your angling vacation truly the trip of a lifetime. Prepare a budget that's comfortable and try to stick to it. When you're interviewing lodge operators, be sure to ask for an estimate of the total cost, including tips, licenses, fees for processing and shipping fish, and extra costs such as bar tabs and charges for flies or lures. Some lodges tout "all inclusive prices." Ask for a written list of what is included and what is not. That way you won't be surprised.

Before you get together to plan the trip, give these questions to each member of the group. That way, when you meet, you'll all have had a chance to think about the answers. The nominal leader of the group (and there's always one), should create an agenda for the meeting — just to make sure that everything gets covered. Near the close of the meeting, write up a list of priorities for your trip. Get each member a copy of the list, and a week later, check with each to see if there are any second thoughts? There should be. What's changed? Revise the priorities and move to do the next step: gather information.

Once you've answered the previous questions, you're ready to move to the next steps.

Gather information. Sources of information about lodges are legion. Magazines, books, the world wide web (a search for "fishing lodges" will keep you online for a week), agents, booths at fishing shows, governmental game and fish agencies, chambers of commerce, and tackleshops are all ready sources. So, too, are your friends and acquaintances who may have fished the area you plan to visit. Ask around.

❖ *About booking agents*

There are two schools of thought about whether to book a trip through an agent. On the plus side: Agents know many more lodges than most of us. They have inspected the lodges and understand the clientele that the lodge serves. And they know about the fishing. In most cases, you'll pay the same price for a week at a lodge whether you book through an agent or do it yourself. (If you book through an agent, the lodge pays the agent a fee; it costs you the same either way.)

On the down side, some agents have exclusive relationships with one or more lodges. There's a quid pro quo in this. In exchange for being the sole representative of a lodge in, say, the U. S., the agent pledges to provide the lodge with so many guests per year. If an agent is the sole representative for a lodge, you can bet that his priority is filling that lodge with guests. Sure, he wants guests to be satisfied. That keeps him and the lodge in repeat business. But rest assured, he's going to try and sell you on that lodge, even though it may not be right for you.

Agents who represent many lodges have a different perspective. Their bread and butter comes from establishing relationships with clients who may not want to go to the same lodge year after year. In the main, their job is to help you find the fishing vacation of your dreams — and then book it. If things go awry on your trip, as they sometimes to do, and if you booked it through an agent, you'll have greater opportunity for redress than you will if you've booked it directly. Agents are generally current on international travel and airline regulations, and will provide you with a wealth of practical information that will facilitate your fishing vacation.

Watch out, too, for "freelance" agents — guys who try to pass themselves off as "representatives" for this agent or that one in a geographic area. Most of these chaps earn a percentage for each trip they sell, and they may get a "free" trip if they can convince six or ten of their nearest and dearest buddies to book a trip with them to Tora Tora. Remember the movie *The Tin Men* with Danny DeVito? Freelance agents are the tin men of the fishing travel business. If you're considering an agent, call the home office of one of the reputable firms listed below. Ask them if there's an agent in your area who can help you, and heed their advice.

Your local travel agent can be helpful, though you'll save money in most cases by booking your own flights. If you know where you want to go, and when, any travel agent can make necessary arrangements. However, few travel agents know anything about fishing. The wise ones defer to professional agencies that deal daily with fishing travel.

You might want to think of a booking agent as a kind of travel consultant. Some, such as Off the Beaten Path, specialize in designing custom angling (and other) vacations. You'll pay an additional fee — about $200 for a single destination trip, or $70 per hour for one that's more complex — but in return you receive a personal itinerary, background on each destination, and savings on airfares, car rentals and en-route lodging. Though they operate only in the northern Rockies, Off the Beaten Path is a master at this, and well worth consideration if your plans take you in that direction.

Even if you're working with an agent, you should talk directly with prospective lodges as well. And woe unto the agent who tries to prevent you from doing it. Remember, it's your trip and your money, and you must satisfy yourself that this trip is going to meet your expectations. At the same time, if you're working with an agent who has recommended a lodge, it's frankly unethical to book the lodge on your own.

Selecting an agent is similar to picking a lodge. We've included a list of some of the best. Call them, ask about their services, discuss their relationships with the lodges they represent, and obtain and use a list of references, particularly people who live near you.

❖ Approvals, endorsements and ratings

We Americans like to rate things . . . our colleges, cities, computers, cake mixes, everything. While no uniform rating system exists for angling lodges, you can get some hints in terms of quality by looking at ratings that do exist. Some tourism agencies in the provinces of Canada rate angling lodges in terms of service, accommodations and food. Stars are awarded. Call the tourism office in the province you're headed to and ask to see a list of the rankings. The North American Fishing Club (612/939-9449) "approves" fishing lodges based on member reports. Also based on subscriber reports, Don Causey's (305/670-1376) newsletter, *The Angling Report*, provides details on lodges and regions, but he does not approve or endorse lodges. Orvis (800/778-4778) endorses a number of angling lodges that meet fairly strict standards and pay a promotional fee. How valuable are the ratings? They add a bit of useful information, but should not be the determining factor in your choice of a lodge.

❖ References, references, references

So when you ask the lodge for a list of references, do you think they're going to give you anything other than a list of their most satisfied customers? Along with the happy campers, ask for two or three folks who may not have been fully satisfied. If the lodge staffer tells you that everyone who fishes there was just delighted, thank the person you're talking to and move on. Lots of folks get lists of references; few check them out thoroughly. Make a list of questions and ask them of each person you call.

BOOKING AGENTS

ANGLING DESTINATIONS
330 N. Main Street
Sheridan, WY 82801
800/211-8530
www.anglingdestinations.com

◆

CABELA'S OUTDOOR ADVENTURES
812 13th Avenue
Sidney, NE 69160
800/346-8747
www.cabelas.com

◆

FISHABOUT
PO Box 1679
Los Gatos, CA 95031
800/409-2000
www.fishabout.com

◆

FRONTIERS INTERNATIONAL
305 Logan Road
PO Box 959
Wexford, PA 15090-0959
800/245-1950
www.frontierstrvl.com

◆

GAGE OUTDOOR EXPEDITIONS
Northstar East Building
10000 Hwy 55
Plymouth, MN 55441
800/888-1601
www.gageoutdoor.com

◆

KAUFMANN'S STREAMBORN
PO Box 23032
Portland, OR 97281-3032
800/442-4359
www.kman.com

◆

BOB MARRIOTT'S FLYFISHING STORE
2700 W. Orangethorpe Avenue
Fullerton, CA 92833
800/535-6633
www.bobmarriotts.com

◆

JIM MCCARTHY ADVENTURES
4906 Creek Drive
Harrisburg, PA 17112
717/652-4374

◆

PAUL MERZIG'S ADVENTURE
SAFARIS LTD.
38 W. 581 Sunset Drive
St. Charles, IL 60175
630/584-6836

◆

OFF THE BEATEN PATH
27 E. Main Street
Bozeman, MT 59715
800/445-2995
www.offbeatenpath.com

◆

OUTDOOR WORLD TRAVEL
1955 S. Campbell Rd.
Springfield, MO 65807
800/422-1321; Fax 417/888-4474

◆

PAN ANGLING TRAVEL SERVICES
5348 W. Vermont
Indianapolis, IN 46224
800/533-4353
www.panangling.com

◆

SHOOTING AND ANGLING
DESTINATIONS
3220 Audley
Houston, TX 77098
800/292-2213
www.detailco.com

◆

THE FLY SHOP
4140 Churn Creek Road
Redding, CA 96002
800/669-3474
www.theflyshop.com

◆

TIGHTLINE DESTINATIONS
248 Spring Street
Hope Valley, RI 02832
800/933-4742
www.tightlinedestinations.com

❖ *Making the final choice*

After you've identified several lodges that appear to meet your criteria, how do you make a final choice? Here's one way that works well. Organize your information, one lodge to a file folder. Then assemble your group and get out your list of priorities, along with the answers to the questions we discussed at the beginning of this chapter. Pass the files around and have each member grade (A, B, C, etc.) each lodge. Then, after everybody's had a chance to review each lodge, sit back and discuss why you graded them as you did. Also, agree on the dates you want to travel. By the end of the evening, you'll have settled on one you like best and a couple of alternatives. Elect one person to contact the agent or lodge, and arrange the booking.

❖ *After you return*

One night, after you return and you've gotten your pictures back, gather everyone together and debrief. Take a look at your priorities when you started preparing for the trip. What was really great? What didn't work? How could the trip have been better? Make notes. Before you know it, you'll be planning for next year.

Turneffe Island Lodge, off the coast of Belize, is a hot spot for anglers intent on honing bonefishing skills.

Tips for Successful Travel

TRY AS I MIGHT, I still take too much gear when I travel. I get away with it because most anglers don't travel with all the camera gear I must lug along. Still, I'm learning to travel light and right. Why? When it comes to baggage for traveling anglers, the times are changing. Recently, the Federal Aviation Agency (FAA) forced domestic and international carriers that operate within the U.S. to define policies for checked and carry-on baggage. Most complied, and in the process tightened procedures that used to make traveling a bit more convenient for us.

Gone, pretty much, are the days when you could bring four-foot fly rod tubes aboard and stow them in the overhead baggage bin. With grace and charm, you may be able to talk a flight attendant into standing these ungainly cases upright in the first-class coat closet (it's easier to do this if you're traveling first class). But don't count on it. Most counter clerks will make you check your rods with your other baggage. True, most of the time everything arrives with you and in fine shape — but we've all heard those horror stories of when it hasn't.

Unfortunately, absolutely no consistency exists among airlines' luggage rules. Best advice: have the airline fax you its baggage policies on its own letterhead well before your flight. If you get hassled by a ticket agent, show 'em their company's policy. This advice comes from Don Causey, publisher of *The Angling Report*. A veteran of the sporting travel wars, Don maintains that ticket agents don't always know their company's rules, and yet, what they say, goes. In your rush to catch your flight, you won't have time to argue with their edict of the moment. But if you show the counter clerk the information from his or her own airline, you may be able to save the day. Don is compiling an inventory of each airline's regulations. For more information, call him at 305/670-1376.

When packing for a trip that involves a flight, check baggage weight and size limitations of the smallest air carrier on your itinerary. While domestic airlines may allow you to check two 70-pound bags and carry-on a pair of 35-pound satchels, Super Cub Air — your bush plane company — may hold your baggage allowance down to 25 pounds per passenger! If you've booked with a lodge or through an agent, he or she should give you the limits — in writing. If not, you'll have to check them out yourself.

THE ESSENTIALS

When packing for a fishing vacation, ask yourself: "What are the most important items I must, and I mean MUST, have with me at all times?" The answer is medication and money. They come first.

❖ Medications and prescription glasses

Lay in two emergency supplies of prescription medications and over-the-counter remedies that work for you. Call your doctor, tell him or her where you're going and why. Ask for permission to fill duplicate prescriptions. If one pain pill works better for you than another, have your doctor give you a prescription for that as well. You may not need it. But if you break an ankle up in the Ungava where you're a day away from any medical help, you'll need the pain medicine. Carry one supply with you, pack the other in your luggage. Be sure to have current copies of prescriptions. Make two copies of your medical history and include at the very top of the page any known allergies you have to prescription medicines. The hospital in San Jose Costa Rica might not know you're highly allergic to penicillin; and there's no way for them to find out quickly, unless it's in a record you're carrying with you. In addition to prescription, polarized sunglasses, take a spare pair of clear glasses and extra sets of contact lenses if you use them. My spare glasses travel in my carry-on.

❖ Money

Traveler's checks, ATM cards and credit cards have reduced the need for cold cash on the road. But not entirely. It's a good rule of thumb to have the equivalent of $200 (U.S.) in local currency and another $300 to $500 in traveler's checks for each week you'll be on the road. In addition, take two or three personal checks. And take only two or three credit cards (American Express, MasterCard or Visa). Many lodges won't take plastic, and those that do rely more on Visa or MasterCard than American Express. Many will accept personal or business checks in payment. Keep $200 in emergency cash and traveler's checks, and a list of all your credit cards (card numbers and phone numbers if you have to cancel them) in a place separate from where you carry your main funds. That way, you won't be out of luck if someone steals your wallet. Pay attention to laws governing the amount of currency you may bring into a country. I used to change money at the airport when I entered a country. Now I forego the money changers, if I can, and use my ATM card. Generally speaking, my bank will get a better rate of exchange that I get in person. Same goes for paying with plastic when you can — unless the vendor adds a percentage (anywhere from three to seven percent) to the price of goods or services bought with a credit card. In those cases, either shop elsewhere, or pay the tab from your supply of local currency.

❖ Identification

If you're traveling out of the U.S., get a passport. Waiting time can be up to five weeks. If you plan to travel sooner than that, you can expedite the process by paying an additional fee and sending along other evidence, such as a copy of your plane ticket, with the application. To initiate the passport process, contact your county courthouse or the largest post office in your county. You may also contact the National Passport Information Center at 900/225-5674. Operated by the U.S. Department of State, the center will give you the name of the closest office where you can apply for a passport and provide information on the status of a passport application. Automated service is available for 35 cents per minute, and live operators, $1.05 per minute.

You don't really need a passport to travel to the Bahamas, Canada or Mexico. A photo ID such as a driver's license and your birth certificate will suffice. Be aware that regulations do vary from country to country. Belize, for instance, wants to see your round-trip plane ticket and proof of sufficient financial resources equal to $50 for each day you plan to be in the country. Half of that must be in cash. The lodge that you are booking into or your travel agent should be able to tell you precisely what's required.

❖ Airline tickets

A flight at the best price is like playing the lottery. Travel agents can sometimes get you a good deal, but increasingly, you can do better on your own. It depends, mainly, on whether you're willing to spend the time to do it. Advance-purchase tickets can save you a bundle, but not if the no-refund, no-alteration policy is so strict as to limit flexibility in case of missed connections due to weather, primarily on the return leg of your trip. Beware of connections that are too tight, particularly at international airports. Though baggage may be checked through, you'll have to take it through customs yourself. Even when entering Canada, two hours between planes isn't too much. Booking agents have shepherded thousands of clients through the intricacies of international travel. If you're new to the traveling angler game, they can be a big help.

Tickets do get lost or stolen. Make copies of them before leaving home; keep one with your stash of emergency cash, the other folded in your wallet. If your ticket vanishes mysteriously, the copy will help you cancel the ticket and may help secure a replacement. And don't carry your ticket sticking out of a travel bag. Sure, it's convenient, but it's also easily swiped.

❖ Insurance

Lodges book far in advance and require payment of up to 50 percent to hold a reservation. In some cases, the balance is due in advance, while others may want it on arrival or just prior to departure. In any event, you will have contracted for services; should you not be able to make the trip, you'll be liable for the full cost. If you cancel more than 60 days in advance, there's a fairly good chance that the lodge or your booking agent will be able to fill the space. (Each lodge has its own refund policies. Check them out thoroughly.) Travel insurance is something to consider, too. Should illness, accident or a death in the family prohibit you from making the trip, the insurance will pay up to the full amount of your obligations. Available coverage varies extensively among insurance companies, as do premiums. Expect to pay about five percent of the total coverage, or roughly $350 for a policy worth $6,500.

If you're traveling to another country, you'll also want to check with your medical insurance carrier to determine coverages. If you're stricken with an acute medical problem while in the bush, will your insurance pay for your evacuation to the closest hospital? It's also a good idea to determine the applicability of automobile insurance and loss/theft provisions of your homeowner's or business insurance in foreign countries.

THE BASICS

If you've taken care of the essentials, you'll survive your trip and most likely won't go broke. But what about luggage, clothing and traveling tackle?

❖ Baggage

Add up all your gear: waders, wading boots, rain jacket, sweaters, rods, reels, etc., etc. None of it's light and most of it's bulky. While baggage weight limits in the U.S. are not too stringently enforced, you can bet that when you fly internationally, you'll be charged for excess weight or size. In some cases, you'll be charged per pound. In others, you'll be charged a flat fee that will vary depending on your destination and length of the flight. Check baggage limits with each carrier that you plan to fly with. If you're headed for a fly-in lodge, the lodge operator can provide weight and size restrictions.

Anglers (and other tourists) are obvious prey for baggage thieves. Use tough, nondescript bags when you plan to check your luggage. Carefully cut-off expensive labels. (You'll still know your bag is a Mulholland, but thieves won't.) Attach a tag with your name, address and phone number on each bag; put one inside as well. Even if you're in love with a long two-piece rod, consider getting shorter travel or packrods. (While three- and four-piece travel rods used to be extremely stiff because of the extra joints, today's graphite rods with plug-style ferrules fish almost as well as their two-piece siblings.) You can hide packrods in your duffel bag, or stow them in carry-on luggage.

Checked baggage does get lost. Because of this, I pack things that I absolutely cannot do without in my carry-on luggage: medications, extra glasses, Gore-Tex hat (wear the jacket), mini-shaving kit, camera, a couple paperbacks, waders, ultralight wading shoes, fingerless gloves, flashlight, extra batteries for camera and light, two reels with floating and sinking lines, and a Ziploc bag with a pair of heavy socks and lightweight polypropylene long underwear. The shortest traveling rod I own, a Thomas & Thomas Vagabond, straps on top, and whatever tackle (nippers, forceps, flies, leaders, etc.) I need, I cram in the side pockets. All this, stuffed into an old large waterproof Fisherman's Kit Bag from Orvis, weighs about 25 pounds and slings comfortably over my shoulder. It fits most overhead bins and can be stowed under most seats.

Wherever I fish, it rains. Instead of a waterproof fishing jacket, I prefer to use a lightweight Gore-Tex parka shell. It's comfortable and attractive enough to wear as a jacket. Rather than packing it, I tend to wear it when I travel. The same is true with my walking boots and, in winter, a heavy Polar fleece or woolen sweater. (Leave cotton sweaters at home. They're bulky, heavy, soak up moisture like sponges, and provide no comfort when even the least bit damp.)

Finally, consider wearing a sport pouch to carry spare medication, emergency money, identification, glasses, small flashlight and a Swiss army knife with scissors, screwdriver, corkscrew and file. Unobtrusive and secure, you'll forget you're even wearing the pouch, but you'll be glad you have it in an emergency.

❖ Clothing

Each lodge will provide you with a list of things to bring. If you have questions, call and talk with the operator. Fashionable clothing at most lodges fits into the old and comfortable category. At some of the more posh places in the states and islands, you may want a jacket for dinner. Here, too, the lodge management can provide guidance. Otherwise, keep it simple. Remember that many lodges have laundries; if they don't, you can always wash clothing in the sink and drape it over tent line to dry.

TRAVEL RODS

When this book first came out, true traveling rods were few. You had the Hardy Smuggler and the Thomas and Thomas Vagabond — both great seven piece rods that fit in a tube so short you can carry it in a brief case. Will they handle big fish? Sure. While fishing for grayling with my five-weight T&T Vagabond, a six pound lake trout took my nymph, and we duked it out for what seemed half an hour.

In the last three years, the multi-piece travel rod has come into its own. With the possible exception of heavy-weight rods for salmon, bonefish and tarpon, there's little reason to choose a two-piece rod over one of four sections or more. But be careful when choosing multi-section rods. Two ferrule systems are commonly found: "tip-over-butt" and "plug." The plug system is the stronger of the two because it flexes more readily, says master rod-builder Dave Lewis of Performance Fly Rods (540/867-0856). And should the plug fail, it can normally be replaced quite easily.

Purists complain that the additional ferrules in multi-piece traveling rods makes such rods over-stiff and more difficult to cast. That's probably true for anglers who cast with such finesse that they can tell the difference. And you are better off with a two-piece rod, simply because ferrules are the weak point in any rod, and the fewer, the better. The secret to avoiding grief with a multi-section rod is to pause every fifteen minutes or so and check to be sure that the pieces are tightly joined. Casting can work them loose.

My battery of traveling rods includes the marvelous seven-piece, five-weight Vagabond from Thomas & Thomas (413/863-9727) and the equally good five-piece, five-weight from Winston (406/684-5674). Winston has five-piece models that run up to 12-weight for sail and other big game fish. And, as this is being written, Orvis (800/541-3541) is entering the fray with a seven-section five weight Trident. Also among my favorites is the heavy-duty Performance six-piece eight-weight that packs down to 22-inches. All fit into my carry-on and employ plug ferrule systems. Scott's (303/728-4191) 10-foot, eight-weight is a four-piece rod that's such a performer on steelhead and Arctic char that I don't really mind the 33-inch aluminum tube. Look for more five- to seven-piece rods on the market in the next few years. And you'll begin to see more multi-piece rods for spinfishers and bait casters, such as those from Bass Pro Shops (800/277-7776).

❖ *Batteries*

So many of our devices are powered by batteries that we hardly give them a thought until they die, which is usually at the worst possible time. Before you leave, replace or charge batteries in everything that you intend to take along (watch, flashlight, tape player, camcorder, camera). Carry spares if you can. Many lodges sell common batteries, but don't count on finding the ones you need for your watch or camera in their supply.

❖ *Insect repellent*

The best times to fish usually occur during the height of insect season, especially in the North, where black flies and mosquitoes grow to bird-like proportions. Don't let them ruin your trip. Carry lots of your favorite insect repellent, and use it liberally when astream. The same applies to suntan lotion and lip balm.

❖ *Tackle*

As with clothing, outfitters will tell you what to bring. Some supply gear, and it's usually in pretty good shape. Still, you'll want to use your own when you can. Take at least two rods, but no more than three (unless you'll be fishing in a number of different situations—fly rodding for grayling, casting for big king salmon, bottom fishing for halibut). Drag systems on reels fail more frequently than rods. A couple of spare reels is very good insurance. Put fresh, new line on all of your reels before your trip. Stock up on leader materials, and don't forget wire leader if you're after pike, blues or other toothsome gamefish. Lures and flies will generally be available from the lodge or guides. Still, take those that have worked for you in similar situations, or which you intuitively feel will catch fish. They don't weigh much.

❖ *Shipping fish home*

With the exception of saltwater and salmon lodges in Alaska and British Columbia, most fishing is now catch-and-release. What you bring home are photos and memories, or perhaps a fishprint (*gyotaku*) made in the Japanese style. Most catch-and-keep lodges will clean and package your fish in insulated boxes. You'll be responsible for additional charges for shipping them home.

❖ *Demon rum*

A toddy at the end of a day's fishing can be very welcome. Most lodges have a BYOB policy, though some have open bars with complimentary drink, while others operate lounges where you pay as you go. If it's important to you to imbibe Laphroig or Kings Crest, you'd best bring it with you. Plastic bottles travel well, but you may want to use aluminum or stainless bottles sold by camping stores for fuel. These are virtually indestructible, do not leak and do not impart significant flavor to your favorite potion.

Vital Statistics

WANT A SNAPSHOT of a lodge? Take a glance at the Vital Statistics column alongside each profile. Here's the nitty gritty in a minute's read. Want to know what kind of fish? Which tackle is preferred? When to come? You'll find it here. This is, of course, a broad brush at very best. And the information may change— not the fishing, but specifics about each lodge — from year to year. Below is a guide to our shorthand. Contact lodges that interest you for the latest data.

❖ *Key Species:*

You may catch fish other than those listed here, but these are the ones that attract anglers to the lodge.

❖ *Tackle:*

Sure, you can use almost any gear at any lodge, but don't expect to get much help with technique unless the tackle you like is noted here.

❖ *Flyouts to remote waters:*

High-end lodges will inlcude this in your trip; others will make it available for an additional fee of $150 to $200 or more. Remember, getting there is half the fun!

❖ *Major Season:*

Some lodges are open all year, but the fishing is best from March through October. You get the point.

❖ *Accommodations:*

Log lodge or Victorian manse, this will give you a clue.

NUMBER OF ROOMS: Lodges come in all styles; some with cabins, others with motel-style rooms. This information may tip you off about the size of the operation.

❖ *Handicapped Accessible:*

More and more often, lodges are able to host guests who have some form of physical handicap. A note here suggests that these lodges make an effort to provide some special assistance.

❖ *Maximum Number of Guests:*

Want to know just how intimate your fishing experience will be? You'll find a hint, but only a hint, here. Some huge resorts still offer one-on-one guiding.

❖ *Meals:*

Anglers don't travel on their stomachs, the way other tourists may. Yet the kind of food is nice to know.

❖ *Conference Groups:*

Almost every lodge will host a business or conference group, but those that say "no" generally don't want to be in the meeting planning business. Others don't mind.

❖ *Rates:*

Numbers here are for 1999 - 2000, and are per person unless otherwise noted. These fees will probably be changing as you read this book. Their use, then, is to give you a relative feeling of what one place costs as opposed to another. More often than not, fees are listed in U.S. dollars, but not always. "Cdn" means "Canadian." When you contact the lodge, ask what currency its prices are quoted in.

❖ *Guides:*

Lodges that are dedicated to fishing often include guiding (two anglers per guide) in their packages. At others, guides are optional. If it's included and you don't want it, you probably can't have the cost removed from your package. So in that case, think of your guide as a cousin who happens to live on the river, and who's honor bound to tell you everything he or she knows.

❖ *Gratuities:*

Tips are earned, not obligatory. If your guide goes out of his way to provide you with a great experience, slip him $20 per day. On the other hand, some guides see this as a very important supplement to their fixed income.

❖ *Preferred Payment:*

More and more lodges are accepting plastic (and raising rates to cover the discounts charged by credit card companies). But some don't. Best bet is to ask.

❖ *Getting There:*

Our assumption, based on the fact that time can be shorter than money, is that most traveling anglers will fly to the pick-up point for the lodge. However, you can drive from Atlanta to Anchorage.

❖ *Other Activities:*

Some fishing lodges do have their own golf courses, but not many. This is a list of things to do in the general area of the lodge.

❖ *Contact:*

Addresses are temporal, thanks to changes in area and postal codes. And staff changes, as do, occasionally, the names of the lodges. If you have difficulty reaching one of the lodges, and telephone information fails to provide requisite clues, call a tackle shop in the closest town. They may be able to give you the right steer.

❖ *Agents:*

Some agents have long-standing relationships with some lodges, and it's those that are listed here.

Beneath the falls on the Gibbon, big browns school and, once in a while, fall prey to well-worked streamers.

EAST

CONNECTICUT, MAINE, MASSACHUSETTS, NEW HAMPSHIRE, NEW JERSEY, NEW YORK, PENNSYLVANIA, RHODE ISLAND, VERMONT

FROM THE PEAKS of the Presidential Range to the rounded foothill plains dimpled by kettle ponds perched on kame terraces, the eastern U.S. shows the work of glaciers. They trapped salmon and char in broad, cold lakes creating the landlocked and lake trout salmon fishing that's always best just after ice-out. Headwaters of rivers once fed by glacial melt swarm with native brook trout, once nearly fished out but now restored, thanks to conservation efforts. In bigger, warmer rivers you'll catch fat browns, and where those rivers become warmer still, smallmouth will tear you up. Along the coast, pitch streamers and poppers for saltwater stripers. The traditions of American freshwater angling were born in the waters of Pennsylvania, New York and Maine. Many of these fisheries have been restored, and near them, you'll find camps, lodges, country inns and bed-and-breakfasts that cater to anglers.

Lodges:
Connecticut
1 THE BOULDERS (23)
2 HOUSATONIC ANGLERS B&B (25)
3 THE OLD RIVERTON INN (26)
Maine
4 BEAR MOUNTAIN LODGE (29)
5 GENTLE BEN'S LODGE (30)
6 GRANTS KENNEBAGO LAKE CAMPS (31)
7 GREENVILLE INN (32)
8 LIBBY SPORTING CAMPS (33)
9 NORTHERN OUTDOORS (34)
10 THE PINES (35)
11 RED RIVER CAMPS (36)
12 WEATHERBY'S (37)
13 WHEATON'S LODGE AND CAMPS (38)
Massachusetts
14 THE WILLIAMSVILLE INN (39)
New Hampshire
15 THE BALSAMS (41)
16 NERELEDGE INN (42)
17 TALL TIMBER LODGE (43)
New York
18 BEAVERKILL VALLEY INN (44)
19 ELDRED PRESERVE (45)
20 THE HUNGRY TROUT (46)
21 K&G SPORTFISHING LODGE 47)
22 LAKE PLACID LODGE (48)
23 LODGE AT THE RIVERS EDGE (49)
24 ROSCOE MOTEL (50)
25 SMITH'S COLONIAL MOTEL (51)

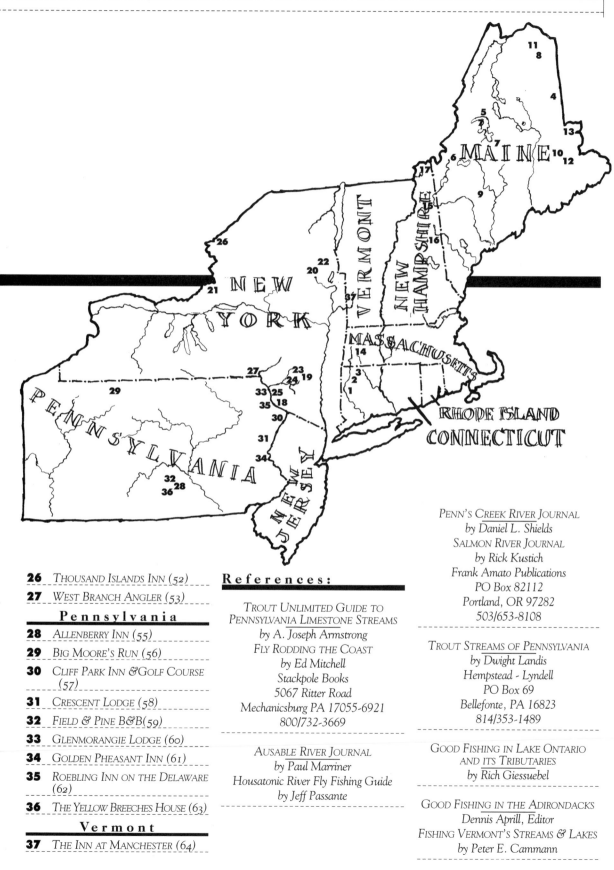

References:

TROUT UNLIMITED GUIDE TO
PENNSYLVANIA LIMESTONE STREAMS
by A. Joseph Armstrong
FLY RODDING THE COAST
by Ed Mitchell
Stackpole Books
5067 Ritter Road
Mechanicsburg PA 17055-6921
800/732-3669

AUSABLE RIVER JOURNAL
by Paul Marriner
Housatonic River Fly Fishing Guide
by Jeff Passante

PENN'S CREEK RIVER JOURNAL
by Daniel L. Shields
SALMON RIVER JOURNAL
by Rick Kustich
Frank Amato Publications
PO Box 82112
Portland, OR 97282
503/653-8108

TROUT STREAMS OF PENNSYLVANIA
by Dwight Landis
Hempstead - Lyndell
PO Box 69
Bellefonte, PA 16823
814/353-1489

GOOD FISHING IN LAKE ONTARIO
AND ITS TRIBUTARIES
by Rich Giessuebel

GOOD FISHING IN THE ADIRONDACKS
Dennis Aprill, Editor
FISHING VERMONT'S STREAMS & LAKES
by Peter E. Cammann

[E A S T]

MID-ATLANTIC TROUT STREAMS
AND THEIR HATCHES
by Charles Meck

MID-ATLANTIC BUDGET ANGLER
by Ann McIntosh
Backcountry Publications
The Countryman Press
Rt. 2, PO Box 748
Woodstock, VT 05091
802/457-4826

NORTHEAST GUIDE TO SALTWATER
FISHING & BOATING
by Vin T. Sparano, Editor
International Marine/McGraw-Hill
Companies
Customer Service Department
PO Box 547
Blacklick, OH 43004
800/822-8158

FISHING MAINE
by Tom Seymour
Falcon Press
PO Box 1718
Helena, MT 59624
800/582-2665

FLYFISHER'S GUIDE TO
NORTHERN NEW ENGLAND: MAINE,
NEW HAMPSHIRE AND VERMONT
Wilderness Adventure Press
PO Box 627
Gallatin Gateway MT 59730
800/925-3339

Resources:

CONNECTICUT DEPARTMENT OF
ENVIRONMENTAL PROTECTION,
WILDLIFE DIVISION
79 Elm St., 6th Floor
Hartford, CT 06106
860/424-3011

MAINE DEPARTMENT OF INLAND
FISHERIES AND WILDLIFE
284 State St., Station #41
Augusta, ME 04333
207/287-8000
web:
www.state.me.us/ifw/homepage.htm

MASSACHUSETTS DIVISION OF
FISHERIES AND WILDLIFE
100 Cambridge St., Room 1902
Boston, MA 02202
617/727-3155
web: www.state.ma.us/dfwele

NEW HAMPSHIRE
FISH AND GAME DEPARTMENT
2 Hazen Dr
Concord, NH 03301
603/271-3422
Fax: 603/271-1438
web: www.wildlife.state.nh.us/

NEW JERSEY DIVISION OF FISH,
GAME AND WILDLIFE
Information & Education Div
PO Box 400
Trenton, NJ 08625-0400
609/292-9450
web: www.state.nj.us/dep/fgw

NEW YORK DEPARTMENT OF
ENVIRONMENTAL CONSERVATION
50 Wolf Rd
Albany, NY 12233
518/457-3521
web: www.dec.state.ny.us

PENNSYLVANIA GAME COMMISSION
2001 Elmerton Ave
Harrisburg, PA 171100-9797
717/787-4250
Fax: 717/772-2411
web: www.pgc.state.pa.us/

RHODE ISLAND DIVISION OF
FISH AND WILDLIFE
4800 Tower Hill Rd
Wakefield, RI 02879-2207
401/789-8281
web: www.state.ri.us/dem

VERMONT FISH AND WILDLIFE
DEPARTMENT
103 South Main St
Waterbury, VT 05676
802/241-3700
Web: www.state.vt.us/anr

The Boulders

New Preston, Connecticut

While not a fishing lodge per se, wise anglers enjoy this luxurious country inn and drive a few miles to stellar angling.

IF YOU'RE LOOKING for an utterly elegant getaway that's close enough to New York City to make a Friday night arrival something less than a frantic hassle, check out this lodge deep in Connecticut's Litchfield Hills. While they put one in mind of the Berkshires, the Litchfield Hills are an hour closer to New York City. Head up to Danbury then turn north on U.S. 202. Depending on traffic, the trip is less than two hours from Manhattan.

Once there, you'll find yourself amidst a tableau of gently rolling hills, smoothed and rounded by glaciers. Drive ten miles north of New Preston on State Route 45 and you'll hit the Housatonic, one of America's 100 best trout streams according to Trout Unlimited. With a bottom of limestone, the Housy is easily wadeable. Browns, generally in the 10- to 15-inch class, constitute the bulk of the fishery, though rainbows up to 18 inches are also encountered. Blue-winged Olives produce from spring through fall; Green and Brown Drakes come off in the Horse Hole in late May and early June. You'll also find Tricos and Sulphurs. Caddis, such a staple on other streams, are limited to May and mid-June on the Housy. Unlike most trout management waters, bait fishing is permitted, logic being that if you can't eat the fish anyway, what's the difference how you catch them? Above the hamlet of Cornwall Bridge runs a 3.5 mile section of fly-fishing-only water. "A western river misplaced in the East," is how guide Rob Nicholas (860/672-4457) describes the river. While this is primarily a trout stream, the mileage from Cornwall Bridge to Kent Falls can produce 30 to 50 smallmouths, many in the 15- to 16-inch range, on a float trip.

There's more than one game in this town. Valleys below the hills carry a number of small rivers: the Appentuck and its East Branch; the Bantam above and below Bantam Lake; and the Shepaug. Most are stocked with trout and provide limited but productive angling. Small lakes offer fishing opportunities as well: Bantam Lake for largemouth and smallmouth bass; the pond in Mount Tom State Park for largemouths and trout; South Spectacle Pond for largemouths; and Waramaug Lake features largemouths and smallmouths. Most of these waters are governed by special regulations.

While it bills itself as a country inn, The Boulders is actually the quintessential lakefront lodge. Native rock defines the deep porch and the massive chimney of the weathered shingle lodge. It sits amidst maples on the slope of a hill. When nights are balmy, dinners are served on a semi-circular terrace and deck with a lovely view of the lake across the road. Meals are exquisite. Start with roasted portobello mushroom with polenta and umbreco cheese. Move on to crisp skinned duck breast with Asian black bean salad. Rooms, some with fireplaces and all with private baths, are furnished with antiques and comfortable overstuffed chairs and sofas for lounging or reading. Directly behind the inn, four guest houses offer lake views, private decks and fireplaces. Fireplaces are also featured in the three rooms in the carriage house. Slip down to the inn's dock early in the morning, untie a canoe and work the shore for smallies. Breakfast will be waiting in your room when you return.

Some might not call the Boulders a fishing lodge, and it isn't per se. But guests who enjoy its elegant rooms and five-star cuisine have been known to match hatches on the Housatonic, a ten mile drive from the Inn.

Housatonic Anglers B & B

West Cornwall, Connecticut

Riverside cabins, great fishing in fall and spring, and just two hours from Times or Scully Squares.

VITAL STATISTICS:

KEY SPECIES:
Browns, rainbows, smallmouth

Tackle:
Fly-fishing, spinning
Major Season:
April 15 through November
Accommodations:
Two riverfront cabins
Number of Rooms: 2
Maximum Number of Guests: 4
Meals: Continental breakfast; dinners in nearby restaurants
Conference Groups: Yes
Rates: From $100 / night / 2
Guides: $225
Gratuities: $25
Preferred Payment:
Cash, check or credit cards
Getting There:
Fly to Hartford and rent a car.
Other Activities:
Canoeing/kayaking/rafting, golf, hiking, horseback riding

Contact:
Rob and Nell Nichols
Housatonic Anglers B & B
PO Box 282
484 Kent Rd.
West Cornwall CT 06796
Ph: 860/672-4457
Fax: 860/672-4457
e-mail:
intern@snet.net

THE HOUSATONIC in the vicinity of West Cornwall resembles, to many, a western river. Wading is not difficult. Limestone ledges provide cover while much of the bottom is cobbly. Vegetation tends not to overpower the stream. The "Housy," as it's called by those who love it, offers excellent fishing for stocked trout — browns and rainbows mainly — and smallmouth bass. Fishing here is strictly catch-and-release. That it is within a couple hours drive of New York City and Boston makes it a popular weekend getaway, yet it's often not crowded.

Most anglers head for the Housatonic River Trout Management Area, roughly nine miles of water, from the Routes 112 and 7 downstream to Cornwall Bridge. Route 7 follows the Trout Management waters and along the way, passes through Housatonic Meadows State Park. Many pools along this run carry names which tell you that this river holds a place in America's angling lore — Push 'em Up Pool, the Doctor's Hole, and the Elms. Browns of 10 to 15 inches make up the bulk of the fishery, yet you'll also find a few rainbows up to 18 inches. If there's a signature fly for this river, it's the Blue-winged Olive, which can be fished virtually year-round. Green and Brown Drakes are prevalent in late May and early June. Tricos and Sulphurs hatch later in the summer. What you won't find are hoards of caddis; they seem restricted to May through mid-June. Bait can be used on this stream — weird logic for catch-and-release water — but the 3.5 mile stretch above Cornwall Bridge is set aside for fly-fishing only.

On their 14 acres along the Housy, Rob Nicholas, a veteran guide/angler on this stream, and his wife Nell run a charming pair of streamfront cabins, each complete with fireplace and private bath. Rob gives several fly-fishing schools during the year and offers float trips down the river in canoes. A continental breakfast is provided with the cabin. Restaurants abound in the area and fine evening dining is less than a 10-minute drive down the road.

VITAL STATISTICS:

KEY SPECIES:
Browns, rainbows

Tackle:
Fly-fishing, spinning
Major Season:
All year
Accommodations:
CLASSIC COUNTRY INN
NUMBER OF ROOMS: 12
MAXIMUM NUMBER OF GUESTS: 28
Meals: Breakfast included, dinners
additional
Conference Groups: Yes
Rates: From $45 / night
Guides: Additional
Gratuities: Angler's discretion
Preferred Payment:
Cash, check or credit cards
Getting There:
Fly to Hartford and rent a car.
Other Activities:
Bird-watching, canoeing/kayaking/
rafting, golf, hiking, skiing,
wildlife photography

Contact:
Mark & Pauline Telford
The Old Riverton Inn
Box 6, Rt. 20
Riverton CT 06065
Ph: 860/379-8678
Fax: 860/379-1006

The Old Riverton Inn

Riverton, Connecticut

With the yellowing of the maples comes some of the finest dry fly-fishing on this quaint stream.

FIRST A STAGE STOP of the Albany Post Road, travelers have sought rest and refreshment in the Old Riverton Inn for more than 200 years. There is no record as to whether they angled or not for the once native brook trout that populated the West Branch of the Farmington. But increasing numbers of visitors to the inn arrive with a rod tucked in a tube and waders bundled in a kit bag in the trunk of their cars.

One of Connecticut's premier trout streams, today the West Branch is a tail-water fishery with flows controlled by releases from Goodwin Dam about a mile upstream from the inn. Four miles downstream in People's State Forest is a four-mile catch-and-release section which, oddly enough, can be fished with bait as well as lures. Fly-fishers should try Church Pool, a half mile of riffles, runs and a long quiet flat. That's the most interesting water according to guide Don Butler (860/583-2446). "Particular" doesn't even begin to describe these browns that range up to 16 inches. There's also good trout fishing across the street from the inn. In midsummer, water temperatures stay in the 60s, thanks to the dam, and that brings trout upstream from warmer waters.

If you ask Don, he'll tell you that the best angling occurs twice during the season. You won't want to miss sulphur hatches in June. But the best fishing comes with tiny Blue-winged Olives, #22s, fished with an eight-foot 1-weight under gray days when it seems the only light comes from maple leaves flaming against the glowering sky. Don't let winter turn you off. Crisp bright mornings often trigger a hatch of black caddis.

If you're interested in history, this inn has more than a bit of it. An enclosed porch is floored with stones quarried 100 years ago in Nova Scotia that were used to grind world-famous Collins machetes made downstream in Collinsville. The Hitchcock Chair Company was founded across the river from the inn. Shoppers will like the company's outlet store and numerous antique shops nearby.

With 12 guest rooms, many with fireplaces and all with private baths, The Old Riverton is small enough to be intimate, yet large enough to offer all the amenities, including a very good restaurant. Licenses are available from the store near the inn and seven miles downstream in New Hartford, you'll find flies, tackle and advice at Up-Country Sportfishing (860/379-1952).

*Roebling Inn on the Delaware is a charming late 19th century
bed-and-breakfast. It's named for John Roebling,
whose earliest surviving suspension bridge spans the river
downstream from the inn, and whose most famous
carries commuters back and forth to Brooklyn.*

*If you're chasing river-run brookies and landlocked salmon
in Maine's northern woods, you'll do well to hang your
waders in the comfortable lodge of Allagash Guide Service.*

Walk down the steps of the West Branch Angler's Wild
Rainbow Lodge, and you're in the main stem of the
Delaware, where rainbows fight like steelhead.

With more than a dram of good sense, Pat Schuler renamed
his highly-regarded lodge after Glenmorangie scotch, which
goes down well after battling the 20-inch-plus
rainbows of the upper Delaware.

Bear Mountain Lodge

Smyrna Mills, Maine

A down-East hunting lodge in spring and fall, but come summer, you'll find the fish bite too.

VITAL STATISTICS:

KEY SPECIES:
Brookies, lake trout, landlocked salmon, pickerel, smallmouth, white perch

Tackle:
Fly-fishing, spinning, trolling
Flyouts to Remote Waters: Yes
Major Season:
May through September
Accommodations:
PRIVATE CABINS OR ROOMS IN THE LODGE
NUMBER OF ROOMS: 4
HANDICAPPED ACCESSIBLE: 2
MAXIMUM NUMBER OF GUESTS: 25
Meals: Family-style
Conference Groups: Yes
Rates: From $125 / week (housekeeping cabins); $400 / week with board
Guides: $100 /day
Gratuities: 10% of total
Preferred Payment:
Cash, bank checks
Getting There:
Fly to Bangor and rent a car.
Other Activities:
Big game, waterfowling, wingshooting, bird-watching, canoeing/kayaking/rafting, skiing, swimming, wildlife photography

Contact:
Carroll P. Gerow
Bear Mountain Lodge
Moro Plantation
RR 1, Box 1969
Smyrna Mills ME 04780
Ph: 207/528-2124

SOME LODGES ARE ALL TRICKED UP with bedspreads that match drapes that are coordinated with wall coverings and carpet on the floor. Meals are epicurean adventures accompanied with wines that cost more per bottle than a jug of good bourbon. On the other side of the coin are those down-home places that are clean, comfortable and somewhat Spartan. You know the kinds of places: a couple of beds in a room or cabin with screened windows and door, a place to hang up your clothes, lights, hot and cold water and a privy that's often, but not always, indoors. Food is basic — turkey, ham, baked beans — and plentiful. At down-home lodges, the operative philosophy is pure Maine: "Make do, do without, use it up, wear it out."

The advantage? These camps tend to be very affordable. A housekeeping cabin may cost only $20 per night per person; room and board for a week will set you back only $400 or so. Here you can hire a guide if you wish (and it's a good idea for a day or two), but you can fish on your own and figure it out for yourself. There's more than a little virtue in that.

Bear Mountain Lodge is one such camp. Run by registered Maine guide Carroll Gerow and his wife, Deanna, most of the year it houses hunters after bear, deer, moose and birds. But from ice-out on the first of May through mid-July when the water warms, the camp fills with anglers in search of brook trout and landlocked salmon. Brookies aren't huge — a 14-incher is a good fish — but they're brightly colored and eager to hit your lure, bait or fly. Dozens of small 10- to 12-acre ponds dimple this country and are often connected by good-size streams that hold fair fish. You can work the ponds and their flowages by using canoes, starting with landlocked salmon that feed on smelt as soon as the ice is out. Troll spoons or flies in Rockabema, Pleasant or Mud lakes or in Shin Ponds for fish up to 20 inches. Carroll will also arrange flyouts to remote lakes and ponds, and he rents canoes.

Anglers at Bear Mountain Lodge stay in four cabins with private baths or in rooms (some with private baths) in the lodge. Buildings are wood with some log, and by no means fancy. You can either do your own cooking or dine family-style in the lodge. Bear Mountain also operates an outpost camp at Rockabema Lakes and another at Skitacook Lakes. Here you'll be heating with wood and cooking with gas. The outhouse is 'round back.

[E A S T]

Gentle Ben's Lodge

R o c k w o o d ,   M a i n e

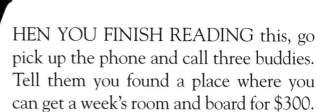

Nothin' fancy about this down-East lodge, 'cept maybe the way them salmon cut up when you hook 'em.

VITAL STATISTICS:

KEY SPECIES:
Brookies, lake trout, landlocked salmon

Tackle:
Fly-fishing, spinning, trolling
Flyouts to Remote Waters: Yes
Major Season:
May through September
Accommodations:
COMFORTABLE, BUT NOT FANCY, LODGE
NUMBER OF ROOMS: 3
MAXIMUM NUMBER OF GUESTS: 12
Meals: Family-style steaks, chops, roasts
Conference Groups: Yes
Rates: From $50 / night
Guides: $225 / day
Gratuities: $25
Preferred Payment:
Cash, check or credit cards
Getting There:
Fly to Bangor and rent a car.
Other Activities:
Big game, wingshooting, bird-watching, boating, canoeing/kayaking/rafting, hiking, swimming, wildlife photography

Contact:
Bruce Pelletier
Gentle Ben's Lodge
PO Box 212
Rockwood ME 04478
Ph: 207/534-2201
Fax: 207/534-2236
e-mail:
info@gentleben.com
Web:
www.gentleben.com

WHEN YOU FINISH READING this, go pick up the phone and call three buddies. Tell them you found a place where you can get a week's room and board for $300. That's three meals a day and a warm and dry place to sleep for a week on Moosehead Lake. Long been a favored angling destination, 175,000-acre Moosehead is known for its populations of landlocked salmon, lake trout and brookies.

Moosehead opens up with ice-out in late April to early May. Ten days after ice-out, smelt run into the mouths of the Moose and Roach rivers that feed the lake. Smelt turn on the salmon. Trolling wobblers or copper and chrome Sutton spoons brings strikes near the surface. Fly-rodders use traditional patterns such as the Grey Ghost or Joe's Smelt. Lake trout are occasionally taken, too, but they tend to be deeper. When Pelletier, the owner of this lodge, has to pick a "best time" to fish these species, he'll tell you early June. After that, the salmon and lake trout move to cooler and deeper water and become less active. If landlocked salmon are your primary interest, you'll want to fish the east outlet of Moosehead Lake. That's the headwaters of the Kennebec and it's one of the best salmon rivers in the state. With good pools, fast riffles and an occasional boulder, the three-mile run down to Indian Pond is the best water. Flow is controlled by releases from the dam at the lake. Under 2,000 cfs, it's wadeable. Above, you'd better float it in canoe or raft.

Maine boasts a fine stock of native brook trout, sometimes called "speckled trout" or "specs." They are feisty from Memorial Day on. Fly-fishing for them in the tributaries can be very productive at this time, as can trolling or casting with spinning gear. Moosehead brookies run up to two-pounds-plus, but your chances of catching a trophy improve if you opt for a flyout to a remote lake. A Cessna or workhorse Beaver will ferry you to one of a number of lakes unreachable by road. Brookies in these are in the three-pound class. The area also provides unlimited stream fishing for brook trout.

With typical Maine practicality, the lakeside lodge is comfortable but not tricked up. Fishing parties will have the run of three bedrooms and a shared bath upstairs in the house. Owners Bruce and Cheryl Pelletier only book up to four fishing guests at one time. "We don't mix parties," says Bruce. "We only have one group at a time." With a weekly rate including meals of $300 per person, Gentle Ben's hosts a lot of families. Family-style meals are served in the dining room downstairs.

Grant's Kennebago Lake Camps

Rangeley, Maine

Here in the eastern mountains, brookies and landlocked salmon don't get up before you do.

VITAL STATISTICS:

KEY SPECIES:
Brookies, browns, landlocked salmon

Tackle:
Fly-fishing
Major Season:
May through September
Accommodations:
NUMBER OF ROOMS: 18
HANDICAPPED ACCESSIBLE: SOME
MAXIMUM NUMBER OF GUESTS: 58
Meals: Sturdy regional cuisine
Conference Groups: Yes
Rates: From $110 / day
Guides: $125 / day
Gratuities: $25
Preferred Payment:
Cash, check or credit cards
Getting There:
Fly to Portland and rent a car, or take the local air shuttle to the airport at Rangeley where you'll be met.
Other Activities:
Bird-watching, boating, canoeing/kayaking/rafting, golf, hiking, swimming, tennis, wildlife photography

Contact:
John Blunt
Grant's Kennebago Lake Camps
PO Box 786
Rangeley ME 04970
Ph: 800/633-4815
Web:
www.grantscamps.com

SPORTSMEN AND WOMEN have been making the trek to Kennebago Lake for its landlocked salmon and brookies since the days of the Civil War. Back then, rumors of six- to eight-pound brookies — caught on a fly — had permeated the Boston fly-fishing community, and those with a penchant for hard travel took the train as far as it would go, switched to a wagon, and finally ended up hiking nine miles to reach a rude shelter at the head of Lake Kennebago.

You don't have to bust your whatsis to reach Grant's Kennebago Camps today. Drive or hook a ride in on a floatplane. Unlimber your gear on the screened porch of your rustic lakefront cabin, walk down the path to your private dock, climb in your Rangeley Lake boat, cast off, fire up the kicker, and head off to that cove where you took that three-pound squaretail last fall. Every cabin includes a dock, but you should make arrangements in advance for a boat for your entire stay. Guides can be arranged. Five miles long and over 100 feet deep in places, Kennebago Lake is ripe with ledges, creek mouths and baitfish that feed landlocked salmon, brookies and a few browns. Fishing is best in June and September, and only flies are allowed. Grant's is the only commercial camp on the lake, resulting in limited angling pressure.

While the lake is the main attraction for guests at the camp, don't forget the river — it's one of the 100 best in America, according to members of Trout Unlimited. You don't have to beat the sun to this water; the river fishes consistently throughout the day. In wet years when there's good runoff, the landlocked salmon will stay in the river all year. However, if summers are hot and flows are low, come July, salmon will move out of the main channel into the depths of the closest, coolest lake. Even then you'll find brook trout, though they may be concentrated near springs or coldwater seeps. After summer heat breaks, usually by mid-August, trout return to the main stream, and salmon will follow a week or two later. During summer and fall, spates of rain will trigger action. Gated roads control access to upper and lower sections of the river, which is wadeable in most spots.

Stretching along a low ridge, Grant's is a picture-book old Maine camp. Wooden cabins roost under firs. Inside are cast-iron stoves and double armloads of split hardwood on the porches. Private baths have plenty of hot water, and in the main lodge you'll dine on the likes of filet mignon and lobster.

Greenville Inn

G r e e n v i l l e ,   M a i n e

Ships' carpenters worked ten years to create this Victorian mansion that sits next to some of Maine's finest angling.

VITAL STATISTICS:

KEY SPECIES:
Brookies, lake trout, landlocked salmon, smallmouth

Tackle:
Fly-fishing, spinning, trolling
Major Season:
May through September
Accommodations:
ELEGANT VICTORIAN MANSION
NUMBER OF ROOMS: 12
MAXIMUM NUMBER OF GUESTS: 28
Meals: Gourmet dinners
Conference Groups: Yes
Rates: From $115 / 2
Guides: $250
Gratuities: 10% - 30%
Angler's discretion
Preferred Payment:
Cash, check or credit cards
Getting There:
Fly to Bangor and rent a car.
Other Activities:
Bird-watching, boating, canoeing/kayaking/rafting, golf, hiking, skiing, swimming, tennis, wildlife photography

Contact:
Michael Schnetzer
Greenville Inn
PO Box 1194
Norris Road
Greenville ME 04441
Ph: 888/695-6000
Fax: 207/695.0335
e-mail:
gvlinn@moosehead.net
Web:
www.greenvilleinn.com

TIMBER CRUISERS, loyal to the King, first trod Maine's endless north woods marking trees with an arrow, a sign that they'd later be felled and floated down surging rivers to be trimmed and turned into masts and spars for the Royal Navy. The new nation, secured finally at Yorktown, needed lumber for its navy and for fast clippers. The forest drew eastern wealth up into Maine's wilderness, and with it came the first of generations of visiting sportsmen who hunted deer, moose and bear; gunned for grouse and ducks; and fished for brookies, lake trout and landlocked salmon.

Accommodations could be as rude as a log hut with windows of waxed paper or as grand as a mansion on the lake. That's where the Greenville Inn comes in. Built in 1895 by lumber baron William Shaw on a hill overlooking Moosehead Lake, this mansion is the epitome of Victoriana. Skilled craftsmen rendered figures and flora in oak, cherry and mahogany. Rich polished paneling adds depth to lamps glowing on period tables. Sun shining through the spruce painted on a leaded window in the stairwell gives you the feeling of climbing the tree itself. Graceful and elegant, the inn is yet, somehow, as easy and comfortable as a well-worn shirt of red plaid wool. Rooms include breakfasts, but most guests stay for gourmet dinners as well: quail with herb sausage stuffing and potato pancakes.

What a spot for a week's angling. Arise in the morning for breakfast in the sunny dining room (or for a quick coffee and roll with the promise of fuller fare when you return), and then head for the headwaters of the Kennebec, 20 miles northeast at the East Outlet of Moosehead Lake. There you'll find some of the finest landlocked salmon in the entire state (it's one of TU's 100 Best Trout Streams) as well as fine brookies. A little farther to the north is the West Outlet, better known for smallmouth bass.

Fishing in Moosehead Lake is improving, as catches of lake trout in the three- to 12-pound range attest. The best angling is right after ice-out in May. So it is, too, with landlocked salmon that run from two to six pounds. And you'll find scrappy smallmouths up to three pounds or so on top in June. But the better fishing is found in the myriad small lakes and streams that connect them. To check them out, contact Maine Guide Service (207/695-2266), one of the best in the state.

Libby Sporting Camps

Ashland, Maine

The fishing's still good at this camp run by the Libby family for more than 100 years.

VITAL STATISTICS:

KEY SPECIES:
Brookies, lake trout, landlocked salmon

Tackle:
Casting, fly-fishing, spinning, trolling
Flyouts to Remote Waters: Yes
Major Season:
May through September
Accommodations:
RUSTIC STONE LODGE OR SPIKE CAMPS
NUMBER OF ROOMS: 8
HANDICAPPED ACCESSIBLE: 1
MAXIMUM NUMBER OF GUESTS: 20
Meals: Scrumptious home cooking
Conference Groups: Yes
Rates: From $115 / day
Guides: $150 / day
Gratuities: $30 / day
Preferred Payment:
Cash, check or credit cards
Getting There:
Fly to Presque Isle and ride the float-plane for $120 / person, round trip.
Other Activities:
Big game, waterfowling, wingshooting, bird-watching, boating, canoeing/kayaking/rafting, horseback riding, hiking, swimming, wildlife photography

Contact:
Matt & Ellen Libby
Libby Sporting Camps
PO Box 810
Ashland ME 04732
Ph: 207/435-8274
Fax: 207/435-3230
e-mail:
matt@libbycamps.com
Web:
www.libbycamps.com

Agents:
Orvis endorsed

WITH A BACK as black as midnight and a belly like sunrise, the brook trout sups on your Mickey Finn. You're fishing a #8 fly, guided by the philosophy that bigger flies catch bigger fish. That's particularly true in the rocky runs and pools of scores of streams that drain the firs and birches of Maine's north woods. You don't need a big rig to fish these waters — a five-weight is plenty. At times drys produce, but often it's more mundane fare — the Woolly Buggers and beadhead Hare's Ears — that bring brook trout to net. They'll run a pound or two in the rivers, but sometimes more. Larger fish are more often caught in Millinocket and other nearby lakes. All told, in these headwaters of the Aroostock drainage, you'll find 46 ponds, 18 lakes, 12 streams and four rivers within 20 miles of Matt and Ellen Libby's main lodge on Lake Millinocket.

No public access exists to the 2,700-acre lake where the camp is located. That's one reason angling is so good here (the other is catch-and-release advocacy). The season begins for lake trout (two to 12 pounds) right after ice-out, generally around May 1. The same goes for landlocked salmon of up to six pounds. Trolling streamers and spoons is the most effective tactic, though casting from shore can sometimes produce results. Brook trout, up to four pounds or so, also open in May, but the fishing doesn't really get going until June and July. Low shallow waters warm earliest while those that are higher and deeper peak last. During August, brookies school up in spring-holes and, when you find them, fishing can be fabulous. As water cools in September, the fishery revives with the onset of the spawn.

For four generations the Libby family has run the camps. Early clients included Teddy Roosevelt and Jack Dempsey. Here you'll find oil lamps, woodstoves, ice cut from the lake, seven up-to-date log guest cabins, and Ellen Libby's scrumptious cooking served in the rustic stone lodge with the open, double-sided stone fireplace. Get a copy of her cookbook. For anglers who seek utter seclusion, the family also maintains eight spike camps on seven other lakes for overnight trips.

Libby's offers various packages. The basic plan includes room, maid service, home-cooked meals and boat, motor or canoe. You can add every-other-day flyouts or overnights at remote spike camps (you'll fly in with your own food, which you'll prepare in fully-equipped log cabins). Guides are also available.

[E A S T]

Northern Outdoors

The Forks, Maine

Do it all at this full-featured resort — whitewater rafting, rock climbing and world-class smallmouth fishing.

VITAL STATISTICS:

KEY SPECIES:
Smallmouth

Tackle:
Fly-fishing, spinning
Major Season:
May through September
Accommodations:
VARIES FROM LODGE ROOMS TO
RUSTIC CAMPS
NUMBER OF ROOMS: 18, PLUS 7 CABINS
HANDICAPPED ACCESSIBLE: 1 CABIN
MAXIMUM NUMBER OF GUESTS: 300
Meals: Full-service restaurant
Conference Groups: Yes
Rates: From $50 / night, double
occupancy
Guides: $200 / day
Gratuities: $10 / day
Preferred Payment:
Cash, check or credit cards
Getting There:
Fly to Bangor and rent a car.
Other Activities:
Big game, canoeing/kayaking/rafting,
hiking, skiing, snowmobiling, tennis,
rock climbing, leadership development

Contact:
Jerry Costa
Northern Outdoors
PO Box 100, Route 201
The Forks ME 04985
Ph: 800/765-7238
Fax: 207/663-2244
e-mail:
info@northernoutdoors.com
Web:
www.northernoutdoors.com

SOME TRAVELING anglers enjoy those rustic places so far back in the woods that you've got to be a registered guide to find them. That's fine for dedicated anglers, but what of those with families — particularly those with young teenagers who may not be overly enthused about the difference between may and caddis flies. That's where Northern Outdoors comes in. It's a full-featured adventure resort that provides such a wide array of activities that kids can do something different and exciting every day for a week.

Located on the Kennebec, one of Maine's premier rivers, *micropterus dolomieui* — smallmouth bass — gets top billing. How come? With their tail-walking and deep runs, smallmouth bring light tackle fans constant action. They thrive in Maine's lakes and rollicking rivers. Both facts aren't lost on outfitter Wayne Hockmeyer, who with his wife, Suzie, created Northern Outdoors and its comfortable resort at The Forks, about 50 miles north of Waterville on Route 201.

Hockmeyer is an angler (he invented the Banjo Minnow lure), and he runs fishing trips for smallmouth only. "We literally turn away trout fishermen," he says. "The trout fishing isn't that good anymore, and I don't want them to be disappointed." In the watersheds Hockmeyer fishes — the Kennebec, Penobscot and Androscoggin — everyone can be successful on smallmouth in the two- to three-pound range.

As you would suspect for a master Maine guide, Hockmeyer knows the area. He guides clients on a number of tributaries to larger and well-known streams. Strictly catch-and-release, protecting the resource is his first concern. Second comes the success of his guests. They fish from bass boats on larger waters, and float tubes or rafts where lakes are small and inaccessible. Small streams are waded. June is the best month, but smallies of size and quantity can be found into the fall. Spinning or fly-tackle is preferred. Hockmeyer is a topwater fan and likes to fish the minnow of his own creation ("a soft plastic jerkbait that swims"). Other effective lures include small Slugos, Rapalas and stickbaits. Northern Outdoors also offers a fly-fishing school.

The Forks Resort Center is a total recreation complex, complete with platform tennis, swimming pool, lounges and bars. (It just opened its own micro-brewery). A variety of accommodations suit different tastes. Choose from modern lodge rooms, or cabins with separate bedrooms, living room, dining area and full kitchen. Or you can rough it in gas-lit cabins, cabin tents and campsites. All have private baths.

The Pines

Grand Lake Stream, Maine

Stay at a serene old camp in Maine's deep woods on a lake where salmon and smallmouth abound.

VITAL STATISTICS:

KEY SPECIES:
Brookies, landlocked salmon, smallmouth

Tackle:
Fly-fishing, spinning
Major Season:
May through September
Accommodations:
OLD GUEST LODGE AND CABINS
NUMBER OF ROOMS: 7
MAXIMUM NUMBER OF GUESTS: 25
Meals: Family-style Yankee fare
Conference Groups: No
Rates: From $65
Guides: $140
Gratuities: Angler's discretion
Preferred Payment:
Cash or check
Getting There:
Fly to Bangor and rent a car.
Other Activities:
Bird-watching, boating, hiking, swimming, wildlife photography

Contact:
Steve Norris
The Pines
PO Box 158
Grand Lake Stream ME 04637
Ph: 207/557-7463
e-mail:
pinespair@juno.com
Web:
www.thepineslodge.com

Off Season:
Ph: 207/796-5006

SINCE THE DAYS when the well-to-do began summering in Maine, folks have been journeying to Lake Sysladobsis, a sibling of West Grand Lake in eastcentral Maine. The only way to reach this bit of tranquility is via gravel road. That helps keep the traffic down. Tucked back from the water on eight-acre Norway Point is the main lodge, built of wood in 1884. An unusual double porch fronts the lodge, and the view of the lake is as restful as the breeze whispering in the lodge's namesake conifers.

Three rooms with shared bath are found in the main lodge. Adjacent are five rustic cabins heated with iron stoves (kindling and cordwood are stacked by your door each day). Cabins contain lavatories but showers are centralized in a cottage constructed for that purpose. If it's total privacy you want, two nearby islands each sport a housekeeping cabin. Here you'll live by lamplight, cooking your own meals on a gas stove. If some night you'd rather not, just boat across to the main lodge and join other guests for Yankee pot roast, baked haddock, or roast pork.

As a fishery, Sysladobsis is quite good. Roughly seven miles long and a mile or so wide, Sysladobsis fishes best from ice-out (about May 1) through June, when the bass leave their beds. One should troll for landlocked salmon with flies or hardware early. Most fish run two to three pounds, with some larger ones likely. Smallmouth action picks up again when waters warm in late June, with fish typically running a pound or two. They are plentiful, though; 30-fish days are not at all unusual. And among the bunch will be one or two in the three-pound-plus category. Crankbaits, spinners, spinnerbaits and topwater plugs all work, as do fly rod poppers, streamers and Woolly Buggers.

In addition to fishing local ponds and flowages for brook trout, fly-fishermen will enjoy a trip over to Grand Lake Stream, where three miles of fly-fishing-only water runs from West Grand Lake to Big Lake. Landlocked salmon, running up to 20 inches in length, readily take streamers and, on occasion, dries. The best fishing is in the last weeks of September when the trees wear more than a hint of color and the fish, as well, don pre-spawn hues.

VITAL STATISTICS:

KEY SPECIES:
Bluebacked trout, brookies, landlocked salmon

Tackle:
Fly-fishing, spinning
Major Season:
May through September
Accommodations:
RUSTIC LOG CABINS
NUMBER OF ROOMS: 15
HANDICAPPED ACCESSIBLE: 2
MAXIMUM NUMBER OF GUESTS: 32
Meals: Hearty beef, turkey, steak
Conference Groups: Yes
Rates: From $80 / day
Guides: $150 / day
Gratuities: $50 / day
Preferred Payment:
Cash or check
Getting There:
Fly to Presque Isle and rent a car.
Other Activities:
Big game, wingshooting, bird-watching, hiking, swimming, wildlife photography

Contact:
Mike & Rhonda Brophy
Red River Camps
PO Box 320
Portage ME 04768
Ph: 207/435-6000
Web:
www.mainerec.com/redriver

Off Season:
PO Box 92
Patten ME 04765
Ph: 207/528-2259

Red River Camps

Portage, Maine

Fish for rare blueback trout in Red River's ponds.

OF SPECIAL INTEREST here is the blueback trout (*Savelinus oquassa*). Left when glaciers melted down about 10,000 years ago, bluebacks are a member of the char family, like brook trout. Once quite common in Maine waters, they seem to be all but extinct. Yet a vigorous population is thriving in a few isolated lakes near Red River Camps. If you catch one, net it carefully. Without removing it from the water, slip the hook (barbless) from its mouth, take its picture, and let it swim gently away. That way, there'll be more next time you visit. The most likely time to catch them is just after ice-out and again in late September, when landlocked salmon are hitting as well.

Anglers have been catching bluebacks, brookies and landlocked salmon for more than a century where the Red River flows out of Pushineer Pond. With buildings made of local log, the camp has grown to 17 buildings. One, a single cottage on a small island, can be used as a honeymoon suite, family getaway or just a place to hide out. The only way to reach this cabin with its big stone fireplace, large living room and bedroom with modern bath and kitchenette, is by canoe. You'll bask in the solitude.

Red River Camps fishes some 15 lakes and ponds ranging in size from 12 to 300 acres. Nine of the ponds are restricted to fly-fishing-only; four permit trolling with spinners; one is artificials only; and one, Togue Pond, allows use of bait. Brook trout, or "speckled trout" in local lingo, are the primary quarry here. Fishing for them is best in late June and July. When air temperatures climb into the nineties and the surface temperature of the water reaches 70°F or so, brookies hug bottom. At this time, successful anglers use high-density sinking lines (weighted nymphs and split-shot on leaders may be illegal; check the regs) and relatively short, stout leaders to get streamers and big nymphs down to spring holes. The mouths of feeder creeks can also produce. Brook trout come back up to feed in September as the water cools. Guides are available but not required. Flyouts to remote lakes can also be arranged.

In addition to the island camp, guests stay in nine other log cabins of varying size. All feature gas lights, woodstoves and private baths. Electricity is provided for three hours in the morning and late evening (bring a flashlight). Guests enjoy family-style dinners, and anglers are sent out with generous packed lunches.

Weatherby's

Grand Lake Stream, Maine

Generations of anglers have been coming back to this Maine lodge for its fine fishing and good food.

VITAL STATISTICS:

KEY SPECIES:
Brookies, lake trout, landlocked salmon, pickerel, smallmouth

Tackle:
Casting, fly-fishing, spinning, trolling
Major Season:
May through September
Accommodations:
HISTORIC COUNTRY INN
NUMBER OF ROOMS: 26
HANDICAPPED ACCESSIBLE: SOME
MAXIMUM NUMBER OF GUESTS: 45
Meals: Lobster, leg of lamb, New England boiled dinners
Conference Groups: Yes
Rates: From $92, double occupancy
Guides: $140 / day
Gratuities: $25 / day
Preferred Payment:
Cash, check or credit cards
Getting There:
Fly to Bangor and rent a car or fly for $125 round trip.
Other Activities:
Wingshooting, bird-watching, boating, canoeing/kayaking/rafting, golf, horseback riding, hiking, swimming, tennis, wildlife photography

Contact:
Charlene Sassi
Weatherby's
PO Box 69
Grand Lake Stream ME
04637
Ph: 207-796-5558
e-mail:
weather@somtel.com
Web:
www.weatherbys.com

Off Season:
RR 1 Box 2272
Kingsfield ME 04947
Ph: 207/237-2911

GRAND LAKE STREAM is one of everybody's favorites in New England. Known for its marvelous stocks of landlocked salmon and brook trout, the river provides plenty of nice-sized fish: trout of a pound or two and salmon, occasionally, of three pounds plus. Public access is ample and anglers of varying skill can find suitable beats. That's why TU included this short three-mile run between West Grand Lake and Big Lake as one of its 100 best streams in the country.

Grand Lake Stream has two distinct seasons when it comes to landlocked salmon. Opening on April 1, smelt imitations including streamers and tube flies fished with sink-tip lines or intermediate lines and a short, three-foot section of 3X tippet will produce. Salmon are foraging on needle smelt, about two inches long. As the season progresses toward May, fish become more active but less interested in streamers. Beadhead Prince, Hare's Ear and stonefly nymphs — even Brassies — work well. Bigger is definitely not better. When summer sun drives water temperatures up to 64° F, salmon return to the depths of Big Lake. Still in the river, though, are brook trout, and they provide gay sport throughout the summer. You'll also encounter great smallmouth action in the lakes. Salmon return to the river in mid- to late August and continue in residence through September. You can find big spawning brookies there too.

For more than 25 years, Ken and Charlene Sassi have owned Weatherby's, a lodge that traces its ancestry back to the turn of the century. This is everything you'd expect a Down East resort to be. A long front porch, some of it open and other parts screened and glassed, wraps three sides of the white clapboard inn. Paneled in pine with hooked rugs on hardwood floors and a mounted salmon above the mantle graced by a pair of oil lamps over the fireplace, this is a fish camp at its finest. Guests stay in cabins (with private baths) of similar decor that are scattered under the trees around the main lodge. The cabins have screened porches and deep Adirondack chairs meant for lazing away the afternoon before a dinner of lobster, lamb or turkey, which is followed by the evening hatch.

Wheaton's Lodge and Camps

B r o o k t o n ,   M a i n e

Smallmouth and salmon go hand in hand at this lodge famed for its "fishin', not wishin'."

VITAL STATISTICS:

KEY SPECIES:
Lake trout, landlocked salmon, perch, pickerel, smallmouth

Tackle:
Fly-fishing, spinning
Major Season:
May through September
Accommodations:
SPORTING CAMP COTTAGES
NUMBER OF ROOMS: 20 rooms in 10 cabins
HANDICAPPED ACCESSIBLE: Some
MAXIMUM NUMBER OF GUESTS: 30
Meals: Crabmeat, turkey, prime rib
Conference Groups: Yes
Rates: From $80 / day
Guides: $120 /day
Gratuities: $20
Preferred Payment:
Cash, check or credit cards
Getting There:
Fly to Bangor and rent a car.
Other Activities:
Bird-watching, boating, canoeing/kayaking/rafting, hiking, swimming

Contact:
Dale Wheaton
Wheaton's Lodge and Camps
HC 81, Box 120
Brookton ME 04413
Ph: 207/448-7723
e-mail:
wheatons1@hotmail.com
Web:
www.mainerec.com/wheatons

Off Season:
PO Box 261
Holden ME 004413
Ph: 207/843-5732

SMALLMOUTH BASS have finally come into their own here in Maine, a state that used to turn its collective nose up at the favorite son of the Mid-Atlantic. It might have been snobbery, pure and simple. It might have been that smallmouth are so plentiful that they offer less of a challenge than landlocked salmon, brookies, lake trout, and the few Atlantic salmon that struggle each year into a few of the state's river. But whatever it was that denigrated bronzebacks into second-class status, it's over now. Smallies are game fish and the relatively isolated lakes and rivers in the Great North Woods offer some of the fastest and finest angling for them in the world.

You won't find the five- to seven-pounders that hang out in the Ozark or Appalachian mountain foothill streams. But there's an abundance of two- to three-pound fish, and four-pounders-plus are not at all rare. Among waters where smallmouth fishing is superb, East Grand Lake is one of the best.

At the east end of the lake you'll find Wheaton's Lodge with its 10 rustic cottages scattered under the pines. "We offer fishin', not wishin'," says owner Dale Wheaton. He and his wife, Jana, have been in the business for 25 years and run one of the finest outfits in the state. Guests stay in quaint cottages scattered in a grove of pines along Grand Lake. Each has a screened porch and private bath. Dining is American plan, but guests order from menus and the food is scrumptious. Reservations should be made early in the year.

Open from ice-out in May through September, Wheaton's offers excellent smallmouth action from June through August. The bass will attack plugs, poppers, small spinners, streamers and nymphs in the shallows early in the season. Later, fish for them at dusk and dawn with crankbaits off points, or down deep with bait. Then, when the first chill of fall spices the air, the bronzebacks go on a feeding binge. Each season, Wheaton's guests catch-and-release 20 smallies that are more than four pounds. In its beginning, salmon season coincides with smallmouth, and you have to choose between the two. Landlocks are caught trolling. Early in the season they hit spoons and flies near the surface, but as the water warms, they too go deep. For fun, tie a bit of ultrathin wire leader to your ultralight or fly leader and cast small spinnerbaits or streamers for pickerel. Take your own boat, rent a boat or hire a guide and his canoe for $120 per day for two.

The Williamsville Inn

West Stockbridge, Massachusetts

Looking for a charming inn where the fishing shines along with the accommodations? Head for the Williams River.

VITAL STATISTICS:

KEY SPECIES:
Bookies, browns, rainbows

Tackle:
Fly-fishing, spinning

Major Season:
April through October

Accommodations:
HISTORIC COUNTRY INN
NUMBER OF ROOMS: 16
HANDICAPPED ACCESSIBLE: SOME
MAXIMUM NUMBER OF GUESTS: 37

Meals: Fresh seasonal foods

Conference Groups: Yes

Rates: From $120 / day / 2

Guides: $200+ / day

Gratuities: Angler's Discretion

Preferred Payment:
Cash, check or credit cards

Getting There:
Fly to Albany, NY, or Hartford, CT, and rent a car.

Other Activities:
Hiking, swimming, tennis

Contact:
Govane Lohbauer
The Williamsville Inn
Rt. 41
West Stockbridge MA 01266
Ph: 413/274-6118
Fax: 413/274-3539
e-mail:
williamsville@taconic.net
Web:
www.williamsvilleinn.com

THE WILLIAMS IS A SECRET RIVER, vastly overshadowed by the Housatonic a few miles to the east. Yet, those who know it, love it. The Williams rises in Shaker Mill Pond north of West Stockbridge and runs under the Mass Pike. Then it breaks to the west and turns south, paralleling but hidden from the Great Barrington Road. Winding through a narrow valley, it's crossed by the Great Barrington Road just north of the Cobb Road intersection. After passing through a small pond, the Williams plays tag with the road until it eventually enters the Housatonic east of Van Deusenville. Public access is limited, but the best is a path across the road from The Williamsville Inn.

Here the river is small, about 25 feet wide. Its bottom is gravel and, in late summer and fall, it can be quite shallow. Some of its pools, however, are 10 feet deep and provide holding areas for trout. While boulders create some pocket water, in the main, the Williams is slow and steady. Wading is the way to fish it. Rick Moon (413/528-4666), who guides and operates an outdoor sports store in Great Barrington, recommends an Elk-Hair Caddis with a green body on a no. 14 or 16 hook. Browns up to 22 inches, small brook trout and a few rainbows inhabit the river, as do rock bass and carp. Because of pollution problems in the past, the Williams has been a kind of self-maintained catch-and-release fishery. In the early 1990s, a new sewage treatment plant went on line in West Stockbridge, and the water quality in the Williams is now suitable for swimming and fishing.

As one would expect here in the Berkshires, the Williamsville Inn is deeply rooted in the region's rich colonial heritage. Prior to the signing of the Declaration of Independence, Christopher French began purchasing parcels between the Williams River and Tom Ball Mountain to the west. After the Revolutionary War, he built the house that in 1952 became the Williamsville Inn. The restaurant, recommended by *Bon Appetit*, serves scrumptious breakfasts and dinners that verge on gourmet. Twelve guest rooms are located in the old house and another four are found in a charmingly remodeled barn.

Is the Williams a destination river? Maybe not. But this corner of western Massachusetts is hard by Connecticut and therein are found a number of reasonably good trout rivers. We can't think of a better place to combine a little fishing with the search for that perfect antique and a romantic night in a lovely country inn.

*Anglers who book into the Beaverkill Valley Inn enjoy
gourmet dining, perhaps attend Joan Wulff's famed fishing
school, and fish a mile of the intensely private reaches
of one of the world's finest trout streams.*

*Of squared limestone and timber, Field and Pine
Bed-and-Breakfast near Shippensburg, Pa., is five minutes
from the best water on Big Spring Creek, and half an hour
from the famed Letort and Falling Spring Runs.*

The Balsams

A grand alpine hotel in the Swiss style offers some fine fishing in the waters north of the White Mountains.

VITAL STATISTICS:

KEY SPECIES:
Brookies, browns, lake trout, landlocked salmon, rainbows

Tackle:
Casting, fly-fishing, spinning, trolling
Major Season:
Late May through October
Accommodations:
ELEGANT MOUNTAIN LODGE
NUMBER OF ROOMS: 204
HANDICAPPED ACCESSIBLE: 9
MAXIMUM NUMBER OF GUESTS: 400
Meals: Continental fare with an American bent
Conference Groups: Yes
Rates: From $132 / night / 2
Guides: $225
Gratuities: Angler's discretion
Preferred Payment:
Cash, check or credit cards
Getting There:
Fly to Portland, ME, or Manchester and rent a car.
Other Activities:
Bird-watching, boating, canoeing/kayaking/rafting, children's programs, golf, hiking, skiing, swimming, tennis, wildlife photography

Contact:
Jerry Owens
The Balsams
Lake Gloriette
Rt. 26
Dixville Notch NH 03576
Ph: 603/255-3400
Fax: 603/255-4221
e-mail:
theBALSAMS@aol.com
Web:
www.thebalsams.com

SINCE 1866, tourists have been finding their way to the tiny Hamlet of Dixville Notch. You know Dixville Notch as the first precinct to report its results during each presidential election. "As goes Dixville Notch, so goes the nation," some pundits proclaim. The pundits are wrong. The good folk of Dixville Notch have been right in their choice of president about as often as they've been wrong.

What residents of Dixville Notch have been able to do is find a way to live in one of the loveliest locales in North America. To the east, the road winds down the mountain to the Androscoggin drainage. Going west runs you to the Upper Connecticut River. Both are well regarded for brown trout. The Androscoggin is closer and thus sees more attention from guests who stay at The Balsams.

The Androscoggin River flows out of the dam impounding Lake Umbagog. The upper section from Bog Brook to the Umbagog dam (about 20 miles) is big pocket water broken by long flats. The flats are deep and hold huge browns. In the heavy water, you'll find brookies, rainbows and browns, as well as smallmouths and a few landlocked salmon. The salmon are thin because the river lacks smelt, the staple of their diet. All but the three-quarters of a mile below the dam can be fished with any tackle during the season, which runs January 1 through October 15. Fly-fishers will enjoy the tailwater of Umbagog Dam, which holds rainbows and brookies up to five pounds. You'll also find some browns. Best spring fishing begins in mid-April.

While the fishing is better than good all summer, Umbagog is big, shallow and warms easily, and that warms the river, turning July and August fishing into early- and late-day propositions. But when fall comes, the waters cool and angling becomes as glorious as the foliage. While the fly-fishing-only section of the Androscoggin commands attention, not to be overlooked are trout in Clear Stream, native brookies in the Swift Diamond River, or browns in the Connecticut River.

Since 1866, travelers have found a warm hearth and friendly lodging in the glacial-carved notch between Dixville Peak and Sanguinary Mountain. Golf has been a mainstay of this lodge since 1897. Scenic doesn't even begin to describe the feeling you get walking these links. The Balsams is one of the last great Victorian resorts (the "New Wing" was completed in 1918), and its rooms and amenities have been continually updated without sacrificing the classic vintage hotel charm.

Nereledge Inn

North Conway, New Hampshire

*Fish freestone rivers and beaver ponds with
a host of presidents looking over your shoulder.*

VITAL STATISTICS:

KEY SPECIES:
Brookies, browns, landlocked salmon, smallmouth

Tackle:
Fly-fishing, spinning
Major Season:
All year
Accommodations:
TRADITIONAL COUNTRY INN
NUMBER OF ROOMS: 11
MAXIMUM NUMBER OF GUESTS: 25
Meals: Scrumptious breakfasts
Conference Groups: Yes
Rates: From $59 / 2
Guides: From $175
Gratuities: $25
Preferred Payment:
Cash, check or credit cards
Getting There:
Fly to Portland, ME, and rent a car.
Other Activities:
Bird-watching, boating, canoeing/kayaking/rafting, golf, hiking, rock climbing, skiing, swimming, wildlife photography

Contact:
Valerie & Dave Halpin
Nereledge Inn
River Road
PO Box 547
North Conway NH 03860
Ph: 603/356-2831
Fax: 603/356-7085
e-mail:
info@nerelegeinn.com
Web:
www.nereledgeinn.com

HOW'D YOU LIKE TO GO FISHING with the president looking over your shoulder? That's just what you do up here in the White Mountains. Only the presidents — Washington, Jefferson, Adams and Monroe — have been dead for a while so you needn't worry about offending them with your lousy casts. These four peaks form the backbone of the Presidential Range. They're high and barren of trees, and capped with snow from November through May.

But all that snow has to go somewhere. There's a spate of runoff in late March and April. Ice generally leaves Winnipesaukee and other big lakes about income tax time, and landlocked salmon and lake trout immediately go on the feed. Troll for them in lakes with long streamers, or fish fast water of the inflows and outlets. By May, brook trouting blooms as well as spring flowers. High mountain ponds are affected by acid rain and may not be particularly productive. But those in low notches and the foothills below have fared better and yield one- to two-pounders to flies as artlessly cast as mine.

When you stay at Nereledge, you'll want to visit Jon Howe of North Country Angler in Intervale (603/356-6000). Jon will take you to fish Sawyer and Mountain ponds. You may fish them in May when the swamp maples are in flower or in early fall when the same maples begin to blush red. He will also take you to the Saco and Ellis rivers, big freestone streams that drain the Presidentials, where brookies, browns and rainbows take Red Quills, caddis and stoneflies. Fish range in the eight- to 12-inch class, but occasionally a 20-incher succumbs to fly or spinner. With his MacKenzie driftboat, Howe will float you down the Androscoggin for browns, brookies, landlocked salmon and rainbows, or run you over to the Connecticut for a drift from West Stewardstown to Colebrook, a great brook trout tailwater.

Good things seldom change in the Granite state. That's certainly the case at the Nereledge Inn, a traditional bed-and-breakfast on the outskirts of North Conway, New Hampshire's biggest ski and mountain tourism resort town. Built in 1787, the inn exudes traditional country charm. You'll find a score of outstanding restaurants in town. And the following morning, in the cozy and sunny breakfast room, you'll have your choice of eggs, pancakes or French toast, topped off with warm apple pie with vanilla ice cream. Think you could get away with that at home?

Tall Timber Lodge

P i t t s b u r g ,   N e w   H a m p s h i r e

For more than 50 years, anglers have been coming here for landlocked salmon and big brown trout.

VITAL STATISTICS:

KEY SPECIES:
Brookies, browns, lake trout, landlocked salmon, rainbows

Tackle:
Casting, fly-fishing, spinning, trolling
Major Season:
April through October
Accommodations:
RUSTIC COTTAGES AND LODGE
NUMBER OF ROOMS: 25
HANDICAPPED ACCESSIBLE: 2
MAXIMUM NUMBER OF GUESTS: 120
Meals:
Trout, escargot, scampi
Conference Groups: Yes
Rates: From $48, double occupancy
Guides: $125
Gratuities: $20
Preferred Payment:
Cash, check or credit cards
Getting There:
Fly to Manchester and rent a car.
Other Activities:
Big game, wingshooting, bird-watching, boating, canoeing/kayaking/rafting, golf, hiking, skiing, snowmobiling, swimming, tennis, wildlife photography

Contact:
David Caron
Tall Timber Lodge
231 Beach Road
Pittsburg NH 03592
Ph: 603/538-6651
e-mail:
info@talltimber.com
Web:
www.talltimber.com

THERE ARE THOSE who know the Connecticut River as that wide, slow river that joins Long Island Sound at Old Lyme, where it's crossed by the Interstate 95 bridge. But about 250 miles to the north, you can plant a foot on each bank and watch the Connecticut flow between your legs. You're standing in the dimple in the top of New Hampshire, and over the ridge runs the Canadian border and the Province of Quebec.

This is a land of big woods and streams the color of under-perked coffee, which gather moisture from thick beds of moss weeping with the melting snow. Beavers turn rivulets into ponds which, if allowed to exist for a few years, soon develop populations of native brookies as brightly colored as summer sunsets. Larger lakes hold stocks of salmon and lakers that try your patience and your rod.

Troll for landlocked salmon and lake trout as soon after ice-out as you can. When water warms in June and July, caddis, mayfly and stonefly hatches provide good dry fly-fishing for browns and brookies. In the dog days of August, dredging nymphs through spring holes will entice big browns. And when the maples reach their glorious reds and yellows in late September, that's the time for equally colorful brookies and browns on the spawn. Salmon return to the rivers then, as well. Anglers who prefer spinning tackle can have a field day here, as ultralight gear is ideal for the rivers and streams.

Located on Back Lake, the lodge is at the threshold of the upper Connecticut River watershed. Its first guests arrived soon after World War II, and anglers have been arriving ever since. Local guides are available for guests who want them, and the lodge's staff provides helpful hints on where to go and what to use. Licenses, tackle and flies are available at the lodge. Seventeen cabins with two to five bedrooms line the lake near the main lodge. All feature private baths and porches. The main lodge includes eight guest rooms, two with private baths. Owners Cindy Sullivan and Judith Caron take their food seriously. You'll find pot roast, steak and pork on the menu with homemade soups, breads and enticing desserts.

Getting to the Tall Timber requires a drive. Manchester, NH is the closest major airport, though fares may be lower if you fly into Boston. Rent a car, drive up Interstate 93 through Franconia Notch, and take Route 3 north. No matter when you do it, the ride is one of the prettiest in the East, so allow yourself a day to enjoy it.

[E A S T]

Beaverkill Valley Inn

Lew Beach, New York

Cross the bridge over the Beaverkill River and find yourself in an 1880s hotel that's got all the modern amenities.

VITAL STATISTICS:

KEY SPECIES:
Brookies, browns, rainbows

Tackle:
Fly-fishing

Major Season:
April through mid-October

Accommodations:
TRADITIONAL COUNTRY INN
NUMBER OF ROOMS: 28
HANDICAPPED ACCESSIBLE: 2
MAXIMUM NUMBER OF GUESTS: 50

Meals: Elegant regional cuisine

Conference Groups: Yes

Rates: From $160 / night

Guides: $225

Gratuities: Angler's discretion

Preferred Payment:
Cash, check or credit cards

Getting There:
Fly to Newburgh and rent a car.

Other Activities:
Bird-watching, boating, cross-country skiing, hiking, skiing, swimming, tennis, wildlife photography

Contact:
Darlene O'Dell
Beaverkill Valley Inn
HCR 136 Beaverkill Road
Lew Beach NY 12753
Ph: 914/439-4844
Fax: 914/439-3884
e-mail:
inn@beaverkillvalley.com
Web:
www.beaverkillvalley.com

BY THE TIME you work your way up the Beaverkill Valley to Lew Beach and beyond, all of this landmark trout stream is privately owned and posted. Here, the Beaverkill is shallow and little more than 30 feet wide. Shaded by a canopy of hardwoods, the river turns through pools, chutes and runs strewn with boulders the size of medicine balls. At times, it hugs the seam between the edge of a meadow and a heavily forested ridge. At other times, the stream runs along a road retained by a sturdy rock wall that provides cover for the baitfish on which browns and brook trout forage. Despite some flooding in years past, the Beaverkill is known for prolific hatches and thus stable populations of wild trout.

Access to this water is limited to say the least. Beaverkill Valley Inn has about a mile of it and that's reason enough to book a room here. Begin fishing the bottom of the long pool and gently work your way upstream, casting to rising trout. On the right runs a rock wall where the water is deeper. Browns of 16-inches-plus use this stretch. Below this pool is a sharp bend where the stream beats against big boulders as it turns into a short hole. Nymphs, particularly at dusk, can produce fish after fish. The upper reaches of the inn's mile is classic pocket water. Overhanging trees make casting challenging. A 7 1/2-foot 3-weight rod is ideal.

Several local fly shops sell patterns specific to the river, and the Catskill Fly Fishing Center and Museum in nearby Livingston Manor displays memorabilia from the legendary flytiers, the Darbees and the Dettes. It also features an extensive collection of Lee Wulff's innovations and many exhibits depicting the angling heritage of the region. If you want to improve your fishing and casting skills, explore programs at the Wulff School of Fly Fishing (914/439-4060), just up the road.

With 20 rooms in the main lodge and another eight at a large farmhouse down the road, the Beaverkill Valley Inn offers gracious lodging and excellent meals (rack of lamb, tuna, filet of beef) in a setting reminiscent of the 1880s. A wide front porch wraps the front of the house — pegs for rods and waders await by the side entrance. Behind the lodge opens a wide meadow where deer brazenly graze all day long. A pond attracts waterfowl and beyond the pond is an indoor pool and self-service ice cream bar. More than one angler has stopped for an ice cream cone on the way to the evening hatch.

Eldred Preserve
Eldred, New York

Fish and game abound on this 3,000-acre preserve that caters to families attuned to rod and gun.

VITAL STATISTICS:

KEY SPECIES:
Brookies, browns, crappie, largemouth, pickerel, rainbows, smallmouth

Tackle:
Casting, fly-fishing, spinning, trolling
Major Season:
All year
Accommodations:
LOG MOTEL
NUMBER OF ROOMS: 26
MAXIMUM NUMBER OF GUESTS: 50
Meals: Trout any way you like it, as well as beef and fowl
Conference Groups: Yes
Rates: From $55 / night
Guides: Available
Gratuities: Angler's discretion
Preferred Payment:
Cash, check or credit cards
Getting There:
Fly to Newburgh and rent a car.
Other Activities:
Big game, canoeing/kayaking/ rafting, horseback riding, sporting clays

Contact:
Bonnie Robertson
Eldred Preserve
1040 Rt. 55
PO Box 11
Eldred NY 12732
Ph: 914/557-8316
Fax: 914/557-8733
e-mail:
eldred@warwick.net
Web:
www.eldredpreserve.com

HERE'S THE QUESTION: Where can you introduce a young angler to the sport where there's little risk and great chance of success. We've all done it with our kids, but that was back when a friendly chat with a farmer gained you access to the blue-ribbon water that flowed through his pastures. Today, places where kids can fish under controlled conditions are few and far between.

And that's one of the aspects that makes this preserve north of the Delaware River near the little town of Eldred, so special. Eldred Preserve offers anglers the opportunity to choose from bass, trout or catfish from a series of carefully managed lakes and ponds. The prime attraction at Eldred is a pair of bass lakes, each offering a different kind of angling. Sunrise Lake contains 75 acres of submerged weedbeds, timber and deep structure. Steges Lake is bigger, 85 acres, shallower and known for rafts of lily pads that hide good fish. A strict catch-and-release policy applies, and that's why largemouths in the four- to six-pound class are not unusual. You'll fish from a 16-foot bass boat powered by a bow-mounted trolling motor. You may also want to check out Eldred's catch-and-release trout ponds. Brown, brook, rainbow, tiger and golden trout to six pounds are more difficult to catch than you think on barbless flies. What a place to introduce kids to the rewards of catch-and-release angling! If it's a mess of fish you're wanting, switch to the catch-and-keep pond and fill your creel with one- and two-pounders. Other ponds are set aside for catfish. Here, any bait that works is legal.

If you come, look into Eldred's guided floats on the Delaware. The middle section between New York and Pennsylvania is dynamite for smallmouth bass and spring shad. You'll also find some walleye in this section. Upper reaches are among the finest rainbow and brown trout water in the country. Costs vary depending on species and whether you want to float or wade.

Air-conditioned rooms in the log-style lodge feature private baths, phones and cable TV. On the menu in the restaurant are trout any way you want them: preserve-style with capers, lemon and tomatoes; amandine; baked with seasoned bread crumbs and herbs; stuffed with crab; fried in cornmeal; blackened; or charbroiled. There's also steak for those who want it. In addition to your appetite and fishing tackle, bring your shotgun and shoot sporting clays.

The Hungry Trout

W h i t e f a c e   M o u n t a i n ,   N e w   Y o r k

For less than a C-note, you get a room, meals, and a day on a private stretch of the West Branch of the Ausable River.

VITAL STATISTICS:

KEY SPECIES:
Brookies, browns, rainbows, smallmouth

Tackle:
Fly-fishing
Major Season:
May through October
Accommodations:
QUALITY MOTEL AND A HIDDEN CABIN
NUMBER OF ROOMS: 20
HANDICAPPED ACCESSIBLE: SOME
MAXIMUM NUMBER OF GUESTS: 80
Meals: Pub grub to fine dining
Conference Groups: Yes
Rates: From $90 / night
Guides: $220
Gratuities: 15%
Angler's discretion
Preferred Payment:
Cash, check or credit cards
Getting There:
Fly to Albany and rent a car.
Other Activities:
Wingshooting, bird-watching, boating, canoeing/kayaking/rafting, golf, horseback riding, skiing, swimming, tennis, wildlife photography

Contact:
Jerry Bottcher
The Hungry Trout
Rt. 86
Whiteface Mountain NY
12997
Ph: 800/766-9137
Fax: 518/946-7418
e-mail:
hungrytrout@whiteface.net
Web:
www.hungrytrout.com

West Branch of the Ausable River deservedly makes TU's ranking of the 100 best trout streams in America. Clean, cold, unpolluted water that's well oxygenated with ample food and good cover, the river supports a very good population of brook, brown and rainbow trout. The upper reaches run through thick meadows where the water is smooth and deep, and trout are reputed to be larger than in other sections. Below NY Route 86, the gradient increases and the river plunges through pools and rapids before rolling off 100-foot falls. From the foam beneath the falls, the Ausable plays the pocket water game, crashing through a gorge and eddying out in a big pool named for Fran Betters, a fly-fishing legend in these parts. At the town of Wilmington, the river is impounded and there's access for handicapped anglers. The pool below the mill-dam is a hot spot for big trout in the spring. From here down to Ausable Forks is classic pocket water and the best dry fly-fishing on the stream.

Fly, spin and bait fishing are permitted, although several sections are governed by special regulations. The Hungry Trout has the only mile of pure catch-and-release, fly-fishing-only mileage on the river. Anglers who fish this most frequently time their visits to early spring and summer, and fall when color riots in maples along the river's course. If you're handy with a 20-gauge, bring it along in October. That's when ruffed grouse are at their peak. Funny, brown and brook trout fishing is hot then as well.

After a morning's cast or blast, settle into R.F. McDougall's, have the barman draw you a pint, watch fishing video's on the giant screen, and work your way through a "Black Jack" burger. If you've got the urge, go to the bench and tie up some patterns for the afternoon's fun and games. Dinners are served in a more formal setting. You must try "An American Bounty," a mixed grill of venison chop, sautéed trout and breast of duck. Rooms are comfortable and the fly shop is open when you get up.

Oh yea, if for some reason the river is high or otherwise misbehaving when you come, Jerry'll take you to a wonderfully rustic cabin on Little Saranac Lake. There you'll fish for smallmouth up to four pounds, wend through little canals between the lakes with old wooden locks operated by hand, and dine on fare that's fine beyond belief. Small wonder that unscrupulous anglers try to book into the Hungry Trout when they know the Ausable is running wild.

K&G Sportfishing Lodge

Oswego, New York

On the shore of Lake Ontario rises a brand new stone and timber lodge where salmon and steelhead abound.

VITAL STATISTICS:

KEY SPECIES:
Browns, king/chinook salmon, lake trout, rainbows, silver/coho salmon, steelhead, walleye

Tackle:
Casting, fly-fishing, spinning, trolling
Major Season:
March through November
Accommodations:
New stone and timber lodge
Number of Cabins: 20
Maximum Number of Guests: 40
Meals: Area restaurants
Conference Groups: Yes
Rates: From $40 / night
Guides: $700 / 4 anglers
Gratuities: 15% - 20%
Preferred Payment:
Cash, check or credit cards
Getting There:
Fly to Syracuse and rent a car.
Other Activities:
Big game, wingshooting, bird-watching, boating, golf, snowmobiling, swimming, wildlife photography

Contact:
Greg Gehrig
K&G Sportfishing Lodge
94 Creamery Road
Oswego NY 13126
Ph: 800/346-6533
Fax: 315/342-1041

LOTS OF ANGLERS IN THE KNOW have headed to K&G Sportfishing Lodge because of the owners' — Greg and Kris Gehrig — penchant for putting clients on Lake Ontario's browns, As of this writing, guests will put up in one of 20 cabins and dine in town. But in 2001, the couple will open its brand new lodge of stone, timber and glass. With 61 rooms, the lodge can handle large groups. Even with a new lodge, Greg and Kris are committed to providing the intimacy and personal service that has made their operation so popular. This is a family resort where fishing is foremost on the agenda.

From spring into the fall, you'll fish Lake Ontario from outrigger and down-rigger equipped 30- to 35-foot sportfishermen. In April, as the surface warms, brown trout averaging six pounds become active at the top of the water column. Use custom noodle rods with reels spooled with 8-pound-test line to troll stickbaits and small flutter spoons. Lake trout and steelhead fall for the same setup when they get going in May. By June, the fish have moved down to 40 or 50 feet, but on still days when there's little wave action to mix temperature layers, Gehrig looks for thermobars, flows of warm water riding on the surface of the cold. When he finds them, you'll find steelhead and lots of them. If thermobars are not present, Gehrig trolls with "jingle bell" rigs on downriggers for lake trout averaging 13 pounds.

In September, focus shifts to the salmon run on the Oswego. Steelhead averaging 10 pounds and browns in the six-pound-plus range follow later in October. You'll fish from jet or driftboat, or wade, depending on your preference and river conditions. The jetboat allows anglers to cover more of the river with greater thoroughness than with other types of watercraft. And it's an incredible aid to fly-fishers because it's easier to follow big fish. Fishing improves as the weather deteriorates, and an enclosed cockpit provides welcome relief from freezing rain. You can also find smallmouths and walleyes in both the river and lake.

[E A S T]

Lake Placid Lodge

L a k e   P l a c i d ,   N e w   Y o r k

After fishing from this fine old Adirondack lodge, you'll understand the roots of all of the great lodges on Western waters.

VITAL STATISTICS:

KEY SPECIES:
Brookies, browns, lake trout, pike, rainbows, smallmouth

Tackle:
Fly-fishing, spinning
Major Season:
April through mid-October
Accommodations:
ADIRONDACK-STYLE LOG LODGE
NUMBER OF ROOMS: 34
HANDICAPPED ACCESSIBLE: 1
MAXIMUM NUMBER OF GUESTS: 75
Meals: Gourmet, featuring regional cuisine
Conference Groups: Yes
Rates: From $300 / night
Guides: $200
Gratuities: Angler's discretion
Preferred Payment:
Cash, check or credit cards
Getting There:
Fly to Saranac Lake and rent a car.
Other Activities:
Bird-watching, boating, canoeing/kayaking/rafting, golf, hiking, skiing, swimming, tennis, wildlife photography

Contact:
Charlie Levitz
Lake Placid Lodge
PO Box 550
Lake Placid NY 12946
Ph: 518/523-2700
Fax: 518/523-1124
Web:
www.lplodge.com

WALK INTO THE INN at Old Faithful in Yellowstone National Park and immediately you'll see the use of unplaned timbers and bent limbs to support floors and railings. Ceilings are high, open and airy. Rock hearths hold roaring blazes. Think this architecture was born in the West? Guess again. It's a natural evolution of a style developed in the late 1800s in upstate New York's Adirondacks.

Artful use of bent twigs and branches is a hallmark of the Adirondack style, and you'll admire its sophisticated application at Lake Placid Lodge. Multi-tiered porches shaded by trees rise above the lake. Sit in a rocker and watch loons bobbing, diving and warbling their eerie call. Inside, overstuffed chairs rest on oriental rugs over gleaming wooden floors before floor-to-ceiling hearths of round river rock. Snowshoes, moose heads and old wicker creels adorn mantles and walls. Guest rooms are found in the lodge or nearby log cabins. Adirondack antiques are found in most, as are massive and working stone fireplaces. Menus are highly evolved. Dining is strictly gourmet and appropriate wines are served.

Brookies, browns, rainbows, lakers, smallmouth and walleye — you'll find them all in Lake Placid. Sculpted by glaciers and filled by icy streams running down the folds of the mountains, the lake is known for large lake trout. Best angling occurs just after ice goes out, usually in late April or early May, or in the few days prior to the close of the season on Oct. 15. Trolling is the most productive tactic. In 1986, the state record laker of 34 pounds, 8 ounces was taken with a deeply trolled spoon. Brook trout also fish best just after ice-out, with small spoons, spinners, streamers and big nymphs all producing. In fall, work the mouths of creeks which they will be running up to spawn. Rainbows seem to come to life in June when the water temperature exceeds 55°F.

Smallmouths in the two- to three-pound range inhale crankbaits cast shoreward in June. But don't be surprised if a four- or five-pounder nails your plug. And, of course, not to be overlooked is the nearby Ausable River with its mix of rainbows and browns, or the waters of nearby Mirror which also yield good trout. Don Jones at Jones Outfitters, Ltd. (518/523-3468), offers guided trips to trout and bass waters in the Lake Placid region. You can make arrangements directly with him or through the lodge. The lodge can also arrange boat rentals.

The Lodge at the Rivers Edge

R o s c o e ,   N e w   Y o r k

You'll find more of TU's top 100 rivers within an hour of Roscoe than any other town besides West Yellowstone.

VITAL STATISTICS:

KEY SPECIES:
Brookies, browns, rainbows

Tackle:
Fly-fishing, spinning
Major Season:
May through September
Accommodations:
CARRIAGE HOUSE APARTMENT
NUMBER OF ROOMS: 3
MAXIMUM NUMBER OF GUESTS: 8
Meals: On your own
Conference Groups: No
Rates: From $40
Guides: $325
Gratuities: 10% - 15%
Angler's discretion
Preferred Payment:
Cash, check or credit cards
Getting There:
Fly to Newburgh and rent a car.
Other Activities:
Hiking, cross-country skiing

Contact:
Rick & Marie Miller
The Lodge at the Rivers Edge
PO Box 277
Roscoe NY 12776-0277
Ph: 914/439-5050
Fax: 914/439-5451
e-mail:
milflyfish@aol.com
Web:
www.rickmillerfly-fishing.com

RICK AND MARIE MILLER have picked up a sweet bit of pasture on the Beaverkill in the hamlet of Craig-e-Clair (extra points are awarded if you can find it on a map). The Miller's spread covers only 14 acres, not very big by most standards, but there's a quarter to a half mile of private water here that you can fish to your heart's desire. Nobody besides you and the member of your party will be on this section during your stay. It's yours, but the trout aren't; you have to release them as soon and as delicately as you can.

Well back from the river, the couple has constructed a carriage house — a large flat of 1,500 square feet over the garage. Comfy but not fancy, these lodgings contain two bedrooms, one with a queen and the other with two twin-sized beds, a steam shower and private bath, full kitchen provisioned with all the staples and equipment, a living room with a sofa that becomes a queen bed for the guy who drew the short straw, and a deck with barbecue. If your group is large, you may want to engage the third room, a den with private entrance, half-bath and futon sofa-bed. Dining is in your hands: grill steaks, warm up some beans, or head to Roscoe where you'll find a number of restaurants.

Clients who've booked with Rick, a veteran guide, are given preference in using the lodge. He fishes all the rivers that have made Roscoe the center of trout fishing in the Catskills. The Beaverkill and Willowemoc rivers are close at hand. Down Rt. 17 a ways is the East Branch of the Delaware. This river, a tailwater issuing from Pepacton, holds truly huge browns that became corpulent by not getting caught. Fish the mileage above the river's junction with the Beaverkill. An hour's drive west will take you to Hancock and the West Branch of the Delaware along with the main stem. Drive east an equal distance and you'll be on the Esopus or the Neversink.

Roscoe Motel

Roscoe, New York

Walk to the famed Junction Pool where the Beaverkill and Willowemoc meet and wrestle the great two-headed trout.

VITAL STATISTICS:

KEY SPECIES:
Brookies, browns, rainbows

Tackle:
Fly-fishing, spinning
Major Season:
All year
Accommodations:
VERY NICE MOTEL ROOMS AND ONE CABIN
NUMBER OF ROOMS: 18
MAXIMUM NUMBER OF GUESTS: 50
Meals: Continental breakfast, restaurants in town
Conference Groups: No
Rates: From $60 / 2
Guides: Available from $200+
Gratuities: Angler's discretion
Preferred Payment:
Cash, check or credit cards
Getting There:
Fly to Newburgh and rent a car.
Other Activities:
Big game, waterfowling, wingshooting, bird-watching, boating, canoeing/kayaking/rafting, golf, horseback riding, hiking, skiing, snowmobiling, swimming, tennis, wildlife photography

Contact:
George & Debra Kinne
Roscoe Motel
PO Box 609
Old Rt. 17
Roscoe NY 12776
Ph: 607/498-5220
Fax: 607/498-4643

I N THE LONG, TEAR-SHAPED POOL, trout are rising. It's early and they are taking Hendricksons. You're standing on the rocky cobble at the foot of the Junction Pool. You've targeted what seems to be a fish that's better than others dimpling in the pool. His snout seems to break the water each time he takes. A cast, the float, he ignores your fly and sups on another six inches to the right. With a mighty effort at self control, you rest him for as long as you can stand it. Then you cast again. No take. Another iron-willed pause. One more cast. Yesss! The fish is heavy. He charges to the left, running up the Beaverkill. No! Shit! He's coming back! Strip, strip, strip, get that loose line in. Whoa. Now he's running up the Willow. Pop goes your tippet. Gongrats, you've just met the legendary two-headed trout of the Junction Pool.

The Beaverkill is *de classe* with the big trout crowd. They'd rather be in Idaho. But you don't make the pilgrimage to Roscoe, the quintessential trout town, on New York's Rt. 17, for big fish. The journey is more spiritual. The upper runs of the river, with the exception of the mileage near the campground at the covered bridge, is essentially private. Yet from its confluence with the Willowemoc, downstream to the junction of the East Branch of the Delaware, is some of the most celebrated trout water in America. Access is easy. Route 17 — the Quickway from New York City to Binghamton — follows the river. Pull-offs for parking abound. Use fly, lure or bait; it's up to you. Every pool, and they're all named, sees heavy concentrations of anglers, particularly those in the no-kill sections. Still, the fishing is good and well worth the trip.

Fly shops and guides are readily available in this little hamlet, but river-front accommodations are few. Among the best values is the barn-red with white-trim Roscoe Motel which sits neat as can be on a maple shaded green alongside the Beaverkill, just less than 100 yards from the Junction Pool. A short stretch of private water flows behind the motel. Rooms are clean and quite reasonably priced. Continental breakfast comes with your room; lunch and dinners are found in the village, a five minute drive or 20 minute walk from the motel. For those who like to cook, rent the efficiency cabin which contains a full-kitchen and sleeps up to four.

Smith's Colonial Motel

Hancock, New York

Spend the night, rent a canoe and have all the fun of fishing the upper Delaware without denting your wallet.

VITAL STATISTICS:

KEY SPECIES:
Brookies, browns, rainbows, shad

Tackle:
Fly-fishing, spinning
Major Season:
May through October
Accommodations:
CLEAN AND COMFORTABLE MOTEL
NUMBER OF ROOMS: 14
HANDICAPPED ACCESSIBLE: 1
MAXIMUM NUMBER OF GUESTS: 50
Meals: Restaurants in Hancock
Conference Groups: No
Rates: From $55 / night / 2
Guides: From $250 +
Gratuities: Angler's discretion
Preferred Payment:
Cash, check or credit cards
Getting There:
Fly to Newburgh and rent a car.
Other Activities:
Canoeing, hiking

Contact:
Jeff Smith
Smith's Colonial Motel
RR Box 172D
Hancock NY 13783
Ph: 607/637-2989
e-mail:
colonial@hancock.net

STAND ON THE DECK of this modest and clean motel and be prepared to have your mind blown. There below you is the best of the main stem of the Delaware River running upstream to Hancock where the East and West Branches of the river come together. Access to this mileage of the Delaware is not as easy as it once was. Landowners are realizing the value of the river in their backyards. Posted signs, sadly, abound.

If you spend the night at this motel — $55 ain't bad — you can hike down the hill, cross the railroad tracks and continue on across the floodplain to the river. This will put you about a mile below the public access and below the water treatment plant just south of the junction of the two branches. The water where the trail from the motel reaches the river is some of the best there is. Here the river comes back together after rounding a big island. You'll find gravel bars, chutes and pools that look for all the world like water from the Bighorn or the South Fork of the Snake.

It's rainbow country with a few browns thrown in for good measure. May, June and July are the most prolific months for hatches — first mayflies and then caddis. But the activity continues well into fall. Don't overlook shad which migrate into this area in May. They're difficult to hook — use a 7-weight, sinking tip line and a small bead-headed two-toned streamer of white and day-glow orange, chartreuse or red. A night at Smith's positions you to fish the West Branch of the Delaware (cooler and smaller than the main stem), the East Branch above its junction with the Beaverkill (below gets pretty warm in summer), and the famed Bea-Moc system around Roscoe, about 50 miles east on Rt. 17.

There's nothing at all pretentious about Jeff and Ingrid Smith's motel. He'll arrange guided trips on the river if you want, and he also rents canoes. Now lots of anglers prefer fishing from drift boats, but to do so you need to lay out bucks for a guide ($300+ per day), or you have to have your own boat. Almost anybody can pilot a canoe down this section of the Big D. There's no whitewater. Pull ashore to fish the water that turns you on. Jeff will pick you up at the end of your float.

Thousand Islands Inn

C l a y t o n ,   N e w   Y o r k

Would you believe that people came for the salad dressing and stayed for the fishing?

VITAL STATISTICS:

KEY SPECIES:
Largemouth, muskie, pike, smallmouth, walleye

Tackle:
Fly-fishing, spinning
Major Season:
May through October
Accommodations:
HISTORIC HOTEL
NUMBER OF ROOMS: 14
MAXIMUM NUMBER OF GUESTS: 25
Meals: Eclectic game and American fare
Conference Groups: Yes
Rates: From $47.50 / day
Guides: $310
Gratuities: Angler's discretion
Preferred Payment:
Cash, check or credit cards
Getting There:
Fly to Syracuse or Watertown and rent a car.
Other Activities:
Waterfowling, wingshooting, bird-watching, boating, canoeing/ kayaking/rafting, golf, horseback riding, hiking, swimming, tennis, wildlife photography

Contact:
Allen & Susan Benas
Thousand Islands Inn
335 Riverside Dr.
PO Box 69
Clayton NY 13624-0069
Ph: 877/544-4241
e-mail:
tiinn@1000-islands.com
Web:
www.1000-islands.com/inn

AS LAKE ONTARIO prepares to discharge into the St. Lawrence River, it becomes shallow. Land, some drier than other, rises above the surface. Broad flats grow stands of flooded grass. In places, the old outlet from a glacial river cuts against headlands and here the river is deep and black. Shallows abound and occur with no seeming rhyme, other than to wreck the props of boats piloted by the unsuspecting. If you are an angler you should be looking for the shallows. That's where you'll find largemouth and smallmouth bass. Drop-offs hold walleye. Additionally, muskies prowl these freshwater flats like she-lions on the savanah.

Tackle is your choice. Fly and spinfishers will find bass and pike in the shallows early in their seasons. Everything goes deep during summer with the exception of smallmouths on the shoals after dark. Best fishing for walleyes and muskies is in fall, and that means jigging and trolling with fairly stout gear. The St. Lawrence fishery is so varied that you'll need an expert to help you sort it out.

Allen Benas, who with wife Susan, owns the Thousand Islands Inn, is a pretty good bet. Since 1978 he's guided anglers for bass and pike on the St. Lawrence. Among the better ways to get to know the water is to book a trip with Benas on his "office," a custom headboat designed to carry a maximum of 15 anglers to drift-fish for walleyes. Benas' office also carries fly-rodders in search of bass and northern pike. Numerous other fishing packages are available, including fall hunts for trophy muskies. Many trips include a shore lunch: appetizer, salad, corn on the cob, boiled potatoes, fresh fish and dessert. The nap afterwards is optional.

Dating from 1897, the inn is one of the few remaining small resort hotels that were once prolific in towns along the St. Lawrence. The hotel has 14 rooms with private baths in turn-of-the-century country style. When dining in the restaurant, check out the venison, quail and walleye entrees. And, in case you didn't know it, the salad dressing of the same name was invented right here. Anglers with their own boats can launch and dock them across the street from the inn. Anglers with the good sense to fish in the fall will also have the opportunity for a bit of pheasant hunting at a nearby preserve.

Remember that frustrated dentist from Manhattan who loved to fish and wrote all those westerns to pay for his vice? Well, you don't need to ride the purple sage to find Zane Grey's home (now museum) on the upper Delaware at Lackawaxen.

West Branch Angler

D e p o s i t ,   N e w   Y o r k

If you can figure out the back cast, you can work this river almost from your front porch.

VITAL STATISTICS:

KEY SPECIES:
Browns, rainbows

Tackle:
Fly-fishing
Major Season:
April through November
Accommodations:
RIVERFRONT CABINS
NUMBER OF CABINS: 22
MAXIMUM NUMBER OF GUESTS: 95
Meals: Steaks, fish and Italian specialties
Conference Groups: Yes
Rates: From $75
Guides: From $225
Gratuities: $25
Preferred Payment:
Cash, check or credit cards
Getting There:
Fly to Binghamton and rent a car.
Other Activities:
Big game, waterfowling, wingshooting, bird-watching, boating, canoeing/kayaking/rafting, golf, hiking, skiing, sporting clays, swimming, wildlife photography

Contact:
Harry Batschelet
West Branch Angler
150 Faulkner Road
PO Box 102
Deposit NY 13754
Ph: 607/467-5525
Fax: 607/467-2215
e-mail:
wbangler@TDs.net
Web:
www.westbranchangler.com

HARRY BATSCHELET, whose West Branch Angler is the most complete fishing lodge on the upper Delaware, has added a new eatery — the River Run Restaurant and Troutskeller Bar. Now, once you wheel into the lodge just off Rt. 17 (soon to become Interstate 86), you'll not have to use your wheels until you leave. And given the fishing in the West Branch, you may not ever want to do that.

Thanks to a landmark agreement with the New York City which draws on the Delaware Watershed for drinking water, the once warm and turgid river now flows cold (most of the time) and fairly clear. The river runs from Stilesville at the base of Cannonsville Reservoir for 16 miles downstream to Hancock, where it joins the East Branch. The confluence forms the main stem of the Delaware. Route 17 follows the course of the river closely and anglers use pull-offs for parking. Easy access can mean crowds, but it's no worse here than popular streams in the West.

No huge rapids or brawling falls are found on the West Branch. Instead, the river threads its way through an utterly bucolic farm valley where agriculture has long since ceased. Meanders are few, but in places the river braids, providing seams and still-water pockets where trout will lie. Cobbles and gravel make up the bottom, providing good spawning grounds as well as easy wading. Browns up to 20 inches predominate in the upper section of the West Branch above Hale Eddy and Hancock, and rainbows of the same size hang out below. Fly and spin fishing are permitted. The section from Hale Eddy south is open year-round, but upstream to the dam, the river is only fished from April 1 through September 30. Hatches are prolific throughout the season.

Harry operates two lodges on the Upper Delaware: West Branch Angler and Sportsman's Resort at Hales Eddy; and Wild Rainbow Lodge a couple miles below Hancock. At West Branch Angler, guests stay in one of 22 riverfront log housekeeping cabins or in the lodge. All rooms have private baths. Meals are served a la carte in the restaurant. Wild Rainbow, which is ideal for a group of anglers, is a log house with four bedrooms and a broad deck on a low terrace just above the river. Nearby is an intimate cabin with two bedrooms. Guest rooms have private baths. Meals will be prepared if desired or they may be eaten in town. At the resort is a fully stocked fly shop, and guides are available for wade or float trips.

Allenberry Inn

Boiling Springs, Pennsylvania

When the Music Man opens on stage, white flies will be hatching on the Breeches.

VITAL STATISTICS:

KEY SPECIES:
Browns, rainbows, smallmouth

Tackle:
Casting, fly-fishing, spinning
Major Season:
April through November
Accommodations:
COUNTRY INN
NUMBER OF ROOMS: 69
HANDICAPPED ACCESSIBLE: SOME
MAXIMUM NUMBER OF GUESTS: 128
Meals: Excellent restaurants
Conference Groups: Yes
Rates: From $125 / 2
Guides: $250
Gratuities: Angler's discretion
Preferred Payment:
Cash, check or credit cards
Getting There:
Fly to Harrisburg and rent a car.
Other Activities:
Swimming, tennis

Contact:
Jere Heinze
Allenberry Inn
PO Box 7
Boiling Springs PA 17007
Ph: 717/258-3211
Fax: 717/960-5280
e-mail:
aberry@epix.net
Web:
www.allenberry.com

THE YELLOW BREECHES RIVER drifts through its valley like a finely gaited horse ambling back to the stable. Moving with style and grace, it knows where it wants to go, and that it will get there in good time. So flows the Yellow Breeches, running down the center of the eastern half of Pennsylvania's Cumberland Valley, bound for the Susquehanna below Camp Hill.

That the Breeches is easily waded exposes its greatest shortcoming. During periods of drought like that of 1999, long stretches of the river were devoid of browns and rainbows. Even those stocked by the commonwealth's Fish Commission high tailed it out of there as fast as their fins could push 'em. That's the bad news. The good news is that virtually all of them found cold water springs and seeps to hole up in until the weather god recharged the river with cool rain. Among the runs where fish concentrate in such times is the mileage between Allenberry Playhouse and Boiling Spring.

The spring is one of the largest in Pennsylvania. Its outflow chills about a mile of the Breeches, insuring a good stock of fish even on the hottest summer day. The signature hatch here is the white fly of August, and anglers from throughout the East flock to the river to get in on the action. As guide Joe Humphreys says, "You may be hooking a fish at somebody else's boot tops, but it's still fun." He advises that midweek angling is always less crowded and suggests that other times of the year (particularly May) can be almost as good. The catch-and-release mile from the springs to Allenberry is open year-round. Joe and his colleagues, Ed Shenk and Norm Shires, run fly-fishing schools at the resort (about $365). Nearby is the Letort, one of the most difficult dry fly spring creeks in America.

Allenberry Resort, located along the Yellow Breeches, includes an equity theatre company. If you come in May, you'll want to reserve tickets for *Phantom of the Opera*; hatches in July play to *Pirates of Penzance*; the white fly action concludes with the *Music Man*. Uphill from an old mill dam on the Breeches are the resort's two major buildings, remodeled limestone barns that date from the late 1700s. In addition, there are a pair of fine restaurants, comfortable but not elegant guest rooms in three lodges, extensive conference facilities, tennis courts, an Olympic-size pool, and extensive manicured lawns that invite one to nap or read in the shade.

Big Moore's Run

Coudersport, Pennsylvania

Clinics and classes from A to Z, and at the end, a final exam proctored by the toughest judges of all: big old trout.

VITAL STATISTICS:

KEY SPECIES:
Brookies, browns, rainbows

Tackle:
Fly-fishing
Major Season:
April through November
Accommodations:
COMFORTABLE LOG LODGE
NUMBER OF ROOMS: 5
HANDICAPPED ACCESSIBLE: 2
MAXIMUM NUMBER OF GUESTS: 25
Meals: Family-style dining
Conference Groups: Yes
Rates: From $200 / double occupancy
Guides: Fishing programs vary
Gratuities: $20
Preferred Payment:
Cash, check or credit cards
Getting There:
Fly to Bradford Regional Airport and rent a car.
Other Activities:
Big game, bird-watching, golf, hiking, wildlife photography, sporting clays, shooting schools

Contact:
Bill or Barb Haldaman
Big Moore's Run
RR 3, Box 204A
2218 Big Moore's Run Rd.
Coudersport PA 16915
Ph: 814/647-5300
Fax: 814/647-9928
e-mail:
bigmoores@out.doors.com
Web:
www.bigmoores.com

Agents:
Orvis endorsed

EVEN THE WORDS — Allegheny Highlands — cool you. Forested with pines, firs and hardwoods, this plateau in northcentral Pennsylvania seems as endless as it is devoid of people. Free-flowing rivers have carved narrow and deep valleys where freestone streams frolic over their boulder-strewn courses. At times, the sun doesn't kiss the valley floors until it's close to its zenith. Trout reproduce well in many of these waters, but fishing for them is not easy.

That's one of the reasons that Bill Haldaman, who founded Big Moore's Run, developed the downstream roll cast and other fancy tricks to present flies to persnickety trout in waters as clear as a drinking glass. Getting the fly to the fish is only half the task. When he takes, you've got to react quickly, yet judiciously, or all you'll have is a flyless tippet to show for your indiscretion. Think of Big Moore's Run as a one-stop shop for folks interested in learning how to fish with flies. Clinics are held almost weekly. Anglers will learn the basics of reading streams, selecting flies, casting and playing fish in group schools held most weekends from the end of March through September. A pair of ponds and a section of stream are managed so students can hook into and play big fish. Advanced students will spend more time on Bill's stream and others nearby learning how to entice lunkers out of tight lies with Haldaman's special brand of headwater's fishing. Personal tutors are also available.

Not only does Big Moore's offer quality instruction, but the waters are pristine. Browns, brookies and Kamloops rainbows propagate naturally. The ponds are incredibly fertile, one of the few places in the East where Specklewing mayflies (*Calibaetis*) hatch with regularity. More common in the West, a Specklewing hatch can last for hours and bring fish to a state of near indiscriminate feeding. At Big Moore's, you have five or six weeks to catch the hatch in early April and May. Bring your Blue Duns or buy them at Haldaman's Orvis shop. Taking eight-pound Kamloops on dries in Pennsylvania is not to be missed.

Bill and wife Barbara's lodge seems to snuggle into a wooded hill overlooking the lake. From the deck, you can see fish rising and deer coming to drink on the far shore. Guest rooms are simply furnished and comfortable; all have private baths. Family-style dinners include duck, pheasant, quail, trout and steaks. There's also a sporting clay's course and golf.

Cliff Park Inn & Golf Course

Milford, Pennsylvania

History and golf stroll hand in hand across this plateau, while below flows one of the best smallmouth rivers in the country.

VITAL STATISTICS:

KEY SPECIES:
Browns, muskie, rainbows, shad, smallmouth, walleye

Tackle:
Casting, fly-fishing, spinning, trolling
Major Season:
May through October
Accommodations:
THREE-STORY WHITE FRAME HOMESTEAD AND CABINS
NUMBER OF ROOMS: 18
HANDICAPPED ACCESSIBLE: 6
MAXIMUM NUMBER OF GUESTS: 36
Meals: Elegant American cuisine with a continental flare
Conference Groups: Yes
Rates: From $93
Guides: $25 / hour
Gratuities: $20
Preferred Payment:
Cash, check or credit cards
Getting There:
Fly to Newburg and rent a car.
Other Activities:
Canoeing/kayaking/rafting, golf, hiking, skiing, swimming

Contact:
Cliff Park Inn & Golf Course
155 Cliff Park Rd
Milford PA 18337
Ph: 570/296-6491
Fax: 570/296-3982
e-mail:
cpi@warwick.net
Web:
www.cliffparkinn.com

AROUND THE TURN of the last century, Harry W., the scion of the Buchanan family, made a fateful decision. The family farm would no longer raise sheep; instead, it would take in tourists. Milford, a charming Pennsylvania town just south of where the state joins with New York and New Jersey, was entering its heyday as a summer vacation resort. Families from New York City took big old Victorian homes for the summer. Gifford Pinchot, pioneering conservationist and pal of Teddy Roosevelt, ran a school for nascent foresters there.

The Buchanan's added a golf course, modeled after links in Scotland, that meanders around the big white-framed lodge and is surrounded by stands of maple, oak and beech. A short walk across the course leads to a trail which climbs a gentle rise. Round the bend and to your left, you can see the land fall away for more than 400 feet down to the valley of the Delaware River below. There are no condos or malls in sight. The land is all included in the Delaware National Recreation Area, set aside for fishing, hunting, hiking, camping and canoeing.

Less than 10 minutes by car from the lodge puts you on the river. The season begins with shad on light spinning or fly-tackle in May. Smallmouth bass become active at the end of the month, lull a bit at the height of summer and turn on in August and September. Winter finds the walleyes hitting, particularly in the deep pool at the Milford access. And muskies, fished either with live suckers or big stickbaits, become vicious feeders from October through December.

The most pleasant way to fish the river is by canoe. Start your float at Tri-State Canoe, and fish the heads of the pools as you drift down. Cast crankbaits that imitate crayfish or minnows into rocky cover and breaks in the grassbeds along the banks. Ultralight spinning tackle with 4-pound-test line is all you need. Fly-fishers will find better success if they pull over and cast Zonkers, Woolly Buggers or crayfish patterns out into the fast water and let them wash down.

While you wouldn't call the Cliff Park Inn a fishing lodge (guides will be arranged on request), many of its guests fish the Delaware and the scores of trout streams in the surrounding Pocono Highlands. The three-story white frame homestead is a classic. If it's a sense of historic country elegance you're seeking, with outstanding fishing nearby, there are few better places so close to New York City.

[E A S T]

Crescent Lodge

C r e s c o ,   P e n n s y l v a n i a

(Psst . . . Don't tell anyone. But the cradle of fly-fishing for trout in America was here in the Poconos.)

VITAL STATISTICS:

KEY SPECIES:
Brookies, browns, rainbows

Tackle:
Fly-fishing, spinning
Major Season:
April through October
Accommodations:
STONE AND FRAME COTTAGES
NUMBER OF ROOMS: 30
MAXIMUM NUMBER OF GUESTS: 60
Meals: Excellent restaurant
Conference Groups: No
Rates: From $85
Guides: Available through
Dunkleburger's
Gratuities: Angler's discretion
Preferred Payment:
Cash, check or credit cards
Getting There:
Fly to Newark and rent a car.
Other Activities:
Bird-watching, golf, hiking, tennis

Contact:
Robert F. Dunlop
Crescent Lodge
Paradise Valley
Cresco PA 18326
Ph: 570/595-7486
Web:
www.crescentlodge.com

BEFORE RAILROADS could carry vacationers all the way to New York's Catskills, fly-fishers set their caps by the Pennsylvania's Brodhead. Rising high on the Pocono Plateau, the Brodhead River collects a myriad number of wee tributaries and channels them into a dainty, freestone stream that has many of the attributes, but not the isolation, of its successor in trouting fame, the Beaverkill. In the mid-1800s, much of the prime water was leased by private clubs, and their descendents still control the upper runs of the river.

But behind the tavern at Analomink, public water begins. It gets better as it makes the run toward Stroudsburg and, thence, through a gorge and into the Delaware. Stocked, you'll find browns and rainbows in the 10- to 15-inch class with some surprises that nudge 20 inches. Among the best water is the run through town and the gorge section. The latter is difficult to access, but well worth the climb down from the railroad bed that runs along the north side of the creek. Here, the water is large and heavy. It is difficult to wade, but not impossible with caution and a wading staff. It's also possible to access the lower end of the gorge via a rutted track that drops down the hill to the south just east of Exit 52 on Interstate 80.

Other streams hold trout in the area. Try Poplar Run, a tributary of the Brodhead that flows through the Delaware State Forest. According to Dwight Landis in *Trout Steams of Pennsylvania* — an excellent and accurate guide that's available from Dunkleburger's Sporting Goods in Stroudsburg (tackle, advice on guides, and licenses too) — wild brookies and browns populate this run. Also worth a look early in the season is Tobyhanna Creek for stocked trout. Don't ignore McMichael or Pocono Creek; both are vastly underrated. Big and Little Bushkill creeks are also about 10 miles up the Delaware from East Stroudsburg.

Most anglers who come to fish this area take potluck with motels. This is the Poconos and you'll find accommodations that suite every taste and budget. However, among the nicest retreats is one about 15 miles up the Brodhead from Stroudsburg in Paradise Valley. The Crescent Lodge is a full-service resort of stone and shingles that caters to folks who want to get away from it all, but don't necessarily want to rough it. Rooms are comfortable and well appointed, and the restaurant leaves nothing to be desired.

Field & Pine Bed-and-Breakfast

Shippensburg, Pennsylvania

Historic and cozy, this inn is a mile from Big Spring Creek, and half an hour from the Letort and Falling Spring Run.

VITAL
STATISTICS:

KEY SPECIES:
Brookies, browns, rainbows

Tackle:
Fly-fishing
Major Season:
April through November
Accommodations:
COUNTRY STONE HOUSE
NUMBER OF ROOMS: 3
MAXIMUM NUMBER OF GUESTS: 8
Meals: Full breakfast
Conference Groups: No
Rates: From $50
Guides: Available
Gratuities: Angler's discretion
Preferred Payment:
Cash, check or credit cards
Getting There:
Fly to Harrisburg and rent a car.
Other Activities:
Bird-watching, golf, hiking, tennis

Contact:
Allan & Mary Ellen Williams
Field & Pine
Bed-and-Breakfast
2155 Rittner Hwy
Shippensburg PA 17257
Ph: 717/776-7179
Fax: 717/776-0076
e-mail:
fieldpine@aol.com

THIS FIRST-CLASS bed-and-breakfast of half stone, half clapboard construction sits just around the corner from the fly-fishing-only section of Big Spring Creek in southcentral Pennsylvania. Big Spring Creek must be one of the major disappointments to the Pennsylvania Fish Commission. Fifty years ago, a lovely limestone spring of memorable dimension pumped clear water of constant temperature into a gentle run that slid with hardly a rapid for four miles to the Conodoguinet Creek below Newville. The bed was shallow and cobbly making for ideal redds. Insect hatches were prolific. Big Spring was likened to the more famous Letort in Carlisle 15 miles east.

But the construction of a state hatchery which utilized the waters from the spring before releasing them into the streambed may have been responsible for the decline of this once wild fishery. Now, only 1.1 miles below the spring is considered really good water. Challenging fishing, you can see the trout — brookies going better than 15 inches. They fin gently in water that seems faintly frosted. They're used to seeing humans. That's not the problem. They're also used to seeing every manner of fly ever tied. Hatches are few. Best success comes with tiny cress bug patterns. Terrestrials also perform, as do midges. Try also Brassies and fine San Juan worms. Angling is year-round.

While in this neck of the woods, you'd be remiss if you failed to drive down to Chambersburg (30 minutes) to fish Falling Spring Run which enters the city from the east. From Interstate 81, take the U.S. 30 exit toward Gettysburg and immediately turn right onto Falling Spring Road. You'll cross the creek and then follow it toward its headwaters. Crossing the stream one more time, you'll see the TU/Orvis greenway project. The best fishing begins here. Falling Spring is best known for its trico hatches. You'll find trout feeding on no. 24 tricos in the mornings from June through October. Perhaps the best hatch on Falling Spring is the sulphur hatch that begins in May, reaches full force in June and early July, and continues into fall. Winter fishing features browns and rainbows of more than 20 inches.

Field & Pine couldn't be a better place to hang your waders. Three rooms, one with private bath, are immensely comforting after a day trying to convince one of those Big Spring brookies to give you a tumble. Rates are little more than you'd pay for a motel. Restaurants provide reasonable dinners.

[E A S T]

Glenmorangie Lodge

S t a r l i g h t ,   P e n n s y l v a n i a

This fine lodge was the Starlight. Now it's the Glenmorangie, and the Delaware River 'bows are hotter than ever.

**VITAL
STATISTICS:**

KEY SPECIES:
Browns, rainbows, shad

Tackle:
Fly-fishing
Major Season:
April through October
Accommodations:
FINE LOG LODGE
NUMBER OF ROOMS: 6
HANDICAPPED ACCESSIBLE: 2
MAXIMUM NUMBER OF GUESTS: 14
Meals: Bed-and-breakfast
Conference Groups: Yes
Rates: From $100 / single
Guides: $275
Gratuities: $25
Preferred Payment:
Cash or check
Getting There:
Fly to Binghampton and rent a car.
Other Activities:
Wingshooting, bird-watching,
canoeing/kayaking/rafting, golf,
skiing, sporting clays

Contact:
Pat Schuler
Glenmorangie Lodge
PO Box 86
Starlight PA 18461
Ph: 570/798-2350
e-mail:
Jlastcast@nep.net

A COUPLE OF YEARS AGO the gents from Glenmorangie made Pat Schuler an offer that sounded right. They wanted a little broader exposure. Starlight underwent a name change, but other than that, it's the same outstanding angler's inn as before, and one of the first devoted to fly-fishing on the Upper Delaware.

Three hours west of New York City and not much farther from Boston and Philadelphia flows the upper Delaware River, one of the best stretches of water in the East. Beginning where the east and west branches meet just south of Hancock, New York, and for about 18 miles south to Hankins, this section is a superb cold-water fishery. Rainbows outnumber the browns. Hatches, all the Eastern standards, are prolific and reasonably consistent, and fish rise readily. And when nothing's coming off, big stoneflies and streamers work well. The rainbows in this run have a reputation for being hotter than any others in the country, unless you count steelhead. Typical fish here run between 14 and 18 inches. Smaller fish are seldom caught. Why? They stay in the tributaries, guesses Pat, or deep in spring holes.

Hancock is an old lumbering town that could be a tourist mecca, but it's not. The fishing's good enough, but there's no skiing and no dude ranches. What there is, is a very good diner, groceries and gas. Anglers meet their guides at the diner. This is the jumping-off point for the Delaware's east and west branches. From Pepacton Dam down to the village of East Branch, the eastern fork of the river is an excellent brown trout fishery. At the village it joins the Beaverkill, which in its lower reaches can be tragically warm in summer. The West Branch is shorter (about 18 miles long compared to 31 miles for the East Branch), and more heavily influenced by dam releases. This, too, is brown trout water.

River guide Pat Schuler's bed-and-breakfast is the place where serious fly-fishers stay when fishing the main stem. Glenmorangie caters to anglers (and increasingly upland bird hunters, too). Pegs hold scores of rods on the walls, decorated with frames of flies tied in classic Delaware style. There's a drying room for waders and boots, and a tier's bench is handy. Rooms are comfortable, but not plush. Breakfast is served on a tiled island in the kitchen. Dinners are not typically part of the deal, nor is a bottle of the namesake single malt. Yet for some, a couple fingers of the latter finds its way into a glass for those so inclined.

Golden Pheasant Inn

Erwinna, Pennsylvania

Anglers will love this historic country inn not only for its cuisine, but for the smallmouth that dance in the river all night.

VITAL STATISTICS:

KEY SPECIES:
Shad, smallmouth, striped bass

Tackle:
Fly-fishing, spinning
Major Season:
April through November
Accommodations:
ELEGANT RIVERFRONT INN
NUMBER OF ROOMS: 6
MAXIMUM NUMBER OF GUESTS: 14
Meals: Gourmet game cuisine
Conference Groups: Yes
Rates: From $75 / night
Guides: $125 / day
Gratuities: Angler's discretion
Preferred Payment:
Cash, check or credit cards
Getting There:
Fly to Newark or Philadelphia and rent a car.
Other Activities:
Wingshooting, bird-watching, boating, canoeing/kayaking/rafting, horseback riding, hiking, swimming, wildlife photography

Contact:
Barbara Faure
Golden Pheasant Inn
763 River Road
Erwinna PA 18920
Ph: 610/294-9595
Fax: 610/294-9882
Web:
www.goldenpheasant.com

ELEGANT ACCOMMODATIONS and exquisite cuisine on a river where the fishing is first rate? Not often found in the East, yet this happy situation occurs on the lower Delaware. And it's within a few hours' drive of both Philadelphia and New York City. Quaint and historic river towns dot the Delaware between Bucks County and Hunterdon County in New Jersey. The Delaware Canal follows the river. Built of brick and stone, many of the circa-1850s houses where mule-pulled barges paused have been reincarnated as country inns. None is more charming than the Golden Pheasant.

You'll find canopied beds, period furniture, electrified oil lamps and fresh flowers in the six bedrooms. Each has a private bath. A fire fills the grate in the stone-walled, open-beamed dining room where colonial decor blends appropriately with French country accents. You have the feeling that Lafayette would be comfortable here, and well he should. His countryman, Michel Faure, from Grenoble, owns the inn with his wife, Barbara. Michel is always at work in the kitchen turning out such entrees as smoked filet of trout, lump crab cake with a light mustard hollandaise, and roast boneless duck with a raspberry, ginger and rum sauce. Folks who put up at the Golden Pheasant do eat well, no?

It's best to book Friday and Saturday nights. Beat it out of work early so you can arrive in time to scout the river, noting water level, clarity and access (not a problem). Plan your approach for the next day's angling. If you go in April, you'll no doubt want to fish shad. Known as "Poor Man's Salmon," they'll hit one-eighth-ounce darts cast out and bumped along bottom or fished behind an anchored boat. Shad are valiant fighters that, after a lightning run or three, settle down to duke it out with you. Striped bass move into the river to spawn in June. Crankbaits and Clousers work on them, for spin and fly-fishers respectively. Smallmouth bass are standard fare, running one to three pounds, with fish of five pounds more than possible. Fish them early in the morning or as the sun sets. And don't pass up muskies up to 12 pounds. Though few and far between, those that smack your plug or bait will bend your rod double before you get it sorted out. Guides are not available at the Golden Pheasant, but you might try J.B. Kasper (215/295-1502). He lives in Morrisville, across the river from Trenton, and knows the Delaware with great intimacy.

[E A S T]

Roebling Inn on the Delaware

L a c k a w a x e n ,   P e n n s y l v a n i a

Visit the old house that Zane Grey loved so well, and then fish his first and favorite river.

VITAL STATISTICS:

KEY SPECIES:
Browns, muskie, rainbows, shad, smallmouth, striped bass/rockfish, walleye

Tackle:
Casting, fly-fishing, spinning, trolling
Major Season:
March through November
Accommodations:
1900s VINTAGE RIVER HOUSE
NUMBER OF ROOMS: 6
MAXIMUM NUMBER OF GUESTS: 15
Meals: Bed-and-breakfast
Conference Groups: No
Rates: From $65
Guides: $200
Gratuities: Angler's discretion
Preferred Payment:
Cash, check or credit cards
Getting There:
Less than 2 hours from New York City.
Other Activities:
Big game, waterfowling, wingshooting, bird-watching, boating, canoeing/kayaking/rafting, golf, horseback riding, hiking, skiing, snowmobiling, swimming, tennis, wildlife photography

Contact:
Don & JoAnn Jahn
Roebling Inn on the Delaware
155 Scenic Dr
Lackawaxen PA 18435
Ph: 570/685-7900
Fax: 570/685-1718
e-mail:
roebling@ltis.net
Web:
www.poconos.org/members/roeblinginn

AN OBSCURE DENTIST, Zane Grey dreamed of the time when he could flee his office in Manhattan and do what he did best: fish. He left the city when he could, heading west to Lackawaxen on the Delware. There he caught smallmouth with his brother Robby, penned a trio of fishing stories: *A Day on the Delaware*, *Mast Hope Brook in June*, and *Lord of Lackawaxen Creek*; fell in love with Dolly, his wife-to-be; wrote *Rider's of the Purple Sage*; and galloped off to become America's best known author of adventure westerns and a foremost pioneer of worldwide angling. Not bad for a guy who cast minnows into the deep holes on the Delaware.

You can too. Maybe not the writing part, but the fishing is still there, although it's quite a different river today than it was in Grey's era. Then it was a free-flowing warm water river known for smallmouth, shad and an occasional striped bass. Trout were a rarity in those days, restricted pretty much to the Lackawaxen, Mast Hope Brook, and other streams that drain the Pocono Highlands to the west. But since the late 1950s, with the construction of New York City water supply reservoirs in its headwaters, the Delaware has become a classic tailwater fishery.

Upstream, above Calicoon, are hard-fighting rainbows that act for all the world like steelhead, yet they feed like trout. In the pool in front of Grey's place, you'll have a field day with shad in the spring and walleyes in autumn. Riffles up and downstream are great for smallmouth in late summer and fall. Lackawaxen Creek, also controlled by an upstream hydro plant, is a poor vestige of what it once was. On summer days, water temperatures can reach the high 70s. Trout fishing here is essentially a marginal put-and-take operation. But the pool at the mouth of the creek continues to yield an occasional striped bass.

Come for the shad and smallmouth, and stay in the Roebling Inn, a white frame Greek revival house dating from 1870. Owners Don and JoAnn Jahn offer six comfortable guest rooms with private baths, and a basic breakfast. An adjacent cottage with kitchen and bath provides accommodations for two. Visit the National Park Service's Zane Grey Museum in the house he once owned. Or walk down to the oldest wire suspension bridge in the U.S. Built in 1849 by John Roebling, this bridge is the precursor to the Brooklyn Bridge. Also nearby is Angler's Roost, source of licenses, tackle, flies, tubes, canoes and rafts for riding the river.

The Yellow Breeches House

Boiling Springs, Pennsylvania

A bed for the night, breakfast with the dawn, and a day on central Pennsylvania's spring creeks. Not bad, eh?

VITAL STATISTICS:

KEY SPECIES:
Browns, rainbows

Tackle:
Fly-fishing
Major Season:
April through November
Accommodations:
1900s Bed-and-Breakfast
Number of Rooms: 5
Maximum Number of Guests: 10
Meals: Restaurants in the town
Conference Groups: Yes
Rates: From $99 / 2
Guides: $295
Gratuities: $40 - $50;
Angler's discretion
Preferred Payment:
Cash, check or credit cards
Getting There:
Fly to Harrisburg and rent a car.
Other Activities:
Bird-watching, hiking, skiing,
swimming, tennis, wildlife
photography

Contact:
Matt Zito
The Yellow Breeches House
213 Front St
PO Box 221
Boiling Springs PA 17007
Ph: 800/258-1639
Fax: 717/258-9882
e-mail:
flyfish@pa.net
Web:
www.pa.net/flyfish/

ACROSS THE STREET from this bed-and-breakfast, you'll see a huge spring that is clear as crystal. Its chill waters beat back the heat of summer and allow trout to thrive in Yellow Breeches Creek below the outlet. When August's dogs pant hot and humid, you'll find trout stacked up like cordwood in the icy outlet from the spring. The cool plume extends a mile downstream creating a Mecca for browns, rainbows and for the fly-fishers who play them. This is fly-fishing-only water, but when the weather is more temperate, trout disperse throughout the Yellow Breeches offering opportunities for spin fishers.

This is, however, not the only game in town. Not half a dozen miles north is the famous Letort Spring Run where Vince Marinaro, Charlie Fox and Ed Shenk pondered the feeding habits of those huge browns lying beneath waving cresses. They experimented with numerous patterns and developed a series of terrestrials — ants, hoppers, jassids, and beetles — and another of sowbugs and scuds that imitate the crustacea on which these browns primarily feed. Their work on the Letort was every bit as important as Gordon's in the Catskills. Unlike the Catskill streams, the Letort retains a good deal of the same character as it did when Messrs. Marinaro et al were unraveling their mysteries. Much of the best water is protected and open to fly-fishing only. You'll see browns sipping in the flows.

The schools run by Matt Zito at The Yellow Breeches House will help you get ready for the Letort and other spring creeks in the region. The Learn to Flyfish Program attracts students of all ages, but never more than six at a time. You'll learn about rods, reels, lines, leaders, and how these components work in harmony to deliver fly to fish. You'll learn to cast — not those long, sinuous casts that look so lovely — but the short practical casts that take fish in nearby streams. You'll learn how to read the water and how to select flies. Advanced schools, two students to an instructor, focus on techniques for success on the Letort.

Matt's bed-and-breakfast also includes a small tackleshop, a fishing library with flytying bench, a guest kitchen where you can whip up a bag lunch, and a 35-foot porch ideal for goofing off. Rooms have been modernized and are comfortable, but not fancy. Two of the five share a bath. A short walk around the lake brings you to Yellow Breeches Outfitters, an outstanding fly-fishing emporium.

[**E A S T**]

The Inn at Manchester

M a n c h e s t e r ,   V e r m o n t

Orvis and the Batten Kill are within easy walking distance of this bed-and-breakfast.

VITAL STATISTICS:

KEY SPECIES:
Brookies, browns

Tackle:
Fly-fishing, spinning
Major Season:
April through November
Accommodations:
Framed Colonial filled with antiques
Number of Rooms: 18
Maximum Number of Guests: 40
Meals: Scrumptious breakfasts; dinners in town
Conference Groups: Yes
Rates: From $129
Guides: From $300 / day
Gratuities: Angler's discretion
Preferred Payment:
Cash, check or credit cards
Getting There:
Fly to Albany and rent a car.
Other Activities:
Canoeing/kayaking/rafting, golf, hiking, skiing, swimming

Contact:
Stan Rosenberg
The Inn at Manchester
Historic Rt. 7A, Box 41
Manchester VT 05254
Ph: 800/273-1793
Fax: 802/362-3218
e-mail:
imahevermonte.com
Web:
www.innatmanchester.com

LIKE ALL NATIVE NEW ENGLANDERS, the Batten Kill River is friendly but reserved. Met halfway, it will gladly show you its treasures: brookies in the upper runs below East Dorset, and browns which become more prominent as the river moves down the valley into and through Manchester. Below this quaint and lovely Vermont town, the water grows with the inflows from Lye, Mill Brooks and Roaring Fork. Yet rather than gaining speed, the Batten Kill deepens and seems to flow like syrup from the maples along its course. This is the water made immortal by generations of writers and a pair of artists: John Atherton and Ogden Pleisner. In the mileage from Dorset down, you want to fish sulphurs in June, Blue-winged Olives from July into August, and tricos and terrestrials well into fall. A three-weight is dandy medicine on this stretch.

Breaking for the west at Arlington, the Batten Kill shallows, widens and turns on the gas. Easy riffles separate long pools with an occasional rocky rapid and undercut or rocky bank. Browns in this run, and that to the New York border, tend to be a bit smaller than the denizens who lie in the dark waters above Arlington. Fish the river all the way to the state line. Spinner fans who toss Panther Martins and little Mepps, and who dredge tiny Rapalas through long slow pools will be quite successful. Ultralight is the name of the game here — two- to four-pound-test line, and lures of 1/32 to 1/8 ounce.

While the Inn at Manchester is not a fishing lodge, per se, it is a place where anglers stay. Why? For one, the Orvis headquarters' store is within walking distance. Check out their three-day fly-fishing schools, a bargain at $395. Also within a stone's throw is the Batten Kill. Walk down Union Street, past the golf course, and you'll come to a bridge spanning the creek. Downstream from the bridge, stretching for almost a mile, is the fly-fishing-only section. Fish through dusk, treat yourself and someone special to dinner in one of the many excellent restaurants in this colonial town, sleep well and be on the stream with the next day's sun.

A white Victorian, The Inn at Manchester dates from the 1880s, when the town was in its prime as a summer vacation resort. With 18 guest rooms (four in the carriage house), all with private baths, the inn offers turn-of-the-century serenity. It is a bed-and-breakfast, to be sure, but in late afternoons tea is served along with such delights as homemade apricot/cheese pound cake and plum cake.

SOUTH

ALABAMA, ARKANSAS, DELAWARE, FLORIDA, GEORGIA, KENTUCKY, LOUISIANA, MARYLAND, MISSISSIPPI, NORTH CAROLINA, SOUTH CAROLINA, TENNESSEE, TEXAS, VIRGINIA, WEST VIRGINIA

THE SOUTH is full of mountain streams with wild brookies painted so bright you'd think they were wildflowers; frigid tailwaters teeming with heavy browns and rainbows; riffle-pool rivers of the foothills alive with smallmouth bass; sprawling lakes and reservoirs with record-class largemouth bass; and flats where bonefish and permit cruise and tarpon wait just to bust your gear. Add landlocked striped bass, muskies, walleyes, sauger and huge blue and flathead catfish. Bluefish, striped bass and sea trout highlight fishing off northern beaches. Snook and redfish predominate around Florida and into the Gulf. Offshore, it's tuna, marlin, cobia, wahoo and sharks. Accommodations vary from quiet marina motels to elegant lodges.

Lodges:

Alabama
1 WHITE OAK PLANTATION (69)

Arkansas
2 ANDERSON HOUSE INN (71)
3 GASTON'S WHITE RIVER RESORT (72)
4 PJ'S LODGE (73)

Florida
5 ANGLER'S MARINA (74)
6 BIENVILLE PLANTATION (76)
7 CHEECA LODGE (77)
8 FARO BLANCO RESORT (78)
9 FLAMINGO LODGE (79)
10 THE FLORIDIAN SPORTS CLUB (80)
11 HAWK'S CAY RESORT AND MARINA (82)
12 ROD & GUN CLUB (83)
13 ROLAND MARTIN MARINA AND RESORT (84)
14 'TWEEN WATERS INN (85)

Georgia
15 BRIGADOON LODGE (86)
16 CALLAWAY GARDENS (87)
17 HIGHLAND MARINA & RESORT (88)
18 THE LODGE AT CABIN BLUFF (89)
19 THE LODGE AT LITTLE ST. SIMON'S ISLAND (90)
20 THE LODGE AT SMITHGALL WOODS (92)

Kentucky
21 LAKE BARKLEY STATE RESORT PARK

Maryland
22 GUNPOWDER B&B (94)

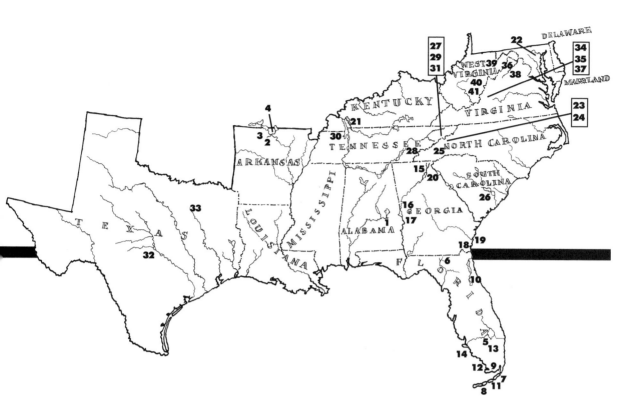

References:

BASS FISHING IN NORTH CAROLINA

FLY FISHING IN NORTH CAROLINA
by Buck Paysour
Down Home Press
PO Box 4126
Asheboro, NC 27204
910/672-6889

NORTHEAST GUIDE TO
SALTWATER FISHING & BOATING

SOUTHEAST GUIDE TO
SALTWATER FISHING & BOATING
Vin T. Sparano, Editor
International Marine/McGraw-Hill
Companies
Customer Service Department
PO Box 547
Blacklick, OH 43004
800/822-8158

SMOKY MOUNTAINS
TROUT FISHING GUIDE
FLY-FISHING GUIDE TO THE
GREAT SMOKY MOUNTAINS
by Don Kirk
Menasha Ridge Press
700 South St., Ste. 206
Birmingham, AL 35233
800/247-9437

THE FLY FISHERMAN'S
GUIDE TO THE GREAT SMOKY
MOUNTAINS NATIONAL PARK
by H. Lea Lawrence
Cumberland House Publishing
431 Harding Industrial Drive
Nashville, TN 37211
615-832-1171

TROUT FISHING IN THE
SHENANDOAH NATIONAL PARK
by Harry W. Murray
Shenandoah Publishing Co
PO Box 156
Edinburg, VA 22824
703/984-4212

[S O U T H]

VIRGINIA TROUT STREAMS
by Harry Slone
TAILWATER TROUT IN THE SOUTH
TROUT STREAMS OF SOUTHERN
APPALACHIA
by Jimmy Jacobs
Backcountry Publications
The Countryman Press
Rt. 2, PO Box 748
Woodstock, VT 05091
802/457-4826

FRESHWATER FISHING IN VIRGINIA
by Gerald Almy
Virginia Heritage Publications
Casco Communications
PO Box 933
Warrenton, VA 22186
540/347-1568

FISHING IN FLORIDA
by Kris Thoemke
Falcon Press
PO Box 1718
Helena, MT 59624
800/582-2665

FLORIDA FISHING :
FLORIDA'S COMPLETE SALTWATER
FISHING GUIDE
by Allen Applegarth, Robin Voshardt, Ed.
Southern Heritage Press
P.O. Box 10937
St. Petersburg, FL 33733
800/282-2823

FLY FISHING THE TEXAS COAST
by Chuck Scates & Phil H. Shook
Pruett Publishing Co
7464 Arapahoe Road, Ste. A-9
Boulder, CO 80303-1500
303/449-4919

Resources:

ALABAMA DEPARTMENT OF
CONSERVATION AND NATURAL
RESOURCES
Div. of Game and Fish, Wildlife Section
PO Box 301456
Montgomery, AL 36130
334/242-3469
web: www.dcnr.state.al.us/agfd

DELAWARE DIVISION OF FISH
AND WILDLIFE
Wildlife Section
Dover, DE 19901
302/739-3441
web: www.dnrec.state.de.us

FLORIDA GAME AND FRESH WATER
FISH COMMISSION
620 S. Meridian
Tallahassee, FL 32399-1600
904/488-1960
web: www.state.fl.us/gfc/

GEORGIA WILDLIFE RESOURCES
DIVISION
2070 U.S. Hwy. 278 SE
Social Circle, GA 30025
770/918-6400
web: www.dnr.state.ga.us/

KENTUCKY DEPARTMENT OF FISH
AND WILDLIFE RESOURCES
#1 Game Farm Rd
Frankfort, KY 40601
502/564-3400
web:
www.state.ky.us/agencies/fw/kdfwr.htm

LOUISIANA DEPARTMENT OF
WILDLIFE AND FISHERIES
Box 98000
Baton Rouge, LA 70898-9000
504-765-2800
web: www.wlf.state.la.us

MARYLAND DEPARTMENT OF
NATURAL RESOURCES
Wildlife & HeritageDivision
E-1 580 Taylor Ave.
Annapolis, MD 21401
410/260-8540
web: www.dnr.state.md.us

MISSISSIPPI DEPARTMENT OF WILDLIFE,
FISHERIES AND PARKS
Box 451
Jackson, MS 39205
601/362-9212
web: www.mdwfp.com

NORTH CAROLINA WILDLIFE
RESOURCES COMMISSION
Division of Wildlife Management
512 N. Salisbury St
Raleigh, NC 27604-1188
919/733-7291
web:
www.state.nc.us/wildlife/management

SOUTH CAROLINA DEPARTMENT
OF NATURAL RESOURCES
Division of Wildlife and Freshwater
Fisheries
Box 167
Columbia, SC 29202
803/734-3889
web: www.dnr.state.sc.us

TENNESSEE WILDLIFE
RESOURCES AGENCY
Box 40747
Nashville, TN 37204
615/781-6500
web: www.state.tn.us/twra

TEXAS PARKS AND WILDLIFE
DEPARTMENT
4200 Smith School Rd
Austin, TX 78744
512/389-4505
web: www.tpwd.state.tx.us/

VIRGINIA DEPARTMENT OF GAME
AND INLAND FISHERIES
4010 W. Broad St
Box 11104
Richmond, VA 23230-1104
804/367-1000
web: www.dgif.state.va.us

WEST VIRGINIA DIVISION OF
NATURAL RESOURCES
Building 3, Room 819
1900 Kanawah Blvd. E
Charleston, WV 25305
304/558-2771
web: www.dnr.state.wv.us

White Oak Plantation

T u s k e g e e ,   A l a b a m a

Well, what's it gonna be? Quail, turkey,
big ol' bucks, or bass with mouths the size of buckets.

VITAL STATISTICS:

KEY SPECIES:
Bream, catfish, largemouth

Tackle:
Casting, fly-fishing, spinning
Major Season:
All year
Accommodations:
BOARD AND BATTEN LODGE
NUMBER OF ROOMS: 9
HANDICAPPED ACCESSIBLE: 2
MAXIMUM NUMBER OF GUESTS: 18
Meals: Hearty southern cooking
Conference Groups: Yes
Rates: From $125 / day
Guides: Optional
Gratuities: Angler discretion
Preferred Payment:
Cash, check or credit cards
Getting There:
Fly to Montgomery and rent a car.
Other Activities:
Big game, wingshooting, bird-watching,
wildlife photography, sporting clays

Contact:
Robert Pitman
White Oak Plantation
5215 County Rd. 10
Tuskegee AL 36083
Ph: 334/727-9258
Fax: 334/727-3411
e-mail:
whiteoakhunts@mindspring.com
Web:
www.americaoutdoors.com/woak

SWEET MUSIC comes from the fencerow, a pair of repeated notes followed by a third that rises and lingers in the soft morning light. As if directed by a grand concert master, bobwhite's fading song cues the raucous laugh of a tom who's advertising his wares with the authority of a prize fighter. You bagged your turkey yesterday morning, a nice bird with a 10-inch beard, and so you're rocking on the front porch, belly full of breakfast. That's when the expanding rings near the rushes by the side of the pond catch your attention. Bass!

You got it right. While most folks don't think of bass when they think of this lodge deep in Alabama's black-belt, there are few hunting lodges down here that offer better fishing. The reason — ponds established for wildlife. The ponds hold largemouths averaging two to four pounds. Once a week, someone gets hot and boats one that pushes eight pounds, and every season a lunker of 10-pounds-plus gets caught-and-released.

When he was building the resort, Bo Pitman put in the eight ponds and stocked them with largemouths. The lakes weren't fished for a while so the bass could become acclimated and grow. Today, the fishing pressure is not what you'd call heavy. Some guests bring rods (or you may rent them at the plantation), and walk the banks in the evening, tossing crankbaits or topwater plugs at the cover. You don't need a boat, but a few with electric motors are available. Along with bass, shellcrackers, bluegills and catfish also live in these waters. Pitman is working closely with biologists from Auburn University to develop a balanced fishery. In addition to casual angling, White Oak also holds schools on fly-fishing for bass.

If you go to White Oak to fish (or plan to fish while you hunt), you might want to take some of those old lures, the one's your daddy and granddaddy used. If you've got an old steel rod and a vintage level-wind reel, take that too. Pitman is into antique tackle. In fact, he's planning a bass tourney wherein gear from the 1950s and earlier will be the only legal tackle. How's that for a backlash?

The lodge, low and long, is not large. This is not a classic Southern plantation house, but its nine paneled rooms give you that warm, down-home feeling. All rooms have private baths and open onto the covered front porch. Good southern meals are served in the restaurant. Various hunting, shooting, youth conservation and fishing packages are available.

Lakefront cabins at Santee State Park on Lake Marion are designed for anglers who want to be close to those big ol' rock fish and largemouth for which this lake is known worldwide.

The Jodi Foster, Richard Gere movie SOMERSBY was filmed at this meticulously restored Greek Revival mansion, which in real life is the Hidden Valley Inn on the upper mileage of the Jackson River, one of TU's 100 best trout streams.

Anderson House Inn

Record book trout and great golf are just minutes away from this quaint bed-and-breakfast.

VITAL STATISTICS:

KEY SPECIES:
Brookies, browns, cutthroat, hybrid bass, rainbows, walleye

Tackle:
Fly-fishing, spinning
Major Season:
All year
Accommodations:
RESTORED COUNTRY VICTORIAN
NUMBER OF ROOMS: 15
MAXIMUM NUMBER OF GUESTS: 36
Meals: Hearty breakfasts and dinners by special arrangement
Conference Groups: Yes
Rates: From $84 / 2
Guides: $225
Gratuities: 15%
Preferred Payment:
Cash, check or credit cards
Getting There:
Fly to Little Rock and rent a car.
Other Activities:
Wingshooting, boating, canoeing/kayaking/rafting, golf, horseback riding, hiking, swimming, tennis

Contact:
Terry Bryant
Anderson House Inn
201 E. Main St
Heber Springs AR 72543
Ph: 501/362-5266
Fax: 501/362-2326
e-mail:
inkeepr@cswnet.com
Web:
www.yourinn.com

HEBER SPRINGS is a bucolic town about an hour north of Little Rock. Less than a mile away rises Greers Ferry dam, and the tailwater that issues forth below holds record breaking brown trout. How big? Well, the world record brown of 40 pounds, 4 ounces was pulled from these waters one May day in 1992. Larger browns are seen during the spawn, but most serious anglers don't fish for them then. Too much pressure can kill a huge old brown and that, most agree, would be a shame.

Arkansas is known for its great tailwaters: the White below Bull Shoals dam and the Norfork near Mountain Home. These two rivers have less aquatic vegetation and are, as a consequence, much easier to fish. The Little Red is rife with coontail moss, a curse for anglers but a blessing for browns and stocked rainbows. Loaded with crustaceans on which trout feed, the moss provides breaks in the current where trout can rest and cover from predators.

Water weeds make presentation of nymphs difficult. Bill Combs of The Ozark Angler (501/362-3597), an Orvis-endorsed outfitter near Heber Springs, claims that the only way to catch big browns on a fly is to perfect a dead-drift technique imitating the natural movement of the sow bugs. You can't swing a nymph or streamer here: too much grass. But no matter. It fishes well all year. In January and February, rainbows make spawning runs upstream toward the dam; then the browns do the same from September through December. March, April and May can bring higher water, but levels drop in May and June. Those are the best months for fishing Blue-winged Olives and caddis. Otherwise, soft hackles and nymphs are the name of this game. Most anglers will fish from rafts or driftboats, as wading access is limited and the water can rise in a hurry. If you prefer lake fishing, switch to hybrid bass, which feed on schooled shad in Greers Ferry Lake above the dam. When you hook up, the bass will race for bottom. Keeping the fish from reaching the submerged treetops is the only way to win the battle.

The Anderson House is a great place to stay whether you're fishing the lake or the river. First the town's theatre and later a school and then a doctor's clinic, this comfortable inn exhibits carefully restored turn-of-the-last-century charm. Your room will be one of 16, all with private baths. Breakfasts are country hearty and dinners can be arranged by advanced request. Non-anglers will enjoy antiquing in town.

[S O U T H]

Gaston's White River Resort

L a k e v i e w ,   A r k a n s a s

Fly your own plane into this quintessential Ozark River resort, then go tussle with the browns.

VITAL STATISTICS:

KEY SPECIES:
Browns, cutthroat, rainbows, smallmouth

Tackle:
Casting, fly-fishing, spinning
Major Season:
All year
Accommodations:
RIVERFRONT COTTAGES
NUMBER OF ROOMS: 74
HANDICAPPED ACCESSIBLE: 10
MAXIMUM NUMBER OF GUESTS: 250
Meals: Full-service restaurant
Conference Groups: Yes
Rates: From $80
Guides: Additional
Gratuities: $10 - $20 / day
Preferred Payment:
Cash, check or credit cards
Getting There:
Fly to Mountain Home and rent a car.
Other Activities:
Bird-watching, boating, golf, hiking, swimming, tennis, wildlife photography

Contact:
Jim Gaston
Gaston's White River Resort
1 River Rd
Lakeview AR 72642
Ph: 870/431-5202
Fax: 870/431-5215
e-mail:
gastons@mtnhome.com
Web:
www.gastons.com

WHEN FOLKS GET TO THINKING about Arkansas' White River, they think of big browns and rainbows in the tailwaters of the dams along the river's course. Fished year-round, these are the waters of record book trout, and the best way to fish for them is in a johnboat, lazily drifting along with the current.

Fishing is taken seriously here. When you book a cottage, you also get a 20-foot johnboat. Rent a 10-horse motor and you're in business for fishing this outstanding tailwater. Releases from Bull Shoals dam, a few miles upstream from the resort, are a constant 55°F. Even in the dog days of summer, the water warms less than 1°F per mile downstream from the dam. That promotes an abundance of aquatic insects and crustaceans on which browns and rainbows feed. Browns of more than 10 pounds are frequent, while rainbows run to five pounds or so. As is the case with most tailwaters, flows can fluctuate quite a bit. Use your johnboat to reach the shallows you want to fish, but if you see the water rising, climb back into the boat, anchor for a while, and eat a sandwich while you give the fish a chance to adjust to the increased flow.

Fishing is generally good here year-round, but most trophy browns are taken in the dead of winter. From November 1 through January 31, from the base of the dam to the downstream boundary of Bull Shoals State Park, brown trout are strictly catch-and-release and may be taken only with artificial lures carrying a single barbless hook. Cress Bugs, Sulphurs and midges work well, as do Woolly Buggers. Hurlers of hardware will find spinners and imitation minnows effective where they are legal. And while you're at it, don't overlook the smallmouth bass. Another year-round fishery, the best months are March through May, and September and October for bronzebacks up to seven pounds.

"Resort" is just the right word to describe Jim Gaston's place on the White River. Seventy-four cottages (some with fireplaces and wood decks, all with private baths), sleeping from two to 10 guests, string along the river, flanking the main lodge with its river-view restaurant, bar, gift shop, tackle shop and game room. Behind the lodge, nestled in a copse of trees, is a pool and, nearby, tennis courts. Across the road from the cottages is a private landing field with a 3,200-foot grass runway. This place gives a different meaning to the idea of roughing it at an Arkansas fish camp.

PJ's Lodge

Norfork, Arkansas

Among the best year-round rivers in the country are the Norfork and the White, both fished from PJ's fine lodge.

IN THIS LAND OF TAILWATERS, the White and the Norfork (that's a local contraction of North Fork of the White) are always top ranked. Conditions in the highly alkaline water couldn't be better for aquatic insects on which trout feed. Baitfish also gorge on insects, and you know what big trout eat. Dragging streamers of various persuasions will always turn up big trout.

But if you're looking for an ultimate challenge, try the winning combo at PJ's Lodge. Take a nine-foot #2 weight and mount it with a reel carrying a weight-forward floating line. Bend on a 12-foot leader that tapers to 6x. Use weighted nymphs, no. 16 and smaller, and cast with finesse. In November and December, spawning 10-pound browns and five-pound rainbows will wear you out. Rainbows spawning in winter? That's right, they're a little precocious, and remember, both the White and Norfork are tailwater fisheries. They're good all year, but come into their prime when leaves turn russet and a chill braces the air.

While you'll find many that are smaller, a good number of 16- to 26-inch rainbows are caught-and-released each week. Browns in this part of the river have tipped the scales at 39 pounds. November through January are especially good for the rainbows, though they crank up again for traditional hatches from March through August. Browns peak from December through January and later in March and April. In addition, you can fish for brook trout and cutthroats year-round (trophy cuts up to 10 pounds have been landed in November through January). You may also want to test your fly tackle against striped bass in the lake from December through March, or catch them on trolled baits year-round. Fly-fishers prefer to wade while baitfishers generally drift the river. Opportunities to freelance, that is to fish without a guide, are legion, but it makes sense to use a guide for a couple of days to get the lay of the water.

PJ's lodge is a perennial favorite with anglers. Wood, glass and vistas overlooking the White River give this 10-guestroom (with private baths) hideaway a distinctly western flavor. This is emphasized with Paul and wife Joyce's expanding interest in raising Pasco Finos, a horse of Spanish and Central American lineage noted for its easy riding and fine gait. Trailer your horse, put him up in one of Paul's new stalls, ride some of the trails in the nearby national forest, and see if you can work out a way to fish the river from horseback.

[S O U T H]

Angler's Marina

C l e w i s t o n ,   F l o r i d a

In this old fishing town, you'll find the best catfish and hush puppies around — and a few darn big bass, too.

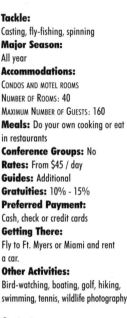

FLORIDA WAS once a farming state with big ranches stretched across palmetto flats. Houses were made of pine board and roofed with tin, and about the only entertainment was listening to the big console radio with the dials that glowed when you tuned in a station. Progress has wiped most of old Florida from the map, except in little towns like Clewiston which perches on the south end of Lake Okeechobee.

Agriculture is still big business here, and ranchers and farmers bump elbows with anglers who come for big bass in the Big O. While smaller Florida lakes may produce bigger bass, Okeechobee's 750 square miles of shallow water grows huge numbers of largemouth. Why? For a bass, the lake is like a huge feed lot. Every patch of lily pads or reeds holds hundreds of baitfish, growing fat in the warm nutritious water. It seems as if there's so much food that all a largemouth has to do is swim around with its mouth open. Average bass run in the three- to five-pound range. That means you'll catch a lot of one- to three-pound bass, but you're bound to pick up one or two in the five- to seven-pound range to equal things out. A 10-pounder is a good fish in Okeechobee, just like it is anywhere else.

Okeechobee fishes well all year, too. During cooler weather, bass are on the move and maybe a little more aggressive. When temperatures climb and south-central Florida can feel like an inferno, bass hang out in the coolest, shadiest water they can find. You can catch bruisers in summer, but they are harder to locate. That's where a good guide and a good map, like the one put out by The Map Maker (941/983-5741), comes in. Most anglers use casting tackle, but fly-rodders find success. Light tackle fans will have field days on bluegills, crappies and shell-crackers.

Angler's Marina offers full boating services, including launch, slips, rentals (14-footers and pontoon boats), sales and service. Tackle and guides are also available. Surrounding the marina are 26 rental condominiums and a dozen efficiency motel rooms, all clean, quiet and tastefully decorated. Condos have two bedrooms and two baths, as well as a kitchen; the motel units include kitchenettes. If you don't feel like cooking, drive over to the Clewiston Inn for dinner or check out the quaint Old South barbecue for its fried catfish and hush puppies.

VITAL STATISTICS:

KEY SPECIES:
Bream, crappie, largemouth

Tackle:
Casting, fly-fishing, spinning
Major Season:
All year
Accommodations:
CONDOS AND MOTEL ROOMS
NUMBER OF ROOMS: 40
MAXIMUM NUMBER OF GUESTS: 160
Meals: Do your own cooking or eat in restaurants
Conference Groups: No
Rates: From $45 / day
Guides: Additional
Gratuities: 10% - 15%
Preferred Payment:
Cash, check or credit cards
Getting There:
Fly to Ft. Myers or Miami and rent a car.
Other Activities:
Bird-watching, boating, golf, hiking, swimming, tennis, wildlife photography

Contact:
Manager
Angler's Marina
910 Okeechobee Blvd
Clewiston FL 33440
Ph: 800/741-3141
Fax: 863/983-4613
e-mail:
info@anglersmarina.com
Web:
www.anglersmarina.com

Anglers at 'Tween Waters Inn, located between the Gulf of Mexico and Pine Island Sound, fish for snook, tarpon and red fish from their base on Florida's Captiva Island.

When Bass Pro Shops founder Johnny Morris went looking for the best bass retreat, he found it at The Floridian Sports Club on the St. John's River.

[S O U T H]

Bienville Plantation

White Springs, Florida

Not far from Stephen Foster's Suwanee sprawls this ultimate fishing and hunting resort.

VITAL STATISTICS:

KEY SPECIES:
Bream, crappie, largemouth

Tackle:
Casting, fly-fishing
Major Season:
All year
Accommodations:
FIVE LAKESIDE LOG HOMES
NUMBER OF ROOMS: 25
HANDICAPPED ACCESSIBLE: 5
MAXIMUM NUMBER OF GUESTS: 50
Meals: Excellent regional cuisine
Conference Groups: Yes
Rates: From $120 / night / 2
Guides: From $200 / 1/2 day
Gratuities: $25 - $100 / group
Preferred Payment:
Cash, check or credit cards
Getting There:
Fly to Jacksonville and rent a car.
Other Activities:
Big game, waterfowling,
wingshooting, trap

Contact:
Manager
Bienville Plantation
County Road 137
White Springs FL 32096
Ph: 904/397-1989
Fax: 904/397-2981
e-mail:
bienville1@aol.com
Web:
www.bienville.com

WITH MORE THAN 15,000 ACRES about an hour and a half west of Jacksonville, there's plenty of room here to do whatever turns you on: fishing for bass or crappie; working pointers for wild and pen-raised quail; sitting in a stand and watching whitetails step gingerly into feed lots; or hunkering down in a duck blind as the morning flights of mallards and teal slice into your spread.

Bass fishing is a year-round proposition here. A half-day on one of more than a dozen lakes will bring 15 to 20 good bass, and that means two pounds and up, to net. Many will be in the three- to five-pound class, and you may even tangle with some better than that. Bream run to a pound plus and crappie two to three times that. You'll name your own poison; casting gear is preferred, but on a number of ponds, working big green fly-fished poppers near the lily pads and hyacinths will provoke strikes that you'll dream about all year.

The deal here is to mix bass fishin' with an afternoon quail hunt. Use Bienville's dogs or your own. Plan it for March or October. Or, what the heck, come down in January and mix in a little duck, deer and hog hunting. A pro shop on site sells everything you need. Guides are available and most use fully-equipped bass boats.

Accommodations can only be called plush. Five log houses are set on points and coves overlooking one of the lakes. Each contains five bedrooms for two guests each. Each room is served by its own private bath. A small kitchen complements a large sitting room with fireplace, and a screened porch opens onto the lake. You don't, of course, have to do your own cooking. The main lodge holds a fine restaurant where the likes of duck with raspberry sauce, veal merlot and fine angus tenderloin are served nightly. Breakfasts are so hearty that you've gotta walk them off before you get in the boat.

Cheeca Lodge

Islamorada, Florida

The breeze blows in from the sea, a perpetual cooling fan, as you fish for bonefish to your heart's delight.

VITAL STATISTICS:

KEY SPECIES:
Bonefish, dolphin/dorado, jack crevalle, mackerel, marlin, permit, redfish, sailfish, sea trout, shark, snook, tarpon, tuna, wahoo, kingfish, cobia

Tackle:
Casting, fly-fishing, spinning, trolling
Major Season:
All year
Accommodations:
RESORT HOTEL AND COTTAGES
NUMBER OF ROOMS: 203
HANDICAPPED ACCESSIBLE: 1
MAXIMUM NUMBER OF GUESTS: 600
Meals: Fine regional cuisine
Conference Groups: Yes
Rates: From $195 / night / 2
Guides: $350
Gratuities: 20%
Preferred Payment:
Cash, check or credit cards
Getting There:
Fly to Miami and rent a car.
Other Activities:
Bird-watching, boating, canoeing/kayaking/rafting, golf, swimming, tennis, diving

Contact:
Manager
Cheeca Lodge
Mile Marker 82
PO Box 527
Islamorada FL 33036
Ph: 305/644-4651
Fax: 305/664-2893
e-mail:
cheecalodge@aol.com
Web:
www.cheeca.com

THEY CALLED IT the overseas highway, that ribbon of concrete that streams south from Florida City. You flew into Miami this morning, a Saturday, and collected the cheapest rental car you could find. After freeing yourself from the airport traffic, you nosed west on the 836 to the parkway, then south through the tolls to U.S. 1. Not far now. Upper Metacumbe is another half an hour south. A glimpse of surf to the left. First good look, though, comes at the first bridge below Plantation. Another bridge, and then the water is with you. Cheeca Lodge is up ahead.

You're about a third of the way down that 100-mile chain of limestone islands that swings west from mainland Florida. It's October. Back in Rochester, leaves are yellow and red and that first day of cold gray rain let you know what's in store. But here it's 85 degrees, with a light wind from the east. Summer and green. By 2:00 you're on the water in a 17-foot skiff poled by a guide who must smell bonefish like a pointer finds quail, because you sure as hell can't see 'em. He tells you to look through the water, not for the fish, but for its shadow. There! Got it. Haul, one back cast, haul again, shoot that Crazy Charlie eight feet ahead of the tailing bone. Good. Watch him come. Get ready. His fins quiver and you think he's got it and eagerly set the hook. Nothing there but a muddy swirl where he was. You wipe your face with a rag. Patience. There'll be other bonefish.

March through June, and August through October, are best for bones on the backcountry flats, plus tarpon. November brings sailfish and kingfish on the Atlantic side and reds in the backcountry. Sailfish peak at the end of the year, but they're still around the reefs in January before moving offshore. Marlin pick up in May and peak in June.

Cheeca Lodge, about halfway down the Keys on Islamorada, is in the center of this fishery. A full day's offshore trip for up to six runs from $700 to $800. A full day for two, for bones, tarpon or reds in the backcountry, is about $350. Or fish for snapper from a party boat for $50 a day. Winner of the AAA's Four Diamond Award, Cheeca is an island of tranquility in the frenzy of the Keys. Rooms, either ocean view or garden view, are located in the main lodge or in island-style villas close by. All are air-conditioned, and many open onto private balconies. Dining is first class, whether in the award-winning Atlantic's Edge or Ocean Terrace Grill.

[S O U T H]

Faro Blanco Resort

Marathon, Florida

Epicenter for flats and offshore angling, Marathon's the place where dedicated anglers go for spring break.

VITAL STATISTICS:

KEY SPECIES:
Bonefish, dolphin/dorado, marlin, permit, redfish, sea trout, shad, snook, tarpon, tuna, snapper, grouper, wahoo

Tackle:
Casting, fly-fishing, spinning, trolling
Major Season:
March through December
Accommodations:
CONDOS, COTTAGES, HOUSEBOATS AND A LIGHTHOUSE
NUMBER OF ROOMS: 99
MAXIMUM NUMBER OF GUESTS: 200+
Meals: Choice of three restaurants
Conference Groups: Yes
Rates: From $79
Guides: $200+
Gratuities:
Angler's discretion
Preferred Payment:
Cash, check or credit cards
Getting There:
Fly to Marathon or Miami and rent a car.
Other Activities:
Bird-watching, boating, canoeing/kayaking/rafting, golf, hiking, swimming, tennis, wildlife photography

Contact:
Faro Blanco Resort
1996 Overseas Hwy
Marathon FL 33050
Ph: 305/743-9018
Fax: 305/743-2918

I T ISN'T JUST COLLEGE STUDENTS who flock to Florida for spring break. It's every mother's son or daughter who's infected with angling wanderlust. You might say that Marathon — half way down Florida's chain of keys — is overrun by anglers in spring. They have just cause. From April through June, there's bonefish and permit on the flats and tarpon in the channels in between. Offshore, dolphin, sailfish, blackfin tuna and a few marlin slam trolled baits. Reefs and wrecks hold snapper and grouper, and an hour's boat ride will cover the 22 miles up to Flamingo in Florida Bay for backcountry snook, redfish, tripletail, weakfish and virtually every member of the snapper family.

Because of the crowds of anglers, flats fishing in the Keys is often disparaged in favor of the Bahamas, a few score miles east and south. There is a difference to be sure: you'll find fewer anglers in the Bahamas, and you'll find more fish, but they are smaller. In the Keys, big schools of bones number 20 to 30, but you'll find many more six- to ten-pounders. And there seems to be ample acreage on the flats so anglers don't have to stand shoulder to shoulder as they do on some trout streams we won't name. In the Keys, your chances of hooking a 10 pound bone are reasonably good; what you do then is another matter. Most anglers fish from flats boats, poled by a guide. In all but a few places, the bottom is too soft to wade with comfort. While resident tarpon are plentiful, bigger fish move onto the flats in spring. Permit are also present, especially over wrecks, but also on the edges of flats. A fly-fisherman out for a grand slam stands about a 25 percent chance, and the odds for spin fishermen are even better.

From quite a distance, you'll see Faro Blanco's tall white lighthouse sticking up above everything else that lines the Overseas Highway that links Florida's Keys. Faintly New England in style, the lighthouse was originally built as a bit of hokey tourist hype which attracted motorists to the resort. Serves the same purpose today. Even so, Faro Blanco's long been a destination for winter-weary anglers. Stay in stuccoed cottages on the Gulf side, or in elegant three-bedroom and two-bath condos, on houseboats permanently moored to the dock or in the lighthouse itself. Some accommodations feature kitchens; all have cable TV, phone and private bath. Three restaurants cater to every palate. At the marina, you can arrange for a guide, buy bait and tackle, or rent a boat and have a go all by yourself.

Flamingo Lodge

Flamingo, Florida

Snook, tarpon, redfish and sea trout (and others) lurk in the flats and mangroves around this lodge in the Everglades.

VITAL STATISTICS:

KEY SPECIES:
Jack crevalle, largemouth, redfish, sea trout, shark, snook, tarpon

Tackle:
Casting, fly-fishing, spinning, trolling
Major Season:
All year
Accommodations:
MOTEL ROOMS AND COTTAGES
NUMBER OF ROOMS: 127
HANDICAPPED ACCESSIBLE: 2
MAXIMUM NUMBER OF GUESTS: 250
Meals: Florida regional cuisine in the lodge restaurant
Conference Groups: Yes
Rates: From $65 / night
Guides: Available
Gratuities: $25 / day
Preferred Payment:
Cash, check or credit cards
Getting There:
Fly to Miami and rent a car.
Other Activities:
Bird-watching, boating, canoeing/kayaking/rafting, hiking, swimming, wildlife photography, houseboat rental

Contact:
Jennifer Huber
Flamingo Lodge
1 Flamingo Dr
Flamingo FL 33034
Ph: 941/695-3101
Fax: 941/695-3921
e-mail:
everglad@ix.netcom.com
Web:
www.flamingolodge.com

HEN THE SEMINOLE WARS ended in the late 1850s, drifters and dreamers began attempting to subdue the Everglades. It was warm all year. Fresh water was in abundance even if dry land was a little limited. You'd think it'd be a great place to grow tomatoes in winter. Ship them down to Key West (then the state's largest city), and put 'em on a boat for New York. Hard work, but the money was good. And if you weren't into farming, or harvesting plumes of egrets, wood storks and spoonbills wasn't your thing, then there was always fishing.

And there still is. Flamingo has it all, save bonefish and blue water species. Snook, tarpon, redfish, sea trout, a dozen different varieties of snapper, jacks and lady fish, and up in the park where the water is fresher, largemouth bass and bream that'll make a believer of you. Inshore waters, often only a few inches deep at low tide, gave birth to the open-decked flats boat. Sportfishermen make longer runs to deeper waters. A dam and lock at Flamingo gives boaters access to a network of canals, including the 99-mile wilderness waterway that wends through a maze of brackish lakes and rivers to Everglades City on the western edge of the national park.

You'll need a boat to fish the area near Flamingo as shore fishing is virtually nonexistent. You can charter a guide for either bay or backcountry fishing. Other options include renting a houseboat, aluminum boat and motor, or canoe. The season for snook, the premiere fish here, is closed from December 15 to January 31 and again from June through August. Sea trout is closed in November and December, but other species are available year-round. Angling for redfish is best from August to December, tarpon from May to August. Sea trout turn on in spring and snapper in fall and winter.

Flamingo Lodge is open all year. You'll find cheerful motel-style rooms that face the bay and a colony of housekeeping cottages. The full-service restaurant in the visitor's center features regional cuisine. A screened pool keeps ever-present mosquitoes at bay, but outside in the summer (when the fishing's best, naturally), you'll be glad you wore long-sleeve light-colored cotton shirts and poplin trousers.

The Floridian Sports Club

W e l a k a ,   F l o r i d a

Bass Pro founder Johnny Morris has a great lodge on the St. John's. Check in and enjoy great largemouth!

FLOWING NORTH for more than 300 miles, St. John's River shadows Florida's Atlantic coast before dumping into the sea at Jacksonville. It is a river of bass, mainly, but snook, shad, crappie and fat bream form the supporting cast. A growing number of cheap flights into Orlando and Jacksonville via various cut-rate carriers make these waters quite accessible. Rental cars are more reasonably priced in Orlando than in many other markets. Here, a fly/drive/fish vacation won't break your bank.

But where to fish the river? If big bass are your meat, and you're not too proud to fish with bait, then a junket to Welaka, Fla. might be in your cards. Roughly 10 miles downstream from the mouth of Lake George, this dot on the map is two hours north of Orlando and an hour south of Jacksonville. In this reach, the St. Johns is swelled with the flow from the Ocklawaha River via Rodman Reservoir and constricts a bit as it flows around Turkey Isles. On the west, the river is bounded by the Ocala National Forest. To the east rises the high bank of the coastal plain, and along its rim, you'll find a number of fishing lodges. The best of them is The Floridian Sports Club, owned by Bass Pro's John L. Morris.

May and June will probably yield the most fish, fall and winter, the biggest. Anglers who insist on using lures will have the most success fishing beds in March and April. If you're fleeing a Yankee winter, try to time your fishing here for the two or three days in advance of a cold front, and avoid the high pressure immediately behind it. Your odds of hooking a behemoth of 10 pounds plus are greater in winter. From Hanukkah to George Washington's Birthday — which more or less signals the beginning of the spawn — big ol' bass are interested in one thing. Drag a seven-inch golden shiner in range of their littoral line, and you're likely to have a customer.

Most of the riverfront motels along the St. John's are children of the 1950s, and many are showing some age. But not The Floridian Sports Club. Set in arboretum-like grounds beneath venerable live oaks and sweet gums draped with Spanish moss, the club's oyster white stuccoed cottages rim a modestly high bluff overlooking Welaka Spring where snook and manatee play in winter. Accommodations border on luxurious. Standard rooms include a pair of queen size beds, separate dressing rooms, and baths with Jacuzzis. Wet bars, fridges, coffee makers and stovetops are typical. Two-bedroom or three-bedroom cottages are available. And if romance is on your card, ask about Johnny Morris' suite with the sauna and private screened porch.

Guest rooms are separated from the main lodges by a gently curving flower-lined walk. Climb the steps to the shady front porch. Open the French doors. Paneled walls carry mounts of gargantuan bass taken with tackle of years gone by. Beneath a row of windows runs a long wooden table where dinners and breakfasts are served family-style (unless you opt to dine in your room). A stone fireplace climbs the wall across from the dining table, and in front of it sits an overstuffed sofa. If it's chilly, this is the place for the day's postmortems. Otherwise, take your libation out on the porch, sink yourself in one of the wicker rockers beneath a lazy ceiling fan, and watch the rises in the lagoon down the hill.

Hawk's Cay Resort and Marina

D u c k   K e y ,   F l o r i d a

$50 million in renovations have made angling and fishing from this Florida Key just ducky.

ITH 60 ACRES on a private island in the midst of Florida's Keys, at Hawk's Cay you can have it all. Five pools, tennis, golf, sailing, diving, beach combing, shopping — here there's never a dull moment. Unless you want one. Just hang out on the screened porch of your condo or under the palms on a shaded deck overlooking the bay. You don't have to go fishing, but if you do, you'll encounter some of the best in the southeast.

Offshore, sailfish of 30 to 60 pounds and kingfish of 10 to 20 are most active in January and February. Yellowtails of one to five pounds hit well from November to March. Cobia up to 80 pounds seem to be best in March and April, while dolphin in the five- to 50-pound range hit year-round, but are best in summer. Rates for offshore angling vary, but a party of four can expect to pay about $700 for a full day.

Flats guiding is a little less expensive, running around $400 per day for two. Using fly, spin or bait casting tackle, you will fish flats for bonefish in the six- to 15-pound range from September through November, and February through April. April through May marks the height of tarpon (40 to 150 pounds) season, with permit (10 to 40 pounds) hitting their stride in May. Late April is the best month to try for a grand slam: a tarpon, bone and permit all in one day. Connecting on all three is incredibly tough. Permit are hard to find and more difficult to catch. For the same price, spend a day in the backcountry casting for snook and redfish. The run from Hawk's Cay to the intricate channels among mangrove islands off Everglades National Park takes only an hour or so, and the fishing can be absolutely first class.

Hawk's Cay Resort and Marina keeps a staff of five skippers and guides on hand for both offshore and backcountry fishing. And when you're not out on the water you can expect to be pampered. The flavor of the Caribbean permeates this tropical inn, its colorful public areas complete with paddle fans, wicker and lush foliage. Your room will include a refrigerator and private balcony that views the Atlantic or the Gulf. The range of accommodations includes inn rooms, villas and suites, and the list of packages is extensive. So, too, are dining opportunities. Four restaurants offer menus ranging from gourmet regional cuisine to quick bites. Check out Hawk's Cay's conference facilities as well. Cheap flights to Miami from many northern cities make this an ideal location for meetings that mix business with pleasure.

VITAL STATISTICS:

KEY SPECIES:
Bonefish, dolphin/dorado, grouper, marlin, permit, redfish, sailfish, sea trout, shark, snapper, snook, tarpon, tuna, wahoo

Tackle:
Casting, fly-fishing, spinning, trolling
Major Season:
All year
Accommodations:
INN ROOMS, SUITES, VILLAS
NUMBER OF ROOMS: 334
MAXIMUM NUMBER OF GUESTS: 700+
Meals: Everything from fine dining to fast food
Conference Groups: Yes
Rates: From $190
Guides: $300 up
Gratuities: 15%
Preferred Payment:
Cash, check or credit cards
Getting There:
Fly to Marathon and rent a car.
Other Activities:
Bird-watching, boating, canoeing/kayaking/rafting, diving, golf, hiking, swimming, tennis, wildlife photography

Contact:
Christopher R. Ferguson
Hawk's Cay Resort and Marina
61 Hawk's Cay Blvd
Duck Key FL 33050
Ph: 305/743-7000
Fax: 305/743-5215
e-mail:
c.ferguson@hawkscay.com
Web:
www.hawkscay.com

Rod & Gun Club

Everglades City, Florida

Take the Tamiami to old-time Florida and some of the finest backcountry saltwater fishing in the world.

VITAL STATISTICS:

KEY SPECIES:
Redfish, sea trout, snook, tarpon

Tackle:
Casting, fly-fishing, spinning
Major Season:
All year
Accommodations:
BUNGALOWS AT A FINE OLD LODGE
NUMBER OF ROOMS: 17
MAXIMUM NUMBER OF GUESTS: 34
Meals: Regional cuisine plus great steaks
Conference Groups: Yes
Rates: From $65 / night
Guides: Available from $200 up
Gratuities: Angler's discretion
Preferred Payment:
Cash or check
Getting There:
Fly to Ft. Myers or Miami and rent a car.
Other Activities:
Bird-watching, boating, canoeing/kayaking/rafting, hiking, swimming, tennis, wildlife photography

Contact:
Pat Bowen
Rod & Gun Club
PO Box 190
Everglades City FL 34139
Ph: 941/695-2101

EVERGLADES CITY is a quiet little village, deeply overshadowed in glitz and glamour by Marco Island and Naples to the west. It sits on a bit of flat ground where the Barron River wanders out of the Everglades and mixes with the salt of Chokoloskee Bay. The river is shallow and tannic and the bay is warm. To the southeast are a fringe of mangrove keys called the Ten Thousand Islands. To the north are more brackish rivers. The region holds some of the finest backcountry saltwater fishing in the world, and much of it is as primitive today as it was a century ago — more so, in fact.

How could it be wilder today than 100 years past? Easy. The turn of the last century brought hordes of schemers and dreamers to the Everglades and its keys. Their visions were huge. They planned to drain the Everglades and convert it to lush fields growing tomatoes and other vegetables for insatiable northern markets. Dredges carved canals, railroad spurs were pushed to the coast, plantations were begun anywhere the land stayed above high tide for most of the year. But in the face of hurricanes and the great depression, such grand plans failed and were quickly forgotten. If you look closely enough, you might find a cement cistern overgrown with vines, but otherwise, there's little trace of development. Nature has a way of healing itself.

Gentle backcountry rivers teem with snook and redfish. Farther upstream you'll find largemouth bass, grown feisty with a dash of saltwater. In shallows, tarpon of 100 pounds or more lie like logs, ready to rise to a carefully presented red and white Deceiver or a well-cast mullet bait. In the passes between the islands, sea trout are common and you'll find snapper and grouper hiding in deep holes. It matters not which gear you use: fly, spinning or bait casting, or whether or not you fish artificial or bait. You'll catch fish in these waters throughout the year. Tarpon fishing picks up in mid-March and continues as long as the water temperature is above 70°F. In spring and fall, snook fishing is unparalleled. Redfish, open all year, and sea trout (season varies, check when you get there) are making comebacks, thanks to new slot limits. Most of the waters you'll fish are included within the Everglades National Park

The old frame hotel of The Rod & Gun Club no longer houses guests, but you'll stay in rooms (private baths) in modern bungalows. Sometimes, breakfasts are served on the long screened hotel porch that fronts the Barron River. You can lunch there, too, but dinners are more formal and served inside the high-ceilinged dining room.

[S O U T H]

Roland Martin Marina and Resort

C l e w i s t o n ,   F l o r i d a

Summertime on the Big O means more fish.
Come fall, they're fewer but bigger.

VITAL STATISTICS:

KEY SPECIES:
Bream, crappie, largemouth

Tackle:
Casting, fly-fishing, spinning
Major Season:
All year
Accommodations:
MOTEL ROOMS AND CONDO UNITS
NUMBER OF ROOMS: 69
MAXIMUM NUMBER OF GUESTS: 150
Meals: Self-catered or full-service restaurant
Conference Groups: Yes
Rates: From $58 / night
Guides: Available
Gratuities: $25+
Preferred Payment:
Cash, check or credit cards
Getting There:
Fly to West Palm Beach or Miami and rent a car.
Other Activities:
Bird-watching, boating, swimming

Contact:
Reservations
Roland Martin Marina and Resort
920 E. Del Monte Ave
Clewiston FL 33440
Ph: 941/983-3151
Fax: 941/983-2191
e-mail:
oson@gate.net

LAKE OKEECHOBEE is a big round hole in the center of southern Florida. There's some speculation that it's the crater of an ancient meteor. Whatever caused the lake to form was a godsend to bass anglers everywhere. And truth be told: the hotter the temperature, the hotter the fishing — within reason that is. Though midday temperatures will near 100°F and the fishery shuts down, early mornings and evenings in July and early August provide fabulous action for bass in the two- to four-pound class. Days of 30 to 40 fish caught-and-released are not all that unusual.

A famed fishery since the turn of the century (commercial anglers would net up to 9,000 pounds of catfish a day), Okeechobee was once extremely shallow. A dike system designed to prevent flooding deepened the lake (maximum about 17 feet) and provided more natural structure. Anglers work grass islands, submerged reefs, flooded stumps, stands of reeds and lily pads. Also productive are manmade structures: boat docks, rocky sides of the dikes, numerous channels and marina mouths.

Tackle for Okeechobee can be as simple or sophisticated as you want. Minnows account for a lot of big bass. So do Baby Zara Spooks, Tiny Torpedoes and other topwater plugs. Black weedless spoons dressed with skirts and Texas-rigged worms are still good producers, as are buzzbaits, spinnerbaits and crankbaits fished with slow jerk/pause cadences. Poppers and hairbody bugs do the job for fly-fishermen. And for those not too proud, a little popper or light-colored stonefly nymph can attract bream that will put a good bend in a 4-weight rod.

While it's tempting to fish worms and crankbaits on relatively light tackle, you do so at risk of overstressing your quarry. Fish that are played too long in warm water frequently expire even after they've been released. It makes better sense to use tackle more appropriate to the job at hand. After all, bass from eight to 10 pounds are relatively common, and you'll need stout gear to horse them out of peppergrass flats.

In this area, hostelries that combine quality lodging, dining, bait and tackle, and a full-service marina are scarce. Among the best is Roland Martin's Resort, which accommodates 128 guests in appealing motel rooms, efficiencies and condos. The dock is steps from your door, and tennis and golf are nearby. RV sites are available as well. And all the lures you need can be found in Roland's store.

'Tween Waters Inn

Captiva Island, Florida

Teddy Roosevelt could have slept here, but he was too busy fishing for snook and tarpon.

VITAL STATISTICS:

KEY SPECIES:
Redfish, sea trout, snook, tarpon

Tackle:
Casting, fly-fishing, spinning, trolling
Major Season:
All year
Accommodations:
Motel rooms, efficiencies, condos
Number of Rooms: 137
Handicapped Accessible: 3
Maximum Number of Guests: 300
Meals: Full-service restaurant
Conference Groups: Yes
Rates: From $100 / day
Guides: Available
Gratuities: 15%
Preferred Payment:
Cash, check or credit cards
Getting There:
Fly to Ft. Myers and rent a car.
Other Activities:
Bird-watching, boating, canoeing/kayaking/rafting, swimming, tennis, wildlife photography

Contact:
Frank Scatbo
'Tween Waters Inn
PO Box 249
15951 Captiva Dr
Captiva Island FL 33924
Ph: 941/472-5161
Fax: 941/472-0249
Web:
www.tween-waters.com

CAPTIVA AND SANIBEL, those islands just northwest of Ft. Myers, are marvelous vacation spots, and they have been since the days of Teddy Roosevelt. Snook, tarpon and redfish brought him to these islands, and were he to return, there are places he'd recognize. Here, particularly in Pine Island Sound and San Carlos Bay, it's possible to recapture a bit of the tranquility of Florida before the boom. Snook fishing is particularly good. These voracious linesides, the saltwater equivalent of smallmouth bass, will top 20 pounds. The fishing is best in April and May, and again in September. Check Florida freshwater fisheries for the seasons and limits.

In May and June, you'll also find tarpon averaging 60 to 80 pounds, with some going to 150 pounds or better. Redfish (seven to 12 pounds) are best in summer. Sight casting to these species is especially exciting. Weakfish or sea trout (closed from November through December) provide fast lighttackle action. As for bottomfish, there are groupers up to 20 pounds. Charters and guides are available through the lodge or call Steve Jones (941/278-3564) who runs trips for tarpon, tripletail, snook, redfish, sea trout or any other game fish that will take your line for a ride.

Far removed from the hustle and hype of high-pressure tourism, but still in the orb of civilized accommodations, is the 'Tween Waters Inn on Captiva Island. A narrow sand spit eroding with each tide, Captiva separates the Gulf of Mexico from Pine Island Sound. To the south, nourished by Captiva's sands, is larger Sanibel Island. Both are known as the best shelling beaches in Florida. If you visit Sanibel, you'll want to spend a day at the wonderful wildlife sanctuary, a memorial to J.M. "Ding" Darling, pioneer conservationist and one-time director of the U.S. Fish and Wildlife Service. Winter months bring thousands of wading birds and waterfowl to the sanctuary.

Anglers have been fishing from 'Tween Waters since 1905, then a private fish camp. In the 1930s, guests began staying at "The School House," now the Old Captiva House restaurant (regional cuisine) at 'Tween Waters. Today, this full-service resort and marina offers a range of gulf- and bay-view rooms and efficiencies with kitchenettes. Boats can be launched and moored at the marina. To sample a bit of "Old Florida," check out the housekeeping cottages at The Castaways at Blind Pass, also operated by 'Tween Waters on the northern tip of Sanibel.

Brigadoon Lodge

Clarkesville, Georgia

Fat browns and rainbows hang out in the Soque,
just upstream from Ted Turner's place.

NORTH GEORGIA is one of those amazing angling locales. Its lakes hold largemouth and stripers, many of the rivers run with wild and stocked trout populations, and high in those little rivulets that trickle out of the hazy blue mountains live colonies of fine native brook trout. In short, this land of rolling foothills is a fishing paradise of sorts.

Rebekah Stewart Gauthier has taken a lovely mile plus of the Soque and stocked it with huge 'bows and browns. Fish of a foot and a half are a matter of course here, and two footers aren't all that rare. You don't keep 'em of course. You test drive them, much the way you'd enter a showroom and check out a BMW for a spin. While you're at the wheel, the car belongs to you, but when you return it to the dealership, it goes back on the lot waiting for the next customer. And that's the way with these trout. Otherwise, Rebekah would never be able to maintain more than 5,000 fish per mile.

Coursing over ledges, the river swings through pools and runs. Never more than 25 yards wide, the blocky rock bottom can provide wading with a little challenge, but in the main it's easily mastered. Only at high noon does sun penetrate the deep valley through which the river runs. Novice anglers are required to use guides — to protect the fish, primarily. Experienced hands are given free reign. But never are there more than six rods on the water per day.

Corporate groups vie for choice spring and fall dates at this lodge of stone, glass and wood overlooking the river. You'll find top brass from Georgia Pacific, Ernst & Young, Paine Weber, Caterpillar and the like booking the whole place. No commercial kitchen here — "We're a fish camp," Rebekah laughs — but she's an absolute master at arranging the very best of catered fare from gourmet cuisine to the rarest of single malt scotches and fine cigars of Cuban leaf. Open only in spring and fall — the river is too low and warm in July and August to play big fish and not fatally stress them — the lodge features four streamside rooms and a two-bedroom cabin nearby. A local airport offers all-weather facilities for corporate jets and Atlanta's Hartsfield is less than two hours away.

You don't have to be a member of a corporate group to fish these waters. Call, make a reservation, pay the daily rod fee and you're in. If you plan to overnight but don't want to spring for a caterer, you'll find good restaurants in Clarkesville.

VITAL STATISTICS:

KEY SPECIES:
Brookies, browns, rainbows

Tackle:
Fly-fishing

Major Season:
April into June; September into November

Accommodations:
STONE AND LOG LODGE, AND CABIN
NUMBER OF ROOMS: 5
HANDICAPPED ACCESSIBLE: SOME
MAXIMUM NUMBER OF GUESTS: 12

Meals: Do you own cooking or arrange for catering

Conference Groups: Yes

Rates:
Lodging: $100 / night
Rod Fee: $250 / day

Guides:
$125 (includes flies and tippet)

Gratuities: $25 - $50;
Angler's discretion

Preferred Payment:
Cash, check or credit cards

Getting There:
Fly to Atlanta or Greenville, SC, and rent a car.

Other Activities:
Big game, waterfowling, wingshooting

Contact:
Rebekah Stewart Gauthier
Brigadoon Lodge
Rt. 3, Box 3158A
Clarkesville GA 30523
Ph: 706/754-1558
Fax: 706/754-2486
Web:
www.brigadoonlodge.com

Callaway Gardens

Pine Mountain, Georgia

Fish early to loosen up the muscles, get in 18-holes on one of three courses, and then hit the ponds again.

VITAL STATISTICS:

KEY SPECIES:
Bream, largemouth, rainbows

Tackle:
Casting, fly-fishing, spinning
Major Season:
All year
Accommodations:
VARIETY OF SUITES, COTTAGES AND VILLAS
NUMBER OF ROOMS: 791
HANDICAPPED ACCESSIBLE: 132
MAXIMUM NUMBER OF GUESTS: 1,500
Meals: Seven restaurants to choose from
Conference Groups: Yes
Rates: From $110 / day
Guides: $175 / half day / 2
Gratuities: Angler's discretion
Preferred Payment:
Cash, check or credit cards
Getting There:
Fly to Atlanta or Columbus and rent a car.
Other Activities:
Bird-watching, boating, golf, hiking, swimming, tennis, water skiing, wildlife photography

Contact:
Reservations
Callaway Gardens
US Hwy 27
Pine Mountain GA 31822-2000
Ph: 800/225-5292
Fax: 706/663-5068
e-mail:
info@callawaygardens.com
Web:
www.callawaygardens.com

GOLF AND FISHING don't often come in the same package, but here in the woods of west Georgia you'll find both, along with lodging that's top-ranked in everybody's book of resorts. Long renowned for its profuse and carefully tended vistas of flowering trees, shrubs and other plants, and for three championship level PGA courses, Callaway Gardens is also achieving a reputation for bass fishing. The largest of its 13 lakes, Mountain Creek, has been open to fishing since the 1960s, but the other dozen have been fished by guests only for the past couple of years.

Catch-and-release fishing is the name of the game here and that ensures good fishing for everyone. The lakes hold good largemouth, including some real hogs upwards of five pounds. Most run three-pounds-plus. You'll also encounter shellcrackers up to three pounds and bluegills that nudge two. For $20 you can rent a johnboat for a half-day and fill a stringer with largemouths that average three pounds. Use artificial lures on spinning, casting or fly tackle. The smaller lakes are used exclusively for fly-fishing schools and privately guided sessions. The angling pro shop at Callaway Gardens' boathouse provides everything you'll need.

Early spring and the shank of fall are traditionally the best months to fish these lakes. Summer evenings produce top water action on deer-hair divers, Sneaky Pets and cork poppers. Winter angling for stocked trout and bass is coming into its own as well.

There's no doubt that Callaway Gardens is a magical place. It all began one July afternoon, some 60 years ago, when Cason Callaway took a walk in the west Georgia woods and came across a bright red azalea. He'd never seen one like it before, and neither had anyone else. It was a rare native species — prunifolia — that grew only within 100 miles of Pine Mountain. Today, thanks to careful management, you'll see it in abundance throughout the 14,000 acres of Callaway Gardens.

The garden is also famous for its collection of butterflies. Add tennis, swimming and hiking. This is one of the most comprehensive resorts in the southeast. Accommodations range from elegant to luxurious in Callaway Gardens Inn (rooms and suites), Callaway Country Cottages (two-bedroom cottages) and private Mountain Creek Villas, which feature large living/dining areas with fireplace, kitchen, washer/dryer, screen porch and private bath for each bedroom.

[S O U T H]

Highland Marina and Resort

L a G r a n g e ,   G e o r g i a

More often than you've a right to expect, West Point Lake yields largemouths of eight pounds or more.

VITAL STATISTICS:

KEY SPECIES:
Crappie, hybrid stripers, largemouth

Tackle:
Casting, spinning, trolling
Major Season:
All year
Accommodations:
FULLY-EQUIPPED COTTAGES
NUMBER OF ROOMS: 34
HANDICAPPED ACCESSIBLE: SOME
MAXIMUM NUMBER OF GUESTS: 59
Meals: Self-catered
Conference Groups: No
Rates: From $59 / day
Guides: Available on special request
Gratuities: Angler's discretion
Preferred Payment:
Cash, check or credit cards
Getting There:
Fly to Atlanta and rent a car.
Other Activities:
Boating, golf, hiking, swimming, water skiing

Contact:
George Marovich
Highland Marina and Resort
1000 Seminole Rd
LaGrange GA 30240
Ph: 706/882-3437
Fax: 706/845-2968
Web:
www.highlandmarina.com

AMONG THE SECRETS of a great bass lake is a profusion and diversity of cover. Sure, largemouth need shady cool hides for protection from the sun and mid-season heat. But deep waters won't do it alone. You have to have warm shallows with grasses and brush where baitfish can breed and thrive. Add inflows of cool creek water with high oxygen content and a prudent management plan, and maybe you'll generate largemouths as plentiful and as large as those in West Point Lake.

When the U.S. Army Corps of Engineers impounded this stretch of the Chattahoochee River, it created a 34-mile-long lake of 27,000 acres. The lake continues to earn kudos from pros and amateurs for its steady production of largemouths in the six- to eight-pound class. Among the best facilities on the lake is Highland Marina and Resort in LaGrange, the major full-service fishing resort.

Like so many other southern bass lakes, West Point fishes best in spring. Later in the year, hot water temperatures drive bass down deep. In those balmy days of February and March, work the drowned valleys of the feeder streams. Highland is located on Yellow Jacket Creek, an arm of the lake that offers outstanding fishing, but because of its proximity to the marina, Yellow Jacket is often crowded. You might be better off running up to the New River, a tributary on the upper end of the lake, or ducking into others such as Veasy, Wehatkee or White Water. While largemouth is the name of the game here, a resident population of hybrid striped bass has also taken root. Live bait is the best bet, but shad-like lures and top water plugs work well too. Hybrids average four pounds or so and can be caught year-round, though February and March are definitely the best months. As you'd suspect, crappies of a pound to a pound and a half are also plentiful, with the catching best in December and February. Recent changes in seasons allow the lake to remain open all year.

Tucked in the woods above the lake, Highland Marina's 34 ranch-like cottages range from one to three bedrooms, all with kitchens, decks and grills, central heat and air, cable TV and phones, and some with private docks. Highland has all the amenities you'd expect at a quality lakefront resort. Rent a fully-equipped bass boat, launch your own, stock up on bait and tackle, have your boat serviced or engage a guide at the marina. The waterfront restaurant offers hearty fare. A shaded campground on the resort's 200 acres provides hookups for the RV crowd.

The Lodge at Cabin Bluff

S e a   I s l a n d ,   G e o r g i a

A fine old sporting club beneath the live oaks offers marvelous angling for tarpon, bonito and sea trout.

VITAL STATISTICS:

KEY SPECIES:
Dolphin/dorado, redfish, sea trout, tarpon, cobia, king mackerel

Tackle:
Casting, fly-fishing, spinning, trolling
Major Season:
All year
Accommodations:
RUSTIC LODGE AND CABINS
NUMBER OF ROOMS: 16
HANDICAPPED ACCESSIBLE: 1
MAXIMUM NUMBER OF GUESTS: 16
Meals: Elegant southern coastal cuisine
Conference Groups: Yes
Rates: From $1,573 / 3 nights, 2 days
Guides: Included
Gratuities: Angler's discretion
Preferred Payment:
Cash, check or credit cards
Getting There:
Fly to Jacksonville and rent a car.
Other Activities:
Big game, wingshooting, bird-watching, boating, canoeing/kayaking/rafting, golf, horseback riding, hiking, swimming, tennis, wildlife photography

Contact:
The Lodge at Cabin Bluff
PO Box 30203
Sea Island GA 31561
Ph: 800/732-4752
Fax: 912/638-5897
Web:
www.cabinbluff.com

YOU HARDLY believe it. Less than an hour since picking up your car at Jacksonville Int'l, you've put the city far behind you. It got better when you crossed the Georgia line and turned off Interstate 95. And when you kept goin' and goin' on that two lane road, 'til you thought you'd gone too far, you worried that you'd missed the gate. Then, there was the two-mile run down the drive between the loden walls of the pine woods, broken here and there by fields of palmetto scrub. At the end of the pavement you found an oasis, so tranquil and laid-back you wondered where the Spanish moss found the energy to wave gently in the onshore breeze. You smelled the salt, and that rich earthy aroma of swamp and tide that means south coast. Across the manicured lawn, you spied the dock, boats and the channel that separates this little neck from historic Cumberland Island, a protected national park. You were shown to your cottage, and told to make yourself comfortable, and then invited to return to the main lodge when you were ready to go out.

Just what "going out" means depends on the season. If its summer, you may rig for tarpon, cobia, false albacore, dolphin, kind mackerel or the like. If you have the good sense to arrive in late fall, you'll fish for redfish or sea trout. How you fish is up to you. Want to toss big deceivers all day looking for tarpon to 100 pounds — that's fine. You can also climb aboard a small cruiser, lay a chum line, and offer old silversides live bunker. You'll catch more tarpon this way than with a fly. Onshore or offshore, it's up to you. There's even a special boat for families who want to take their kids out for whiting and other fine frying fish. Saltwater not your bag? Ponds on the grounds hold bass of a couple of pounds that have been known to inhale poppers without the slightest provocation.

Smart sports plan their trips here for November. That's when quail hunting hits its stride and the sea trout fishing peaks. After you've chased Mr. Bob and nailed a few four-pound trout, settle down in the lodge before the crackling fire. Meals are utterly exquisite and built around fish, venison, and other regional fare. Six cabins of rustic wood are scattered in an arc on either side of the main lodge. All front the narrow reach of the intercoastal waterway that separates this forested neck from the national seashore preserve across the way. To the north of the main lodge is a completely equipped conference center and beyond that a championship golf course.

[S O U T H]

The Lodge at Little St. Simons Island

L i t t l e   S t .   S i m o n ' s   I s l a n d ,   G e o r g i a

When the back of summer breaks, head for
this barrier island and its historic and rustic lodge.

VITAL STATISTICS:

KEY SPECIES:
Flounder, redfish, sea trout, tarpon

Tackle:
Casting, fly-fishing, spinning
Major Season:
September through January
Accommodations:
MAIN LODGE AND CABINS BENEATH THE OAKS
NUMBER OF ROOMS: 15
MAXIMUM NUMBER OF GUESTS: 30
Meals: Marvelous country/regional cuisine
Conference Groups: Yes
Rates: From $325 / day / 2
Guides: $100
Gratuities: Angler's discretion
Preferred Payment:
Cash, check or credit cards
Getting There:
Fly to Jacksonville and rent a car.
Other Activities:
Bird-watching, boating, horseback riding, hiking, swimming, wildlife photography, nature talks

Contact:
Maureen Ahern
The Lodge at Little St.
Simon's Island
PO Box 21078
Little St. Simon's Island GA
31522-0578
Ph: 888/433-5774
Fax: 912/634.1811
e-mail:
lssi@mindspring.com
Web:
www.littlestsimonsisland.com

BARRIER ISLANDS ARE MAGIC PLACES for me. In the southeast, the Atlantic surf bounces along beaches of fine quartz sand, behind which rise low dunes, not the massive hills of Kitty Hawk in North Carolina, but rolling hummocks fringed with grasses and sedge that struggle to hold the sand in place. Behind the dunes are ponds fed by rainwater, for downpours are frequent through spring and summer and into the fall. Scrubby oak, pine, palmetto and flowering vines and shrubs grow with a vigor we could only wish for our gardens. In those places where the land floods with high tides, salt marshes emerge. Barrier islands are vibrant habitat for all things of temperate clime.

Little St. Simons Island is a private and secluded 10,000-acre barrier island, a nip off the tip of its larger sibling. Scores of tidal creeks drain marshes and forests behind the dunes. They deepen as they flow bayward and they brim with a rich stew of small fish. From August through November, and sometimes as late as the end of January, redfish, weakfish and flounder come into the mouths of these creeks to feed. Redfish of up to six pounds are found in the deeper holes of the creeks and in their mouths. At times, you will see them tailing in the shallows. Stalk them, then cast ahead so your Clouser or Deceiver strips across their noses. You will also encounter redfish in the surf, but will need a bigger rod, like a 10-foot 8-weight, to reach them. Fishing for reds is best in September and October.

Weakfish show up in mid-summer, schooling up in holes in the creeks and cruising the beach. By September, the concentrations are dense enough to provide good fishing. While tarpon are not as large or as plentiful as they are farther south, they are occasionally caught in summer in Altamaha Sound to the north. And flounder can be picked up in the island's creeks and surf much of the year.

The lodge provides guides, gear and Carolina skiffs, or you may fish from the beach if you wish. Many guests contract for guides before they arrive and over the phone hatch a plan to fish these inshore waters. Upon arrival, guest and guide fine-tune their schemes, based on the dictates of tide and weather. Many anglers time their arrival to coincide with fly-fishing schools held in late summer and fall.

Owned by the Berolzheimer family since the early 1900s, the island has been left largely as nature made it. A few shell roads wind through the trees, passing ponds where herons and wood storks fish, on their way to the beach. Dating from 1917, the Hunting Lodge is the heart of guest activities on Little St. Simon's. Heads of deer and other game adorn the richly paneled walls of the rustic, yet elegant, living room. If you come in late October or November, a fire will be crackling in the hearth, and the chef may have prepared a hearty chowder to open dinner, which features fine regional cuisine. Two guest rooms, each with private bath, are located in the Hunting Lodge. A nearby bungalow, Michael Cottage, is light and airy, and has a pair of bedrooms served by a private bath, as well as a living room with fireplace. This is a favorite with families and honeymooning couples. Helen House, Cedar House and River Lodge round out the accommodations. Each has four bedrooms with private baths, living room with fireplace and a screened porch.

[S O U T H]

The Lodge at Smithgall Woods

H e l e n , G e o r g i a

Seldom can the vision and generosity of one person create such a fine and public paradise for anglers.

VITAL STATISTICS:

KEY SPECIES:
Brookies, browns, rainbows

Tackle:
Fly-fishing, spinning
Major Season:
All year
Accommodations:
ELEGANT LOG CABINS
NUMBER OF ROOMS: 14
HANDICAPPED ACCESSIBLE: 1
MAXIMUM NUMBER OF GUESTS: 28
Meals: Fine regional cuisine
Conference Groups: Yes
Rates: From $135 / day
Guides: Available
Gratuities: 20%
Preferred Payment:
Cash, check or credit cards
Getting There:
Fly to Atlanta and rent a car.
Other Activities:
Big game, bird-watching,
canoeing/kayaking/rafting, golf,
horseback riding, hiking, nature
programs, tennis, wildlife
photography

Contact:
John Erbele
The Lodge at Smithgall
Woods
61 Tsalaki Trail
Helen GA 30545
Ph: 706/878-3087
Fax: 706/878-0301
e-mail:
sgwoods@stc.net
Web:
www.smithgallwoods.com

YOU MAY THINK you're in *Deliverance* country and that those notes drifting on the spring breeze are the opening bars of "Dueling Banjoes." But rest assured, it's nothing more than the happy chatter of squirrels in the tops of old-growth hickories and oaks in the 5,604-acre tract of mountains and streams that a media entrepreneur sold to the state of Georgia for half of its developable value. Acquired in 1994, the land was immediately protected as a Georgia Heritage Preserve, and its web of trails offers utter solitude.

Through Smithgall Woods runs the best mile of Duke's Creek, a freestone stream that members of Trout Unlimited selected as one of the 100 top trout waters in the country. Fishing here is like visiting your rich uncle's estate. Only 15 anglers are permitted on the stream during each of the two, six-hour fishing sessions daily. Once there, you'll either walk or be driven to the mileage you wish to fish. And, on the stream, you'll cast nymphs to some of the largest trout in the mountains. Jim Harris, who runs Unicoi Outfitters in nearby Helen, talks of a 28-inch rainbow that he had to return to the stream. All fish are returned, and rules call for barbless hooks on artificial lures. The fee for all this hospitality, a mere $2 for a parking permit. It'll be the best $2 you'll ever spend.

The fishery is divided into four sections of approximately equal length. The upper mileage runs through a bit of a gorge with lots of cascades and plunge pools. Hemlock, laurel and pine overhang the waters, clutching at backcast lures and flies. On the middle two sections, the gradient lessens and the stream flows past abandoned farmland. The bed contains some gravel, and limited hatches of caddis and sulfurs occur. In the lower section, the river again enters a tight gorge that's difficult to fish. Spinners and nymphs are on the menu here. Woolly Buggers, Prince, Tellico, Pheasant Tail, Hare's Ear, Beadheads — they'll all do the job. You may provoke strikes with parachute Adams and Wulffs.

The Lodge is an assemblage of five mountain houses (too grand to be called cabins) clustered around the head-end of a charming narrow valley. Décor is not country, but rather Appalachian elegant. Rich fabrics are coordinated with furniture and art, creating an ambiance that at once is rustic yet sophisticated. Prints of native flora and fauna decorate walls. Cottages have their own kitchens, but guests do not miss family-style dinners artfully whelped from regional staples.

Lake Barkley State Resort Park

Cadiz, Kentucky

Among state park resorts where largemouth reign, this one's a diamond that's not the least bit rough.

VITAL STATISTICS:

KEY SPECIES:
Bream, catfish, crappie, largemouth

Tackle:
Casting, fly-fishing, spinning
Major Season:
All year
Accommodations:
NUMBER OF ROOMS: 135
HANDICAPPED ACCESSIBLE: 5
MAXIMUM NUMBER OF GUESTS: 500
Meals: Regional dishes from full-service restaurant
Conference Groups: Yes
Rates: From $40
Guides: Available through the marina
Gratuities: Angler's discretion
Preferred Payment:
Cash, check or credit cards
Getting There:
Fly to Nashville and rent a car.
Other Activities:
Waterfowling, bird-watching, boating, golf, hiking, swimming, tennis, wildlife photography

Contact:
Bill Stevens
Lake Barkley State
Resort Park
PO Box 790
Cadiz KY 42211
Ph: 502/924-1131
Fax: 502/924-0013

STATE PARK RESORTS offer good fishing at reasonable rates, and in the constellation of state-run properties, this one is a real gem. The 3600-acre Lake Barkley State Resort Park has earned the American Automobile Association's Four Diamond Award. Guests stay either in Barkley Lodge, a rambling contemporary hotel of cedar with 120 rooms and four suites, or in nearby Little River Lodge with 10 rooms and one suite. In addition, 13 two-bedroom cabins, four of them log and all with screened porches or decks, are available. The resort also includes a convention center.

A full-service restaurant complements the lodge and among perennial favorites are the Kentucky Hot Brown — a hot open faced sandwich of turkey and baked ham and cheese with bacon and tomato served en casserole — and Derby pie. A half-mile from the lodge is the 172-slip marina where boats may be launched and rented. In addition, the resort includes a trap range, tennis courts and year-round campground with 78 sites complete with utility hookups.

But what of the fishing? Lake Barkley is the impoundment of the Cumberland River, and it's kissin' cousin is Kentucky Lake over on the Tennessee River. They're separated by Land Between the Lakes, a 170,000-acre wilderness area managed by the Tennessee Valley Authority in cooperation with the state wildlife agencies of Kentucky and Tennessee. The two lakes cover nearly 250,000 acres, but they are different. Kentucky is broad, shallower and tends to be more turbid. Barkley at 57,920 acres is smaller, narrower, a little deeper and a bit clearer. Of the two, there are those who say Barkley is the better bass fishery.

Barkley is known for largemouth and Kentucky bass that run in the four- to five-pound range. You'll also find crappies of a pound or more, catfish and plenty of bluegills. Bigger bass begin hitting in March as the water starts to warm. Fish the stumps and brushpiles, and the north side of the bank. Bass begin to move to spawning areas in April, and that's the best time for consistent action. Look for flooded Buttonball willows. From the bow of your boat, flip a jig and pig against the bank and work it through the submerged brush. They're still in the shallows during May and June, but retreat into deeper pockets from mid-June to September, when water temperatures reach the eighties.

[S O U T H]

Gunpowder Bed & Breakfast

M o n k t o n ,   M a r y l a n d

Fish the famed Gunpowder River from the home of the author of TU's "Budget Angler" column.

VITAL STATISTICS:

KEY SPECIES:
Browns, rainbows

Tackle:
Fly-fishing

Major Season:
All year

Accommodations:
CHARMING FARMHOUSE
NUMBER OF ROOMS: 2
MAXIMUM NUMBER OF GUESTS: 4

Meals: Bed & Breakfast

Conference Groups: No

Rates: $85 / night / 2

Guides: $200

Gratuities: Angler's discretion

Preferred Payment:
Cash or check

Getting There:
Fly to Baltimore/Washington and
rent a car.

Other Activities:
Bird-watching, canoeing/kayaking/
rafting, horseback riding, hiking

Contact:
Gunpowder Bed & Breakfast
3810 Beatty Road
Monkton MD 21111
Ph: 410/557-7594
Fax: 410/692-2355
e-mail:
annmcintosh@compuserve.com

ANN MCINTOSH KNOWS FISHING, and she knows lodging, and she pulls them together at her quaint and charming farmhouse of yellow clapboard a few minutes from one of the finest trout streams in the mid-Atlantic States. Convenient? I'll say it is. Blow into Washington, D.C. or Baltimore for a meeting, wrap it up as soon as you can, and be fast to a nice brown in the Gunpowder two hours later.

Ambling through the countryside of northcentral Maryland, the Big Gunpowder Falls River is a tailwater that fishes well throughout the year. Angling begins below Prettyboy Dam, and wading to fish these shaded jade pools is a piece of cake. Water temperature is fairly consistent. The browns — some of them very respectable — are fairly picky. Precision presentation is a must. The first seven miles of the river are managed as catch-and-release water. Farther down, it becomes a trophy trout fishery. The river has not been stocked since 1990.

Spring comes fairly early here and by mid-May, most of the trees are in full leaf. That's when good hatches of sulphurs trigger the first top-water feeding. Other effective patterns, each in its season, include Little Black Stoneflies early in the year; Blue-winged Olives, Hendricksons, and March Browns in April and May; light Cahills in May and June; and various caddis from mid-May through August. In the river's lower meadow runs, terrestrials can be extremely effective. In winter, haul out the usual suspects: Clousers, Woolly Buggers, Hare's Ears, Pheasant Tails, and Prince.

Ann will tell you what she knows of the river over breakfast of homemade muffins, freshly squeezed juice and hot coffee. But if you want a guide, call Wally Vait at On the Fly (410/329-6821), an excellent tackle shop in nearby Hereford. Located on the edge of Maryland's famed hunt country, you'll find lots of great restaurants just a few minutes from the inn.

Fontana Village Resort

Fontana Dam, North Carolina

Sliding along the backside of the Smokies is a 29-mile lake, marvelous tailwater and a handful of trout streams.

VITAL STATISTICS:

KEY SPECIES:
Brookies, browns, catfish, largemouth, rainbows, smallmouth, walleye

Tackle:
Casting, fly-fishing, spinning, trolling
Major Season:
All year
Accommodations:
CABINS AND MOTEL ROOMS
NUMBER OF ROOMS: 250
HANDICAPPED ACCESSIBLE: 5
MAXIMUM NUMBER OF GUESTS: 376
Meals: Country-style cafeteria and restaurant fare
Conference Groups: Yes
Rates: From $49 / night
Guides: $200
Gratuities: Angler's discretion
Preferred Payment:
Cash, check or credit cards
Getting There:
Fly to Knoxville and rent a car.
Other Activities:
Boating, canoeing/kayaking/rafting, horseback riding, hiking, swimming, tennis

Contact:
Scott Waycaster
Fontana Village Resort
Hwy. 28, PO Box 68
Fontana Dam NC 28733
Ph: 800/849-2258
Fax: 828/498-2209
Web:
www.fontanavillage.com

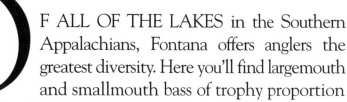

F ALL OF THE LAKES in the Southern Appalachians, Fontana offers anglers the greatest diversity. Here you'll find largemouth and smallmouth bass of trophy proportion and plenty of walleye. The normal array of panfish play in coves, much to children's delight. And across the lake, in an area of the Great Smoky Mountains National Park, rises a trio of trout streams that only those who boat across the lake, or hike or ride horseback can reach. Add a healthy dollop of mountain history — about timber barons and moonshiners and those rugged families who struggled to make a go of it — and you have one of the most interesting angling locales in the country.

Rising 480 feet above the Little Tennessee River, Fontana Dam was built to generate electricity for aluminum plants and to power research at Oak Ridge, where America's first atomic bomb was developed. Anglers fishing the tailwater below the dam can't help being awed by this grey wedge of concrete jammed in a narrow gorge. But the river is clear and cold, and browns respond to flies, spinners and bait throughout the year.

The best time to fish the lake is spring. When the sun climbs the ridge, it warms your back as you cast gray and brown jigs, spinnerbaits and crawdad imitations to the rocky shore exposed by the fluctuating lake pool. Guides, gear and boat rentals can be found at the lodge's marina. If you want to fish where the history is, hire a boat (about $40) for the run over to Hazel Creek. It'll drop you off on an old road which crosses the stream near the lost town of Proctor. What's left now is a graveled railroad grade that follows the stream, allowing anglers easy access to some of the best fishing in the Smokies. In summer, you'll find lots of anglers here, but there's ample stream to absorb them all.

It was up this stream that Horace Kephart lived. In the early 1900s, Kephart blew into Hazel Creek wreathed in moonshine fumes, lived there in a rude mountain cabin, and later wrote *Our Southern Highlanders*, a book that helped create the park and an absolute must-read for those who fish these streams and Fontana.

A family resort, Fontana Village is headquarters for exploring this Mecca. Cottages that once housed construction workers have been remodeled and augmented by attractive motel-style accommodations, close to the main stone lodge, where meals are served in both cafeteria and a la carte manner.

[S O U T H]

Hemlock Inn

B r y s o n   C i t y ,   N o r t h   C a r o l i n a

This friendly mountain retreat is as fine for families as it is for anglers bent on fishing the best of Old Smokey's trout streams.

**VITAL
STATISTICS:**

KEY SPECIES:
**Browns, rainbows,
smallmouth**

Tackle:
Fly-fishing, spinning
Major Season:
All year
Accommodations:
MOTEL-STYLE LODGE
NUMBER OF ROOMS: 26
HANDICAPPED ACCESSIBLE: 3
MAXIMUM NUMBER OF GUESTS: 60
Meals: Family-style southern
mountain cooking
Conference Groups: No
Rates: From $113 / night
Guides: $200
Gratuities: Angler's discretion
Preferred Payment:
Cash, check or credit cards
Getting There:
Fly to Asheville or Knoxville, TN, and
rent a car.
Other Activities:
Bird-watching, canoeing/kayaking/
rafting, horseback riding, hiking

Contact:
Mort White
Hemlock Inn
PO Drawer EE
Bryson City NC 28113
Ph: 828/488-2885
Fax: 828/488-8985
e-mail:
hemlock@dnet.net
Web:
www.innbook.com/hemlock

ON A KNOB overlooking the Oconaluftee Valley is a well established, yet unpretentious, motel-style lodge that has families coming back year after year. The draw is the southern side of Great Smoky Mountain National Park. While you'll encounter an abundance of outlet malls, amusement parks and fast food and motel franchises in Gatlinburg and Pigeon Forge on the Tennessee side to the north, the southern, or North Carolina, side is more tranquil and secluded.

The Eastern Band of the Cherokee owns much of the land that borders the park near the tourist town of Cherokee. They manage a network of 30 miles of first-class trout water in the middle mileage of the Oconaluftee River. In addition to the river down to the reservation border, check out Raven Fork, Bunches Creek, Soco Creek, and the ponds in Big Cove. These waters are stocked with large fish from the Cherokee hatchery quite often. Rod fees of $7 per day are levied, but nobody who's fished out west will wince at these prices.

Above the national park boundary, there is no stocking and no special fee to fish. You'll find smaller browns and rainbows in this stretch. Fish the section behind the visitor's center north of the junction of the Blue Ridge Parkway and U.S. 441, the park's sole trans-mountain road.

Better fishing, and almost as convenient, can be found near Bryson City in Deep Creek. This is one of the finest streams in the Smokies with good wild populations of both brown and rainbow trout. The lower run is heavily favored by tubers, but trout are used to them, and thus not as wary of humans as they might be. Fish this mileage early in the morning or at dusk. An upstream hike of a couple miles will take you to water that sees only anglers. Hatches are excellent.

Among the nice features of Hemlock is a little library of 300 volumes or so tucked in a room near the office. Not only will you find books on the mountain's flora, fauna and history, but current novels and some of those old standards you've been meaning to read. There's no phone, television, air-conditioning or noisy pool for kids. Just good mountain food, rockers on the porch overlooking the valley, and an occasional fly-fishing school for those whose skills need sharpening.

High Hampton Inn and Country Club

Cashiers, North Carolina

With grace and dignity, this grand dame of mountain hotels knows a thing or two about making guests real comfortable.

VITAL STATISTICS:

KEY SPECIES:
Brookies, browns, rainbows, smallmouth

Tackle:
Fly-fishing, spinning
Major Season:
April through October
Accommodations:
COMFORTABLE LODGE AND COTTAGES
NUMBER OF ROOMS AND CABINS: 48
MAXIMUM NUMBER OF GUESTS: 200+
Meals: Fine southern cooking
Conference Groups: Yes
Rates: From $75
Guides: $250
Gratuities: Angler's discretion
Preferred Payment:
Cash, check or credit cards
Getting There:
Fly to Asheville and rent a car.
Other Activities:
Bird-watching, boating, canoeing/kayaking/rafting, golf, horseback riding, hiking, swimming, tennis, wildlife photography

Contact:
**High Hampton Inn
and Country Club**
PO Box 338
Cashiers NC 28717-0338
Ph: 828/743-2411
Fax: 828/743-5991
Web:
www.highhamptoninn.com

FORGET GLITZ AND GLITTER. If the McKee family that's owned and run High Hampton for the last 75 years has learned anything at all, it's that, when it comes to quality, simple mountain traditions count for much more than color-coordinated drapes and duvets. Here, curtains are cotton, bedspreads may be handmade quilts, and the air-conditioning blows in through windows thrown open to catch the hemlock-scented breeze. You won't be kept awake by your neighbor's television. He doesn't have one and neither do you. A wooden booth by the front desk holds public phones for the 31-room main lodge and 17 outlying cabins.

For generations, families have been coming to High Hampton. They came first for the golf, back in the days when greens were of sand and golfers wore knickers. This is still a family lodge. During their week's stay, guests have their own table in the dining room and a personal waiter. From 9:00 a.m. until 2:00 p.m., the Kid's Club offers activities for youngsters from five to 12. Organized playgroups are also available for toddlers from two to four. Rooms in the lodge are basic: double beds, nightstand, bureau, private bath. Similarly appointed rooms and suites available in cottages may be a bit fancier.

More and more guests come to fish as well as play golf and tennis. Brookings (828/743-3768), an anglers' shop up the road in Cashiers, provides guides and runs fly-fishing schools at the inn's practice pond. Between the lush green links and heavy forest rising to 4300-foot granite-faced Rock Mountain are two lakes. With bait and bobbers, kids catch rainbows, bream and an occasional largemouth up to four pounds. The kitchen will gladly prepare your fish for lunch or dinner.

Sophisticated anglers should not overlook the lakes. Nearby, they'll also find a plethora of trout water, mostly freestone mountain streams and small rivers. Some high mountain creeks, hidden by laurel slicks, hold bright native brookies. Nearby are the Davidson and the Nantahala, both among Trout Unlimited's 100 best rivers. Also tempting are the South Mills and Whitewater rivers, with their populations of browns and rainbows. A two hour drive takes you into the Smoky Mountains and its best trout waters: Forney, Deep and Hazel creeks. The best months are September / October and April / May. If there are better months to fish anywhere, I couldn't hazard a guess as to what they might be.

Santee State Park

S a n t e e ,   S o u t h   C a r o l i n a

*Take I-95 across South Carolina to
Lake Marion where the stripers play.*

VITAL STATISTICS:

KEY SPECIES:
Bream, catfish, crappie, largemouth, striped bass/rockfish

Tackle:
Casting, fly-fishing, spinning, trolling
Major Season:
All year
Accommodations:
OCTAGONAL LAKEFRONT CABINS
NUMBER OF CABINS: 30
MAXIMUM NUMBER OF GUESTS: 180
Meals: Self-catered
Conference Groups: Yes
Rates: From $70 / day
Guides: $200
Gratuities: Angler's discretion
Preferred Payment:
Cash, check or credit cards
Getting There:
Fly to Columbia and rent a car.
Other Activities:
Bird-watching, boating, canoeing/kayaking/rafting, golf, hiking, swimming, tennis, water skiing, wildlife photography

Contact:
Mike Spivey
Santee State Park
251 State Park Rd
Santee SC 29142
Ph: 803/854-2408
Fax: 803/854-4834
Web:
www.travelsc.com/welcome/index

INTERSTATE 95 HUSTLES ALONG a southwesterly course, well inland from the coast of South Carolina. About midway across the state, the highway sails across a long causeway over the waters of Lake Marion. On the south bank is the quiet little town of Santee, the location of as fine a fishing-focused state park as you'll find anywhere in the country. Thirty octagonal lakeside housekeeping cabins sleep six each. Ten, built on piers over the water, have private docks. The 20 land-based cabins have decks and grills. All are fully furnished with cooking utensils, linens, cable TV and private baths. From June through August, cabins are rented for periods of not less than one week. At other times, they may be engaged on a nightly basis.

The draw here is striped bass. In these two lakes, Marion being the long, northernmost of the pair and Moultrie the round cousin lying to the southeast, are found the oldest population of landlocked striped bass in the country. It happened this way. To spawn, stripers would come up the Santee River from its mouth on the Atlantic below Georgetown. But the closing of Santee dam and the filling of the lakes in 1939 trapped some of the bass in the river channel. How they adapted to freshwater is one of those miracles that anglers everywhere praise. Thanks to this happy accident, freshwater striped bass, often called rockfish, and their many hybrid strains are found in warm water impoundments throughout the country.

Lake Moultrie, about half the size of Marion, is the better of the two lakes for stripers. The diversion canal between the two lakes is a favorite spot for striper anglers, particularly during the spawn. Drift a big shiner where your fish finder tells you and be prepared for one heck of a fight. After the spawn, the fish disperse throughout the lakes, and trolling becomes the most effective tactic. In fall, flights of feeding sea gulls will often signal striper activity near the surface.

Marion is a steadily improving largemouth bass fishery. Spreading hydrilla, vast forests of flooded cypress and plentiful submerged stumps and logs provide excellent cover. And fishing pressure for black bass, according to state biologist Miller White, "is relatively light. We have more big fish than other lakes with similar fish densities." Cast spinnerbaits and crankbaits as close to cypress as possible. In late spring, don't bypass weedbeds, and in summer, fish worm rigs, except early and late when top-water can pay off big time. Bass ranging from six to eight pounds are common.

Blackberry Farm

Walland, Tennessee

Tastefully elegant with its own stream and ponds, this lodge may be the finest in the South.

VITAL STATISTICS:

KEY SPECIES:
Browns, rainbows, smallmouth

Tackle:
Fly-fishing, spinning

Major Season:
April through November

Accommodations:
SECLUDED CABINS AROUND A COMFORTABLE AND QUIET LODGE
NUMBER OF ROOMS: 44
HANDICAPPED ACCESSIBLE: Some
MAXIMUM NUMBER OF GUESTS: 88

Meals: Gourmet, but bring your own wines

Conference Groups: Yes

Rates: From $395 / night / 2

Guides: From $200 / day

Gratuities: Angler's discretion

Preferred Payment: Cash, check or credit cards

Getting There: Fly to Knoxville and rent a car.

Other Activities:
Bird-watching, canoeing/kayaking/rafting, golf, horseback riding, hiking, swimming, tennis, wildlife photography, wildflower walks

Contact:
Kreis & Sandy Beall
Blackberry Farm
1471 W. Millers Cove Rd
Walland TN 37803
Ph: 423/984-8166
Fax: 423/681-7753
e-mail:
info@blackberryfarm.com
Web:
www.blackberryfarm.com

Agents:
Relais & Chateaux

SO LULLED ARE YOU by the pastoral scene as you make your way up the unpretentious, verdant valley, that you're quite unprepared for the white board fence and the rambling two-story house with its stone chimneys and French doors on the ridge above the road. A small sign, the only one you'll ever see, announces Blackberry Farm, and a macadam drive leads you into a complex of utterly charming cottages stained a soft dove grey. The valet loads your bags onto a green golf cart, which then whisks you silently to your cabin down the hill in among the hemlocks and mountain laurel. You notice that none of the cabin's doorways quite faces another, and that if you choose to sit and rock on the porch, you can do so in relative seclusion. Each cabin is decorated with antiques in a style that could be called opulent were it not so deftly executed — fireplaces, private baths with Jacuzzi, dressing rooms, fresh flowers, a fainting couch beneath the window and a stout four-poster with feather queen size bed. For dinner, asparagus and crayfish soup with lemon crème fraiche, grilled Smithfield veal chop with vanilla red plum sauce, and chocolate berry cobbler. Lighting is low, and tables are spaced far enough from each other that conversations don't intrude. The wait staff is confident and genuinely helpful. There are full-service conference facilities if you need them. This is a retreat.

A free fly-fishing lesson comes with your room, and fishing schools are offered throughout the year. There's a fly shop on premises, courtesy of Little River Outfitters. Ponds provide catch-and-release angling for trout and bass. A good run of Hesse Creek flows through the 1,100 acres for those who wish to fish a well-stocked stream. A fifteen minute drive takes you to the gates of the Great Smoky National Park at Townsend and miles and miles of wild trout water. Day trips to the region's great tailwaters — Clinch, Hiwassee, South Holston — are easily arranged. Tennis, wildflower walks, hikes in the fall woods — all can be found here, thanks to the vision of Kreis and Sandy Beall, founders of the inn.

Located on an isolated knob near Cherokee, NC, Hemlock Inn's guests dine on scrumptious country cooking and fish the wonderful streams of the southern Smoky Mountains.

In the spring, you can't hunt turkey all day at Ft. Lewis Lodge, down in Virginia's hot springs district. So, come afternoon, you must go tickle the trout.

Hiwassee Outfitters

Reliance, Tennessee

Right on the bank of Tennessee's finest trout tailwater is this handy outdoor resort.

VITAL STATISTICS:

KEY SPECIES:
Browns, rainbows

Tackle:
Fly-fishing, spinning
Major Season:
March through October
Accommodations:
RUSTIC RIVERFRONT CABINS
NUMBER OF CABINS: 14
MAXIMUM NUMBER OF GUESTS: 55
Meals: Restaurant on site
Conference Groups: No
Rates: From $79 / cabin
Guides: $275
Gratuities: 15%
Preferred Payment:
Cash, check or credit cards
Getting There:
Fly to Chattanooga or Atlanta and rent a car.
Other Activities:
Bird-watching, boating, canoeing/kayaking/rafting, hiking, swimming, wildlife photography

Contact:
Michael Smith
Hiwassee Outfitters
PO Box 62
Reliance TN 37369
Ph: 800/338-8133 or
423/338-8115
Fax: 423/338-1261
Web:
www.hiawasseeoutfitters.com

EAST TENNESSEE is positively wealthy with fine trout tailwaters. Three — the Hiwassee, the Clinch and the South Holston — are among Trout Unlimited's 100 best trout streams. The Watauga, up in the northeasternmost corner of the state, is almost as good. If you've got two weeks of vacation, you could do worse, much worse, than planning to fish all four.

But if you only have a week, focus on the Hiwassee. It's probably the best of the bunch. Its flows are slightly warmer than those of the others, and that may be the reason for the river's excellent hatches of mayflies, caddis and stoneflies. Four impoundments warm the Hiwassee before it vanishes into the tunnel at Apalachia dam. Ten miles downstream, it flows through a powerhouse and regains its strength. The next 15 miles or so are prime trout country. The river is wide and reasonably shallow. Rock ledge after rock ledge traverse the river. You'll find some pocket water. A three mile section is regulated for trophy trout where lures must be artificial. Otherwise, any legal bait or lure can be used. Hatches, while very profuse, are not as predicable as on other rivers. April and May sees good Blue-winged Olives, Quill Gordons, Hendricksons, Sulphurs, Slate Olive Duns, and Light Cahills. Tiny Psuedocloeons emerge from July through August. Slate Drakes are prevalent in June and July and again in late October and November. Various caddis are represented throughout the year.

You'll find the best fishing for large trout when the river is "on," that is, running heavily. That also brings out canoeists, rafters and kayakers. You'll rub elbows with them at Hiwassee Outfitters, which also boasts a very good fly and tackle shop, and provides guided float trips. Overnight guests stay in comfortable cabins. Four cabins have one bedroom and sleep four, five hold two bedrooms and can sleep six, and the tenth can put up twelve. Hard-core anglers might opt for the bunkhouse. A small restaurant on site provides breakfast, lunch and dinner — nothing fancy. More substantial chow can be found in Cleveland, Tennessee, about 30 miles to the southwest.

[S O U T H]

Little Greenbrier Lodge

S e v i e r v i l l e ,   T e n n e s s e e

All of Wear Cove lies beneath this lodge high on the northern flank of the Great Smoky Mountains.

VITAL STATISTICS:

KEY SPECIES:
Browns, rainbows

Tackle:
Fly-fishing, spinning
Major Season:
April through November
Accommodations:
COUNTRY INN WITH STUNNING MOUNTAIN VIEWS
NUMBER OF ROOMS: 10
MAXIMUM NUMBER OF GUESTS: 20
Meals: Wonderful breakfasts
Conference Groups: Yes
Rates: From $75
Guides: Available
Gratuities: Angler's discretion
Preferred Payment:
Cash, check or credit cards
Getting There:
Fly to Knoxville and rent a car.
Other Activities:
Bird-watching, hiking, snowmobiling, swimming, wildlife photography, wildflowers

Contact:
Charles & Susan Lebon
Little Greenbrier Lodge
3685 Lyon Springs Rd
Sevierville TN 37862
Ph: 423/429-2500
Fax: 423/429-4093

GATLINBURG, Sevierville, Pigeon Forge: those are the towns that tourism built at the northern entrance to the Great Smoky Mountains National Park. But there are other ways into the park that allow you to avoid most of the tourist hubbub. One of the best is the road from Wear Cove over Little Mountain into Metcalf Bottoms. Just before you crest the gap where the boundary of the park runs, there's a steep little drive to the east that leads to a charming bed-and-breakfast. It's small, quiet and convenient. Its views of Wear Cove are stunning, and ten minutes over the hill are the streams of the park where fishing is generally better than good.

Through Metcalf Bottoms flows a branch of the Little River, the hallmark Smoky Mountain trout stream. But it is more than a single river. The largest fork is the East which draws its waters from the flanks of a quartet of 6,000-foot-plus mountains along the Old Smoky's backbone. But so, too, does the Middle Prong which passes through the environmental center at Tremont, and the West Prong with rises on ridges named "Defeat" and "Doghobble" on the slopes of Thunderhead. Not stocked in more than 20 years, the streams of the park are seeing a tremendous renaissance. Fishing for wild browns and rainbows with artificial lures-only is excellent. Though patience is required — you'll share these waters with picnickers and swimmers — fishing early or late generally avoids most others.

In cooperation with the fisheries staff in the park, TU's Great Smoky Mountain and Little River chapters are heavily involved in gathering data on acid deposition in a number of high altitude creeks, restoration projects, clean-up, and ongoing monitoring of the status of various species in the river. The prognosis for trout streams in the Great Smokies: good and getting better. Area fly shops can help you match each hatch, but you'll do almost as well if your fly box contains Adams, caddis, ants, green inch worms, Gold-ribbed Hare's Ears of beadhead and non-beaded varieties, and a sampling of olive and black Woolly Buggers. Spinning anglers will find success with the tiniest of Mepps, Rooster Tails, and Panther Martins.

Charles and Susan Lebon, owners of Little Greenbrier, have done a fine job in creating a place that reflects the mountain heritage and the Victorian era without going overboard. Breakfasts are a bit eclectic. Try the artichoke bake with biscuit, gravy and country ham. Most rooms have private baths.

Mansard Island Resort & Marina

Springville, Tennessee

Everybody wants to catch bass, and at this laid-back resort on Kentucky Lake, they do.

VITAL STATISTICS:

KEY SPECIES:
Bream, catfish, crappie, largemouth

Tackle:
Casting, fly-fishing, spinning
Major Season:
March through October
Accommodations:
CABINS, COTTAGES AND MOBILE HOMES
NUMBER OF ROOMS: 40
MAXIMUM NUMBER OF GUESTS: 175
Meals: You'll do your own cooking
Conference Groups: No
Rates: From $38
Guides: $175
Gratuities: Angler's discretion
Preferred Payment:
Cash, check or credit cards
Getting There:
Fly to Nashville and rent a car.
Other Activities:
Big game, waterfowling, wingshooting, bird-watching, boating, golf, hiking, skiing, swimming, tennis, wildlife photography

Contact:
J. D. Koenig
Mansard Island Resort & Marina
60 Mansard Island Dr
Springville TN 38256
Ph: 901/642-5590
Fax: 901/642-3120
e-mail:
mansardisland@wk.net
Web:
festivalusa.com/mansard-island

WARM AND SHALLOWER than neighboring Lake Barkeley, Kentucky Lake's 2,400 miles of shoreline is jam-packed with structure. Largemouth bass love it. So, too, do smallmouth. Along this 180-mile-long impoundment of the Tennessee River, you'll find a number of marinas. About a third of the way down the lake, just across the Tennessee line, is a laid-back, home-style, affordable resort that offers accommodations and facilities that will suite a wide range of tastes and interests. And the fishing is good not five minutes from the marina. Fishermen with families make tracks for Mansard Island.

The resort caters to anglers. Largemouths, the lake's premiere fish, run up to 10 pounds, but stringers of two- to three-pounders are more normal. Gravel points, creek mouths, brush piles, drowned timber and stumps, and other structure are all worth fishing. In spring, work the shallows when bass are bedding. Don't overlook weedy shorelines. May is usually a top month for bass; worms, jig 'n pigs, crankbaits and buzzbaits all produce. Try points, channels of old river channels, and islands near the mouths of creeks. As the water heats — and the weather does get hot in west Tennessee — bass go deep. Fish them early and late. You may find topwater action at night. Come fall, they'll feed a little more aggressively, but the best fishing is generally in spring.

While bass is definitely the main event, don't pass up crappies from one to three pounds in the spring, bluegills (real treats on a fly rod and great fun for kids), catfish and sauger, a cousin of the walleye that is prized table fare. Sauger fish best in winter.

Situated on the Big Sandy River arm of the lake amidst the trees, Mansard Island Resort offers everything from townhouses, cottages and private rooms, to a campground for recreational vehicles and tents. Along with a laundromat and a grocery and general store, you'll also find tennis, a swimming pool, and a playground with a stocked pond for kids. Fishing and pontoon boats can be rented from the full-service marina, which can accommodate boats up to 30 feet long. A launch ramp and covered slips are available. A number of guides work out of the marina, which also sells licenses and bait. You'll find restaurants in nearby Paris, Tennessee, and Murray, Kentucky.

[S O U T H]

Wonderland Lodge

S e v i e r v i l l e ,   T e n n e s s e e

A sad story gives birth to a new hotel on the back porch of the Great Smoky Mountain National Park.

VITAL STATISTICS:

KEY SPECIES:
Browns, rainbows

Tackle:
Fly-fishing, spinning
Major Season:
April through November
Accommodations:
MODERN YET RUSTIC LODGE OF LOG
NUMBER OF ROOMS: 29
HANDICAPPED ACCESSIBLE: 2
MAXIMUM NUMBER OF GUESTS: 98
Meals: Country fare
Conference Groups: No
Rates: From $50
Guides: Can be arranged on request
Gratuities: Angler's discretion
Preferred Payment:
Cash, check or credit cards
Getting There:
Fly to Knoxville and rent a car.
Other Activities:
Bird-watching, hiking, wildlife photography

Contact:
Jim & Becki Claypool
Wonderland Lodge
3889 Wonderland Way
Sevierville TN 37862
Ph: 877/428-0779
Fax: 423/774-5011

ONCE UP IN THE SMOKIES at Elkmont there was a wonderful old pine board hotel. Built in the early 1900s, it housed, first, lumbermen who'd come to strip hemlock and hardwoods from the mountain sides. But when the logging was finished and the tract became part of the Great Smoky Mountain National Park, the hotel was operated for tourists. Meals were simple country food. Anglers often stopped for lunch and perhaps to overnight. Everyone enjoyed sitting in the rockers looking off across the valley. Fifty years after creating the park, the lease on the hotel expired, as it did for all of the private cabins in the Elkmont area. Much to the sadness of those who knew the hotel and wondered why it could not be allowed to operate like those in Yellowstone, the old hotel was closed in the late 1980s.

A new hotel with the old name now graces the flank of a mountain nose outside the park on the road from Wear Valley into Metcalf Bottoms. Thoroughly modern yet rustic in appearance, you'll find private baths and all the amenities that the old hotel lacked. The hotel restaurant serves good country-cooked meals based on fresh local produce and meats. And a wide front porch is just as comfortable as the old.

Less than 15 minutes will put you on the mileage of the East Prong of the Little River, the Wonderland's traditional home waters. In its uppermost reaches, the East Prong bounces from pool through chute to pool, working through a maze of mammoth boulders left from an earlier geologic age. Fish Camp Prong joins the East Prong about 4 miles upstream from Elkmont, and at this junction, the river becomes a consistently good fishery. You'll find dainty rainbows of seven to 10 inches willing to take Adams, Caddis or little Grey Hare's Ears. Tiny Mepps or Rooster Tails also get results, but they are better fished in the larger waters below. Jake's Creek adds its waters to the East Prong at Elkmont. The lower section of the river is matched with paved road all the way to the park entrance at Townsend. Despite high numbers of tourists who camp at Elkmont and picnic along the stream, it is an amazingly good fishery. While browns upwards of five pounds are caught each season, as are rainbows of two to four pounds, more normal fare is around 10 inches. You can spend a whole season fishing the East Prong of the Little River from Metcalf Bottoms up, and never get to know it well. That's why anglers keep coming back.

777 Ranch

Hondo, Texas

With the Gemsbok and largemouth, you could be on the South African veldt. But then comes the biscuits and gravy.

VITAL STATISTICS:

KEY SPECIES:
Catfish, crappie, largemouth

Tackle:
Casting, fly-fishing, spinning
Major Season:
All year
Accommodations:
WELL FURNISHED MOTEL-STYLE ROOMS
NUMBER OF ROOMS: 25
MAXIMUM NUMBER OF GUESTS: 50
Meals: Good ol' Southern cooking
Conference Groups: Yes
Rates: From $ 250 / night, double occupancy
Guides: $200
Gratuities: $30
Preferred Payment:
Cash, check or credit cards
Getting There:
Fly to San Antonio and rent a car.
Other Activities:
Big game, wingshooting, bird-watching, boating, golf, hiking, swimming, tennis, wildlife photography

Contact:
Kevin Christiansen
777 Ranch
Private Road 5327
Hondo TX 78861
Ph: 830/426-3476
Fax: 830/426-4821
e-mail:
777 ranch@ranch.com
Web:
www.777ranch.com

HUNTERS KNOW WELL the 15,000-acre 777 Ranch, an hour or so west of San Antonio. More than 50 species of big game — eland, oryx, gemsbok, zebra, blackbuck antelope — wander these hills that roll with prairie grasses, mesquite and acacia. If you didn't know better, you'd think you were on the savanna or the veldt, but no. This here's Texas. And it's dry. So when Kevin Christiansen started the game ranch, he made sure that there were plenty of stock tanks (read that ponds) to water the big animals. Of course, those water holes can't sit there empty. That's where the largemouth come in.

Ranging from ponds so small that you can chuck a stone across them to lakes of 100 acres or so, these waters hold largemouths averaging six to eight pounds. Florida-strain bass were planted here about 20 years ago, and the 777 has been practicing catch-and-release ever since. You'll fish for them from 16-foot Carolina skiffs pushed by electric trolling motors. The time of year doesn't make much difference in terms of catching bass on the ranch, but the tactics and lures will vary. Bassassassins and Slugos in pumpkinseed and chartreuse are effective when the wind has made the water a little dingy. So too are white, yellow and chartreuse spinnerbaits. When the water's clear, darker colors perform better. In spring, you'll do well with buzzbaits cast toward shore early and late in the day. In summer and fall, go deeper with Rat-L-Traps. Booking is by advance reservation only, and a week before you come, the ranch staff calls, confirms and tells you what plugs are hot. That's smart service! And the ranch maintains a fully stocked pro shop.

Big game hunting is the bread and butter of this ranch. You'll find species from Africa, Europe and India, along with American whitetails and elk. Not to be overlooked are turkeys, quail, ducks, geese and sandhill cranes when in season. Fill your big game tag and then chill out with an afternoon of bassin' in one of the ponds. Some ponds hold catfish, and others perch or crappie.

Accommodations in the ranch's main California cedar lodge are as comfortable and well appointed as any of the country's first-rate motels. Corporate groups can have the run of the place and they'll find the facilities conducive to business — as long as they stay indoors. Food is good and stick-to-your-ribs solid. A large pool and outdoor barbecue are very popular when the fishing's done.

[**S O U T H**]

Lake Fork Lodge

A l b a ,   T e x a s

When it comes to record largemouth, it's hard to beat this, the best little hog lake in Texas.

VITAL STATISTICS:

KEY SPECIES:
Bream, catfish, crappie, largemouth

Tackle:
Casting, fly-fishing, spinning
Major Season:
All year
Accommodations:
MODERN MOTEL ROOMS WITH ALL THE AMENITIES
NUMBER OF ROOMS: 7
HANDICAPPED ACCESSIBLE: ALL
MAXIMUM NUMBER OF GUESTS: 30
Meals: Use one of several barbecue grills, or eat in nearby restaurants
Conference Groups: Yes
Rates: From $75
Guides: $250
Gratuities: 15%
Preferred Payment:
Cash, check or credit cards
Getting There:
Fly to Dallas / Ft. Worth and rent a car.
Other Activities:
Waterfowling, wingshooting, bird-watching, golf, swimming, wildlife photography

Contact:
Kyle Jones
Lake Fork Lodge
PO Box 160
Alba TX 75410
Ph: 903/473-7236
e-mail:
lakefork@koyote.com
Web:
www.lakeforklodge.com

WRESTLIN' HOGS. That's what fishing this 28,000-acre lake is all about. About an hour east of Dallas, Lake Fork has produced 19 of the state's 25 biggest largemouth. That includes the state's 18 pound, 3 ounce record. Not only are the fish good sized, but you'll also catch lots of them. Days of 20 to 30 fish aren't all that unusual. How come? About two decades ago Texas' fisheries folk thought that Lake Fork could support largemouth of trophy proportions. To get things started, they dumped 800,000 Florida-strain largemouth in the waters.

Habitat couldn't have been better. Lake Fork is not particularly deep, averaging between 12 and 18 feet except at the dam, and it offers a wide variety of structure. Flooded timber, reefs, grass beds, abandoned road rights-of-way and stream channels, rocky points and some drop-offs abound. Cover for baitfish is plentiful. These largemouth fingerlings settled in and grew in a big way. Now their progeny are ripe for harvest.

While the season is open year-round, the most productive months are March through May, October and November. Spawning generally occurs from mid-February to mid-March. Night fishing during the height of summer is very effective. Try the popular Zara Spook or other topwater plugs. For general fishing, locals recommend a jig and crawl rig. While largemouths get most of the attention on this trophy lake, you might want to factor in a little fishing for crappies, which fish best in spring and late fall. And if you feel up to the task, try tussling with some big blue cats (five to 70 pounds) in early summer.

Motel/marinas and guide services are plentiful here. But if you're looking for something different, try Kyle and Debbie Jones' contemporary brick lakeside "Bass & Breakfast." Book in the night before and have dinner at a nearby restaurant. Then, early in the morning, before sun-up, have a small breakfast — just enough to tide you over — before hitting the water. Fish 'til 10:00 or so, then beat it back to the lodge and satisfy your horrible hungries with eggs, grits, biscuits and gravy, and anything else you can imagine. Go nap, you'll need it. After the evening's fishing, come back, whip a steak on the grill, open a bottle of cabernet and toast your good fortune. A soak in the hot-tub completes the day. Dinners are not included in the price of the room, but they can be catered on special request.

Ft. Lewis Lodge

Milboro, Virginia

Here, everybody fishes the Cowpasture River and, thanks to a little help from a friend, they do very well.

THOSE HARDY SCOTCH-IRISH who settled these western Virginia valleys in the mid-1700s sometimes got carried away with place names. Where else do you find rivers named Calfpasture, Bullpasture and Cowpasture. It works this way. The Bullpasture flows into the Cowpasture, which seems logical enough. But the Calfpasture is a couple valleys to the east and draws its water from neither the Cow nor the Bull. Our forebears had a better understanding of biology than that.

Just as long as you understand the geography, the rest doesn't matter. In spring and fall, rivers in moderate floodplains between the forested ridges run cool. In summer, save deep holes or seeps where spring waters feed in, they warm a bit. You can fish for trout then, but the fishing is better from April through June, and in September and October. There's one exception to this: smallmouth bass. On the 2.5 miles of the Cowpasture owned by Ft. Lewis Lodge, you'll find loads of bronzebacks, some up to three pounds. Anglers don't come here for the smallmouth, though. They come for browns and rainbows in the 12-inch-and-up size stocked by owner John Cowden. Broken into two sections, the lower mile and a half is bigger, with a run, riffle, pool persona. Upstream, the river is smaller, better shaded and fishes well later into the summer. Use the tackle that suits you, but catch-and-release is the rule.

Among the best time to fish this river is during spring gobbler season. When hunting turkey, you can only climb around on those hardwood ridges above the lodge 'til noon. After lunch, and maybe a few winks, most hunters grab fly or spinning rods and head for the stream. Deer hunting archers may also wile away midday on the river, but most prefer to either stay out all day or rest their eyes a bit before going out again that afternoon.

This is a working farm of 3,400 acres. Even so, accommodations in the main lodge and two cabins are strictly first class, with color-coordinated drapes and spreads, private baths and a sitting room with overstuffed furniture fronting a rock hearth where a fire burns. Opt for one of the cabins if you can, and you'll sleep at night lulled by the embers of your dying fire. Meals are served in a remodeled mill. You'll dine on heavenly roasts, grilled steaks, veggies and homemade pastries and pies.

Hidden Valley

Warm Springs, Virginia

If you yearn for the days of Rhett and Scarlet, you can actually live them here, and enjoy fine trout fishing to boot!

VITAL STATISTICS:

KEY SPECIES:
Browns, rainbows

Tackle:
Fly-fishing, spinning
Major Season:
April through October
Accommodations:
ELEGANT HISTORIC PLANTATION
NUMBER OF ROOMS: 3
MAXIMUM NUMBER OF GUESTS: 9
Meals: Breakfast only
Conference Groups: No
Rates: From $105 / 2
Guides: Available
Gratuities: Angler's discretion
Preferred Payment:
Cash or check
Getting There:
Fly to Roanoke and rent a car.
Other Activities:
Bird-watching, hiking, wildlife photography

Contact:
Pat Stidham
Hidden Valley
PO Box 53
Warm Springs VA 24484
Ph: 540/839-3178
Fax: 540/839-3178

DEEP IN THE George Washington National Forest is an 8,000-acre plantation on the Jackson River that was assembled by Bath County judge James Warwick. The house is of brick, a fine example of Greek Revival architecture. The entry porch carries the classical pediment supported by four Doric columns. A narrow line of transom and side lights surround the front door, and the side lights are echoed in the second story window. Lift the tarnished brass door knocker and innkeeper Pat Stidham will bid you welcome. As you step into the center hall, you know in an instant that this is the real McCoy. To the left is the music room and to the right is the parlor, each with fireplaces and antiques from the 1850s to the 1870s. Unlike museums, you're encouraged to sit and touch; this is, after all, a bed-and-breakfast.

If it looks familiar to you, maybe it should. You may have seen the house and the surrounding countryside in the Civil War movie *Sommersby*, starring Jodie Foster and Richard Gere. You may also have caught glimpses of the river. The Jackson flows past the front door of the mansion. Fewer than 100 yards puts you on the stream. The mansion is owned by the U.S. Forest Service and the river is public water. It's stocked in spring and fall. But the real action occurs a mile and a half upstream where the trophy trout water begins. Pools are slow, long and shady. You'll find some riffles, and a few patches of boulders with deep holes downstream. It's artificials-only water, fly or spin. Mayfly and caddis hatches are regular and trigger feeding by browns of 10 to 14 inches. Terrestrials work brilliantly in late summer and early fall. Anglers may keep a brace of fish over 16 inches, but all others must be released unharmed. Nobody brings out the big fish.

If your soul thirsts for immersion in history, check into this fine old plantation house. Dinner is not served here unless by prior arrangements made well in advance. Though you'd never know it from the fields and mountains you see from your windows, you're in the heart of one of Virginia's most historic resort areas. Warm Springs and Hot Springs have been drawing tourists since the late 1700s, and in those towns you'll find wonderful fine dining or fast food, depending on the state of your palate.

Inn at Narrow Passage

Woodstock, Virginia

In front of this historic lodge flows a run of the Shenandoah's North Fork that's loaded with smallmouth.

VITAL STATISTICS:

KEY SPECIES:
Smallmouth

Tackle:
Fly-fishing, spinning
Major Season:
March through November
Accommodations:
HISTORIC LOG COUNTRY INN
NUMBER OF ROOMS: 12
HANDICAPPED ACCESSIBLE: 1
MAXIMUM NUMBER OF GUESTS: 30
Meals: Wonderful breakfast;
dinners in town
Conference Groups: Yes
Rates: From $75
Guides: $175
Gratuities: Angler's discretion
Preferred Payment:
Cash, check or credit cards
Getting There:
Fly to Dulles and rent a car.
Other Activities:
Bird-watching, canoeing/kayaking/
rafting, golf, hiking, tennis, wildlife
photography

Contact:
Ed Markel
Inn at Narrow Passage
PO Box 608
Woodstock VA 22664
Ph: 540/459-8000
Fax: 540/459-8001
e-mail:
innkeeper@innatnarrowpassage.com
Web:
www.innatnarrowpassage.com

THERE MAY BE BETTER smallmouth rivers than the Shenandoah, but for the life of me, I can't imagine them. Oh, sure, you'll find some that consistently produce bigger fish, but here 100-fish days are routine. Other rivers are wider and deeper and boast heavier rapids, but the North Fork is a gentle stream, ideally suited for lazy drifting in a canoe, or wading. Add a heavy dose of scenery — steep mountains that terminate in rock bluffs cut by the river, gentle bends that swing around farms that have been in the same families since George Washington's era, amd deer and hawks who seem little perturbed by your presence — and you'll see that the Shenandoah can be an angler's idyll.

Rock ledges give way to bouldery gravel runs fringed by beds of grass, some submerged and others not. Baitfish and crawdads thrive in the warmish waters. All you'll need is a 6-weight rod, a weight-forward floating line and a few streamers, poppers and big nymphs. Or use ultralight spinning gear. A five-foot rod, a little reel spooled with 4-pound-test line and a half dozen three-inch black-and-silver floating and diving crankbaits will keep you in smallmouths all day. If you've a mind to, pack along a couple of crawdad imitations. Perhaps the best month on this river is October.

Public access to the river is plentiful. Just north of Woodstock, Route 665 turns east from U.S. 11 toward Green Mountain. In a couple of miles it joins Route 758 and crosses the North Fork below an old mill dam. The plunge pool at the dam holds fish, but the better fishing is downstream along the rocky shoals and ledges. Several state and county roads cross the river as it meanders down the valley. Each bridge has a parking pull-off. For local patterns and advice on where to use them, drop in on smallmouth guru Harry Murray (540/984-4212) in his pharmacy turned tackle shop, south on U.S. 11 in Edinburg. Murray is a gregarious guy whose fly-fishing schools (two days for $275) for Shenandoah smallmouths are frequent and well attended. Murray employs a staff of guides.

The Inn at Narrow Passage was once Stonewall Jackson's headquarters. The log inn has been lovingly restored by Ed and Ellen Markel, who run it as a bed-and-breakfast. Choose from Jackson's room in the original inn that dates from 1740, or pick a newer room with a private door onto the front porch. All 12 rooms include private baths. Breakfast is served in front of a stone fireplace. And if the Civil War piques your curiosity, you're right in the heart of Jackson's Valley Campaigns of 1862.

[S O U T H]

Meadow Lane Lodge

W a r m   S p r i n g s ,   V i r g i n i a

Solitude and fish thrive deep in the folds of the western mountains of Virginia.

VITAL STATISTICS:

KEY SPECIES:
Brookies, browns, rainbows, smallmouth, McConaughy trout

Tackle:
Fly-fishing

Major Season:
March through November

Accommodations:
DIVERSE IN STYLE BUT ALL ELEGANT ROOMS IN A CLASSIC LODGE

NUMBER OF ROOMS: 14

MAXIMUM NUMBER OF GUESTS: 30

Meals: Breakfast and lunch (dinner by special request)

Conference Groups: No

Rates: From $105 / night / 2

Guides: $250 / day

Gratuities: Angler's discretion

Preferred Payment:
Cash, check or credit cards

Getting There:
Fly to Roanoke and rent a car.

Other Activities:
Bird-watching, golf, horseback riding, hiking, nature tours, swimming, tennis, wildlife photography, cross-country skiing

Contact:
Carter and Michelle Ancona
Meadow Lane Lodge
HCR 01, Box 110
Warm Springs VA 24484
Ph: 540/839-5959
Fax: 540/839-2135
e-mail:
meadowln@va.tds.net
Web:
www.meadowlanelodge.com

IN ITS WESTERNMOST PARTS, Virginia is scrunched up like a hooked rug pushed against the wall. Ridge repeats ridge while valleys are verdant or not depending on the season. Sometimes they're tawny like the flanks of the cougar that roamed the hills when George Washington came through with his rod and chains. In early summer, the valleys are so green that they can't help buoy your heart. To stand there amidst the fields is to know that you have come home even if you've never been there.

Such is the feeling of Meadow Lane Lodge, the 1600-acre homestead of the Hirsch family. Just as the twenties began to roar, Allan Hirsh bought the land, built the lodge, and set about raising thoroughbreds. It's owned by the same family today. With its double porch stacked one atop the other, the white clapboard lodge is framed by hardwoods and looks out across the valley of the Jackson River. Down by the river is the granary, an 1890s grain barn that retained its fascinating character during its conversion into a first-class, three-bedroom guest house ideal for families. In all of the lodge's 14 rooms you'll find honest antiques, comfortable quilts, and private baths. Breakfast and lunch are provided, but not dinner unless you make a special request.

Riding, hiking, swimming, canoeing and croquet are among the most popular pastimes here. So, too, is the fishing. Meadow Lane owns 2.5 miles of the Jackson. Throughout the season, it is stocked with rainbows, brooks and browns to augment a growing population of wild trout. Angling is strictly catch-and-release. Fishing here is best in the spring when hills bloom, first with redbud, then dogwood and finally azalea. In July and August, the river warms and slows, and angling is better in nearby lakes or in the Jackson tailwater below Garthwright Dam which impounds Lake Moomaw. As fall progresses from Labor Day on, fishing picks up, peaking with the vivid reds, oranges and yellows of maple and beech. Fishing schools are frequent and guides can be arranged if anglers so desire. So can anything else within reason, for that matter. Innkeepers Carter and Michelle Ancona, the third generation to manage the farm, are those kind of folks.

Meadow Lane Lodge in southwest Virginia is one of those places where you can fish, ride, walk the woods for wild flowers, or just hang out in a rocker and read.

Tucked away in the mountains of north Georgia is the Lodge at Smithgall Woods, where accommodations are utterly without peer, as is the fishing in Duke's Creek, one of TU's best.

Shenandoah Lodge

L u r a y ,   V i r g i n i a

The South Fork of the Shenandoah is longer and wider than the North Fork, and demands a different approach.

VITAL STATISTICS:

KEY SPECIES:
Smallmouth, brookies

Tackle:
Fly-fishing
Major Season:
April through October
Accommodations:
WOOD-SIDED LODGE ABOVE THE RIVER
NUMBER OF ROOMS: 5
MAXIMUM NUMBER OF GUESTS: 12
Meals: Excellent regional cuisine
Conference Groups: Yes
Rates: From $595 / 3 days
Guides: Included
Gratuities: $50 - $100 / trip;
Angler's discretion
Preferred Payment:
Cash, check or credit cards
Getting There:
Fly to Washington Dulles and rent
a car.
Other Activities:
Bird-watching, biking,
canoeing/kayaking/rafting, golf,
horseback riding, hiking, swimming,
wildlife photography

Contact:
Alec Burnett
Shenandoah Lodge
100 Grand View Dr
Luray VA 22835
Ph: 800/866-9958
Fax: 540/743-1916
e-mail:
flyfish@shentel.net
Web:
www.shenlodge.com

IN A WAY, there are three Shenandoah Rivers. At Front Royal, beneath the prominent nose of Massanutten Mountain, the north and south forks come together to form the main river. The North Fork meanders — and I mean like ribbon candy — up the valley that everyone calls by the name of the river, and through which Interstate 81 runs. The South Fork flows through the valley between Massanutten Mountain and the mountains of Shenandoah National Park. Follow U.S. Route 340 from Front Royal through Luray (Caverns), and beyond and you'll trace its course.

The South Fork drains a large area and carries more water than the North Fork. It's a little less easily waded, but floats better. Nobody knows which produces more or bigger fish. But the South Fork has been plagued by industrial pollution. Most caught smallmouths are released. On the South Fork, 100-fish floats are the norm. Most will run a pound or so, yet you never know. Shenandoah smallmouths are rapacious like hawks. In April and May, they'll nail small spinnerbaits, plastic grubs, worms and floating-diving minnow plugs. Don't overlook Mepps spinners: a no. 1 silver bucktail can be a killer. In summer, poppers work at dusk. Fishing is best in September and October when the bigger fish are more aggressive.

While spinfishers do well, the river was made for fly-fishing. Flies are big and you'll need at least a five-weight rod to throw them effectively. Among the best water on the South Fork is the lodge's six-mile home stretch of riffled shallows and a run or two that harbor big bronzebacks and an errant trout. Trout in the Shenandoah? That's right. Scores of trout streams drain into the South Fork. It stands to reason that rainbows and browns can live in the colder and better oxygenated sections of the river and run up small creeks to spawn. However, they are few and far between. In the main, trout fishing means angling in Shenandoah National Park with a fly for native brookies in the six- to 12-inch range, or on private creeks.

Bass and trout anglers share the same dinner tables at Shenandoah Lodge, so conversation regarding the relative merits of each is apt to be lively. So is the menu: chilled gazpacho, roast Cornish game hens, vidalias and mushrooms in herb sauce. Of five guest rooms, two are in the main lodge and three in log cabins on the hillside. All have private baths.

When it comes to sporting resorts, Bienville Plantation near White Springs, FL, has it all — big bass, ducks, deer, and lord love us, quail.

Trout may be fly fishers' preferred quarry, but wise anglers toss streamers for smallmouth in the cool waters of the foothills of the Appalachians.

*If it's big largemouth you're wanting, book into The Floridian
Sports Club on the St. Johns River an hour or so southwest
of Jacksonville. Accommodations and food are excellent,
and so are its guides like Gramme Chennell.*

*Lush and elegant native flora surround cabins at
Blackberry Farm, an exquisite retreat where dinners are
served with candlelight and silver, and anglers chase
wild trout on the Tennessee side of the Smokies.*

Blackwater Lodge

D a v i s ,   W e s t   V i r g i n i a

Deep in the gorge are good browns and rainbows, and above, on the rim, sits a fine log and stone lodge.

VITAL STATISTICS:

KEY SPECIES:
Brookies, browns, rainbows

Tackle:
Fly-fishing, spinning

Major Season:
March through October

Accommodations:
RUSTIC STONE LODGE AND CABINS
NUMBER OF ROOMS: 54
NUMBER OF CABINS: 25
HANDICAPPED ACCESSIBLE: 3
MAXIMUM NUMBER OF LODGE GUESTS: 108

Meals: Restaurant fare in southern tradition

Conference Groups: Yes

Rates: From $60

Guides: $150

Gratuities: Angler's discretion

Preferred Payment:
Cash, check or credit cards

Getting There:
Fly to Pittsburgh and rent a car, or drive from Washington, D.C.

Other Activities:
Bird-watching, boating, canoeing/kayaking/rafting, golf, hiking, swimming, tennis, wildlife photography

Contact:
Lois Reed
Blackwater Lodge
PO Drawer 490
Davis WV 26260
Ph: 304/259-5216
Fax: 304/259-5881
e-mail:
blackwater@access.mountain.net

LODGES IN STATE PARKS can provide accommodations that are quite good at a price that won't wear a hole in your hip pocket. One is Blackwater Lodge near Davis, West Virginia, where a single room will set you back $60 a night. That's not bad for a hotel of rock and log that has much of the same ambiance of the great lodges in Yellowstone, and the fact that it's only a three-hour drive from Washington, DC, is a real plus.

Amidst 1,700 acres of spruce and hemlock, the lodge overlooks the Blackwater Canyon near the falls that drop the river down into the canyon. From the falls downstream are four miles of catch-and-release water where browns and rainbows run in the 12- to 16-inch range. Some are bigger. The most challenging aspect of fishing here is the half-mile hike down into the gorge. Other than that, the angling is fairly straight forward. Nymphs and streamers of beadhead persuasion — Hare's ear, Woolly Bugger, etc. — in sizes from #12 to #14 will do the job. This is not especially dry fly water, though anglers whose fly boxes carry a standard assortment of Adams, Sulfurs, and Blue-winged Olives will get by just fine. Spin fishing is permitted here as well. A river of pools among big boulders with runs and riffles, the Blackwater fishes best from April into June, and again in mid-fall, assuming waterflows are appropriate.

While in the area, you'll want to check out nearby rivers. The North Branch of the Potomac below Jennings Randolph Dam is known as the Madison of the East for its stocks of browns, rainbows and cutthroat. Dry Fork is a limestone river with very good rainbows and some fine wild brookies in its headwaters. While no guides are affiliated with the lodge, Tory Mountain Outfitters (304/259-5853) is a full-fledged fly shop in Davis, a couple of miles from the gorge. Darrell Hensley and Steve Douglas, the two anglers behind Tory Mountain, offer guided trips and instruction.

Rooms at the lodge are very comfortable, but not overly fancy. Meals — often with a southern flair — are served in a large dining room with glass windows that look out into the gorge. Along with fishing, an extensive trail network is great for hiking or riding on horseback. If you want to be off by yourselves, book one of the 25 cabins which contain kitchens and private baths.

[S O U T H]

Cheat Mountain Club

D u r b i n ,   W e s t   V i r g i n i a

By-passed by the ravages of progress, Cheat Mountain offers fine trout fishing in an aura of historic elegance.

A PRIVATE RETREAT set on 187 acres in the midst of the Monongahela National Forest, the Cheat Mountain Club has pretty much avoided the 20th century. So hidden is it among nine of West Virginia's highest mountains that you have to know where you're going to get there, and even then — map from the club in hand — you may not be too sure. And when the gravel lane brings you, at last, to the rustic pine board lodge, you wouldn't be too surprised to see Messrs. Ford, Edison and Firestone chatting on the porch as they did in 1918.

Past the front porch flows Shavers Fork of the Cheat River; more than a mile and a half runs through the property. Owners of the hotel stock the river with 12- to 14-inch rainbows, and only those who stay at the hotel may fish it, catch-and-release, of course. The upper Shavers Fork is not big water, but rather riffles and runs with a stony bottom. Maples, beech and some spruce line its banks. Occasional undercut banks, heavy with grass, hang over the stream, sheltering browns, rainbows and a few brookies. The water warms in midsummer, sending trout into spring holes or shady mouths of cold water tributaries. The best time to fish this stream is in April, May and June, when the water is cool. Then you'll fish among blooming dogwoods and, later, laurel and rhododendron. In September and October, the river revives with autumn temperatures. This is the time for terrestrials.

Fish the shadows as that's where trout hold in this low, clear water. The lower part of the river offers smallmouth bass fishing. Two- to three-pounders are frequently released. Also within striking distance is Seneca Creek to the north and the Cranberry River to the south. Both are among TU's 100 best trout streams in America.

The Cheat Mountain Club is a day's drive from Atlanta, Cleveland, New York and Washington DC. The trip is well worth it. At the end of the lane, you'll find that what this retreat lacks in modern amenities (only one room has a private bath, the others share as they have since its earliest days), it more than makes up for in pure, traditional warmth. Guest rooms are softly paneled. On the third floor, there's a special bunkroom for children. Downstairs, handmade sofas and chairs are grouped in front of the fieldstone fireplace and in corners just made for casual conversation or a stint with a good book. Candles and crystal complement china of the club's own pattern for full-course, family-style dinners.

VITAL STATISTICS:

KEY SPECIES:
Browns, rainbows

Tackle:
Fly-fishing
Major Season:
April through September
Accommodations:
RUSTIC TURN-OF-THE-CENTURY LODGE
NUMBER OF ROOMS: 12
HANDICAPPED ACCESSIBLE: 2
MAXIMUM NUMBER OF GUESTS: 32
Meals: Elegant country, yet casual
Conference Groups: Yes
Rates: From $80 / night / 2
Guides: $150
Gratuities: $20;
Angler's discretion
Preferred Payment:
Cash, check or credit cards
Getting There:
Fly to Lewisburg and rent a car.
Other Activities:
Bird-watching, boating, canoeing/kayaking/rafting, horseback riding, hiking, skiing, wildlife photography

Contact:
Sherry Yates
Cheat Mountain Club
PO Box 28
Durbin WV 26264
Ph: 304/456-4627
Fax: 304/456-3192
e-mail:
cheatmc@newmedia.net
Web:
www.cheatmountainclub.com

Class VI River Runners

L a n s i n g ,   W e s t   V i r g i n i a

Smallies are on the bite, but the only way to reach them is via a crazy raft ride through the New River Gorge.

VITAL STATISTICS:

KEY SPECIES:
Muskie, smallmouth

Tackle:
Fly-fishing, spinning
Major Season:
April through November
Accommodations:
RIVER CAMPS OR CABIN
NUMBER OF ROOMS: 4 IN CABIN
MAXIMUM NUMBER OF GUESTS: 8 IN CABIN
Meals: Streamside
Conference Groups: Yes
Rates: From $400 / boat
Guides: Included
Gratuities: Angler's discretion
Preferred Payment:
Cash, check or credit cards
Getting There:
Fly to Charleston and rent a car.
Other Activities:
Big game, bird-watching, canoeing/kayaking/rafting, horseback riding, hiking

Contact:
Dave Arnold
Class VI River Runners
Ames Heights Rd
PO Box 78
Lansing WV 25862
Ph: 800/252-7784
Fax: 304/574-4906
e-mail:
classvi@raftwv.com
Web:
www.raftwv.com

EVER THE ANGLER, you're scanning the deep olive-colored river as you cast your crayfish crankbait here and there, probing for smallmouth. At the end of the pool, a half-mile or so downstream, you see flashes of white. A questions forms in the back off your mouth, but then a smallmouth of a pound plus inhales your lure and you concentrate on the fish. Releasing it, you hear Brian, your guide, yell, "Hang on!" as the white raft noses into a caldron of steaming, spinning froth. Bucking like a bull, the raft surges up, standing on its stern. Brian is screaming, "Cast left, Cast left!" and somehow you manage to fire the plug into a moment's still water where what must have been a five-pounder slapped your plug, played with you for a heartbeat, and them broke off as you vanished into a wall of foam. This is extreme fishing!

The New River is a tailwater known for some of the highest quality smallmouth fishing in the country. However, even die-hard anglers would not take a boat into the gorge. Water there is dangerously rough for anything other than a reinforced raft. But you can fish from a raft, so why not? Day trips of six miles, and longer overnight expeditions, down the New are something of a specialty for Dave Arnold, a whitewater nut who owns Class VI River Runners. Class VI rafts have rigid floors with padded pedestal seats. Personal gear is stowed in dry bags. All you have to do is plug pockets behind the boulders and hang on!

Smallmouth fishing is best in May, June and August, while your best shot at muskies up to 45 inches comes in August and September. This is a spin fisher's game, so bring plenty of plugs — spinner baits and Rebel lures — but also slip in a 6-weight with a sink tip line and a bunch of big Woolly Buggers. Why not?

Unless you stay in Class VI's new cabin for eight (four bedrooms, two baths), you'll want to take your own tackle and camping gear. If you need to rent tents, pads or sleeping bags, you can from Class VI. Equipment for overnight treks — tents, sleeping bags, dry clothing, food — is carried in a supply raft. Day trippers will marvel at the gourmet lunch spread beside the river. Overnighters will welcome hors d'oeuvres and wine that precede dinner. If you'd rather have a hot shower at the end of the day, the staff at Class VI will make arrangements for your stay at one of more than a dozen hostelries, ranging from the elegant Greenbrier at White Sulphur Springs, an hour and a half from the river, to bed-and-breakfasts or rustic cabins nearby.

MIDWEST

ILLINOIS, INDIANA, IOWA, KANSAS, MICHIGAN, MINNESOTA, MISSOURI, NEBRASKA, NORTH DAKOTA, OHIO, OKLAHOMA, SOUTH DAKOTA, WISCONSIN

THERE'S A TENDENCY to think of those great plains that run from the Allegheny's to the Rockies as boringly the same. Don't fall into that trap. While the lay of the land may be fairly flat, it varies with the subtlety of an intricate tapestry and contains hidden surprises for those willing to give it more than scant attention. Sure, you know about the great trout and steelhead streams of Michigan and Arkansas and the walleye and smallmouth of the Great Lakes. But what do you know of the wild browns in the Driftless Area or walleye that can be caught on a fly in the Missouri or Mississippi. In keeping with the plain sense of the sweeping prairies, fishing lodges are few. Rather, anglers hole up in tidy motels or restored Victorian B&Bs and take their meals in country restaurants where everything is good.

References:

AU SABLE
by Bob Linsenman
GREAT LAKES STEELHEAD GUIDE
by Mike Modrzynski
PERE MARQUETTE RIVER
by Matthew A. Supinski
Frank Amato Publications
P.O. Box 82112
Portland, OR 97282
503/653-8108

WISCONSIN & MINNESOTA TROUT STREAMS
by Jim Humphrey & Bill Shogren
GREAT LAKES STEELHEAD: A GUIDED TOUR FOR FLY-ANGLERS

MICHIGAN TROUT STREAMS
by Bob Linsenman & Steve Nevala
Backcountry Publications
The Countryman Press
Rt. 2, P.O. Box 748,
Woodstock, VT 05091
802/457-4826

FLY FISHING FOR TROUT IN MISSOURI
by Chuck & Sharon Tryon
FOzark Mountain Fly Fishers
1 Johnson St., Rolla, MO 65401
573/364-5509

Resources:

ARKANSAS GAME AND FISH COMMISSION
Information Section
2 Natural Resources Dr.
Little Rock, AR 72205
501/223-6300
800/364-4263 ext. 6351
web: www.agfc.state.ar.us

ILLINOIS DEPARTMENT OF NATURAL RESOURCES
Lincoln Tower Plaza
524 S. Second St
Springfield, IL 62701-1787
217/785-0067
web: http://dnr.state.il.us

INDIANA DIVISION OF FISH AND WILDLIFE
402 W. Washington St., Room W-273
Indianapolis, IN 46204
317/232-4080
web:
www.dnr.state.in.us/fishwild/index.html

[M I D W E S T]

IOWA DEPARTMENT OF
NATURAL RESOURCES
Wallace State Office Building
East Ninth and Grand Ave
Des Moines, IA 50319
515/281-5145
web: www.state.ia.us/wildlife

KANSAS DEPARTMENT OF
WILDLIFE AND PARKS
900 SW Jackson St., Suite 502
Topeka, KS 66612-1233
913/296-2281
web: www.kdwp.state.ks.us

MICHIGAN DEPARTMENT OF
NATURAL RESOURCES
Wildlife Division
Box 30444
Lansing, MI 48909
517/373-1263
web: www.dnr.state.mi.us

MINNESOTA DEPARTMENT OF
NATURAL RESOURCES
Division of Fish and Wildlife
500 Lafayette St
St. Paul, MN 55155-4001
612/297-1308
web: www.dnr.state.mn.us/

MISSOURI DEPARTMENT
OF CONSERVATION
2901 W. Truman Blvd., Box 180
Jefferson City, MO 65102-0180
573/751-4115
web: www.conservation.state.mo.us

NEBRASKA GAME AND
PARKS COMMISSION
2200 N. 33rd St., Box 30370
Lincoln, NE 68503
402/471-0641
web: www.npgc.state.ne.us

NORTH DAKOTA STATE GAME
AND FISH DEPARTMENT
100 North Bismarck Expy
Bismarck, ND 58501
701/328-6300
web: www.state.nd.us/gnf/

OHIO DIVISION OF WILDLIFE
1840 Belcher Dr
Columbus, OH 43224-1329
614/265-6300
web: www.dnr.state.oh.us/odnr/wildlife

OKLAHOMA DEPARTMENT OF
WILDLIFE CONSERVATION
1801 N. Lincoln
Box 53465
Oklahoma City, OK 73152
405/521-3851
web: www.state.ok.us/~odwc

SOUTH DAKOTA DEPARTMENT OF
GAME, FISH AND PARKS
523 E. Capitol
Pierre, SD 57501-3182
605/773-3387
web:
www.state.sd.us/state/gfp/index.html

WISCONSIN DEPARTMENT OF
NATURAL RESORUCES
PO Box 7921
Madison WI 53707
608/266-2121
web: www.dnr.state.wi.us

Which fly? The choice on the fine stream that flows through Dogwood Canyon near Big Cedar Lodge makes little difference. Here you'll find hefty rainbows, brookies and browns of three to five pounds and sometimes more.

Starved Rock Lodge

Utica, Illinois

What's the finest tasting freshwater fish in the country? Walleye fishermen will tell you it's sauger.

A MONG THE least known species of game fish in North America is the sauger. Nobody's burning up the sauger tourney circuit or getting rich endorsing sauger boats or marketing special scents to attract this cousin of the walleye. Yet when it comes to eating, sauger is fine fare indeed and that's the secret of Starved Rock Lodge on the Illinois River.

Sauger are similar to walleye, but they are smaller, averaging a pound or two. They can be easily identified by the round spots on the membranes between the dorsal spines. They can stand water with a heavier silt content than walleyes, and like their more popular cousins, prefer deep water. In fact, walleyes like shallower water than sauger. In the Midwest, some of the best sauger waters are those below dams. That's the case at this lodge hard by a dam that impounds a short section of the river.

At Starved Rock, you'll find four times as many saugers as walleyes. Typical fish run between 14 and 18 inches. Walleyes tend to be a little larger, though not as plentiful. Best fishing is from April through June, and again from September through November. Fall fishing, because water levels are more stable, is more predictable. Anglers working jigs and minnows, minnows under slip bobbers, and spinnerbaits should do well. Some anglers may be disappointed that they're catching sauger and not walleye, but that only lasts until their first mouthful of broiled sauger filet.

Above the dam, the Illinois River takes on the character of still water. Fish the mouths of feeder creeks for smallmouth bass of 12 inches or so in the spring. Scrappy white bass, also called striped bass (which they're not), hit jigs and spinners with abandon in spring. Throughout summer, you'll find a profusion of panfish made for kids with light spinning tackle. Channel cats can go into the double digits, and they're the favorite quarry of some anglers. Fishing information, licenses and guides are available from Starved Rock Bait & Tackle (815/667-4862).

As you'd expect, anyplace with a name like Starved Rock has to have a bit of lore behind it. In the 1760s, members of the Illiniwek slew the noble Pontiac, chief of the Ottawas. In revenge, the Ottawas and their allies, the Potawatomi, surrounded a high bluff to which the Illiniwek had retreated, and starved them to death. Today, no one starves at this state park resort. The restaurant is open year-round and has something of a local reputation for fine fish. Guests stay in rooms in the lovely old hotel, built by the CCC in the 1930s, or in nearby cabins.

VITAL STATISTICS:

KEY SPECIES:
Catfish, sauger, walleye, white bass

Tackle:
Casting, spinning, live bait
Major Season:
All year
Accommodations:
Historic lodge and cabins
Number of Rooms: 94
Handicapped Accessible: All
Maximum Number of Guests: 280
Meals: Full-service restaurant
Conference Groups: Yes
Rates: From $60 / day
Guides: $250 / day
Gratuities: Angler's discretion
Preferred Payment:
Cash, check or credit cards
Getting There:
Fly to Chicago and rent a car.
Other Activities:
Bird-watching, boating, canoeing/kayaking/rafting, golf, horseback riding, hiking, skiing, swimming, wildlife photography

Contact:
Jackie Just
Starved Rock Lodge
PO Box 570
Rts. 71 & 178
Utica IL 61373
Ph: 815/667-4211
Fax: 815/667-4455
e-mail:
srlodge@ivnet.com
Web:
www.starvedrocklodge.com

Gates Au Sable Lodge

G r a y l i n g ,   M i c h i g a n

These holy waters hatched Trout Unlimited, and insects upon which browns and rainbows feed with abandon.

VITAL STATISTICS:

KEY SPECIES:
Brookies, browns, rainbows

Tackle:
Fly-fishing
Major Season:
April through October
Accommodations:
Clean and comfortable motel rooms
Number of Rooms: 16
Handicapped Accessible: 8
Maximum Number of Guests: 36
Meals: Fine homestyle cooking
Conference Groups: Yes
Rates: From $80 / 2
Guides: $195
Gratuities: 20% - 30%
Preferred Payment:
Cash, check or credit cards
Getting There:
Fly to Traverse City and rent a car.
Other Activities:
Bird-watching, canoeing/kayaking/
rafting, golf, hiking, swimming,
wildlife photography

Contact:
Rusty Gates
Gates Au Sable Lodge
471 Stephan Bridge Rd
Grayling MI 49738
Ph: 517/348-8462
Fax: 517/348-2541
e-mail:
gator@gateslodge.com
Web:
www.gateslodge.com

RISING JUST WEST of Interstate 75 near the town of Grayling, the Au Sable ranks along with the streams of New York's Catskills as America's most hallowed trout waters. It was on this river in 1959 that George Griffith, a passionate angler and conservationist, adapted the principles of Ducks Unlimited to cold water fisheries. He'd been pleased with how TUers had labored to maintain the river he loved. And you can bet that were he still alive, he'd enjoy its fishing.

In the headwaters above Grayling, you'll find some small but wild brookies, browns and rainbows. After cutting through the town, gathering water from the confluence with its East Branch and ducking under the highway, the Au Sable assumes the persona that sustains it through the Holy Water — eight miles of fly-fishing only, no-kill angling. Riffling a gravel and sand bottom, tufted here and there with waving strands of aquatic grasses, the river here is quite wadeable and fish hold in easily seen lies. (They can see you, too!) Hendricksons garner the most interest from early season anglers. Later, in May, come the Sulphurs. Hexigenia limbata is the signature hatch of the river's next run from Wakley Bridge to Mio Pond. From late May into mid-June, nymphal forms will prove successful if fished late in the day and into the evening. Duns emerge in June and early July, and fishing for hoggish browns in the dark of night is as challenging as it is exciting. Numerous sections of this long river are governed by special regulations. Spinfishers as well as fly-fishermen will enjoy themselves.

If the eight miles of the Au Sable below Grayling is called "the Holy Water," then its church is the fly shop at Gates Au Sable Lodge, and its high priest is Rusty Gates. He knows the river like no one else. For more than a quarter of a century, he's guided anglers, tied patterns specific to the river and fought like a pit bull to ensure that development, pollution and politics do not upset the balance of this world-class stream. As for the lodge, 16 spacious rooms, efficiencies and a suite (all with private baths) face the river. So, too, does the dining room where Rusty's wife, Julie, runs the restaurant. Together they operate one of the most complete shops in the Midwest and it is well stocked with flies proven on the river. Fish free-lance or hire a guide and float the river in a slim, canoe-line Au Sable River boat. That's the time honored way, and you'll love it.

Johnson's Pere Marquette Lodge

Baldwin, Michigan

It's hard not to be seduced by salmon and steelhead, but focus on monster browns if you can.

VITAL STATISTICS:

KEY SPECIES:
Browns, chinook & coho salmon, rainbows, steelhead

Tackle:
Fly-fishing, spinning
Major Season:
May through September
Accommodations:
Cedar lodge and cabins
Number of Rooms: 34
Handicapped Accessible: 1
Maximum Number of Guests: 70
Meals: Outstanding game dinners
Conference Groups: Yes
Rates: From $39
Guides: $225 / day
Gratuities: Angler's discretion
Preferred Payment:
Cash, check or credit cards
Getting There:
Fly to Grand Rapids and rent a car.
Other Activities:
Canoeing/kayaking/rafting, golf

Contact:
Jim Johnson
Johnson's Pere Marquette Lodge
Rt. 1, Box 1290
Baldwin MI 49304
Ph: 616/745-3972
Fax: 616/745-3830

Agents:
Orvis endorsed

THE PERE MARQUETTE is a river of varying species and looks. From late fall into mid-spring, steelhead run up into the river from its mouth at Ludington on Lake Michigan's shore. Chinook enter the system in August and continue into October. Browns and rainbows, with the former predominating, are the mainstays of the river. Most anglers, such as author Bob Linsenman, divide the Pere Marquette into three sections.

The upper river, east of Route 37 and south of Baldwin, offers fine angling for browns for about nine miles up to Rosa Road, where it becomes a bit small to fish comfortably. In this section, the river is narrow, averaging about 20 feet, and shallow, seldom more than three feet deep. From the Rt. 37 bridge eight miles west to Gleason's Landing is the most famous reach of the river and it's restricted to fly-fishing only. The fishing does not end at Gleason's; it's just that the river is bigger, deeper and more dicey to wade. But it also hides its share of mature browns and rainbows, as well as salmon and steelhead in their seasons.

But according to Bob Linsenman and Steve Nevala, authors of *Michigan Trout Streams*, too many anglers concentrate on the Pere Marquette's glamour fish, salmon and steelhead, and give short shrift to "its everyday citizens, beautiful and healthy brown trout." Sure, everyone loves to see a nine-pound steelhead slam a Wiggler pattern, slash off 75 feet of line and somersault upstream. But browns are the mainstay of this river, and you can avoid the crowds by fishing where most others don't. Linsenman recommends attractors: Royal Wulffs, Adams and Rusty's Spinners; black and brown stonefly nymphs, sizes 8 to 10; and terrestrials, especially small 'hoppers for those days when puffs of summer wind blow them onto the water and turn on trout like nothing else.

Orvis-endorsed Johnson's Lodge is on the fly-fishing-only section of the river where it's crossed by Route 37 just below Baldwin. Built of cedar with a rustic fieldstone fireplace and log stair banister, the main lodge has 10 rooms, each with a large whirlpool tub. Five fishing cabins and two houses round out accommodations at Johnson's. The lodge has added a wonderful restaurant whose award-winning chef turns out cherry glazed duck, grilled elk steak, and stuffed salmon. Flies Only, a full-service tackle shop, supplies local patterns and plenty of information about stream conditions. You can arrange guides and floats here as well.

Angle Outpost Resort

A n g l e   I n l e t ,   M i n n e s o t a

Where's the northernmost land in the contiguous U.S.? If you said "Alaska," you blew it!

VITAL STATISTICS:

KEY SPECIES:
Muskie, pike, sauger, smallmouth, walleye

Tackle:
Casting, fly-fishing, spinning, trolling
Major Season:
May through November
Accommodations:
FULLY-EQUIPPED CABINS
NUMBER OF ROOMS: 30
HANDICAPPED ACCESSIBLE: 15
MAXIMUM NUMBER OF GUESTS: 65
Meals: Homestyle ribs, fish, chicken
Conference Groups: No
Rates: From $36 / day
Guides: $185 / up to 4 anglers
Gratuities: Angler's discretion
Preferred Payment:
Cash, check or credit cards
Getting There:
Fly to Winnipeg, Manitoba, and rent a car.
Other Activities:
Big game, waterfowling, wingshooting, boating, golf, horseback riding, hiking, snowmobiling, swimming

Contact:
Jessica Fandrich
Angle Outpost Resort
RR 1 Box 36
Angle Inlet MN 56711
Ph: 800/441-5014
Fax: 218/223-8101
e-mail:
angleoutpost@means.net
Web:
www.fishandgame.com

THERE'S A CHUNK OF THE U.S. that's totally separated from the rest of the country, but it's not an island. It's frequently the coldest spot on weather maps, and you'll find it jutting into Manitoba above the rest of Minnesota. Yep, Lake of the Woods is an isolated place, a peninsula that pokes into a lake that's roughly 66 miles long and 52 miles wide. Lake of the Woods contains 14,000 or so rocky islands wearing caps of spruce and fir. The peninsula carries the Red Lake Indian Reservation, and it's also known as the Northwest Angle.

As freshwater fisheries go, this is one of the finest in North America. Flattened and gouged by glaciers, the land is low and rocky. Boulders by the millions pave the shores of all the islands. Submerged reefs are everywhere. Some bays and backwaters are sandy, silt-bottomed and fringed with beds of reedy grass. The habitat is ideal for smallmouths, walleyes, pike and muskies. Bronzebacks are plentiful, though they seldom exceed two pounds. Fishing is best for them in July and August. Use crankbaits or unlimber that fly rod and work poppers or streamers along the bouldery shore. Walleyes, also abundant, generally run in the two- to three-pound class, but may top seven. Action with them begins in mid-May and peaks in June and July. Northern pike average five to eight pounds, but bruisers of 20 pounds or more take spoons or spinners often enough to keep you on your toes. Your best chance for a trophy is just after ice-out in May. And if you're after muskellunge, you'll find lots of 15-pounders, and many between 20 and 30. Fish for them from July through September. Don't forget ice fishing for walleyes and sauger.

Angle Outpost is one of the few full-service resorts serving anglers who want to fish Lake of the Woods. Numerous packages are available, from straight rental of one of 12 modern housekeeping cabins to a deluxe American plan that includes boat, motor and guide. The cabins are warm and homey, cheerfully decorated and scattered among the trees near the main lodge. Each has a fully-equipped kitchen (coffee maker and microwave) and most feature fireplaces or wood stoves. In addition to the restaurant, you'll find a camp store that sells groceries as well as bait, tackle and gifts. You can launch or rent a boat at the marina.

Birch Knoll Ranch

Lanesboro, Minnesota

Southeastern Minnesota offers outstanding angling for wild trout with very little pressure.

VITAL STATISTICS:

KEY SPECIES:
Brookies, browns, rainbows

Tackle:
Fly-fishing, spinning
Major Season:
April through September
Accommodations:
CLASSIC BED-AND-BREAKFAST
NUMBER OF ROOMS: 3
MAXIMUM NUMBER OF GUESTS: 6
Meals: On your own
Conference Groups: No
Rates: From $185 / night / up to 6
Guides: Available
Gratuities: Angler's discretion
Preferred Payment:
Cash or check
Getting There:
Fly to Rochester and rent a car.
Other Activities:
Big game, biking, bird-watching,
canoeing/kayaking/rafting

Contact:
Duke Hust
Birch Knoll Ranch
Box 11
Lanesboro MN 55949
Ph: 507/467-2418

Off Season:
820 Old Crystal Bay Rd
Wayzata MN 55391
Ph: 612/475-2054
Fax: 612/341-9363

WHEN IT COMES TO sheer numbers of fine trout streams, it's very hard to beat southeastern Minnesota and southwestern Wisconsin. On any given day during the season from April through September, you'll find at least half a dozen streams with hatches, but no anglers. And we're not talking little fish either. Browns range into the upper teens with regularity, while fish measuring more than 20 inches are not common, but not unheard of either.

How come the fishing's so good and nobody knows about it? Three reasons: geology; the partnership among landowners, TU and FFF chapters, and the state fisheries folk; and walleye. For reasons not fully understood, continental glaciers flowed around — not over — this area. So, unlike other regions, the steep and narrow valleys here were not filled up with sand and cobble. Along valley floors flow freestone, spring-fed creeks. The region, too, has benefited from more than a generation of cooperation from farmers and anglers facilitated by state agencies. The result is an abundance of easements along high-quality trout waters. What of walleye? It's simple. Most Minnesota anglers put down their trout tackle when walleye season opens in May, leaving the streams to catch-and-release trouters.

Lanesboro is a charming old mill village in the center of the state's finest trout waters. The South Fork of the Root River flows through town. Nearby is Trout Run, which made TU's list of the best streams in the country. You'll also find Beaver Creek and the Whitewater (fine winter fishing, would you believe it?). An hour's drive to the east opens up all the similar streams in Wisconsin. Hatches are prolific. But a fly box containing Elk-Hair Caddis (no. 14 to 18), Blue-Winged Olives (no. 16 to 18), Adams (no. 14 to 18) and a stock of Gold-Ribbed Hare's Ears, Woolly Buggers and Pheasant Tail Nymphs will suffice. Guide Wayne Bartz (507/289-7312) can be helpful to first-time visitors.

In the village are a number of bed-and-breakfasts and a couple of really good restaurants. But among the most congenial hostelries for weary anglers is Birch Knoll Ranch, a bed-and-breakfast owned by Duke Hust, a Twin Cities trout activist. You and your friends will be the only ones at the house when you book it. Breakfast is a do-it-yourself affair: all the fixings for blueberry French toast and similar fare are delivered (with instructions) each day. Cook when you want.

125

[M I D W E S T]

Eagle Ridge at Lutsen Mountain

L u t s e n , M i n n e s o t a

*Big 'bows and brookies feed after dark
on little lakes near this stylish lodge.*

VITAL STATISTICS:

KEY SPECIES:
Brookies, king/chinook salmon, lake trout, pike, rainbows, silver/coho salmon, steelhead

Tackle:
Fly-fishing, spinning, trolling
Major Season:
May through September
Accommodations:
MODERN STUDIOS AND CONDOMINIUMS
NUMBER OF ROOMS: 75
HANDICAPPED ACCESSIBLE: 6
MAXIMUM NUMBER OF GUESTS: 300
Meals: Full-service restaurant or whip up your own gourmet delights
Conference Groups: Yes
Rates: From $49
Guides: $250 / day
Gratuities: $20 / day
Preferred Payment:
Cash, check or credit cards
Getting There:
Fly to Duluth and rent a car.
Other Activities:
Bird-watching, boating, canoeing/kayaking/rafting, golf, hiking, skiing, swimming, wildlife photography

Contact:
Reservations
Eagle Ridge at
Lutsen Mountain
Box 106
Lutsen MN 55612
Ph: 800/360-7666
Fax: 218/663-7699
Web:
www.lutsen.com/eagleridge

THINK "MINNESOTA" and what pops into mind? Walleyes and *Grumpy Old Men*? That may be true in the state's endless prairies and forested plains, but when you hit the North Shore, you're talking trout, salmon and steelhead. It's as if somebody transplanted the best of coastal Maine to the Midwest, only the waves lapping the stony shore are fresh, not salt. You do have the impression of being on the ocean here; Superior is the world's largest freshwater lake. You're also in the mountains, or so it seems. Rocky headlands rise 300 feet above the lake and climb steadily to nearly twice that high a few miles west of the beach. Myriad little streams, and some major ones, too, cut down through the highlands to the lake. Headwaters teem with native brook trout, while the rivers are more brown trout water. And at the base of falls and impassable cataracts, you'll find steelhead and chinooks.

Flowing by the lodge is the Poplar River, a tannin-water brook trout stream. But better and easier fishing is to be found in numerous lakes up in the hills. Inland lakes, heavily stocked by Minnesota's Department of Natural Resources, produce healthy catches of 12- to 14-inch rainbows and brook trout. Best fishing is in early summer, from the opening of the season in mid-May to the end of June. September is also good. However, you could be in for a treat if you schedule your trip for late June or early July. Some of these inland lakes see good Hexagenia hatches, and that means stellar fishing from dark until midnight. That's when rainbows of six or seven pounds and brookies of up to five pounds come out to feed. The North Shore steelhead and chinook fisheries are in decline as of this writing. While there is some fishing in the Arrowhead Brule, numbers of fish entering the river are falling off.

Eagle Ridge is not a fishing lodge in the conventional sense. Rather, there's the nearby Superior National Golf Course and excellent hiking and sailing all in an environment that feels and looks like the Maine coast. For guests who want to fish, the helpful staff will make a call to Granpa Woo who runs fishing charters on Lake Superior, or to Smith Bait and Tackle, a sport shop that offers guide service for spin and fly anglers. Located at one of the North Shore's finest ski complexes, Eagle Ridge offers a range of modern and well-appointed lodgings, from studios with fireplaces, Jacuzzi, microwaves and refrigerators to one- to three-bedroom condominiums, many with fireplaces or Jacuzzi and all with complete kitchens.

Golden Eagle Lodge

Grand Marais, Minnesota

On Flour Lake, smallmouth have made a miraculous recovery!

VITAL STATISTICS:

KEY SPECIES:
Lake trout, pike, smallmouth, walleye

Tackle:
Fly-fishing, spinning
Major Season:
May through September
Accommodations:
FULLY-EQUIPPED CABINS OR CAMPSITES
NUMBER OF ROOMS: 11
HANDICAPPED ACCESSIBLE: 2
MAXIMUM NUMBER OF GUESTS: 64
Meals: Self-catered in summer
Conference Groups: No
Rates: From $99 / day / 2
Guides: $90 / day
Gratuities: $20 - $30
Preferred Payment:
Cash, check or credit cards
Getting There:
Fly to Duluth and rent a car.
Other Activities:
Wingshooting, bird-watching, boating, canoeing/kayaking/rafting, hiking, skiing, swimming, wildlife photography

Contact:
Dan Baumann
Golden Eagle Lodge
468 Clearwater Rd
Grand Marais MN 55604
Ph: 218/388-2203
Fax: 218/388-9417
e-mail:
sports@golden-eagle.com
Web:
www.golden-eagle.com

THE BIG NEWS HERE on Flour Lake, just south of the Boundary Waters Canoe Area in northern Minnesota, is the phenomenal resurgence of the smallmouth bass population. Three years ago, when faced with declining size and populations, Minnesota's DNR established 11 inches as the maximum size for keepers. You can get a couple of nice filets from a 10- or 11-incher, but everything larger had to be returned unharmed to the lake. Did it make a difference? You bet. The number of three and four pound smallies caught-and-released in Flour is rising annually and, for the first year in a long time, several five-pounders were boated and returned. That's great news!

Flour Lake is not unusual. It's like hundreds along the watery border between Minnesota and Ontario. Shores are rocky. Boulders are strewn about the bottoms. Small, secret rivers, often caroming down tight, narrow channels, link one to the next. Rocky reefs rise underneath, but do not break the surface. Low ridges thick with pine and spruce separate the lakes, channeling any winds. Flour is small as these lakes go, only three miles long and not a mile at its widest spot. Though powerboats are allowed, this is canoeing water at its best.

When ice leaves the lake in May, lake trout up to 26 inches, walleye in the three- to five-pound range and northern pike go on the feed. Lake trout are rapacious, falling for crawlers and Rapalas cast from shore or fished from a boat. Use a canoe to troll the lake. Rest your rod on the gunwale with the grip cocked behind one leg and the butt section braced against the front of the other. Tie your paddle to the thwart with a thin, eight-foot line. When a fish hits the lure, you can drop the paddle without losing it overboard and grab the rod. June to September is best for smallmouth. Walleyes become predatory at dusk, moving out of the depths and into shallow water. You'll also find perch available year-round. The outflow of Flour Lake leads into the Boundary Waters Area, accessible only by canoe.

Golden Eagle Lodge is not massive by resort standards. Eleven cabins spread out from the lodge along Flour Lake. The cabins (all with kitchens, fireplaces and private baths) can sleep two to six comfortably. New in 1999 was a nine-site campground, with electric and water hookups and a shower. The Golden Eagle provides meals for cross-country skiers and ice fishermen, but during summer, guests either cook in their cabins or avail themselves of the chow at nearby restaurants.

VITAL STATISTICS:

KEY SPECIES:
Perch, pike, walleye

Tackle:
Casting, spinning, trolling
Major Season:
May through February
Accommodations:
LAKEVIEW CABINS
NUMBER OF ROOMS: 51
HANDICAPPED ACCESSIBLE: All
MAXIMUM NUMBER OF GUESTS: 150
Meals: Hearty country fare
Conference Groups: Yes
Rates: From $345 / 2 days,
3 nights, double occupancy
Guides: $225
Gratuities: $20 - $40
Preferred Payment:
Cash, check or credit cards
Getting There:
Fly to Bemidji and rent a car.
Other Activities:
Waterfowling, wingshooting, bird-
watching, boating, golf, horseback
riding, hiking, snowmobiling,
swimming, tennis

Contact:
Ron or Sharon Hunter
Judd's Resort
52 W. Winnie Estates Dr. NE
Bena MN 56626
Ph: 218/665-2216
Fax: 218/665-2237
e-mail:
captron@judds-resort.com
Web:
www.judds-resort.com

Judd's Resort

B e n a ,   M i n n e s o t a

*Winter or summer, the walleyes on
Winnibigoshish are willing, but are you?*

DEEP IN THE HEART of the Leech Lake
Indian Reservation and surrounded by the
Chippewa National Forest, lies the headwa-
ters lake of the Mississippi River (formed of
course, when Babe the Blue Ox got rambunctious and upset Paul Bunyon's water
wagon). This is walleye water without peer. It's a favorite of "Mr. Walleye" — Gary
Roach — and his Roach Rigs are very popular. Guides on this lake also like
Northland Tackle's eight-ounce Fireball jigs in either two-tone chartreuse/lime
green or glow-in-the dark shades. They also give the nod to Loomis rods, Trilene
XL, and Lund Pro V boats pushed by Yamaha outboards.

Lake Winnibigoshish differs from such walleye waters as Mille Lacs. Far
fewer cabins rim Winnibigoshish. Angling pressure is lighter in the summer.
There's a really good chance of landing six- to eight-pound fish in the summer.
Northerns from nine to fifteen pounds attack Dardevles in spring and summer.
Fishing slows in the fall while everything freezes. But by the first of December,
Judd's is pulling its ice houses out on the ice, and anglers are lining up to catch
buckets of yellow perch of up to a pound and a half. The action is nonstop, and
anglers can take up to 100 fish. This is where folks from Wisconsin and Iowa come
to fill their freezers. Judd's will clean your catch at 20 cents per perch. That's the
best deal in town. Winter also brings out the black shacks for anglers who like to
spear northerns.

Judd's offers a number of packages, ranging from rental of housekeeping cottages (great if you have your own boat, know the lake, and like to cook), to full-
service guided trips. Launches are available for larger groups who want to fish
together, for anglers who want to fish at night, and for individuals who don't care
to fish from a small boat. Prices are reasonable.

Food at Judd's is basic — steaks, ribs, chicken, fish (yours if you want) —
and accommodations are comfortably utilitarian. Ten cabins overlook the lake
and another 10 are spread under the trees near the main lodge. Two of the cabins
are really full-size houses, ideal for families. Some of the cabins offer private baths
with each bedroom; others share. All have kitchenettes. No need to stock up on
lures, bait or licenses. Along with a fleet of rental boats and motors, Judd's has a
good supply of everything you need.

Rockwood Lodge

Grans Marais, Minnesota

*Fish the Gunflint Trail from canoes
and see it as the Voyageurs did.*

**VITAL
STATISTICS:**

KEY SPECIES:
Brookies, lake trout, pike,
rainbows, smallmouth,
walleye

Tackle:
Casting, fly-fishing, spinning, trolling
Major Season:
May through September
Accommodations:
CLASSIC LOG LODGE
NUMBER OF ROOMS: 7
HANDICAPPED ACCESSIBLE: SOME
MAXIMUM NUMBER OF GUESTS: 31
Meals: Self-catered or dine in fine
restaurants nearby
Conference Groups: Yes
Rates: From $125
Guides: $175 / day
Gratuities: $20+
Preferred Payment:
Cash, check or credit cards
Getting There:
Fly to Duluth and rent a car.
Other Activities:
Bird-watching, boating,
canoeing/kayaking/rafting, hiking,
swimming, wildlife photography

Contact:
Val or Gail Roloff
Rockwood Lodge
50 Rockwood Road
Grand Marais MN 55604
Ph: 800/942/2922
Fax: 218/388-0117
e-mail:
rockwood@boreal.org
Web:
www.rockwood-bwca.com

WHEN YOU SLIP YOUR CANOE into Poplar Lake in front of Rockwood Lodge, you've entered a land of more than a million acres, a thousand lakes and as many or more streams and connecting rivers. This is the Boundary Waters Canoe Area, a web of thin channels, jewel-like ponds and some big waters where, if the wind is blowing against you, you'll know you've put in a day's paddling. Here, granite of the Canadian shield plays leapfrog with dark tannic-rich waters. Loons shield their young from your passing canoe and their tremulous cries hang with your dreams.

Seven sporting species dominate these waters. When the season opens in mid-May, walleyes (one to three pounds), brook trout (one to three pounds), splake (one to three pounds; a naturally occurring brook trout/lake trout hybrid) and lake trout (two to eight pounds) will be ready for your lures. No need to go deep as these fish find forage near the top of the water column in spring. Trolling is a good strategy now, as is casting from boat or shore. As summer warms, they will go deeper and you'll have to dredge or jig them up. In August and September, they move back into the shallows for a final feed before winter. Northern pike go three to 10 pounds, and can exceed 20. They hit well all season. Fly-fishermen will enjoy them best when they are shallow and can be sight-fished in May and early June. In the height of summer, big rainbows can be taken from lakes and feeder streams, as can smallmouth bass.

Rockwood Lodge is one of the original lodges that sits astride the Gunflint Trail. Use it as your portal to this ageless land. Built in the 1920s of pine logs, the lodge is revered by those who know it for its eclectic and rustic atmosphere. Guests stay in comfortable cabins with private baths and full kitchens. Bring your own filet mignon and salmon with vintages to match. Or you can hie yourself to one of the many restaurants nearby. Rockwood also outfits parties for three- to seven-day canoe and fishing treks. Packages range from economical aluminum canoes to ultralight Kevlars for extended trips with many portages.

If you head to this country, read Sigrud Olson's *Rune's of the North* or *Open Horizons* before you come. These books will whet your spirit; bring one or the other with you. Read a little each night and again in the morning. If you do this, Mr. Olson — the greatest of the northwoods writers — will whisper his secrets in your ear as you paddle down the trail.

[M I D W E S T]

Big Cedar Lodge

R i d g e d a l e ,   M i s s o u r i

You'll find it all — bass, trout, par-three golf — at this ultimate outdoors resort.

VITAL STATISTICS:

KEY SPECIES:
Crappie, largemouth, smallmouth, trout

Tackle:
Casting, fly-fishing, spinning

Major Season:
All year

Accommodations:
HOTELS AND COTTAGES
NUMBER OF ROOMS: 247
HANDICAPPED ACCESSIBLE: 7
MAXIMUM NUMBER OF GUESTS: 750

Meals: Choose from three restaurants

Conference Groups: Yes

Rates: From $79

Guides: $215 / day

Gratuities: Angler's discretion

Preferred Payment:
Cash, check or credit cards

Getting There:
Fly to Springfield and rent a car.

Other Activities:
Bird-watching, boating, canoeing/kayaking/rafting, golf, horseback riding, hiking, skiing, swimming, tennis

Contact:
Reservations
Big Cedar Lodge
612 Devil's Pool Rd
Ridgedale MO 65739
Ph: 417/335-2777
Fax: 417/334-3956
Web:
www.big-cedar.com

JOHNNY MORRIS founded the world's largest retail sporting goods company — Bass Pro Shops — and is now in the process of developing the National Fishing and Wildlife Center adjacent to Bass Pro headquarters in Springfield, Missouri. Springfield is located on the cusp of the Ozarks. A few miles south of town the land begins to fall away into deep valleys and steep limestone hills. This terrain is part of the White River watershed. A number of dams impound the river, creating a chain of stellar bass lakes and wonderful tailwaters for trout below. Among the best of the fishing lakes is Table Rock.

On this lake, known for largemouth, crappie and some smallmouth, Morris created Big Cedar Lodge. Don't be put off by the number of potential guests. On a pair of hillside points, he's laid out seven (at this counting) separate lodges and cabin communities that offer lodging for virtually every taste and wallet. There's Valley View Lodge that sits atop its own ridge. Accommodations here range form standard rooms to palatial suites. Adjacent is the new Falls Lodge where each of the 65 rooms has its own balcony and Jacuzzi. In the style of an old Adirondack sporting resort, Spring View Lodge faces a charming series of waterfalls and provides guests with a measure of seclusion and tranquility. Add four clusters of cabins that range from elegant private vacation residences to the fishing cabins of Thunderhead Point, and you get the picture. Many cabins offer kitchen facilities but, of course, there's the Devil's Pool restaurant with its elegant country cuisine.

One of the first lakes to adopt a 15-inch limit on largemouths, 43,000-acre Table Rock produces its share of good-size bass. You'll find some flats in the upper end, but flooded timber and aquatic vegetation is minimal. Rocky bluffs line the shore. The best action is at creek mouths and their channels in winter. Then try crankbaits over spawning beds in spring; heavy spinnerbaits through deep schools of forage fish in summer; and back to the creeks in fall. You'll also find spotted bass near bluffs, and once in a while, pick up a smallmouth.

Trout anglers might want to check out Morris' Dogwood Canyon Nature Park about 20 minutes west of the main lodge. Flowing through 10,000 acres of mixed hardwoods is a carefully maintained spring-fed trout stream stocked with rainbows up to eight pounds. Fishing is fully catch-and-release. The park includes a few cabins for anglers who seek a bit more seclusion.

Chateau on the Lake

Branson, Missouri

So, what's this country music capital most famous for? Trout and Bass!

VITAL STATISTICS:

KEY SPECIES:
Browns, crappie, largemouth, rainbows, smallmouth

Tackle:
Basting, fly-fishing, spinning, trolling
Major Season:
All year
Accommodations:
GRAND HOTEL
NUMBER OF ROOMS: 301
HANDICAPPED ACCESSIBLE: 8
MAXIMUM NUMBER OF GUESTS: 650
Meals: From fine dining to sandwiches
Conference Groups: Yes
Rates: From $119
Guides: $220
Gratuities: Angler's discretion
Preferred Payment:
Cash, check or credit cards
Getting There:
Fly to Springfield and rent a car.
Other Activities:
Boating, canoeing/kayaking/rafting, golf, horseback riding, swimming, tennis

Contact:
Chateau on the Lake
415 N. State Hwy 265
Branson MO 65616
Ph: 417/334-1161
Fax: 417/339-5566
Web:
www.jqh.com/chateau

AT ONE TIME, Branson was a sleepy town along the banks of Lake Taneycomo. Not much happened there, except that a few good 'ol boys snagged bass out of a thin little lake backed up by a power-generating dam. But in 1958, the Corps of Engineers completed Table Rock Dam, and the cold water that issued from its base transformed this reach of the White River into one of the nation's finest coldwater fisheries. Then in the 1980s, somebody got the bright idea to bring in live country music shows, and soon, stars like Andy Williams and the Osmonds were opening theatres to the hills overlooking the tranquil river valley.

Table Rock Lake, with its 745 miles of shoreline, is known for stands of flooded cedar and oak. Kentuckies, largemouth and smallmouth are the prime sport fish here, but you'll also encounter excellent crappie in the spring. Since the reservoir was not cleared prior to impoundment, structure is abundant. You'll also fish rocky points, steep bluffs, gravel banks, submerged channels and creek mouths. Spring and fall fish better than high summer. Winter's good, too.

Below the dam flows a mile and a half of cold tailwater which draws fly-fishers from all over the U.S. When the generators are off, this water is easily waded. Most park at the Shepherd of the Hills fish hatchery on the Branson side of the river and fish around two outflows from the rearing station. Browns and rainbows up to 20 inches are the draw here, and you can find them all season. However, angling is best in this run of catch-and-release water during late fall and winter. There's little native propagation going on; what you're catching are stocked fish that gorge on bait in Lake Taneycomo and then run up to the shallows driven by the innate urge to spawn. Taneycomo itself is great for large rainbows and browns, fished with bait or lures from boats. A year-round fishery, the lake is home to a number of fishing marinas where guides, boats and bait are readily available.

John Q. Hammon's Chateau-on-the-Lake has all the earmarks of one of those great Swiss resort hotels, plus the best location in Branson as far as angling is concerned. This grand hotel overlooks the lake and the tailwater below the dam. There's a full-service marina and the catch-and-release section of the tailwater is less than a half-mile walk downhill. Fly-fishers should make it a point to stop into Chuck Gries' Anglers and Archery (417/335-4655) for advice on fishing Taneycomo.

[M I D W E S T]

Taylormade River Treks

T e c u m s e h ,   M i s s o u r i

*The river above Norfork Lake is without peer
when it comes to wild trout, fly-fishing and solitude.*

**VITAL
STATISTICS:**

KEY SPECIES:
**Browns, rainbows,
smallmouth, striped
bass/rockfish**

Tackle:
Fly-fishing
Major Season:
All year
Accommodations:
RIVERFRONT BED-AND-BREAKFAST
NUMBER OF ROOMS: 2
HANDICAPPED ACCESSIBLE: 1
MAXIMUM NUMBER OF GUESTS: 4
Meals: Breakfast, with dinners by
special request
Conference Groups: No
Rates: From $65 / night / 2
Guides: $250 / day
Gratuities: $25 - $50
Preferred Payment:
Cash or check
Getting There:
Fly to Springfield and rent a car.
Other Activities:
Bird-watching, canoeing/kayaking/
rafting, swimming, wildlife
photography

Contact:
Shawn & Chris Taylor
Taylormade River Treks
HC-1, Box 1755
Tecumseh MO 65760
Ph: 417/284-3055
e-mail:
tarpon3@juno.com

MOST OF THE BEST FISHERIES in the Ozarks are the famed tailwaters. Yet there's another, where flows aren't regulated by power demand, that's truly outstanding — so much so that Trout Unlimited named it one of the 100 best in the country. On maps it's called the North Fork of the White River, but most folks here just call it the North Fork. Rising east of the little town of Mountain Grove, the Norfork runs almost due south into the Mark Twain National Forest where it takes on nourishment from numerous tributaries before getting a real shot in the arm from two big springs – North Fork and Rainbow.

It is here where the most interesting water begins. From the springs south, classic freestone pocket water characterizes the river. A few limestone ledges transect the channel. And along the way you'll find pools fed by long smooth gravel runs and mileage where the river surges over and around big boulders. Canoes, johnboats and small drift boats provide the most convenient access to the river. Access is limited for foot-bound anglers until you reach Blair Bridge. Then you'll find numerous places to get into the water. The Norfork is the only major river in Missouri with a substantial population of wild rainbow trout. Some go seven pounds, but most average 19 inches. Browns are stocked.

This is primarily a river for nymphs or emergers says Shawn Taylor, impresario of Taylormade River Treks, a guide service cum bed-and-breakfast on the river near Tecumseh. While you'll find the usual mayflies and stoneflies, nymphs and streamers that imitate hellgrammites, crayfish and scuds also perform well. Floating and occasionally stopping to wade is the best way to fish the North Fork. Winter fishing may be better than summer, especially if you want to catch large 'bows and browns. Spring and summer feature dry fly action for trout, but don't overlook the smallmouths or hybrid striped bass. Trips to the White and Red in Arkansas are also available.

The Taylors offer two rooms in the lower level of their log home. The first boasts a fireplace, oak paneling, decorations of antique rods, reels, flies and related equipage, a library of old fishing books and a bristle dart board. Off the room is a private bath. The second room is similarly appointed sans fireplace and private bath. The inn serves breakfast with the price of the room, and provides a streamside lunch if you're fishing with one of the guides. Dinner can be arranged by special request.

WindRush Farms

Two cabins and a wild little log home offer an angler's getaway that's beyond compare.

VITAL STATISTICS:

KEY SPECIES:
Browns, largemouth, rainbows

Tackle:
Fly-fishing, spinning
Major Season:
Mid-February through November
Accommodations:
QUAINT CABINS AND A LOG HOME
NUMBER OF ROOMS: 9
MAXIMUM NUMBER OF GUESTS: 36
Meals: Be your own chef
Conference Groups: Yes
Rates: From $75 / night
Guides: $175 / 2
Gratuities: Angler's discretion
Preferred Payment:
Cash, check or credit cards
Getting There:
Fly to St. Louis and rent a car.
Other Activities:
Bird-watching, boating, canoeing/kayaking/rafting, golf, horseback riding, hiking, nature trails, swimming, wildlife photography

Contact:
Quint & Cicely Drennan
WindRush Farms
Cook Station MO 65449
Ph: 573/743-6555
Fax: 573-743-6888
e-mail:
windrush@misn.com
Web:
www.misn.com/windrush

A DOZEN YEARS AGO, the protagonists in this yarn found themselves with 400 acres drained by a stream so warm and shallow it wouldn't support a bluegill, let along trophy trout. Sure, it was fed by a lovely spring, but so choked was it with weeds and muddied by cattle that only a couple with vision or a knack for accepting reality would have looked at the mess and thought "trout."

Well, Quint and Cicely have never been much for conventional wisdom. They forged ahead and now WindRush Farm has earned a great reputation as a booming trout fishery. You need to understand up front that you'll pay $30 per day to fish the two miles of spring creek at WindRush or a similar mileage on SpringRise, their 500 acres half an hour to the east. What you get is angling over some of the finest spring-fed creeks in the Midwest less than 90 minutes from downtown St. Louis. Typical rainbows and browns run 14-inches-plus and a number of 20-inchers are taken each year. On both properties, the streams have been rehabilitated with pools, gravelly runs, lots of cover and a variety of fish-holding structures. Limited natural propagation is occurring.

Guests have their choice of accommodations. A pair of 1840s vintage log cabins contain four suites apiece. Each suite has a log bedroom and modern bath, living room and kitchen. You'll do your own cooking. A mile upstream is a lovely two acre spring pond where a funky, eccentric, but oh-so-comfortable log home sits. If you book into the home, you'll have the pond to yourself — lots of trout, largemouth to three pounds, and a few grass carp that will make believe they're salmon should you catch one on your four-weight. You'll do you own cooking here because Cook Station and nearby St. James aren't close to much besides antique shops, lots of outdoors and the headwaters of the Meremac, one of the Show-Me state's best trout fisheries. In a year or two, look for a new lodge at SpringRise, and perhaps rentals in vacation homes being built on five-acre lots in the rolling hills overlooking the stream.

[M I D W E S T]

Gayle's Bed & Breakfast

P u t - i n - B a y , O h i o

Smallmouth, walleye, perch and, when October rolls around, some of the best duckin' in the Midwest.

**VITAL
STATISTICS:**

KEY SPECIES:
**Smallmouth, walleye,
yellow perch**

Tackle:
Casting, spinning, trolling
Major Season:
All year
Accommodations:
FRAME BED-AND-BREAKFAST
NUMBER OF ROOMS: 4
MAXIMUM NUMBER OF GUESTS: 12
Meals: Scrumptious breakfasts
Conference Groups: No
Rates: From $40 / night, double
occupancy
Guides: $400+ / 6
Gratuities: Angler's discretion
Preferred Payment:
Cash, check or credit cards
Getting There:
Fly from Port Clinton.
Other Activities:
Waterfowling, boating, swimming

Contact:
Hank Polcyn
Gayle's Bed & Breakfast
85 Cessna Dr
Box 564
Put-in-Bay OH 43456
Ph: 419/285-7181

PAT CHRYSLER likes to put his clients onto fish. We're not talking about a few fish, but lots of fish — like limits of 30 fat yellow perch, or walleyes of 16- to 18-inches-plus, or smallmouth in the four- to six-pound range. Additionally, when the water cools down and fronts from Canada become more frequent, ducks of every description begin to sail across these islands in Lake Erie due north of Sandusky. That happens in October, and there's no better time to hang out in Put-in-Bay.

Put-in-Bay is a tiny community at the tip of a natural marina on South Bass Island. To get there, drive to Port Clinton and catch the six-seat Piper Cherokee to the island. It'll set you back all of $40 round trip. Once there, no matter what the season, you'll be up to your ears in fish. Chrysler will run you in his new air-boat out to the most active of his ice shanties in winter. You'll stay warm enough in a snowmobile suit. Though small, there's plenty of room in each shanty for two men, two holes, a fish-finder and a Thermos of hot coffee. Walleyes, averaging 14 to 18 inches, will be frozen for your trip home. Perch will be fileted for an on-the-ice fish fry. Jigging is the name of this January to mid-March game.

Come spring, Chrysler goes to work on walleyes with jig and minnow rigs. Later, in May and June, the smallmouth action heats up, first with minnows and later with Berkeley Power Baits and Power Tubes. Soft crayfish also produce. The Ohio state record of 9 pounds, 8 ounces came from these waters. When water temps hit 60°F, bass move onto spawning beds and fly cast poppers and crankbaits fished with light spinning tackle generate explosive strikes. That's why most of the major pro-bass circuits hold tourneys at Put-in-Bay. Average smallies run in the 15- to 17-inch range. Bass action moves deeper as summer progresses and then heats up again in fall. As the waters cool, walleyes form pre-spawn schools that can yield the biggest fish of the year. You'll find Pat Chrysler at 419/285-4631 or www.patchrysler.put-in-bay-com.

Gayle's Bed-and-Breakfast is located in a 1900s vintage frame house. Three bedrooms have private baths, and two are fitted with lavatories but share showers. Also on the property is a two-bedroom cabin with bath. Killer breakfasts are apt to include French toast soaked overnight in a batter of milk, eggs, corn flakes and coconut. To this you can add bacon, sausage and eggs. Dinner is not served at the B&B.

Lake Texoma Resort

Kingston, Oklahoma

Rebounding striped bass and a healthy stock of smallmouth and catfish draw anglers from all over to Lake Texoma.

VITAL STATISTICS:

KEY SPECIES:
Catfish, crappie, smallmouth, striped bass/rockfish

Tackle:
Casting, fly-fishing, spinning, trolling
Major Season:
All year
Accommodations:
HOTEL ROOMS AND CABINS
NUMBER OF ROOMS: 177
HANDICAPPED ACCESSIBLE: 13
MAXIMUM NUMBER OF GUESTS: 800
Meals: Extensive restaurant menu
Conference Groups: Yes
Rates: From $40 / night
Guides: $100
Gratuities: Angler's discretion
Preferred Payment:
Cash, check or credit cards
Getting There:
Fly to Dallas/Ft. Worth and rent a car.
Other Activities:
Bird-watching, boating, canoeing/kayaking/rafting, golf, horseback riding, hiking, swimming, tennis, water skiing, wildlife photography, nature programs, children's programs

Contact:
Lake Texoma Resort
PO Box 248
Kingston OK 73439
Ph: 580/564-2311
Fax: 580/564-9322
e-mail:
texomaresort@onenet.net
Web:
www.oklaresorts.com

GARTHRIGHT DAM backs up 93,000 acres of the Red River between the border of Oklahoma and Texas. Like the claws of a crab, its arms spread north and south from U.S. Rt. 70 east of the town of Durant, Oklahoma. Just across the bridge on the road from Durant sprawls Lake Texoma Resort, one of the finest combinations of state park, golf course, fishing and accommodations in the country.

The draw for anglers is striped bass, catfish and crappie. While the hogs that once made the hook and bullet press are not as frequently caught, the odds favor filling your stringer with fish in the three- to five-pound range. They'll put a bend in your rod for sure. Seldom does anyone go home empty handed. Guide Phil Jones (580/564-2037) says that April, May and June are the best months to fish for stripers on Texoma, and October and November are the second-best months. In spring, stripers move inshore. Fish shad-imitating crankbaits hard against the flooded brush. Top water plugs can work too. As the season ages, stripers head for deeper water. Fish finders will pinpoint schools anywhere from 20 to 40 feet down. Hookups come from drifting live shad two feet below a barrel sinker. Sometimes, in the hot summer months, stripers will chase bait to the surface. You can see swarms of gulls in the air, and as you get close, a flotilla of anglers who have the same idea you do. If you're first on the scene, action can be fun, particularly if you're using light casting rigs spooled with 8-pound test. Check out the lodge's striper package.

Anglers from Dallas/Fort Worth, about 60 miles south, flock to Lake Texoma to fill coolers with crappie. Big catfish are popular with fishermen who want to go mano y mano with blue and flathead of up to 10 pounds. Rumor also has it that the population of smallmouth is burgeoning. Three- to five-pound fish are not the least bit unusual. Bigger fish, well over seven pounds, have been taken.

With its full-service marina with tackle, bait and guides, comfortable hotel and spacious guest cabins, Lake Texoma State Resort is the place to stay when you're fishing the lake. In the hotel, you'll find standard rooms, terrace rooms with sundecks, and cabanas with pool-side patios, sitting areas and wet bars. Two-bedroom cottages sleep four to eight and include kitchenette and living area. Similar amenities are found in one-bedroom "studio" cottages. The hotel restaurant offers standard American cuisine. Guests also enjoy a fine golf course, tennis courts and trail rides.

[M I D W E S T]

Cedar Shore

C h a m b e r l a i n ,   S o u t h   D a k o t a

A full-featured resort and marina on what may be the best springtime walleye fishery in the country.

VITAL STATISTICS:

KEY SPECIES:
Smallmouth, walleye

Tackle:
Casting, fly-fishing, spinning
Major Season:
Late April through November
Accommodations:
RESORT HOTEL
NUMBER OF ROOMS: 99
HANDICAPPED ACCESSIBLE: 4
MAXIMUM NUMBER OF GUESTS: 250
Meals: Full restaurant menu or
diners in town
Conference Groups: Yes
Rates: From $59
Guides: $225
Gratuities: $25
Preferred Payment:
Cash, check or credit cards
Getting There:
Fly to Sioux Falls and rent a car.
Other Activities:
Waterfowling, wingshooting, bird-
watching, boating, golf, hiking,
swimming, tennis, wildlife
photography

Contact:
Angeliq Bosworth
Cedar Shore
PO Box 308
101 George S. Mickelson
Shoreline Dr
Chamberlain SD 57325
Ph: 605/734-6376
Fax: 605/734-6854
e-mail:
cedar@easnet.net
Web:
www.cedarshore.com

BEATING WEST ACROSS South Dakota on Interstate 90 would bore you out of your skull were it not for the visions of walleye that fill your mind. An hour or two after leaving the Minnesota line, you find the exit for Chamberlain and taking it, drop down off the prairie. You're not alone on this trek; there's a convoy of 4x4s hauling Lunds, and most of them are headed for this fishing town on the Missouri. Many make the stop in motels lining the main street, but you've got your sights set on the resort across the river. You speed across the bridge over Lake Francis Case, a 107-mile stretch of the Missouri River impounded by Ft. Randall Dam, and follow the road into the resort.

Best fishing here is the bite in late April before walleye go on the spawn. They've come up from the 30- to 40-foot depths where they've held semi-dormant all winter. Fish the rip-rap bank on the Chamberlain side, or along the approaches to the new bridge that carries I-90 over the river. Also try the rocky bank below St. Joseph's School. If the angling is too crowded, motor upstream to Crow Creek. The river belongs to those who fish from boats during the day. At night, small bonfires dot the shore, warming anglers who fish bait and wait. They're successful too. Early in spring, almost everyone fishes a jig and minnow, vertically. As the water warms to 40°F, the walleye move up onto the shoals. Crankbaits, stickbaits and spinnerbaits can all be effective now. Trolling is popular. And, as outlandish as it seems, now is the time when walleyes can be taken on a fly rod. Use a 6- or 7-weight with six- or seven-foot 6-pound tippet to cast to the bank. Fish are in the two-pound range. A slot limit imposed recently allows anglers three fish between 15 and 18 inches and one over 18. Anything smaller must be released unharmed. After the initial walleye blitz, smallmouth turn on. They'll run from two to four pounds and are caught on bait or plugs. This fishery holds up as long the river is getting consistent cold water releases from Big Bend Dam.

At Cedar Shore's marina, you can rent a boat and motor or hook up with a guide. One of the best in the area is Jim Ristau (605/734-4240), who runs a fully-equipped 1900-series Lund. For about $225 per day, he'll provide everything you'll need. The hotel sits on a low bank above the Missouri. A full-service resort with an eye to the conference trade, here you'll also find a very good restaurant, a sporting clays course and easy access to the scenic Missouri Breaks.

VITAL STATISTICS:

KEY SPECIES:
Brookies, browns, rainbows

Tackle:
Fly-fishing, spinning
Major Season:
May through September
Accommodations:
CEDAR-SIDED LODGE AND CABINS
NUMBER OF ROOMS: 15
HANDICAPPED ACCESSIBLE: 4
MAXIMUM NUMBER OF GUESTS: 30
Meals: Killer breakfasts and lunch;
dinner on your own
Conference Groups: Yes
Rates: From $42 / night
Guides: $200
Gratuities: Angler's discretion
Preferred Payment:
Cash, check or credit cards
Getting There:
Fly to Green Bay and rent a car.
Other Activities:
Bird-watching, boating,
canoeing/kayaking/rafting, hiking,
skiing, swimming, wildlife
photography, cooking classes, art
classes, nature programs

Contact:
Bear Paw Inn
N3494 Hwy 55
White Lake WI 54491
Ph: 715/882-3502
Fax: 715/882-2100
e-mail:
bearpaw@newnorth.net
Web:
www.bearpawinn.com

Bear Paw Inn

White Lake, Wisconsin

Comfortable cedar cabins, a varied program of kayaking/canoeing/hiking, and fishing on the Wolf.

NORTHERN WISCONSIN is a land of many great trout rivers, the Bois Brule and the Wolf being the finest. The Brule flows north and enters Lake Superior east of Duluth. The Wolf rises northwest of Pearson and flows to the southeast toward Appleton. For 60 miles, to the southern boundary of the Menominee Indian Reservation, the Wolf is first-class trout water. The upper 34 miles of the river is accessible to all anglers, while the remainder of the mileage is reserved for the native Indians.

In its upper reaches, the Wolf is slow and cold. Slate drakes come off in mid-July drawing scores of anglers to the stream. Farther downstream, the Wolf begins to hustle along over submerged boulders, skipping through pocket water, and sliding down deep runs. Occasionally boulders — erratics left by glacial ice — break the river's flow, as do infrequent islands. Where flats widen and shallow the river, braided channels form. The Wolf wades easily and access, thanks to the Wisconsin Department of Natural Resources, is assured and not overly difficult for those willing to walk a bit on bridgeheads over the river. The Soo Line Railroad Bridge, about seven miles north of Langlade, marks the upper reach of five miles or so of catch-and-release water restricted to artificial lures with single barbless hooks.

About a mile and a half from the river near the little hamlet of White Lake rises the Bear Paw Outdoor Adventure Resort. That moniker conjures up visions of hiking, biking and whitewater kayaking. To be sure, this is a resort that takes its nature seriously (but with a substantial grain of salt as well). Cedar-sided on the outside and pine-paneled within, cabins host most of the guests, though there are six rooms in the main lodge. Breakfast and lunch are included with the room, and the price is right! The Wolf is either a mile and a half walk through the pines and popple, or two miles by car. Guides are available through the lodge, which also sells tackle. And, if you come, don't overlook spring-fed ponds hidden deep in the woods. Fishing here from kick-boats can be awesome for native brookies.

Jamieson House Inn

P o y n e t t e ,   W i s c o n s i n

Combine 1890s charm with browns and brookies in a stream that flows right through town.

VITAL STATISTICS:

KEY SPECIES:
Bream, browns, largemouth, pike, rainbows, smallmouth, walleye

Tackle:
Casting, fly-fishing, spinning, trolling
Major Season:
April through September
Accommodations:
CLASSIC VICTORIAN ROOMS
NUMBER OF ROOMS: 12
MAXIMUM NUMBER OF GUESTS: 30
Meals: Elegant breakfasts with the room. Gourmet dinners in restaurant.
Conference Groups: Yes
Rates: From $75
Guides: $225 / 2
Gratuities: Angler's discretion
Preferred Payment:
Cash, check or credit cards
Getting There:
Fly to Madison and rent a car.
Other Activities:
Bird-watching, boating, hiking, skiing

Contact:
Heidi Hutchinson
Jamieson House Inn
407 N. Franklin St
Poynette WI 53955
Ph: 608/635-4100
Fax: 608/635-2292
Web:
www.jamiesonhouse.com

I**F THERE'S ONE THING** that immediately attracts your attention about this lovely country inn, it is its aura of elegance. Three historic buildings — two brick mansions and a schoolhouse — make up the inns. The mansions reflect the Victorian era of the 1880s, with arched bay windows running from floor to ceiling. Rooms are furnished with antiques and period reproductions. Most have sitting areas and queen beds; all have private baths. Two French country suites with cable TV and whirlpools are located in the schoolhouse. Breakfast is served in the sunny conservatory, and at night, Emily's Cafe offers elegant cuisine.

The inn is located in Poynette, a charming village of true Victorian persona, about 30 miles north of Madison via Interstate 94. Trout fishers need look no farther than the center of town to find angling. Rowan Creek cuts through Poynette from east to west, eventually ducking under the interstate and flowing into Lake Wisconsin (good for walleyes and smallmouths). Public access to Rowan Creek is ample. A mile of special regulation water runs east of town through property owned by the state's Department of Natural Resources. Access, of course, means other anglers, so odds are against having it to yourself. However, many who fish it are fair-weather fishers. When it's cloudy or drizzly it may be deserted, and that's often when hatches are best. Brown and brook trout here hit the standard nymphs — Hare's Ears and Pheasant Tails — and the usual dries — Adams and Griffith's Gnats.

This stream provides some diversion for guests at Jamieson House. Serious anglers will cram their copies of Humphrey's and Shogren's *Wisconsin and Minnesota Trout Streams* into their pockets and head for Rocky Run, particularly the section east of the Highway 51 bridge. The Mecan, about 40 miles north near Richford, is also worth a tumble, as is the Fox at Princeton. While you're in the neighborhood, check out the Black Earth which follows U.S. 14 west of Madison, and Mount Vernon Creek just off U.S. 151 at Mt. Vernon. According to Humphrey and Shogren, Mt. Vernon Creek is a "jewel," known for hatches of spring creek mayflies and its "hex" hatch in June. Good-size browns can be caught from these clear waters. The Rowan eventually winds its way into Lake Wisconsin where walleye, sturgeon, smallmouth, and pike are found. A number of marinas operate on the lake, and guides like Ron Barefield (608/838-8756) can show you the lake or the streams, depending on your mood.

Serendipity Farm

Viroqua, Wisconsin

Stay at a working farm, and catch big browns in the pasture.

EST FORK of the Kickapoo River is seeing a tremendous rejuvenation. A nine mile section, from the bridge at State Route 82 upstream to Bloomingdale (no department stores, sorry), now produces browns of 16 to 18 inches. This is catch-and-release water, and it is fairly small, ranging from 15 to 30 feet in width. For the most part, it flows through grassy pasture shaded by occasional century-old cottonwoods and willows. The main channel was terribly exposed to the sun until a number of lunker structures were installed by the West Fork Sportsman's Club to provide cover for trout. In many spots, the river is easily wadeable, but often stealthy casting from the bank is more effective. Patience can bring some of those phenomenal days of a dozen fish no smaller than 12 inches.

Try March Browns in May and Sulphurs in June; Light Cahills, Yellow Sallies, or Caddis (Elk Hair Caddis) are good almost throughout the season. Terrestrials from July on are very important. Hoppers, beetles, crickets and ants plopped right next to the bank will often draw strikes even on the stillest of days. Fish big nymphs or streams — muskrats, grey Woolly Buggers, or muddlers — as dark settles into the valley. You don't need a guide, though the nearby town of Coon Valley in the heart of Wisconsin's Coulee Region, is home to a couple of good ones. Try Dennis Graupe (608/452-3430) at Spring Creek Angler, an Orvis dealer.

Building on pioneering work by the West Fork Sportsman's Club, with an assist from TU's Blackhawk and Timber Coulee chapters, is more than $200,000 that's been raised under TU's Home Waters Initiative to fund a thorough baseline study of the watershed, accelerate enhancement of in-stream and riparian habitat, and provide educational and informational outreach to area residents, school children, tourists and anglers.

Astride the West Branch are the lands of Serendipity Farm. The main house sits on a low bluff overlooking the river. A rooster awakens anglers who want to fish early. Hearty breakfasts — eggs gathered that morning, sausage, homemade breads and jams — are the rule. Guests stay in three bedrooms in the Garret's house or in a cottage nearby. The cottage has a private bath; guest rooms in the main house share.

VITAL STATISTICS:

KEY SPECIES:
Browns

Tackle:
Fly-fishing
Major Season:
May through September
Accommodations:
Farmhouse and cabin
Number of Rooms: 3
Maximum Number of Guests: 12
Meals: Fresh country breakfast
Conference Groups: No
Rates: From $60
Guides: $200
Gratuities: Angler's discretion
Preferred Payment:
Cash, check or credit cards
Getting There:
Fly to LaCrosse and rent a car.
Other Activities:
Bird-watching, canoeing/kayaking/
rafting, hiking, wildlife photography

Contact:
Forrest & Suzanne Garret
Serendipity Farm
RR 3 Box 162
Viroqua WI 54665
Ph: 608/637-7708

NORTHERN ROCKIES

IDAHO, MONTANA, WYOMING

THE WISH IS in all of us: a summer to spend fishing the blue-ribbon waters that flow from the crests and calderas of the northern Rockies. Begin on great tailwaters — the Missouri, the Bighorn, the Beaverhead — then move onto the Snake, the Salmon, and the Yellowstone. Pause for a moment on Armstrong and Nelson's spring creeks, then ride horseback to high ponds where cutthroat have never seen your fly. Easy or toughly technical, these waters take on all comers. Fly shops and fishing lodges abound, as do motels, dude ranches and campgrounds. The overlooked seasons are spring and fall, and that's when angling is usually best.

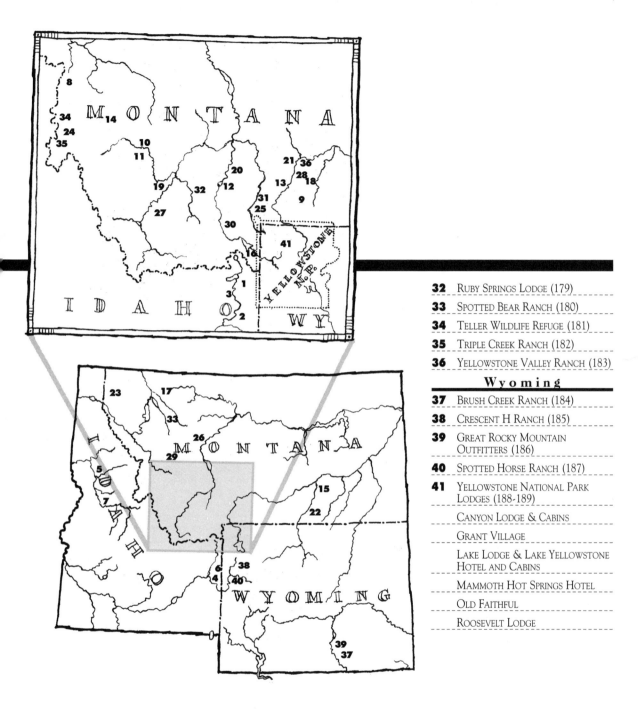

References:

RIVER JOURNAL:
YELLOWSTONE NATIONAL PARK
by Bruce Staples

IDAHO BLUE-RIBBON
FLY FISHING GUIDE
by John Shewey

YELLOWSTONE RIVER
AND ITS ANGLING
by Dave Hughes

SNAKE RIVER COUNTRY:
FLIES AND WATERS
by Bruce Staples

MADISON RIVER JOURNAL
by John Holt

- -

SILVER CREEK
by W. David Joye &Jeff Findley, Editor

HENRY'S FORK
by Larry Tullis

BIG HOLE RIVER
by Steve Probasco

CLARK FORK RIVER
by Greg Thomas
Frank Amato Publications
PO Box 82112
Portland, OR 97282
503/653-8108

- -

FISHING IDAHO, AN ANGLER'S GUIDE
by Joe H. Evancho
Cutthroat Press, PO Box 1471 Boise ID
83701; 800/390-5907

- -

FLY FISHING THE
ROCKY MOUNTAIN BACKCOUNTRY
by Rich Osthoff
Stackpole Books, 5067 Ritter Road,
Mechanicsburg PA 17055-6921;
800/732-3669

- -

FISHING MONTANA
by Michael S. Sample

FISHING THE BEARTOOTHS
by Pat Marcuson

FISHING GLACIER NATIONAL PARK
by Russ Schneider

FISHING WYOMING
by Ken Graham

FISHING YELLOWSTONE
NATIONAL PARK
by Richard Parks
Falcon Publishing Co
PO Box 1718
Helena, MT 59624
406/442-6597

- -

THE MONTANA ANGLING GUIDE
THE WYOMING ANGLING GUIDE
by Chuck Fothergill and Bob Sterling
Stream Stalker Publishing Co
PO Box 238Woody Creek, CO 81656
970/923-4552

- -

FLY FISHER'S
GUIDE TO IDAHO
by Ken Retallic & Rocky Barker

FLY FISHER'S
GUIDE TO WYOMING
by Ken Retallic

FLY FISHING THE
YELLOWSTONE RIVER
by Rod Walinchus & Tom Travis

FLY FISHING
THE NORTH PLATTE
by Rod Walinchus
Wilderness Adventure Press
PO Box 627
Gallatin Gateway MT 59730
800/925-3339

- -

Resources:

IDAHO FISH AND GAME DEPARTMENT
Box 25, 600 S. Walnut St
Boise, ID 83707
208/334-3700
web: www.state.id.us/fishgame

- -

MONTANA DEPARTMENT OF FISH,
WILDLIFE AND PARKS
1420 E. 6th Ave
Helena, MT 59620
406/444-2535
web: fwp.state.mt.us

- -

WYOMING GAME AND FISH
DEPARTMENT
5400 Bishop Blvd
Cheyenne, WY 82006
307/777-4600
web: www.gf.state.wy.us

- -

*Rafting the Big Hole is high art for Craig Fellin,
whose lodge on the Wise River is a favorite with
anglers who also enjoy gourmet dining.*

Elk Creek Ranch

Island Park, Idaho

Hospitality reigns within this old weathered ranch on the headwaters of Henry's Fork.

VITAL STATISTICS:

KEY SPECIES:
Brookies, cutthroat, rainbows

Tackle:
Fly-fishing
Major Season:
June through mid-October
Accommodations:
RUSTIC RANCH
NUMBER OF ROOMS: 18
MAXIMUM NUMBER OF GUESTS: 30
Meals: Family-style
Conference Groups: Yes
Rates: From $75 / day
Guides: Available for $200 + / day
Gratuities: 15%
Preferred Payment:
Cash, check or credit cards
Getting There:
Fly to Idaho Falls and rent a car.
Other Activities:
Bird-watching, hiking, wildlife photography

Contact:
**Gary Merrill
Elk Creek Ranch
PO Box 2
Island Park ID 89429
Ph: 208/558-7404**

Off Season:
**Box 3000 MS 614
Patrump NV
Ph: 775/727-9144
Fax: 775/727-9528**

AMONG TROUT UNLIMITED members, Henry's Fork is the most popular trout stream in the country, and with good cause. In the main, TUers love it because of the sheer difficulty of seducing its corps of 20-inch-plus 'bows from the spring creek waters. Even the least skilled angler can catch trout in Henry's Fork, but only at the right time. The easy water on Henry's Fork lies just below the dam at the head of the Box Canyon. When water is not being released, anglers of modest skill can catch smallish brookies and rainbows, and maybe a cutthroat. A bit farther downstream, the river constricts, the current picks up, the fish get bigger, and the angling tougher.

To some degree, Henry's Fork is a classic tailwater. Flows are controlled by releases from Island Park Dam. In spring and fall, when downstream irrigation needs are minimal, the famed Box Canyon is wadeable. As canyons go, the Box isn't very deep, but boulders, deep holes and lots of good pocket water hold many large rainbows, as well as cutthroats, browns and brookies.

After leaving the Box, the river broadens and slows, taking on the spring creek characteristics for which it is so highly regarded. Rapids end at aptly named Last Chance. Below that, Henry's Fork flows silky and supine through the flat meadows of Harriman Ranch. Matching the hatch is essential if you're to take 'bows here. Hatches are prolific from early Iron Blue Quills in March, through Green Drakes in late June, to tiny Callibaetis in September. At times, the insects are so profuse that they look like lint on the water. Below the ranch, the river picks up speed as the gradient steepens. Conditions are similar to the Box.

Special regulations govern fishing on the Henry's Fork and you'll want to check on these at Henry's Fork Anglers (208/558-7525) in Last Chance. The history of Henry's Fork has been checkered, plagued with low flows and agricultural pollution. Thanks to the savvy of Mike Lawson and others, a model private-public partnership for river preservation and sport fishing — the Henry's Fork Foundation — was created more than a decade ago. It's work is telling. Today, Henry's Fork is indeed one of the best trout streams in the nation.

Up on the river's headwaters, you'll find Elk Creek Ranch and its private trout-filled lake. Comfortable and laid-back in western tradition, Elk Creek puts its guests up in log cabins, each with private bath, living and bedrooms.

[N O R T H E R N   R O C K I E S]

Fish Creek Lodging

A s h t o n ,   I d a h o

VITAL STATISTICS:

KEY SPECIES:
Browns, cutthroat, rainbows

Tackle:
Fly-fishing, spinning
Major Season:
June through October
Accommodations:
RUSTIC LOG CABIN
NUMBER OF ROOMS: 2
MAXIMUM NUMBER OF GUESTS: 6
Meals: You are your own gourmet chef
Conference Groups: No
Rates: From $80 / night
Guides: Available
Gratuities: Angler's discretion
Preferred Payment:
Cash or check
Getting There:
Fly to Idaho Falls / Jackson, WY, and rent a car.
Other Activities:
Bird-watching, horseback riding, hiking, wildlife photography

Contact:
Janet Keefer
Fish Creek Lodging
PO Box 833
Ashton ID 83420
Ph: 208/652-7900
Fax: 208/652-7990
e-mail:
elynch@fremontnet.com

If you want to avoid the crowds on Henry's Fork, fish the runs below Mesa Falls.

HENRY'S FORK IS MANY RIVERS in one. Originating in Henry's Lake up near the Montana border (a float-tuber's paradise for rising brown trout), the river flows from the lake as a thin trickle. When joined by the icy waters from Big Springs, where huge rainbows, browns and cutthroats fin in the boiling spring, the fork becomes a stream of note. But it's only after impoundment in Island Park Reservoir that it emerges as a much-storied fishery. Now a full-fledged tailwater, it clatters through Box Canyon, slows and weaves through the Harriman Ranch (here resembling a spring creek), and picks up speed again below Osborne Bridge as it begins its descending run to Upper and Lower Mesa Falls.

The falls mark the edge of the caldera through which the upper river flows. Below the falls, Henry's Fork works its way through a deep valley that opens where the Warm River flows in from the east. As gradient diminishes, Henry's Fork becomes more like the cobble bottom sections of the Madison and the South Fork of the Snake. Long runs are punctuated by gravel riffles. Just below the U.S. Route 20 bridge north of Ashton, the river is again impounded. Above the lake, the fishing is good, but the lake itself is small. The tailwater below the dam holds huge rainbows, and the fishing can be outstanding all the way down to the junction with the South Fork.

The lower mileage of Henry's Fork is much less heavily fished than the upper section. While hatches are not as prolific, they are still good. If you are staying in the Island Park area, you'll probably not drive down to the lower area to fish, but if you are lodged near Ashton, you'll be doing yourself a disservice if you forsake the lower Henry's Fork (and the Warm and Fall rivers nearby). All have excellent populations of browns and rainbows, with a few cutthroats on the side. Flows are heavy in spring and summer, but tail off in the fall as irrigation needs lessen. The fishing is at its best then. Spinning and fly-fishing are permitted, but regulations change, so you'll want to check them thoroughly when you buy your license.

Close to the confluence of the Warm River and Henry's Fork, about five miles below the falls, Janet Keefer rents out a private log guest cabin — Fish Creek Lodging — that offers all the conveniences of home. Use the cast-iron woodstove to steal the chill from cool evenings. You'll whip up your own gourmet dinner. Sleep deeply in comfortable beds, and if it rains, listen to it patter on the tin roof.

To lure tourists to Glacier National Park, railroads built the Prince of Wales Hotel from which anglers seek wild and native cutthroat in clear rivers and jewels of alpine lakes.

Henry's Fork Lodge

I s l a n d   P a r k ,   I d a h o

Overlooking the Henry's Fork is this award-winning lodge with a wonderful twist.

SOME 600,000 years ago a mountain blew its top, forming a huge caldera through which the North (or Henry's) Fork of the Snake River flows. To the north and east is another great caldera, this one holding the Yellowstone drainage and all of those marvelous rivers — the Firehole, Gibbon, Upper Madison and the Yellowstone itself — that you know so well. They're but an hour's drive from the front porch of Henry's Fork Lodge.

Even though you've come to Henry's Fork to fish it, you'll want to spend a couple of days or more poking around Yellowstone. That is if you can pry yourself away from the river that runs past the lodge. The main event here is the stretch that winds gracefully through the Harriman Ranch, now a state park. Here the river flows as luxuriously as silk. Laminar waters slide up to occasional riffles. But don't be misled. Devilish micro-currents will twist your tippet, dragging your fly to the distraction of the trout. Hatches are heavy, consistent and well-posted at Henry's Fork Angler's (208/558-7525), where fly-fishers gather to drink Mike Lawson's terrible coffee and tell lies that are even worse.

While the Harriman Ranch section is the most challenging mileage of the upper river, you'll want to spend some time in the Box Canyon upstream. From the outflow of Island Park Dam to the hamlet of Last Chance, the river runs through a canyon that's not very deep. The bottom is blocky with squared off boulders and ledges, providing great water for rainbows in excess of 20 inches. Float it in a drift boat if the river is running; wade it if it's not. Below the Harriman Ranch to Hatchery Ford runs a stretch of river that's similar to that in the Box. Float trips are the most popular mode of fishing this section, though it's possible to wade.

The best time to fish Henry's Fork is any time between late May and the end of November. Numerous anglers aim for the famed Green and Brown Drake and salmonfly hatches in June and early July. Next come terrestrials on the flat runs in the ranch and nymphs in Box Canyon for midsummer. If you're seeking solitude, forget about spring and summer. Instead, come in the fall when the people are gone.

As befitting this fine trout stream (#1 in a recent TU survey) is one of the best of the western fishing lodges. Exquisite accommodations are blended with an elegant and eclectic cuisine. After dinner, settle back with a cordial and listen to informal chats by local naturalists, artists and authors. Fishing schools are also hosted.

VITAL STATISTICS:

KEY SPECIES:
Brookies, browns, cutthroat, rainbows

Tackle:
Fly-fishing, spinning
Major Season:
May through October
Accommodations:
FINE WESTERN LODGE
NUMBER OF ROOMS: 14
HANDICAPPED ACCESSIBLE: 1
MAXIMUM NUMBER OF GUESTS: 28
Meals: Elegant and hearty cuisine
Conference Groups: Yes
Rates: From $250 / day
Guides: $325 - $350 / day / 2
Gratuities: $35 - $50 / day
Preferred Payment:
Cash, check or credit cards
Getting There: Fly to Idaho Falls, ID, and rent a car, or arrange for the free van from the lodge.
Other Activities: Big game, waterfowling, wingshooting, bird-watching, boating, canoeing/kayaking/rafting, golf, horseback riding, hiking, nature programs, tennis, wildlife photography

Contact:
Nelson Ishiyama
Henry's Fork Lodge
HC66 Box 600
Island Park ID 83429
Ph: 208/558-7953
Fax: 208/558-7956
e-mail:
hflodge@ida.net

Off Season:
465 California St., Suite 800
San Francisco CA 94104
Ph: 415/434-1657
Fax: 415/392-1268
e-mail:
nelsoni@ix.netcom.com

Agents:
Off the Beaten Path: 800/445-2995
Kaufmann's: 800/442-4359
The Gilly: 914/632-2634
Fishing International: 800/950-4242

The Lodge at Palisades Creek

Irwin, Idaho

If you had to choose to fish only one spot this year, you could do worse than the South Fork of the Snake. Much worse.

VITAL STATISTICS:

KEY SPECIES:
Browns, cutthroat, rainbows

Tackle:
Fly-fishing
Major Season:
June through late October
Accommodations:
MODERN YET RUSTIC PINE CABINS
NUMBER OF ROOMS: 9
MAXIMUM NUMBER OF GUESTS: 15
Meals: Very good regional recipes
Conference Groups: Yes
Rates: From $412.50 / person, double occupancy
Guides: Included
Gratuities: $50 / boat
Preferred Payment:
Cash, check or credit cards
Getting There:
Fly to Idaho Falls / Jackson, WY, and rent a car.
Other Activities:
Boating, canoeing/kayaking/rafting, golf, horseback riding, hiking, swimming, wildlife photography

Contact:
The Lodge at Palisades Creek
PO Box 70
Irwin ID 83428
Ph: 208/483-2222
Fax: 208/483-2227
e-mail:
palisades@tlapc.com
Web:
www.tlapc.com

Agents:
Pan Angling

MOST ANGLERS who find their way into southeastern Idaho's Swan Valley make a huge mistake. They treat the South Fork as one of those "been there, done that" rivers. They give it a day, maybe two, and in the process fail to unlock its secrets. In a sort of perverse way, that's fine. Bigger fish and more of them come to anglers who invest the time to learn the wiles of the big browns and cutthroats cruising this tailwater.

Issuing forth from Palisades Dam near the Wyoming Border, the South Fork flows westward nearly 60 miles to its junction with Henry's (North) Fork of the Snake. All of it is good, albeit different, trout water. For the first 14 miles from the dam to Conant, the river runs through the Swan Valley, a narrow floodplain. Beyond the plain rise palisades capped with basalt, a precursor to the forest which strives to climb Teton-like peaks. Below Conant, the Snake enters the section called the "Canyon," but in reality, this mileage passes a number of small 300- to 400-foot canyons — Dry, Ladder, Black, Bums — before emerging at Byington launch ramp near the town of Poplar. In the upper and middle sections, the riverbed is similar, characterized by gravel bars, slick runs, and backwater eddies. Twenty-fish days are not at all unusual on the upper and middle reaches.

Dry flies are the favorite game here: Sulfur duns all year, Blue-winged Olives early and late, and when it's cloudy and rainy, stoneflies, golden stones, and yellow sallies in late June and July when runoff begins to recede. Caddis show up from August through September and terrestrials fish well into the fall. When all else fails, you can pound the water with nymphs, weighted or not, depending on flow. Despite incessant variation in releases from Palisades Dam, the river has a reputation for producing lots of browns, cutthroat and rainbows, most in the 12- to 16-inch range.

The Lodge at Palisades Creek, with its Orvis-endorsed tackle shop, is known for guided all-day float trips from the runs below the dam on the upper section to the canyon stretch. Don't pass up a visit to Henry's Bathtub or Brown Town below the canyon. Trout season opens on Memorial Day and closes on November 30. For sheer beauty (and good fish), the first week of October is hard to beat.

Five rustic cabins and an A-frame chalet nestle in the cottonwoods along the bank of the river. All are modern with private baths. Uphill from the cabins is the lodge proper and fish pond. Cuisine features ample portions of fish, fowl or beef.

The Lodge at Riggins Hot Springs

R i g g i n s ,   I d a h o

Steelhead rumble in this river when cottonwoods and larch blaze gold in the fall.

VITAL STATISTICS:

KEY SPECIES:
Steelhead, sturgeon

Tackle:
Casting, fly-fishing, spinning, trolling
Major Season:
All year
Accommodations:
ELEGANTLY RUSTIC LODGE AND CABINS
NUMBER OF ROOMS: 10
HANDICAPPED ACCESSIBLE: 1
MAXIMUM NUMBER OF GUESTS: 22
Meals: Fine dining
Conference Groups: Yes
Rates: From $265 / night / 2
Guides: $150
Gratuities: $20
Preferred Payment:
Cash, check or credit cards
Getting There:
Fly to Boise and rent a car.
Other Activities:
Big game, wingshooting, boating,
canoeing/kayaking/rafting, golf,
horseback riding, hiking, swimming

Contact:
Tony Bradbury
The Lodge at Riggins
Hot Springs
PO Box 1247
Riggins ID 83549
Ph: 208/628-3785
Fax: 208/628-4129
e-mail:
rhslodge@cybershighway.net
Web:
www.rhslodge.com

COLD AND GREEN, the waters of the Salmon River rush down to the lodge, pause and pool up for a moment, and then break hard against the bank in their chase downstream. It's kind of nifty to stand on the suspension bridge and look down into the pool it spans. Once in a while you'll see dark shapes deep in the hole. Those are steelhead. Smaller shadows are most likely cutthroat.

For the nine miles down to Riggins where the Little Salmon comes in, and upstream as far as you can ride a boat, the steelheading can be excellent. Best fishing occurs in the fall when water levels are lower and the river is clearer. These are glorious days. Cottonwoods, aspen and larch blaze like fat yellow candles against the brooding deep green of firs and pine that climb steep, heavily forested slopes. Catch it right in October and you'll hear elk bugling as you cast. You can wade then, working the depths and tails of pools with various streamers. Best technique is to hire a drift boat and ride down from pool to pool, casting into likely holds. Typical steelies that take flies run between 6 and 12 pounds, a real handful on your typical eight-weight.

If fly-fishing is not your game, hook up with a guide who runs a jet boat. He'll set you up with a heavy-duty spinning rod with a Hot Shot or other crankbait as your lure. The guide will run the boat headed upstream at just less than the speed of the current; the force of the water will carry your lure downstream where it will dance (you hope) in front of the nose of a big steelhead. This method is called "back trolling," and fish up to 20 pounds are taken this way. Sturgeon, up to nine feet in length, can be taken from April through September.

In the summer, steelheading is pretty slow, but cutthroat abound in numerous small creeks and rivers. And there's a pond at the lodge, loaded with trout of two-pounds-plus, where you can work the kinks out of your casting. When you're finished fishing, you'll slip out of your waders, don some swim shorts, and slide into the hot spring for a therapeutic dip. Your room may be in the main lodge or a cabin, but you can bet that either way it's a fine spot to take a night's rest. Dinner includes the likes of tenderloin or pork with blackberry port wine sauce, or grilled halibut with cilantro lime butter. The Nez Perce believed Riggins Hot Springs to be a place for healing the soul, and in this, there was no argument.

Teton Valley Lodge

Driggs, Idaho

Since 1938, this fine old lodge on the back side of the Tetons has been offering anglers the finest of wild trout.

THE FRIENDLY cabins of Teton Valley Lodge has been welcoming anglers for more than half-a-century. With more than 18 different floats on three main rivers — the Teton, Henry's Fork, and the South Fork of the Snake — guides from this lodge can create an angling vacation that fits your interest and skills with precision.

Henry's Fork and its sibling, the South Fork, get all the press. But if you stay at this lodge, you'll want to spend the bulk of your time fishing the Teton. Rising on the back side of the Teton Range, this river looks like a big spring creek. After clearing in June, the river sees continual hatches of mayflies starting with big Green Drakes. In this run, the bottom is silt and wading is difficult. Farther, with flows like molten glass, unnatural waves disturb fish and put them off their take. That's why the lodge developed its own style of drift boat — a 20-footer with swivel chairs mounted fore and aft. You cast while sitting in the chair, lest the fish see you standing or your casting motion rock the boat — either of which will spook the fish. This is dry fly water. Nymphs are simply not as effective. Rainbows, browns, and cutts in the 16-inch-plus range provide ample exercise for anglers. Days of 25 or more good fish are not at all uncommon

Downstream from the lodge, the Teton enters The Narrows, a tight canyon with some heavy white water. Rugged and virtually inaccessible except by a drift boat oared by a guide who really knows the water (you'll walk around the roughest rapids), here you'll find the kind of isolation and pristine environment — as well as very nice fish — that everyone seeks. Other sections of the Teton, particularly the island mileage, is comfortably wadeable and favored by those who like to stalk individual fish like they were hunting trophy elk.

Perched on the bank of the river, Teton's guest cabins — all 10 of them — are larger than those at most other western lodges. The schedule is civilized. The first hatches begin to come off around 10:00 a.m. and continue to dark. That's when you'll fish. Dinner (exceptional prime rib preceded by Dijon gumbo) is served about 9:00 p.m.. Hearty box lunches help you make it through the day. If you fish here, you'll want to rent a car. Driggs is a quaint village, somewhat off the tourist path. An hour north or south puts you on the Snake or Henry's Fork, and a little farther can take you over the mountains into Jackson or up into West Yellowstone.

VITAL STATISTICS:

KEY SPECIES:
Browns, cutthroat, rainbows

Tackle:
Fly-fishing

Major Season:
Mid-June through October

Accommodations:
RUSTIC LOG CABINS
NUMBER OF CABINS: 10
HANDICAPPED ACCESSIBLE: 2
MAXIMUM NUMBER OF GUESTS: 46

Meals: Excellent regional fare

Conference Groups: Yes

Rates: From $900 / day / 2

Guides: Included

Gratuities: $75 / boat;
Angler's discretion

Preferred Payment:
Cash, check or credit cards

Getting There:
Fly to Jackson, WY, or Idaho Falls and rent a car.

Other Activities:
Waterfowling, wingshooting

Contact:
Teton Valley Lodge
379 Adams Rd
Driggs ID 83422
Ph: 800/455-1182
Fax: 208/354-3190
e-mail:
rbarry@if.rmc.net
Web:
www.tetonvalleylodge.com

[N O R T H E R N   R O C K I E S]

*"Off the beaten path" describes Tim Linehan's
(host of TU's television series) lodge at Yaak, way up
in the northwest corner of Montana, where rainbows
and cutts play in the nearby Kootenai River.*

*Spend the night in Kingfisher Lodge which caters to
serious anglers who are headed for the Bighorn, one of
the West's finest all season tailwaters.*

Wapiti Meadow Ranch

Cascade, Idaho

East meets West on the doorstep of the River of No Return.

VITAL STATISTICS:

KEY SPECIES:
Bull trout/Dolly Varden, cutthroat, rainbows

Tackle:
Fly-fishing, spinning
Major Season:
Mid-July through mid-September
Accommodations:
STONE AND LOG LODGE
NUMBER OF ROOMS: 9
MAXIMUM NUMBER OF GUESTS: 14
Meals: Hearty cuisine with a flare
Conference Groups: Yes
Rates: From $2,250 / week
Guides: Included
Gratuities: Angler's discretion
Preferred Payment:
Cash or check
Getting There:
Fly to Boise and rent a car, or catch
an air taxi for $120 each way.
Other Activities:
Big game, bird-watching,
canoeing/kayaking/rafting, horseback
riding, hiking, wildlife photography

Contact:
Diana Bryant
Wapiti Meadow Ranch
HC 72
Cascade ID 83611
Ph: 208/633-3217
Fax: 208/633-3219
e-mail:
wapitimr@aol.com
Web:
www.wapitimeadowranch.com

THE Frank Church/River of No Return Wilderness is a rugged land known for absurdly steep mountains, huge elk and bear, brawling whitewater and lakes high above the treeline. Folks here are hardy common-sense people, more apt to knock back a belt or two of whisky and eat steak and beans from a tin plate than accompany a dinner of game hen with a fume blanc. At Wapiti Meadow Ranch, the rugged West collided with the blue-blooded East, and the result is a delightful working guest ranch appointed with honest colonial antiques

Horse talk is taken seriously, and trail rides are *de rigueur*. But increasingly, those treks head for high mountain lakes where fly and spin anglers battle native cutthroats. Overnight pack trips take guests deep into the wilderness to fish waters only accessible by horse. Wild rivers abound in this terrain, so rugged that a 1935 National Geographic expedition to explore the deep canyon of Middle Fork of the Salmon River was forced to return without achieving its goal. Today, anglers fly a short 15-minute hop from the ranch to an airstrip on the Middle Fork for two days of fishing for cutthroats and rainbows at an overnight camp. Also nearby is the South Fork of the Salmon.

Cutthroats and rainbows here range from 12 to 20 inches, and bull trout (a subspecies of the Dolly Varden) can top 24 inches. The best fishing on flowing waters is after July 15, when spring meltwater has washed through the system and rivers have returned to clear summer levels. Still waters are fishable earlier, and the ranch's stocked pond provides trout for those of catch-and-eat persuasion. Orvis-endorsed, the ranch offers complimentary fly-tackle to guests booking fishing packages and rents spinning gear to those more conventionally inclined.

Scattered along the fringe of the South Meadow, four guest cabins reflect the history of the area: Ponderosa Bungalow, for the logging of its namesake pine; Lafe Cox's Cache, for a pioneer outfitter who helped explore the wilderness; Thunder Mountain Cabin, after Zane Grey's novel about gold miners; and The Rendezvous, a bow to those rugged hunters and trappers. All include two bedrooms (except Thunder Mountain, which has only one), a spacious sitting room, woodstove, kitchenette and private bath. An executive suite with sitting room, two bedrooms and bath is located in the main lodge. Candlelight dinners are elegant, with gourmet specialties.

Blackbird's Lodge

V i c t o r ,   M o n t a n a

At this charming lodge half-way down the Bitterroot, fall fishing can be a blast.

RISING ON THE FLANKS of the Bitterroot Mountains to the west and the Pintlar Peaks of the Sapphire Mountains to the east, the Bitterroot watershed contains more than 2.5 million acres of wilderness — superb country for elk, mule deer, bear and cougar. Headwaters carry cutthroat and brook trout. The main stem of the Bitterroot begins at Conner and runs north about 70 miles to Missoula. A thrashing brawling stream above Conner, it changes tune below the town, becoming much more placid and suitable for floating and wading. The bottom becomes gravel which shifts with each spring's meltwater runoff. Riffles, runs and pools predominate. Deadfalls from cottonwoods along the bank provide additional cover. Runs of riprap stabilize banks offering good holds for baitfish and big browns and rainbows that feed on them.

You might liken the main run of the Bitterroot to the Madison from Quake Lake to Ennis. The broad valley is bucolic and looks tailor-made for whitetail deer (which it is). From mid-March to mid-April, local fly-casters fish the skwala hatch, an olive stone fly in sizes #8 to #12. Runoff surges through in May and June, but tributary and headwater streams clear first and provide decent angling. Blackbird guides will take anglers over the mountain to fish the Beaverhead or Missouri tailwaters if nothing in the immediate area suits. In summer, the Bitterroot is known for its stellar caddis. Late summer is terrestrial time. Tricos come off in September, and the cooling weather also brings out October Caddis, marvelous baetis hatches and lots of mahoganies. This lodge tends to lean toward upland game when cottonwoods yellow-up in the fall; it's a great spot to combine wingshooting and angling.

Blackbird's is small as fishing lodges go in this corner of Montana. The main lodge holds four rooms and an annex (a small cabin) carries another. Only one party of up to eight books the main lodge, while a second group of no more than four may hole up in the cabin. If one of the four likes to cook (and the others like his cooking), you can save a buck or two. Dinners in the main lodge are custom prepared to menus set by each group.

VITAL STATISTICS:

KEY SPECIES:
Browns, cutthroat, rainbows, cutbows

Tackle:
Fly-fishing
Major Season:
March through November
Accommodations:
Rustic lodge and cabin
Number of Rooms: 5
Handicapped Accessible: All
Maximum Number of Guests: 12
Meals: Excellent regional cuisine
Conference Groups: Yes
Rates: $425 / day, double occupancy
Guides: $325 / 2
Gratuities: 15% - 20%
Angler's discretion
Preferred Payment:
Cash, check or credit cards
Getting There:
Fly to Missoula and rent a car.
Other Activities:
Waterfowling, wingshooting, canoeing/kayaking/rafting, golf, horseback riding, hiking, skiing

Contact:
Mark Bachik
Blackbird's Lodge
PO Box 998
1754 Highway 93 North
Victor MT 59875
Ph: 406/642-6375
Fax: 406/642-6393
e-mail:
blackbrd@bitterroot.net
Web:
www.blackbirds.com

Agents:
Frontiers
Off the Beaten Path

Chico Hot Springs Lodge

P r a y ,   M o n t a n a

*Let the waters of the hot springs soak your
trout-weary bod and mellow your mood for dinner.*

**VITAL
STATISTICS:**

KEY SPECIES:
Browns, cutthroat, rainbows

Tackle:
Fly-fishing, spinning
Major Season:
May through September
Accommodations:
HISTORIC, YET MODERN HOTEL
NUMBER OF ROOMS: 89
HANDICAPPED ACCESSIBLE: 2
MAXIMUM NUMBER OF GUESTS: 270
Meals: Scrumptious regional
cuisine
Conference Groups: Yes
Rates: From $39 / night
Guides: $275 / day
Gratuities: 15%
Preferred Payment:
Cash, check or credit cards
Getting There:
Fly to Bozeman and rent a car,
though shuttles are available on
request.
Other Activities:
Canoeing/kayaking/rafting, horse-
back riding, hiking, skiing, swimming

Contact:
Colin Davis
Chico Hot Springs Lodge
Drawer D
Pray MT 59065
Ph: 406/333-4933
Fax: 406/333-4694
e-mail:
chico@chicohotsprings.com
Web:
www.chicohotsprings.com

Agents:
Off the Beaten Path
Travel Montana
Grizzly Hackle

IN THE EARLY 1900s, hot springs were all the rage. Warmed by the same fires that breed volcanoes, hot springs bubble forth issuing a faintly sulphuric flow. In the old days, folks drank the water which was reputed to cure cancers, gout and, according to romantics, affairs of the heart. Whether the waters are actually therapeutic is moot — they sure feel good at the end of a day's fishing. It's something not to miss if you're staying at Chico Hot Springs Lodge.

As you'd suspect, the lodge grew up around the spring. Today it's a fine resort that caters to upscale anglers and other guests who seek the quintessential western experience with few rough edges. Located midway up the Paradise Valley from Livingston, the lodge is enough off the well trod thoroughfare for quiet and tranquility, but close enough to put you on angling hot spots with only a few minutes drive. Cutthroats, browns and rainbows in the one- to eight-pound class are the main event here. Fish Armstong's and Nelson's spring creeks, the Yellowstone both in and out of the park, Lamar River and Slough Creeks. And if you're willing to invest an hour or more behind the wheel, you'll reach the Firehole, Gibbon, and Upper Madison. There's enough fishing here to keep you busy for months.

Guides generally aren't required unless you plan to float one of the major streams. Anglers new to this area might find that investing in a day's guided fishing ($300 or so) will pay off handsomely when you fish later on your own. Think of it as continuing education. The lodge will make arrangements for you if you wish. Then, too, there's the lodge's own pond, filled with brook trout. It's a great place for kids to learn the ropes. Though meltwater swells the Yellowstone in late May and June, you'll always be able to find fishable waters. Among the best fishing is the pre-melt period, and late in the season when the aspen's turned yellow.

Accommodations reflect the evolution of the resort. Guests in the main lodge stay in rooms of period decor and, in keeping with the era, share baths. More modern motel rooms, as well as rustic cabins, houses and condominiums, are also available. Dinners befit the lodge. Open with smoked trout, served with cream cheese, lemon and tomato. Move on to a spinach salad. Choose from aged beef, Mediterranean chicken, Thai shrimp or a dozen other entrees. Hearty eaters may want to check out the buffalo steak. After such meals, all sleep well.

The Complete Fly Fisher

W i s e   R i v e r ,   M o n t a n a

To be wise is a quality much admired but more often found in fish than anglers, except for those who stay at this lodge.

VITAL STATISTICS:

KEY SPECIES:
Brookies, browns, cutthroat, rainbows

Tackle:
Fly-fishing
Major Season:
May through October
Accommodations:
OPEN, AIRY AND MODERN RIVERFRONT LODGE
NUMBER OF ROOMS: 7
HANDICAPPED ACCESSIBLE: 1
MAXIMUM NUMBER OF GUESTS: 14
Meals: Elegant regional cuisine
Conference Groups: Yes
Rates: From $2,250 / week, double occupancy
Guides: Included
Gratuities: $40 - $60 / day
Preferred Payment:
Cash or check
Getting There:
Fly to Butte and rent a car.
Other Activities:
Bird-watching, canoeing/kayaking/ rafting, horseback riding, hiking, wildlife photography

Contact:
David & Stuart Decker
The Complete Fly Fisher
PO Box 127
Wise River MT 59762
Ph: 406/832-3175
Fax: 406/832-3169
e-mail:
comfly@montana.com
Web:
www.completeflyfisher.com

THE BIG HOLE rises on the eastern flank of the Bitterroot Mountains and flows about 125 miles to Twin Bridges, where it joins the Beaverhead to form the Jefferson. Once down from the high peaks, it courses through the Big Hole Basin, a deep valley surrounded by mountains, before plunging into a set of canyons and cuts below Dickey Bridge where the fishing, water permitting, can be awesome.

The upper reaches contain brook and cutthroat trout. The population of rainbows, many in the 14- to 18-inch range, increases in the canyon, while the lower section belongs to brown trout. Dry fly-fishing is at its peak in July and early August. The only significant population of Montana grayling, remnants of arctic stock left over from the last glacial advance, are found in the river's upper sections. "Their numbers are dwindling," co-owner Stuart Decker says. "We'll pull the boat over to watch them feed, but otherwise we leave them alone."

That pretty much sums up the philosophy of this lodge. It's different from others. You'll find little of the braggadocio associated with the Cuban cigar and single malt crowd — who cares who caught the most fish on the smallest flies? Think of a sojourn at The Complete Fly Fisher as a kind of Chatauqua. Here the guiding philosophy goes beyond providing guests with a first-class experience, though when it comes to angling and accommodations, The Complete Fly Fisher has few peers. The lodge exists to help every guest learn more about fly-fishing — casting, fly selection, river reading, fish playing — and about some of the environmental issues affecting wild trout in the Big Hole watershed. Guides will help improve your fishing. You'll fish the rivers, and you'll talk about the fishing. And you'll come away with new skills and maybe a few new understandings, not just about yourself, but about how you relate to your environs.

Nestled behind a screen of cottonwoods, The Complete Fly Fisher fronts the Big Hole. Low and long, yet open and airy, natural wood and big glass windows help the lodge blend into its surroundings. Dinner on some nights when the hatch is great may not be served until 10:00 p.m. Breakfast and lunch are at your convenience. You have a choice of accommodations from two rooms in the lodge, rooms in five cabins near the lodge, or Spring Creek Cabin, a cottage with two bedrooms a mile from the lodge. All rooms have private baths.

Craig Fellin's Big Hole River Outfitters

Wise River, Montana

Think of this lodge as being like a smooth pool at the foot of a long and difficult series of rapids.

VITAL STATISTICS:

KEY SPECIES:
Brookies, browns, cutthroat, grayling, rainbows

Tackle:
Fly-fishing
Major Season:
June through September
Accommodations:
CHARMING LOG CABINS
NUMBER OF ROOMS: 4
MAXIMUM NUMBER OF GUESTS: 8
Meals: If not gourmet, it's pretty close
Conference Groups: Yes
Rates: From $2,250 / week
Guides: Included
Gratuities: $50
Preferred Payment:
Cash or check
Getting There:
Fly to Butte and rent a car or get picked up by the lodge van for free.
Other Activities:
Golf, hiking

Contact:
Craig Fellin
Craig Fellin's Big Hole River Outfitters
Box 156
Wise River MT 59762
Ph: 406/832-3252
Fax: 406/832-3252
e-mail:
wsr3252@montanna.com
Web:
www.flyfishinglodge.com

Agents:
Frontiers

CUTTING DOWN from the foothills of the Pioneer Mountains is a little, vest pocket sort of river that offers very good rainbow fishing, as well as an occasional grayling or cutthroat. Freestone and of consistent riffle character, you need no guide to fish this. All you have to do is slip on your waders, pick up your rod from the peg where it hangs, and amble off across the meadow and through the trees. Fish it to your heart's content. Fish it solo. There are times when it's nice to be alone on a piece of water which you do not know.

And there are times when it's great to have somebody around who'll suggest the right fly, recommend a particular placement of the cast, and then clap you on the back after you've released that 17-inch rainbow. The nice thing about Craig Fellin, who owns this lodge, and his guides is that they're pretty adept at knowing when to help and when not to. Craig's guides will help you get what you want from the Wise and the Big Hole which it feeds. Most guests come to float the Big Hole, as fine a trout river as there is. 150 miles of water ranges from the thin upper reaches where you'll catch brookies and grayling in meadow meanders, to the rumbling, tumbling torrents and swift runs of the river below the hamlet of Wise River. Here the gradient steepens, and the river swirls around boulders, chuffs through deep pockets, and crashes between the walls of Maiden Rock Canyon. Fish here are bigger and there tend to be more browns than rainbows. Below Glen, the river paces through braided channels, good brown trout water, on its way to the Jefferson at Twin Bridges. If this isn't enough, there's the Beaverhead and the Ruby within easy striking distance.

Small and intimate is the best way to describe Craig Fellin's Big Hole River Outfitters on the Wise River. Booking only six to eight guests per week, Craig's mission is to help his guests slow down and take it easy. The main lodge and two spacious log guest cabins (each with two rooms) nestle up against a hillside timbered with lodgepole pine. The dining room, where the likes of baked eggs with asparagus spears greet you at breakfast, looks across a deeply green valley. The lodge maintains a small fly shop where you can stock up on the pattern du jour and purchase all those things you left at home. You can hear the river sing through the open window of your tastefully appointed log cabin.

Diamond J Ranch

E n n i s ,   M o n t a n a

How could you not stay at the Diamond J and miss fishing Jackass Creek?

VITAL STATISTICS:

KEY SPECIES:
Browns, rainbows

Tackle:
Fly-fishing, spinning
Major Season:
May through September
Accommodations:
LOG GUEST CABINS
NUMBER OF ROOMS: 12
HANDICAPPED ACCESSIBLE: 1
MAXIMUM NUMBER OF GUESTS: 35
Meals: Hearty fish, fowl and beef
Conference Groups: Yes
Rates: From $1,150 / week
Guides: $275 / day
Gratuities: $40
Preferred Payment:
Cash, check or credit cards
Getting There:
Fly to Gallatin and rent a car.
Other Activities:
Wingshooting, bird-watching, canoeing/kayaking/rafting, horseback riding, hiking, swimming, tennis

Contact:
Peter & Jenny Combs
Diamond J Ranch
PO Box 577
Ennis MT 59729
Ph: 406/682-4867
Fax: 406/682-4106
e-mail:
totalmgt@3rivers.com
Web:
www.diamondj.com

Agents:
Orvis endorsed

TWELVE MILES DUE EAST of Ennis up a lovely valley flanked by peaks of the Madison Range is the well-known and highly regarded Diamond J Ranch. For owners Peter and Jinny Combs, the ranch is a labor of love. For nearly two generations, their ranch has been highly regarded for its rustic and comfortable cabins; excellent food; and a range of activities that include riding, hiking, square dancing, bird hunting and fly-fishing. Of special note are programs for children, including riding, games and storytelling in front of a blazing fire in the stone hearth; there are also special playing and dining facilities for children. Service to guests is what this ranch is all about. That and helping them get the better of at least one jackass.

We're talking about the creek, a little stream that flows through the ranch and offers fishing for rainbows. Angling on this stream can be quite challenging, and rewarding too. Also on the ranch is a two-acre pond that's used during free fly-fishing schools (every Monday afternoon). Orvis-endorsed, the Diamond J employs a fishmaster to help guests become successful anglers on the ranch waters. Ranch personnel will also hook you up with guides from the Tackle Shop at Ennis for trips to the Madison and other blue-ribbon streams and lakes within striking range.

An hour's drive accesses most of the Madison. Running 52 miles from Quake Lake to Ennis, the Madison has a reputation of not being too difficult to wade. Rainbows, browns and cutthroats are the quarry here. Below Ennis Lake, the river drops into wild Bear Trap Canyon (Class III to V rapids), where fishing — particularly in the fall when water is low and cool — can be tremendous for browns up to five pounds. Fishing here isn't for the faint of heart. A 35-mile two-day float with an overnight in a log cabin on the river is a great way to survey the Madison. Add another half an hour to your car ride and you can hit half a dozen of the best trout streams in the country, including Henry's Fork, the Gallatin, Gibbon, Firehole and, if you push your ride a bit, the Yellowstone. Go west for the Ruby, Beaverhead and Big Hole. Ah, so many streams. Guess you'll have to stay longer.

At the Diamond J, you'll sleep in spacious log cabins, each with private bath, fireplace and front porch. Meals with a southwestern flare are served in the main dining room. Fare is hearty as well as healthy. Outdoor barbecues are a weekly feature, and breakfast trail rides are often held in the summer.

Dome Mountain Lodge at Point of Rocks

E m i g r a n t , M o n t a n a

Under new ownership, this ranch is well on its way to becoming a great outdoors resort.

VITAL STATISTICS:

KEY SPECIES:
Browns, cutthroat, rainbows

Tackle:
Fly-fishing, spinning
Major Season:
May through November
Accommodations:
CABINS AND FOUR GUEST HOUSES
NUMBER OF CABINS: 8
HANDICAPPED ACCESSIBLE: 8
MAXIMUM NUMBER OF GUESTS: 30
Meals: Self-catered or breakfast only, unless by special arrangement
Conference Groups: Yes
Rates: From $60 / day
Guides: $250 / day
Gratuities: 25%
Preferred Payment:
Cash, check or credit cards
Getting There:
Fly to Bozeman and rent a car.
Other Activities:
Big game, waterfowling, wingshooting, bird-watching, boating, canoeing/ kayaking/rafting, horseback riding, hiking, swimming, wildlife photography, archery, roping

Contact:
J.B. Klyap
Dome Mountain Lodge
at Point of Rocks
2017 US 89 South
Emigrant MT 59027
Ph: 406/333-4361
Fax: 406/848-7222
e-mail:
dmrlodge@hotmail.com

YOU KNEW THIS LODGE AS Point of Rock's Ranch, and you thoroughly enjoyed its four plus private miles of the Yellowstone River, 20 miles south of the park. A year or so ago, the ranch changed hands. There's the same rolling 5,000 acres that climbs into the Abasroka-Beartooth Wilderness with its millions of acres of wilderness. Next door is the 4,000-acre Dome Mountain Wildlife Refuge. Opportunities to see elk, bear and moose abound.

What's new here besides the owner, Frederick Smith, and his manager J.B. Klyap, are four new guest houses. With five bedrooms, Cedar House sleeps 12 and comes appointed with Jacuzzi, full-kitchen, and satellite television. High on a ridge overlooking the valley is Alpine House, ideal for small families or groups. The Log House sleeps 10 and its pool room (billiards, not swimming) provides evening entertainment. The Studio is a comfy single-bedroom cottage warmed by a woodstove. You may also stay in cabins near the ranch house. If you rent one of the houses, you'll rely on your own culinary talents or those of restaurants in Paradise Valley. Cabins without kitchens operate as bed-and-breakfasts. Dinners are available on special request.

Most guests find themselves fishing the private reach of the Yellowstone. Above the ranch is fast pocket and pool water, below it's more riffles and runs. By this point on the Yellowstone, brown trout have become dominant, and they are big. A leviathan of 23-plus pounds was once pulled from a pool behind the ranch, which each year yields a four-pounder or two. Caddis and salmonfly hatches are particularly good on this section, but the best chance of landing a trophy brown comes after September 15. Big streamers and nymphs can really pay off. Not only do anglers who hang their waders here have access to the mileage on the Yellowstone, but there are two lakes on the ranch that hold good trout, and all of Yellowstone National Park is less than an hour away. Heading for the park leads you to Slough Creek above Gardiner for its cutthroats or, farther, into the headwaters of the Gallatin and Gibbon. Drive a little longer and you're on the upper Madison or the Firehole. A half-hour north of the lodge are Nelson's and Armstrong's spring creeks. Unlike many guest ranches that cater to anglers, you need not hire a guide when you stay at Dome Mountain.

Double Arrow Resort

S e e l e y   L a k e ,   M o n t a n a

A half an hour drive from this charming golfing ranch puts you on the river that Norman Maclean made famous.

VITAL STATISTICS:

KEY SPECIES:
Bull trout, cutthroat, rainbows

Tackle:
Fly-fishing
Major Season:
May through September
Accommodations:
Cabins and rooms in the log lodge
Number of Rooms: 30
Handicapped Accessible: Some
Maximum Number of Guests: 70
Meals: Gourmet with a continental twist
Conference Groups: Yes
Rates: From $70
Guides: $300
Gratuities: 15%
Preferred Payment:
Cash, check or credit cards
Getting There:
Fly to Missoula and rent a car.
Other Activities:
Boating, canoeing/kayaking/rafting, golf, horseback riding, hiking, swimming, tennis, wildlife photography

Contact:
Ed Beazanson
Double Arrow Resort
PO Box 847
Seeley Lake MT 59868
Ph: 406/677-2777
Fax: 406/677-2922

THE IMAGE OF BRAD PITT standing on the rock casting that long and lovely line is an image as indelible as any in angling. Redford's film — *A River Runs Through It* — hatched in some of us a dormant human yearning for a simple and better life that could somehow be fulfilled by fishing with a fly. The film was, of course, not filmed on the river that author Norman Maclean had in mind when he wrote the book. But that doesn't make any difference. You can fish the river he fished, and if you re-read his book (and avoid watching the movie), your trip to his river — the Blackfoot — will be richer for it.

Not far from the hustle of Missoula, the Blackfoot is known as a family river. A 30-mile long corridor along the river provides campgrounds, access, and protection for this, one of Montana's finest rivers. This is good trout water and it's improving thanks to cooperation among a host of private and public organizations. It's a great river for new anglers. Wading is reasonably easy. Runoff normally clears the river before the hatch of salmon and Golden Stone flies in June and July. Autumn (late summer was the setting of *A River*) is among the best times to fish this river. Floating boats are largely gone from the water and trout are gorging on grasshoppers. Rainbows predominate, browns are frequent, and bull trout show up often enough to steal the breath from anglers not ready for their girth or ferocity. The rep of this river suggests that dries take more trout than wet patterns.

Because of its utter reliability, Double Arrow, 20 miles north in Seeley Lake, uses the Blackfoot as its home river. Guided fishing packages can be arranged through the lodge, and many guests who book into this charming resort with its antique-style brass beds and thick comforters with matching duvets, spend a good deal of time behind a fly rod. But they also swing woods and irons on a gem of a nine-hole (soon to be 18-hole) course tucked among the pines in a gentle valley. The golf course is open until October 1, depending on weather. If fishing and golf are your passion, book into this resort in September. Aspens are yellowing, morning air has a touch of a nip to it and the fire on the hearth feels so good when the sun slides behind the mountains.

Eagle Nest Lodge

Hardin, Montana

If the browns and rainbows in the Bighorn don't get you, you can have a crack at sharptails and Huns.

VITAL STATISTICS:

KEY SPECIES:
Brookies, browns, cutthroat, rainbows

Tackle:
Fly-fishing
Major Season:
April through November
Accommodations:
Stylish log lodge
Number of Rooms: 7
Handicapped Accessible: 2
Maximum Number of Guests: 14
Meals: Excellent beef, fowl and fish
Conference Groups: Yes
Rates: From $1,000 / 3 days, 2 nights
Guides: Included
Gratuities: $50 - $100 / day
Preferred Payment:
Cash, check or credit cards
Getting There:
Fly to Billings and rent a car.
Other Activities:
Waterfowling, wingshooting, bird-watching, hiking, wildlife photography

Contact:
Scott Moscato
Eagle Nest Lodge
PO Box 509
Hardin MT 59034
Ph: 406/665-3711
Fax: 406/665-3712
e-mail:
eaglenestlodge@mcn.net
Web:
www.eaglenestlodge.com

Agents:
Orvis endorsed

EAGLE NEST LODGE was one of the first fishing lodges in the Bighorn Valley upstream from Hardin. It's still one of the best. Until the construction of Yellowtail Dam up at Fort Smith, the Bighorn was one of those western rivers you love to hate. Spring meltwaters rampaged through the canyon above the dam and flooded the valley below. Their ebbing in July and the droughts of August and September left the river low and warm. Quality trout fishing was restricted to the upper reaches of the river.

But with the closing of Yellowtail Dam in 1965, all that changed. The Bighorn became a tailwater fishery and that meant reasonable water flows all year long, thanks to an afterbay constructed below the main impoundment. For 13 miles below the dam — the stretch that fishes best — the river flows clear and reasonably cold year-round. Brown trout outnumber rainbows in sizes up to 22 inches. If you happen to hook a larger trout, odds are it will be a big 'bow. Rainbows tend to school up in tight pods at those junctions between riffles and deep, slow pools. Good guides will find those holding areas and fish them hard. While the river is open all year, fishing starts with the first hatches in March and continues into October.

Fly-fisherman should bring an assortment of midges, Blue-winged Olives, Pale Morning Duns, tricos and caddis. Hoppers may produce in late summer and fall. And don't forget a stock of standard nymphs. Spinfishermen will find success with Mepps, Rooster Tails and Rapalas. Most anglers drift until they spot feeding fish or likely-looking water, then pull ashore and wade. Neoprenes are needed in spring and fall.

You won't find verdant green farmlands here, rather acre upon acre of wheat stubble and grass. It's prime pheasant country. Gunning for ringnecks gets under way in October. Add Hungarian partridge, sharptails and chukar, and you're really rolling. Waterfowl seasons also overlap trout fishing. Eagle Nest offers the ultimate casts and wingshooting, and take it from me, it's a blast.

Founded by Alan Kelley, the lodge was sold to Scott Moscato in early 1999. It remains the flagship of Orvis-endorsed sporting lodges. The reddish log lodge provides guests with tastefully decorated rooms, all with private baths. Hungarian partridge and pheasants find their ways onto the menu, as do filet mignon and pork tenderloin. Located on the Bighorn, Eagle Nest is inside the Crow Reservation, and thus serves no alcohol. It's okay to bring your own.

[N O R T H E R N   R O C K I E S]

Firehole Ranch

W e s t   Y e l l o w s t o n e ,   M o n t a n a

Small, intimate, excellent — the Firehole Ranch may be the quintessential western hideaway.

VITAL STATISTICS:

KEY SPECIES:
Browns, cutthroat, grayling, rainbows

Tackle:
Fly-fishing
Major Season:
June through October
Accommodations:
RUSTIC CABINS
NUMBER OF ROOMS: 10
MAXIMUM NUMBER OF GUESTS: 20
Meals: Gourmet western cuisine
Conference Groups: No
Rates: From $1,200 / 4 nights
Guides: $295 / day
Gratuities: 15%;
Angler's discretion
Preferred Payment:
Cash or check
Getting There:
Fly to West Yellowstone and rent a car or let the lodge collect you.
Other Activities:
Bird-watching, boating, canoeing/kayaking/rafting, horseback riding, hiking, swimming, wildlife photography

Contact:
Stan Klassen
Firehole Ranch
Box 686
West Yellowstone MT 59758
Ph: 406/646-7294
Fax: 406/646-4728
e-mail:
info@fireholeranch.com
Web:
www.fireholeranch.com

Agents:
Orvis endorsed

THE DAY HAS BEEN GOOD. Well rested from a good night's sleep, you filched a pair of muffins from the kitchen. After charging your go-cup with more coffee, you rode with your guide out the lane and down into Last Chance. You stopped off at Mike Lawson's fly shop, just for the hell of it. You always stop there when you're in West Yellowstone. An hour later you were fishing the Box on Henry's Fork. The water was down and you could work the holds behind the rocks and it was, this time finally, like picking pockets. Not every cast, of course, brought a 'bow. But after a couple hours you'd played a dozen rainbows, the biggest of which thumbed his nose at you when you tried to horse him. "Gotta watch that," you told yourself.

Ever the fan of diner fare, you chowed down on chili, a burger and fries and a couple of Heinekens at the A Bar, and then drove back upriver. You were thinking of tubing in Hebgen Lake, but naw, all that float tube stuff seemed too much trouble. Why not scout the Firehole? An hour later, you were there. Little rings were regularly appearing in the dark water near the burbling mud pots and fumaroles, smoking in the mid-afternoon sun. You rigged a three weight — you'd been using a six in the Box — and tied on a 7x tippet. What a hero, you laughed at yourself. And for once you managed to tie that #22 Adams on without fumbling for the magnifier buried somewhere in you vest. Your guide was watching all of this and, because he was a good guide, he knew enough to rig his own gear and not talk too much. You went down to the stream together, watching the water for a rising 'bow. You didn't know what the hatch was, the Adams was close enough. And the guide had a little ant on, in case terrestrials were in vogue.

Later, you enjoyed a shower, fresh slacks and wool shirt against the chill, Bombay martini with a twist, stuffed chair by the fire — hard to pry you out for a dinner of braised veal chop and garlic potatoes. And while conversations swirled around you, your mind was there on the Firehole. Would you go back in the morning or would it be the Madison or the Gibbon below the falls, or a float tube and the monster trout in the lake? In your cabin's stone fireplace, the fire you'd lit while changing for dinner was smoldering. You added a thin log to keep it alive, avoided a night cap, and climbed into bed watching the flames flutter in the hearth. Where to fish tomorrow? The morning would tell you what to do.

Camouflage is not required to fool trout on the Bighorn.
But if helps if you've come to shoot a few ducks as well.

[**N O R T H E R N   R O C K I E S**]

Glacier National Park Hotels

E .   G l a c i e r ,   M o n t a n a

Glory in the splendor of grand railway hotels, and fish for wild trout in waters as clear as any you'll ever see.

VITAL STATISTICS:

KEY SPECIES:
Bull trout, cutthroat, grayling, Kokanee salmon, lake trout, rainbows

Tackle:
Fly-fishing, spinning
Major Season:
Late May through September
Accommodations:
GRAND OLD HOTELS, MOTELS, COTTAGES
HANDICAPPED ACCESS: SOME
NUMBER OF ROOMS: VARIES
MAXIMUM NUMBER OF GUESTS: VARIES
Meals: Several restaurants offering fine to casual fare; some cottages have kitchens
Conference Groups: Yes
Guides: $295 / 2
Gratuities: Angler's discretion
Preferred Payment:
Cash, check or credit cards
Getting There:
Fly to Kalispell and rent a car.
Other Activities:
Big game, wingshooting, bird-watching, boating, canoeing/kayaking/rafting, golf, horseback riding, hiking, swimming, wildlife photography

Contact:
Reservations
Glacier National Park Hotels
PO Box 147
E. Glacier MT 59434
Ph: 406/226-9311
Web:
www.glacierparkinc.com

Off Season:
1850 N. Central Ave
Phoenix AZ 85077
Ph: 602/207-2850
Fax: 602/207-5589

SHARP PEAKS, PLUCKED BY GLACIERS, pierce the sky and long sinuous lakes stretch forever blue down fir-rimmed valleys. Waterton/ Glacier International Peace Park, as it's formally called, covers more than a million acres in the United States and Canada. Faces of active glaciers glow gray and faintly blue, charging streams with melt that's murky with rock flour. But the finely ground stone settles out in scores of little lakes and ponds, and their outflows are as clear as ether. Cataracts splash down steep slopes blending into rivers that hold up in big lakes, and then move on toward the Pacific or Atlantic as is their bent.

With more than 200 lakes and countless miles of streams, you'd think that Waterton/Glacier would be an angler's delight. It is, but not the way you'd imagine. Many lakes here are sterile; they've never been stocked and may have had no viable populations of trout or char to begin with. And in the mid-70s, the National Park Service discontinued stocking, a wise and welcome move. Natural populations of brook, cutthroat, bull (sometimes called Dolly Varden), grayling and some rainbows inhabit the park's waters. Lake trout, Kokanee salmon and pike are relatively common in the larger lakes.

Probably the best fishing is in high alpine lakes such as Quartz, Glenns and Loggin. Cutthroat and bull trout in the 10- to 14-inch range readily strike spinners and flies cast from shore. There's one caveat: a two- to three-mile hike precedes the fishing. But that's the case with most of the park's better waters. For lake trout, trolling just after ice-out is the most effective strategy. Don't forget to work the mouths of creeks flowing into the larger lakes. The North and Middle Forks of the Flathead River make up much of the western boundary of the park. Floats in driftboats result in catches of cutthroats of 10 to 15 inches and rainbows that are a little larger. Fish fly or spinning gear. Generally speaking, the park's fishing season runs from the third Saturday in May through November 30. However, Lake McDonald is open for lake trout fishing from April 1 to December 31. The best time to fish streams in the park is from mid-July after melt has passed into September. Check park regulations before wetting a line.

Lodging as exquisite as the scenery is available through three historic hotels and a quartet of inns operated as concessions by Glacier Parks, Inc:

PRINCE OF WALES HOTEL: Centered high on a bluff looking down Waterton Lake, the Prince of Wales hotel is as regal as its namesake, Prince Edward. Opened in 1927, this hotel maintains an air of British, yet rustic, gentility. Take tea in the lobby and dine on the best of English fare in Garden Court. Should sightseeing and angling pale, there's golf and tennis. Eighty-one rooms from $212 for two per night.

MANY GLACIER HOTEL: Built in 1914 and 1915 on the shore of Swiftcurrent Lake, the hotel is best known for its stunning views of Grinnel Point and Mt. Hinkel, prime habitat for mountain goats, bighorn sheep and bear. Reminiscent of Swiss mountain resorts (flags of Swiss Cantons decorate the dining room), this is the largest hotel in the park with 208 rooms. From $103 for two per night.

GLACIER PARK LODGE: Constructed by the Great Northern Railway to promote passenger traffic to the park, this lodge hosts presidents and kings and is known as "The Last Best Place." See the sights from horseback or historic red jammer busses and steep yourself in western mountain culture. Rooms from $131 for two per night.

SWIFTCURRENT MOTOR INN:. A mile from the hotel at the base of Mt. Hinkel is this complex of 26 cabins (shared baths) and 62 modern hotel rooms. Meals are served in the coffee shop. Cabins without baths from $40 for two; inn rooms from $75 for two.

LAKE MCDONALD LODGE: Once John Lewis' grand hunting retreat, these accommodations date from 1913 and reflect the height of early western elegance. The main lodge, motor inn and cottages combine to offer 100 rooms. A restaurant and coffee shop round out the complex. From $81 for small cottage rooms to $130 for rooms in the main lodge.

THE VILLAGE INN: On the opposite end of Lake McDonald is this small motel that contains 36 rooms, 12 of which have kitchens. View the lake from the window of your room or wade its chilly waters from the beach below. From $90 per person per night, single occupancy.

THE RISING SUN MOTOR INN: Near the east entrance to the park and close to St. Mary Lake, you'll find three motel buildings with a total of 72 rooms and 36 cottage rooms. Views of "The Land of Shining Mountain" are stunning. From $81 for two.

[N O R T H E R N   R O C K I E S]

Hawley Mountain Guest Ranch

McLeod,   Montana

With a horse, a fly rod, and a warm and comfortable cabin, who needs a cell phone?

VITAL STATISTICS:

KEY SPECIES:
Brookies, cutthroat, rainbows

Tackle:
Fly-fishing
Major Season:
June through September
Accommodations:
RUSTIC LOG LODGE
NUMBER OF ROOMS: 7
MAXIMUM NUMBER OF GUESTS: 24
Meals: Family western fare
Conference Groups: Yes
Rates: From $1,420 / week
Guides: Included
Gratuities: 15%
Preferred Payment:
Cash or check
Getting There:
Fly to Bozeman or Billings and rent a car.
Other Activities:
Bird-watching, canoeing/kayaking/ rafting, horseback riding, hiking, wildlife photography

Contact:
Ellen Marshall
Hawley Mountain Guest Ranch
PO Box 4
McLeod MT 59052
Ph: 406/932-5791
Fax: 406/932-5715
e-mail:
Bblewett@aol.com
Web:
www.hawleymountain.com

Off Season:
1335 Crown Dr
Alameda CA 94501
Ph: 510/523-4053
Fax: 510/523-5188

HIDDEN DEEP in the Absaroka-Beartooth Wilderness, the Boulder River doesn't have the cachet of the Madison or Yellowstone. However, the native cutthroats and wild rainbows here don't know the difference. After you've fished both, you'll notice one thing: there are fewer angler's on the Boulder because it's buried well away from the tourist routes.

Headquarters for fishing the upper mileage of the river is Hawley Mountain Guest Ranch, 22 miles from McLeod at the end of a gravel road. The Boulder here is beautiful, a fact not lost on filmmakers who shot scenes of *A River Runs Through It* on these waters. Less than 40 feet wide at the ranch, the river's slippery name-sake makes it difficult to wade in places. Yet, once you're in position, you'll discover that cutthroats and rainbows in the one- to four-pound class are not overly shy. Neither are the brookies up toward the headwaters. While the more productive fishing runs from July through October, the best months are August and September. Throughout, nymphs are the flies of choice, though caddis come off in fair profusion after May, and 'hoppers appear in August. Sculpin patterns work well on bigger fish. Ultralight anglers should consider Panther Martins, Rooster Tails and Mepps; check stream regulations regarding number of hooks.

Also on the angling agenda at Hawley Mountain are horseback trips up to high alpine ponds where cutthroat and rainbows slash eagerly at almost any pattern tossed from shore. Fishing is strictly catch-and-release, except in the ranch pond that's stocked with good-sized 'bows. If you ask nicely, and who would do otherwise, the chef will fix your pond-caught trout just the way you want it. Other meals are built around steaks, fried chicken and lasagna. The main lodge has four guest rooms with stunning views from private balconies, and three nearby cabins, scattered under the pines, boast living rooms, bedrooms and sleeping lofts. All have private baths.

You'll find no television, radio, fax or data linkup here. "Even your cell phone won't work," laughs manager Ellen Marshall. One thing that will work is your horse, which comes with your room. The horse, of course, must stay in its stall.

Healing Waters Fly Fishing Lodge

Twin Bridges, Montana

Half-a-dozen of the country's top streams are a short ride from this very interesting inn.

VITAL STATISTICS:

KEY SPECIES:
Brookies, browns, cutthroat, grayling, rainbows

Tackle:
Fly-fishing
Major Season:
April through October
Accommodations:
CHARMINGLY ECCENTRIC STONE HOUSE AND CABINS
NUMBER OF ROOMS: 6
MAXIMUM NUMBER OF GUESTS: 12
Meals: Family-style steak and sea bass with ginger
Conference Groups: No
Rates: From $525 / day
Guides: Included
Gratuities: $50
Preferred Payment:
Cash, check or credit cards
Getting There:
Fly to Butte or Bozeman and rent a car.
Other Activities:
Waterfowling, bird-watching, horseback riding, hiking, wildlife photography

Contact:
Greg & Janet Lilly
Healing Waters
Fly Fishing Lodge
270 Tuke Lane
Twin Bridges MT 59754
Ph: 406/684-5960
Fax: 406/684-5180
e-mail:
glilly@3rivers.net
Web:
www.flyfishing-inn-montana.com

HEALING WATERS IS AN IDEAL home base for fishing southwest Montana. Just upstream from Twin Bridges, the Ruby meets the Beaverhead. A few miles downstream from town, the Big Hole comes in from the west and helps form the Jefferson. The most popular area on the Big Hole — between Divide and Glen — is an easy drive from the lodge, as is the Ruby. It doesn't take much time to run up the Big Hole to reach the Wise, or to follow up the Beaverhead to Dillon. Too, you can head east on 287, cross the divide at Virginia City, and drop down into Ennis on the Madison.

The upper Ruby is very productive when it comes to rainbows, while browns predominate on the lower reaches. A reservoir at the headwaters retards some of the meltwater, but you'll still experience high flows in early summer. Plan to fish it early in the season from July on. Special months here include August and September when terrestrials are blooming; fishing hoppers can be such delightful madness. Much of the lower Ruby is private and access can be a problem. That's where a guide like Greg Lilly comes in; not only do he and his wife, Janet, own the lodge, but he can get you on waters not open to most folks. While your warming your waders in this neck of the woods, don't pass up a visit to the Jefferson below Twin Bridges. At times, the Jefferson is greater than the sum of its parts. With a riffle and pool personality, the river is almost tranquil in comparison to its sources. The upper section has a reputation for fishing as well as the Madison and isn't nearly as crowded. If you're willing to fish nymphs and streamers for bigger fish, consider the beginning or end of the season.

A welcome diversion from typical angling retreats of lodgepole pine, Healing Waters is an eclectic combination of American architecture. Its broad eaves give this stone and stucco two-story the feeling of the Prairie style. Yet the front dormer with its three, four-over-four windows are Craftsman. The main house contains one guest room while four additional rooms are located in adjacent guest cabins of similar style. The master suite in the main house contains its own free-standing fireplace, and the exterior stone motif is echoed in the treatment of the hearth and the walls flanking the Jacuzzi. Other rooms are a little less grand; queen-size beds and private baths are standard. Family-style meals include dinners of filet mignon and twice-baked potatoes or pastas.

[N O R T H E R N   R O C K I E S]

High Country Outfitters

P r a y ,   M o n t a n a

Your own cabin, fine fishing on a lake a few yards from your door, excellent cuisine, and all of Yellowstone on the horizon.

VITAL STATISTICS:

KEY SPECIES:
Browns, cutthroat, rainbows

Tackle:
Fly-fishing
Major Season:
May through September
Accommodations:
PRIVATE LOG CABIN
NUMBER OF ROOMS: 1
MAXIMUM NUMBER OF GUESTS: 4
Meals: Elegant creations of fresh vegetables and fine meats
Conference Groups: No
Rates: From $3,140 / 5 nights / 2
Guides: Included
Gratuities: Angler's discretion
Preferred Payment:
Cash or check
Getting There:
Fly to Bozeman and rent a car.
Other Activities:
Bird-watching, hiking, wildlife photography

Contact:
Chip Rizzotto
High Country Outfitters
158 Bridger Hollow Rd
Pray MT 59065
Ph: 406/333-4763
e-mail:
rizzotto@mcn.net
Web:
www.mcn.net/~rizzotto

SOME PLACES ARE TOO GOOD to change, and that's the case with Chip and Francine's lodge in Paradise Valley. Imagine an intimate cabin. Hudson Bay blankets warm log frame beds. Daily baskets of fresh fruit and flowers grace rustic furniture. Books on angling fill the library, a tier's bench awaits, and rods of every description grace the wall. Across the breezeway, Francine is at work in the kitchen. She does not wear a toque, though her culinary creations suggest that she might. Spicy corn salsa may accent the lamb; the salmon may be gingered. Meanwhile Chip — husband, chief guide and major domo — plots the next day's fishing.

The Rizzottos cater to one party of up to four anglers at a time. Frequently, though, their guests are a couple who rent the single cabin for the five-night minimum with four days of guided fishing. It is as if you have these wonderful friends with a fabulous place: 20 acres of solitude with trout stream and pond adjoining the Absaroka Beartooth Wilderness. You are their guests for a week, and they won't let you lift a finger to help. Your job is to soak up the scenery and fish the streams of Paradise Valley.

That means the Yellowstone and its tributaries. The Yellowstone is the longest free-flowing river in the U.S. And it is wild. A heavy rainstorm high in the mountains may raise and discolor the river. Ice and spring flows are continually rearranging pools and runs. What you fished so well last year might not be there this year. Spring melt swells the river from May through June, and in normal years, the water becomes optimal by mid-July. Despite frequent flooding, the river supports prolific hatches (caddis and salmonfly) and extensive populations of cutthroats, rainbows, browns and whitefish. Cutthroats and browns predominate in the upper river from Gardiner south to Livingston. Fish are not huge — 12 to 14 inches are normal — but they are plentiful. The most popular way to fish the river is to float it, and Rizzotto runs a MacKenzie driftboat for that purpose.

In addition to the Yellowstone, Rizzotto guides anglers on Armstrong Spring Creek, arranges horseback pack-in trips to the buffalo meadows of Slough and Pebble creeks, and offers float tube adventures on high mountain lakes for big rainbows. Increasing in popularity are "Not for men only" fly-fishing schools, where women and men in groups from two to four can enjoy three days of personal on-stream instruction.

Jumping Rainbow Ranch

Livingston, Montana

The angler who slips into the Yellowstone in April beats the runoff and nails fine browns.

VITAL STATISTICS:

KEY SPECIES:
Browns, cutthroat, rainbows

Tackle:
Fly-fishing, spinning
Major Season:
April through October
Accommodations:
RUSTIC LOG LODGE
NUMBER OF ROOMS: 9
MAXIMUM NUMBER OF GUESTS: 20
Meals: Near gourmet dining
Conference Groups: Yes
Rates: From $100 / day / 2
Guides: $275 / 2
Gratuities: 15%
Preferred Payment:
Cash, check or credit cards
Getting There:
Fly to Bozeman and rent a car.
Other Activities:
Bird-watching, horseback riding, hiking, wildlife photography

Contact:
Charles Lakovitch
Jumping Rainbow Ranch
110 Jumping Rainbow Rd
Livingston MT 59047
Ph: 406/222-5425
Fax: 406/222-5508

Agents:
Off the Beaten Path

PARADISE VALLEY, that long run through which the Yellowstone runs on its way north from the national park, can be just that — paradise. Runoff swells the river from late May through June, and only in early July does it really return to levels where wading is comfortable. Sure, there's some great driftboat fishing when the water's up, especially if you plug the bank with heavy nymphs.

However, the Yellowstone has a little secret. In April, depending on temperatures, massive hatches of caddis are triggered and they last into May. Also at that time, virtually any bead-headed nymph or streamer will provoke strikes. Typical fish run in the 12- to 14-inch range, but big browns and 'bows of 18 to 22 inches don't earn much more than a polite "good fish" from local anglers. Along with the benefit of catching trout just as they commence their spring feeding frenzy, there's the fact that you'll find few other anglers working your stretch of river. No hoards of driftboats jousting for position over the best runs. You've got them to yourself. To lesser degree, the same applies in the autumn, the best time of all to fish the Yellowstone. Hatches continue, and Blue-winged Olives and the ilk present some of the best dry fly action of the year. Streamers fished deep will draw attention from big browns.

Charles Lakovitch and Galen Ibes own the Jumping Rainbow Ranch on 300 acres that border a mile of the Yellowstone in the vicinity of Armstrong and Nelson spring creeks. Armstrong, perhaps better known by names of the ranches through which it flows — O'Hair and DePuy — is across the river. Nelson's is upstream. On the ranch are six stocked ponds, and a section of challenging spring creek flows through the property. From there, you can arrange to float the Yellowstone, take a pack trip to lakes high in the Absaroka Wilderness, or explore the great streams on the north end of Yellowstone National Park, particularly Slough Creek.

Accommodations at the Jumping Rainbow are delightfully rustic. Furniture is made of log, floors are wood and trophies hang high on the walls. Double or queen-size beds are the order of the day in the guest rooms, each of which has a private bath. A full-time chef turns out exquisite meals served family-style on the long pine table. A number of meal plans are available. And the Jumping Rainbow rents out a pair of guest cabins that include fully-equipped kitchens.

Kingfisher Lodge

F t .   S m i t h ,   M o n t a n a

You don't really need a 12-gauge to fish the Bighorn; a three-inch 20 will do fine.

VITAL STATISTICS:

KEY SPECIES:
Browns, rainbows

Tackle:
Fly-fishing
Major Season:
All year
Accommodations:
Long, low, wooden motel-style lodge
Number of Rooms: 8
Handicapped Accessible: 2
Maximum Number of Guests: 14
Meals: Nicely done regional fare
Conference Groups: Yes
Rates: From $250 / day
Guides: Included
Gratuities: Angler's discretion
Preferred Payment:
Cash or check
Getting There:
Fly to Billings and rent a car.
Other Activities:
Waterfowling, wingshooting, bird-watching, boating, horseback riding, hiking, wildlife photography

Contact:
George Kelly
Kingfisher Lodge
Bighorn Country Outfitters
Box 7524
Ft. Smith MT 59035
Ph: 406/666-2326

AMONG THE WESTERN tailwater fisheries, few can compare with Montana's Bighorn. Sure the fishing in the others can be, and often is, stunning. But when fall rolls around, the Bighorn proffers anglers a special treat — an abundance of ducks and pheasants. This is the time of year for which George Kelly, impresario of Bighorn River Outfitter's Kingfisher Lodge and author of *Seasons of the Bighorn*, lives.

He'll launch his driftboat and summon his Lab, and you'll climb in and take the seat in the bow. It'll be dark and cold enough to freeze irrigation ditches and scores of pothole ponds so loved by wigeon, gadwall and mallards. As you drift along, you'll hear ducks gabbling as they're flushed from the still waters behind the islands you pass. George has a special place in mind. Grounding the boat, he heaves two bags of decoys over the side, and then runs the boat on around a hidden slough at the base of the island. No sooner have the dekes been set than the first ducks come in and you see them clearly from your spot under the Russian olive trees. By midmorning, you've bagged a brace of drake mallards and that's enough. Sip coffee and eat a sandwich as you rig your six-weight. For the rest of the trip, you work the seams between fast and still waters around the islands. Not, by god, a bad day.

Though open all year, the season generally begins in March with midges and dark Blue-winged Olives. Standard nymph patterns — Gold-ribbed Hare's Ears, Prince, Pheasant Tail — produce better than dries. The fishing holds up into June when the river typically rises a bit with meltwater. Still quite fishable in June, nymphs, streamers and scuds carry the day. In July, caddis activity begins and in late August, tricos begin to come off. Later in the season, nymphs and streamers become an angler's mainstays. Bait fishing is limited to a short section just below the dam, but spin fishers can ply hardware and plugs the length of the best trout water. Crimping barbs on hooks (and replacing treble hooks with singles) will facilitate required release of rainbows. This section of the river has two to three times as many trout per mile than other premiere streams in Montana. Fish tend to be in the 14- to 18-inch range. Among larger fish, rainbows seem to be more prevalent than browns.

Kingfisher Lodge is a half-mile from the Bighorn River. Modern and comfortable, you'll find fly-tying benches in every room. All but one have private baths. George, who's a pretty good cook, now offers dinners in his new dining room.

Linehan Outfitting

Yaak, Montana

Fish the Kootenai with the host of Trout Unlimited's widely acclaimed television series.

VITAL STATISTICS:

KEY SPECIES:
Cutthroat, rainbows

Tackle:
Fly-fishing

Major Season:
Mid-June through October

Accommodations:
THREE CHARMING LOG CABINS
NUMBER OF ROOMS: 8
MAXIMUM NUMBER OF GUESTS: 8

Meals: Self-catered

Conference Groups: No

Rates: From $125 / night / 2

Guides: $300 / 2

Gratuities: 20%

Preferred Payment:
Cash, check or credit cards

Getting There:
Fly to Spokane or Kalispell and rent a car.

Other Activities:
Wingshooting, bird-watching, horseback riding, hiking, skiing, wildlife photography

Contact:
Tim Linehan
Linehan Outfitting
472 Upper Ford Rd
Troy MT 59935
Ph: 406/295-4872
Fax: 406/295-6038
e-mail:
linehan@libby.org
Web:
www.fishmontana.com

IF THE NAME OF THE OWNER of this lodge rings a bell, it's because you've seen his face as the genial host of Trout Unlimited Television (TUTV). Tim, poor soul, travels throughout the U.S. filming 30-minute shows that feature great waters — Arkansas' White, The Beaver Kill, Colorado at Lees Ferry — and the great guides who fish them. Tim's been around, an Easterner who moved West heading for Alaska but got stuck when passing through the uppermost corner of northwest Montana.

There is not much here, save mountains filled with red cedar and lodgepole pine. Larch, aspen and black cottonwood all turn brilliant yellow in the fall. Libby is a lumber town with a number of motels and fast food franchises. Troy is little more than a speed zone on U.S. Route 2 between Libby and Bonner's Ferry, Idaho. Farther north, the land belongs to British Columbia.

The angling game in this neck of the woods is the Kootenai River, especially the tailwater section from Libby Dam. The river itself rises in Kootenai National Park in the Canadian Rockies across the ridge from Banff. But the closing of Libby Dam impounded the lake, and brought to an end the annual flooding that ravaged Libby. A by-product of the dam was the marvelous tailwater. Rainbows and cutthroat to 20 inches cruise its clear green depths. The bottom is rocky, a blend of deep pools with boulder-strewn bottoms and shallower gravely runs. Runoff fills the river in May and June, but because of the upstream lake, the tailwater remains fishable. The best angling occurs from August into October. That's when you'll find better hatches and more aggressive fish. In the past, the Kootenai was plagued by wildly fluctuating discharges, but a new partnership among the Corps of Engineers, anglers and Montana's Department of Natural Resources has made flows more predictable.

Coming into this country, Tim and his wife, Joanne, looked for a location to erect their lodge that had tranquility, lots of space, and reasonable access to the river. The found it in Yaak, a crossroads about 30 miles from Libby on a scenic forest service road. The couple built three charming log cabins, each with a broad front porch and private bath. The cabins contain complete kitchen facilities or guests can sample the more than adequate chow at the Red Dog Saloon. If you plan a venture to this wilderness, time it for October when you can catch trout and chase grouse.

The Lodge

Hamilton, Montana

You won't encounter other anglers as you fish for big browns and rainbows here.

VITAL STATISTICS:

KEY SPECIES:
Browns, cutthroat, rainbows

Tackle:
Fly-fishing
Major Season:
Mid-March through October
Accommodations:
RUSTIC ONE-STORY RIVERFRONT LODGE
NUMBER OF ROOMS: 3
MAXIMUM NUMBER OF GUESTS: 6
Meals: Near gourmet regional cuisine
Conference Groups: Yes
Rates: From $750 / 4 nights
Guides: $300 / day
Gratuities: $75 - $100 / day
Preferred Payment:
Cash or check
Getting There:
Fly to Missoula and rent a car.
Other Activities:
Hiking, skiing, wildlife photography

Contact:
John Talia
The Lodge
PO box 302
Hamilton MT 59840-0302
Ph: 406/363-4661
Fax: 406/363-6964
e-mail:
bitterrootriver@msn.com

Agents:
Off the Beaten Path

SNOWS THAT CLING to the Bitterroot and Sapphire mountains melt and feed the west and east forks of the Bitterroot, draining more than 2.5 million acres of wilderness. High lakes hold populations of cutthroat and brook trout. You'll find them in the upper reaches of the river, and yes, they are worth fishing. The main stem of the Bitterroot really begins below the hamlet of Conner and runs some 70 miles almost due north through a widening valley to Missoula. Below the town, the river assumes a modest demeanor that makes it as popular to wade as to float.

Riffle, pool, riffle, run, pool, riffle again. That's the song of the Bitterroot. Cut-banks are held in place by roots of old cottonwoods, aspen and fir. Fish pools beneath log jams. Cutthroat up to 20 inches are making a huge recovery in the river above the town of Victor, and a similar resurgence of bull trout (Dolly Varden) is also being seen. The Bitterroot tends to discharge its load of snow runoff more rapidly than many other rivers in the same part of the state, thus it tends to fish better in late June than most. Fish are not finicky here. Royal Wulffs and Adams are ever productive, as are many caddis patterns and nymphs. You'll catch cutthroats, rainbows and browns, and cuttbows too. Those are a hybrid of cutthroats and rainbows that "eats like a cutthroat and fights like a rainbow," says John Talia, co-owner of The Lodge.

The Lodge is hard by the river. You can spend a week wading and fishing the Bitterroot in front of the lodge and never cover it all; or you can float the river. In either case, you'll come off the river at the door to your room. Soak in the hot tub and take a nap before dinner. Yours will be one of three guest rooms, all with private baths and beds with thick down comforters. Evening meals — butterflied leg of lamb, carne asada with chili rellenos, grilled salmon — are frequently held in the boardroom, which offers stunning views of the Bitterroot Mountains and the river. For the inspired, a tier's bench is in the corner. For the less compulsive, sofas before the fireplace in the great room can be very inviting.

Seldom will you encounter other anglers. The lodge is a mile and a quarter beyond paved road, and four or five miles from public river access. With no more than five other guests per week, The Lodge is private indeed.

Lone Mountain Ranch

Big Sky, Montana

*Four rivers in one: that's
the story on the Gallatin.*

**VITAL
STATISTICS:**

KEY SPECIES:
Browns, cutthroat, grayling,
rainbows

Tackle:
Fly-fishing
Major Season:
June through October
Accommodations:
LOVELY AND IMMACULATE LOG CABINS
NUMBER OF ROOMS: 30
HANDICAPPED ACCESSIBLE: 1
MAXIMUM NUMBER OF GUESTS: 85
Meals: Fine dining
Conference Groups: Yes
Rates: From $3,850 / week / 2
Guides: $260
Gratuities: $20
Preferred Payment:
Cash, check or credit cards
Getting There:
Fly to Bozeman and rent a car (you'll
want it to fish other rivers).
Other Activities:
Bird-watching, canoeing/kayaking/
rafting, horseback riding, hiking,
skiing, wildlife photography

Contact:
Nancy Norlander
Lone Mountain Ranch
PO Box 160069
Big Sky MT 59716
Ph: 406/995-4644
Fax: 406/995-4670
e-mail:
lmranch@imr.com
Web:
www.lmranch.com

RISING IN THE NORTHWEST CORNER of Yellowstone National Park, the Gallatin holds something for anglers of all skill levels. Though the Gallatin flows through the next valley west of the Yellowstone, it lacks much of the popularity and development of Paradise Valley. Here you'll find tranquil vistas, unspoiled to large degree, with no road-side shops and other detritus of the tourist trade. However, U.S. 191 follows its course from West Yellowstone to Bozeman. Much of the river is easily accessible because it flows through national forest lands in its lower reaches, and then the acreage of the national park.

Coming out of the park where it's first crossed by U.S. 191, the Gallatin winds through meadows. Pools are separated by shallow runs while little stream-side brushes reach out to snag errant back casts. A 12-inch rainbow is a good one. Yet they and their cousins, the cutthroat, seem willing to forgive inexpert presentation. This section fishes best from late June, and it's better if the day's sun has warmed it a bit. Downstream at Cinnamon Station, the Gallatin enters a short canyon about three miles long. You'll find chutes and plunge pools here, and some water that holds bigger fish. The canyon opens up into a valley called the Lower Basin at the turn off to Big Sky. At the northern end of the valley, the West Fork enters and, immediately, the river crashes into a 22-mile canyon of turbulent runs and pools. This mileage produces bows of 12 to 18 inches. The best run of the river is the five miles downstream from the bottom of the canyon. Gravel runs lead to pools that undercut banks creating holds for larger rainbows, cutthroat and cutt-bows – a hybrid of the two. Browns are present, but rare.

Lone Mountain Ranch, about 4.5 miles from the Gallatin, is headquarters for fishing the river. Scattered on a bench in the pines, 24 log cabins — pine log furniture, carpeted floors, private baths, woodstoves or fireplaces — host two to nine guests. Just under the brow of the ridge sits the main lodge with six luxuriously appointed guest rooms. Nearby is a third lodge, also of log, that contains a ranch shop that sells Orvis tackle, a watering hole known as "the saloon" and a very good restaurant. You'll dine by candlelight on fresh fish, fowl or heavy steaks. A well-stocked cellar complements dinner. Packages vary depending on the guests' desires. Float trips, fly-fishing schools, treks and packtrips are all available.

Russ and Karen Kipp's Montana High Country Tours
is known for great excursions on the Beaverhead
and surrounding waters.

Bring your rods and some grub and move into this cabin
on the lower reaches of Henry's Fork. You'll find fish aplenty,
and a dose of healthy solitude at Fish Creek Lodges.

Missouri River Trout Shop and Lodge

Craig, Montana

Browns revel in the Holter tailwater that looks like the largest spring creek in the world.

VITAL STATISTICS:

KEY SPECIES:
Browns, cutthroat, rainbows

Tackle:
Fly-fishing
Major Season:
All year
Accommodations:
ROOMS AND CABINS
NUMBER OF ROOMS: 7
MAXIMUM NUMBER OF GUESTS: 15
Meals: Breakfast included with some rooms; others have kitchens
Conference Groups: Yes
Rates: From $55 / double occupancy
Guides: $300
Gratuities: 20%
Preferred Payment:
Cash, check or credit cards
Getting There:
Fly to Helena or Great Falls and rent a car.
Other Activities:
More fishing

Contact:
Jerry Lappier
Missouri River Trout Shop and Lodge
110 Bridge St
Craig MT 59648
Ph: 406/235-4474
Fax: 406/235-4090
e-mail:
flyshop@thetroutshop.com
Web:
www.thetroutshop.com

BORN OF GREAT trout rivers — the Gallatin, Jefferson, and Madison — the Missouri has all the ancestry it needs to be famous. But its upper reaches run across a high, flat and arid steppe where it suffers heavy sedimentation as torrents dash down the mountains and drop their silt. Four dams transform the river from a slow, tepid, prairie stream to first-class trout tailwater, that is, increasingly, a year-round destination for anglers.

Below Holter Dam, the most downstream of the impoundments, the river breaks forth with all the attributes of a massive spring creek. If you're eager to get the jump on western fishing in spring, or don't want to hang it up after the leaves fall, this should be your destination. The Missouri fishes quite well for rainbows in the 17-inch range in early May. And from mid-October to mid-November, when the famous streams in the mountains of southwest Montana are threatened by heavy snow, the Missouri remains accessible. This is truly one of America's blue-ribbon trout rivers, and headquarters for fishing it is Jerry Lappier's trout shop, cafe and lodge in Craig, just off Interstate 15.

With more than 5,300 trout per mile (80 percent of which are larger than 10 inches), the 10-mile section between Craig and Holter Dam is a prolific, flat-water dry fly fishery. Melt swells the river from mid-May to mid-June, but as it begins to go down, hatches of caddis appear and continue into fall. You'll find Pale Morning Duns as well. In July, it's tricos in the morning, Pale Morning Duns in the afternoon and caddis for two hours before dark. August is problematic. A tremendous hatch of Pseudocloen, called the "green curse" by locals, blankets the river. At times it seems as if every square inch is covered, and trout are rising every-where. You can barely distinguish your fly from the thousands of naturals. Fish a parachute pattern with a tiny nymph as a trailing fly and keep at it. In fall, when the "curse" leaves the river, small Baetis hatch and no. 18 Blue-winged Olives can be effective, as can 'hoppers with a little bead-head nymph as a trailing fly.

Accommodations vary at the lodge. You'll find seven rooms with two beds each that share three baths. Breakfast is included with the price of these rooms. A studio apartment with kitchen facilities and private bath is upstairs over the fly shop. Two modern cabins for four to six guests are nearby. And, of course, the best restaurant in Craig is the cafe at the trout shop.

Montana High Country Tours

D i l l o n ,   M o n t a n a

From his lodge at the head of Grasshopper Valley, this native leads anglers to waters he's known since he was a kid.

VITAL STATISTICS:

KEY SPECIES:
Browns, cutthroat, rainbows

Tackle:
Fly-fishing, spinning

Major Season:
May through September

Accommodations:
Newly expanded log lodge
Number of Rooms: 8
Maximum Number of Guests: 20

Meals: Fine country cooking

Conference Groups: Yes

Rates: From $75 / night

Guides: $250 / day

Gratuities: 10%

Preferred Payment:
Cash, check or credit cards

Getting There:
Fly to Butte and rent a car.

Other Activities:
Big game, waterfowling, wingshooting, bird-watching, boating, canoeing/kayaking/rafting, horseback riding, hiking, skiing, snowmobiling, swimming, wildlife photography

Contact:
Russ Kipp
Montana High Country Tours
1036 E. Reeder St
Dillon MT 59725
Ph: 406/683-4920
Fax: 406/683-4920
e-mail:
montana@mhct.com
Web:
www.mhct.com

HAILING FROM the area around Dillon in southwest Montana, Russ Kipp knows all the best rivers and lakes. He's been told that he thinks like a fish, but that's only in the summer. Come fall, elk weigh heavily on his mind. Mainstays for Russ' angling adventures are the Beaverhead and the Big Hole, both world-class trout rivers.

Flowing from the base of Clarks Canyon Reservoir 20 miles south of Dillon, the Beaverhead runs north-by-northeast for more than 50 miles before joining the Big Hole below Twin Bridges to form the Jefferson. The upper stretch from the reservoir down to Barrett's diversion dam is considered to be prime rainbow water. Below the dam, the river warms and brown trout predominate. In effect, the Beaverhead is two different rivers. Runoff peaks in June, then the river settles down to fairly steady flows above the diversion dam. Most anglers float this stretch and fire weighted Woolly Buggers and similar patterns into the brush. That strategy works, but you'll also encounter lovely hatches of Blue-winged Olives in spring and early summer. Later come hatches of caddis (July and August) and Pale Morning Duns, Yellow Sallies and Golden Stones. Craneflies begin coming off in mid-August and continue through the end of September. From July on, Barrett's dam cuts flows in the lower river by half. You'll find fewer big fish in these waters than on the upper reaches, but the number of anglers will be much reduced.

A second source of behemoth trout is 6000-acre Clark Canyon Lake itself. Rainbows top seven pounds and browns, though fewer, can break into double digits. Prime time is right after ice-out. As water warms, fish go deeper, but the mouth of Red Rock River will continue to provide action on both dry and wet flies into fall. Grasshopper Creek is a feast-or-famine stream. After heavy rains, it silts terribly and irrigation can draw the creek down to a trickle. But sections of the Grasshopper can fish well. If they don't, Kipp keeps a few high mountain lakes in reserve. Here you'll find cutthroats and rainbows that aren't huge, but the scenery alone is worth the trip.

Expanded in 1998, Russ and wife Karen's lodge at the head end of the upper Grasshopper Valley is located on the road from Polaris to Wise River. Built of heavy log and framed by pine and spruce, the lodge boasts a stone fireplace, gleaming board floors, and easy chairs and couches. You'll find digital TV, an indoor Jacuzzi, and wonderful country cooking.

Nelson's Spring Creek Ranch

Livingston, Montana

"Challenging" describes this spring creek which anglers love to hate.

I F, IN AUGUST, you looked only at the aquatic grasses undulating with the languid currents of this icy cold spring creek, you might think you were on the Letort or maybe a chalk stream in England. But no. The Absarokas rise behind you while across the way is the Gallatin Range, and just across a narrow throat of land flows the Yellowstone. This little spring creek is as small as the Yellowstone is broad, and its rainbows and browns are as picky as they come.

Successful anglers here come in two flavors. Most are supreme technicians. They've made a science out of presenting the tiniest of nymphs, scuds and emergers on tippets of 6x and 7x. To watch these angler's fish is like viewing a chess match. Each move is studied. No cast is rushed. From the opening gambit, nothing is left to chance. The other group of anglers who raise one of the leviathans in this mileage are those who were borne under lucky stars. It is not over with the take. That's when the hard work begins. You see the fish is angry because it allowed itself to be fooled. So it sulks deep in the weeds. It's your job to root it out and preserve that faint thread that connects him to you. It is a game of patience, and he who blinks first, loses.

It is not all the time that Nelson's Spring Creek fishes this way. Early in the season, in April and May, and late, in October and November, the weeds are diminished. The fishing is easier then, and the daily rod fee (about $100) is lower. Only six rods are permitted on the stream on any given day. But one day on Nelson's is not enough. Two or three make more sense. Wise anglers book one of the three cabins with bath and cooking facilities maintained by Ed and Helen Nelson. When compared to the fancy places along the Yellowstone, these are fairly spartan. On the other hand, one wants to focus on the fishing and not on getting back to the lodge in time for dinner. Here, since you're slinging your own hash, you won't eat until you're done fishing.

VITAL STATISTICS:

KEY SPECIES:
Browns, rainbows

Tackle:
Fly-fishing

Major Season:
All year

Accommodations:
MODERN EFFICIENCY CABINS
NUMBER OF ROOMS: 3
MAXIMUM NUMBER OF GUESTS: 9

Meals: You're on your own

Conference Groups: No

Rates: From $100 / night / 2

Guides: Available from trout shops in Livingston

Gratuities: Angler's discretion

Preferred Payment:
Cash or check

Getting There:
Fly to Gallatin Field and rent a car.

Other Activities:
Hiking, horseback riding, wildlife viewing

Contact:
Edwin & Helen Nelson
Nelson's Spring Creek Ranch
90 Nelson's Spring Creek Rd
Livingston MT 59047
Ph: 406/222-2159

[N O R T H E R N   R O C K I E S]

North Fork Crossing

H e l e n a ,   M o n t a n a

Here's a twist — thanks to angling pressure, Maclean's home river is once again worth fishing!

VITAL STATISTICS:

KEY SPECIES:
Browns, cutthroat, rainbows

Tackle:
Fly-fishing

Major Season:
May through mid-October

Accommodations:
Excellent canvas cabins
Number of Cabins: 6
Maximum Number of Guests: 12

Meals: Fine regional cuisine and seafood

Conference Groups: Yes

Rates: From $1,230 / 3 days, 4 nights / person, double occupancy

Guides: Included

Gratuities: $50 / day

Preferred Payment:
Cash, check or credit cards

Getting There:
Fly to Missoula and the lodge van will collect you for $50 or so.

Other Activities:
Wingshooting, bird-watching, canoeing/kayaking/rafting, horseback riding, hiking, swimming

Contact:
Paul Roos
North Fork Crossing
c/o Paul Roos Outfitting
PO Box 621
Helena MT 59624
Ph: 800/858-3497
Fax: 406/449-2293
e-mail:
probek@hdmaster.com
Web:
www.prooutfitters.com

Agents:
Off the Beaten Path

RISING BETWEEN Scapegoat Mountain and Olson Peak in some of Montana's finest elk country, the North Fork of the Blackfoot is vastly overshadowed by the main stem which it joins a little southeast of Ovando. You know the Blackfoot as Norman Maclean's river. And since Robert Redford's film made the Maclean's novella popular, lots of folks have headed here. Contrary to what you might expect, the river's fame was not its undoing. To the contrary, efforts by a number of conservation groups have been effective in improving the fishery.

In the Blackfoot, you'll catch westslope cutthroats, browns, rainbows and bull trout. The bulls are on the endangered species list. However, they don't know it. Every once in a while, when some sport is playing a 10-inch cutt, a big old bull trout will rise from its lair and swallow the cutt. Yes, that will put a bend in your three-weight. Typically rainbows run between 14 and 17 inches; browns go a little bigger as do the cutts. You'll find the same species in the North Fork where the best fishing is in the mileage where it breaks free of the mountains and starts across the meadows bound for the bigger river below. There's never really a bad time to fish here. When spring melt swells the system in May and early June, spring creeks and headwaters are clear and productive. So, too, are the five ponds at the lodge. And Paul Roos, who was the first to earn Orvis-endorsed outfitter of the year honors, also runs trips on the Smith, the Missouri, and a bunch of creeks named Tomahawk just to confuse those too curious about their precise locations.

North Fork Crossing, itself, is something of an anomaly among western angling lodges. Each of six tents sleeps two. Slab of foam on a plywood platform? Not here. Hotel grade mattresses grace custom beds, screened windows keep bugs out but let the breeze in, and your private bath is around the corner. Nobody feels crowded here. Meals are served family-style in the main lodge. You'll dine on the likes of lamb in a mustard and herb sauce and for dessert, pears poached in champagne with homemade cinnamon ice cream drizzled with a dash of chocolate sauce. Good wines accompany dinner.

The Old Kirby Place

C a m e r o n ,   M o n t a n a

Jim Bridger would have enjoyed this log lodge,
and the vittles and vintages served therein.

FROM THE FRONT, this looks like a place where you would just want to be. No modern hype in the architecture, no California chic. Hand-squared logs dovetail into each other in that old, sturdy time-tested way. A front porch wraps around the side. Close to, but not crowding it, are a pair of cabins, each with two rooms and private baths. Upstairs in the main lodge are a pair of bedrooms, again with private baths.

The first floor is one open room. A massive bar with racked wines dominates one corner, a commercial stove the other. The maitre de, cum chef and bottle washer — Walter Kannon — whips up gourmet dinners to suit his guests' tastes. You'll eat on a long table of pumpkin pine in the lodge's great room near a fat old woodstove that'll be glowing if frost is nipping your tippets.

The Old Kirby Place fronts the Madison River. Fothergill and Sterling describe the Madison as "one tire skid mark" of consistent width and depth, pretty much from Quake Lake south 80 miles to its mouth at Three Forks. For most of its run, the Madison's bottom is flat and pools are seldom more than six feet deep. Among the exceptions is the mileage from below Quake Lake to the mouth of the West Yellowstone. Here, the Madison holds more pools, a nice contrast to the rest of the river, which has been described as "the world's longest riffle." The lodge sits at the downstream end of the pool water.

That gives its anglers certain advantages. The character of the river above the lodge contains more classic water for fishing dry flies morning and evenings. The upper river, too, holds more rainbows than browns. Yet downstream from the lodge at the head of the riffles, trout have less time to inspect an offering and seem to feel the need to nail a fly before it's gone. This relative lack of selectivity has given the Madison a rep as a good beginner's river. Anglers using ultralight tackle can have a ball with gold-bladed Mepps and Panther Martins. While the Madison is catch-and-release, anglers staying at The Old Kirby Place can fill their frying pans in the West Fork of the Madison just downstream. You can also catch dinner in the lodge's stocked pond. The famous streams near the western edge of Yellowstone Park — the Gibbon, Firehole and Henry's Fork — are only an hour from The Old Kirby Place. A couple days of guided fishing will introduce you to the river, then you can fish it on your own for the rest of the week.

[N O R T H E R N   R O C K I E S]

Rainbow Ranch Lodge

B i g   S k y ,   M o n t a n a

Some come to fish, some come to eat, and some just come to pass the time away.

VITAL STATISTICS:

KEY SPECIES:
Browns, cutthroat, rainbows

Tackle:
Fly-fishing, spinning
Major Season:
Mid-June through October
Accommodations:
Elegant rooms with western decor
Number of Rooms: 16
Handicapped Accessible: 1
Maximum Number of Guests: 40
Meals: Gourmet dining
Conference Groups: Yes
Rates: From $115 / night / 2
Guides: $250
Gratuities: Angler's discretion
Preferred Payment:
Cash, check or credit cards
Getting There:
Fly to Bozeman and rent a car.
Other Activities:
Big game, golf, horseback riding,
hiking, skiing, snowmobiling,
swimming

Contact:
Rainbow Ranch Lodge
PO Box 160336
Big Sky MT 59716
Ph: 406/995-4132
Fax: 406/995-2861
e-mail:
rainbow_ranch@gomontana.com
Web:
www.rainbowranch.co

WHAT A DAY. It began with all those cholesterol laden delights that doctors warn us to avoid (OK, you could have had fresh fruit, granola and yogurt, but hey . . . this is a vacation). You went back to your room and picked up your three-weight. You tucked a couple of boxes of nymphs and one of basic drys — a few caddis, Blue-winged Olives, Adams, and a smattering of ants, crickets and hoppers — in your vest. You checked to be sure you had tippet, floatant, nippers and a hemostat. You slipped into your rental car, drove a couple of miles upstream to where the Gallatin breaks into gentle runs through a wide open meadow. You opened the trunk and found with some chagrin that you'd left your waders in the room. Rather than admit defeat, you opted to wade wet — the water isn't deep. And during the course of the morning you picked up a dozen small rainbows and a couple of cutthroat as wild and beautifully colored as they were ever meant to be.

That afternoon, after retrieving your waders, you headed south on U.S. 191, into West Yellowstone where you haunted the fly shops for a moment. The Firehole had always been on your mind, ever since you saw that picture of steaming fumaroles at Mule Shoe Bend, and you decided that's where you'd spend the afternoon. After all, you could always fish the Madison and Henry's Fork another day.

Choice of great fishing is what Rainbow Ranch Lodge is all about. Located about midway between Bozeman and West Yellowstone on U.S. 191, you have your choice of waters. Within easy striking distance are the upper and park sections of the Madison, and the Gibbon and Firehole which feed it. A short run west from West Yellowstone takes you to float tubing on Hebgen Lake. Another hour south is the famed Henry's Fork. And Armstrong's and Nelson's are but a couple hours from the lodge. Or, if you want to play it close to home, there's the Gallatin in your back yard. A number of excellent guides — including those from Gallatin Riverguides (406/995-2290) — are available for float or wade trips.

You'll enjoy the accommodations at Rainbow Ranch. All rooms feature Jacuzzi's, some have fireplaces and all are tastefully decorated. Dining here is without peer. Try the sesame crusted yellowfin tuna with ginger soy glaze, or the smoked venison and quail. Lots of folks drive to this ranch just for the food; wise travelers stay here and avoid the after dinner drive.

Ruby Springs Lodge

S h e r i d a n ,   M o n t a n a

At Ruby Springs, you'll have seven miles of private access to grasshopper heaven.

VITAL STATISTICS:

KEY SPECIES:
Browns, rainbows

Tackle:
Fly-fishing
Major Season:
June through September
Accommodations:
Charming cabins
Number of Rooms: 6
Maximum Number of Guests: 12
Meals: Regional cuisine with a flare
Conference Groups: Yes
Rates: From $550 / day
Guides: Available
Gratuities: $40 - $50
Preferred Payment:
Cash, check or credit cards
Getting There:
Fly to Butte and rent a car.
Other Activities:
Wingshooting, golf, horseback riding, hiking

Contact:
Paul & Jeanne Moseley
Ruby Springs Lodge
2487 Hwy. 287
Sheridan MT 59749
Ph: 800/278-7829
Fax: 406/842-5806
e-mail:
info@rubyspringslodge.com
Web:
www.rubyspringslodge.com

AT TIMES IT SEEMS AS IF every angler from New York to Denver has descended on Montana's great trout rivers. Parking can be at a premium along certain stretches of the Madison. Drift boats seem as prolific as salmon flies during their hatch on the Yellowstone. The wait at launch ramps rivals that of arriving planes at Atlanta's airport. Some of us go fishing to get away from crowds, yet we journey to the same destinations as everyone else.

That's where the Ruby comes in. Rising between the Snowcrest and the Gravelly ranges in the Beaverhead National Forest, the Ruby is an unpretentious stream on the mileage above Ruby Reservoir. Rainbows from the lake come into the upper reaches to spawn and feed. Otherwise, you'll have a ball with small cutts and rainbows here. Below the lake, the river takes on a more mature character. It meanders through open meadows and occasional woods. Best time to fish it is in May and early June before sediment-laden meltwater spills over the dam. Meltwater discolors the creek in June, but by mid-July it fishes fine. Come back again in late July and stay through September. Fish caddis in May. Pale Morning Duns in July and tricos in August also draw strikes, but it's the 'hoppers in mid-July through late September that turn on the browns like nothing else.

While you're in the area, check out Clear Creek, a tributary to the Ruby. When the Ruby warms in late summer, Clear Creek's cool spring waters, deep and shaded by a tangle of willows, attract big browns of up to 22 inches that feed on 'hoppers. While anglers normally fish with Ruby Springs' guides (included in the basic package), they may freelance if they wish. Float trips are possible farther down, but the name of the game here is stalking fish from the meadow and planning your approach. An eight-foot 4-weight rod is ideal for these waters.

Rustic elegance is one way to describe Ruby Springs' accommodations. Six cabins sleep two and feature private baths. After fishing, have a cocktail in the River Room that overlooks the home pool. You'll see fish rising. If you can't stand it, grab one of the rods by the door and make a cast or two. But beware. Other guests may save you no dinner (grilled prawns, beef tenderloin with thyme - Dijon glaze with twice-baked potatoes and waxed beans). Breakfasts are grand. Forget the boxed lunch, you won't need it.

[N O R T H E R N   R O C K I E S]

Spotted Bear Ranch

K a l i s p e l l ,   M o n t a n a

If you want to fish where other folks ain't, head upstream for a float on the South Fork of the Flathead.

VITAL STATISTICS:

KEY SPECIES:
Cutthroat

Tackle:
Fly-fishing
Major Season:
Mid-June through mid-September
Accommodations:
RUSTIC CABINS WITH PRIVATE BATHS
NUMBER OF CABINS: 5
HANDICAPPED ACCESSIBLE: 5
MAXIMUM NUMBER OF GUESTS: 20
Meals: Homestyle western fare
Conference Groups: No
Rates: From $1,995 / 5 days, 6 nights
Guides: Included
Gratuities: $60 - $80
Preferred Payment:
Cash, check or credit cards
Getting There:
Fly to Glacier Park International (Kalispell) and rent a car.
Other Activities:
Big game, horseback riding, hiking, wildlife photography

Contact:
Kirk Gentry
Spotted Bear Ranch
115 Lake Blain Dr
Kalispell MT 59901
Ph: 406/755-7337
Fax: 406/755-7336
e-mail:
sbr@cyberport.net
Web:
www.spottedbear.com

A NATIONAL Scenic and Wild River, the South Fork of the Flathead is paralleled by no roads, gravel or otherwise. There's only a trail for hikers and horseback riders. No towns discharge effluent and no agricultural interests siphon off the flow. The only thing upstream is water clear as mountain air. The river caroms through narrow canyons, streams across gravel flats, races through runs shaded by heavy stands of lodgepole and ponderosa pine, and placidly glides through meadows bright with wildflowers. This is native cutthroat water, pure and simple. Oh, you'll encounter bull trout and some of them may be huge (more than four pounds), but bull trout are on the endangered species list. It's a violation to fish for them. If caught, they must be released unharmed.

The best way to get to know this river, and the wilderness and valley that run up into the famed Bob Marshall Wilderness, is to saddle up at the Spotted Bear Ranch for a five-day pack and float on the South Fork of the Flathead. You'll ride for two days upriver, stopping in the evening to fish sections that virtually never see flies. With gear loaded in inflatables, you'll then drift back downstream, pulling ashore when you feel like it. Thirty-fish days are not uncommon. Elk, deer and mountain goats will watch your progress.

Spotted Bear also offers shorter floats on the South Fork and Spotted Bear rivers. You can float a different section, below the upper wilderness area, each day and return to your rustic log cabin each night. Each cabin contains two bedrooms, a fireplace, private bath and central heat. Daily maid service is provided. You'll find the main lodge on a bluff with a stunning view of the South Fork. Club chairs surround an open fire pit and game mounts decorate the walls. Meals are family-style, and on Wednesday nights the barbecued ribs are not to be missed. And while you're there, talk to owner Kirk Gentry about guided hunts for deer and elk in the fall.

Gateway to this paradise is Kalispell, or more correctly the hamlet of Hungry Horse at the base of the dam on the South Fork by the same name. A 15 minute drive northeast from this little town puts you in Glacier National Park, an absolute must see if you haven't been there.

Teller Wildlife Refuge

Corvallis, Montana

*Rent your own 1870s farmhouse and fish
four miles of the blue-ribbon Bitterroot.*

**VITAL
STATISTICS:**

KEY SPECIES:
Browns, cutthroat, rainbows

Tackle:
Fly-fishing
Major Season:
May through November
Accommodations:
THREE HISTORIC HOMESTEADS AND CABINS
NUMBER OF ROOMS: 20
HANDICAPPED ACCESSIBLE: SOME
MAXIMUM NUMBER OF GUESTS: 22
Meals: Custom tailored to your
needs
Conference Groups: Yes
Rates: From $230 / night
Guides: $290 / day
Gratuities: $20
Preferred Payment:
Cash or check
Getting There:
Fly to Missoula and rent a car.
Other Activities:
Waterfowling, wingshooting, bird-
watching, golf, horseback riding,
hiking, skiing, wildlife photography

Contact:
Mary Stone
Teller Wildlife Refuge
1292 Chaffin Lane
Corvallis MT 59828
Ph: 800/343-3707
Fax: 406/961-8316
e-mail:
teller@bitterroot.net
Web:
www.bitterroot.net/teller/lodging

THIS WAS ONE OF OTTO TELLER'S dreams. Past president and founding member of Trout Unlimited and the Trout and Salmon Foundation, the late Mr. Teller was one of the first to fight what's come to be known as urban sprawl. He established the 1,300-acre Teller Wildlife Refuge as a private nonprofit initiative to protect agricultural land from subdivision. The refuge is among the first of its kind in Montana and a model for similar initiatives in other states. Seasonal wildlife populations contain white-tailed deer, occasional moose and elk, beavers, foxes, geese, ducks, owls and more than 200 other bird species.

The refuge lies a few miles downstream from Hamilton in the Bitterroot Valley. Four miles of the Bitterroot River, one of the 100 best in the country according to TU members, flows through the preserve. Here the river breaks into numerous braids with small channels separating islands. It comes back together in long cobbly channels only to divide again farther down. Heavy meltwaters of spring shift channels, bars and pools. Lodged deadfalls and the undercutting stream create new pockets that hide browns, rainbows and cutthroats.

Big streamers begin taking fish in March and April. Then snowmelt pushes through, although the high water is still fishable. Trout, often less cautious in the dingy water, take big streamers fired into holds along brushy banks. Late June and July are the months of caddis, and 'hoppers come into their own in August and stay around through late September. If you seek a change of pace from the Bitterroot, spend a day or two on the no-name spring creek that winds through the refuge. You might dance with browns and rainbows up to 20 inches. Anglers who arrive in mid-October should pack a side-by-side shotgun to hunt pheasants and ducks. At this ecologically-aware lodge, conservation and preservation go hand in hand.

On the refuge are three homesteads, two of which — Teller Lodge and Slack House — operate as full-service lodges. Meals are not served at the third, Burrough's House. The refuge also houses guests in two cabins and a small house 14 miles upstream, halfway between Hamilton and Darby. These contain kitchen facilities where you can prepare your own meals. Teller and Slack, with wrap-around screened porches, are gracious farmhouses that date from the 1870s. The refuge only books one party into each house or set of cabins at a time.

[N O R T H E R N   R O C K I E S]

Triple Creek Ranch

D a r b y ,   M o n t a n a

This Relais & Chateau guest ranch draws rave reviews from romantics and anglers alike.

VITAL STATISTICS:

KEY SPECIES:
Browns, cutthroat, rainbows

Tackle:
Fly-fishing

Major Season:
May through November

Accommodations:
ELEGANT LOG CABINS
NUMBER OF ROOMS: 22
HANDICAPPED ACCESSIBLE: 2
MAXIMUM NUMBER OF GUESTS: 28

Meals: Gourmet regional cuisine

Conference Groups: Yes

Rates: From $510 / night / 2

Guides: $295 / day / 2

Gratuities: 10% - 20%

Preferred Payment:
Cash, check or credit cards

Getting There:
Fly to Missoula and rent a car.

Other Activities:
Bird-watching, canoeing/kayaking/rafting, golf, horseback riding, heli-skiing/hiking, hiking, skiing, snow-mobiling, swimming, tennis, wildlife photography

Contact:
Triple Creek Ranch
5551 West Fork Stage Route
Darby MT 59829
Ph: 406/821-4600
Fax: 406/821-4666
e-mail:
trc@bitterroot.net
Web:
www.triplecreekranch.com

Agents:
Relais & Chateau: 212/856-0115

ELEGANCE AND LUXURY are the hallmarks of this well-established lodge high in the Bitterroots. Let's start with dinner: a breast of pheasant rubbed with fresh ground peppercorns, then pan roasted and served with a sauce of dried cherry, balsamic vinegar and port. Your appetizer might be the pungent and spicy Thai chicken satay or seared sea scallops, and the salad, fresh greens with pears and hazelnuts. Strombili highlights the lunch menu along with shrimp crepe. Breakfast can be fancy — try the omelet with smoked salmon, cream cheese and green onions — or plainly stout — oatmeal with brown sugar and raisins.

Then there are the cabins, 19 of them secluded beneath lodgepole pine. Each features a fireplace and many include private hot tubs. Décor is modern, yet rustic, with a muted and tasteful western flavor. Sit on your porch and let the clear mountain air soak into your bones. A guest ranch, riding is high on the agenda here, but so too is tennis and hiking. Helicopters carry guests high into the mountains for treks above tree line. And, of course, there's the fishing.

The road to Triple Creek follows the West Fork of the Bitterroot River. This is very comfortable water to wade and fish. Between 40- and 50-feet wide and with a fairly even cobble bottom, this river holds cutthroat, rainbow, brook and bull trout (protected under current Montana regs). The lower section can be floated in spring. At Conner, the West Fork joins the East Fork to form the main stem of the Bitterroot. Not as pristine as the West Fork, the East Fork above Sula holds wild brook trout, small rainbows and cutthroats. Below the junction, cutthroats, rainbows and browns predominate. You'll find traditional riffles, runs and pools, and undercut banks and pockets — all those lies which hold trout. While the ranch will provide transfers from Missoula airport ($200 round-trip per vehicle), you'll want to rent a car to get to the fishing.

The Bitterroot sheds its load of spring melt in mid-June, earlier than many of the other blue-ribbon streams in southwestern Montana. And it's not as quick to cloud as others. But if for some reason it doesn't suit, you've only to cross into Idaho to fish the Selway and Salmon rivers, head east through Chief Joseph Pass to strike the Big Hole at Wise, or arrange with a guide to fish any number of alpine lakes near the lodge. There's also a trout pond at Triple Creek.

Yellowstone Valley Ranch

L i v i n g s t o n ,   M o n t a n a

Lean back in your chair on the terrace, sip the last of the dinner's wine, and watch the river slide slowly past the lodge.

VITAL STATISTICS:

KEY SPECIES:
Brookies, browns, cutthroat, rainbows

Tackle:
Fly-fishing, spinning
Major Season:
June through September
Accommodations:
Log cabins with stream views
Number of Rooms: 10
Handicapped Accessible: Some
Maximum Number of Guests: 20
Meals: Delightful game and other regional cuisine
Conference Groups: Yes
Rates: From $2,195 / week, double occupancy
Guides: Included
Gratuities: $30 - $50 / day
Preferred Payment:
Cash, check or credit cards
Getting There:
Fly to Bozeman and rent a car.
Other Activities:
Bird-watching, canoeing/kayaking/rafting, golf, horseback riding, hiking, swimming, wildlife photography

Contact:
Nancy Boisvert
Yellowstone Valley Ranch
3840 US Hwy. 89 South
Livingston MT 59047
Ph: 406/333-4787
Fax: 406/333-4787
e-mail:
destinations@mcn.net
Web:
www.destinations-ltd.com

Off Season:
422 S. Main St
Livingston MT 59047
Ph: 800/626-3526
Fax: 406/585-3526

Agents:
Destinations

RISING IN A MAGNIFICENT CALDERA of paint pots and smoking fumaroles, the Yellowstone tumbles out of the national park at Gardiner and sprints through Yankee Jim Canyon into Paradise Valley. This river's bound for Livingston about 60 miles downstream. Cutthroats and rainbows ply the upper river above Yankee Jim Canyon. In the gorge, deep water holds browns of sizes that can only be imagined. From the foot of the canyon north, rainbows reclaim most of the river, but you'll find occasional browns and cutthroats here, too. Runoff swells the river with silty water from mid-May well into June and often July, depending on the snowpack. But thereafter, the river runs clear, except when torrential thunderstorms muddy up the Lamar and Gardner. Then the Yellowstone will take a day or two to clear. The Yellowstone is one of TU's 100 best trout streams and so too are a handful of its siblings in the neighborhood.

If you haven't fished this area before, Yellowstone Valley Ranch's "Montana Sampler" is an offer not to be bypassed. About 14 miles south of Livingston, the ranch is an ideal jumping-off point for exploring Paradise Valley. The legendary Armstrong and Nelson's spring creeks are 10 minutes down the road from the ranch. Counterpoint to the rocky Yellowstone, these spring creeks are slow affairs lush with weed beds, hatches and trout. DuPuy and O'Hair ranches control access to Armstrong. Rod fees are charged, and reservations must be made well in advance. In addition, the north gate to Yellowstone National Park is an hour south. Head for the lower Gardner, Gibbon and upper Madison. No trip to Yellowstone is complete without a stop at Muleshoe Bend on the Firehole — fumaroles blow off steam and mudpots percolate as you fish in this geyser basin just north of Old Faithful. If you haven't done it before, a quick trip to these park waters is certainly worth it. Another must is a float trip on the Yellowstone through Paradise Valley, where you will find cutthroats, browns and rainbows.

As you'd suspect, Yellowstone Valley Lodge is first class in all aspects. Rooms, two to a cabin, are spacious, comfortably furnished and offer views of the river. Meals are truly outstanding: mixed game grill of red deer and antelope, grilled tuna with wasabi, herbavorian pasta. Dine on the terrace, nurse another bottle of wine and watch dusk creep up the mountains.

Brush Creek Ranch

S a r a t o g a ,   W y o m i n g

An easy ride in the saddle carries you to this creek where browns and brookies spawn in the fall.

VITAL STATISTICS:

KEY SPECIES:
Brookies, browns, cutthroat, rainbows

Tackle:
Fly-fishing
Major Season:
May through October
Accommodations:
WESTERN RANCH HOUSE AND GUEST CABIN
NUMBER OF ROOMS: 11
HANDICAPPED ACCESSIBLE: 1
MAXIMUM NUMBER OF GUESTS: 15
Meals: Hearty fare for hardy anglers
Conference Groups: Yes
Rates: From $175 / night
Guides: Included
Gratuities: 15%;
Angler's discretion
Preferred Payment:
Cash, check or credit cards
Getting There:
Fly to Denver and rent a car.
Other Activities:
Big game, bird-watching, hiking, snowmobiling, wildlife photography, dog sledding, cross-country skiing

Contact:
Kinta & Gib Blumenthal
Brush Creek Ranch
HCG 3 Box 10
Saratoga WY 82331
Ph: 307/327-5241
Fax: 307/327-5384
e-mail:
kinta@brushcreekranch.com
Web:
www.brushcreekranch.com

Agents:
Orvis endorsed

THE VALLEY between the Sierra Madre and the Medicine Bow mountains resembles a series of low, bench-like plateaus. In early summer, they're carpeted in heavy grasses, green with the waters of spring snowmelt. With each week, they turn progressively tawny, taking on the color of an aged lion by fall. Plan your trip to this country for late July or August (if you're bringing kids who have to be back in school) or September if you're coming with others. Fishing generally improves as the season progresses.

With 6,000 acres bordering the Medicine Bow National Forest at the foot of the Snowy Range, Brush Creek Ranch is the place to be to fish the upper reaches of the North Platte River and three private miles of the stream from which the ranch took its name. Spawning in the fall, browns and brookies move up into the creek and provide pretty good fishing. Browns range up to 18 inches; the brook trout, 10 inches or so. You'll also find rainbows and cutthroats in the 12- to 14-inch range. The entire length of Brush Creek is fishable, but its name is no lie. Portions are thick with stunted cottonwoods and willows (and these, naturally, hold the better trout), but much of the creek is open. Angling can be a challenge, but taking a 20-inch brown on a #18 Caddis does have its rewards. Much less challenging, but almost as much fun, is the casting pond. Here's a perfect place to introduce children to fly-fishing, the only method allowed on the ranch.

Downstream from the ranch, Brush Creek flows into the North Platte, the premiere trout river in southeast Wyoming. A favorite to float down to Saratoga, the North Platte is populated mainly with rainbows and browns. Some of these top four pounds, but most are smaller. Also of interest is the nearby Encampment River with its browns, rainbows and occasional brook trout. Though limited public access exists on both rivers, better fishing is found on private waters. Great Rocky Mountain Outfitters, Orvis-endorsed as is the ranch, leases several stretches of the upper North Platte and Encampment rivers.

If you time your trip right, you can help Gib Blumenthal and his hands move cattle on the ranch. You'll stay in the lodge, which dates from the early 1900s. Exposed logs grace some of the guest rooms in the main lodge and outlying cottages. At Brush Creek, everybody — staff and guests included — gathers for family-style dinners. Afterwards, go for a walk, or settle into a rocking chair on the front porch.

Crescent H Ranch

Wilson, Wyoming

The Snake's the thing at the base of the Grand Tetons, but wise anglers diversify options.

VITAL STATISTICS:

KEY SPECIES:
Browns, cutthroat

Tackle:
Fly-fishing
Major Season:
June through September
Accommodations:
RUSTIC LOG LODGE AND CABINS
NUMBER OF ROOMS: 10
MAXIMUM NUMBER OF GUESTS: 25
Meals: Western fare with a flair
Conference Groups: Yes
Rates: From $385 / day
(the 7 night fishing package for
$3,000, double occupancy, is quite
popular)
Guides: $385 / day if not booked
as package
Gratuities: 15%;
Angler's discretion
Preferred Payment:
Cash, check or credit cards
Getting There:
Fly to Jackson Hole Airport and the
lodge van will meet you.
Other Activities:
Canoeing/kayaking/rafting, golf,
horseback riding, hiking, tennis

Contact:
Barbara Beaton
Crescent H Ranch
PO Box 347
Wilson WY 83014
Ph: 307/733-3674
Fax: 307/733-8475
Web:
www.crescenth.com

Agents:
Orvis endorsed

ONLY A FEW HUNDRED YARDS separate the headwaters of the Snake and the Yellowstone rivers, high in the southeast corner of Yellowstone National Park. The waters of the Yellowstone cascade across a marvelous caldera, stream across Montana, join the Missouri and eventually reach the Gulf of Mexico. It is America's finest free-flowing river. The Snake is a different story. It heads for the Pacific, and though impounded a number of times, it too is a stunning fishery. Anglers from the Crescent H work the upper end of the river.

Floats are arranged in the short section between Yellowstone National Park and Grand Teton National Park. Braided and easily fished (floating this run is a real challenge because of deadfalls and log jams), cutthroat to 16 inches abound. Chuck bead-headed streamers against the bank and presto, there's a hookup. The scenery is as spectacular as the fishing. Below Jackson Lake, the Snake is big, braided and best fished from a drift boat. North of the town of Jackson, the Gros Ventre enters the Snake. This too is cutthroat water. Nearby is Flat Creek, a special-regulation stream that meanders through the National Elk Refuge. Most successful anglers here crawl on their hands and knees to reach the grassy bank and pray that an errant gust doesn't blow their dry flies astray. The reward: cutthroats up to 14 inches. Below Jackson, the Snake cuts through a canyon, floatable in the fall, down to Palisades Reservoir on the Idaho border.

As comfortable as an old woolen fishing shirt, the Crescent H is an ideal headquarters for angling in these waters. If you're willing to invest a couple hours in a car, you can make it to and from such famed locales as Henry's Fork, the upper Green River, and the Lewis and Firehole in Yellowstone National Park.

Located south of Jackson, the ranch's 1,300 acres rise gently from the Snake River. Tributaries such as Fish Creek and a number of others, carry populations of rainbows. Highly regarded for its relaxed atmosphere and excellent horses and trails, Crescent H offers guests rustic pine cabins with every amenity. In the main house, also of log, guests chat around the wagon wheel coffee tables or rest in an elk-horn rocker near one of the two huge stone fireplaces. Dinner might be a hearty western barbecue or venison tenderloin with sun-dried fruit sauce, gratin potatoes, broccoli and yellow squash.

VITAL STATISTICS:

KEY SPECIES:
Browns, rainbows

Tackle:
Fly-fishing
Major Season:
June through September
Accommodations:
CHARMING COTTAGE
NUMBER OF ROOMS: 3
MAXIMUM NUMBER OF GUESTS: 10
Meals: Self-catered
Conference Groups: No
Rates: From $125 / night
Guides: $325
Gratuities: $50
Preferred Payment:
Cash, check or credit cards
Getting There:
Fly to Laramie or Denver and rent
a car.
Other Activities:
Big game, bird-watching,
canoeing/kayaking/rafting, hiking,
skiing, snowmobiling, wildlife
photography

Contact:
Robert Smith
Great Rocky Mountain
Outfitters
216 E. Walnut
PO Box 1677
Saratoga WY 82331
Ph: 307/326-8750
Fax: 307/326-5390
e-mail:
GRMO@union-tel.com
Web:
www.grmo.com

Great Rocky Mountain Outfitters

S a r a t o g a ,   W y o m i n g

A tasteful cottage centers you on the finest trout water in southeast Wyoming.

ALREADY 30 MILES OLD when it enters Wyoming, the North Platte is one of three world-class trout rivers in the state. Borne of runoff and melt in the Medicine Bow Mountains, the North Platte enters the high plains where it's joined by the Encampment, another fine trout river, about 10 miles south of Saratoga. Like a stallion, the river runs free for another 70 miles or so before being penned up in Seminoe Lake and Kortes below it. Yet the tailwater of the latter begins the famed "Magic Mile," which offers fabulous year-round angling for record book browns.

Rainbows and browns dominate the river — estimated at 4,500 fish per mile — in the high plains section south of Saratoga. Much of the bottom is cobble and easily waded where there's access. Below the town, much of the land is devoted to ranching, bridges are few, and formal public access is very limited. Floats are the answer. More fish per mile are caught south of the Interstate 80 bridge than north of it.

For nearly 20 years, Robert Smith has been running Great Rocky Mountain Outfitters and guiding on the river. He arranges excursions to the headwaters of the North Platte and Encampment, and to the Magic Mile as well. He'll even show you where to fish right in town. Fly-fishing schools and individual instruction are always on tap, and he and his guides have a reputation for helping novice anglers catch that first wild fish that sets their drags a screaming. He's arranged private access with many landowners. He'll guide you in a McKenzie drift boat or rent you one (or, better for novice anglers, a canoe) if you want to try it on your own. As for accommodations, there's a charming riverfront housekeeping cottage available by the night or week, or for full-service stays, he'll recommend Brush Creek Ranch, an Orvis endorsed fishing lodge a ways south of town. You'll find all the gear you need at his fly shop.

Spotted Horse Ranch

Jackson Hole, Wyoming

Over the years, the folks at this riverfront ranch have learned that your success is their success.

VITAL STATISTICS:

KEY SPECIES:
Browns, cutthroat, rainbows

Tackle:
Fly-fishing, spinning
Major Season:
May through October
Accommodations:
Log cabins
Number of Rooms: 10
Handicapped Accessible: Some
Maximum Number of Guests: 30
Meals: Hearty western fare
Conference Groups: Yes
Rates: From $190, double occupancy
Guides: $300
Gratuities: $20 - $50
Preferred Payment:
Cash, check or credit cards
Getting There:
Fly to Jackson and rent a car.
Other Activities:
Big game, bird-watching, canoeing/kayaking/rafting, golf, horseback riding, hiking, snowmobiling, wildlife photography

Contact:
Clare Berger
Spotted Horse Ranch
12355 S. Hwy 191
Jackson Hole WY 83001
Ph: 307/733-2097
Fax: 307/733-3712
Web:
www.spottedhorseranch.com

DEEP IN Hoback Canyon, 16 miles south of Jackson, lies an elegant little ranch heavily steeped in the traditions of Rocky Mountain fishing. Though tiny when it comes to the size of most spreads in the west, this 46-acre ranch is long on angling reputation. From its private mile-long frontage on the Hoback to its easy access to the Snake, Salt and Green rivers, the Spotted Horse offers anglers an almost infinite range of fishing. Both neophyte and pro will find success on these waters.

The Hoback earns a modest rating from Fothergill and Sterling in their comprehensive *The Wyoming Angling Guide* because it is apt to color excessively with runoff from rains. Primarily a cutthroat river, its fish tend to be a bit smaller than those downstream in the Snake below Hoback Junction, where the two rivers meet. In the ranch's mileage, you can expect cutts in the 12- to 14-inch class, though fish up to 22 inches have been taken. Better angling is found in the upper Green — one of TU's top 100 trout streams — a 45-minute ride through the scenic Gros Ventre Range. This is primarily rainbow and brown trout water, and it fishes quite well once the spring melt has flushed through by mid-July. Rubber rafts with casting chairs are the conveyance of choice for all-day floats on the Green. Fish average about 14 inches, but it's not uncommon for a three-pounder to hit your fly or spinner. Equidistant from the ranch is the Salt River, which flows north out of the mountain range of the same name and joins Palisades Reservoir just east of the Wyoming/Idaho line. Like the Hoback, this is principally a cutthroat river, except that spawning browns move into the stream in August. Not to be forgotten, of course, is the Snake and its indigenous fine-spotted cutthroats averaging 14 inches. Floats on the section below Hoback Junction offer grand scenery as well as top-notch angling.

Spread along the river under a stand of aspen, the ranch's main lodge and cabins have an inviting feeling. On the front porch, wooden rockers face the river inviting you to sit a spell. Dinners, simple and scrumptious featuring staples such as steak, turkey and Mexican entrees, leave little room for anything more. You'll walk in the evening chill back to your log cabin, furnished with all amenities including private bath. All activities of the ranch except float trips are included in the American plan fee.

[N O R T H E R N   R O C K I E S]

Yellowstone National Park Lodges

Y e l l o w s t o n e ,   W y o m i n g

Among the best bargains for traveling anglers are the historic lodges in Teddy Roosevelt's first national park.

VITAL STATISTICS:

KEY SPECIES:
Cutthroat, brook trout, brown trout, rainbows

Major Season/Meals/Rates:
Varies with location; see next page

Guides:
Available throughout the park, the managers of each of Yellowstone's Hotels can provide names and phone numbers of those familiar with the waters in the vicinity. Expect to pay between $250 and $300 per day for two. Tips should average 15%.

Weather:
Snows come early to the high caldera that is the floor of park. You can expect temporary closures of all roads after October 1. And as of November 1, all roads within the park are closed, with the exception of the road between Mammoth and Cooke City. Again, regulations for travel and fishing within the park vary from season to season. If you plan a late or early season expedition, you'll want to check with the park in advance.

Other Activities:
In addition to its wonderful and varied fishing, Yellowstone teems with deer, elk, sheep, bears, antelope, bison, moose, and birds of every description. You'll see fumaroles and sputtering mud pots along with geysers. Here, in every season, the wilderness is on display. The park service and concessionaires have developed a number of interpretative activities, from instructional multi-media presentations in visitors centers, horseback rides , and fairly arduous hikes to see flora, fauna, and fascinating geology first hand. In addition, particularly in the Mammoth area, special waters are set aside for children to fish, one more way that the park service is committed to propagating the species.

Contact:
Yellowstone National Park Lodges
PO Box 165
Yellowstone National Park WY, 82190
Ph: 307/344-7901
Fax: 307/344-7456
Web:
www.travelyellowstone.com

MUD POTS BUBBLE YELLOW, red and white; fumaroles vent sulphurous steam; geysers spray boiling water hundreds of feet in the air. Herds of elk and bison amble through meadows; you glimpse a grizzly in the woods; moose graze with utter contentment in the shallow reeds. This is Yellowstone National Park, America's caldera park, where the scenery and wildlife are only eclipsed by trout fishing. You'll find more first-class trout water of similar yet diverse character within the park's bounds than anywhere else in North America. Tally the list yourself: Falls, Firehole, Gallatin, Gardner, Gibbon, Lamar, Lewis, Madison, Slough Creek, Snake and the Yellowstone itself. And don't forget Shoshone and Yellowstone lakes. West Yellowstone is the Mecca for fly-fishers and Paradise Valley is just what it says.

And unlike most national parks, Yellowstone boasts a wealth of fine old hotels, each with its own ambiance and personality. At rates that are very reasonable in comparison to those charged by facilities on the fringes of the park, one can stay the night, eat well, and fish to heart's content. Guides are available, but you don't really need them. Much has been written about fishing in Yellowstone: go buy a book, ask a ranger, and then get your line wet. The current concessionaire operating the hotels is AmFac Parks and Resorts of Aurora, Colorado. Reservations at any of the Yellowstone hotels may be made by calling 307/344-7311. Seasons may vary slightly at each.

CANYON LODGE & CABINS: Canyon Village is in the center of the park, where the Yellowstone River breaks off to the northwest and enters the Grand Canyon of the Yellowstone. From the falls down to Inspiration Point, the river is closed to fishing, but below, for anglers willing to hike 1,500 feet down to its waters, the river offers excellent cutthroat fishing. 609 rooms, restaurant, $51 to $105.

GRANT VILLAGE: Near West Thumb, Grant is on Yellowstone Lake, home of pure-strain cutthroat trout. Covering 150 square miles, the lake is more than 300 feet deep in spots. Use of motors is restricted in some sections of the lake. Fishing is often very good near shore and in feeder creeks. Float tube and wading anglers can do as well as boaters. Check regulations carefully; streams open later than the lake. 300 rooms, restaurant, marina, $83 to $96.

LAKE LODGE AND LAKE YELLOWSTONE HOTEL AND CABINS: Just west of the outlet and on Yellowstone in Lake Village, you'll find extensive accommodations close to the first fishable section of the Yellowstone River, beginning a mile downstream from the lake. Yellowstone cutthroats of 16 to 18 inches are the prime attraction. Wading — dicey at times — is the best way to fish it. As with elsewhere in the park, things change. Check regulations before wetting a line. Lake Lodge: 186 rooms, restaurant, $48 to $110; Lake Yellowstone Hotel and Cabins: 194 rooms, 102 cabins, restaurant, $77 to $373.

MAMMOTH HOT SPRINGS HOTEL: Fans of massive 1890s military-post architecture will love Mammoth Hot Springs, headquarters for the park. While it receives some pressure, the Gardner River below Osprey Falls holds nice browns that migrate up from the Yellowstone River in fall. You'll also find cutthroats here. 96 rooms in the hotel, 126 in cabins, restaurant, $48 to $245.

OLD FAITHFUL: Here are three large lodges and adjacent cabins — The Inn; Lodge Cabins; and Snow Lodge & Cabins. Of massive logs with its towering interior, The Inn is the park's signature hotel. Nearby is Snow Lodge & Cabins, and a little beyond, Lodge Cabins. All three are convenient to the Firehole, Gibbon and upper Madison. In the heat of summer, try Iron Spring and Sentinel creeks, cool havens for hot Firehole browns. Inn: 325 rooms, restaurant, $52 to $325; Lodge Cabins: 132 rooms (85 with private baths), $32 to $58; Snow Lodge & Cabins: 31 rooms in lodge, 34 cabins (some with private baths), $101 to $121.

ROOSEVELT LODGE: The road from Cooke City at the northwest entrance to the park follows Soda Butte Creek to its junction with the Lamar River. Both are good fisheries. The Lamar has nice populations of cutthroats and rainbows. When the Lamar muddies, the Soda Butte is often clear, though fish average only 10 inches. At Tower, the Yellowstone flows out of its Grand Canyon, through relatively gentle terrain, and then into the Black Canyon of the Yellowstone. Fishing is quite good, but once in the canyon, the river becomes difficult to wade. Slough Creek, another fine stream known for cutthroats, receives more than moderate pressure than other streams in the park, but can be reached by the road to Slough Creek Campground, north of the Tower-Cooke City Road. 80 rooms (17 with private baths), restaurant, $40 to $77.

SOUTHERN ROCKIES

ARIZONA, COLORADO, NEW MEXICO, UTAH,

JUST AS RUGGED, but a bit drier than their northern siblings, the southern half of the Rockies has its share of marvelous fisheries. The South Platte sits on Denver's doorstep; the Gunnison, Fryingpan, White, and Colorado drain the west slopes. Famed tailwaters — the Green in Flaming Gorge, the Colorado at Lees Ferry, the San Juan in New Mexico — draw anglers year-round. Here, too, high mountain lakes attract pack-trip anglers, and the gentle streams of southernmost central Colorado and northcentral New Mexico hide browns and cutthroat of surprising size. Lodges, ranches, and motels cluster where the fishing's best, and some are as elegant as they come.

References:

*ARIZONA TROUT:
A FLY FISHING GUIDE*
by Rex Johnson Jr.

UTAH'S GREEN RIVER
by Dennis Breer

GREEN RIVER JOURNAL
by Larry Tullis

RIVER JOURNAL: RIO GRANDE
by Craig Martin
Frank Amato Publications
PO Box 82112
Portland, OR 97282
503/653-8108

FLY FISHING THE SOUTH PLATTE
by Roger Hill

FLY FISHING ROCKY MOUNTAIN
NATIONAL PARK

FLY FISHING COLORADO'S FRONT
RANGE
by Todd Hosman

FLY FISHING THE COLORADO RIVER
by Al Marlowe

FLY FISHING SOUTHERN COLORADO
by Craig Martin, Tom Knopick,
& John Flick
Pruett Publishing Co
7464 Arapahoe Road, Ste. A-9
Boulder, CO 80303-1500
303/449-4919

- -

FLYFISHER'S GUIDE TO COLORADO
by Harry Bartholomew
Wilderness Adventure Press
PO Box 627
Gallatin Gateway MT 59730
800/925-3339

- -

FISHING IN NEW MEXICO
by Ti Piper

FLY FISHING IN NORTHERN NEW
MEXICO
by Craig Martin

FLY FISHING IN SOUTHERN
NEW MEXICO
by Rex Johnson Jr. & Ronald Smorynski
University of New Mexico Press
1720 Lomas Blvd. NE
Albuquerque, NM 87131-1591
505/277-2346

- -

THE COLORADO ANGLING GUIDE
by Chuck Fothergill and Bob Sterling
Stream Stalker Publishing Co.
P.O. Box 238
Woody Creek, CO 81656
970/923-4552

- -

Resources:

ARIZONA GAME AND FISH
DEPARTMENT
2221 W. Greenway Rd
Phoenix, AZ 85023
602/942-3000
web: www.gf.state.az.us

- -

COLORADO DIVISION OF WILDLIFE
6060 Broadway
Denver, CO 80216
303/297-1192
web: www.dnr.state.co.us/wildlife

- -

NEW MEXICO DEPARTMENT OF
GAME AND FISH
Box 25112
Santa Fe, NM 87504
505/827-7911
800/862-9310

- -

UTAH DIVISION OF WILDLIFE
RESOURCES
1594 W. North Temple, Ste. 2110
Salt Lake City, UT 84114-6301
801/538-4700
web: www.nr.state.ut.us/dwr

- -

[S O U T H E R N   R O C K I E S]

Lees Ferry Lodge

M a r b l e   C a n y o n ,   A r i z o n a

A little funky, a lot laid-back, but if you fish the Colorado, you gotta stay here.

VITAL STATISTICS:

KEY SPECIES:
Rainbows

Tackle:
Fly-fishing, spinning
Major Season:
All year
Accommodations:
MOTEL ROOMS
NUMBER OF ROOMS: 11
MAXIMUM NUMBER OF GUESTS: 32
Meals: Hearty with an eclectic twist
Conference Groups: No
Rates: From $53
Guides: $275
Gratuities: 10%;
Angler's discretion
Preferred Payment:
Cash, check or credit cards
Getting There:
Page is the closest airport with commercial flights, but you'll find better fares if you fly to Las Vegas or Flagstaff and rent a car.
Other Activities:
Bird-watching, boating, canoeing/kayaking/rafting, hiking, wildlife photography

Contact:
Maggie Sacher
Lees Ferry Lodge
Vermilion Cliffs
HC67-Box 1
Marble Canyon AZ 86036
Ph: 520/355-2231

ENTERTAINMENT IN THE HAMLET of Marble Canyon, where the Vermilion Cliffs rise high above the wine-bottle green Colorado tailwater, depends a lot on local talent. Yet, at times, its effect is positively inspired. Take the evening when the gang at Maggie's bar took to singing that old back-seat classic, "99 Bottles of Beer." After the crew lost count somewhere in the 30s, one enlightened wag suggested that it'd be cool if Maggie stocked 99 different brands of beer. Were this drinkery located in San Francisco or Philadelphia or Milwaukee, it would have been a piece of cake. But Marble Canyon is a good 125 miles from anywhere you've ever heard of. Maggie persevered, though, and this watering hole with its 11 rooms now boasts 145 different brews. Even if you popped a can or two of suds with your green eggs and ham at breakfast, you'll need at least a week to sample them all.

That probably wouldn't help your fishing, but who knows. Sinuous, cold and very green from deep and life-giving beds of aquatic mosses, the Colorado flows past 1,000 foot cliffs of rugged red sandstone on its 15.5 mile journey from Glen Canyon dam to Lees Ferry, where it descends into the Grand Canyon. Here the Colorado is as fine a tailwater as you'll find in the U.S. Most anglers hire a guide at Lees Ferry Anglers (800/962-9755), a quintessential outfitter for fly-fishers run by Wendy and Terry Gunn, next door to the motel. The guide motors fishers upstream past scores of shallow-water bars that cut the river. No matter what season, midge patterns seem to be the most effective dries, and the usual array of nymphs — Hare's Ear, Pheasant Tails, Prince, often fished with a tiny Brassie as a dropper — turn the trick here. Rainbow water pure and simple, 'bows run in the 12- to 24-inch range. If you don't want a guide, you can rent a boat, or you can fish a very productive half-mile of walk-in water near the boat launch.

Lees Ferry is the departure point for most of the raft trips through the Grand Canyon, and the region is known for its absolutely stunning beauty. Condors sail above the cliffs and antelope dance across the broad plain that runs to the lip of the canyon. History abounds. And the river-rock, motel-style Lees Ferry Lodge is part of it all. Looking for all the world like the set from a grade B western, you'll discover that the rooms (all with private baths) are very comfortable and reasonably modern. The bar offers very substantial chow.

Elktrout Lodge

Kremmling, Colorado

Troublesome is the name of the creek, and so are the trout, unless you're a sneaky cuss.

VITAL STATISTICS:

KEY SPECIES:
Browns, cutthroat, rainbows

Tackle:
Fly-fishing
Major Season:
Mid-May through mid-October
Accommodations:
RUSTIC LOG LODGE AND CABINS
NUMBER OF ROOMS: 11
HANDICAPPED ACCESSIBLE: 2
MAXIMUM NUMBER OF GUESTS: 22
Meals: Excellent western cuisine
Conference Groups: Yes
Rates: From $1,600 / 3 days
Guides: Included
Gratuities: $50 - $75 / day
Preferred Payment:
Cash, check or credit cards
Getting There:
Fly to Denver and rent a car.
Other Activities:
Big game, bird-watching, canoeing/kayaking/rafting, golf, horseback riding, hiking, wildlife photography

Contact:
Marty Cecil
Elktrout Lodge
PO Box 614
Kremmling CO 80459
Ph: 970/742-3343
Fax: 970/742-9063
Web:
www.elktrout.com

Agents:
Orvis endorsed

ANGLERS WHO FISH ELKTROUT GO looking for trouble. They're searching for those skittish 12- to 20-inch browns and rainbows that lie in a spring run that goes by the name of Troublesome Creek. It's aptly named. Water as clear as ether slides along and undercuts banks of grass. A hands and knees approach isn't always necessary, but remember: If you can see these big 'bows, they can see you too. Precise casting is a must.

Along with caddis and terrestrial imitations, Muddlers, particularly those heavily greased and skittered across the surface, can ignite savage strikes. And you really need to talk with Marty Cecil about fishing "water boatman" beetles. Hatching under the clear blue skies of late August, these beetles rise to the surface, spread their wings and paddle for the grassy pond bank as if their lives depend on it. They do. Trout here like nothing better than a few boatmen for breakfast.

Along with the lower Troublesome Creek and the larger waters of the Blue and Colorado rivers, Elktrout Ranch holds four ponds where bellyboaters and bank-stalkers catch cutthroats, browns and rainbows, the girths of which are as long as many river-run fish. Easily wadeable, the Blue and Colorado are freestone waters which offer runs and pools and the usual repertoire of hatches. Also on the agenda here is upper Troublesome, a delightful creek that plunges, pools and beats around boulders before emptying into the lower mountain section.

Not all of these waters fish well all of the time, but what waters do? Throughout Elktrout's five-month season, you can bet that two or more of the ranch's fisheries will be hot at a given time. Much depends on water levels and irrigation needs. If the Blue and Colorado are flowing between 250 and 400 cfs, angling will be quite good. Fish will not be big, generally in the 12- to 18-inch range, but they will be plentiful, and there's a reasonably good chance of playing a 16- to 18-inch fish.

At Elktrout, the fishing day begins around 8:30 a.m. with a trip to one of a dozen ponds. After lunch, you may fish one of the rivers. Dinner is around 6:30 p.m., where everybody stuffs themselves on charred rack of lamb, smoked prime rib or steak au poivre. You'll have a tendency to head for the porch, sit back, prop your feet on the rail and watch the sunset while others fish the evening rise. Don't give in to the temptation. Orvis-endorsed, the lodge maintains a small but well-stocked tackle shop.

193

[S O U T H E R N   R O C K I E S]

Mt. Blanca Game Bird & Trout Lodge

B l a n c a ,   C o l o r a d o

The mountains of southern Colorado offer surpassingly good trout fishing. Just ask Liz Taylor!

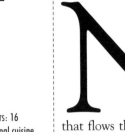

VITAL STATISTICS:

KEY SPECIES:
Brookies, browns, cutthroat, rainbows, steelhead

Tackle:
Fly-fishing
Major Season:
May through September
Accommodations:
ELEGANTLY MODERN LODGE
NUMBER OF ROOMS: 8
MAXIMUM NUMBER OF GUESTS: 16
Meals: Exquisite regional cuisine with wines to match
Conference Groups: Yes
Rates: From $99 / night; fishing and meals additional
Guides: Included
Gratuities: Angler's discretion
Preferred Payment:
Cash, check or credit cards
Getting There:
Fly to Alamosa and rent a car.
Other Activities:
Big game, waterfowling, wingshooting, golf, horseback riding, hiking, skiing, wildlife photography

Contact:
Mt. Blanca Game Bird & Trout Lodge
PO Box 236
Blanca CO 81123-0236
Ph: 800/686-4024
Fax: 719/379-3843
e-mail:
mblanca@fone.net
Web:
www.mtblanca.com

Agents:
Orvis Endorsed

NOW ELIZABETH TAYLOR isn't Joan Wulff, but she did, on extremely rare occasions, trod a trout stream while in the company of Malcomb Forbes. It's on Ute Creek that flows through the Forbes Ranch where fly-fishing and Miss Taylor's travels crossed paths. There's no record of the specifics of the meeting, but the stream still carries fine stocks of cutthroat, and it's one of the loveliest places to fish on the planet. Swinging through a gentle meadow of wildflowers, Ute Creek moves from sun to shade beneath stands of aspen, cottonwood and pine. A half-mile changes the terrain into a maze of canyons and tight valleys. Most anglers throw nymphs such as Pheasant Tails, Hare's Ears, and the like. Terrestrials work well in late summer. You'll also connect with Royal Wulffs and caddis.

Ute Creek isn't the only water in the neighborhood. There is the Trinchera with its browns, rainbows and cutthroat, and its tributary, the Little Trinchera, which would be considered an ugly stream did its browns not push 22 inches. Sangre Creek, too, is worth a look for its cutthroat, and if you're poking around in this neck of the woods, you'll want to spend a little time on the Rio Grande.

Along with these wild trout fisheries, Mt. Blanca stocks a number of ponds on its 1,200 acres with leviathans dead set on busting up your tackle. That's fun, of course, but it's nothing like pushing through a willow thicket and stepping into a mountain stream where you can see trout rising against the far bank.

Fishing holds up well into the fall, and that makes Mt. Blanca a special place to visit. Bring a doublegun and toss shot at wild doves, ducks or released pheasant, chukar, quail or Hungarian partridge. Accommodations in this modern lodge of glass and wood leave nothing to be desired. Neither do the meals, or the wine list, or the hot tub. The lodge, however, lies at an elevation of 8,000-feet-plus. Better plan to spend a week to get acclimated.

Seven Lakes Lodge

Meeker, Colorado

When Henry Kravis decided to start a fishing lodge, he went all the way!

VITAL STATISTICS:

KEY SPECIES:
Brookies, browns, rainbows

Tackle:
Fly-fishing
Major Season:
Mid-June through early October
Accommodations:
ELEGANT LOG LODGE
NUMBER OF ROOMS: 11
HANDICAPPED ACCESSIBLE: 1
MAXIMUM NUMBER OF GUESTS: 22
Meals: Exquisite gourmet cuisine
Conference Groups: Yes
Rates: From $6,140 / 6 nights
Guides: Included
Gratuities: 15% of stay
Preferred Payment:
Cash, check or credit cards
Getting There:
Fly to Grand Junction and the lodge van will meet you.
Other Activities:
Archery course, big game, bird-watching, horseback riding, hiking, swimming, tennis, wildlife photography

Contact:
Steve Herter
Seven Lakes Lodge
PO Box 39
Edwards CO 81632
Ph: 970/926-7813
Fax: 970/926-7815
e-mail:
info@sevenlakes.com
Web:
www.sevenlakes.com

WHEN INVESTOR Henry Kravis goes about a task, he does it absolutely first class. And that was the game plan when he bought and redid Seven Lakes Lodge in 1996. Before he took the reins, Seven Lakes Lodge had been a modest place with a little mileage on a better than average trout stream. Today, Seven Lakes is in the top tier of the nation's finest angling retreats, all because of Henry's vision.

Take the White River. Seven Lakes bought and reconstructed three miles of it, adding 29 pools, homes for the deep-bellied rainbows and cutthroats that were stocked later. Average fish run between 18 and 20 inches, although 24-inch rainbows are common. If these guys seem too small, there's a bunch of 10-pounders in the lodge's lakes. And, of course, there are other nearby trout waters. In the Flat Tops National Wilderness Area are scores of small lakes, and a few good-size ones like Trappers and Marvine. Trappers Lake is accessible by vehicle, but even so it retains the pristine qualities associated with isolation: stunning vistas, superlative native cutthroats and a litter-free environment. In the other lakes, many reachable only by horse or foot, you'll find rainbow, brook and cutthroat trout. It's worth a day or two to explore these stillwater fisheries. And a little time spent on the White below the lodge will offer yet another challenge, this one for smaller stream trout.

Among the many aspects that distinguish Seven Lakes from other angling lodges are its guides. You'll have your own guide for a week. He or she will learn your likes and dislikes, what you can do and what you want to do, and will bend over backwards to keep you happy. It would be a mistake not to ride one of the lodge's gentle horses to a remote pond or stream. And if you're a shotgunner, you'll do yourself a disservice if you don't shoot a rounds of sporting clays on the Michael Rose-designed course.

Sprawling over 15,000 square feet, the main stone and timber lodge is as grand inside as the panoramas you see through countless picture windows. A giant rock fireplace commands the great room and attracts the attention of guests in the lounge and dining room. Little is more delightful than having breakfast or dinner (gourmet with good wines, as you'd expect) on the large glass-enclosed porch. Eight guest suites are upstairs in the main lodge. A private, executive log cabin contains three bedrooms. Seven Lakes also includes an exercise center, spa and full conference facilities.

*Condors ride thermals at the crest of Vermilion Cliffs. At their
base is the Colorado at Lees Ferry and a wonderfully
funky motel and restaurant favored by anglers in the know.*

*Quiet and clean, the San Juan River Lodge provides spacious
rooms with tying tables. Navajo Dam serves as
jump-off point for fishing for the river's legendary rainbows.*

Wit's End Guest Rance

Bayfield, Colorado

Jump off into the backcountry where trout play in high mountain lakes that only you and your wrangler can find.

VITAL STATISTICS:

KEY SPECIES:
Brookies, browns, cutthroat, rainbows

Tackle:
Fly-fishing, spinning
Major Season:
March through November
Accommodations:
LOG CABINS
NUMBER OF ROOMS: 54
HANDICAPPED ACCESSIBLE: SEVERAL
MAXIMUM NUMBER OF GUESTS: 180
Meals: Fine western cuisine
Conference Groups: Yes
Rates: From $725 / day
Guides: Included
Gratuities: 10% - 15%
Preferred Payment:
Cash, check or credit cards
Getting There:
Fly to Durango and rent a car.
Other Activities:
Boating, canoeing/kayaking/rafting, golf, horseback riding, hiking, swimming, tennis

Contact:
Chad Hughes
Wit's End Guest Rance
254 CR 500
Bayfield CO 81122
Ph: 970/884-4115
Fax: 970/884-3261
e-mail:
weranch@aol.com
Web:
www.ranchweb.com/witsend/

Off Season:
4207 North 19th St
Phoenix AZ 85015
Ph: 602/263-0000
Fax: 602/234-0298

THE CORNER OF COLORADO just east of Durango is a land of steep and forested mountains, tranquil glades and mountain lakes. At the head of one of these lakes, Vallecito, sprawls a guest ranch that's among the West's most historic: Wit's End. Nothin' major happened here, except a lot of kids and horses got raised, and kin of the Patricks, who established the ranch in 1859, came for visits. There began the tradition for hospitality. The ranch grew and by the mid-1880s, it had pooled the waters from creeks feeding the lake and established a hatchery for native trout. Abutting the 425,000-acre Wimenuche Wilderness, Wit's End tells its share of stories, about the Dalton gang, Teddy Roosevelt, and of millions from lost mines stashed in the high hills.

A week at Wit's End may be just the prescription. The ranch offers fishing for browns, cutthroat and rainbows in more than half a mile of the Vallecito River. You can saddle-up and ride out to high mountain lakes where native cutts and brook trout, stocked long ago, play tag with equally venerable rainbow transplants. Overnight pack trips are available as well. The lake itself offers some fishing for pike, trout and Kokanee salmon. The famed San Juan is a couple hours south with its willing 'bows and, lower down in the river, bigger browns. Through Durango, an hour or so west, flows the Animas. Both rivers are rated among the top 100 in the country by members of Trout Unlimited.

Wit's End is a family-focused guest ranch. After breakfast, children may take part in riding, hiking and games supervised by trained counselors, or they may spend time with their moms and dads. As you'd expect, many activities revolve around riding and instruction is available for all from beginners who've never touched a horse, to those who are quite advanced. Guests stay in sturdy log cabins, many with fireplaces, and enjoy fine dining and buffets in the main lodge — the old barn that John Patrick built in 1870.

Blackfire Flyfishing Guest Ranch

A n g e l   F i r e ,   N e w   M e x i c o

It's as if your rich uncle had this great fly-fishing retreat and he left it to you.

VITAL STATISTICS:

KEY SPECIES:
Browns, cutthroat, rainbows

Tackle:
Fly-fishing
Major Season:
May through October
Accommodations:
COMFORTABLE LODGE FOR ONE GROUP AT A TIME
NUMBER OF ROOMS: 3
MAXIMUM NUMBER OF GUESTS: 12
Meals: Southwestern cuisine
Conference Groups: Yes
Rates: From $990 / 3 nights / 2
Guides: $200
Gratuities: 20%
Preferred Payment:
Cash or check
Getting There:
Fly to Albuquerque and rent a car.
Other Activities:
Bird-watching, canoeing/kayaking rafting, golf, horseback riding, hiking, tennis, wildlife photography

Contact:
Mickey & Maggie Greenwood
Blackfire Flyfishing Guest
Ranch
PO Box 981
Angel Fire NM 87710
Ph: 505/377-6870
Fax: 505/377-3807
e-mail:
blackfire@newmex.com
Web:
www.newmex.com/blackfire

IMAGINE A PRIVATE FLY-FISHING RESORT that's all yours for a week. Maybe you and a few guys from the office, or a week for women fly-fishers; a couple of couples, or just you and a significant other. However you want to do it, this place high in the heart of New Mexico's alpine district caters to one group at a time. As few as two or as many as 12 will enjoy the comforts of a modern three-bedroom ranch with two baths. Meals are served when you want them and they're tuned to the desires of each guest. In the main you'll dine on exquisite southwestern cuisine: chicken breasts with cranberry sage sauce, fajitas, and the like.

The draw, aside from the charming house, great chow and infinite solitude, is a five-acre lake where rainbows grow as big as largemouth, and cutts and browns come just slightly smaller. Handling an eight-pound rainbow on a five- or six-weight will make anyone's day. Catch a dozen and your arm's ready for a trip to the chiropractor. Don't think of fighting these fish like weight-training. Call it trout training! After a week here, you're ready for anything.

The ranch season opens in June and continues through October, with June through August providing the best action. While trout will hammer dries on occasion, most of the lake's denizens fall to streamers and nymphs. Fish a five-weight with a sink-tip line from a float tube, canoe or the shore — your choice. Around the lake are stands of pine and hills that roll upward to mountains in the distance. There's nothing else, except for bald and golden eagles and maybe an elk to keep you company. For as little as $1,200 apiece, you and a buddy can have the lake and its lodge to yourselves for a week.

If fishing the lake pales, and everyone gets tired of five-pound 'bows running deep into the backing day after day, a short drive will take you to the Red River, Rio Grande or Cimarron. These rivers and several smaller streams drain the Sangre de Cristo Mountains. Runoff inhibits fishing until mid-June, but it picks up after that, peaking in early fall. A guide isn't necessary to fish the lake, but you may want one if you plan on exploring other water in the area. You also may want to check out the lodge's fly-fishing schools. A small but excellent fly shop is located at the ranch.

High up in Colorado's White River country, Henry Kravis'
Seven Lakes Lodge offers anglers four-star accommodations and
outstanding angling in ponds, stocked streams and wild rivers.

[S O U T H E R N   R O C K I E S]

The Lodge at Chama

C h a m a ,   N e w   M e x i c o

This lodge has a number of great lakes, and the wild streams of northern New Mexico will inspire your dreams.

VITAL STATISTICS:

KEY SPECIES:
Browns, cutthroat, rainbows

Tackle:
Fly-fishing, spinning
Major Season:
June through September
Accommodations:
ELEGANT LODGE ROOMS WITH WESTERN FLARE
NUMBER OF ROOMS: 11
HANDICAPPED ACCESSIBLE: ALL
MAXIMUM NUMBER OF GUESTS: 22
Meals: Gourmet regional cuisine
Conference Groups: Yes
Rates: From $225 / day
Guides: $200
Gratuities: Angler's discretion
Preferred Payment:
Cash, check or credit cards
Getting There:
Fly to Albuquerque and rent a car.
Other Activities:
Big game, bird-watching, horseback riding, hiking, sporting clays, swimming, wildlife photography

Contact:
Frank Simms
The Lodge at Chama
PO Box 127
Chama NM 87520
Ph: 505/756-2133
Fax: 505/756-2519
e-mail:
reservations@lodgeatchama.com
Web:
www.lodgeatchama.com

WANT WILD TROUT? Want to tussle with behemoths that'll sip your little caddis ever so daintily and then scream your reel 'til it smokes? Or do you just want to hammer away with Mr. Woolly B. catching fish after fish after fish. You can do it all here at the Lodge at Chama. It's a 32,000-acre outdoor playground.

Chama is a tiny little hamlet hard by the Colorado border. Not far outside the town limits begins the ranch land — roughly 50 square miles of it. That's plenty of territory in anyone's book. The water is as varied as the anglers who fish it. Experts will enjoy runs that look for all the world like spring creeks. Those whose skills are more modest will find success on numerous ponds and lakes stocked with browns, brookies, cutthroats and rainbows. The rainbows are the heavyweights, tipping the scales at 10 to 12 pounds. Cutthroats follow in the four- to five-pound range, with brookies and browns running two pounds or more. A private fishery, no licenses are required here, and anglers may use spinning as well as fly-tackle as long as lures have single barbless hooks. Some of the ponds are designated catch-and-release water, but from others, anglers may keep up to four fish per day.

Ranch ponds aren't the only game in town though. Rio Chama flows through the center of the village, and much of it is public water. Stocked rainbows predominate, but you'll also catch some wild browns. The tailwaters below Heron Dam and El Vado Reservoir — about 20 miles south of the lodge — provide some action, with big browns below El Vado being the better alternative. Roughly two hours west is the famed San Juan, and it's well worth the drive. Guides from the lodge occasionally float guests down the San Juan, or they can make arrangements with colleagues in the town of Navajo Dam to guide guests on the river. The San Juan is one of the four or five top tailwaters in the U.S., and a chance to fish it for rainbows that consistently exceed 18-inches must not be missed.

Overlooking the valley at Chama is the 13,500-square-foot lodge. Under cathedral ceilings, guests warm themselves by the 20-foot-long fireplace or enjoy sitting watching the sunset from rockers on the comfortable veranda. Guest rooms are huge by most lodge standards. Some have fireplaces, and most are so comfortable you really hate to leave them. Dinners are elegant yet traditional featuring steaks and roasts as well as buffalo, trout and fowl often prepared with New Mexican flare.

Rizuto's San Juan River Lodge

Navajo Dam, New Mexico

Little, laid-back, clean and very comfortable — this lodge is all you need after a day on the San Juan.

VITAL STATISTICS:

KEY SPECIES:
Browns, cuttbows, rainbows, smallmouth

Tackle:
Fly- fishing, spinning
Major Season:
All year
Accommodations:
WOODEN CABINS
NUMBER OF ROOMS: 8
MAXIMUM NUMBER OF GUESTS: 18
Meals: At restaurants in town
Conference Groups: Yes
Rates: From $75 / night / two
Guides: $225
Gratuities: $25
Preferred Payment:
Cash, check or credit cards
Getting There:
Fly to Farmington or Durango, CO and rent a car.
Other Activities:
Big game, hiking (although there's absolutely no reason to go to Navajo Dam other than to fish)

Contact:
Chuck Rizuto
Rizuto's San Juan
River Lodge
PO Box 6309
1796 Highway 173
Navajo Dam NM 87419
Ph: 505/632-3893
Fax: 505/632-8798
e-mail:
driftboat@worldnet.att.net
Web:
www.rizutos.com

Agents:
Marriott's

WHAT STRIKES YOU when you pull into the one-time construction town of Navajo Dam is that you can tell it was, well, a construction town. But when you park at Chuck Rizuto's lodge, you're immediately greeted with a sense of quiet. Two rows of neat grey cabins face each other. Shaded and cool, even in midsummer, the walkway between the cabins is landscaped with flowers and bushes in bloom. Hang your waders on the porch, slip inside the air-conditioned room, and make yourself at home. There's a tying bench on the wall, or stock up on local patterns from the fly shop at the lodge. Meals are found in a funky bar at the top of the hill.

The San Juan below Navajo Dam is one of the finest tailwaters in the world, and one of TU's 100 best trout streams in America. Chuck Rizuto owns the lodge and guides when you twist his arm. Almost everybody hooks 20-inchers every day or two. Bigger fish are possible. It's also possible that you'll break off your first few fish. These guys like their flies small (no. 18 to 22), and their tippets fine (5x to 6x). Rods should be long, limber and light. Not only are the fish of good size, but they readily take artificials. Baetis duns and midge clusters produce consistently on top. Under the surface, use the San Juan Worm or a Brassie.

In June, flows may be high because of snow melting in the mountains to the north in Colorado. Don't worry. Rainbows move into back channels and you can find them there. This is one of the most challenging kinds of trouting there is. When the water is running its normal flows, anglers will average 20 to 30 fish on a day's float over the 3.5 mile flies-only stretch. Below, in the next 13 miles where bait and spinfishing is legal, the number of hookups will be about half that (still not bad). Clearly, the highest concentrations of fish are closer to the dam. And the closer to the dam, the greater the percentage of rainbows to browns. Above the dam, you'll find excellent and virtually ignored smallmouth.

There's no off-season at this lodge. Sure, in winter the temperature drops and skies turn gray, and it may even snow. But the water comes out of the dam at a consistent 42°F. By the time it reaches the midpoint of the 3 1/2-mile-long no-kill/flies-only stretch, the flow has warmed only to the mid-50s. Cold days in winter stay below freezing, but they are as rare as fishless days on the river. Normally the mid-day temperature hovers in the 40s and 50s, and sunny days in the 60s are common.

[S O U T H E R N   R O C K I E S]

Step Back Inn

A z t e c ,   N e w   M e x i c o

The spirit of the Anasazi watches over the San Juan from a fort which you'll pass when you float the river.

VITAL STATISTICS:

KEY SPECIES:
Browns, rainbows

Tackle:
Fly-fishing, spinning
Major Season:
All year
Accommodations:
LODGE WITH HISTORIC THEME
NUMBER OF ROOMS: 39
HANDICAPPED ACCESSIBLE: 2
MAXIMUM NUMBER OF GUESTS: 80
Meals: In restaurants
Conference Groups: Yes
Rates: From $58
Guides: $265
Gratuities:
Angler's discretion
Preferred Payment:
Cash, check or credit cards
Getting There:
Fly to Farmington and rent a car.
Other Activities:
Big game, waterfowling, wingshooting, bird-watching, boating, canoeing/kayaking/rafting, golf, horseback riding, hiking, skiing, snowmobiling, tennis, wildlife photography

Contact:
T. Blancett
Step Back Inn
103 W. Aztec Blvd
Aztec NM 87410
Ph: 505/334-1200
Fax: 505/334-9858
e-mail:
stepback@cyberport.com
Web:
www.aztecnm.cyberport.com

THE "ANCIENT ONES," the Anasazi, knew the river long before there were trout in it. They knew it because it was a source of water for their crops, fish and shellfish. Game abounded in cane breaks along the channel. It was their water of life. When you float the San Juan, you'll drift by a long abandoned Anasazi fort and beneath petroglyphs they etched on the bluffs that rise from the channel. Your guide will point them out if you ask.

Knowing a bit of history always makes a trip more intriguing. But you come for the fishing and what fishing there is. For about four miles below San Juan dam, the river flows cold and fairly clear through what's come to be known as "the quality waters." This is fly-fishing only, no-kill country. Guide Jerry Freeman, with his wife Nancy, operates Anasazi Anglers (970/385-4665) out of Durango, Colorado, about 50 miles northwest. He lives on the river and knows it well.

Cold and consistent, except when it's a bit higher in June, the river holds some of the finest rainbows in the west. Fish of 18 to 20 inches are common. When they reach 22 to 26 inches, things get interesting. A smattering of 28- and 29-inchers are landed each year, and in 1996, two 30-inchers tied the shop record. Generally, the smaller the fly, the bigger the fish: San Juan Worms, size 16, are about as large as Freeman goes. Except, that is, for a few magic days in early July when black carpenter ants swarm. You never know when it will happen, but when it does, the fish go bonkers. You'll throw a no. 6 Black Ant dressed to float high. You can skate it across the water and a big old rainbow will chase it like a beagle after a rabbit. Nine-foot rods are the order of the day on the San Juan, and anglers seldom need anything heavier than a no. 4 or 5. The softness of the lighter rods tends to protect the 5x and 6x tippets required for fishing all but the Black Ants.

Diehard fly-casters will probably hole-up in the town of Navajo Dam. But if you want something that's a cut above, drive 30 minutes west to Aztec and book into the Step Back Inn. Of deep blue-gray wood, with a full-length front porch, the inn projects the motif of an Old West Main Street hotel. Each of the rooms is named for a locally prominent pioneer, the famous and infamous alike. With turn-of-the-century ambience, rooms also contain all key modern amenities. Guests awaken to the smell of freshly perked coffee. Breakfast and dinner are available in the restaurant downstairs. It's quaint and a little quirky, but very, very comfortable.

Flaming Gorge Lodge

Dutch John, Utah

When the Green River is bad, it's still very, very good, and when it's great, it can't be beat.

IN MANY WAYS, the Colorado below Glen Canyon dam and the Green River downstream from Flaming Gorge are similar tailwaters. Both are year-round fisheries. Dry fly angling is without peer. The deep canyons that contain them are stunning. But there are a couple of important differences: the only way to fish most of the Colorado is to boat up it and float back down. On the Green, an 11-mile foot path follows the length of the north side of the river. You don't need a drift boat to fish here. In the Colorado, you'll catch rainbows predominantly. On the Green, you'll find browns and cutthroat as well.

Most who fish the Green River do float it. The most popular trip is the upper 7.5 miles from the dam down to Little Hole. Fish this section from June through August, and pay no heed to exuberant rafters and canoeists — the fish don't seem to mind, so why should you? Casting toward the bank can turn up browns averaging 16-inches and rainbows and cutthroats that are slightly smaller. If you're a buff of western history, make the run from Little Hole down to Browns Park where Butch Cassidy and the Wild Bunch used to play. The Green is reasonably predictable for constant flows. The river runs between 2,500 cfs and 3,000 cfs during the winter, rising to about 4,000 cfs in May. In late June or early July, flows drop back to about 1,800 cfs, where they are maintained throughout the fall.

Most of the anglers you'll meet on the Green will be pushing fly rods. But spin-fishers can do well with 1/4 and 1/8 ounce lead-head jigs in black and ginger. Midges start the fly-fishing season in February and March, then it's Blue-winged Olives from March into May, big cicadas in May, and finally terrestrials — hoppers, crickets, ants. Sizes tend to be small — #16 to #26s.

Flaming Gorge Lodge has new owners and you can look for improvements in their many motel rooms and condos, rented on a daily or weekly basis. Condos include one queen, one single and a hide-a-bed, and a fully-equipped kitchen. Motel rooms are furnished with a pair of twin beds with a rollaway available on request. Some are handicapped accessible. Meals are served in the main restaurant. There's also a full-service tackle shop which is headquarters for area guide services.

WEST

CALIFORNIA, NEVADA, OREGON, WASHINGTON

W HEREVER YOU find mountains and seashores, you'll find great fishing. And the west coast of the U.S. is no exception. Golden trout, cutthroat, rainbows and browns swim in alpine ponds, spring creeks and mountain streams of the Sierras. Coastal rivers from San Francisco (striped bass) north run with steelhead and salmon. Rivers in the interior of Oregon are renowned for steelhead and trout. Commercial angling and habitat destruction have taken their toll on several of these fisheries, and intensive efforts — closed seasons, dam removal, slot limits — are underway to save them. Still, many are exceptional and worth a visit from prudent anglers. In southern California, there are trophy bass to be caught in lakes Casitas and Castaic north of Los Angles and in the ponds around San Diego. And the lower reaches of marvelous steelhead rivers often hold find smallmouth.

References:

ANGLING ALPINE
by J.E. Warren
J.E. Warren c/o Sorensen's Resort
14255 Hwy. 88
Hope Valley, CA 96120
800/423-9949

DESCHUTES
by Dave Hughes
FISHING THE LOWER COLUMBIA
by Larry Leonard

FISHING IN NEW MEXICO
by Ti Piper

FLY FISHING IN NORTHERN
NEW MEXICO
by Craig Martin
University of New Mexico Press
1720 Lomas Blvd. NE
Albuquerque, NM 87131-1591
505/277-7564

Resources:

CALIFORNIA DEPARTMENT
OF FISH & GAME
Wildlife and Inland Fisheries Division
1416 9th St., Box 944209
Sacramento, CA 95814
916/324-7243
web: www.dfg.ca.gov/

NEVADA DIVISION OF WILDLIFE
Box 10678
Reno, NV 89520
702/688-1500
web: www.state.nv.us/cnr.nvwildlife

OREGON DEPARTMENT OF FISH
AND WILDLIFE
Box 59
Portland, OR 97207
503/872-5268
web: www.dfw.state.or.us/

WASHINGTON DEPARTMENT OF
FISH AND WILDLIFE
600 Capitol Way North
Olympia, WA 98501-1091
360/902-2515
web: www.wa.gov/wdfw/

When the finicky trout of the Williamson tie your psyche into
knots, you can switch from Lonesome Duck's private run of the
river to its tranquil pond where the trout are more willing.

Clearwater House on Hat Creek

Cassel, California

Study at the feet of one of fly-fishing's true gurus,
and then go out and let the trout teach you a lesson.

VITAL STATISTICS:

KEY SPECIES:
Browns, rainbows

Tackle:
Fly-fishing
Major Season:
May through November
Accommodations:
STUCCO COUNTRY FARMHOUSE
NUMBER OF ROOMS: 7
HANDICAPPED ACCESSIBLE: 3
MAXIMUM NUMBER OF GUESTS: 14
Meals: Thai shrimp, filet mignon, pork loin
Conference Groups: Yes
Rates: From $165 / day
Guides: Optional
Gratuities: $50 / day
Preferred Payment:
Cash, check or credit cards
Getting There:
Fly to Redding and rent a car.
Other Activities:
Bird-watching, canoeing/kayaking/ rafting, golf, horseback riding, hiking, swimming, tennis, wildlife photography

Contact:
Dick Galland
Clearwater House on Hat Creek
PO Box 90
21568 Cassel Rd
Cassel CA 96016
Ph: 530/335-5500
Fax: 530/335-5500
e-mail:
info@clearwatertrout.com
Web:
www.clearwatertrout.com

Off Season:
310 Sunset Way
Box 274
Muir Beach CA 94965
Ph: 415/381-1173
Fax: 415/383-9136

Agents:
Orvis endorsed

MOVE OVER West Yellowstone — Cassel, a little wide spot just north of Mt. Lassen, may be the best trout town in the West. It sits well within striking distance of a welter of fine trout rivers — the Pit, Fall, Upper Sacramento, McCloud — and famed Hat Creek flows through the center of town.

Rising on the slopes of Lassen Volcanic National Park, Hat Creek is a bustling little freestone stream that hustles down the mountain and breaks into the valley floor. Inflows from bubbling springs of the Rising River which joins Hat Creek just south of Cassel, cool the river to consistent temperatures and change its nature from a freestone meadow stream to a spring creek. Highly alkaline, the water supports a wealth of aquatic life, resulting in myriad hatches and substantial populations of crustacea.

Cassel sits astride the creek. Upstream of the town is a long shallow forebay impounding the intake for the Hat #1 generating plant for Pacific Gas & Electric. That water's very good, but it's the Trophy Trout mileage below Hat Powerhouse #2 that draws the raves. The first 200 yards below Lake Baum is a classic freestone riffle, a fine piece of water that can be fished so easily as to make every nimrod a pro. After the Powerhouse Riffle, Hat Creek slows and comes into its own. Sandy bottomed with beds of aquatic mosses and grasses that wave in the steady current, the creek dons the trappings of the quintessential spring creek. The trophy trout section of Hat Creek and, to lesser degree, the three miles above it are some of the most technically challenging water in the west. Hat Creek's quality is no accident. Thirty years ago, the Burney and San Francisco chapters of Trout Unlimited joined forces with Pacific Gas & Electric and the California Department of Fish and Game to create this trophy trout fishery.

Clearwater House is a light-gray stucco farmstead on the bank of Hat Creek. A sunny porch is draped with waders and rods, testimony to it's angling lineage and the number of fly-fishing schools held throughout the summer. Spacious guest rooms are all served by private baths. Dinners (shrimp pasta with green curry, sea bass with tomatillo relish) are accompanied by good wines and served on a round table under open beams. Orvis-endorsed, Clearwater offers a range of packages from bed-and-breakfast to full American plan with guided fishing.

[W E S T]

Henderson Springs

B i g   B e n d ,   C a l i f o r n i a

A new lake with huge rainbows and browns adds zest to this private angler's delight.

**VITAL
STATISTICS:**

KEY SPECIES:
Brookies, browns, rainbows

Tackle:
Fly-fishing
Major Season:
February through November
Accommodations:
Log lodge with lots of glass
Number of Rooms: 8
Handicapped Accessible: 1
Maximum Number of Guests: 12
Meals: Lamb, beef and pork
Conference Groups: Yes
Rates: From $205 / day
Guides: Optional
Gratuities: $20 / day
Preferred Payment:
Cash, check or credit cards
Getting There:
Fly to Redding and rent a car.
Other Activities:
Bird-watching, hiking, wildlife
photography

Contact:
Mark Henderson
Henderson Springs
PO Box 220
Big Bend CA 96011
Ph: 530/337-6917
Fax: 530/337-6257
e-mail:
mark@hendersonsprings.com
Web:
www.hendersonsprings.com

SECLUSION IS VALUED almost as much as fine and aggressive fish by trout anglers. Here in Mt. Shasta country resides a small ranch of 500 acres where rainbows and browns grow huge, and where no more than a dozen people will ever fish at a time. Four blue-water lakes rimmed with pine, spruce and oak, range in size from seven to 20 acres. Floating peat islands drift slowly in the spring-fed currents of the lake. The mats are rich with aquatic life. Big trout of up to 10 pounds cruise the dark green shade underneath. They feed as their hunger tells them, or when offered a morsel that's too good to pass up.

That's where you come in. Think of your fly boxes as a deli for trout. What will entice a strike. A Woolly Bugger or bead-head nymph on a medium sinking line? A scud? A muddler?

Sometimes, a bit of split-shot is needed to get the fly down fast, though casting with such combinations is cumbersome. Fishing is from pontoon boats or float tubes — no other watercraft allowed. Don't become mesmerized by the lakes; there's half a mile of fine spring creek that flows from one of the lakes to the Pit River. Like the lakes, this spring creek mileage is stocked with rainbows and browns.

At Henderson Springs, most guests do not use guides, though they are available. So is fly-fishing instruction. It's best to pick up tackle before you arrive, though float tubes and fins can be rented. Fishing is strictly catch-and-release, barbless hook and fly-fishing. And you'll find that these waters fish best early in the season (April, May) and late, in October.

The lodge is masterful. Framed by towering peaks on three sides, the lodge marries local log architecture with lots of glass. Its five bedrooms and three baths, two living rooms, and a huge deck provide inspiring vistas of the creek, rolling hills and the mountains beyond. Breakfast and dinner are served family-style; heart healthy and vegetarian meals are available, and meals are timed to miss major hatches. Anglers are sent out with boxed lunches. In addition to the main lodge, the ranch includes a housekeeping cottage with a single bedroom, sleeping loft for four and fully-equipped kitchen.

VITAL STATISTICS:

KEY SPECIES:
Browns, rainbows

Tackle:
Fly-fishing, spinning
Major Season:
April through October
Accommodations:
Quaint Craftsman-style lodge
Number of Rooms: 18
Handicapped Accessible: 6
Maximum Number of Guests: 56
Meals: Exceptional fare in the restaurant
Conference Groups: Yes
Rates: From $40 / night
Guides: $275
Gratuities: 20%
Preferred Payment:
Cash, check or credit cards
Getting There:
Fly to Redding and rent a car.
Other Activities:
Big game, waterfowling, wingshooting, bird-watching, boating, canoeing/ kayaking/rafting, golf, horseback riding, hiking, swimming, water skiing, wildlife photography

Contact:
Gary York
Pit River Lodge
PO Box 920
Pit One Power House Road
Fall River Mills CA 906028-0920
Ph: 530/336-5005
Fax: 530/336-5013
e-mail:
pitriverlodge@msn.net
Web:
www.pitriverlodge.com

Pit River Lodge

Fall River Mills, California

A night in this classic California Craftsman-style inn puts you in fine shape to fight the Pit's big 'bows.

AFTER WORLD WAR I, the nation's thirst for electricity fueled a race to build power plants, and the rivers of northeastern California were prime candidates. A dam and powerhouse were under construction in the area, and the contractor needed housing for its workers. And so it was that this lodge came to be built on 44 acres along the Pit River, one of California's blue ribbon trout streams. California pioneered the Craftsman architectural style: wide eaves and deep porches with small-paned windows tucked beneath. The style is comfortable, connoting a kind of place that makes you feel good going to it.

Two wings branch out from the white-columned entrance to the lodge. Inside are 11 guest rooms decorated with period antiques and featuring private baths. The lodge also holds a fine restaurant. Anglers gravitate to the Annex, an adjacent cottage of similar style with five bedrooms and two shared baths. Rooms include only one twin bed, but after a day on the Pit or Fall River, that's all you need. Also on the grounds are three cottages with kitchen facilities for families or groups of anglers who want to do their own thing.

The fishing is as varied as it is superb. Choose from Hat Creek at nearby Cassel with water for novice and expert alike. The spring-fed Fall River joins the Pit at Fall River Mills. The Fall is rainbow water of peerless quality, but it flows largely through private land. Access is limited. Most anglers fish dry flies and float the river in john-boats powered by a pair of electric trolling motors. Carpeted with undulating aquatic weed, the Fall is rich with rainbows and browns. The Pit River, too, offers fine angling, but it's often filled with canoeists and rafters in the summer. Don't let that bother you. Fish get used to seeing bouncing watercraft filled with boisterous vacationers. They continue to feed and if you can steel yourself to ignore the chatter, you'll catch some very good fish. If you're looking for quieter water, you can reach the McCloud and the Upper Sacramento and still be back in time for a late dinner.

Pit River Lodge is one of those places that's near activities for the whole family. Golf is a short cart-ride away. Biking and hiking, as well as canoeing, are on the agenda here; so ,too, is day tripping to Lassen Volcanic National Park and Mount Shasta. Everybody can find something to do here and that's fine, 'cause it means you're free to fish.

Rippling Waters Resort

Hat Creek, California

Stop in this wide spot in the road, soak up the shade, and do your best to seduce Hat Creek's browns and 'bows.

VITAL
STATISTICS:

KEY SPECIES:
Browns, rainbows

Tackle:
Fly-fishing, spinning
Major Season:
May through September
Accommodations:
RUSTIC CABINS UNDER THE TREES
NUMBER OF CABINS: 6
MAXIMUM NUMBER OF GUESTS: 23
Meals: Self-catered
Conference Groups: Yes
Rates: From $70 / night / 2
Guides: Available on special
request
Gratuities: Angler's discretion
Preferred Payment:
Cash, check or credit cards
Getting There:
Fly to Redding and rent a car.
Other Activities:
Big game, waterfowling, wingshooting,
bird-watching, boating, golf, hiking,
skiing, swimming, tennis, wildlife
photography

Contact:
Ann or Don Johnson
Rippling Waters Resort
16241 Hwy 89
Hat Creek CA 96040
Ph: 530/335-7400
e-mail:
ripplingwaters@norcalis.net
Web:
www.ripplingwaters.com

HAT CREEK LOPES ALONG Route 89 as it flows through Lassen National Forest on its way to fame as one of the most technical of all trout streams in the mileage below Cassel. Above Cassel, Hat Creek traces a winding path through pastures, tawny with grasses that wave in the afternoon breeze. Some of this water is lined with willows and brush, and feels like a spring creek. But the further up the valley you go, the greater the gradient and the more the creek takes on the character of a free stone stream. At the little hamlet of Hat Creek, seven miles south of Cassel, Hat Creek River becomes shaded, and under the trees lies Rippling Waters Resort.

Through the resort flows more than a section of Hat Creek. Mostly pocket water here, the creek holds good populations of trout — some stocked and others that are bred in the stream. Three other creeks wind through the property, and there's also a trophy pond where children can tussle with monster trout and adults can give their light rods a real workout. Not only are the premiere runs of Hat Creek within a few minutes drive, but so too are the wonderful runs of the Pit and Fall rivers.

Rippling Waters is a family resort with half-a-dozen housekeeping cabins scattered under lofty pines. Staying here won't break your bank, especially if one of your party is a culinary whiz and the other can uncork the wine. You won't find a staff of macho guides here, but the resort's store carries patterns that work and basic tackle should you have forgotten something. Should you require expert assistance, Don or Ann Johnson, who own the resort, will call one of a number of outstanding guides in the area.

Sorensen's Resort

H o p e   V a l l e y ,   C a l i f o r n i a

A potpourri of nature talks, music, and history add zest and depth to fishing the Carson.

VITAL STATISTICS:

KEY SPECIES:
Brook, brown, cutthroat, rainbows

Tackle:
Fly-fishing, spinning
Major Season:
May through September
Accommodations:
SCANDINAVIAN-STYLE CABINS
NUMBER OF ROOMS: 30
HANDICAPPED ACCESSIBLE: 1
MAXIMUM NUMBER OF GUESTS: 100
Meals: Cook your own or dine in the new restaurant
Conference Groups: Yes
Rates: From $80 / night / 2
Guides: $50 / hour
Gratuities: Angler's discretion
Preferred Payment:
Cash, check or credit cards
Getting There:
Fly to Reno, NV, and rent a car.
Other Activities:
Bird-watching, hiking, skiing, swimming, wildlife photography, family activities

Contact:
John & Patty Brissenden
Sorensen's Resort
14255 Hwy. 88
Hope Valley CA 96120
Ph: 800/423.9949

NOT MORE than 25 miles south of Lake Tahoe lies a year-round resort where the flavor is more than faintly Scandinavian and the fishing is far better than fair. Add a diverse program of evening talks by authors, demonstrations and exhibits by artists, and concerts, and you've got a resort that is really something special. And there's also the new restaurant with its marvelous eclectic fare.

First the fishing. The eastern slope of the Sierra Nevada's is drier and more sparsely vegetated that the west. Low willows and banks of grass line meadow waters that pick up shade as they trip through canyon runs. In this neck of the woods, the East Fork of the Carson River gets most of the play and, to be sure, it has its moments. However, the West Fork, including the mileage that runs through Sorensen's Resort, can be exceptional. The resort waters are stocked with rainbows in the one- to two-pound range. Wild brookies up to 12 inches or so readily take almost any well-presented pattern. Browns are larger than the rainbows but less populous. This is not big water at all. Less than 50 feet in many places, the river features riffles, pocket water, plunge pools and deep holes.

In late April and early May, the West Fork runs high with meltwater, making wading somewhat of a challenge. Yet anglers score well using sinking-tip lines and weighted nymphs or sculpin patterns. Later, from the end of May into October, standard dries and wets produce consistently. The ideal rod is an eight-foot six-inch 4-weight, according to Judy Warren, author of *Alpine Angling* and master of Horse Feathers Fly Fishing School at the resort. In September, grasshoppers play an important role in trout diets, and October brings caddis. Fish West Fork headwaters for brook trout or a number of the ponds for cutthroats, Mackinaw (lake trout) and at least three species of rainbows: golden, Paiute and Kamloops. Rimmed with stately Jeffrey pines and fringed with mock peach, the ponds are float-tube water that can also be fished from shore or boat.

Woodstoves in Sorensen's quaint log cabins take out the chill of early summer mornings, and their kitchenettes allow a quick bite before hitting the river. After fishing, amble over to the restaurant for breakfast or, if the fishing has been really good, for lunch. Sorensen's 30 cabins and main lodge lie dotted under the pines, and each cozy cabin provides private baths.

The Big K Guest Ranch

E l k t o n ,   O r e g o n

Sinuous, the Umpqua slides through the foothills carrying a mother lode of smallmouth, steelhead and salmon.

VITAL STATISTICS:

KEY SPECIES:
King/chinook salmon, shad, silver/coho salmon, smallmouth, steelhead, sturgeon, striped bass/rockfish

Tackle:
Casting, fly-fishing, spinning, trolling
Major Season:
All year
Accommodations:
CABINS OF LOG OVERLOOKING THE RIVER
NUMBER OF ROOMS: 20
HANDICAPPED ACCESSIBLE: All
MAXIMUM NUMBER OF GUESTS: 80
Meals: Hearty ranch fare
Conference Groups: Yes
Rates: From $115 / night
Guides: $200
Gratuities: 15% - 20%; angler's discretion
Preferred Payment:
Cash, check or credit cards
Getting There:
Fly to Eugene and rent a car.
Other Activities:
Big game, waterfowling, wingshooting, bird-watching, horseback riding, hiking, swimming, wildlife photography

Contact:
Kathie Williamson
The Big K Guest Ranch
20029 Highway 138 W
Elkton OR 97436
Ph: 800/390-2445
Fax: 541/584-2395
e-mail:
aparrish@jeffnet.org
Web:
www.big-k.com

BELOW THE FORMED NORTH FORK, the Umpqua settles down. It winds gently among forested ridges of the valley between the Cascade Range to the east and the Coast Range to the west. You wouldn't call the river tranquil, yet its long pools and gentle riffles offer a kind of respite from the hustling, brawling water that characterizes its passage through the mountains.

In the middle mileage near Elkton, about 20 miles west of Interstate 5, the Umpqua's reputation is built on smallmouth bass. Buzz and spinnerbaits, thrown deep into shadows cast by dark firs looming over the banks, generate ferocious strikes from smallies of three to five pounds. Fat streamers — Woolly Buggers and Zonkers — serve fly rodders well. This is a summer game, best played from May through September.

Those who cast streamers may find themselves in for a rude shock. Summer steelhead ply the same runs as smallmouth from June through September. But don't worry, if one takes your streamer, you'll know it. The better steelhead angling comes in the winter under leaden, fretful skies. Fish of 25 inches or so are not rare. Chinook make spring and fall runs in the river, and coho pick up where summer steelies leave off. Striped bass use this water from March into June, and sturgeon appear throughout the year.

Though driftboats are the most popular conveyance for anglers, much of the water near the ranch is wadeable. And though fly is the tackle of choice for all but sturgeon, spinfishermen do well. The middle Umpqua is good-size water and The Big K, a 2500-acre working ranch that's been in the Kesterson family for decades, fronts on ten miles of it. The ranch employs a staff of guides, but guests may freelance if they wish. Boxed lunches are available for anglers out on the water all day. Fishing seasons overlap big game, upland bird and waterfowl seasons. Check the dates and bring an appropriate firearm or bow.

Twenty log guest cabins climb the gentle hill behind the main lodge that overlooks the river. All rooms have private baths, and all are handicapped accessible. Dinners feature hearty cuts of beef and lamb, as well as quail, duck and salmon.

C&J Lodge

Maupin, Oregon

Red-side trout and steelhead make the Deschutes the place to fish in September and October.

VITAL STATISTICS:

KEY SPECIES:
Red-side trout, steelhead

Tackle:
Fly-fishing
Major Season:
February through November
Accommodations:
RUSTIC RIVERSIDE INN
NUMBER OF ROOMS: 11
HANDICAPPED ACCESSIBLE: 1
MAXIMUM NUMBER OF GUESTS: 24
Meals: Bed-and-breakfast with
dinners by special arrangement
Conference Groups: Yes
Rates: From $55
Guides: $200 walk in; $450 / drift
for two
Gratuities: Angler's discretion
Preferred Payment: Cash, check
or credit cards
Getting There: Fly to Portland or
Redland and rent a car.
Other Activities: Wingshooting,
bird-watching, canoeing/kayaking/
rafting, hiking, wildlife photography

Contact:
Carrol & Judy White
C&J Lodge
304 Bakeoven Rd
PO Box 130
Maupin OR 97037
Ph: 541/395-2404
Fax: 541/395-2494
e-mail:
cnjlodge@centurytel.net
Web:
www.deschutesriver.com

OREGON'S TWO TOP steelhead rivers — the North Fork of the Umpqua and the Deschutes — rise on opposite sides of the divide in the Mount Thielsen Wilderness north of Crater Lake National Park. In their headwaters, both are better than fair trout streams. But the North Fork of the Umpqua quickly becomes steelhead water, and on the 100 mile-run of the Deschutes, it's the lower third that captures the hearts of die-hard steelheaders.

Good fishing begins below the town of Madras. Here you'll find runs of "red-side" trout — that hybrid of rainbow and cutthroat which is native to this river. Fast growing (four to five inches a year), red-sides fight more fiercely than their length (12 to 16 inches) or weight (average one to two pounds) would suggest. To fish them, use both dries (midges, little Blue-winged Olives, Pale Morning Duns and Pale Evening Duns, Salmonflies and Golden Stoneflies) and wets. Angling for red-sides picks up in February and trails off in November.

Red-sides would perform in the center ring were they encountered in any other than a river with steelhead. But here, chrome-sided, sea-run rainbows of both hatchery and wild persuasion take the spotlight. Starting by the end of June and running into December, steelhead use the river. Fish with clipped adipose fins (behind the dorsal) may be, and should be, kept. While the state stocks these fish to satisfy those who like to catch-and-eat, it's not interested in diluting the wild gene pool with hatchery strains. Wild fish run smaller (four to six pounds) than stocked fish (six to nine pounds). Best months for steelhead are September and October.

The odds of taking steelhead in the Deschutes are probably better than in the Umpqua, simply because the river is bigger and there's more fishable water. Among the best trips is the float through the canyon below Maupin. You'll have to get out of the boat to fish; that's the law. Guides like John Smeraglio of the Deschutes Canyon Fly Shop (541/395-2565) advise anglers to not be in too great a hurry to fish the center of the river. Often, at dawn, fish are holding under the junipers and aspens along the bank. "You'll never need to wet your knees," says Smeraglio.

Attractive and comfortably furnished, C&J Lodge provides rooms with private baths. During steelhead season, breakfast fixings are delivered the night before to anglers' rooms as they like to head for the stream by 5:00 a.m.

Little Creek Lodge

La Grande, Oregon

While the Grande Ronde isn't as big as the Deschutes, its steelhead and smallmouth don't seem the least bit subdued.

VITAL STATISTICS:

KEY SPECIES:
Rainbows, smallmouth, steelhead

Tackle:
Casting, fly-fishing, spinning
Major Season:
April through November
Accommodations:
RUSTIC LOG LODGE AND GUEST HOUSE
NUMBER OF ROOMS: 4
MAXIMUM NUMBER OF GUESTS: 8
Meals: Hearty family fare
Conference Groups: Yes
Rates: From $175 / double occupancy
Guides: Included
Gratuities: $20
Preferred Payment:
Cash, check or credit cards
Getting There:
Fly to Lewiston, ID, and rent a car.
Other Activities:
Wingshooting, bird-watching, canoeing/kayaking/rafting, hiking, wildlife photography

Contact:
John Ecklund
Little Creek
1505 L Ave
La Grande OR 97850
Ph: 541/963-7878
Fax: 541/963-7878
e-mail:
littleor@vcinet.com

Agents:
John Eustice & Associates
Kaufman's

RISING in the Wallowa/Whitman National Forest, the Grande Ronde tumbles off the slope of the Blue Mountains and turns north as it enters Rich Valley. Roads trace its course until it picks up the waters of the Wallowa, northeast of Elgin. There it enters a 40-mile canyon where the only access is to raft the Class III rips. At Troy, the surging river breaks out of the gorge for 20 miles or so. During this run, it's followed by country roads and crosses into Washington. Just downstream from Rt. 129, the river dives into another canyon which carries it to the Snake River, 30 miles away. Much of the Grande Ronde wears the federal "wild and scenic river" designation, and it is justly deserved. John Eklund's Little Creek Lodge is located on the mileage just northeast of Troy, and from the lodge, he runs a number of fishing excursions for steelhead, smallmouth and rainbows.

A mixture of wild and stocked steelhead run in the Grande Ronde. One of the best introductions to fishing for these finicky sea-run rainbows is through six-day schools featuring Bill McMillan, author of *Dry Line Steelhead*. The curriculum covers topwater steelheading (dry fly, skated fly, walking flies), as well as wet fly presentations. Morning instruction on the first two days is followed by fishing on the lodge's half mile of river. On the last two days, you'll spend all your time streamside with McMillan and your guide. Tuition: $1,850 per angler. You'll find rainbows in the 14-inch range in the water near the lodge during summer. Little Creek runs guided floats on the Grande Ronde, where you may encounter bull trout as well. Fish the hatches in the morning, and muddlers and leeches after midday. The price is from $1,375 per person for a five-day trip. For smallmouth, John shifts operations to the John Day, Oregon's longest free-flowing river. Four or five-day float trips put anglers on some of the best bronzeback fishing in the states. Action is best between June and September. Introduced to the river in 1971, smallmouth bass thrive in these waters. Days of 100 fish with several in the two to three pound class are normal. The price is from $1,100 per person for a four-day trip.

Built in 1984, the full-timbered lodge combines creature comforts with traditional western ambience. Sit on the back porch and view the river and its canyon beyond. Your room may be in the lodge or one of four in the cedar guest house. Prime ribs, pasta and seafood will greet you when you walk down the hill for dinner.

Lonesome Duck

Chiloquin, Oregon

The Williamson is one of those creeks that you hate to love.

VITAL STATISTICS:

KEY SPECIES:
Browns, rainbows

Tackle:
Fly-fishing

Major Season:
Late May through October

Accommodations:
Three log guest homes
Number of Rooms: 8
Maximum Number of Guests: 18

Meals: Be your own gourmet cook
or arrange for catered meals

Conference Groups: Yes

Rates: From $160 / night / 2

Guides: $260

Gratuities: $30

Preferred Payment:
Cash, check or credit cards

Getting There:
Fly to Klamath Falls and rent a car.

Other Activities:
Bird-watching, boating,
canoeing/kayaking/rafting, golf,
horseback riding, hiking, skiing,
snowmobiling, swimming, tennis,
wildlife photography

Contact:
Steve Hilbert
Lonesome Duck
32955 Hwy 97 W
Chiloquin OR 97406
Ph: 800/367-2540
Fax: 541/783-2994
e-mail:
steveh@lonesomeduck.com
Web:
www.lonesomeduck.com

Off Season:
PO Box 8164
Incline Village NV 89452
Ph: 800/367-2540
Fax: 702/831-3039

THE MADNESS OF IT. You see the rises and, every once in a while, the roll of a dorsal fin a second or two after the take. So crystalline is the water that even the most delicate of leaders seems like a hawser to the leviathan 'bows cruising below. You go as light as you dare, and then one size smaller. The fly, of course, is as precise an imitation of a mayfly or caddis as a human can make. And the cast, well, micro currents play hob with even the best presentations. Your best will have to do.

To say that the Williamson is a technical fishery is like saying that a Ferrari is a sports car. Ledges, choppy riffles, glassy glides, aquatic fronds waving in the current. Willows crown grassy undercut banks. Rainbows run up the Williamson from Upper Klamath Lake to spawn. The largest of them slide into the river when summer sun and air temperatures warm the lake to intolerable levels, sometime in late June or early July. In some cool wet seasons they may not move in at all. Under those circumstances, you can attempt to seduce smaller, resident fish. They, too, can prove very stubborn.

That's what guides will tell you about this river in southcentral Oregon. Take it with a grain or two of salt. Anglers wedded to dry fly-fishing may not be as successful here as those willing to chuck nymphs and other subsurface patterns. Most effective are streamers such as Woolly Buggers, Zonkers and big nymphs. Fished across and down on a sink-tip line, with a slow pull-and-pause retrieve, these flies can be deadly. Try them also in the subsurface film. The glory hatch must be *Hexagenia limbata* in the mileage below Chiloquin. Cast drys or subsurface variations toward the bank. And don't overlook hoppers in August and early September.

All of this, of course, wasn't news to Steve Hilbert when he put up a resort of three log homes under the pines. Arrowhead Cottage boasts two bedrooms, single bath, dining room, living room, fireplace, kitchen and front porch where you can watch the river roll by. Rivers Edge and Eagle's Nest are larger, having additional sleeping lofts and baths. Eagle's Nest is a non-smoking cabin, and the view from the front porch across a pond to the mountains is stunning. Bring your own food or arrange for the Hilberts to provide meals in your dining room. Steve's resort includes a private mile-and-a-half of the river. Boats to fish the river are available at the lodge and licenses and tackle can be found at Williamson River Anglers.

Morrison's Rogue River Lodge

M e r l i n ,   O r e g o n

*Fight a steelhead "half-pounder" on a light rod
and don't be surprised if it goes 12 pounds.*

**VITAL
STATISTICS:**

KEY SPECIES:
**King/chinook salmon,
silver/coho salmon,
steelhead**

Tackle:
Fly-fishing, spinning
Major Season:
Late August through November
Accommodations:
GRACEFUL LODGE AND CABINS
NUMBER OF ROOMS: 13
MAXIMUM NUMBER OF GUESTS: 40
Meals: Regional gourmet
Conference Groups: Yes
Rates: From $300 / night / 2;
(numerous packages)
Guides: $255
Gratuities: $30 - $80
Angler's discretion
Preferred Payment:
Cash, check or credit cards
Getting There:
Fly to Medford and rent a car.
Other Activities:
Boating, canoeing/kayaking/rafting,
golf, hiking, swimming, tennis

Contact:
Michelle Hanten
**Morrison's Rogue River
Lodge**
8500 Galice Rd
Merlin OR 97532
Ph: 800/826-1963
Fax: 541/476-4953
e-mail:
info@morrisonslodge.com
Web:
www.morrisonslidge.com

Agents:
Orvis endorsed

IF YOU HAD TO CHOOSE one place to spend every October for the rest of your natural born days, you could do worse, much worse, than the Rogue near Merlin. The Rogue is well known. It rises west of Crater Lake National Park and then dances down the mountains to Medford where it rather abruptly breaks off to the west. You can follow its course on State Route 62 and thence from Medford on Interstate 5. A side road off the Interstate will run you through Merlin, past Hellgate Canyon and Indian Mary Park, and through the village of Galice, beyond which the Rogue rages through the Coast Range to its destiny with the Pacific at Wedderburn.

The Rogue is a river for steelhead and salmon. Its steelhead are not huge by the standards set by writers of articles published in fly-fishing magazines. Most range between 12 and 18 inches. They're called "half-pounders" for reasons that are completely obscure. These fish actually weigh a pound to two, but they fight like scalded dogs and are as stubborn as hickory. Hook one on your five-weight and watch it peel your backing down to nothing. Five or six of these will leave you with one of those dumb grins on your face. Of course, running in the same water are steelhead of six to eight pounds, and fall runs of chinook and coho. Most times salmon are only taken on lures or bait, but not always. If you're working light gear for half-pounders and one of these big guys slams your fly, you're in for a treat, or heartbreak, and maybe both. Chinooks also run the Rogue from mid-May through June. The upper river can provide good summer trout fishing, particularly during the June salmon fly hatch. And a little travel will put you on the Wood or Williamson for trout in the height of summer.

Tucked across a little meadow from the river, Morrison's continues to be a destination of choice for anglers who are a bit laid-back. Framed by deep woods, this lodge has been hosting fisher folk for more than 50 years. It wears its age with grace and *joi de vive*. The main lodge contains four comfy guest rooms; cottages with fireplaces contain nine more. It's renowned for gourmet regional cuisine (poached salmon with saffron beurre blanc sauce is a favorite) and a good cellar of imported, as well as California and Northwest vintages. And at this Orvis-endorsed lodge, you'll find a complete fly shop that rents and sells whatever you need.

Steamboat Inn

Steamboat, Oregon

Experience the last of Zane Grey's rivers from a lodge established for steelheading anglers.

VITAL STATISTICS:

KEY SPECIES:
Steelhead

Tackle:
Fly-fishing
Major Season:
March through December
Accommodations:
WONDERFUL CABINS HIGH ABOVE THE RIVER
NUMBER OF ROOMS: 19
HANDICAPPED ACCESSIBLE: 2
MAXIMUM NUMBER OF GUESTS: 60
Meals: Regional gourmet cuisine
Conference Groups: Yes
Rates: From $130 / night / 2
Guides: $175
Gratuities: 10%;
Angler's discretion
Preferred Payment:
Cash, check or credit cards
Getting There:
Fly to Eugene and rent a car.
Other Activities:
Bird-watching, canoeing/kayaking/
rafting, hiking, swimming

Contact:
Jim Van Loan
Steamboat Inn
42705 N. Umpqua Hwy
Steamboat OR 97447-9703
Ph: 800/840-8825
Fax: 541/498-2411
e-mail:
stmbtinn@rosenet.net
Web:
www.thesteamboatinn.com

IN THE LANGUAGE OF the Yoncalla Indians, Umpqua means "thundering water." Right they are. When snow melts on the Calapooya Mountains and the back side of Crater Lake National Park, the river fills and roars, crashing into bluffs, ripping over ledges, spinning wildly like a leaping steelhead at the end of your line. Rambunctious as a teenager, this river will never grow up, though in summer periods of low flows, its frothy jade shoots and emerald pools appear almost benign.

The North Fork of the Umpqua was the last river that Zane Grey loved. He found it on the way to fish for king salmon on Campbell River. That was in 1932. He returned annually, drawn by heavy runs of summer steelhead. While in camp in 1937, he suffered the stroke that would kill him two years hence. The river is much changed from Grey's time, yet it is the same. Though lakes have been impounded in its headwaters, the river still flows cold and green through the black rock canyon where he fished. Steelhead, fewer now, still make annual runs. Summer fish start in June and are in the system until October. The winter run begins in January and reaches its peak in February before tailing off in March. The 32 miles from Rock Creek upstream to Soda Springs Dam is fly-fishing-only, catch-and-release water.

The river is narrow in the mileage upstream from Rock Creek. It flows through a gorge of slab rock, chutes, occasional gravel bars and runs so deep that, though the water is very clear, you'll never see the bottom. It is good water, ideal for an eight-weight. Most of the pressure on the river comes in summer when the steelhead are a little smaller, and approximately 2,400 wild fish and twice that number of stockers are found. The best fishing, though, comes in winter, when gray skies and blustery days drive snow in your eyes as you cast. The steelhead of winter run larger, and anglers are many times fewer.

Among the best locales for picking up info is during dinner at the Steamboat Inn. The inn's wide sugar-pine table has hosted fishermen for more than 60 years. On the table today you'll find the superb regional cuisine of co-owner Sharon Van Loan and her colleague, Pat Lee (also an outstanding steelhead guide). A range of accommodations is available: eight pine-paneled streamside cabins; five modern cottages in the woods with soaking tubs, fireplaces, lofts and mini-kitchens; two luxurious and romantic river suites; and a quartet of three-bedroom homes.

Williamson River Club at Crystalwood Lodge

F t .   K l a m a t h ,   O r e g o n

Eagles, elk, rainbows so large they look like pike, and a lodge of the highest caliber — who could wish for more?

VITAL STATISTICS:

KEY SPECIES:
Browns, rainbows, steelhead

Tackle:
Fly-fishing
Flyouts to Remote Waters: Yes
Major Season:
May through September
Accommodations:
REMODELED HOMESTEAD
NUMBER OF ROOMS: 7
HANDICAPPED ACCESSIBLE: SOME
MAXIMUM NUMBER OF GUESTS: 14
Meals: Elegant regional cuisine
Conference Groups: Yes
Rates: From $1,050 / 3 days,
double occupancy
Guides: $325
Gratuities: $30
Preferred Payment:
Cash, check or credit cards
Getting There:
Fly to Medford and rent a car.
Other Activities:
Waterfowling, wingshooting, bird-
watching, boating, canoeing/kayaking/
rafting, golf, hiking, tennis, wildlife
photography

Contact:
Rich McIntyre
Williamson River Club at
Crystalwood Lodge
PO Box 469
Ft Klamath OR 97626
Ph: 541/381-2322
Fax: 541/381-2328
e-mail:
salmo99@aol.com
Web:
www.fbn-flyfish.com/crystalwoodlodge

Agents:
Frontiers

IF STALKING some of the largest rainbows in North America (and by large we're talking Alaska-sized and better) lies deep in your dreams, it's time to wake up and beat a path to Crystalwood Lodge on Crystal Creek near the Klamath National Wildlife Refuge. Located on a ranch of 130 acres, the lodge also fishes a second ranch of 230 acres nearby. Both contain a number of spring creeks and ponds managed for trophy rainbows and steelhead. A short walk from the lodge puts you onto fish you'll remember for ever.

Within a few minutes' drive of the lodge are the Wood and Williamson rivers. The Wood, a trophy spring creek, holds resident populations of browns in the five- to six-pound category. You'll also find two races of migratory rainbows, reportedly a unique strain with genetic links to the steelhead that spawned in these waters before dams were built downstream. Fish here are huge for the lower forty-eight; 15-pounders are taken every year. Similar to, but larger than, the Wood, the Williamson River holds a resident population of rainbows, and hosts two migratory strains that come into the river from Upper Klamath Lake. Fish range between three and 12 pounds. Both the rivers have the reputation for being somewhat technical, meaning hatch-matching and precise casting are the surest way for trophy fish. The best times to fish them is in July (trico and a hexagenia hatch) and in August and September, when 'hoppers dot the surface and big rainbows are there to feed on them.

Summer steelhead are also on the docket. The fabled North Fork of the Umpqua is within an hour's drive, as is the Rogue. Steelhead run in the five- to eight-pound class, but some monsters of 15 pounds and more have been taken by Crystalwood guests. And when you're not fishing, cast your Swarovski's toward the sandhill cranes and other avian species on the refuge. Bird-watching here is among the best in the world.

Crystalwood Lodge began its life as the homestead on the ranch. Over the years, it's seen several renovations, the most recent at the hands of Rich McIntire and wife, Karen Greene. You'll find seven bedrooms with private baths. Dinners are elegant (fine wines, crystal and china) and somewhat exotic (prime rib of buffalo). Rates include lodging and meals. Guests may fish without a guide if they wish, but most hire one from the staff employed by the ranch.

Brightwater House

Forks, Washington

Deep in the lush Olympic Peninsula lies this lovely B & B, with the Sol Duc's steelhead right in the back yard.

VITAL STATISTICS:

KEY SPECIES:
Cutthroat, king/chinook salmon, silver/coho salmon, steelhead

Tackle:
Fly-fishing
Major Season:
All year
Accommodations:
COMFORTABLE ROOMS IN A TRADITIONAL BED-AND-BREAKFAST
NUMBER OF ROOMS: 3
HANDICAPPED ACCESSIBLE: 1
MAXIMUM NUMBER OF GUESTS: 7
Meals: Varied breakfast menu; dinners in town
Conference Groups: No
Rates: From $70 / night
Guides: $200
Gratuities: Angler's discretion
Preferred Payment:
Cash, check or credit cards
Getting There:
Fly to Port Angeles or Seattle and rent a car.
Other Activities:
Biking, bird-watching, boating, canoeing/kayaking/rafting, hiking, swimming

Contact:
Richard Chesmore
Brightwater House
PO Box 1222
Forks WA 98331
Ph: 360/347-5453
Web:
www.northolympic.com/brightwater

RIVERS RUN THROUGH MANY PLACES, but often they're accompanied by hordes of tourists. But here on the western flanks of the Olympic Mountains, steelhead run in so many seasons that you can avoid the masses and have stretches of river almost to yourself. Richard Chesmore does. For 200 days a year he fishes the Sol Duc, which for two-thirds of a mile cuts around the lush 60 acres where he and wife, Beth, have their modern bed-and-breakfast, Brightwater House.

The Sol Duc River rises in Olympic National Park and pushes through deep forest toward the Pacific. It's a year-round river. In June and July, sockeye salmon move up the river to spawn in it and in Lake Pleasant near its headwaters. Three distinct runs keep the river in steelhead all year. And if year-round steelheading isn't enough, you'll find fall and spring runs of chinook and silvers in July. Naturally, cutthroats up to 24 inches follow the salmon, just like rainbows in Alaska.

Steelhead are the premiere species. In October, hatchery stock begins to work its way upstream. In mid-January, native spawners enter the system. These are the biggest, some reaching more than 20 pounds. As that run passes, a final surge of slightly smaller (six- to 15-pound) fish enters in late May and remains through September, when the cycle begins again. Despite their prevalence, they are not easily caught. The Sol Duc is not a big stream and it is easily waded. But seldom is there room for long backcasts. (Spinfishing is permitted on much of the river, but Brightwater House caters to fly-fishers.) Rollcasting is a refined art here. That complicates matters because as water levels fall in summer, steelhead get spooky. Along with the Sol Duc, there's the Bogachiel, Hoh, Queets and Quinault — all rivers that drain the high volcanic mountains. These rivers, too, carry runs of steelhead and salmon.

Flowers riot around the entrance to Brightwater House and tall windows bring them right into the living room. Upstairs are three very comfortable rooms for guests. One is a small suite with a private bath; the other two share a bath. Breakfast is the only meal of the day — quiche and fritattas — but custom gourmet dinners are available on request. And in the town of Forks, you'll find a number of funky restaurants. Among the best guides in the area is Bob Pigott (360/327-2554). Book two days with him; the first to float the Sol Duc and the second to wade other rivers.

ALASKA

LASKA FIRES OUR dreams: five species of salmon — kings, silvers, reds, pinks, chums — will each burn line off your reel while you keep a weather eye peeled for b'rer griz who may want to fish your hole. Add rainbows reaching double digits, smokin' steelhead, arctic char, and ubiquitous Dolly Varden to your dance card. Float-toting Beavers and Cessnas land you on waters so remote it would take weeks to reach them on foot. Elsewhere, you can fish within 15 feet of your parked car. Alaska built its angling reputation on wild salmanoids, but there's halibut aplenty, as well as other bottom fish for anglers who so prefer. Accommodations range from utterly first-class abodes with gourmet chefs and matching wine cellars, to housekeeping cabins where you see the cook with every glance in a mirror. Waters of Iliamna and Bristol Bay draw most of the crowds. Yet there's excellent angling on Kodiak and Afognak islands, in the Aleutians, and the wild fjords of the state's southeast tail.

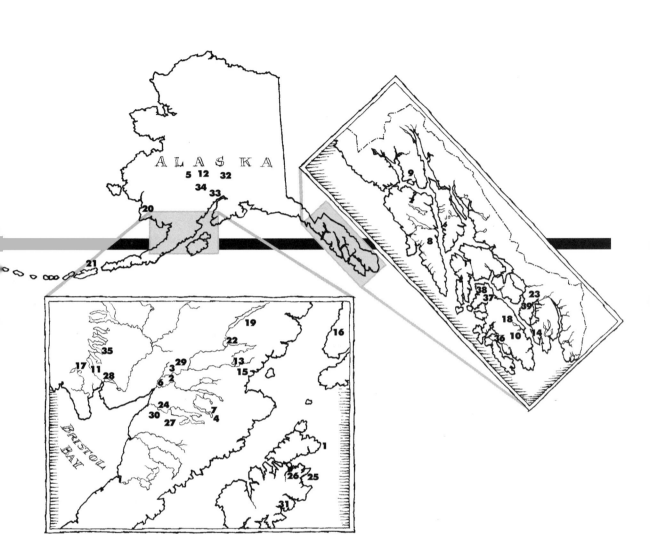

References:

FLY-FISHING ALASKA'S
WILD RIVERS
by Dan Heiner
Stackpole Books
5067 Ritter Road
Mechanicsburg PA 17055-6921
800/732-3669

FISHING ALASKA
by Evan and Margaret Swensen
Falcon Publishing Co.
PO Box 1718
Helena, MT 59624
406/442-6597

ROADSIDE GUIDE
TO FLY FISHING ALASKA
by Anthony J. Route
Johnson Books
1870 S. 57th Court
Boulder, CO 80301
800/258-5830

KENAI RIVER
by Anthony J. Route
Frank Amato Publications
PO Box 82112
Portland, OR 97282
800/541-9498

HOW TO CATCH
ALASKA'S TROPHY SPORTFISH

FISH ALASKA
ON DOLLAR$ A DAY

CHRIS BATIN'S
20 GREAT ALASKA
FISHING ADVENTURES

HOW TO CATCH
TROPHY HALIBUT
(W/TERRY RUDNIK)
by Christopher M. Batin
Alaska Angler Publications
PO Box 83550
Fairbanks, AK 99708
907/455-8000

Resources:

ALASKA DEPARTMENT OF
FISH AND GAME
Box 25526
Juneau, Alaska 99802
(907) 465-4100
web: www.fishgame.state.ak.us

Massive spruce beams support the high ceiling of the
great room in Bear Track Lodge, one of the finest
in southeastern Alaska's panhandle.

Afognak Wilderness Lodge

Seal Bay, Alaska

A pioneer husband and wife team runs an elegant family-style lodge on Afognak Island.

VITAL STATISTICS:

KEY SPECIES:
Bull trout/Dolly Varden, cod, halibut, pink salmon, rainbows, red/sockeye salmon, silver/coho salmon

Tackle:
Fly-fishing, spinning
Major Season:
June through September
Accommodations:
LOVELY LOG CABINS
NUMBER OF ROOMS: 6
MAXIMUM NUMBER OF GUESTS: 15
Meals: Hearty meals featuring regional seafood
Conference Groups: No
Rates: $450 / day
Guides: Included
Gratuities: $20 - $50 / day
Preferred Payment:
Cash, Check or Visa/MasterCard
Getting There:
Fly to Kodiak, AK, and catch the air taxi (about $100 round trip).
Other Activities:
Big game, waterfowling, wingshooting, boating, canoeing/kayaking/rafting, horseback riding, hiking, skiing, swimming

Contact:
Shannon Randall
Afognak Wilderness Lodge
Seal Bay AK 99697
Ph: 907/486-6442
Fax: 907/486-2217
e-mail:
afognak@usa.net
Web:
www.afognaklodge.com

YOU MIGHT CALL THIS the American Family Randall. These hearty pioneers, who came to the wilds of Afognak with little more than chainsaws, an old Jeep, an engine-powered winch and gin pole, and plenty of ingenuity. They hand built one of the finest lodges in Alaska. Three two-bedroom cabins of heavy, honey-toned log sit on a spruce-capped point that juts into Seal Bay. The main lodge presides over a cusp in the shore. Cabins are delightfully furnished and include private baths.

In the main lodge, spiral log stairs climb to the second story, which the Randalls have occupied since the cabins were built. Meals, well, you don't know the meaning of hearty until Shannon feeds you a breakfast of sourdough pancakes, eggs and halibut fingers. At Afognak, everyone — family and guests — eats together at a long spruce table with stumps for chairs.

Guests come to Afognak, a low and brooding island to the northeast of Kodiak, to photograph wildlife — deer, bear, seals, walrus and waterfowl of every description. While Afognak lacks the big rivers of its sibling Kodiak Island, you'll find scores of clear streams draining the island's low mountains, with boggy lakes in between. Each of these streams is a magnet for spawning salmon. First come the sockeyes, from June 10 to the middle of July. They're followed by pinks that run through the end of August. Silvers hit full stride from August 1 through September 15. You'll find rainbows up to 20 inches all summer. Because the streams are small and generally shallow, the salmon are accessible not only to you, but to brown bears as well. When fishing the salmon runs, Randall carries a .375 H&H for insurance.

If you prefer to fish the salt, the lodge's fleet of cabin cruisers and Makos can take you trolling for king salmon (up to 40 pounds) or put you to work lifting halibut of up to 300 pounds from the ocean floor.

[A L A S K A]

Alagnak Lodge

K i n g   S a l m o n ,   A l a s k a

Stay at a comfortable, basic lodge, and fish for salmon, rainbows and grayling in any weather.

VITAL STATISTICS:

KEY SPECIES:
Arctic char, chum salmon, grayling, king/chinook salmon, pink salmon, rainbows, silver/coho salmon

Tackle:
Casting, fly-fishing, spinning
Flyouts to Remote Waters: Yes
Major Season:
June through September
Accommodations:
MODERN TWO-STORY FRAME LODGE
NUMBER OF ROOMS: 14
HANDICAPPED ACCESSIBLE: 2
MAXIMUM NUMBER OF GUESTS: 27
Meals: Steak, crab, and salmon
Conference Groups: No
Rates: From $1,790
Guides: Included
Gratuities: $30 - $40 / day
Preferred Payment:
Cash or check
Getting There:
Fly to King Salmon and meet Tony's float plane.
Other Activities:
Wildlife photography

Contact:
Tony Behm
Alagnak Lodge
505 Ward Ave. #207
Honolulu HI 96814
Ph: 800/877-9903
Fax: 800/320-8993
e-mail:
tonybehm@hotmail.com
Web:
www.alagnaklodge.com
Off Season:
4055 Mineral Springs Lane #28
Glen Allen VA 23060
Ph: 800/887-9903
Fax: 800/320-8993

"WILD AND SCENIC" is the National Park Service designation for the Alagnak River. It flows for some 66 miles from a pair of lakes through a string of gravel runs, brushy islands, sandbars and pools into Bristol Bay, the mother lode of Alaskan salmon. Alagnak Lodge sits on a low bluff 45 feet above the river near the upper end of its tidal zone.

Two stories and painted white, the lodge is as modern as it is clean and comfortable. Second-floor guest rooms offer panoramic views. Baths are shared. Screened windows let in the breeze but keep mosquitoes at bay. Downstairs is the spacious dining room and lounge where everyone gathers around for steaks, prime rib and salmon. No tents crammed with wet waders and sweaty fleece here. New owner, Tony Behm, understands that creature comforts complement good fishing.

And you'll discover excellent fishing right at the lodge. Most guests take advantage of at least two of the three daily angling sessions: morning, afternoon and evening. Skiffs ferry anglers to good fishing. A crank of the outboard will take you and your guide up the river. Seven or eight miles upstream is the boundary of Katmai National Park. A few miles beyond you'll find the braided zone (four miles of channels and little islands with good fly-fishing water when fish are running), and another 20 minutes will bring you to some of the best rainbow and grayling water on the Alagnak.

The river carries all five species of Pacific salmon: kings (20 to 60 pounds) from late June through August; silvers (eight to 17 pounds) from late July into September; sockeyes (four to nine pounds) from mid-June through mid-July; chums (eight to 17 pounds); and pinks (two to eight pounds) from mid-July through late August. Rainbows up to 10 pounds and grayling up to four run from the second week in June through September. The best time to be there is in early June when rainbows are ravenous, or in September, when they are gorging on salmon spawn.

Flyouts to remote waters are available at additional cost, normally about $270 per person for groups of three or more. The lodge also offers a variety of packages, some of which include flyouts on alternating days. And if after you've returned from a flyout and have had dinner and you have yet to fish your fill, borrow a boat and work the pools in front of the lodge.

Alaska Rainbow Lodge

King   Salmon,   Alaska

*Fly or float to big rainbows and salmon
in the Iliamna area.*

VITAL STATISTICS:

KEY SPECIES:
Chum salmon, grayling, king/chinook salmon, pink salmon, rainbows, silver/coho salmon

Tackle:
Fly-fishing, spinning
Flyouts to Remote Waters: Yes
Major Season:
June through August
Accommodations:
LONG, LOW WOODEN LODGE
NUMBER OF ROOMS: 6
HANDICAPPED ACCESSIBLE: 1
MAXIMUM NUMBER OF GUESTS: 12
Meals: Regional seafoods served with gourmet flare
Conference Groups: No
Rates: $5,150 / week lodge; $2,450 / week float trip
Guides: Included
Gratuities: $300 - $500
Preferred Payment:
Cash or Check
Getting There:
Fly to King Salmon and one of Ron's Cessnas or Beavers will collect you.
Other Activities:
Big game, wildlife photography

Contact:
Ron Hayes
Alaska Rainbow Lodge
PO Box 39
King Salmon AK 99613
Ph: 800/451-6198
Fax: 817/236-1696

Off Season:
PO Box 10459
Ft. Worth TX 76114
Ph: 817/236-1002
Fax: 817/236-1696

WITH RON HAYES, major domo of this operation, you have two choices. Either you hole up at his long, low and comfortably plush lodge that overlooks the river, or you sleep in a tent on a gravel bar. The former wins hands down, you say? Well, it ain't bad. Private baths, china and silver, overstuffed couches for lounging with an after dinner drink as you watch eagles soar. If the rigors of daily flyouts to wrestle with some of the biggest rainbows and salmon in Alaska's Iliamna region get you down — or if you, like me, enjoy a hot shower and maybe a nap before dinner — the lodge may just be the place for you. You'll arise each morning thoroughly refreshed and ready for new water, more fish, and a flight over some of the most spectacular country in the world.

On the other hand, there are 35 miles of exquisite fishing in the upper reaches of the Alagnak River in Katmai National Park. If you want to see it all, first hand, sign up for the week-long float. You and three other anglers will be air-lifted to the headwaters of the river, spend the first evening working the kinks out of your fly lines and casting arms, and prepare for the morning's departure. Riding large rubber rafts — two anglers and a guide in each — you'll laze your way down the river, stopping where and when the spirit and the fishing moves. See rainbows or grayling working drys? Pull over, grab your six-weights and have a ball. Are those kings stacked up in that run? Hand me my eight-weight and let me at 'em. During your shore lunch, the third staffer assigned to the trip will float past with the raft full of gear. By the time you reach the end of the day's run, you'll find your tents erected and dinner ready to go. You'll sit with a libation, swapping stories like the one of that bear by the falls.

Whether you fly out or drift the river, you'll find king salmon averaging between 22 and 28 pounds. They run between the middle of June and the end of July. Sockeyes enter the system in the fourth week of June and fish well through July. Chums of two to eight pounds come in during the first week of July and are followed by pinks. Chum fishing fades in early August, but that's when eight- to 12-pound silvers show up. They'll hang around all fall. In the first three weeks of June, you can fish for trophy rainbows, kings and sockeyes. In the last three weeks of August, silvers and trophy rainbows overlap. And all during the season, you'll find arctic char, Dolly Varden, arctic grayling, northern pike and lake trout.

Alaska's Enchanted Lake Lodge

K i n g   S a l m o n ,   A l a s k a

Utter luxury located in the heart of trophy rainbow country.

VITAL STATISTICS:

KEY SPECIES:
Arctic char, chum salmon, king/chinook salmon, pike, pink salmon, rainbows, silver/coho salmon

Tackle:
Fly-fishing
Fly-outs to Remote Waters:
Yes
Major Season:
June through September
Accommodations:
ELEGANT HILL-TOP LODGE
NUMBER OF ROOMS: 7
MAXIMUM NUMBER OF GUESTS: 14
Meals: Prime rib and fine regional cuisine
Conference Groups: No
Rates: $5,600 / week
Guides: Included
Gratuities: Angler's discretion
Preferred Payment:
Cash or check
Getting There:
Fly to King Salmon and catch one of Dick's float planes.
Other Activities:
Wildlife photography

Contact:
Dick Matthews
Alaska's Enchanted Lake Lodge
PO Box 97
King Salmon AK 99613
Ph: 907/246-6878
e-mail:
enchantedlake@msn.com
Web:
enchantedlake.com
Off Season:
PO Box 52785
Bellevue WA 98015-2785
Ph: 425/557-1004
Fax: 425/557-1009

HOW DOES IT FEEL to know you're miles and miles from anything that closely resembles civilization, and yet you are awakened with a fresh pot of coffee or tea? That's how it is here at this first-class lodge surrounded by Katmai National Park. Tough, huh? After a sumptuous breakfast, you and your guide board a deHavilland Beaver. By then, you'll have made your choice of which of the dozens of rivers in the Iliamna area you'd like to fish. Maybe you'll opt for salmon, rainbow, grayling, arctic char or northern pike fishing.

The season begins in June when rainbows gang up to feed on eggs of spring spawning salmon and salmon smolts from the year before. Kings enter the system also in June and provide steady action for anglers who want to go toe-to-toe with a 50 pound fish. July brings the sockeyes, those hard-fighting red salmon that are great on the grill. They take wet flies readily, but that's the end of the easy part. Once hooked, they'll strip your backing in nothing flat, tailwalking all the way. In August, the streams fill with pink, coho and chum salmon. Of inelegant name, chums try to get even by busting your tackle. September may be the best month on Nonvianuk and the nearby Kulik.

Bring 5/6- and 8-weight systems, suggests Dick Matthews, pilot and owner of Enchanted Lake. While a weight-forward, floating line is standard, you may find use for a second spool loaded with a sink tip. One hundred yards of 20-pound backing is essential, and reels should have good drags as well as rims that can be palmed. Among standard flies, bring Royal Wulffs, Elk-Hair Caddis, Humpies and Adams in no. 14 to 18; leeches and sculpins (Woolly Buggers and Rabbit Fur Leeches, no. 4 to 8); and a variety of nymphs including Hare's Ears, Pheasant Tails and Princes, sizes 12 to 18. Bring egg patterns if you wish, but the lodge stocks patterns that Matthews and sons, Mike and Steve, have found productive over the years.

You come here to fish, of course, but you'll remember the eating. For lunch, the guide bakes fish you caught that morning, pulls fresh vegetables, fruits and homemade cookies from the cooler, and serves it with a properly chilled white wine or imported beer. A nap restores the soul before afternoon fishing and the flight back to the lodge. A few minutes in the sauna readies you for cocktails and hors d'oeuvres preceding a gourmet dinner.

Alaska's Northwoods Lodge

Skwentna, Alaska

A four-day float, flyouts from the lodge, or fishing in sight of your cabin — these are the secrets of Northwoods Lodge.

VITAL
STATISTICS:

KEY SPECIES:
Chum salmon, grayling,
king/chinook salmon, pink
salmon, rainbows, red/
sockeye salmon, silver/coho
salmon

Tackle:
Casting, fly-fishing, spinning
Major Season:
May through September
Accommodations:
MODERN SPRUCE LODGE
NUMBER OF ROOMS: 6
MAXIMUM NUMBER OF GUESTS: 16
Meals: Festive fowl and fish recipes
Conference Groups: Yes
Rates:
From: $3,399 / week
Guides: Included
Gratuities: $25 - $40 / day;
$15 / day, wait staff
Preferred Payment:
Cash, check or credit cards
Getting There:
Fly to Anchorage and take the float
plane.
Other Activities:
Canoeing/kayaking/rafting,
horseback riding, skiing, water skiing,
wildlife photography

Contact:
Shan Jonson
Alaska's Northwoods Lodge
PO Box 56
Skwentna AK 99667
Ph: 800/999-6539
Fax: 907/733-3742
e-mail:
fish@northwoodslodge.net
Web:
www.northwoodslodge.net
Agents:
Alaska Outdoor Adventures
Outdoor Connection

CAPPED BY ICE FIELDS, the mountains of Denali National Park spawn hundreds of streams that run milky with glacial melt for much of the summer. Not so Lake Creek, the stream where Eric Johnson leads floats for rainbows, grayling, lake trout and salmon. Chelatna Lake, the headwaters for this stream, acts as a basin where sediment settles. The river creek runs clear most of the year. Rafting along in rubber boats, you'll bounce through Class III rapids, slide over chattering runs, and eddy out in long slow pools where salmon stack up.

Start in late May for grayling, pike and rainbows. In June, chinook (king) salmon come into the Yenta River and Fish Lakes Creek, the homewaters of Northwoods. July brings pinks, and August cohos (silvers) and chums. The best fishing, according Eric, may be in the first few weeks of June when rainbows, grayling and king salmon are at the height of their runs. The northern pike fishing is also excellent at this time.

While fly-fishing is spoken here — there's a fully equipped tying bench for working out local patterns — one need not be a purist to hook into good sport. Spinning tackle is the weapon of choice for chinooks up to 50 pounds, and casting gear is preferred for silvers, pinks and chums. All anglers fish with guides (on staff) and boat to hotspots on the Yenta and Sustina rivers. Tackle and hip boots are provided as part of the package price, and the lodge will obtain licenses for guests. There is no tackle shop here, however, so anglers should bring their own equipment and stock up on miscellaneous gear ahead of time. Northwoods encourages catch-and-release fishing, but will filet and package salmon for the trip home.

Set among the trees above a bend on the creek, the main log lodge is surrounded by six cabins that can accommodate 16 clients, though 12 is more typical. A log-sided chalet (with queen-size bed, living room with a sofa bed, and private bath) is popular with couples. Two smaller cabins contain two bedrooms each and a shared bath. Two one-bedroom cabins and a bunkhouse for up to 10 make use of a bathhouse nearby. The food, according to guests, is something to write home about. Shan Johnson and daughter, Julie, turn out the likes of grilled chicken with mustard and rosemary, festive tortellini and marinated orange salmon. And guides pack a shore lunch that's apt to include local salmon or caribou.

[A L A S K A]

Angler's Alibi

K i n g   S a l m o n ,   A l a s k a

Tents on the Alagnak put you in the park for a grand slam on Alaskan salmon.

VITAL STATISTICS:

KEY SPECIES:
Chum salmon, king/chinook salmon, pike, pink salmon, rainbows, red/sockeye salmon, silver/coho salmon

Tackle:
Casting, fly-fishing, spinning, trolling
Flyouts to Remote Waters: Yes
Major Season:
June through mid-August
Accommodations:
WEATHERPORT TENTS
NUMBER OF ROOMS: 4
MAXIMUM NUMBER OF GUESTS: 9
Meals: Hearty prime rib and fowl
Conference Groups: No
Rates: $3,300 / week
Guides: Included
Gratuities: 10%
Preferred Payment:
Cash or check
Getting There:
Fly to King Salmon and take the float plane.
Other Activities:
Bird-watching, wildlife photography

Contact:
Karl Storath
Angler's Alibi
PO Box 271
King Salmon AK 99613
Ph: 907/439-4234
Off Season:
605 Poplar Beach
Romulus NY 14541
Ph: 607/869-9397
Fax: 607/869-9656

THERE ARE TENTS and then there are tents, and among the best are the Weatherports out of which Karl Storath has built his famed Angler's Alibi lodge on the Alagnak River. You know the river. It drains a large chunk of the Katmai region surrounding Nonvianuk Lake, about 225 air miles southwest of Anchorage. Located on the lower tidal reaches of the river, every day the camp sees fresh runs of salmon headed upstream to spawn.

All five Alaskan salmon — kings, sockeyes, silvers, chums and pinks — use the river, along with rainbows, arctic char, grayling and pike. The last week in June and the first week in July are choice for kings and sockeyes. Kings normally run better than 30 pounds, and fish from 45 to 50 pounds are common. Sockeyes in the 7- to 14-pound range provide good sport on fly rods or medium-weight spinning gear. Chums start running in the second week of July. The last week in July is the best time to hit a salmon grand slam — all five species in one week. By then, silvers have entered the river and the first pinks have shown up as well.

Fish incoming tides whenever they occur. Wading is easy in front of the camp, but you'll need to keep an eye on the rising water. If you tire of salmon, you can run up the Alagnak in one of the camp's power boats to water where rainbows of three to five pounds, char, grayling and pike are found. The camp also offers flyouts ($200 to $300 additional cost) to nearby Katmai National Park, where rainbows up to 10 pounds can be caught, especially in August.

Your home away from home, here, is a high, green-roofed 16 x 12-foot tent with screen doors, heaters and carpeted floors. Two or three anglers share each of three tents, and they dine well on Cornish game hens, prime rib and salmon in a jumbo 16 x 25-foot Weatherport. A log bathhouse offers hot showers (slip a pair of thongs into your duffel) that are so welcome after a day's fishing, and laundry facilities.

Angler's Paradise Lodges: *Grosvenor and Kulik*

For salmon, char and rainbow trout, choose from a pair of fine retreats.

VITAL STATISTICS:

KEY SPECIES:
Arctic char, chum salmon, grayling, king/chinook salmon, pink salmon, rainbows, silver/coho salmon

Tackle:
Casting, fly-fishing, spinning, trolling
Flyouts to Remote Waters: Yes
Major Season:
June through October
Accommodations:
MODERN, YET RUSTIC CABINS
NUMBER OF ROOMS: 12
MAXIMUM NUMBER OF GUESTS: 28
Meals: Beef and seafood with homemade breads
Conference Groups: No
Rates: From $1,900 / 3 days
Guides: Included
Gratuities: $200 / week
Preferred Payment:
Cash or check
Getting There:
Fly to Anchorage and Katmai takes care of you for the rest of your trip.
Other Activities:
Flight-seeing, wildlife watching

Contact:
Kip Minnery
Angler's Paradise Lodges
4550 Aircraft Dr.
Anchorage AK 99502
Ph: 800/544-0551
Fax: 907/243-0649
e-mail:
katmailand@alaska.net
Web:
www.katmailand.com

KATMAILAND INC., out of Anchorage, operates these two fine old lodges that offer similar fishing, but in different settings. Located on the river and lake of the same name, at Kulik you'll encounter some of southwest Alaska's best water for rainbows. The water is clear (the bottom consists of gravel) and the wading is easy. In its upper reaches, the Kulik is relatively small. Rainbows peak in June, taper off slightly in July, then come on strong in August and September. Fish are big — in the five-pound-plus range — and the latter part of the season is when to get them. On Kulik and nearby Nonvianuk lakes, you'll catch lake trout, sockeyes, char and pike. The sockeyes run in June and early July. With 12 spruce cabins accented by forest-green porches and all with private baths, Kulik is the flagship lodge. Close to the cabins is the main lodge, also of spruce. Family-style meals of fresh seafood and cuts of beef are served on long pine tables. One corner of the room is devoted to complimentary libations, and another attractive grouping of chairs offers views of the lake.

Grosvenor is a bit more rustic and ideal for a group of fishing friends. Three cabins share a bathhouse. The lodge is smaller, but as comfortable. With menus similar to those at Kulik, you'll overlook the lake as you dine. Trout, char and sockeyes run through the lake's narrows adjacent to the lodge. Two nearby rivers feeding the lake hold the largest concentrations of spawning sockeyes in the Naknek drainage. You'll reach these and smaller streams by jetboat. Should catching and releasing trout and salmon wear thin (you can keep a few salmon to take home), you may want to cast spoons, spinnerbaits or flies for northern pike.

All fishing packages include licenses and use of rods, reels and waders if needed. Angler's Paradise also has boats cached on many lakes and rivers within a 100-mile radius of the lodges. Flyouts to fish all five species of salmon and trout in isolated waters are available at $275 per person. In addition, you may want to check out their week-long guided and unguided float trips on the Alagnak.

Katmai Inc. also operates Brooks Lodge in Katmai National Park. In addition to good fishing on the Brooks River, this lodge offers flight-seeing trips to view active volcanoes, and numerous opportunities to photograph huge brown bears as they fish. Park rangers provide interpretive programs. Brooks closes in mid-September.

*Sockeye salmon pour into thin Alaskan rivers like the Saltery
on Kodiak Island. Your job is to whip them with your fly-rod,
haul them out, and savor their filets when you get home.*

Baranof Wilderness Lodge

Sitka, Alaska

What's good about a little white house on a remote island in the panhandle? If you have to ask, please turn the page.

VITAL STATISTICS:

KEY SPECIES:
Bull trout/Dolly Varden, chum salmon, halibut, king/chinook salmon, pink salmon, rainbows, red/sockeye salmon, silver/coho salmon

Tackle:
Casting, fly-fishing, spinning, trolling
Flyouts to Remote Waters: Yes
Major Season:
June through October
Accommodations:
PRIVATE CABINS; TENT CAMPS ON SAFARIS
NUMBER OF ROOMS: 7
MAXIMUM NUMBER OF GUESTS: 14
Meals: Regional cuisine with loads of fresh vegetables
Conference Groups: No
Rates: From $1,100 / 2 days
Guides: Included
Gratuities:
Angler's discretion
Preferred Payment:
Cash, check or credit cards
Getting There:
Fly to Sitka and you'll be flown to the lodge.
Other Activities:
Bird-watching, boating, canoeing/kayaking/rafting, hiking, whale watching, wildlife photography

Contact:
Mike Trotter
Baranof Wilderness Lodge
PO Box 2187
Sitka AK 99835
Ph: 800/613-6551
Fax: 530/582-8139
Web:
flyfishalaska.com
Off Season:
PO Box 42
Norden CA 95724
Ph: 800/613-6551
Fax: 530/582-8139

Agents:
Fishabout — 800/409-2000
Hunters & Anglers — 214/363-2525

RUSSIAN ALASKA: explored but never settled by merchants of the Czar. They came for whales and fur. You, too, will see whales, but from a seat in an Avon inflatable boat, skipping across the bay en route to waters where salmon are stacked up waiting to move into spawning grounds. The whales aren't far from the front porch of Mike Trotter's little white house, where Warm Springs Bay cuts into Baranof Island, 20 miles by air from Sitka.

The lodge overlooks sheltered Chatham Passage. Salmon run the passage: kings (20 to 50 pounds) from May through July; chums (nine to 17 pounds) and sockeyes (five to eight pounds) in July and August. Later, in July, silvers (eight to 15 pounds) and pinks (two to five pounds) come in. Pinks phase out in September, but the silvers hang on into October. You'll fish saltwater (halibut are a bonus), and freshwater streams where salmon spawn. In other streams and ponds on Baranof and nearby islands, you'll find rainbows, Dolly Varden and cutthroat. Saltwater gear is provided; bring your own spinning or fly-tackle for the strictly catch-and-release freshwater species.

You have your pick of accommodations. Choose cozy cabins set back under tall firs. Cabins are tastefully decorated and feature private baths. Your own front porch overlooks the passage. Local seafood complemented by herbs and vegetables from the garden makes up dinner. You'll also find an extensive list of fine wines. After dinner soak in the hot tub or mineral springs, much as the Tlingit Indians did centuries ago.

Those of hardier stripe may want to check out Mike's seven-day float trips on rivers in the Togiak National Wildlife Refuge north and east of Bristol Bay. He runs The Chosen (late July through late August) and Tikchik (mid-July), both noted for excellent runs of salmon. Accommodations are tents with bunks, but you'll find hot showers, gourmet food, great wines and outstanding fishing. Closer to home are the expeditions to Kelp Bay, a tent camp that's a short flight from Sitka.

Seniors should think about the University of Southeast Alaska's Elderhostel, hosted by Baranof during the first week in June. There's also a great wildlife photography workshop with John Hendrickson, whose work has appeared in *National Geographic* and *Audubon*. And don't overlook the fly-fishing school with Ken Hanley either. Baranof Wilderness Lodge is, indeed, a special place.

231

[A L A S K A]

Bear Track Inn

G u s t a v u s ,   A l a s k a

Made of huge spruce logs, this lodge offers scores of heli-tours, fishing, and wildlife viewing opportunities.

VITAL STATISTICS:

KEY SPECIES:
Bull trout/Dolly Varden, chum salmon, cutthroat, halibut, king/chinook salmon, pink salmon, rainbows, red/sockeye salmon, silver/coho salmon, steelhead

Tackle:
Fly-fishing, spinning, trolling
Flyouts to Remote Waters: Yes
Major Season:
All year
Accommodations:
Substantial log lodge with all the comforts
Number of Rooms: 14
Maximum Number of Guests: 28
Meals: Regional cuisine
Conference Groups: No
Rates: From $393 / 1 night, 2 days
Guides: Additional
Gratuities: 5% - 10%
Preferred Payment:
Cash, check or credit cards
Getting There:
Fly to Juneau and catch the ferry.
Other Activities:
Bird-watching, boating, canoeing/kayaking/rafting, golf, hiking, skiing, wildlife photography, glacier viewing, whale watching

Contact:
Mike Olney
Bear Track Inn
PO Box 6440
Ketchikan AK 99901
Ph: 800/939-2477
Fax: 907/225-8530
e-mail:
beartrac@aol.com
Web:
www.beartrackinn.com

Agents:
Alaska's Inside Passage Resorts: 800/926-2477

I N THE UPPER REACHES of southeast Alaska's panhandle, the Chilkat Range pokes down between the Lynn Canal to the east, and Glacier Bay to the west. Across Glacier Bay rises the Fairweather Range, capped by Brady Glacier and its numerous lobes that ooze down toward the sea. Most of the rugged terrain is preserved in Glacier Bay National Park, and the jump-off point for exploring this year-round winter wonderland is the hamlet of Gustavus.

That's where John and Jane Olney built their lodge, a massive structure of thick spruce log that's reminiscent of the wilderness resorts in Yellowstone. A huge great room extends around an open firepit. Suede couches and end tables made of slabs of ancient trees provide intimate groupings for casual conversation. Fence-railed stairs climb to second floor guest rooms (each with two queen beds and private bath) where the views of the park are spectacular. Cuisine is regional, hearty and prepared with a special flair. Don't pass up the salmon in parchment.

This is one of those lodges where you can do as little or as much as you want. A small creek runs through the Bear Track's 17 acres, and it carries stocks of spawning salmon. A better bet are flyouts to seldom fished streams in the National Park where rainbows, cutthroat, Dolly Varden, and the salmon du jour will be running. Fishing boats carry anglers into Icy Strait and its many coves for all five Alaskan salmon. Come in late May for kings and in September for cohos. Guided fishing is paid by the session, with daily trips running in the $300 range.

Extremely popular here are day trips to view whales that migrate with the salmon. Choose from a three-hour trek on a 78-foot catamaran or design your own excursion with a personal guide. Another cruise takes you into the park's fjords to see calving glaciers, and bear and moose along the shore. A nine-hole golf course challenges players to keep eyes on the ball and not on the stunning views of the Fairweather Mountains. At this lodge, there's lots to do.

Boardwalk Wilderness Lodge
T h o r n e   B a y ,   A l a s k a

For early spring steelhead, it's hard to beat the waters that feed Thorne Bay.

VITAL STATISTICS:

KEY SPECIES:
Chum salmon, cutthroat, halibut, king/chinook salmon, pink salmon, silver/coho salmon, steelhead

Tackle:
Fly-fishing, spinning, trolling
Flyouts to Remote Waters: Yes
Major Season:
April through September
Accommodations:
RUSTIC LOG LODGES
NUMBER OF ROOMS: 6
HANDICAPPED ACCESSIBLE: 1
MAXIMUM NUMBER OF GUESTS: 12
Meals: Chops, regional seafood, rack of lamb
Conference Groups: No
Rates: From: $2,420 / 3 days, double occupancy
Guides: Included
Gratuities: 11%
Preferred Payment:
Cash, check or credit cards
Getting There:
Fly to Ketchikan and meet your float plane.
Other Activities:
Bird-watching, boating, canoeing/kayaking/rafting, caving, hiking, whale watching, wildlife photography

Contact:
Doug Ibbetson
Boardwalk Wilderness Lodge
PO Box 19121
Thorne Bay AK 99919
Ph: 907/828-3918
Fax: 907/828-3367
Web:
www.boardwalklodge.com

Agents:
Orvis endorsed

YOU KNOW WHAT A STEELHEAD IS: a sea-run rainbow that's hell-bent on stripping every inch of line from your reel and busting your rod if you do something really dumb. Flies or spinning gear, it doesn't make any difference. Their sole purpose in life is to make yours miserable. There's no better place to come to wrestle steelies than the Thorne River and Stanley River on the northeast end of Prince of Wales Island, about 40 miles north of Ketchikan.

April, May and June are the prime steelhead months on Prince of Wales, the third largest island in the U.S. Eighty-five of the island's rivers have been documented as steelhead streams. Early in the season, it's reasonable to assume hookups with two to four steelhead per day. Though the island is 135 miles long and 45 miles wide, mountains provide its backbone and watersheds tend to be modest in size. That means plenty of small rivers that are relatively easy to fish. About a dozen, including the Karta, have runs of both spring and fall steelhead. Rivers on the island also hold cutthroats, and virtually all see salmon runs.

Your guide will help you select your species for the day from among 23 different waters. Fish steelhead in the morning when you're fresh, then board one of the lodge's cabin cruisers to go deep for halibut, cod, salmon or rockfish. Mooching — drifting a strip of herring for kings on medium-weight tackle — is pure fun. You stand by the rail, working the bait up and down, when suddenly your rod does a little tango and dives for the bottom. Kings run in the 30- to 40-pound-plus range. Best king fishing is in June. Cohos show up in July and stay through September; the end of the run offers better fishing.

An Orvis-endorsed lodge, Boardwalk Wilderness is top rated by its guests. This hand-built lodge of stripped and notched spruce logs, with porches and balconies and deep overhanging eaves, blends well with the verdant hillsides. Inside are cozy, hand-hewn log walls complemented by antiques and reproductions from a variety of periods. Lounge in the cathedral-ceilinged great room, feet pointed toward the glowing woodstove. It'll be hard to lever yourself up for the short walk through the arched door into the dining room, where dinner of shrimp, halibut or Cornish hen awaits. Half of the guest rooms are upstairs in the main lodge and half are in a second lodge nearby. After dinner, watch Sitka deer from the hot tub on the deck.

233

[A L A S K A]

Bristol Bay Lodge

Dillingham, Alaska

For the ultimate Alaskan angling challenge, set your sights on netting one of every species available from this lodge.

VITAL STATISTICS:

KEY SPECIES:
Arctic char, bull trout/Dolly Varden, chum salmon, grayling, king/chinook salmon, pike, pink salmon, rainbows, red/sockeye salmon, silver/coho salmon

Tackle:
Fly-fishing, spinning
Flyouts to Remote Waters: Yes
Major Season:
June through September
Accommodations:
MODERN, YET RUSTIC LOG LODGE
NUMBER OF ROOMS: 10
Maximum Number of Guests: 24
Meals: Prime rib, seafood
Conference Groups: No
Rates:
From $5,250 / week
Guides: Included
Gratuities: 10%
Preferred Payment:
Cash or check
Getting There:
Fly to Dillingham and catch the free shuttle.
Other Activities:
Bird-watching, hiking, wildlife photography

Contact:
Ron McMillan
Bristol Bay Lodge
Box 1509
Dillingham AK 99576
Ph: 907/842-2500
Fax: 907/842-2599
e-mail:
bristol@eburg.com
Web:
www.bristolbaylodge.com
Off Season:
2422 Hunter Road
Ellensburg WA 98926
Ph: 509/964-2094
Fax: 509/964-2269

Agents:
Several

IT CAN PROBABLY BE DONE. It's possible to catch all 12 of the primary species available from this lodge, 40 air miles north of Dillingham on Lake Aleknagik. Since 1972, Ron McMillan has been hosting anglers here in the center of some of the best trout, salmon and char water in southwestern Alaska. You'll find all five Pacific salmon, Dolly Varden of fresh and sea-run persuasion, arctic char, rainbows, grayling, lake trout and northern pike.

Fishing begins in June with early rainbows, char and grayling, and for these, angling stays good through August. King and chum salmon, also known as dog salmon, enter the river systems in June. Generally speaking, the sockeyes and pinks (every other year) arrive at the end of June and early July, and silvers show up in August. Kings and sockeyes fish best in the last week of June and the first two weeks of July. Prime time for pinks is late July and early August. Silvers hit their peak after the first week in August. If you're going to try for the weekly dozen, the best time is the second or third week of July.

Spin-fishermen will want to bring light and medium-weight systems, matching reels with 6- and 10-pound-test lines and a variety of spinners and spoons. Two systems are required for fly-fishers as well: an 8 1/2-foot for a 6-weight, and a 9- or 10-foot for a 7- or 8-weight. Black and olive Woolly Buggers are the most versatile flies. The lodge has a well-stocked shop with lures, flies and other tackle.

Headquarters is a weathered lodge of wood and glass set high on a knoll overlooking the lake. Flyouts are the order of the day. Within a short hop via Bristol Bay's fleet of three six-passenger Beavers are the fertile waters of the Wood, Tikchik, Nusagak, Togiak and Goodnews rivers. Most flights are 30 minutes or less, unless anglers specifically want a bit of flight-seeing. On each lake or river, the lodge has stashed boats with outboard jet or prop motors. In addition, Bristol Bay maintains several spike camps. You'll fly-in late in the afternoon, fish, have dinner, sleep in comfy Weathersport tents, breakfast and then spend the rest of the day on the water. Pick-up is late in the afternoon and you'll return to the lodge for dinner. Only four anglers are in camp at a time and their needs are looked after by a cook and a pair of guides. If weather grounds the aircraft, fish the Agulawak River and Youth, Icy and Sunshine creeks, all trophy trout streams accessible by boat from the main lodge.

Chelatna Lake Lodge

Anchorage, Alaska

Spinning or fly-fishing, take your choice. The salmon don't care.

VITAL STATISTICS:

KEY SPECIES:
Grayling, king/chinook salmon, lake trout, pike, rainbows, red/sockeye salmon, silver/coho salmon

Tackle:
Casting, fly-fishing, spinning, trolling
Flyouts to Remote Waters: Yes
Major Season:
June into September
Accommodations:
CEDAR CABINS
NUMBER OF ROOMS: 8
MAXIMUM NUMBER OF GUESTS: 17
Meals: Fish with an Italian twist, prime rib
Conference Groups: Yes
Rates: From $2,450 / 3 days, double occupancy
Guides: Included
Gratuities: 10%
Preferred Payment:
Cash, check or credit cards
Getting There:
Fly to Anchorage, take a cab to float plane row, and you're on your way.
Other Activities:
Big game, boating, canoeing/kayaking/rafting, hiking, swimming, bear-watching

Contact:
Becky Bertke
Chelatna Lake Lodge
3941 Float Plane Dr
Anchorage AK 99502
Ph: 907/243-7767
Fax: 907/248-5791
e-mail:
chelatna@alaska.net
Web:
www.alaska.net/chelatna

HIGH AND FRONTED WITH GLASS, the main lodge sits on a spruce-ringed knoll overlooking four cedar guest cabins down by the lake. Aircraft — those hardy deHavilland Beavers and speedy Cessnas — are tethered to the dock, as are a number of vee-hulled fishing boats. All is ready for the morning's merriment. The only question is what it will be, and that, you and your guide are discussing in the warm afterglow of dinner.

Here are the choices: fly out to remote rivers and lakes for salmon with the primary species depending on when you arrive, or float Lake Creek in a stable rubber raft and cast flies or spinners for rainbows or grayling. The lake yields fine lake trout, best trolled up with chartreuse and red wobbling spoons, or you can cast the grassy shallows for wolf-like pike. The best fishing is in the rivers and streams, and the month with the greatest diversity of species is July. If you want to go for 25- to 60-pound kings, arrive before the tenth. After the 15th, silvers and sockeye are legal. Lake trout and grayling also reach their peaks in July. Bring spinning and/or fly-fishing gear, whichever you prefer. The salmon hit spoons (Pixies and Daredevils), while the trout and grayling go after lures and spinners (Mepps, Rooster Tails and so on). The lodge employs a full staff of guides, obtains licenses for guests and provides some tackle if you need it.

Though the fishing is better than superb, even the hardest core angler works in a flight or two above Denali National Park. They forego trout and salmon to observe grizzlies, moose and Dall sheep. Guests also enjoy watching bruins from a protected platform a few minutes' walk from the main chalet. And almost everyone finds themselves up to their respective necks in the wood-fired hot tub at the edge of the lake. That's after the fishing and before a dinner of grilled salmon with lime and ginger sauce with jasmine rice, or halibut *grenobloise* with fettuccine. The chef can accommodate a variety of diet restrictions including heart healthy, vegetarian and MSG/salt free. After dinner, linger with the last of your wine in the twilight and watch the lake and the mountains beyond. Then it's off to bed in one of the chalets. Each contains two bedrooms and a private bath.

Chris Goll's Rainbow River Lodge

I l i a m n a ,   A l a s k a

On the Copper River, a novice can fish like a pro, and a pro may land a lifetime trophy.

VITAL STATISTICS:

KEY SPECIES:
Arctic char, chum salmon, grayling, king/chinook salmon, pike, pink salmon, rainbows, red/sockeye salmon, silver/coho salmon, steelhead

Tackle:
Casting, fly-fishing, spinning
Flyouts to Remote Waters: Yes
Major Season:
June through September
Accommodations:
CEDAR CHALET
NUMBER OF ROOMS: 6
HANDICAPPED ACCESSIBLE: 6
MAXIMUM NUMBER OF GUESTS: 16
Meals: Steak, turkey, prime rib and salmon
Conference Groups: Yes
Rates:
From $3,800 / 6 days
Guides: Included
Gratuities: 5% - 10%
Preferred Payment:
Cash, check or credit cards
Getting There:
Fly to Iliamna and you'll be met.
Other Activities:
Big game, waterfowling, wingshooting, bird-watching, boating, canoeing/kayaking/rafting, hiking, wildlife photography

Contact:
Chris Goll
Rainbow River Lodge
PO Box 330
Iliamna AK 99606
Ph: 907/571-1210
Fax: 907/571-1210
Off Season:
PO Box 1070
Silver City NM 88062
Ph: 505/388-2259
Fax: 505/388-2261

A retired fish biologist, Mack Minnard, calls the Copper River a "beautiful piece of water." He should know. He worked in the drainage for 18 years. It's one of the few Alaska rivers that sees hatches of mayflies, stoneflies and caddis. Stoneflies — mahogany in #6 and #8 and lime greens in #16s and #18s — begin to come off in mid-June. They're followed by yellow sallies (#14s and #16s) toward the end of the month. Caddis appear in the full range of colors and sizes. But by early July, mayflies and stoneflies have faded, yet there's caddis activity into the end of the month.

By the third week of July, top water action virtually ceases. Sockeye are the first of Alaska's five salmon species to spawn in the river, and their eggs attract the interest of rainbows. Soon they're feeding on the bottom like hogs at a trough. So guess which patterns are most effective? Eggs. In virtually any color. And flesh flies, combed out strips of orange yarn tied on a hook. You may also stir up some action with mouse patterns, big Matukas, and Muddlers. Most rainbows run in the 12- to 20-inch range, but the number of 24-inch fish is large enough that most anglers play one or two while they're on the river. The further the season goes, the fatter the fish. July and August are peak months for salmon, but that, too, begins to pale as the weeks slide into September when the 'bows are at their largest.

Thirteen miles of the Copper, from its mouth on Intricate Bay up to a set of 50-foot falls, are navigable. As the river seems to impart its namesake color to its fish, it infects those who fish it as well. Wading is not difficult. Casts need not be of tournament winning length. Sometimes, the trout are so hungry they'll race another fish to a bit of feathers, floss and steel in the water. A novice can feel like a pro here, and an experienced angler will have chance after chance to learn how to play and release huge fish. The Copper is restricted to fly-fishing, but spinfishers will find ample opportunity to tackle kings or troll for huge lake trout. Flyouts to other waters are also available.

Lodge owner Chris Goll received the Conservationist of the Year award in 1980 from the National Wildlife Federation for his work on the Copper River. His guests also toss him kudos for the quality of the lodge. It is immaculate, with snug and secluded cabins of cedar, all with private baths. Meals of near gourmet quality are served in the contemporary, cathedral-ceilinged log lodge.

Classic Alaska Charters

Ketchikan, Alaska

Ever want to captain your own ship? Here's your chance, with great fishing to boot.

VITAL STATISTICS:

KEY SPECIES:
Halibut, king/chinook salmon, pink salmon, coho/silver salmon

Tackle:
Fly-fishing, spinning, trolling
Flyouts to Remote Waters: Yes
Major Season:
May through September
Accommodations:
40-FOOT CABIN CRUISER
NUMBER OF ROOMS: 3
MAXIMUM NUMBER OF GUESTS: 6
Meals: The freshest "catch of the day" in the world
Conference Groups: No
Rates: $1,875 / 5 days, double occupancy
Guides: Included
Gratuities: $25 / day
Preferred Payment:
Cash or check
Getting There:
Fly to Ketchikan where Rob will meet you.
Other Activities:
Big game, bird-watching, hiking, wildlife photography

Contact:
Capt. Rob Scherer
Classic Alaska Charters
PO Box 6117
Ketchikan AK 99901
Ph: 907/225-0608
e-mail:
ClassicAlaskaCharters.Scherer@gte.net
Web:
www.ktn.net/cac

WHAT SPECIES turns you on? Halibut, yelloweye, lingcod, king, silver, pink and chum salmon, black rockfish, cutthroats . . . the choice is yours. Salmon are generally best from late May through late September. So where's the fishing best? In channels through which salmon are surging? At the mouths of creeks where salmon are schooling up, ready for spawning runs? Your tackle preferences — fly, spinning, trolling — will all play a role in your decision.

Once you've got all this figured out, it's time to find a lodge and a guide. Lots of places offer flyouts. Some are located on great water that you can fish from your doorstep. In most cases, you go from the lodge to the fishing. But in some, such as Classic Alaska Charters, you take the lodge *to* the fishing. Rob Scherer, skipper of the Saltery "C," figured that if anglers could fish from a boat, eat on a boat and sleep on a boat, then a boat could be a lodge. Makes sense. And it gets better: You're the admiral. Scherer will tell you what's hot, then you pick the species and how you want to fish for them.

Fish the salt from April through October. Jig deep water — 180 to more than 420 feet — for big halibut with lures weighing 16 to 32 ounces. Fights with fish can last an hour or more. Use medium-weight tackle (20- to 40-pound-test line) and vertical jig for cod, halibut and some salmon. If light tackle is your bag, fish massive schools of rockfish and yelloweye over pinnacles, reefs and kelp beds. You can also troll and drift for salmon and halibut. Run up the spectacular channels of the Misty Fjords National Wilderness Channel or the deep cuts in Revillagigedo Island. Put ashore at the mouths of clear, unnamed rivers teeming with salmon on the spawn. You'll see no other anglers, just pods of killer whales, hundreds of frolicking dolphin, and brown bears and eagles who take their fishing much more seriously than you do.

The Saltery "C" is a 40-foot motor yacht with two heads. It sleeps six, four in the forward cabin and two in the dinette. Meals are prepared from that day's catch: halibut, cod, salmon, Dungeness crab and shrimp. Breakfasts open with homemade cinnamon rolls and coffee on deck, and then things get serious. Fish from the stern cockpit, and later, grill your catch. Not, as they say, a rough life.

[A L A S K A]

Copper River Fly Fishing Lodge

I l i a m n a ,   A l a s k a

Small groups of fly fishers will enjoy booking this lodge and playing 'bows up to 20 pounds.

VITAL STATISTICS:

KEY SPECIES:
Arctic char, bull trout/Dolly Varden, grayling, rainbows, red/sockeye salmon

Tackle:
Fly-fishing
Major Season:
June into October
Accommodations:
LOG LODGE W/SHARED BATHS
NUMBER OF ROOMS: 4
MAXIMUM NUMBER OF GUESTS: 6
Meals: Pork and prime rib
Rates:
$3,200 / week
Guides: Included
Gratuities: 10%
Conference Groups: No
Preferred Payment:
Cash or check
Getting There:
Fly to Iliamna and catch the free shuttle flight.
Other Activities:
Bird-watching, wildlife photography

Contact:
Jeff and Pat Vermillion
Copper River Fly Fishing Lodge
PO Box PVY
Iliamna AK 99606
Ph: 907/571-1464
Off Season:
411 S 3rd St.
Livingston MT 59047
Ph: 406/222-0624

SOME LODGES ARE LARGE, with lots of guests and a sense of hustle and bustle. Others are small and laid-back. So it is with the Copper River Fly Fishing Lodge on the famed river of the same name. Rustic and handbuilt of spruce log, the lodge rides a low hill above a back channel of the Copper, about half a mile from the river's mouth.

To most anglers, the Copper needs no introduction. It's one of those freshwater streams selected by members of Trout Unlimited as among the 100 best cold water fisheries in the country. There's good reason for that. The Copper rises in two creeks — Silver and Ptarmigan — that join at the head of Meadow Lake. Below the lake, the river takes on definition, but it is still very small. It pools up in two more lakes before crashing over a falls and becoming the stream that angler's love worldwide.

West of the last lake in the chain, the Copper broadens. Its bottom is gravel and its current fairly fast, an ideal incubator for eggs of salmon and rainbows, and a marvelous fishery for those who come to angle. Neither wide nor particularly deep, the river is easily waded. Each morning you'll climb aboard a skiff pushed by jet outboards to race upstream into the best fishing. And what fishing it is. In 1975, the state of Alaska restricted the Copper to fly-fishing only, and in 1989 mandated it a catch-and-release fishery for wild trout. In the Copper, rainbows grow fat on salmon spawn. Average summer fish run from three to five pounds. Trophy summer trout reach eight pounds or more. But in fall, as they gorge on salmon eggs, the rainbows will average twice their summer weight, and a lunker will tip the scale at 20 pounds. Fight that on your 5-weight!

Summer also sees a splendid run of four- to 12-pound sockeyes. To catch them, you'll want to be in camp between the Fourth of July and the first week of August. For big rainbows, forget about salmon and come in September. For variety, you'll also catch grayling and arctic char. Bring 5- and 8-weight systems. Three anglers share a guide. Accommodations are in cabins adjacent to the lodge. Baths are shared. Wonderful meals — garlic-roasted pork tenderloin, mashed potatoes, salads, chocolate mousse — are served family-style. No flyouts here; you'll spend your time fishing.

Creekside Inn

Ninilchik, Alaska

Nothing fancy about this budget inn except the fishing and the service, but what else is there?

VITAL STATISTICS:

Key Species:
Halibut, king/chinook salmon, rainbows, red/sockeye salmon, silver/coho salmon, steelhead

Tackle:
Casting, fly-fishing, spinning, trolling
Flyouts to Remote Waters: Yes
Major Season:
April through October
Accommodations:
MOTEL STYLE ROOMS
NUMBER OF ROOMS: 20
HANDICAPPED ACCESSIBLE: 1
MAXIMUM NUMBER OF GUESTS: 42
Meals: Bed and box lunch provided
Conference Groups: Yes
Rates:
From $55 / night (room only); packages from $1,650 / 4 nights, 5 days
Guides: Included in packages
Gratuities: Angler's discretion
Preferred Payment:
Cash, check or credit cards
Getting There:
Fly to Anchorage and rent a car.
Other Activities:
Big game, bird-watching, boating, horseback riding, hiking, swimming, wildlife photography

Contact:
Bill Avarell
Creekside Inn
PO Box 236
Ninilchik AK 99639
Ph: 907/338-1234
Fax: 907/336-2211
e-mail:
creekside-inn@worldnet.att.net
Web:
www.kenaipeninsulacharters.com
Off Season:
PO Box 6009
Crestline CA 92325
Ph: 909/338-3333
Fax: 909/336-2211

AN OLD TOWN settled by Russian traders and missionaries, Ninilchik is about two thirds down the Kenai Peninsula. To get there, some folks fly to Kenai, 45 minutes north. But the better option is to rent a car and drive down from Anchorage, 190 miles north. You'll travel through the Kenai National Refuge, pass the inspiring Portage Glacier, and chance seeing moose, caribou, bears and eagles.

The Kenai Peninsula, separated from most of Alaska by Cook Inlet, is a well-known destination for salmon, rainbows and halibut. The Creekside Inn at Ninilchik offers all three. Bill Avarell, a retired school teacher from the Los Angles area, owns the inn and Kenai Peninsula Charters. Under his care, you can have the best of freshwater and saltwater fishing. Most packages include flyouts to remote lakes and rivers on the peninsula, and across Cook Inlet into the areas of Lakes Clark and Iliamna. These flights traverse the famed Lake Clark Pass, with its spectacular views of glaciers and wildlife. You'll also wade or drift the Kenai and Kasilof rivers, as well as the Ninilchik, Anchor and Deep Creek.

The season opens with halibut in April. At the start of May the first run of kings moves up the peninsula from Anchor Point and reaches Deep Creek a week or so later. By the middle of the month, they've entered Deep Creek and begun migrating up past the inn. Building steadily, numbers increase until fishing reaches its prime in mid-June. A second run of kings enters the creek in early July. The farther up the inlet, the later the peak fishing.

The inn is located near the mouth of Deep Creek, which has runs of all five species of salmon. The river also hosts rainbows and Dolly Varden. Not known as a sockeye stream, they do begin running in late June. Silvers make their appearance near the first week of August, and September through mid-October brings the best runs. Don't forget the pinks, which debut in late July. While the Kasilof River, 19 miles to the north, and the Kenai, a dozen miles farther, are bigger rivers and floatable, Deep Creek will surprise you.

Creekside Inn is not one of those pretentious high-dollar places. Its trademarks are comfort and service. All but three of the 20 guest rooms have private baths. Packages include breakfast and a packed lunch; dinner is on your own. Here you won't be "lodge-bound;" if you drive, you can hop in your car and go exploring.

[A L A S K A]

Crystal Creek Lodge

L a k e   N u n a v a u g a l u k ,   A l a s k a

Fly out to fabulous fishing in 6 million acres of protected wilderness.

VITAL STATISTICS:

KEY SPECIES:
Arctic char, bull trout/Dolly Varden, grayling, king/chinook salmon, rainbows, silver/coho salmon

Tackle:
Casting, fly-fishing, spinning
Flyouts to Remote Waters: Yes
Major Season:
June through September
Accommodations:
LOVELY MODERN WOODEN LODGE
NUMBER OF ROOMS: 13
HANDICAPPED ACCESSIBLE: 1
MAXIMUM NUMBER OF GUESTS: 20
Meals: Choice of different cuisines
Conference Groups: No
Rates: $5,500 / week
Guides: Included
Gratuities: 5% - 15%
Conference Groups: Yes
Preferred Payment:
Cash or check
Getting There:
Fly to Dillingham and meet the lodge's float planes.
Other Activities:
Wingshooting

Contact:
Dan Michels
Crystal Creek Lodge
Box 92170
Anchorage AK 99509
Ph: 907/245-1945
Fax: 907/245-1946
e-mail:
crystal@alaska.net
Web:
www.crystalcreeklodge.com

Agents:
Orvis endorsed

EVERY MORNING AFTER BREAKFAST you hear it. The firing of the cylinders of those big radial engines. It's ragged at first, but it smoothes, and after five minutes — when head temperatures reach working limits — these mighty steeds are ready to lift you off the placid waters of the lake, heading into the hinterlands where there are lots of fish and darn few people. For access to streams where no floatplane can land, there's a meticulously maintained Sikorsky S-55 helicopter.

With a deft touch, pilots will land on secluded lakes where a jet boat may be cached, ready to ferry you up a river to the best wading stretches or to fish deeper waters. You may fish the Goodnews River system to the west, or Katmai off to the east. Other rivers include the Agulawak River. In Alaska, you'll find two Agulawak Rivers. One of them is famous, the other unknown. Crystal Creek fishes the latter: a gravel-bottom stream that provides outstanding spawning habitat for sockeyes. The river fills with them in July and from later that month through August, this is an outstanding fishery for rainbows, char, sea-run Dolly Varden and grayling that move into the river to feed on eggs of spawning sockeyes.

If you've set your sights on a trophy rainbow or grayling, try fishing Oxbow Creek. Resembling a meadow creek with few streamside or underwater obstructions, Oxbow's biggest rainbow topped 34 inches. Average fish are two feet long. Grayling exceed four pounds. Only 50 feet at its widest, this is an easy wading and casting creek. It's hard to imagine a river only 100 feet wide, but that's the story of another fine water, the North. After July 10, it receives a late run of king salmon; easy to wade, it may be the best place to catch a king on a fly rod.

Surrounded by deep green mountains that take on a golden cast with the dusk, the lakefront lodge is modern. Each room has a private bath. Sauna and spa await anglers whose bodies are strained from fighting fish. There's a fly tying bench and a heated room to dry waders for the next day's festivities. Each day's menu offers guests the choice between nouvelle and hearty-homestyle cuisine.

Deer Creek Cottages

T h o r n e   B a y ,   A l a s k a

This do-it-yourself vacation is complete
with boat, motor, salmon and steelhead.

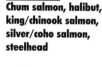

VITAL STATISTICS:

KEY SPECIES:
Chum salmon, halibut, king/chinook salmon, silver/coho salmon, steelhead

Tackle:
Fly-fishing, spinning
Major Season:
February through November
Accommodations:
Two frame cottages
Number of Rooms: 5
Maximum Number of Guests: 10
Meals: Self-catered
Conference Groups: No
Rates: From $500 / day / 4 anglers
Guides: Additional
Gratuities: Angler's discretion
Preferred Payment:
Cash, check or credit cards
Getting There:
Fly to Thorne Bay.
Other Activities:
Big game, bird-watching, boating, hiking, wildlife photography

Contact:
Steve Scheldt
Deer Creek Cottages
PO Box 19475
Thorne Bay AK 99919
Ph: 907/828-3393
Fax: 907/828-3438

ARE ALASKA FISHING VACATIONS only for the well heeled? Not necessarily. Thanks to Steve Scheldt's ingenuity, you can find a week's worth of lodging for less than $1,000. Sound too good to be true? Read on; here's the deal. Steve built two modern cottages, one with two bedrooms, the other with three, equipped them with kitchens as well as charcoal grills and smokers, and added a 19-foot skiff and motor for your use. You and three pals will share the two-bedroom cottage; with two more, you can each save a couple hundred bucks and hang out in the cottage with three bedrooms. This is self-catered. You do the cooking, but you don't have to fly in all of your provisions. You can pick up staples right in the town of Thorne Bay. (If you want great steaks or a sip of single malt, you'd best bring them along, packed in the cooler you'll use to take home your salmon.)

Armed with charts, maps, boat and a van, you can set off to fish the rivers on Prince of Wales Island or the sheltered saltwater around it. Mountainous with deep, fjord-like inlets, the island is drained by scores of small rivers and streams. It's traversed with a road system of sorts. From January through May, and again in November and December, steelhead move into 85 of the rivers and larger streams. Depending on the size of the water, spinning gear or fly rods are favored tackle, but it's all catch-and-release. Steelheading is best in April and May (and the climate is more hospitable). You'll also find silvers in the streams in August through October.

Bigger action occurs in the saltwaters of the Inside Passage. King salmon from 12 to 60 pounds arrive in December, with June and July traditionally the best months. Silvers start their runs in June, and the fishing peaks from late summer to early fall. Chums also make an appearance and are best in July. Best months for deep jigging for halibut (25 to 300 pounds) are July through September. You can also catch cod and yelloweye rockfish.

As do-it-yourself camps go, this one has all the right pieces. If you book in, your group might consider hiring a guide for a day or two ($300 for freshwater, $450 for salt) to pick up a little local intelligence before heading out on your own.

[A L A S K A]

Fishing Unlimited Lodge

A n c h o r a g e ,   A l a s k a

How'd you like your own plane, your own pilot
and the ability to fish anywhere you can fly?

SO VARIED IS THE ANGLING in the Iliamna region — rainbows of more than 10 pounds, five species of salmon, arctic char, grayling, and lakes, rivers and tumbling mountain streams — that you just can't begin to fish it all, let alone even get to it from most wilderness lodges. Lorane Owsichek has the answer, and she's demonstrated it for more than 20 years. The way to sample the best of all that the region has to offer is to fly out every day to waters where fish are active.

Other lodges have flyouts, you say, and indeed they do. But at Fishing Unlimited, every three or four anglers has sole use of a plane every day of their stay. The plane's pilot is a qualified fishing guide, and another guide accompanies the group just to ensure that each guest receives appropriate attention. Spinning and fly-fishing are spoken with equal fluency at this lodge. Your destination may be anywhere in the 30,000-square-mile Bristol Bay watershed, the huge Iliamna/Kvichak drainage, Katmai or Lake Clark National Parks, or even Kodiak Island. When you land, you may be wading or you may board strategically cached boats to reach rivers where the plane can't land. If you want, you'll have the choice of flying into the headwaters of a river and floating down to a point where the plane will meet you at day's end.

The first two weeks of June and the last week of August through the first week of October will give you your best shot at trophy rainbows of six to eight pounds and up. Kings run from mid-June through mid-July. Reds and chums start in the second week of June with reds tapering off a week earlier than chums in late July. Silvers come in the first week of August and remain through October, and pinks make a cameo appearance from late July through mid-August. Char, grayling, lake trout and northern pike are available all season. Packages include flights from Anchorage to Fishing Unlimited, licenses and stamps, and processing of salmon for your trip home.

Tucked in an isolated cove, Fishing Unlimited's two modern wood and glass lodges offer stunning views of Tanalian Peak, where Dall sheep are often sighted. Guests stay in spacious cedar cabins, scattered under the trees, with private baths. Wooden boardwalks connect the cabins to the lodges, where you'll find a sauna and hot tub, lounges with fireplaces and the dining room where the cuisine is excellent.

VITAL STATISTICS:

KEY SPECIES:
Arctic char, chum salmon, grayling, king/chinook salmon, pink salmon, rainbows, red/sockeye salmon, silver/coho salmon

Tackle:
Fly-fishing, spinning
Flyouts to Remote Waters: Yes
Major Season:
June through September
Accommodations:
ELEGANT CABINS
NUMBER OF ROOMS: 9
MAXIMUM NUMBER OF GUESTS: 16
Meals: Fine cuisine
Conference Groups: Yes
Rates: From $3,100 / 3 days
Guides: Inlcuded
Gratuities: 10% of package
Preferred Payment:
Cash or check
Getting There:
Fly to Anchorage and catch the shuttle.
Other Activities:
Flight-seeing, hiking, wildlife photography

Contact:
Lorriane Owsichek
Fishing Unlimited Lodge
PO Box 190301
Anchorage AK 99519
Ph: 907/243-5899
Fax: 907/243-2473
e-mail:
info@alaskalodge.com
Web:
www.alaskalodge.com

*While Waterfall Resort was once a cannery, you'll
find excellent accommodations, food
and service — and lots of salmon, of course!*

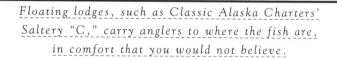

*Floating lodges, such as Classic Alaska Charters'
Saltery "C," carry anglers to where the fish are,
in comfort that you would not believe.*

[A L A S K A]

Goodnews River Lodge

A n c h o r a g e ,   A l a s k a

Surrounded by the Togiak National Wildlife Refuge, you'll have fine fishing here no matter what the weather.

VITAL STATISTICS:

KEY SPECIES:
Dolly Varden, chum salmon, grayling, king/chinook salmon, pink salmon, rainbows, red/sockeye salmon, silver/coho salmon

Tackle:
Fly-fishing, spinning, trolling
Major Season:
Late June through mid-September
Accommodations:
WEATHERPORT TENTS
NUMBER OF ROOMS: 10
HANDICAPPED ACCESSIBLE: 1
MAXIMUM NUMBER OF GUESTS: 20
Meals: Hearty fare with multiple entrees
Conference Groups: Yes
Rates: From $3,950 / 8 days, 7 nights (float trips are $2,995)
Guides: Included
Gratuities: 5% - 10% of trip
Preferred Payment:
Cash, check or credit cards
Getting There:
Fly to Anchorage and catch the private charter to Goodnews Bay.
Other Activities:
Bird-watching, boating, hiking, wildlife photography

Contact:
Scott Gala
Goodnews River Lodge
PO Box 111810
Anchorage AK 99511-1810
Ph: 800/274-8371
Fax: 888/274-9778
e-mail:
grlcamp@aol.com
Web:
www.akgoodnewsriverlodge.com

SOME OUTFITS IN ALASKA rely on floatplanes and choppers to fly anglers to waters where salmon and rainbows run. Not so with Ron Hyde and his crew at Goodnews River Lodge. The lodge is located just upstream from the tidal section, ensuring that clients will have first shot at "fresh" salmon starting their upstream spawning runs. Runs of king and, particularly, silver salmon in this drainage are astounding. The other three salmon species — sockeyes, pinks and chums — play supporting roles. Rainbows open the show in June and bring down the curtain in late August, and Dolly Varden constitute the chorus in the second and third acts. Grayling, ever ready to take small dry flies or spinners, abound as well.

From the time when the season opens in late June to its close in the end of September, the Goodnews and its tributaries fish well. Smaller than many rivers in the area and with numerous pools, runs and riffles, the Goodnews is less than 50 yards wide. The gravel bottom makes for easy wading. Guests ride jetboats as far as 15 or 20 miles to select fishing sites. But you don't have to go far from the lodge for good fishing. When the silvers (12 to 20 pounds) are running in August and early September, the pool just downstream and around the bend can produce 50 fish a day. In fact, silvers are so plentiful in this system that they force rainbows into the back seat. Yet every day, big rainbows hit flies fished for silvers, and once in a while, anglers connect with huge 'bows of 10 pounds. Just skate a deerhair mouse across the surface and see what happens. Kings are fewer than the silvers, but they make up for it in size, averaging between 35 and 50 pounds.

Standing on a high bank, the lodge's two-man Weatherport tents line the river. Each is heated, equipped with electricity, and boasts a front porch for rods and gear. Anglers bed down on comfortable cots fitted with flannel sheets and thick comforters. A special drying room readies waders and boots for the morning. Guests awake to a fresh pot of hot coffee. At dinner, there's always a choice of entrees, and afterward, if you haven't fished your fill, you can head for the gravel bar below the lodge.

For a special treat, ask Ron about his float trips for two to six anglers. You'll rough it where the fish are, spending a full week on the Goodnews. Not only will the fishing be excellent and varied, but you'll see moose and bear up close and, well, pretty personal.

The Grand Aleutian Hotel

Dutch Harbor, Alaska

Takes a hell of a halibut to raise an eyebrow here, but these flat fish aren't the only game in town.

VITAL STATISTICS:

KEY SPECIES:
Bull trout/Dolly Varden, cod, halibut, pink salmon, red/sockeye salmon, silver/coho salmon

Tackle:
Casting, fly-fishing, spinning, trolling
Flyouts to Remote Waters: Yes
Major Season:
April through October
Accommodations:
COMFORTABLE HOTEL
NUMBER OF ROOMS: 133
HANDICAPPED ACCESSIBLE: 6
MAXIMUM NUMBER OF GUESTS: 260
Meals: Regional cuisine
Conference Groups: Yes
Rates: From $150 / day / 2
Guides: $165 / 1/2 day
Gratuities: 15% - 20%
Preferred Payment:
Cash, check or credit cards
Getting There:
Fly to Dutch Harbor and catch the shuttle bus.
Other Activities:
Bird-watching, boating, hiking, wildlife photography, archaeology dig

Contact:
Tour Coordinator
The Grand Aleutian Hotel
Po Box 921169
Dutch Harbor AK 99692-1169
Ph: 907/581-3844
Fax: 907/581-7150
e-mail:
grand.aleutian@unisea.com

FRESH HALIBUT is among the most prized of seafoods; if you're not sure, just check the menu in a great restaurant or price a couple pounds in the fish market. The flesh is firm, not unlike tuna, and the flavor is delicate. Charcoal it with a marinade of fresh ginger and garlic. However, before you can chuck a slab on the grill, you've got to catch it. And the best place for that is a little-known town far out in the Aleutians, that tail of volcanic islands that points to Kamchatka.

In these bitter cold waters, halibut grow to phenomenal size. Fish of 100 to 200 pounds hardly attract notice. Those of 300 pounds plus are considered "big." That's because fish of 400 pounds plus have been brought to boat on rod and reel. Halibut requires not so much finesse, as stamina. A no. 12/0 hook, baited with herring, is dropped over the side from a stiff boat rod with enough weight to hold it near bottom. You sit in the stern of the comfortable Sportfisherman, rod in hand, rising and falling on the gentle swell, waiting for a halibut to bite. You can do nothing but wait. But when a halibut hits, you know it. You rear back on the rod for all you're worth, hoping that you've driven the hook home. That's when the halibut makes his first run and you find out whether your reel's drag is worth the money you paid for it. Then it's you and the fish. Take up five yards of line, give back three. When the skipper shouts "we've got color," you know that the end is near. With shotgun-launched harpoon or flying gaff, the halibut will be brought aboard.

Along with halibut, fly out to Volcano Bay with its beaches of black sand and fish the freshwater streams that charge the sound. There you'll fish for silvers, pink and sockeye salmon, and Dolly Varden. Use fly or spinning gear, as is your choice.

The Aleutians are a bit off the main stream for tourists. You'll enjoy this land — rolling foothills, green and lush, and sprinkled with wildflowers. Mountains capped with snow loom behind the city. On a charming cove sits the Grand Aleutian, a first-class hotel. Modern rooms are well appointed and offer water and mountain views. Works by local artists adorn the walls. Elegant dining features regional cuisine, and the piano in the bar knows all the good old tunes.

Iliaska Lodge

I l i a m n a ,   A l a s k a

On the shore of the lake that gave Alaskan rainbows their fame, you'll find more than fishing.

VITAL STATISTICS:

KEY SPECIES:
Arctic char, grayling, rainbows, red/sockeye salmon, silver/coho salmon

Tackle:
Fly-fishing
Flyouts to Remote Waters: Yes
Major Season:
June through September
Accommodations:
WEATHERED WOODEN LODGE
NUMBER OF ROOMS: 6
MAXIMUM NUMBER OF GUESTS: 14
Meals: Prime rib, lobster, king crab
Conference Groups: No
Rates: $5,200 / week
Guides: Included
Gratuities: $400 / week
Preferred Payment:
Cash or check
Getting There:
Fly to Iliamna and meet the lodge van.
Other Activities:
Waterfowling, wingshooting

Contact:
Ted Gerken
Iliaska Lodge
PO Box 228
Iliamna AK 99606
Ph: 907/571-1221
e-mail:
iliaska@alaska.net
Web:
www.alaska.net/~iliaska

Off Season:
6160 Farport Dr
Anchorage AK 99507
Ph: 907/337-9844
Fax: 907/337-9844

PICTURE THIS, piscators: five million rainbow trout! Migrating behind spawning salmon, these 'bows swim up Kvichak from Bristol Bay and pause for a while in Lake Iliamna. This is the largest freshwater lake in Alaska, and it's fed by more tributaries than anyone's really taken time to count. Each of these streams holds excellent fish.

Ted Gerken, former city manager of the town of Kodiak and founder of Iliaska Lodge, is a rainbow kind of guy. If they're hitting drys anywhere within a reasonable flight, he'll know it. Among the rivers fished by Gerken's guests is Lower Talarik, one of the best 100 trout streams in the U.S., according to Trout Unlimited.

Lower Talarik Creek is short and sweet. It flows into Lake Iliamna about a half-hour's flight west of the lodge, but it is not much to look at. A channel of maybe three-quarters of a mile divides a pair of lagoons. The channel is a feed trough and these rainbows are hogs. They gorge on sockeye salmon flesh and eggs, and almost anything else you care to throw at them. They're big, passive fish used to having the current bring them dinner. Get there at the right time on virtually any day from mid-August into September, and you'll catch so many five- to nine-pound 'bows that you'll wonder whether you'll ever be happy again on your home stream.

Alaska's five salmon each run in their season through the waters fished by Iliaska Lodge. So, too, do char, grayling, lake trout and rainbows. The lodge focuses on trophy rainbows and char, but it does not ignore the salmon. Quite the contrary. You will fly out daily with a guide to fish rivers or lakes where the bite is on. The region offers virtually every kind of water: plunge pools beneath waterfalls; bouldery pocket water; and long gravel slicks and runs. Most is wadeable, but no matter. The floatplane will put down next to one of Gerken's cached boats with motor.

Roofed with tin and grayed by the weather, Iliaska Lodge looks more like it belongs on the Maine coast. It sits on a tundra point, open to winds off the lake. After you've returned from a day's fishing and showered, you'll wander into the living room for the pre-dinner "Liar's Hour." Here you're bound to catch a whopper even if you didn't on the stream. Meanwhile, the kitchen crew is putting the finishing touches on an exquisite dinner. Afterwards, owner Ted Gerken taps a glass and lays out plans for the next day. Rooms are simply furnished and ready whenever dreams overtake you.

Island Point Lodge

Kupreanof Island, Alaska

Fish 18 hours a day for salmon and halibut at this self-guided lodge.

VITAL STATISTICS:

KEY SPECIES:
Bull trout/Dolly Varden, cutthroat, halibut, king/ chinook salmon, rainbows, red/sockeye salmon, silver/coho salmon

Tackle:
Casting, fly-fishing, spinning, trolling
Flyouts to Remote Waters: Yes
Major Season:
May through October
Accommodations:
RUSTIC CABINS
NUMBER OF ROOMS: 7
MAXIMUM NUMBER OF GUESTS: 20
Meals: Hearty family fare
Conference Groups: No
Rates: From $1,325 / week, triple occupancy
Guides: Additional
Gratuities: $50 - $100
Preferred Payment:
Cash, check or credit cards
Getting There:
Fly to Petersburg and take the boat.
Other Activities:
Big game, waterfowling, wildlife photography

Contact:
Frank Stelmach
Island Point Lodge
195 West St
Douglas MA 01516
Ph: 800/352-4522
e-mail:
iplak@vltranet.com
Web:
www.ultranet.com/niplak

LOCATED IN MIDST OF 16.7 million acres of wilderness that includes the Tongass National Forest, Island Point Lodge sits along the Wrangell Narrows on Kupreanof Island, about 90 miles south of Juneau and 14 miles from Petersburg. Tides pump through the narrows with amazing velocity carrying with them pods of salmon.

Island Point Lodge offers anglers a week of self-guided salmon, halibut and trout fishing for a price that's hard to beat. Here's what you get: five and a half days of fishing, use of an Alaskan Lund side-console boat, bait, gas, three meals a day and a bunk. The digs aren't fancy — wood-sided cabins or rooms in the main lodge proper, with shower and toilets in the rear of the lodge and power that goes off between 10:00 p.m. and midnight — but you can fish to your heart's content.

Summer dawns break between 3:00 and 4:00 a.m. and twilight fades at 11:00 p.m. Many Island Point anglers get in three or four hours of fishing before breakfast (often the best time). Lunches are of the do-it-yourself brown bag variety, which you'll probably wolf down in the boat. Naturally, you can fish after dinner.

You'll arrive at the lodge on Saturday, and after orientation by the staff, you're on your own until you return home the following Friday. Depending on which species are running, staff will show you good locations, load your bait cooler with frozen herring, and point you in the right direction. You'll find all five salmon running in the Wrangell Narrows: kings (20 to 30 pounds) from May through July; sockeyes (five to seven pounds) in July; chums (eight to 20 pounds) in July and August; pinks (three to six pounds) in July and August; and silvers (eight to 18 pounds) in August and September. Rivers flowing into the Narrows and adjacent straits hold steelhead in April and May, and char and cutthroats from June through September. Cod and halibut are available throughout the season.

Bring your own fishing gear, including a fairly stiff rod and a medium-heavy reel loaded with 25-pound-test line. Slip a lightweight spinning system into your duffel for char and cutthroats. Fly-fishers will be happy with an 8- or 9-weight system and a 5-weight for trout. This is definitely a catch-and-keep operation. Load your gear into two coolers. Pack along a duffel bag. You'll fill the coolers with filets, and stuff your baggage into the duffel for the trip home. Don't forget a box of heavy-duty freezer bags in which to pack your fish and duct tape to seal the coolers.

[A L A S K A]

King Ko Inn

King Salmon, Alaska

You don't have to rough it to find great salmon and trout. Matter of fact, you can stay in town.

VITAL STATISTICS:

KEY SPECIES:
Chum salmon, grayling, king/chinook salmon, rainbows, silver/coho salmon

Tackle:
Casting, fly-fishing, spinning, trolling
Flyouts to Remote Waters: Yes
Major Season:
April through October
Accommodations:
HOUSEKEEPING EFFICIENCIES
NUMBER OF ROOMS: 24
HANDICAPPED ACCESSIBLE: 2
MAXIMUM NUMBER OF GUESTS: 75
Meals: Eat in restaurants or cook for yourself
Conference Groups: Yes
Rates: $175 / day / 2
Guides: Additional
Gratuities:
Angler's discretion
Preferred Payment:
Cash, check or MasterCard/Visa
Getting There:
Fly to King Salmon, and walk across the street.
Other Activities:
Big game, waterfowling, wingshooting, bird-watching, boating, hiking, wildlife photography

Contact:
Matt Norman or Paul Koval
King Ko Inn
PO Box 346
King Salmon AK 99613
Ph: 907/246-3377
Fax: 907/246-3357
e-mail:
kingko@alaska.net
Web:
www.kingko.com
Off Season:
3340 Arctic Blvd Suite 201
Anchorage AK 99503
Ph: 907/562-0648
Fax: 907/563-7238

The hamlet of King Salmon is the gateway to the famed Bristol Bay area of southwest Alaska, the port of entry for the Kvichak, Alagnak and Nonvianuk watersheds. Daily jet service ferries hundreds of anglers over from Anchorage. There they clamor aboard Beavers and Otters and Cessnas for flights into the bush. It seems as if everyone is going somewhere else, that is, except those intrepid souls who know the secret of the King Ko Inn.

More than 50 years ago, when the Army Air Corps was building a base along the Naknek River which flows past King Salmon, the King Ko opened its doors. The lodge — nothing fancy, mind you — earned a reputation for good service at a fair price. A fire in 1993 destroyed the original structure, but shortly the inn was rebuilt. Modern cabins contain two efficiencies complete with kitchenette and private bath. Adjacent is the main lodge with restaurant and bar featuring live entertainment. Units may be rented with American plan or without meals.

You'll find no daily flyouts or staff of guides at King Ko. There are no boats bobbing at the dock. Managers Matt Norman and Paul Koval will arrange air charters, guides, float trips or anything else (well, almost anything else) you want. They'll refer you to guides who live in King Salmon. Most of King Ko's anglers will spring for a day or two of guided fishing early in the week — just to see where the fish are and learn successful techniques — and then they'll rent a boat and motor (about $125 / day) and head out to try their luck sans guide. You can also rent a car that will take you to some of the small creeks — King Salmon and Pauls in particular — that may hold stocks of spawning salmon.

However, most anglers drift fish or troll the Naknek River for kings. In the general vicinity of the lodge, you'll find four species of salmon. Kings (up to 60 pounds) are best in June and July; chums (four to 20 pounds) and reds (four to 15 pounds) in July; and silvers (four to 15 pounds) in August. Grayling in the two- to three-pound range open the season in May, and rainbows (two to 10-pounds-plus) bring it to a close in September and October.

Think of the King Ko Inn as do-it-yourself Alaska. If you don't need fancy and are willing to do your own cooking, you can enjoy salmon fishing for less than $200 per person per day.

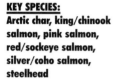

Kodiak Island River Camps

Kodiak, Alaska

For more than a decade, Dan's river trips on Alaska's Emerald Isle have received rave reviews.

VITAL STATISTICS:

KEY SPECIES:
Arctic char, king/chinook salmon, pink salmon, red/sockeye salmon, silver/coho salmon, steelhead

Tackle:
Fly-fishing
Major Season:
June through October
Accommodations:
VARIES FROM IN-TOWN B&B TO TENTS
NUMBER OF ROOMS: 4
MAXIMUM NUMBER OF GUESTS: 6
Meals: Hearty regional seafood plus beef
Conference Groups: No
Rates: From $1,295 / week
Guides: Included
Gratuities: Angler's discretion
Preferred Payment:
Cash or check
Getting There:
Fly to Kodiak.
Other Activities:
Bird-watching, hiking, wildlife photography

Contact:
Dan Busch
Kodiak Island River Camps
Box 1162
Kodiak AK 99615
Ph: 907/486-5310
Fax: 907/486-5310

KODIAK ISLAND is a welter of contrasts. While it ought to be cold, the island's climate is moderated by the Japanese Current. Just to the north, across the narrow Shelikof Strait, volcanic mountains spew sulphurous smoke, but on Kodiak, the mountains are old and worn, relics of an earlier time. The northeastern third of Kodiak is heavily forested with Sitka spruce, but the rest of the island is covered with low willows, alder and wild rose. And the fishing? You can drive to a number of pretty good streams, or you can fly out to rivers that are as isolated as any on the mainland.

Dan Busch is a master of angling on Kodiak and nearby Afognak. He runs fly fishing trips and guides anglers out of his home base in Kodiak. Home base is a two-room (private baths) bed-and-breakfast on the outskirts of this quaint town. From his headquarters, Busch runs four week-long fishing programs:

• PAUL'S LAKE CAMP ON AFOGNAK: Fly to Afognak Island, about half an hour by air from Kodiak, to an island camp on this mile-long lake. The river connecting the lake to Paul's Bay is only a few hundred yards long. From the second week in August through the middle of September, silver salmon run up the channel into the lake. Four anglers fish from inflatables or float tubes, or wade the lake, river or tidal shore under the eye of a guide. Accommodations are utilitarian — three unheated cabins — but the dining cabin is warmed by its gas stove and oven.

• KARLUK FLOAT FOR KING SALMON: After flying into the Karluk, you, a guide and up to three other anglers will drift down the Karluk for six days camping and fishing where the fishing is best. You'll sleep on a cot in a pop-up tent and eat hearty in the stove-equipped cook tent.

• KARLUK FOR STEELHEAD: On this trip, anglers fly into a different section of the river where Koniag, Inc., a cooperative of native associations, maintains four cabins that sleep up to six in bunk beds. They're warm and dry and when steelhead are running in the last two weeks of October, who cares about anything else?

• KODIAK ROAD SYSTEM: In August and the first two weeks of September, silvers show up in many of the rivers along Kodiak's 100-mile-plus road system. Guests stay at Dan's B&B and drive out daily to the American, Olds or other rivers. Anglers booking this trip can also fly out to a remote river or lake at no extra charge. You'll stay in the B&B and eat lovely family-style dinners.

[A L A S K A]

Kodiak Wilderness Outfitters

P o r t   L i o n s ,   A l a s k a

A new lodge, private baths, great salmon, fewer anglers — how's that for starters?

I N 1999, KEVIN AND KATHRYN ADKINS opened their new lodge in Port Lions. It's a sturdy affair built of cedar with three private rooms with two beds in each. Rooms have their own baths — a real plus in my book — and there's plenty of room to hang up gear. "The new lodge is bigger than the old one, but now we take only six anglers per week instead of eight," says Katy. That makes for more elbow room and personal service.

Port Lions rises up from Settler Cove off Kizhuyak Bay. It's not a long boat ride from the town of Kodiak, so if the weather goes south, as it occasionally does, you can still reach the lodge. A tiny road system rims the cove, and it crosses a number of streams that carry salmon. If the town's fogged in on a day you'd planned a flyout, hitch up your socks, pick up your five- and eight-weights, and set off down the road. You'll find plenty of interesting water to fish. Or, slip a sea kayak into the sheltered cove and cast for silvers or sockeye right in front of the lodge.

That, of course, isn't the main event. Kodiak Wilderness Outfitters prides itself on its ability to put clients on big kings on the Karluk in June, and steelhead when scrub alders and cottonwoods yellow up in the fall. Equally popular is the short run across Marmot Bay to Afognak Island and its namesake river for sockeyes and early pinks in July. Halibut are plentiful on the north side of Whale Island, a 20-minute boat trip from the lodge.

The four-day/four-night flyout package includes your choice of two flyout trips to rivers in the region, or an overnight float trip on the Karluk. Go for the float. Operator Kevin Adkins takes four to six guests who drift the river, famous for kings but also heavy with late-summer silvers and sockeyes, and spend the night at a tent camp at the midway point. Tent camp is a bit of a misnomer, as the tents are erected on plywood platforms and heated with stoves. One provides sleeping accommodations for guests. Activity centers around the other, equipped with a full-size cookstove and oven. No canned food here. Everything's flown in fresh, including Katy Adkins' homemade pastries. Dining family-style in the kitchen tent is a cozy end to the day, especially if you've been fighting steelhead in the chill of October.

VITAL STATISTICS:

KEY SPECIES:
Halibut, king/chinook salmon, silver/coho salmon, red/sockeye salmon, steelhead

Tackle:
Fly-fishing, spinning, trolling
Flyouts to Remote Waters: Yes
Major Season:
Late May through October
Accommodations:
NEW CEDAR LODGE
NUMBER OF ROOMS: 3
HANDICAPPED ACCESSIBLE: 3
MAXIMUM NUMBER OF GUESTS: 6
Meals: Prime rib and seafood, plus wickedly good breads and pastries
Conference Groups: No
Rates: From $2,300 / 5 days
Guides: Included
Gratuities: Angler's discretion
Preferred Payment:
Cash, check or MasterCard/Visa
Getting There:
Fly to Kodiak and catch the boat to Port Lions.
Other Activities:
Waterfowling, bird-watching, wildlife photography

Contact:
Kevin Adkins
Kodiak Wilderness Outfitters
PO Box 29
Port Lions AK 99550
Ph: 888/454-2418
Fax: 907/454-2418
e-mail:
fishekwo.kodiak@worldnet.att.net
Web:
www.kodiakwilderness.com

Agents:
Fishing International: 800/950-4242

Mike Cusack's King Salmon Lodge

N a k n e k   R i v e r ,   A l a s k a

Come for the fishing, for the food, for celebrity anglers, and to see bears snatch salmon right out of the air.

VITAL STATISTICS:

KEY SPECIES:
Bull trout/Dolly Varden, grayling, king/chinook salmon, rainbows, red/sockeye salmon, silver/coho salmon

Tackle:
Fly-fishing, spinning, trolling
Flyouts to Remote Waters: Yes
Major Season:
June through mid-October
Accommodations:
RUSTIC YET MODERN LOG LODGE
NUMBER OF ROOMS: 22
HANDICAPPED ACCESSIBLE: 17
MAXIMUM NUMBER OF GUESTS: 44
Meals: Crab and filet mignon
Conference Groups: Yes
Rates: $6,100 / week
Guides: Included
Gratuities: 8%
Preferred Payment:
Cash, check or credit cards
Getting There:
Fly to King Salmon and the lodge van will meet you.
Other Activities:
Big game, biking, boating, waterfowling, wingshooting

Contact:
**Mike Cusack's
King Salmon Lodge
3601 C. St, Suite 1350
Anchorage AK 99503
Ph: 907/277-3033
Fax: 907/563-7929**

IF AMERICAN LODGES were rated, this would earn five stars. Here on the Naknek is a world-class lodge that started out as a getaway, riverfront cabin. Today it's known worldwide. Short flyouts carry guests to the finest fishing offered by the Wild Trout Management Area around Iliamna Lake. Nearby are the bounteous waters of Katmai National Park, and on the way, you can sail through the Valley of 10,000 Smokes and wing past glaciers of milky turquoise. It's little wonder that King Salmon Lodge attracts such folks as Bob Hope, Norman Schwarzkopf, Chuck Yeager, Olivia Newton-John, Tom Weiskopf and John Riggins.

Just which species draw anglers is a matter of personal preference. All five species of Pacific salmon migrate up the Naknek. Kings up to 50-pounds-plus arrive in mid-June and complete their run by August. Sockeyes from four to 12 pounds play a short but intense engagement from late June to mid-July. If you want to test your skills against the biggest and scrappiest members of the salmon clan, book the first week in July. And speaking of duos, what about rainbows averaging six pounds and silver salmon of eight to 16 pounds? If you hit them in early September, as the rainbows gorge on salmon eggs, you will have truly been there and done it all.

Angling is via boat, wading, floatplane or whatever works. Often, two anglers share a guide, but sometimes you may fish one-on-one. If you don't have the tackle you think you'll need, don't worry. King Salmon Lodge will supply everything, not just flies or lures, but rods, reels, waders, you name it.

There's a real advantage to booking a trip late in the season. Ptarmigan (the same bird is called a red grouse in Scotland) are plentiful, and not as dumb as they're made out to be when you hunt them with a skilled pointer. You'll find loaner shotguns at the lodge, but the wise gunner packs a 20-bore in his duffel. You might want to make that a 12-gauge. September's duck season also overlaps with the height of rainbows and silvers.

Quality service isn't just a slogan at King Salmon Lodge, it's a way of life. Owner Mike Cusack grew up here, at his mother's "cabin on the river." As second-generation lodgekeepers, Mike and family know what appeals. Guest rooms (with private baths) are country comfy but informal, homey, and not the least overdone. Along with fine regional cuisine, you'll enjoy the weekly pig roast.

Halibut are Alaska's "other" fish, as eagerly sought by guests at Yes Bay Lodge as the salmon that swim the surging tides.

Mission Lodges: Mission; Alaska West; Kingfishers

Dillingham, Alaska

No matter your interest or your wallet, one of these three lodges may suit your 'druthers.

VITAL STATISTICS:

KEY SPECIES:
Chum salmon, grayling, king/chinook salmon, rainbows, silver/coho salmon

Tackle:
Casting, fly-fishing, spinning, trolling
Flyouts to Remote Waters: Yes
Major Season:
June through September
Accommodations:
MISSION: CALIFORNIA WOOD AND GLASS
ALASKA WEST & KINGFISHERS:
PLATFORM TENTS
NUMBER OF ROOMS / GUESTS:
MISSION: 20 / 20
ALASKA WEST: 9 / 18
KINGFISHER: 4 / 8
Meals: Alaska gourmet
Conference Groups: Yes
Rates:
MISSION: $5,200 / week
ALASKA WEST: $3,450 / week
KINGFISHERS: $2,750 / week
Guides: Included
Gratuities: $500 / week
Preferred Payment:
Cash, check or Master Card/Visa
Getting There:
Fly to Dillingham and take the lodge van or boat.
Other Activities:
Big game, waterfowling, wingshooting, bird-watching, hiking, wildlife photography, bear-watching

Contact:
Guy Fullhart
Mission Lodge
11201 SE 8th St. Suite 100
Bellevue WA 98004
Ph: 800/819-0750
Fax: 425/452-9351
e-mail:
info@missionlodge.com

FOR THE PAST DECADE and a half, Dale De Priest has been refining a trio of angling lodges that make the most of salmon, rainbow, grayling and char in the area north of the head of Bristol Bay. From upscale wilderness tent camps to the almost-elegant resort north of Dillingham, these accommodations offer wide ranging opportunities that should suit varying interests and wallets.

MISSION LODGE: Long and many-gabled, the flagship two-story lodge is replete with ample windows affording spectacular views of the Aleknagik River. Inside, the carpeted interior with free standing fireplace and modern furnishings has a distinctly California feel. Each guest enjoys a private and cheerful room. With the exception of two rooms, baths are shared. Steak, seafood and prime rib are on the menu at dinners served family-style. Guest here fly out daily to hot fishing on the numerous rivers and lakes in the Nushagak Basin. All five species of Pacific salmon — kings, sockeyes, silvers, chums and pinks — spawn in these waters. Rainbows, Dolly Varden, arctic char and grayling are thick in specific locales known to the pilots and guides. Beginning with kings and rainbows in June, angling winds up with trophy rainbows in the fall. You'll fish from aluminum skiffs or wade as conditions and fish dictate. Truly a first-class operation.

ALASKA WEST: Nine wood-floored tents outfitted with heaters and beds with linens, a drying tent for wet waders and gear, a dining tent with a tying bench, and a tent with hot showers make up accommodations on the Kanetok River, which flows into Kuskokwim Bay at Quinhagak. Salmon, trout, char and grayling are found here, with July and August the better months for rainbows of five-pounds-plus. Fly-fishing for kings in the 50-pound-plus range and tossing Polliwogs (big pink deer-hair poppers) for silvers are the prime sports. Two anglers and their guide set off every morning in an 18-foot boat. And at night, after dinner, you can fish in front of the camp until dark, if you've got the stamina.

ALASKA KINGFISHERS: If monster king salmon feed your dreams, then this eight-angler tent camp on the Nushagak River may be for you. With similar accommodations to Alaska West, the camp boasts 22-foot big river sleds pushed by 60-horse motors augmented with 9.9-horse trolling motors. The camp is only open for a few weeks during the height of king and chum salmon runs.

[A L A S K A]

No See Um Lodge

King Salmon, Alaska

Got the plane, got the pilot, got a group of buds and you're flying out to fish. Does it get any better?

WHAT JACK HOLMAN, owner of this lodge, likes to do is load up his Cessna with four anglers and head out to the best rivers in the Iliamna Wild Trout area. There are scores (actually, more than that), so many that it'd take years to fish them all. There are the old standbys that everyone knows (and where you find collections of floatplanes from other lodges), as well as those hidden secret places that are Jack's favorites. Where you fish depends on the weather, the movement of the fish, and your mood.

At some lodges, when the weather turns to gradu, you're stuck. Oh, there might be some trolling in the lake, but otherwise, it's a day for books and long looks at the drizzling sky. Not so at No See Um. You'll encase yourself in Gore-Tex, climb aboard a jet boat, and run up the Kvichak to that run where the guide thinks there just may be a few silvers and kings. Before noon, you'll have had half a dozen hookups and landed three, one of them a 40-pound king on a fly. Not bad for a washed out day, eh?

Fishing at No See Um Lodge is like that. Plans change. But with a floatplane and pilot/guide for every two to four anglers, you've got your choice of where and what to fish. Rainbows are available all season and average three to 10 pounds. In August and September, when they're cramming themselves full of salmon eggs, 13-pounders are occasionally caught. Salmon start their runs in June. Kings average 30 pounds; sockeyes, six pounds; chums, 10; humpies (pinks), three to five pounds; and silvers, 10 pounds but frequently up to 18 pounds. Char (three to 14 pounds), grayling (one to three pounds) and Dolly Varden (three to six pounds) are fishable all season. Though the season opens in early June, best fishing for salmon is generally in July and August. Rainbows become absolutely fabulous later in the season.

To provide such personal services, No See Um Lodge is small and intimate with no more than 10 guests at any given time. Of five guest rooms, all but one are in the cedar guest house on the bank of the river. The other is in a cabin. The guest house commands a sweeping view of the Kvichak River. The day begins at dawn with breakfast. After fishing, you'll return between 5:00 and 6:00 p.m., visit the hot tub or sauna, enjoy cocktails and hors d'oeuvres, and dine at 7:00 p.m. Then, should you still have strength in your casting arm, try fishing right in front of the lodge.

Reel M Inn

King Salmon, Alaska

Salmon and rainbows aren't the only things that you'll get a kick out of at this Bristol Bay country lodge.

VITAL STATISTICS:

KEY SPECIES:
Grayling, king/chinook salmon, rainbows, coho/ silver salmon

Tackle:
Casting, fly-fishing, spinning, trolling
Flyouts to Remote Waters: Yes
Major Season:
June through October
Accommodations:
MODERN LODGE OF WOOD AND GLASS
NUMBER OF ROOMS: 4
HANDICAPPED ACCESSIBLE: 2
MAXIMUM NUMBER OF GUESTS: 8
Meals: Seafood and steaks
Conference Groups: Yes
Rates: From $2,975 / week
Guides: Included
Gratuities: 15%
Preferred Payment:
Cash or check
Getting There:
Fly to King Salmon and meet the van from the lodge.
Other Activities:
Big game, bird-watching, boating, canoeing/kayaking/rafting, hiking, skiing, snowmobiling, swimming, wildlife photography

Contact:
Nanci Morris
Reel M Inn
PO Box 221
King Salmon AK 99613
Ph: 907/246-8322
e-mail:
fishingb@bristolbay.com

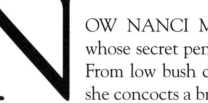

NOW NANCI MORRIS is a classy lass, whose secret penchant is filling your glass. From low bush cranberries and other fare, she concocts a brew — drink it if you dare. Some years it's dry and others a bit fruity, but after landing that salmon, downing a dram is not difficult duty.

Local libations aside, Reel M Inn (despite the horrid pun) is a wonderful lodge hard by the Naknek River near King Salmon. Famed for its five salmon, huge rainbows, deeply colored char and subtle-hued grayling, the river drains the lake of the same name, part of which is encompassed by Katmai National Park.

In front of Reel M Inn, the river is big water, 100 yards wide at the lodge. Much of it is wadeable, but some of it is not. To get around on the river, Nancy uses beamy 20-foot skiffs especially designed for fly-fishers (that means little hardware to snag a cast). Rainbows up to 10 pounds fish best in June and August through October. Kings in the 20- to 40-pound class enter the system in mid-June and fade by the end of July. Sockeye, chum and pink salmon are scattered through midsummer (late June through mid-August), and silvers up to 12 pounds are prevalent from mid-August through early September. Numerous fishing packages from one through seven days are available, and longer stays can be arranged. Those who plan to fish four days or more can fly out to smaller, isolated streams for arctic char and grayling, as well as salmon and rainbows.

Completed recently was Reel M's stunning new lodge of log and timber for up to eight guests. Facing west to catch the afternoon sun, tall windows bring views of the river into the great room dominated on the far wall by a massive stone fireplace. The north wing contains guest rooms, all with private baths, and the south features the dining room. Dinners here are sturdy works featuring regional cuisine and, even if you didn't nail that 30-inch rainbow that hammered your Muddler, a snifter of Nanci's cranberry liquor, served very cordially, of course.

[A L A S K A]

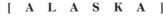

Saltery Lake Lodge

K o d i a k ,   A l a s k a

Sockeyes fill the creek, and at night, you can catch them right behind the lodge.

VITAL STATISTICS:

KEY SPECIES:
Arctic char, king/chinook salmon, pink salmon, red/sockeye salmon, coho/silver salmon, steelhead

Tackle:
Fly-fishing, spinning
Major Season:
June through mid-October
Accommodations:
WOODEN LODGE
NUMBER OF ROOMS: 4
MAXIMUM NUMBER OF GUESTS: 12
Meals: Hearty meat and potatoes
Conference Groups: No
Rates: From $350 / day
Guides: Included
Gratuities: $20 / day
Preferred Payment:
Cash or check
Getting There:
Fly to Kodiak and take the floatplane.
Other Activities:
Boating, bird-watching, canoeing/rafting/kayaking, wildlife photography

Contact:
Doyle Hatfield
Saltery Lake Lodge
1516 Larch St.
Kodiak AK 99615
Ph: 800/770-5037
Fax: 907/486-3188
e-mail:
saltery2@ptiacaka.net
Web:
www.salterylake.com

A BATTERED SUBURBAN JOUNCES down a rutted road, through grassland of a once prominent but now failed dairy farm. With a heave, Doyle Hatfield wrestles the beast out of the deep tracks and onto an obscure path toward the alders and stunted willows along the creek. You climb out and, as you rig your 7-weight, you notice that those pink flowers on the bushes by the stream are wild roses. Nice touch. Now for the salmon.

Saltery Lake Lodge is the only one on Kodiak Island that's located on a freshwater lake. That puts anglers in the catbird seat for a number of reasons. Flowing out of the lake is the Saltery River, seldom more than 50 yards wide. It chatters over gravel bars and slides through long pools on its way to Ugak Bay. All five salmon species use the river. So, too, do Dolly Varden, rainbows and steelhead. When the spawn is on, fresh waves of salmon work their way upstream. They hold in pools, waiting for that primeval trigger to impel them over the next shallows.

You'll find that you can easily see them lying in the pools. Cast a big Mepps against the far bank, let it flutter and sink down to where the salmon lie. Work it slowly through the pool in short jerks. Getting quickly to bottom is important to fly-fishers as well. Use sparsely dressed and weighted patterns, tied on a six- or seven-foot leader and aided by a couple of small split-shot. When a salmon strikes, the Saltery is shallow and open enough so you can chase the fish downstream. Spawning salmon and steelhead school in the lake before moving on up Saltery Creek, which flows behind the lodge. After dinner, as Alaskan twilight hangs over Bread Loaf Mountain, walk down to the mouth of the creek, stand on the gravel bar and cast to sockeyes until you're tired and ready for bed.

You'll sleep in one of four cabins: two share baths while two deluxe cabins have private baths. Accommodations are a bit on the spartan side and meals are hearty, but not gourmet. Hosts Bill and Diane Franklin, and Doyle and Charlotte Hatfield, are warm, friendly and know Kodiak fishing inside and out. They'll bend over backwards to make your stay everything you want it to be.

In addition to fishing the Saltery system, you can arrange to fly out to other watersheds: saltwater fishing for halibut, kings, silvers and cod; and a four- or five-day raft drip down the Karluk for kings, sockeyes and steelhead.

Stephan Lake Lodge

E a g l e   R i v e r ,   A l a s k a

This is where clients dance with salmon and the not-infrequent grizzly in an occasionally personal way.

VITAL STATISTICS:

KEY SPECIES:
Grayling, king/chinook salmon, lake trout, rainbows, red/sockeye salmon, coho/silver salmon

Tackle:
Fly-fishing, spinning
Flyouts to Remote Waters: Yes
Major Season:
June through September
Accommodations:
MELLOW LOG LODGE WITH LOTS OF GLASS
NUMBER OF ROOMS: 7
MAXIMUM NUMBER OF GUESTS: 14
Meals: Beef, chicken and fish
Conference Groups: Yes
Rates: From $1,500 / 3 days
Guides: Included
Gratuities: Angler's discretion
Preferred Payment:
Cash, check or MasterCard/Visa
Getting There:
Fly to Anchorage and take an air taxi (no additional charge).
Other Activities:
Big game, waterfowling, wingshooting, bird-watching, hiking, wildlife photography, bear-watching

Contact:
Jim Bailey
Stephan Lake Lodge
PO Box 770695
Eagle River AK 99577
Ph: 907/696-2163
Fax: 907/694-4129
Web:
www.stephanlakelodge.com

SURROUNDED BY the Talkeetna Mountains lies Stephan Lake, a five-mile-long jewel on the doorstep of Denali National Park. Built of native spruce, now mellowed with age, the lodge sits up on a hill with a commanding view of Stephan Lake and the forest beyond. On chill evenings, a fire burns in the circular hearth and near-perpetual twilight filters through the cathedral window and glows softly on the highly polished floor. Meals are simple and substantial. While baths are shared, sinks with hot and cold water are built into each guest room. The site is the stuff of picture book dreams.

Its reputation, however, is based on more than scenery and creature comforts. For more than 30 years, Stephan Lake Lodge has been putting guests onto fine rainbows, kings and silvers, and showing them spectacular shovel-racked moose and grizzlies. Make that lots of grizzlies. When the kings run up a nearby river, the grizzlies come down, between 70 to 100 of them, and gorge on spawning salmon. If you want, you can look at a grizz up close and very personal. "Never lost a client," muses owner and master guide Jim Bailey. After a moment's reflection he chuckles, "We have had . . . adventures."

Kings run from the first of July to about the thirteenth. You'll need a 10-weight rod for these bruisers, or stout spinning or casting gear to handle hookups of 10 to 20 fish per day. Before it's time for kings, check out the rainbows. The first two weeks of June and the last two weeks of August can bring 40-fish days. We're talking 18- to 24-inch fish here. In August, rainbows are feeding on eggs from spawning king salmon and virtually any egg pattern will work. Before 'bow fishing reaches its peak, silver salmon enter the system, and you'll catch them in the six- to eight-pound range.

While the lodge is on Stephan Lake, Bailey's pretty secretive about the specific names of the rivers he fishes. They're all accessible by floatplane, and he has a fleet of Cessnas and Super Cubs that he uses to ferry guests to trophy water. He also has boats and motors cached on some of the more isolated lakes and rivers. Plus, he has a pair of cabins for anglers who want to overnight at spots that are really secluded. Bring your own tackle, lures and flies, though in an emergency, loaner gear is available. And you can get your fishing licenses at the lodge.

[A L A S K A]

Talaheim Lodge

T a l a c h u l i t n a   R i v e r ,   A l a s k a

Seeking isolated back country rivers where no boat or plane can go? Just spend 30 minutes in a chopper.

VITAL STATISTICS:

KEY SPECIES:
Bull trout/Dolly Varden, grayling, king/chinook salmon, rainbows, coho/silver salmon

Tackle:
Fly-fishing, spinning
Flyouts to Remote Waters: Yes
Major Season:
Mid-June through August
Accommodations:
Log lodge and cabins
Number of Rooms: 3
Maximum Number of Guests: 6
Meals: Family style
Conference Groups: No
Rates: From $3,450 / week
Guides: Included
Gratuities: 5%
Preferred Payment:
Cash or check
Getting There:
Fly to Anchorage and catch the air charter.
Other Activities:
Bear-watching, hiking, wildlife photography

Contact:
Mark Miller
Talaheim Lodge
PO Box 190043
Anchorage AK 99159-0043
Ph: 907/248-6205
Fax: 907/248-6205
e-mail:
talaheim@alaska.net
Web:
www.talaheimlodge.com

BEATING A TATTOO THAT ECHOES from gaunt spruce and rugged rock on the ridge, the rotor lifts you over the rise, and below you opens the channel of the river, winding through dwarf willow and alder. For the last half-hour, you haven't seen any semblance of a road — no ATVers have found their way this far into the bush. And there's no place to land a Cessna or Super Cub, let alone a Beaver.

Gesturing with his left hand while his right grips the column, your pilot points down at a long green pool. You can see salmon, tapered shadows of olive, in the yellowish emerald water. These puppies are big enough to be kings and so early in the season. With a delicate bank around the bend, the pilot flares the 'copter and sets it down on a gravel bar at the head of the pool. You're grin tells the pilot enough.

Since 1988, Talaheim Lodge has been one of the few resorts in Alaska to make extensive use of helicopters to ferry guests to great fishing. While Cessnas and Beavers require somewhat smooth and straight waterways, choppers can drop in anywhere there's a few square yards of treeless, level terrain. Flyouts in rotary-winged aircraft place anglers on waters that are normally only fished by bears.

Just 85 miles west of Anchorage in the foothills of the Alaska Range, Talaheim Lodge is about halfway up the Talachulitna River. Draining into Cook Inlet, the river is a bit off the beaten path. From late June through the second week in July, king salmon averaging 20 pounds run the river. Anglers take four-day, five-night floats through wilderness devoid of other humans. From mid-July through early August, the fishing focuses on rainbows running from two to six pounds, grayling of one and a half and Dolly Varden of three or four pounds. You'll ride the chopper to small streams ideal for medium-weight fly rods. Salmon, this time silvers, return to the picture for the last three weeks of August. Most average between six and 15 pounds. Trout are bigger, more aggressive and are found with the salmon. You'll fly out or ride jetboats to areas where the angling is hot.

Mark and Judi Miller own and run the lodge. It's a family affair; you'll enjoy their kids, Katie and Luke. The number of guests is limited to six per week, and occasionally a couple will have it all to themselves. You'll either stay in a two-bedroom log cabin with shared bath or in a one-bedroom cabin, also log, with a private bath. Meals are simple, hearty, excellent and accompanied by good conversation.

Talstar Lodge

Chugiak, Alaska

*Women anglers love to fish at Talstar,
and so do a few wise guys.*

VITAL STATISTICS:

KEY SPECIES:
Chum salmon, king/chinook salmon, pink salmon, rainbows, red/sockeye salmon, coho/silver salmon

Tackle:
Fly-fishing, spinning
Major Season:
Mid-June through mid-September
Accommodations:
MODERN LOG CABINS
NUMBER OF ROOMS: 3
MAXIMUM NUMBER OF GUESTS: 8
Meals: Elegant regional cuisine
Conference Groups: Yes
Rates: From $400 / day
Guides: Included
Gratuities: $20 / day
Preferred Payment:
Cash, check or MasterCard/Visa
Getting There:
Fly to Anchorage and ride in on a floatplane.
Other Activities:
Bird-watching, boating, wildlife photography

Contact:
Claire Dubin or Dave Scheer
Talstar Lodge
22481 Mirror Lake Drive
Chugiak AK 99567
Ph: 907/688-1116
Fax: 907/688-1117
e-mail:
lodge@tal-star.com
Web:
www.tal-star.com

FOR THE PAST HALF-CENTURY and more, fishing in Alaska has been a man's sport. Heavy waders, beefy rods, lots of wet wool, damp tents, musty sleeping bags and mattresses of willow or spruce boughs. Everything was cooked over a smoky fire in a single skillet — eggs, beans, canned spaghetti — which was washed with sand if it got washed at all. A little grit in your pancakes added digestion, what the hell. We loved it, or more correctly, the magazines told us we did.

Women, of course, knew better. "Why does fishing have to be uncivilized?" they pondered. Enter Claire Dubin, who owns Talstar Lodge. She knew that women enjoy fly-fishing just as they eat up riding, golf and tennis. She also suspected that women would love to fish pristine Alaskan rivers, if only someone would show them how. So she hooked up with fly-fisher Pudge Kleinkauf and, in 1996, hosted a school for women at this lodge on the Talachulitna River. It was a bonzo success!

Kleinkauf and fellow guide, Sandie Arnold, went through the usual stuff — casting, knot tying, leader construction, river reading and fly selection. Classmates cheered good casts and commiserated when line piled at an angler's feet. Kleinkauf and Arnold were always available to help. As the school progressed, students began to help each other too. When one hooked into a fish, congratulatory cries rang over the river. Now Dubin includes at least one school for women anglers each year at Talstar.

It is okay, of course, for men to fish at Talstar as well. The Talachulitna River is 65 miles northwest of Anchorage in the foothills of the Alaska Range. It's a high-quality fishery for all five species of salmon. Kings up to 60 pounds run from mid-June through mid-July. Sockeyes enter the river in mid-July, and chums, pinks and silvers show up by the end of that month. If a grand slam on salmon isn't your dream, think about fishing the Tal in late August or early September with light tackle — fly or spinning — for rainbows up to six pounds, and silvers. Wading is the name of the game here, though sometimes anglers will work a pool from one of the lodge's 18-foot riverboats. One guide is provided for every four anglers.

Talstar is a modern log lodge surrounded by tall stands of ferns in a spruce forest. Two cabins can sleep a total of eight, and guests share three bathrooms. Dining is close to gourmet. Nobody starves; everyone gains weight.

[A L A S K A]

Tikchik Narrows

D i l l i n g h a m ,   A l a s k a

Seeking the ultimate angling challenge? Give the Tikchik ultimate grand slam your best shot.

VITAL STATISTICS:

KEY SPECIES:
Arctic char, bull trout/Dolly Varden, chum salmon, grayling, king/chinook salmon, lake trout, pike, pink salmon, rainbows, red/sockeye salmon, silver/coho salmon

Tackle:
Casting, fly-fishing, spinning, trolling
Flyouts to Remote Waters: Yes
Major Season:
June through September
Accommodations:
RUSTIC, FIRST-CLASS CABINS
NUMBER OF ROOMS: 12
MAXIMUM NUMBER OF GUESTS: 24
Meals: Elegant regional cuisine
Conference Groups: Yes
Rates: $5,400 / week
Guides: Included
Gratuities: Angler's discretion
Preferred Payment:
Cash or check
Getting There:
Fly to Dillingham and meet your Beaver.
Other Activities:
Waterfowling, wingshooting, bird-watching, hiking, wildlife photography

Contact:
Bud Hodson
Tikchik Narrows
PO Box 690
Dillingham AK 99576
Ph: 907/596-3511
Fax: 907/596-3510
e-mail:
info@tikchik.com
Web:
www.tikchiklodge.com
Off Season:
PO Box 220248
Anchorage AK 99522
Ph: 907/243-8450
Fax: 907/248-3091

I N 1998, ANDREW HARPER'S Hideaway Report said it all when it awarded Bud Hodson's Tikchik Narrows its sport fishing lodge of the year award. Such awards aren't easily come by. Reviewers travel incognito, book rooms as typical guests, pay full rates for their stay, and receive no complimentary services. No stayola here.

Tikchik Narrows is a spit of brushy cobble that juts into the slim flowage between Tikchik and Nuyakuk lakes about 60 miles northeast of Dillingham. Lands of the Wood-Tikchik State Park and the Togiak National Wildlife Refuge surround the lodge with more than six million acres of wilderness, more than 13 major lakes and three major river systems. Much of it is accessible only by float-plane. Each morning you'll breakfast as hearty or as healthy as you wish, and then climb aboard a meticulously maintained deHavilland Beaver for the flight to the waters du jour. There, you and your pilot/guide will cast for a dozen species, including all five Pacific salmon, rainbows of trophy proportions, char, Dolly Varden, grayling and lake trout.

If you're the kind of angler who thrives on challenges, plan your visit in the last week of July or early August. That's when you stand the best chance of netting the Tikchik grand slam — one each of the major species available in these waters. This is the ultimate grand slam of fishing and it's a tough go. Cohos are just entering the systems and Kings are on their way out. Can it be done? You could be the first.

Accommodations leave absolutely nothing to be desired. Circular rooms flanking the main core of the lodge contain a lounge and a world-class restaurant. You'll dine on Alaskan seafood for sure, but also on rack of lamb and filet mignon accompanied by abundant fresh vegetables and fruit. Guest cabins overlook the narrows and contain two large and comfortable bedrooms, each with a private bath. Rich native woods and colonial colors set off floral bedspreads and color coordinated carpets. As you'd suspect from the Hideaways rating, this isn't your typical me and Joe fishing lodge.

Waterfall Resort

P r i n c e   o f   W a l e s   I s l a n d

Remember all those salmon patties you had to eat as a kid? Now you can get even!

VITAL STATISTICS:

KEY SPECIES:
Cod, halibut, king/chinook salmon, pink salmon, coho/silver salmon

Tackle:
Casting, spinning
Major Season:
May through September
Accommodations:
Quaint cottages once used by workers
Number of Rooms: 40
Maximum Number of Guests: 84
Meals: Alaskan cuisine
Conference Groups: Yes
Rates: From $1,795 / 3 nights, 4 days
Guides: Included
Gratuities: $30 / day
Preferred Payment:
Cash, check or credit cards
Getting There:
Fly to Ketchikan and ride the floatplane.
Other Activities:
Boating, hiking

Contact:
Mike Dooley
Waterfall Resort
PO Box 6440
320 Dock St
Ketchikan AK 99901
Ph: 800/544-5125
Fax: 907/225-8530
e-mail:
waterfall@ktninet
Web:
www.waterfallresort.com

SO RICH WAS THE LODE OF SALMON in the waters on this side of Prince of Wales Island, that a cannery was founded here in 1912. Then, salmon were caught in floating traps as they migrated, and the tonnage was so large that The Atlantic and Pacific Tea company — that's right, your friendly A&P — bought the fledgling cannery in the 1920s and ran it through the boom years of the 30s and 40s, and into the 60s. By then, the runs of salmon were so reduced that the cannery closed in the 1970s.

It was reborn as a resort in the early 1980s and has been gaining ground ever since. At docks where commercial fishing vessels once emptied their holds of salmon, today boats of happy anglers display catches of king and coho salmon, halibut and lingcod. Unlike resorts on the Inside Passage, Waterfall is on the western shore of Prince of Wales Island. Though sheltered from the north Pacific by Suemez Island, the resort fronts on Ulloa Channel, a marine thoroughfare for salmon migrating fresh from the ocean.

Fishing is from new 25-foot cruisers with heated cabins. Skippered by a guide, four guests will fish from about 7:00 a.m. to 5:00 p.m. each day. Quarry and tactics depend on what fish are running and, of course, the weather. King salmon are most prized. You'll fish bait, perhaps with a flasher, on a long mooching rod. Average kings run 30 pounds but the Waterfall record is 78 pounds. Best fishing is in May and June. Coho average five to 18 pounds and are hot in July through September. Halibut, a popular fish with Waterfall guests, frequently exceed 100 pounds, but those more than that weight are normally released; they're usually females heavy with eggs. Lingcod and red snapper (a member of the rockfish family, not the one from the Gulf of Mexico) round out the range of species.

Old factory towns have a fascination about them, and none more so than Waterfall. Massive metal-sided cannery buildings house the resort store, tackle room and raingear room. Twin ranks of thoroughly modernized frame guest bungalows (with private baths) face the channel. Four luxury beachfront town houses with two bedrooms and baths feature fireplaces, kitchens, and washer/dryers, as well as a shared spa for relaxing. Meals (Alaskan seafood and traditional fare) are served in the former home of the cannery manager, and another building nearby holds the cocktail lounge and meeting rooms.

[A L A S K A]

Whales Resort

Prince of Wales Island, Alaska

Salmon and cutthroat, fished from boats or ashore, give this little resort a big name.

VITAL STATISTICS:

KEY SPECIES:
Bull trout/Dolly Varden, cutthroat, halibut, king/chinook salmon, pink salmon, coho/silver salmon

Tackle:
Casting, fly-fishing, spinning, trolling
Flyouts to Remote Waters: Yes
Major Season:
May through September
Accommodations:
COMFORTABLE MODERN LODGE
NUMBER OF ROOMS: 12
MAXIMUM NUMBER OF GUESTS: 24
Meals: Prime rib and poached salmon
Conference Groups: Yes
Rates: From $700 / day
Guides: Included
Gratuities: $50 / day
Preferred Payment:
Cash, check or credit cards
Getting There:
Fly to Ketchikan and meet your float plane.
Other Activities:
Bird-watching, canoeing/kayaking/rafting, wildlife photography

Contact:
Shawn Fannemel-Ahnee
Whales Resort
PO Box 9835
Ketchikan AK 99901
Ph: 907/846-5300
Fax: 907/846-5303
Web:
www.whalesresort.com
Off Season:
6359 West Donald Dr.
Glendale AZ 85310
Ph: 800/531-9643
Fax: 602/561-5605

WHALE PASSAGE sweeps around Thorne Island on the northeast tip of Prince of Wales Island, and in the currents, kings, silvers, chum, and pink salmon play. Occasionally, when it's very calm and silvers are near the surface, you can see their tell-tail tracks from the glass windows of the lodge. Whales frequent this stretch of aquatic highway, as they do in the Kashevarof Passage to the west.

After breakfast, the dock in front of the lodge becomes the scene of frenetic activity. Jetboats speed away, headed for that little unnamed stream loaded with cutthroats. A 25-foot Bayliner climbs up, headed for the area around Exchange Island where salmon are running. Another Bayliner ferries anglers out to drift for halibut in the Clarence Strait. In the parking lot, a 4x4 is pulling out with a group of anglers bound for a mountain lake. It's all in a morning's work at Whales Resort.

Tides flow vigorously through Clarence Strait, which separates Prince of Wales Island from smaller islands next to the mainland. The strait flows with salmon returning to home streams to spawn. Species are season-dependent: kings (20 to 50 pounds) show up in May and fish best in the first two weeks of June. Pinks of five pounds or so come in July (best fishing is then) and leave in August. Silvers up to 10 pounds run from July through September, with August being the best month. Mooching and trolling are the most popular methods for taking salmon, though silver and pinks may be taken with flies. Steelhead up to 10 pounds are very good early in the season: try April and early May. Halibut from 30 to 100-pounds-plus are available from May through September, with the end of the season producing more big halibut of "barn door" dimension.

While not large as resorts go, Whales does provide a full range of outdoor activities, fishing and non-fishing alike. If fishing isn't your gig, take a jetboat to Anan Creek to watch bears feed. Otters skitter down the boardwalk to bask in the sun on the dock and eagles cruise overhead. And inside the cedar-paneled recreation room you'll find pool, fooseball and electronic shuffleboard. Dinners are very good — salmon Florentine, halibut stuffed with crab — and served in a cozy restaurant. Rooms are carpeted, modern and tasteful. Standard rooms include two twin beds; superior rooms add double beds and TV/VCRs; and suites have spacious separate sitting rooms along with everything else. All have private baths, of course.

Wooden Wheel Cove Lodge

P t .   B a k e r ,   A l a s k a

Fish for steelhead and salmon on a remote island with scores of unnamed streams.

VITAL STATISTICS:

KEY SPECIES:
Chum salmon, halibut, king/chinook salmon, pink salmon, red/sockeye salmon, coho/silver salmon, steelhead

Tackle:
Fly-fishing, spinning, trolling
Major Season:
Late April through September
Accommodations:
RUSTIC LODGE
NUMBER OF ROOMS: 4
MAXIMUM NUMBER OF GUESTS: 8
Meals: Alaska seafood and beef with fresh veggies
Conference Groups: Yes
Rates: From $1,975 / 3 days, 4 nights
Guides: Included
Gratuities: 15%
Preferred Payment:
Cash, check or MasterCard/Visa
Getting There:
Fly to Ketchikan and the float plane will pick you up.
Other Activities:
Bird-watching, boating, hiking, wildlife photography, whale-watching

Contact:
Robert & Patty Gray
Wooden Wheel Cove Lodge
PO Box 118
Pt. Baker AK 99927
Ph: 888/489-9288
Fax: 907/489-2288
e-mail:
wwclodge@aol.com
Web:
www.woodenwheellodge.com

WHEN ROBERT AND PATTY GRAY went looking for a place to put down some outdoor roots, they looked around for a bit and then settled on Prince of Wales Island in southeast Alaska. It's a neat place. Most of the land is part of the Tongass National Forest. Blessing or curse though that may be, the island is webbed with a network of roads of sorts, and that provides access to scores of creeks and rivers where steelhead and salmon run.

None of the flowing water is large; seldom is it wider than 90 feet across. Nor is it particularly deep. Most bottoms are hard gravel, which is good for wading anglers and good for salmon and steelhead. Steelhead run in spring and fall, with the best fishing from mid-April to mid-May. Spinning tackle (seven-foot rods, reels spooled with 12-pound test) works well because of tight quarters on many of the streams. Try a no. 4 or 6 Blue Fox and you'll start catching fish right away. Fly-fishermen will get results with sink-tip lines and black and purple marabou flies. Polar Shrimp and various egg patterns also work well.

From his lodge on Port Protection just south of Pt. Baker on the northern tip of the island, Bob ferries anglers to the mouths of the island's streams on 22-foot boats. The craft are also used to fish for salmon in waters close to the shore. Salmon run through the pass in front of the lodge. Kings, pinks and sockeyes are best in May and June. Cohos turn up in July and peak in August and September. Jigging is the most popular method for taking salmon in salt water. After fish have entered the river, use spinners or flies. And while at Wooden Wheel Cove, don't overlook halibut up to 150 pounds.

The modern wooden lodge sits back under the spruce and looks out through the trees onto Sumner Strait. When the air is chilled, a fire crackles in the stone hearth in the sitting room. Bedrooms are cozy and decorated with antique pine reproductions. Two have private baths and the other two share. Meals are hearty and built around fresh seafood and beef.

[A L A S K A]

Yes Bay Lodge

Tongass National Forest, Alaska

Steelhead or kings, what a choice.
Oh heck, let's do both!

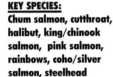

VITAL STATISTICS:

KEY SPECIES:
Chum salmon, cutthroat, halibut, king/chinook salmon, pink salmon, rainbows, coho/silver salmon, steelhead

Tackle:
Fly-fishing, spinning, trolling
Flyouts to Remote Waters: Yes
Major Season:
May through September
Accommodations:
Lovely wood and glass lodge
Number of Rooms: 15
Handicapped Accessible: 15
Maximum Number of Guests: 24
Meals: Alaska cuisine plus beef and chicken
Conference Groups: Yes
Rates: From $1,865 / 3 days, 4 nights
Guides: Included
Gratuities: $30 / guide; $30 / house staff
Preferred Payment:
Cash, check or credit cards
Getting There:
Fly to Ketchikan and meet the lodge's floatplane.
Other Activities:
Bird-watching, boating, canoeing/kayaking/rafting, hiking, wildlife photography

Contact:
Stacey Hallstrom
Yes Bay Lodge
1515 Tongass Ave
PO Box 8660
Ketchikan AK 99901
Ph: 800/999-0784
Fax: 907/247-3875
e-mail:
yes@visit.ktninet
Web:
www.yesbay.com

AT THIS WELL-APPOINTED LODGE, far up the west arm of the Behm Canal — a twisting circular fjord-like channel that separates Revillagigedo Island from the mainland — the season opens with steelhead in late May. King Salmon begin running in mid-June just as steelhead is peaking. With only three days of fishing, you gotta make a choice. Will it be sea-run rainbows (steelheads to you) of double digits in smallish streams with tackle that's probably too light? Or will you troll for heavy kings? My vote gives two days to the steelies and one day to the kings. After all, just how much salmon do you want to take home?

Commanding a grassy point, the timbered Yes Bay Lodge spreads its wings like a totem of the native peoples. A long, elevated boardwalk runs down from the lodge to its floating dock where twelve 20-foot soft-top boats are moored, along with a deHavilland Beaver. From the dock, you can go anywhere, for there are no set fishing programs at Yes Bay Lodge. Troll or mooch for salmon. Jig bottom for halibut or rockfish. Hike or fly out to streams and lakes for steelhead or trout. It all depends on the weather, and what's hot.

Steelheading in the rivers tumbling off the intensely forested slopes can be nothing short of fantastic. With fish averaging eight to 10 pounds, steelheading is best in the second and third weeks of May. At a price that's less than their normal rate, Yes Bay Lodge offers a special May steelhead package that includes a flyout to streams and lakes where these bright, tailwalking fighters run.

If it's diverse angling you want, there's no time better than the second week of July at Yes Bay. Kings are still running, and rainbows and cutthroats are strong. Averaging six pounds, sockeyes are just hitting their stride, and pinks to five pounds and chums to 12 are getting good. Halibut up to 100 pounds and various rockfish up to five pounds are also on the bite. Chums and pinks peak in the fourth week of July, and cohos from late August into September.

Accommodations at Yes Bay are gracious. Large guest rooms are bright with great views of the bay or forest. All have private baths. If you didn't get enough exercise on the boat, you can work out in the weight room complete with Soloflex, nautilus, treadmill and stationary bike. Dinner, a healthy menu of Alaskan seafood, poultry, pasta and prime rib, is served in an open and airy room overlooking the marina.

Afognak Wilderness Lodge on the island northeast of Kodiak is the jumping off point for salmon and rainbow fishing, eco-tours for waterfowl and walrus, and hunts for bear and black-tail deer.

CANADA-WEST

ALBERTA, BRITISH COLUMBIA,
NORTHWEST TERRITORIES, NUNAVUT,
SASKATCHEWAN, YUKON

B OREAL FOREST drained by dark rivers flowing into black-water lakes, beds of limestone thrust a mile or more above valley floors that run with utterly pristine creeks, rivers that tumble down from the mountains into the cold Pacific where salmon and steelhead spawn — the provinces and territories of western Canada have it all. Canada's west gave us rainbows. Here, too, are cutthroat, grayling and char in the rivers that flow into the Arctic Ocean, along with monster lake trout and pike in glacial lakes seen by none other than native peoples and the few anglers lucky enough to fish them.

Walleye abound for succulent lunches ashore, followed by handfuls of wild blueberries for dessert. The scenery is as grand or subtle as you like, and people as hospitable as the climate is not. Seasons in the Arctic are short — eight weeks in July and August. Glacial melt swells streams in the Canadian Rockies, but the much vaunted Bow in Alberta may be fished most of the year. Traveling here means long hours in the air, but the incredible fishing makes all that seat-time worthwhile.

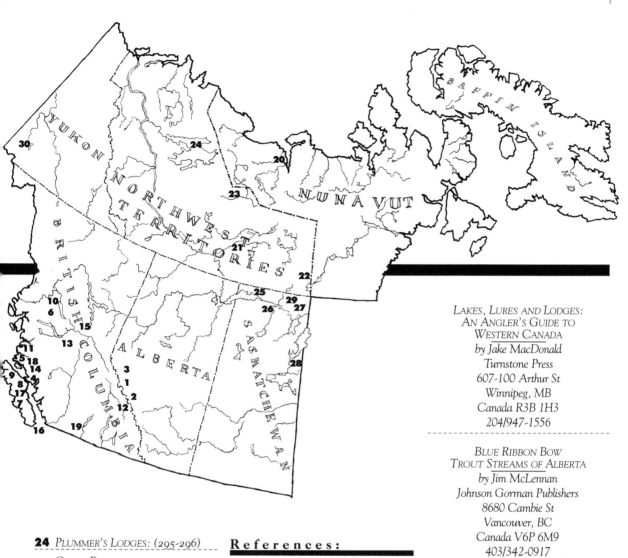

References:

ANGLING IN THE SHADOW
OF THE ROCKIES
by Jeff Mironuck

THOMPSON RIVER
by Art Lingren

FLY FISHING IN THE NORTHWEST
TERRITORIES OF CANADA
by Chris Hanks

STEELHEAD RIVER GUIDES:
DEAN SKEENA
Frank Amato Publications
PO Box 82112
Portland, OR 97282
800/541-9498

LAKES, LURES AND LODGES:
AN ANGLER'S GUIDE TO
WESTERN CANADA
by Jake MacDonald
Turnstone Press
607-100 Arthur St
Winnipeg, MB
Canada R3B 1H3
204/947-1556

BLUE RIBBON BOW
TROUT STREAMS OF ALBERTA
by Jim McLennan
Johnson Gorman Publishers
8680 Cambie St
Vancouver, BC
Canada V6P 6M9
403/342-0917

DUE NORTH OF MONTANA
by Chris Dawson
Johnson Books
1880 S. 57th St
Boulder, CO 80301
303/443-9766

FISHING IN THE WESTERN CANADA
by David Carpenter
Douglas & McIntyre
1615 Venables St
Vancouver, BC
Canada V5L 2H1
604/254-7191

[C A N A D A   W E S T]

BC FISHING:
FRESHWATER DIRECTORY AND ATLAS

BC FISHING: SALTWATER
DIRECTORY AND ATLAS
by Neil Cameron, Editor
BC Outdoors
OP Publishing Ltd
780 Beatty St., Suite 300
Vancouver, BC
Canada V6B 2M1
604/606-4644

Resources:

DEPARTMENT OF
ENVIRONMENTAL PROTECTION
Petroleum Plaza, South Tower
9945 108 St., 9th Floor
Edmonton, Alberta
T5K 2G8, Canada
780/944-0313
web: www.gov.ab.ca/env/

TRAVEL ALBERTA
300-10155 102nd. St.
Edmonton AB
T5J 4G8 Canada
800/661-8888; web: explorealberta.com

MINISTRY OF ENVIRONMENT
WILDLIFE BRANCH
PO Box 9374
Station Provincial Gov't
Victoria, British Columbia
V8W 9M4, Canada
250/387-9731
www.env.gov.bc.ca

TOURISM BRITISH COLUMBIA
865 W. Hornby St.
Vancouver BC
V6Z 2G3 Canada
604/660-2861
800/663-6000
web: www.travel.bc.ca

DEPARTMENT OF RESOURCES
WILDLIFE AND ECONOMIC
DEVELOPMENT
GOVERNMENT OF THE
NORTHWEST TERRITORIES
Box 2668
Yellowknife, Northwest Territories
X1A 3P9, Canada
867/873-7184
web: www.rwed.gov.nt.ca

NWT ARCTIC TOURISM
PO Box 610
Yellowknife NT
X1A 2N5 Canada
800/661-0788
web: www.nwttravel.nt.ca

NUNAVUT TOURISM
P.O. Box 1450
Iqaluit NT
X0A 0H0, Canada
800/491-7910; fax 867/979-1261
email: nunatour@nunanet.com
web: www.nunatour.nt.ca

SASKATCHEWAN ENVIRONMENT AND
RESOURCE MANAGEMENT
524-3211 Albert St.
Regina, Saskatchewan
S4S 5W6, Canada
306/787-2931
web: www.gov.sk.ca/govt/environ/

TOURISM SASKATCHEWAN
500-1900 Albert St.
Regina SK
S4P 4L9 Canada
web: www.sasktourism.com

DEPARTMENT OF RENEWABLE
RESOURCES
Fish & Wildlife Branch
Box 2703
Whitehorse, Yukon Territory
Y1A 2C6, Canada
867/667-5715
web: www.gov.yk.ca/

TOURISM YUKON
Box 2703
Whitehorse, Yukon Territory
Y1A 2C6, Canada
867/667-5340
web: www.touryukon.com

*Helicopters ferry anglers in British Columbia to rivers in the
Coast Range which cannot be reached any other way.*

VITAL STATISTICS:

KEY SPECIES:
Brookies, bull trout/Dolly Varden, cutthroat, pike, rainbows

Tackle:
Fly-fishing, spinning, trolling
Major Season:
All year
Accommodations:
FROM LOG COTTAGES TO MODERN SUITES
NUMBER OF ROOMS: 446
HANDICAPPED ACCESSIBLE: 20
MAXIMUM NUMBER OF GUESTS: 1000
Meals: Elegant gourmet cuisine
Conference Groups: Yes
Rates: From $600 (Cdn) / night, double occupancy / 2 night minimum
Guides: $250
Gratuities: Angler's discretion
Preferred Payment:
Cash, check or credit cards
Getting There:
Fly to Edmonton and rent a car.
Other Activities:
Bird-watching, canoeing/kayaking/ rafting, horseback riding, hiking, snowmobiling, swimming, tennis, wildlife photography

Contact:
Jasper Park Lodge
Box 40
Jasper AB
T0E 1E0, Canada
Ph: 780/852-3301
Fax: 780/852-5107
Web:
www.fairmont.com

Jasper Park Lodge

J a s p e r ,   A l b e r t a

Fish the disappearing lake for rainbows beneath the jutting peaks of Canada's Rockies.

ITH TEETH THAT LOOK like those of a logger's crosscut, the serrated tops of the Canadian Rockies erupt more than a mile over the valley below, verdant with lodgepole pine — the Provincial Tree of Alberta — and stands of engleman, white spruce and larch. It is in the fall that Medicine Lake, south and east of Jasper, struts its stuff. For most of the year, the lake receives little more than an "oh that's nice" look from thousands of tourists streaming south to Maligne Lake, one of the most picturesque in the Rockies. And the stream flowing through the valley below Medicine Lake attracts little attention as well. It's narrow, not very deep or well watered, and seldom fished by anyone other than local anglers in the know.

As you pass Medicine Lake, you'll notice that it's fed by a good-sized river (nice brookies and rainbows here). And, should you have your wits about you (who does during vacation), you may wonder about the fate of all the water that flows into Medicine Lake with its miniscule outlet. The secret is an extensive karst system lying beneath the floor of the lake. Water pours heavily into the lake in spring, and it leaks out throughout the summer until, in mid-fall, the normally 70-foot-deep lake comes only up to your thighs. That's when its rainbows concentrate in the old stream channel that winds through the lakebed. They're fat from feeding on minnows, and bright, like steelhead. These are the feistiest rainbows you'll ever catch. Hire a guide like Loren Currie for a trip or two. Bring a five-weight, and he'll make your day.

Maligne Lake is known for its rainbows up to three or four pounds and brook trout of similar size. Most anglers rent boats and row or motor up to the narrows, or fish at the mouth of one of the many feeder streams. Best angling comes in June just after ice is out, but it's good through August.

Jasper is a tourist town. Hotels and rest camps abound. The finest, though, is the Jasper Park Lodge, which fronts Lac Beauvert across the Athabasca from the town of Jasper. From modern suites to quaint cabins, the lodge offers a wide range of accommodations, all of which are served by the marvelous dining room that annually rates four stars or better in everyone's book. You can fly or drive to the hotel, but savvy travelers take the domed-observation cars of the Canadian Pacific. There's no better way to reach this, one of Canada's stellar railroad hotels.

[C A N A D A   W E S T]

VITAL STATISTICS:

KEY SPECIES:
Bull trout/Dolly Varden, cutthroat

Tackle:
Fly-fishing, spinning
Major Season:
June through September
Accommodations:
FIRST-CLASS MODERN, YET
TRADITIONAL, HOTEL
NUMBER OF ROOMS: 98
MAXIMUM NUMBER OF GUESTS: 250
Meals: Gourmet with a fine and
extensive cellar
Conference Groups: Yes
Rates: From $200
Guides: $200
Gratuities: Angler's discretion
Preferred Payment:
Cash, check or credit cards
Getting There:
Fly to Calgary and rent a car.
Other Activities:
Bird-watching, canoeing/kayaking/
rafting, golf, horseback riding, hiking,
skiing, snowmobiling, swimming,
wildlife photography, rock climbing

Contact:
Post Hotel
200 Pipestone Rd
Lake Louise, AB
T0l 1E0, Canada
Ph: 800/661-1586
Fax: 403/522-3966
e-mail:
posthotl@telusplanet.net
Web:
www.posthotel.com

Post Hotel

L a k e   L o u i s e ,   A l b e r t a

Elegant and serene, this lovely streamside hotel is hard by a trout stream which a few smart guests fish.

LET'S FACE IT. Few anglers travel to the glorious Canadian Rockies to fish. Sure the Bow River below Calgary is one of the world's premiere streams for browns and rainbows, and the upper Bow to the falls at Banff offers excellent fishing for browns and bull trout (which must be released immediately and unharmed). Upriver from Banff, the Bow gets little attention. It's cold, generating little by way of nutrients to nourish populations of aquatic insects needed to support bait and game fish.

But the upper mileage of the Bow is very special. While most of the other big rivers in the Canadian Rockies run grey and then, finally, aquamarine in fall as ground rock flour from the marvelous glaciers settles out, the Bow is normally clear. The reason? Though fed by melt from the Wapta Icefield and Crowfoot Glacier, runoff surges into a deep lake. There sediments drift to the bottom. The Bow River heads in this lake, but the waters are really too cold to support much of a sportfishery.

South of the junctions of routes 93 and 1 — the road to Yoho National Park — the Bow becomes fit to fish. Trout hide in miles of gentle stretches of chattering riffles, an island here or there and wide sweeping bends with deep runs on the outside curve where the current has undermined stands of lodgepole pine and toppled trees into the river. Bottom is of cobble with finer sediments flooring deeper pools. You'll catch cutthroat, mostly, and a few rainbows. Size will run between 10 and 12 inches. A big trout in these waters will top 15 inches, but not by much.

No better accommodations can be found for fishing the uppermost Bow than the Post Hotel. It's small, as resorts go — fewer than 100 rooms. Rooms and service are first class and the meals are beyond gourmet, just what you'd expect from a Relais & Chateau hotel. If you want to avoid crowds, this is the place to stay. Lounge in the sun on the terrace that overlooks the Pipestone River which flows past the lodge and joins the Bow a little way downstream. Sit there and sip a cool drink for as long as you can. Then, give in, unlimber your rod, and go fish it. Its cutts are small but spunky.

*Painter's Lodge in Campbell River,
British Columbia, hosts anglers who troll
the Discovery Passage for salmon.*

*Lodges like Camp Grayling, on Saskatchewan's
Black Lake, put anglers over pike
from ice-out in late May to early September.*

[C A N A D A   W E S T]

Sheep Creek Backcountry Lodge

G r a n d e   C a c h e ,   A l b e r t a

*A jouncing ride in an old Jeep carries you across
a shallow creek to the quaintest lodge in Alberta.*

**VITAL
STATISTICS:**

KEY SPECIES:
**Brookies, bull trout/Dolly
Varden, cutthroat, grayling,
rainbows, whitefish**

Tackle:
Casting, fly-fishing, spinning
Major Season:
July through September
Accommodations:
RUSTIC WOODEN CABINS FURNISHED WITH
ANTIQUES
NUMBER OF ROOMS: 5
MAXIMUM NUMBER OF GUESTS: 10
Meals: Stout family-style fare
Conference Groups: No
Rates: From $875 / week
Guides: Included
Gratuities: 10%
Preferred Payment:
Cash, check or credit cards
Getting There:
Fly to Edmonton or Grand Prairie
and rent a car.
Other Activities:
Big game, wingshooting, bird-watching,
canoeing/kayaking/rafting, horseback
riding, hiking, snowmobiling, wildlife
photography

Contact:
Vic Stapleton
**Sheep Creek Backcountry
Lodge**
Box 195
Grande Cache AB
T0E 0A0, Canada
Ph: 780/827-2829
Fax: 780/827-4838

IN THE EASTERN SLOPE REGIONS of Alberta — that slice of land running north and east from the Montana border and flanked by Canada's great Banff and Jasper National Parks — the Bow River and the Crownsnest get all the press. These are absolutely world-class trout rivers, but the angling doesn't stop there. Hundreds of creeks, rivers and lakes carry good populations of cold water species, particularly bull trout, rainbows, cutthroat and browns. You'll also find some arctic grayling, brookies, and mountain whitefish.

As it goes with the popularity of the Bow and Crownsnest, tourists flock to the national parks and seldom poke around in the great mountain forests to the east. Scores of rivers cascade out of these mountains, and they're fed by hundreds of tributaries, each carrying reasonable stocks of fish. The upside is that angling is not the least bit crowded. But the downside is that many of the rivers drain the headwalls of glaciers, and thus run milky much of the year. Those that aren't fed by glaciers swell with melt from heavy snow packs, and stay high into mid-summer. However, high mountain lakes offer good angling most of the season, and when streams clear in mid- to late-July, fishing can be dynamite.

You'll catch bull trout, rainbow and grayling, with some brookies thrown in on the side. Bull trout must be released immediately as they're endangered in Alberta. You may keep up to five of the other species. Most folks release their catch, except, perhaps, enough for a meal. Fly or spinning gear works well; these fish are not persnickety. Many have never seen fly or lure.

Among my favorite wilderness lodges is Vic and Elaine Stapleton's cabins on Sheep Creek north of Grand Cache. Constructed of log, each cabin contains a comfortable bed, a wood stove and a washstand. You'll draw your water from the spring, and tote it to your cabin (or Vic will do it for you). Fire up your wood stove the moment you arrive and put on a kettle. That's your hot water. (Showers are also available.) Meals built around beef, pork or chicken are accompanied by excellent soups, plenty of salad and good desserts.

Sheep Creek, which drains a portion of the Willmore Wilderness Park, flows past the lodge and its numerous pools and runs of pocket water can keep you busy for a week or more. Ride a horse, canoe, Jeep or your own two feet to the fishing. There's so much water and, as always, so little time.

April Point Lodge

Campbell River, British Columbia

*Savor a bit of old-time Pacific Northwest
in this rustic lodge where salmon roam.*

**VITAL
STATISTICS:**

KEY SPECIES:
**King/chinook salmon,
silver/coho salmon**

Tackle:
Trolling
Flyouts to Remote Waters: Yes
Major Season:
May through August
Accommodations:
CABINS AND MOTEL-STYLE ROOMS
NUMBER OF ROOMS: 52
HANDICAPPED ACCESSIBLE: 15
MAXIMUM NUMBER OF GUESTS: 110
Meals: Seafood and steaks
Conference Groups: Yes
Rates: From $99 (Cdn) / night
Guides: From $248 (Cdn) / 1/2 day
Gratuities:
Angler's discretion
Preferred Payment:
Cash, check or credit cards
Getting There:
Fly to Campbell River and the lodge
van will collect you.
Other Activities:
Hiking

Contact:
Manager
April Point Lodge
PO Box 248
Campbell River BC
V9W 4Z9, Canada
Ph: 250/285-2222
Fax: 250/285-2411
Web:
www.aprilpoint.com

Other Contact:
Oak Bay Marine Group
1327 Beach Dr
Vancouver BC
V8S 2N4, Canada
Ph: 800/663-7090
Fax: 250/598-1361

IT WAS ONCE CALLED POVERTY POINT, this nub of Quadra Island that pokes into the Discovery Passage across from the town of Campbell River on Vancouver Island. In the 1930s and 40s, Poverty Point was the refuge of hard-bitten hard-liners who lived off (read that, drank up) what they caught from the bay. What they caught were salmon, lots of them, and that's what drew the Peterson clan to the point in the days immediately after World War II. The Peterson's built April Point, creating one of the most eclectic lodges in the region.

In 1998, the Oak Bay Marine Group bought April Point and undertook a major renovation campaign. All rooms and cabins have been redone, yet the slightly laid-back and homey flavor of the original lodge remains. And though times have changed, the salmon are the same. Chinooks (six to 50 pounds) and cohos (eight to 18 pounds) run from May through September. Sockeyes (four to eight pounds) and pinks (three to eight pounds) show up in July and August. Chums (10 to 20 pounds) move through these waters from September to November. And what waters! Heavy tides course between stark cliffs and around jagged rocks in Seymour Narrows a few miles north of the lodge. Salmon school up in the deep rocky bays, riding the currents to the streams of their birth. Most of the fishing here is done out of Boston Whalers and similar craft, with Hoochies and flashers downrigged for depth if necessary. In June and July, chinooks are close to the surface. Then you can fish with flies. April Point also offers heli-tours to rivers for summer and winter steelhead, and bottomfishing for lingcod.

With it's sibling lodge a 20-minute ride across the bay, guests have their choice of fine restaurants and easy access to shopping in Campbell River, one of the finest resort communities on the Pacific Coast. If you come here — and you should — rent a car so you can explore the soaring peaks of Strathcona Provincial Park and fish the Campbell River for cutthroat, salmon and steelhead. Park your car at Painters and take the free water taxi across to April Point. Have dinner, and then settle back in your cabin under the firs, and listen to the waves lap on the rocks below your door.

[C A N A D A   W E S T]

Buck's Trophy Lodge

R i v e r s   I n l e t ,   B r i t i s h   C o l u m b i a

Fish for salmon from sun up to sun down, then retire to your floating cabin and let your dreams drift with the tide.

VITAL STATISTICS:

KEY SPECIES:
Cod, halibut, king/chinook salmon, pink salmon, silver/coho salmon

Tackle:
Trolling
Major Season:
June through September
Accommodations:
FLOATING CABINS
NUMBER OF ROOMS: 10
MAXIMUM NUMBER OF GUESTS: 20
Meals: Regional cuisine
Conference Groups: No
Rates: From $1,850 / 4 days, 3 nights
Guides: $100
Gratuities: $50; Angler's discretion
Preferred Payment:
Cash, check or credit cards
Getting There:
Fly to Vancouver and catch the free shuttle.
Other Activities:
Bird-watching, wildlife photography

Contact:
Shelly Lawrence
Buck's Trophy Lodge
PO Box 8000-312
Sumas WA 98295-8000
Ph: 604/859-9779
Fax: 604/859-1661
Web:
www.buckstrophylodge.com

BUCK'S TROPHY LODGE has a simple goal: get guests out on the water and over fish ASAP. Soon after you set foot on the docks at this lodge that floats on Finn Bay in Rivers Inlet due north of the Queen Charlotte Strait from Port Hardy on Vancouver Island, you'll get a crash course on small boat handling. That's because you're the captain and your partner's the mate of a fiberglass skiff powered by a 40-horse outboard. The boat carries ship-to-shore radios, depth finders and rain or sun tops. Tackle is provided — generally an 8- to 11-foot mooching rod — with a direct drive reel loaded with 20-pound-test mono. You'll learn how to make a herring bait or jig and skirt-dance with such seduction that no salmon can resist. You'll be given a map of the waters surrounding the lodge, and then it's up to you. Trolling is the name of the game in these waters, though silvers can be near the surface and may be played on conventional fly, casting or spinning gear.

Bright as silver, chinook (king) salmon begin their run into the bay in June. Fifty- to 70-pounders are frequently caught, and monsters of 80 pounds have been landed. The best months for chinooks are July and August. Silvers from six to 28 pounds enter the estuary in June as well, but the best angling for these slashing fighters occurs in August and September when bigger fish make their appearance. Other species include halibut up to 100 pounds, lingcod to 50 pounds and a variety of other bottomfish. What you fish for is pretty much your choice. During the day, Buck's "Go Go" boat will bring you hot meals, fresh bait and assistance if you need it. Other than the fact that you gotta return in time for dinner, your schedule is your own.

Most guests race back to the dock at the end of the day. Nobody wants to miss the family-style dinners of salmon, halibut, prawns and Dungeness crab. After dinner, most of the 20 guests at Buck's are content (meaning too stuffed to move) to sit and tell lies as the sun settles behind the far mountains of Vancouver Island. A few insatiable souls pick up their rods and head back out. Daylight here lingers, and rumor has it that sometimes the biggest fish hit at dusk. Whichever your choice, you'll catch your zees in a floating cedar cabin complete with a twin and a double bed, private bath, shower and drying room. At the conclusion of your stay, your cleaned catch will be packaged for shipment home.

P.S. Pack carefully; luggage is restricted to 25 pounds per person.

Bulkley River Lodge

C a m p b e l l   R i v e r ,   B r i t i s h   C o l u m b i a

A new lodge by the owner of The Dolphin's Resort puts anglers on big steelhead.

VITAL STATISTICS:

KEY SPECIES:
King/chinook salmon, rainbows, steelhead

Tackle:
Casting, fly-fishing, spinning
Flyouts to Remote Waters: Yes
Major Season:
July; September through late October
Accommodations:
MODERN, YET RUSTIC CABINS
NUMBER OF CABINS: 4
MAXIMUM NUMBER OF GUESTS: 10
Meals: Fine regional cuisine
Conference Groups: No
Rates: From $3,500 / 7 nights,
6-1/2 days fishing
Guides: Included
Gratuities: $200 - $400 / trip
Preferred Payment:
Cash, check or credit cards
Getting There:
Fly to Smithers and you'll be met.
Other Activities:
Hiking, wildlife photography

Contact:
Clint Cameron
Bulkley River Lodge
231 Anne Ave
Campbell River
V9W 3L1, Canada
Ph: 250/287-3244
Fax: 250/287-3281

CLINT CAMERON has made quite a reputation for himself with The Dolphins, a truly first-class lodge at Campbell River. You know Campbell River, the home waters of Roderick Haig-Brown, where big chinooks, pinks, silvers and steelhead come to spawn in one of the shortest and sweetest stretches of fly-fishing water in the world. Over the years, Clint has been indulging his passion, and that's prospecting for outstanding steelhead rivers where action will be fast and other anglers reasonably few.

He's found it on the Bulkley, a not so isolated river that crashes its way out of the highlands north of Francois Lake in the center of the province, picks up waters from the Morice and Telkwa, rattles through a forested gorge, and then joins the Babine to form the Skeena at New Hazelton. There's 110 miles of steelhead river all together, and Clint runs eight different floats. Some involve overnights in camps, most do not.

Under normal circumstances, steelhead anglers consider themselves lucky with two of three hookups per day. But on the 15 miles stretch of the Bulkley which Clint favors, you'll double or triple that number. Typical fish run in the 26- to 32-inch class, fine steelhead in anyone's book. Dries — bombers and Bulkley Mice — are favored in the height of the season from September 1 through October 25. Streamers also produce, particularly sparse dark patterns of blue and black. Egg sucking leeches also are effective. You'll want at least an eight-weight rod; a 10-foot eight is probably the best medicine.

While fall, with its glorious colors and sometimes challenging weather, goes hand in hand with fine steelheading, the river also sees fine runs of springs (early chinook in local lingo) in July. And a number of lakes and rivers in the region offer summer angling for rainbows.

The lodge consists of four modern cabins for two anglers, each with its own private bath, clustered around a larger log lodge containing the kitchen, dining room and lounge. As of this writing, Dave Evans is the fish master. He knows the river intimately and does a fine job in matching anglers of varying skill and agility with appropriate guides. You'll not find this an inexpensive trip. But keep in mind one thing: Every rainbow in Alaska wishes it could grow up to be a Bulkley River steelhead.

[C A N A D A   W E S T]

VITAL STATISTICS:

KEY SPECIES:
Bottom fish, halibut, king/chinook salmon, silver/coho salmon

Tackle:
Casting, trolling
Major Season:
April through September
Accommodations:
STATEROOMS ABOARD SHIP OR HOTEL ROOMS
NUMBER OF ROOMS: 72
HANDICAPPED ACCESSIBLE: 20
MAXIMUM NUMBER OF GUESTS: 144
Meals: Fine seafood and steak
Conference Groups: Yes
Rates: From $219 / 2 nights, double occupancy
Guides: Included in fishing packages
Gratuities: Angler's discretion
Preferred Payment:
Cash, check or credit cards
Getting There:
Fly to Tofino and catch the shuttle, or drive from Victoria.
Other Activities:
Whale-watching

Contact:
Canadian Princess
Ucluelet, BC
Canada
Ph: 800/663-7090
Fax: 250/598-1361
e-mail:
obmg@pinc.com
Web:
www.obmg.com

Other Contact:
Oak Bay Marine Group
1327 Beach Dr
Victoria BC
V8S 2N4, Canada
Ph: 800/663-7090
Fax: 250/598-1361

Canadian Princess

U c l u e l e t ,   B r i t i s h   C o l u m b i a

Stay aboard a fine old steamer moored at the foot of a great hotel and wrestle with salmon of the wild Pacific.

ABOUT A THIRD OF THE WAY UP Vancouver Island, the Pacific pinches in from the west, forming Barkley Sound. Just to the north, a long spit swings down the coast forming a tranquil bay at the foot of the mainland mountains. The town is called Ucluelet, meaning "safe harbor" in the tongue of the Nuu-cha-nulth, the native peoples of the region.

Ucluelet is the third largest port for landing fish in British Columbia. It is the departure point for scores of whale-watching and other nature cruises, particularly during the period from mid-March to mid-April when Pacific grey whales migrate from Mexican waters to those of the Arctic. The Long Beach unit of Pacific Rim National Park runs north from the base of the spit to Tofino and the airport, with regularly scheduled service to Victoria and Vancouver.

Fishing lodges abound here, but none is finer or more interesting than the Canadian Princess, an old steamship moored to a dock by a small hotel that carries the ship's name. An Oak Bay Marine Group property (you can see similarities between the hotel's architecture and that of Painter's, another Oak Bay property in Campbell River), adventure experiences are well organized and can be mixed or matched in an almost endless variety of packages.

You and a handful of other anglers will board cabin cruisers of 43-feet to 52-feet in length to fish for king salmon, cohos or sockeye with mooching gear. Morning salmon trips leave at 6:00 a.m. (you can snooze 'till you fish) and return at 1:00 p.m. Afternoons are reserved for bottom fishing for cod and snapper. In the evening, there's the option of salmon again or halibut which can top 200 pounds. You may fish in the open Pacific or back in Barkley Sound amidst its many islands.

At the end of the day you'll return to your stateroom on the ship or in the modern lodge on the spit. Meals are first class, as you'd expect, and so is the service. You can fly to this lodge, or drive. Opt for the latter. The run over the mountains from Victoria is breathtaking.

The Dolphins Resort

Campbell River, British Columbia

With two lodges, the Dolphins offers anglers after salmon or steelhead a number of thrilling options.

VITAL STATISTICS:

KEY SPECIES:
Bull trout/Dolly Varden, chum salmon, cod, cutthroat, king/chinook salmon, pink salmon, silver/coho salmon, steelhead

Tackle:
Casting, fly-fishing, spinning, trolling
Flyouts to Remote Waters: Yes
Major Season:
DOLPHINS: March through October
DOLPHINS NORTH: July through Sept.
Accommodations:
DOLPHINS: 14 CABINS WITH KITCHENS BENEATH THE TREES
DOLPHINS NORTH: FLOATING LODGE
NUMBER OF ROOMS / GUESTS
DOLPHINS: 24 / 50
DOLPHINS NORTH: 7 / 14
HANDICAPPED ACCESSIBLE: SOME
Meals:
DOLPHINS: Catering by special arrangement
DOLPHINS NORTH: Elegant regional fare
Conference Groups: Yes
Rates:
DOLPHINS: From $535 / 3 days
DOLPHINS NORTH: From $2,075 / 4 days
Guides: $380
Gratuities: $25 - $50
Preferred Payment:
Cash, check or credit cards
Other Activities:
Big game, bird-watching, boating, canoeing/kayaking/rafting, golf, hiking, skiing, swimming, tennis, wildlife photography

Contact:
Clint Cameron
The Dolphins Resort
4125 Discovery Dr
Campbell River BC
V9W 4X6, Canada
Ph: 250/287-3066
Fax: 250/286-6610
e-mail:
fish@dolphinsresort.com
Web:
www.dolphinsresort.com

CAMPBELL RIVER, a medium-sized town on the eastern coast of Vancouver Island, is an excellent jumping off point for salmon, steelhead, cutthroat and Dolly Varden. Here you have it all. Heavy tides that reach 14 knots push up and down the Discovery Passage. In the current ride tens of thousands of coho, pink, chum and chinook salmon. The Campbell River itself sees runs of summer and winter steelhead, as well as carrying stocks of cutthroat and Dolly Varden. Rent a car and you can drive to a score of isolated mountain rivers, some with populations of rainbows. The town is an eclectic brew of old fishing and mining, and new, upscale restaurants, shops, galleries and museums. This is a town that you won't mind passing through on your way to great fishing.

For more than 20 years, The Dolphins has been the place for small groups of anglers who like solitude and the ability to do their own thing. In addition, owner Clint Cameron has expanded his operations to include a new resort, Dolphin's North, high up on the Work Channel between Prince Rupert and Ketchikan, Alaska.

THE DOLPHINS RESORT: Tucked among the firs on Vancouver Island overlooking the Discovery Passage, fourteen wooden cabins of one to four bedrooms are scattered beneath the evergreens. Each is comfortably decorated. In several, brick fireplaces are the focal point, and all have broad decks, delightful for lounging. Most have kitchens. The resort lacks a restaurant, but its chef and staff will prepare meals tailored to your specifications and deliver them to your cabin door. Or you may cook for yourself. Typical packages include meals, guides and fishing from Boston Whalers in the passage. Others include a day or two of heli-fishing.

DOLPHINS NORTH: The place for bruiser salmon up near B.C.'s border with Alaska. A max of 14 anglers (seven rooms with private baths) hold forth on this floating lodge moored to the edge of the forest. Lightweight mooching gear delivers jigs of cut plugs of herring down 20 feet or so to where the kings and cohos swim. Only three to six ounces of weight are required. You know it when a fish hits. Springs (local term for kings or chinooks) average 30 pounds. Their runs start in June while in mid-July the cohos arrive. In August, you can fish for them with standard fly tackle. Clint also knows how to catch halibut so there's more sport to it than carrying a piano up to a third floor studio. Great grizzly viewing; whales too.

[C A N A D A   W E S T]

Farewell Harbour Resort

Telegraph Cove, British Columbia

Salmon enter the famed Discovery Passage at the doorstep of this fine lodge.

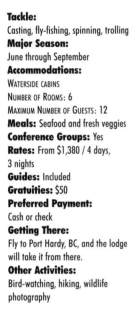

VITAL STATISTICS:

KEY SPECIES:
Halibut, king/chinook salmon, silver/coho salmon

Tackle:
Casting, fly-fishing, spinning, trolling
Major Season:
June through September
Accommodations:
WATERSIDE CABINS
NUMBER OF ROOMS: 6
MAXIMUM NUMBER OF GUESTS: 12
Meals: Seafood and fresh veggies
Conference Groups: Yes
Rates: From $1,380 / 4 days, 3 nights
Guides: Included
Gratuities: $50
Preferred Payment:
Cash or check
Getting There:
Fly to Port Hardy, BC, and the lodge will take it from there.
Other Activities:
Bird-watching, hiking, wildlife photography

Contact:
Paul Weaver
Farewell Harbour Resort
Box 2-4
Telegraph, BC
V0N 3J0, Canada
Ph: 250/928-3115

Off Season:
PO Box 130010
Carlsbad CA 92013-0010
Ph: 760/438-3681
Fax: 760/431-2688

A LOOK AT THE GEOGRAPHY reveals a simple truth: Discovery Passage is a highway. Salmon, migrating to the waters of their birth, enter the passage at its northernmost point and ride monstrous tides up into the fjord-like bays fed by icy streams draining mountains that climb to 8,000 feet and more. Caught in the ebb and flow are millions of baitfish, fodder for cruising salmon. Pitch a chunk of herring overboard, or a jig and hoochie skirt, and hang on. If you're near a pod of salmon, something will slam your lure.

June opens the season. A few winter chinooks are still around, but an early run of bluebacks (cohos) brings out light-tackle anglers who use spinning or fly gear. Hookups are plentiful. Following the bluebacks is the first run of younger chinooks, called springs, in the 25- to 30-pound class. On their tails comes a wave of mature chinooks in the 40- to 50-pound range. By mid-July the action has gone deep. Quick-release down-riggers hold lines bearing white lures or plug-cut herring in the search for resident cohos and chinooks. Also down deep are halibut. At the same time, a few pinks move in and are caught along with cohos. In late August, pinks arrive in full force. They'll stay around until the end of September and provide steady action. The final party begins with the arrival of northern cohos. Fishing is wild — bucktails, buzz bombs, lures, herring — it's hard to miss with these slashing fighters. When chinook fishing fades, everyone's focused on the cohos until a 40-pounder grabs a bait. That's when you remember that up here, big chinooks are called Tyee.

The day begins early at Farewell Harbour. Grab a cup of coffee, fruit, rolls and juice, don your fishing gear (provided if its foul out) and you're away from the dock before 5:30 a.m. Four hours later, you're heading back for brunch. (If the fishing's great, you may be late, but don't worry; there'll be plenty to eat when you do get in.) Fight off the late morning sleepies if you can. You can sleep anytime, but you can't always fish for salmon. The sun officially crosses the yard-arm at 6:30 p.m. That's when the cocktail pennant flies and dinner — whitefish Florentine and cheesecake tarvana — follows an hour later. You'll be down in one of six guest rooms, which run, *en echelon*, down the deck over the waves lapping at the rock below.

Frontiers Farwest

Telkwa, British Columbia

Thoroughly redecorated, this long-time lodge on the Bulkley is as eclectic as the river's steelhead are wild.

VITAL STATISTICS:

KEY SPECIES:
Steelhead

Tackle:
Fly-fishing
Major Season:
Late August through October
Accommodations:
REMODELED CREAMERY
NUMBER OF ROOMS: 7
MAXIMUM NUMBER OF GUESTS: 14
Meals: Elegant dinners with good wines
Conference Groups: Yes
Rates: From $3,280 / 7 nights, 6 1/2 days
Guides: Included
Gratuity: 10%
Preferred Payment:
Cash or check
Getting There:
Fly to Smithers and you'll be collected.
Other Activities:
Hiking, wildlife photography

Contact:
Colin Schadrech
Frontiers Farwest
PO Box 250
Telkwa, BC
V0J 2X0, Canada
Ph: 250-846-9153
Fax: 250/846-5065

Off Season:
2840 Vance Place
Prince George, BC
V2N 4X5, Canada
Ph: 250/562-9257
Fax:250/562-9244

DATA SHOWS THAT more than half of the steelhead that enter the Skeena find their way into the Bulkley, one of British Columbia's premier rivers for these huge sea-run rainbows. Hard by the river in the little town of Telkwa is Frontiers Farwest, one of the premier steelhead lodges in the region. You'll find here folks that are dedicated to angling; great food (try Evelyn's rum cake); comfortable accommodations; and personal attention to the needs of anglers that is without peer.

The major domo of this operation, Colin Schadrech, is an old steelheader from way back. He's plotted more than 1,000 steelhead holds on the 86 miles of river that he and his guides fish. Colin uses a beat system to distribute anglers on the river. Two clients are served by a single guide and each day they work stretches that range from five miles to eleven miles of water. You'll find a number of different looks: tumbling rapids; runs through gravel bars; transverse ledges which hold steelies in between; and long slow pools where fish lie behind submerged boulders.

Most fishing is from Mackenzie drift boats or self-bailing rubber rafts. You'll quarter dries or streamers as is your temperament, skill or preference over water that holds fish. Dries, particularly Bombers and mice, are effective patterns most of the season. Streamers, especially those that are blue or dark purple, work well too. Typical fish run in the 10- to 12-pound range. Steelhead enter the system in the latter weeks of August and the fishing improves steadily into early October. Day trips from the lodge are the norm, but overnights with an intervening stop at a camp with permanent platform tents are also available. Take the overnight float if you can. There's something about setting that second cup of morning coffee down on the cobbly shore as you cast to holds where steelies may be lying. On this river that sees some competition, the first anglers to a pool get first shot at the fish.

Colin's lodge is a converted creamery; you'll see some traces of its former equipment inside. Tastefully redecorated with new carpeting, more washrooms, a fireplace, and a screened porch that overlooks the river, this lodge is one that a number of international anglers come back to year after year. There's a tying table where you can try out new patterns suggested by guides, and enough books and videos to keep you occupied should a case of insomnia strike. It never does, of course. Most anglers tumble into the sack like kids filled up with milk and cookies.

VITAL STATISTICS:

KEY SPECIES:
Bottom fish, halibut, king/chinook salmon, silver/coho salmon

Tackle:
Casting, trolling
Major Season:
June through September
Accommodations:
TIMBER CABINS
NUMBER OF ROOMS: 14
MAXIMUM NUMBER OF GUESTS: 28
Meals: Seafood with style
Conference Groups: Yes
Rates: From $1,345 / 3 nights, 4 days
Guides: Not needed
Gratuities: Angler's discretion
Preferred Payment:
Cash, check or credit cards
Getting There:
Fly to Vancouver and catch the free air shuttle.
Other Activities:
Wildlife-watching

Contact:
King Salmon Resort
Rivers Inlet, BC
Canada
Ph: 800/663-7090
Fax: 250/598-1361
e-mail:
obmg@pinc.com
Web:
www.obmg.com

Other Contact:
Oak Bay Marine Group
1327 Beach Dr
Victoria BC
V8S 2N4, Canada
Ph: 800/663-7090
Fax: 250/598-1361

King Salmon Resort

R i v e r s   I n l e t ,   B r i t i s h   C o l u m b i a

From cabins under the firs, you see the smoky mist rise from Shotbolt Bay, and you know the salmon are in.

TOWERING BEHIND THIS LODGE are a pair of mountains that push through 10,000 feet as if it were nothing. On their flanks are glaciers that feed meltwater into streams that cascade down the mountains until they pause in lakes. There, they drop their loads of chalky rock flour before dancing on to the rivers that merge with the sea. For centuries, Rivers Inlet, one of the fjords that probe back toward the mountains from Fitz Hugh Sound, has been known for its stocks of chinook salmon. A decade ago, the Oak Bay Marine Group opened King Salmon Lodge on Shotbolt Bay, an arm of Rivers Inlet.

So good is the water here for salmon that the Oak Bay Marine Group and a consortium of other lodges have banded together to operate a hatchery to enhance stocks of king salmon. Smolts are released in the streams, go to sea, and return to spawn. Fishing here is a fairly straight-forward affair. You and your partner will be given a vee-hulled skiff with an outboard and all the tackle and bait you need. The fishmaster will suggest locations where you'll likely encounter fish, and then off-you go, jigging or trolling depending on the species you're after. Along with fishing in the waters near the resort, you'll have the option of taking day-trips on a cruiser to areas where fish may be more active. The cruiser tows skiffs. Once on location, you'll climb aboard your boat and get to work. The cruiser, of course, remains nearby, ready with bait, tackle repairs or other assistance should you need it.

Comfortable cabins, each with a deep front porch where you can hang rain gear and boots, rim a pentagonal boardwalk plaza. Clean and spacious rooms contain double beds and private baths. A short stroll down one of the wooden walkways from the plaza brings you to a hot tub with a stunning view of the inlet and the mountains beyond. Soak in the hot tub with a libation, go to dinner in the lodge and stuff yourself with halibut and crab, and then amble back to your cabin. All you have to think about is sleep.

Kootenay Park Lodge

Vermillion Crossing, BC

Over the mountain from the tourist Mecca of Banff is a little known lodge with a bit of great fishing down the road.

VITAL STATISTICS:

KEY SPECIES:
Cutthroat

Tackle:
Fly-fishing, spinning

Major Season:
June through September

Accommodations:
CHARMING HISTORIC CABINS
NUMBER OF ROOMS: 10
MAXIMUM NUMBER OF GUESTS: 20

Meals: Fine regional cuisine with a continental flare

Rates: From $59

Guides: $150

Gratuities: Angler's discretion

Preferred Payment:
Cash, check or credit cards

Getting There:
Fly to Calgary and rent a car.

Other Activities:
Bird-watching, canoeing/kayaking/
rafting, horseback riding, hiking,
swimming, wildlife photography

Contact:
Paul V. Holscher
Kootenay Park Lodge
PO Box 1390
Banff AB
T0L 0C0, Canada
Ph: 403/762-9196
Web:
www.kootenayparklodge

Off Season:
Ph: 403/283-7482
Fax: 403/283-7482

THE CONTRAST SIMPLY COULDN'T BE more dramatic. To the east of the Ball Range, that serrated spine of 10,000 footers which separates Alberta from British Columbia, lies the hustling, bustling four-season tourist town of Banff. On the doorstep of the stunningly spectacular Canadian Rockies, Banff has it all: gourmet restaurants, grand hotels, smart shops, and fast food franchises. What Banff doesn't offer is solitude. That you find on the other side of the ridge in one of the loveliest old-fashioned motor lodges remaining on this continent.

A two-hour drive along a spectacular slice of highway carries you from Banff up the Bow River through Vermillion Pass and down into the virtually unknown Kootenay National Park. The river flows under the road at Vermillion Crossing and there, under a stand of ancient pines and cedar, lies the dark log cabins of Kootenay Park Lodge. Built in 1923 by the Canadian Pacific Railroad, this may be the last of the small lodges that the railroad established to promote tourism in the region.

Furnished with queen or double beds, most of the 10 cabins boast fireplaces and all have private baths. Some have modest kitchen facilities, but there's no reason to do your own cooking. Within the main lodge is a fine restaurant. The innkeeper's mother combines the best fresh meats, fish and vegetables into substantial entrees, flanked by tempting homemade soups and salads, and lush desserts. You'll want to eat hearty here. Most guests hike or climb and bring huge appetites to the table. Afterwards, many linger in the library.

Some guests return to their cabins to ready their gear for the morrow's angling. While the Vermillion carries a good population of bull trout, they are endangered and not to be fished. And the Vermillion is most apt to be discolored with rock flour from glaciers in the headwalls of the valley. The secret is the Kootenay (the spelling changes to Kootenai when it crosses into the U.S.) which rises in a series of beaver ponds and not at the foot of a glacier. Consequently, it's clear, meandering through mountain meadows and patches of forest. Each bend holds a pool, and in the pools are native cutthroat up to 16 inches or so. No need to get fancy with a hatch-matching pattern. Use a Woolly Bugger. Drift it past each log. You may find a few footprints in the streamside sand if you fish in August. But come September, it's all yours.

[C A N A D A   W E S T]

MacKenzie Trail Lodge

T s a c h a   L a k e ,   B r i t i s h   C o l u m b i a

Hey, wanna catch some rainbows? How 'bout a 50- or 100-trout day for less than a grand a week?

VITAL STATISTICS:

KEY SPECIES:
Bull trout/Dolly Varden, lake trout, rainbows

Tackle:
Casting, fly-fishing, spinning
Flyouts to Remote Waters: Yes
Major Season:
June through August
Accommodations:
RUSTIC CABINS
NUMBER OF CABINS / GUESTS:
MACKENZIE TRAIL: 12 / 2 - 6
BLACKWATER: 8 / 2 - 10
CHINE FALLS: 1 / 4
Meals:
MACKENZIE TRAIL: Fine dining
BLACKWATER: Self-catered with cook optional
CHINE FALLS: Self-catered
Conference Groups: No
Rates:
MACKENZIE TRAIL: From $1,699 / 4 nights, 5 days
BLACKWATER: From $125 / night, plus $200 airfare from Nimpo Lake per person
CHINE FALLS: From $ 1,995 for four anglers / 4 nights, 5 days w/airfare from Nimpo Lake included
Guides: Included at MacKenzie Trail
Gratuities: $15
Preferred Payment:
Cash, check or credit cards
Getting There:
Fly to Vancouver and catch the shuttle included in the base price.
Other Activities:
Big game, bird-watching, boating, canoeing/kayaking/rafting, horseback riding, hiking, wildlife photography

Contact:
Mike VanWormer
MacKenzie Trail Lodge
27134 NW Reeder Rd
Portland OR 97231
Ph: 888/808-7688
Fax: 503/621-3551
Web:
www.mackenzietraillodge.com

RISING ON THE EASTERN slopes of the Coast Mountains, the Blackwater (also known as the West Road River) flows some 54 miles before joining the Nazko and, ultimately, the Fraser north of the town of Quesnel. The river flows through a number of lakes — Eliguk, Tsacha, Euchiniko — and in between alternates between fast rapids and runs with long pools. Prolific hatches of caddis, mayflies and stoneflies come off with regularity. Novice anglers will find the fishing easy. Rainbows, all natives, pounce on Royal Wulffs and Woolly Buggers. A 20-fish day is considered so-so; 50- to 70-fish days are the norm. Skilled anglers hook-and-release more than 100, and it's said that a real type A angler — working at it from dawn to dusk — could get close to 200. The season on Tsacha Lake opens June 1, and fishing in the rivers becomes legal a month later. Jean Groth owns three lodges on the Blackwater River, one of British Columbia's finest wild rainbow rivers.

MACKENZIE TRAIL LODGE: Headquartered on Tsacha Lake, this is the flagship lodge offering quaint cabins (some with private baths) with daily maid service, a number of scrumptious entrees for dinner accompanied by appropriate wines, and a pot of hot coffee or chocolate outside your door in the morning. Flyouts to seldom fished lakes are high on the roster here, as are floats via pontoon craft over waters teeming with rainbows. Other waters are an easy hike. Or you can wade where the plane leaves you.

BLACKWATER LODGE: Located on the head of Tsacha Lake, Blackwater includes eight housekeeping cabins for two to 10 anglers, and shares cooking facilities in the main lodge. Bring your own food or order it though Jean and have it delivered when you arrive. A cook can be obtained if none of you wants to wash dishes. You'll have a boat and motor, and total freedom to set your own schedule.

CHINE FALLS CAMP: This may be the best deal for truly wild rainbow trout. Here the Blackwater combines deep flows with good pocket water and the beauty of Kluskoil Lake. A pair of other lakes nearby contain rainbows up to eight pounds (bring your belly boat). You'll bring in your own chow and sleeping bag too, do your own cooking, and use a runabout to work the lake or areas on the river. Round up three buddies and each of you will pay $500 for a four-night, five-day stay.

Nimmo Bay Resort

N i m m o   B a y ,   B r i t i s h   C o l u m b i a

With your own helicopter and pilot, you can fish anywhere you can fly.

VITAL STATISTICS:

KEY SPECIES:
Bull trout/Dolly Varden, cutthroat, king/chinook salmon, pink salmon, rainbows, red/sockeye salmon, silver/coho salmon, steelhead

Tackle:
Fly-fishing, spinning
Flyouts to Remote Waters: Yes
Major Season:
April through October
Accommodations:
RIVERFRONT CHALETS WITH EVERY AMENITY
NUMBER OF ROOMS: 18
HANDICAPPED ACCESSIBLE: 6
MAXIMUM NUMBER OF GUESTS: 18
Meals: Gourmet regional cuisine
Conference Groups: Yes
Rates: From $6,295 / 4 days / person
Guides: Included
Gratuities: $300
Preferred Payment:
Cash, check or credit cards
Getting There:
Fly to Pt. Hardy and you'll be collected.
Other Activities:
Bird-watching, canoeing/kayaking/ rafting, hiking, swimming, wildlife photography, heli-touring

Contact:
Craig Murray
Nimmo Bay Resort
1978 Broughton Blvd
Box 696
Port McNeill BC
V0N 2R0, Canada
Ph: 800/837-4354
Fax: 250/956-2000
e-mail:
heli@nimmobay.bc.ca
Web:
www.nimmobay.bc.ca

COLD AND FAINTLY GREEN, the river sprints around a boulder-capped wedge of glacial gravel and hustles into a pool where it mills about for a moment before beating it on downstream. Pines and firs reach above the banks, which may hold a few aspens, stunted because of the altitude. You've fished this pool for a couple hours. At first it was good, a pair of steelhead in the 12-pound range. Damn good, in fact. But for the last hour, nothing in the first pool or the two you tried below. Were this a typical trip, you'd climb into the drift boat and push off with the current.

But this is not your garden variety getaway. On the gravel bar sits your chariot, a helicopter. When it's time to move, you're up and away, climbing over a ridge that's above the treeline. There's a patch of snow to your left. Was that a ram? Below, far below, is another river. In a trice, you're touching down on another gravel bar by water that's seen no anglers for weeks, and maybe not so far this season.

Heli-fishing. With speed and agility, rotary-winged aircraft can ferry angler's anywhere that there's a clearing. You can fish half-a-dozen different creeks a day — though normally the angling is so good, you won't move more than twice. Steelhead up to 25-pounds-plus run from April to May. Cutthroats of two to three pounds are plentiful from April into mid-October. The time for six-pound pink salmon is late July through August. Silvers of 10 to 20 pounds enter the rivers in August, and chinooks, averaging 30 but running up to 60 pounds, follow in September. Fish for them both through mid-October, when the lodge closes. Each day, you and your party helicopter to water unreachable any other way. Fly and spinning tackle will be provided by the lodge, or bring your own. A wide range of heli-fishing options is available

Tides wash through the pilings that support the lodge and each of its red-roofed chalets, nestled against a backdrop of deep and towering spruce. Sunlight streams through half-moon windows, creating an aura of natural openness in the sitting rooms of each chalet. Sliding doors lead out onto a private deck, and a curving boardwalk joins them all with the lodge. Dinners are gourmet: prawns, halibut, salmon and lamb, with fresh baked pies and homemade ice cream. Often, groups of eight or more book the entire lodge and ensure themselves of exclusive use of its helicopters and facilities. No wonder this lodge has earned kudos from *Harper's Hideaway Report* and, saints be praised, *The New Yorker*.

[C A N A D A   W E S T]

Northern Woodsman Wilderness Resort

W e s t b a n k ,   B r i t i s h   C o l u m b i a

Nobody carps about the size of the rainbows in this remote provincial park lake.

VITAL STATISTICS:

KEY SPECIES:
Rainbows

Tackle:
Fly-fishing, spinning
Major Season:
May through September
Accommodations:
RUSTIC CABINS
NUMBER OF ROOMS: 10
MAXIMUM NUMBER OF GUESTS: 16
Meals: Hearty family-style
Conference Groups: Yes
Rates: $1,499 / week / person
Guides: Included
Gratuities: $100 or Angler's
discretion
Preferred Payment:
Cash, check or credit cards
Getting There:
Fly to Prince George and rent a car.
Other Activities:
Bird-watching, boating,
canoeing/kayaking/rafting, hiking,
swimming, wildlife photography

Contact:
Les Allen
Northern Woodsman
Wilderness Resort
Box 26025
Westbank BC
V4T 2G3, Canada
Ph: 250/769-7642
Web:
http://www.northernwoodsman.com

ERE IN CENTRAL BRITISH COLUMBIA, the land carries much less relief than on the flanks of the province. It feels more like a high table, cut by various lakes and rivers that give birth to some of the finest angling for rainbows in the world. So why, then, would a lake be named for carp? It was explorer Simon Fraser's doing. In passing through the area, he noted in his journal that Indians would take "immense numbers of fish of the carp kind" from the lake. By the way, Fraser founded a fort on Trout Lake. We can only guess what fish inhabited that body of water.

Etched into the landscape by glaciers, Carp Lake encompasses about 15,000 acres. Shaped roughly like an "H," the lake is known for its many coves, reefs and islands. That's what makes the rainbow population so strong — there's more than ample shallows and cover for bait fish and aquatic insect life. These 'bows are healthy. Typical fish top two pounds and feed with abandon on Woolly Buggers, sculpins and dark wet patterns. Some guests troll gang rigs; others cast small silver and gold spinners on ultralight. A big fish here runs over five pounds, while behemoths going better than eight pounds are not infrequently caught.

When you fish out of Les Allen's camp (which he wisely did not name for the lake), you'll also have a shot at nearby MacIntire, a lake of about a mile by a mile-and-a-half. Don't pass up a trip, either, to a third lake where fish are fewer but run larger. The rivers that connect the lakes offer some wading for anglers tired of sitting in a boat. Fishing is best from June through September.

Northern Woodsman Wilderness Resort is the only lodge on Carp Lake, though the Provincial government does operate a campground. You can drive to the lake, and then it's a short boat ride to the rustic lodge. Guests stay in two rooms in the main lodge, a pair of bunkhouses with two bedrooms each, or in a family cabin that was added in 1999 and which contains a private bath and separate bedroom for parents so they won't disturb their kids. (Or the other way around.) Other rooms share a shower house, and outhouses are located at opposite ends of the camp. Home-cooked meals are served on a long pine table near a window that seems to bring the mixed forest of aspen, spruce and lodgepole pine right indoors.

Rivers of northern Nunavut yield thick arctic char,
a cousin of the brook trout, that dance in the high mountain
streams of the southern Appalachians.

A driftboat from Frontiers Farwest shoots rapids
on the Bulkely, one of British Columbia's
premier steelhead rivers.

[C A N A D A   W E S T]

Oak Bay Marine Vessels

V i c t o r i a ,   B r i t i s h   C o l u m b i a

What do a minesweeper, a scientific survey ship, and a one-time light ship have in common? Salmon!

VITAL STATISTICS:

KEY SPECIES:
Bottom fish, halibut, king/chinook salmon, silver/coho salmon

Tackle:
Casting, trolling

Major Season:
May through September

Accommodations:
CLASSIC SHIPS
NUMBER OF ROOMS / GUESTS
M.V. SALMON SEEKER: 17 / 28
M.V. MARABELLE: 13 / 26
M.V. CHARLOTTE PRINCESS: 26 / 30

Meals: Exquisite regional cuisine

Conference Groups: No

Rates: M.V. SALMON SEEKER: From $1,575 / 3 nights, 4 days
M.V. MARABELLE: From $1,575 / 3 days, 4 nights
M.V. CHARLOTTE PRINCESS: From $1,845 / 3 nights, 4 days

Guides:
M.V. SALMON SEEKER: Included
M.V. MARABELLE: Not needed
M.V. CHARLOTTE PRINCESS: Not needed

Gratuities: Angler's discretion

Preferred Payment:
Cash, check or credit cards

Getting There:
Fly to Vancouver and catch the connecting charter.

Other Activities:
Bird-watching, boating, whale-watching

Contact:
Oak Bay Marine Group
1327 Beach Dr
Victoria BC
V8S 2N4, Canada
Ph: 800/663-7090
Fax: 250/598-1361
e-mail:
obmg@pinc.com
Web:
www.obmg.com

OAK BAY MARINE GROUP is one of the largest operators of fishing resorts in North America. You'll find write-ups about their other lodges — April Point, Canadian Princess, Painters, Cape Santa Maria, and King Salmon — elsewhere in this guide. As with four of the five above, salmon is the name of the game. So it is with three luxury yachts run by Oak Bay. They're scattered around the west and north costs of Graham Island, the northernmost and largest of the Queen Charlottes, a chain of islands across Hecate Strait from Prince Rupert.

M.V. SALMON SEEKER: At 180 feet, this retrofitted seismic survey ship began life as a freighter sailing the waters of the Baltic. It is the largest of Oak Bay's vessels. With home waters in the Kano area on the western coast of Graham Island, the Salmon Seeker gives anglers a shot at chinook, cohos, halibut and bottom fish from 20-foot center-console Boston Whalers. Staterooms are paneled with native woods and utterly first class. They accommodate two adults. Baths are shared. Meals are excellent, and there's a hot tub for soaking.

M.V. MARABELL: Once a war-time minesweeper, the Marabell has been redone, yet it retains its classic lines. You'll find plenty of varnished wood, polished brightwork, and, in the main salon, mirrors that hark back to an earlier and more graceful age of travel. Cabins open onto a pair of decks, and from your windows you can see the forested mountains merge with the icy waters of Langara Island. Later in the season, the Marabell moves south, down the Hecate Strait to an anchorage in a pass off the Hakai Recreation Area on British Columbia's west coast. Either location yields fine salmon, chinook and cohos. You'll fish from 17-foot Whalers, without a guide. The Marabell's fishmaster will tell you all you need to know.

M.V. CHARLOTTE PRINCESS: Unless you're a naval architect, you'd never believe that the Charlotte Princess was once a light ship stationed for weeks on end off the Pacific coast. Today, she's as modern as the come, renovated by Columbia Music to entertain guests and groupies of popular musicians. No wonder this vessel feels like a first-class hotel. Cabins boast highly waxed woodwork, single and double bunks, and private baths. Meals are superb. And fishing (self-guided) is outstanding for salmon and halibut.

Painter's Lodge

C a m p b e l l   R i v e r ,   B r i t i s h   C o l u m b i a

Surging tides ensure a healthy flow of salmon in the channel fronting this grand hotel.

VITAL STATISTICS:

KEY SPECIES:
Chum salmon, king/chinook salmon, pink salmon, red/sockeye salmon, silver/coho salmon

Tackle:
Trolling

Major Season:
April through November

Accommodations:
LUXURIOUSLY MODERN RESORT WITH A VICTORIAN FLARE
NUMBER OF ROOMS: 94
HANDICAPPED ACCESSIBLE: 3
MAXIMUM NUMBER OF GUESTS: 200

Meals: Excellent regional flare

Conference Groups: Yes

Rates: From $110 / night

Guides: Numerous packages

Gratuities: $25 / day

Preferred Payment:
Cash, check or credit cards

Getting There:
Fly to Vancouver and catch the shuttle.

Other Activities:
Bird-watching, boating, golf, hiking, swimming, tennis, wildlife photography

Contact:
Manager
Painter's Lodge
1625 McDonald Rd
Campbell River BC
V9J 1H9, Canada
Ph: 250/286-1102
Fax: 250/286-0158
Web:
www.obmg.com

FLOWING NORTH THEN EAST out of a range capped by the mountain called Golden Hinde, the Campbell once plunged over Elk Falls, rushed through the remnants of a deeply forested gorge, and joined the surging tides of the Discovery Passage near the middle of Vancouver Island. In its adolescence, the river crashed and roared with runoff of melting glaciers, spilling its load of boulders, cobbles and sand, and building the spit which hooks north, separating its freshwater from the passage's saltwater. Today, the river is hobbled by dams, its flows choked and low and warm in summer. Still, the four miles downstream between the falls and the strait are prime spawning grounds for chinook.

Most anglers troll for salmon from downrigger-equipped Boston Whalers loaded with fish-finding electronics. Others prefer simpler tackle pioneered by none other than Zane Gray. An oarsman rows a fiberglass copy of a wooden boat, designed by Joe Painter, for whom this lodge is named. He judges wind and current, and rows at a precise speed that keeps your spoon or plug fluttering just above the boulders at the base of the pool where the Tyee (local lingo for chinooks of more than 30 pounds) lie. Catch one on this old-time tackle and you become a member of a very elite club. If this appeals, book your trip in July or early August.

To be sure, most anglers at Painter's don't fish this way. They sign-up for half-day fishing packages that leave the dock and return as regular as a time-clock. Fishing here is a straightforward affair. Two anglers to a boat. Guides know where the fish are running and boats tend to fish together, trolling with downriggers or not, depending on the species and their depth. Cohos run from June through October and may be taken near the surface early in the season. Sockeyes also come in June, fish best in July, and fade in August. Pinks pass up the channel in July, their best month, and August. Chinooks show up in April and are still in the waters come November.

Painter's is a thoroughly modern and upscale resort with the capacity of fishing for 200 or more guests per day. Accommodations vary from rooms to suites to cabins. Sauna, fitness center, swimming pool and golf all mark this as a full-service resort. Cuisine is near-gourmet and served banquet-style in the large dining room in the main lodge. Linger over the last of the wine and watch the setting sun turn the mainland mountains from apricot to plum.

[C A N A D A   W E S T]

Salmon King Lodge

D e l t a ,   B r i t i s h   C o l u m b i a

Committed to restoring salmon runs in streams that feed the fjords, this one-time cannery brings good hope to anglers as well.

VITAL STATISTICS:

KEY SPECIES:
Chum salmon, king/chinook salmon, pink salmon, silver/coho salmon

Tackle:
Trolling
Major Season:
July through September
Accommodations:
PRIVATE SUITES IN A REMODELED CANNERY
NUMBER OF ROOMS: 14
HANDICAPPED ACCESSIBLE: ALL
MAXIMUM NUMBER OF GUESTS: 28
Meals: Excellent regional cuisine
Conference Groups: Yes
Rates: From $1,995 / 4 days, 3 nights
Guides: $200
Gratuities: 10%
Preferred Payment:
Cash, check or credit cards
Getting There:
Fly to Port Hardy and take the air taxi.
Other Activities:
Bird-watching, boating, hiking, swimming, wildlife photography

Contact:
Lisa Killick
Salmon King Lodge
PO Box 1237
Delta BC
V4M 3T3, Canada
Ph: 800/665-0613
Fax: 604/244-8754
Web:
www.salmonking.com

IN 1895, CREWS BEGAN DRIVING PILINGS for what would become one of the most productive canneries on the British Columbia coast. Netters hauled tons of coho, sockeye, chum, chinook, and hump-backed salmon to its rough wooden docks over the next three quarters of a century. But in 1968, the handwriting was on the wall. The icy flows of the tides in Rivers Inlet, a vast fjord north and east of the tip of Vancouver Island, were no longer sustaining a commercially viable salmon population.

That year, the conversion of the cannery to a fishing lodge began. Fourteen guest suites were created, paneled with natural woods and equipped with queen or two single beds. All offer private baths. A spacious lounge offers a variety of games. And the restaurant is widely known for its delightful dinners of not only the freshest seafood in the world, but also excellent prime rib.

This, to some degree, is a self-guided fishing vacation. When you arrive, you and your partner will be assigned a 16-foot soft-top boat with a quiet, electric start four-cycle motor. Each boat is equipped with fish finder, VHF radio, and all the fishing tackle and bait you need. After a short orientation on boat and tackle operation, you're on your own. Prudent guests will invest in one day's guiding just to learn the locations and technique. Normally, you'll drift over waters where your fish finder locates salmon. Mooching with long rods and single-action reels loaded with 20- to 45-pound-test mono, is the name of the game here. You'll bait up with a plug of cut herring, and add enough weight to get it down to where the fish are. If everything works well, and it usually does, you'll drift through schools of kings. Then you'll be busy. Like giant shock absorbers, the long rods bow deeply with every run, easing strain on terminal tackle. While the average king tips the scales between 25 and 30 pounds, 40-pounders are commonplace, 60-pounders are not unheard of, and even bigger fish are taken each year. Kings run first in July. They're followed by pinks (average five pounds), cohos (eight to 26 pounds) and chums (10 to 18 pounds). Bottom fishing for halibut up to 200 pounds (most are much lighter) is another option. All gear, including rain clothes, are provided, which makes it easier to keep your luggage under the 25-pound maximum.

Vaseux Lake Lodge

Oliver, British Columbia

Bighorns and eagles entertain you as you drift this silent lake for salmon and smallmouth.

IF BIGHORN SHEEP, eagles and osprey, wild geese, ducks and songbirds of every description fire the engine that drives your soul — and you want a bit of good fishing on the side — then this lodge on Vaseux Lake may the place for you. Vaseux Lake is an impoundment of the Okanagan River (Okanogan in the U.S.), which crosses into the U.S. just south of Osoyoos (trace the route of U.S. 97 and you'll find it).

Vaseux is known for cutthroat, kokanee salmon and largemouth bass. Cutts run in the one- to two-pound range and are best fished either in May or June, or September through November. Kokanees, up to four pounds, do best in August and September. Largemouth and smallmouth hit best in May and June, slump somewhat in the height of summer, and then pick up in September and October. Whitefish follow a similar pattern, as do perch. The lake is relatively small and narrow, only 1.8 miles long and .4 miles wide, and British Columbia authorities permit no outboards. You'll have to make do trolling or casting from a canoe while you watch bighorn sheep scamper on the rocky crags above the lake. In addition, you'll find cutthroats in many of the small streams that flow into the lake and river.

The fishing can be good, but the wildlife viewing can be excellent, and that's *raison d'etre* for Vaseux Lake Lodge. If you visit the lodge between June and July, you are apt to see ewes leading their young from the lambing cave on Eagle Bluff. Marmots cavort among the bluff's boulders. Golden and bald eagles soar over the lodge, osprey plunge into the lake for fish, and 305 other bird species have been recorded in the area. At night, coyotes serenade you to sleep. This lodge is a naturalist's dream. So plentiful is the wildlife that lodge owners Peter and Denise Axhorn have placed field guides in every room.

Vaseux Lake laps at the beach in front of the lodge, which is made up of four two-story attached townhouses that are staggered to provide privacy. On the main floor of each, the dining/living area with sleeper sofa looks out, through floor to ceiling windows, to the mountains across the lake. You'll enjoy the view as well through the cathedral windows upstairs in the master bedroom. Or you can slide open the windows and sit on your private balcony outside. A fully-equipped kitchen lets you whip up breakfast and lunch. Restaurants for dinner are nearby in Oliver or Penticton.

[C A N A D A   W E S T]

Bathurst Inlet Lodge

B a t h u r s t   I n l e t ,   N u n a v u t

Learn firsthand of the people, flora and fauna of the Arctic, and catch very good fish, too.

VITAL STATISTICS:

KEY SPECIES:
Arctic char, grayling, lake trout, pike

Tackle:
Fly-fishing, spinning, trolling
Flyouts to Remote Waters: Yes
Major Season:
July and August
Accommodations:
CABINS
NUMBER OF ROOMS: 15
HANDICAPPED ACCESSIBLE: 3
MAXIMUM NUMBER OF GUESTS: 30
Meals: Hearty family fare
Conference Groups: Yes
Rates: All trips are custom packaged and priced. (There is no set minimum)
Guides: Included or not as you choose
Gratuities: Angler's discretion
Preferred Payment:
Cash, check or credit cards
Getting There:
Fly to Yellowknife and catch the bush plane.
Other Activities:
Big game, bird-watching, boating, canoeing/kayaking/rafting, wildlife photography

Contact:
Boyd Warner
Bathurst Inlet Lodge
Box 820
Yellowknife NT
X1A 2N6 Canada
Ph: 867/920-4330
Fax: 867/920-4263
e-mail:
bathurst@bathurstinletlodge.com
Web:
www.bathurstinletlodge.com

MOST, BUT NOT ALL, of the lodges in this book focus on fishing. Every other pursuit is strictly secondary. That's not the case at Bathurst Inlet lodge. For more than a generation, Glen and Trish Warner and their son, Boyd, have been catering to amateur naturalists who want to become acquainted, firsthand, with the marvelously beautiful Arctic and the gentle native peoples who inhabit it. If you ask them, the Warners will tell you that life spreads across the rocky old shoulders of the tundra like a green shawl. Embroidered with wildflowers of red, yellow and cream — the colors of the spring and summer — the tundra hosts thousands of caribou and muskox which you'll see during your visit.

Your guides here know the names of the wildflowers — lupines, saxifrages, cinquefoils, arctic poppy, mountain avens — and can tell peregrine falcons from rough-legged hawks. If you're interested, they'll show you the difference between rock bluffs of igneous diabase, born of the earth's molten magma, and algal limestones deposited in seas like those of Florida Bay. And you'll meet (and get to know if you wish) the Inuit families whose lives have been linked to this land since the glaciers departed thousands of years ago.

Fishing can be as high on your agenda as you want it. Bathurst Inlet, which probes the mainland south from the Arctic Ocean, is fed by a variety of rivers. Some are shallow and cobbly, carrying fine stocks of grayling which you can catch one after another with flies or spinners. Other rivers crash and brawl through fissures in the rock. These powerful streams see runs of arctic char, a cousin of the brook trout, and some lake trout as well. Flies and hardware are most effective with these species. Reedy shoals in pristine blackwater lakes hold lunker pike, and on gravel bars, you're apt to connect with lake trout. Trolling is the main angling method on still waters, but when the wind dies and the surface shines like a mirror, look for rising fish.

Built around a historic Oblate mission and a Hudson's Bay Co. Trading Post, the lodge houses guests in modern cabins. Working with Boyd, you can set whatever schedule you like. The Warners operate a number of camps ranging in size from two to six cabins in a variety of locations depending on what you want to do. Camps can be staffed or not; supplied with boats, motors or other equipment; and stocked with food — it's all your choice. Prices vary, of course, based on your choices.

Frontier Fishing Lodge

Snowdrift (Kutsel K'e), NWT

Lake trout, lake trout, and more lake trout lure anglers to the wilds of the Great Slave Lake.

VITAL STATISTICS:

KEY SPECIES:
Grayling, lake trout, pike

Tackle:
Casting, fly-fishing, spinning
Major Season:
Mid-June through mid-September
Accommodations:
LODGE AND CABINS
NUMBER OF ROOMS: 13 PLUS CABINS
MAXIMUM NUMBER OF GUESTS: 35
Meals: Family-style
Conference Groups: Yes
Rates: From $1,400 / 3 days
Guides: Included
Gratuities: $20
Preferred Payment:
Cash or check
Getting There:
Fly to Yellowknife and catch a floatplane.
Other Activities:
Big game, bird-watching, wildlife photography

Contact:
Wayne Witherspoon
Frontier Fishing Lodge
PO Box 32008
Edmonton AB
T6K 4C2, Canada
Ph: 403/465-6843
Fax: 403/466-3874
e-mail:
frontier@compusmart.ab.ca
Web:
www.compusmart.ab.ca/frontier.index/html

THIS LODGE GETS RAVE REVIEWS from guys who ought to know. "In 3-1/2 hours, I hooked 17 lake trout and succeeded in boating eight," writes Keith Gardner of *Fishing World.* "The five waters — Great Slave, Stark and Murky lakes, and the Stark and Snowdrift rivers — one can reach from Frontiers must be ranked among the world's greatest angling waters," says Tom McIntyre, formerly of *Sports Afield.* "The only thing one wishes for is more time," laments that great angling author A.J. McClane.

Great Slave is one of a pair of huge lakes in the Northwest Territories (the other being Great Bear) known throughout the world as one of the perennial hotspots for lake trout. The biggest allegedly ran 74 pounds, while the lodge record is 58 pounds. Roughly 285 miles wide and more than 2000 feet deep in places, Great Slave stays icy cold even in the height of summer. That keeps the lake trout near the surface but slows their growth. A 20 pound fish, a little better than average, may be 20 years old, and a 50-pounder older than 40. Anyone can catch lake trout here (a 9-year-old landed a 35-pounder) and lots of them.

Trolled hardware catches most fish and the largest. Want to hazard a guess at the most popular lure? It's the Five 'O Diamonds with its five red diamonds on a bright yellow background. Other color combos work well too. Lake trout feed on ciscoes, and those who like to cast crankbaits will find success with almost any five or six-inch-long deep diving wobble lure.

Rivers hold grayling and you can catch scores of them in a day on drys of #12 to #16 size. These fish are not particular in the least. Any darkish pattern will do. Really exceptional, the Stark River is a grayling angler's ideal. Easily waded, every eddy seems to hold a handful and each, in turn, seems willing to take flies or ultralight spinners. Grayling run about two pounds each. Lake trout (and a few whitefish) hold in the lower reaches of the river. Pike don't grow as large here as they do in lakes farther south, but still, a 20-pounder will hold your attention.

Located on a little bay a quarter mile from the mouth of the Stark River, six comfortable guest rooms and a lounge with fireplace are found in the main lodge. Seven more bedrooms are attached to a second large building, and six log cabins provide accommodations for anglers desiring more privacy. Baths are shared. Meals are served in a third building. Food is hearty and abundant.

[C A N A D A   W E S T]

VITAL STATISTICS:

KEY SPECIES:
Grayling, lake trout, pike

Tackle:
Casting, fly-fishing, spinning, trolling
Flyouts to Remote Waters: Yes
Major Season:
June through August
Accommodations:
WOODEN CABINS
NUMBER OF ROOMS / GUESTS:
KASBA LAKE: 12 / 45
SOUTH SNOWBIRD: 3 / 9
NORTH SNOWBIRD: 1 / 6
TABANE: 1 / 6
Meals: KASBA LAKE: American
plan with steak, turkey, chicken
SNOWBIRD and TABANE: You'll do
your own cooking
Conference Groups: Yes
Rates:
KASBA LAKE: From $2,395 / 5 days
SNOWBIRD: From $1,495 / 5 days
TABANE: From $1,995 / 5 days
Guides: Included at Kasba
Gratuities: $100 / boat
Preferred Payment:
Cash, check or credit cards
Getting There:
Fly to Winnipeg, Manitoba, and catch
the jet flight to the lodge.
Other Activities:
Bird-watching, boating,
canoeing/kayaking/rafting, hiking,
wildlife photography

Contact:
Doug Hill
Kasba Lake Lodge
PO Box 96
Parksville BC
V9P 2G3, Canada
Ph: 250/248-3572
Fax: 250/248-4576
e-mail:
rhill@island.net
Web:
www.kasba.com

Kasba Lake Lodge

K a s b a   L a k e ,   N o r t h w e s t   T e r r i t o r i e s

After dinner, there's four hours of daylight — plenty of time to grab a boat and chase more lakers or pike.

THE SOUTHERN TIP of Kasba Lake seems to grow out of the point where four Canadian provinces meet: The Northwest Territories, Nunavut, Manitoba and Saskatchewan. The land here is isolated. There are no roads for miles, only endless conifer forest, stunted by the high winds of bitter winters. Here and there are rock outcrops, but in the main, the terrain rises gently from the lakes, rolls on for a bit, and then settles back into water. A handful of rivers feed Kasba: the Snowbird comes in on the west; the Hasbela from the south; and the Schwandt — known for early season lake trout — also from the west. The lake's outflow is the Kazan River which heads north.

Structures offer clues to the location of fish. Waters off rocky points and bars are prime lake trout terrain. Pike congregate in the weedy backs of sandy bays. Grayling favor the fast water of inlets or outlets. Most lake trout are caught trolling big spoons and spinners. Pike like spoons, spinnerbaits and buzzbaits thrown with conventional casting gear. Ultralight anglers will find that grayling love small spinners, while fly-fishermen take them with wets and dries. Three lodges are operated from Kasba Lake. Trip packages all include air transportation from Winnipeg:

KASBA LAKE LODGE: Consisting of 11 cabins, each furnished with all the basics and private baths, this is a full-service lodge located near the mouth of the Snowbird River. Morning begins when the pot of hot coffee is delivered to your door. A short walk brings you to the dining room for breakfast. Down the hill, boats and motors await you and your guide for the day's fishing. All species — lake trout, pike, grayling and walleye — are caught from this lodge.

SNOWBIRD LAKE: Two camps on a lake 24 miles west of Kasba. Known for big lakers, Snowbird has yielded record book fish, one estimated to weigh more than 65 pounds. Forty pounders occasionally come to net. Three guest cabins and a kitchen and dining room make up South Camp. Up to nine guests handle their own cooking chores. The drill is similar at North Camp, on Snowbird, but there's only one cabin for six. Solar energy powers lights; a propane fridge keeps cold stuff cold; kitchens are fully equipped; and there are hot showers.

TABANE LAKE: More of a river fishery than a lake, but known for super lake trout and grayling with some pike. A single cabin sleeps six, with facilities similar to North Camp. This is the retreat for anglers who relish doing their own thing.

*In the Northwest Territories, fat lake trout are most often
taken while trolling. But don't overlook the mouths of rivers
where a cast plug often brings surprising results.*

*You'll find native cutthroat in the Pipestone River, a tributary
of the upper Bow, that flows past the Post Hotel in
Lake Louise, Alberta. The Post Hotel is world-renowned for
its fine dining and excellent accommodations.*

[C A N A D A   W E S T]

Mackay Lake Lodge

Y e l l o w k n i f e ,   N o r t h w e s t   T e r r i t o r i e s

Check out this lodge for lake trout and grayling, and come back later for record caribou.

VITAL STATISTICS:

KEY SPECIES:
Grayling, lake trout, pike

Tackle:
Casting, fly-fishing, spinning, trolling
Flyouts to Remote Waters: Yes
Major Season:
July through mid-August
Accommodations:
STICK BUILT CABINS
NUMBER OF ROOMS: 6
MAXIMUM NUMBER OF GUESTS: 24
Meals: Hearty family-style
Conference Groups: Yes
Rates: From $995 / 3 days /
person, double occupancy
Guides: Available
Gratuities: $200 / week
Preferred Payment:
Cash, check or credit cards
Getting There:
Fly to Yellowknife and catch the free
charter.
Other Activities:
Big game, boating, canoeing/
kayaking/rafting, hiking, wildlife
photography

Contact:
Gary Jaeb
Mackay Lake Lodge
3919 School Ave
Yellowknife NT
X1A 2J7, Canada
Ph: 867/873-8533
Fax: 867/920-4834
e-mail:
tnsafari@internorth.com
Web:
www.truenorthsafaris.com

ORE THAN 100 MILES LONG, Mackay Lake stretches toward the border with Nunavut. It differs from Great Bear and Great Slave in that Mackay has more island structure, more shoals, and more rocky drop-offs. In short, more cover for lake trout, its prime species. Vee-hulled 18-footers with 40-horse outboards make reasonably short work of runs to such hot spots as the Snake, Cosack Bay, Portage Bay and the Narrows where steep rock bluffs rise 50 to 100 feet above the water. While peregrine falcons swoop among the cliff tops, you'll troll for lakers in the 20- to 40-pound range. Spoons and wobbling plugs in chartreuse and red work wonders here. In the spring, soon after ice-out in June, lakers move into the shallows and feed with the aggressiveness of pike. Later, they haunt gravel bars and drop-offs.

Along with very good lake trout fishing, you'll find that feeder streams teem with grayling. Cast a little Mepps spinner or a little dry (a #12 or #14 Adams with a fluorescent parachute works well), and play with these sailfish of the north for as long as you can stand it. The trick is to catch only those that go more than three pounds.

You'll also find some pike in grassy backwaters on Mackay Lake. But if it's true trophies you're after, consider one of the other packages offered by Gary Jaeb, owner of the lodge. He'll arrange for you to spend three days on Great Slave before hopping the charter to Mackay Lake. Or if you prefer, you can do it on your return.

Cabins at the lodge boast toilets and running water. Showers are shared, except in a duplex which has private baths. Meals are simple and solid, with good salads as well as meat and potatoes. Gary maintains a number of outpost camps, primarily for hunters seeking trophy caribou. Talk with him about booking a combined hunting and fishing trip for early fall, when trophy lake trout return to the surface and hundreds of caribou migrate near camp.

Plummer's Lodges

N o r t h w e s t   T e r r i t o r i e s

With five lodges on either side of the Arctic Circle, you'll catch huge fish in a land of unspoiled beauty.

VITAL STATISTICS:

KEY SPECIES:
Arctic char, grayling, lake trout, pike

Tackle:
Casting, fly-fishing, spinning, trolling
Flyouts to Remote Waters: Yes
Major Season:
June through September
Accommodations:
GREAT SLAVE: MAIN LODGE WITH 5 CABINS
GREAT BEAR: MAIN LODGE WITH 8 - 10 CABINS
TREE RIVER: DINING ROOM/KITCHEN WITH PLATFORM TENTS
TROPHY: MOTEL-STYLE LODGE
NEILAND BAY: MOTEL-STYLE LODGE
NUMBER OF GUESTS:
GREAT SLAVE: 44
GREAT BEAR: 45
TREE RIVER: 8
TROPHY: 30
NEILAND BAY: 16
Meals: Excellent breakfasts and dinners with shore or boxed lunches
Conference Groups: Yes
Rates:
GREAT SLAVE: From $1,995 / 3 days
GREAT BEAR, TROPHY, and NEILAND BAY: From $3,795 / 7 days
TREE RIVER: From $445 / overnight from GREAT BEAR
Guides: Included
Gratuities: Angler's discretion
Preferred Payment:
Cash, check or credit cards
Getting There:
Fly to Winnipeg and meet the chartered jet.
Other Activities:
Bird-watching, hiking, wildlife photography

Contact:
Plummer's Lodges
 950 Bradford St
Winnipeg MB
R3N 0N5, Canada
Ph: 204/774-5775
Fax: 204/783-2320
e-mail:
plummers@canadianarcticfishing.com
Web:
www.plummers.mb.ca

BOREAL FOREST GIVES WAY to tundra in the region of the Northwest Territories that surrounds Great Bear and Great Slave lakes. Hills rounded and smoothed by glaciers, but still rugged and rocky, rise 100 to 200 feet above big water lakes that are cut by reefs and drop-offs where lake trout feed. Low stands of conifers back away from grassy bays where pike play. Cheerful open rivers chatter over cobbles, and in each pocket lies two or three grayling. It's hard for the mind to take it all in — the muskox standing in the flat gazing into endless time; a caribou feeding quietly on an island; peregrine falcons cheeing among the cliffs; a season where all the wildflowers of spring and summer are compressed into one month.

The country is stunning and so is the fishing. Check the IGFA book of world-record fish: Plummer's on Great Bear Lake is the place for lake trout, arctic grayling and arctic char. The all-tackle world records for these three species are held by anglers fishing from Plummer's. So, too, are all of the line-class records for arctic grayling, and seven out of 10 for lake trout. The all-tackle record for lake trout, set by Rodney Hartback's 66.5-pounder in 1991, may not stand. Bill Dodson landed a 70-pound behemoth in July, 1996. Big fish are common in the waters surrounding Chummy Plummer's five lodges.

GREAT SLAVE: The southernmost of the five is a short flight west of Yellowknife. Great Slave produces huge lake trout, grayling and pike from July through September. They migrate through the narrows in front of the lodge. Here, you'll fish with another angler and a guide in a boat, trolling or casting spinners or spoons. Fly-fishers have fun with grayling on dries and dark nymphs. Modest cabins with private baths provide accommodations, while the main lodge includes the dining room for substantial meals, a trading post with proven lures and other tackle, and a bank of leather easy chairs for relaxing.

GREAT BEAR: This is the signature lodge on the Dease arm of the NWT's largest lake. Lake trout, trolled up on spoons or wobble plugs, can top 60 pounds. Fishers of flies will find success with full sinking lines, trolling long Clousers and lime-green eels made for striped bass.

Grayling in the mouths of rivers run in the two- to three-pound range. Here, fly-fishers have the advantage; grayling will nail almost any darkish pattern and the flight on a light rod is more fun than a barrel of monkies. Ride vee-hulled boats to a number of bays and passes, or opt for daily flyouts to reaches too far for the outboard. Guest cabins are well maintained and feature hot showers. Chow is uniformly as excellent as it is plentiful. Guides know the water, and they know how to meet a client's needs. Tackle shop on site. Departure point for trips to the Tree River.

TREE RIVER: Located 150 miles northeast of Great Bear Lake Lodge. Ride the 1943-vitnage DC 3 to this utterly charming spot where the Tree breaks free of its gorge and runs seven miles to Coronation Gulf, an arm of the Arctic Ocean. Arctic char fill the river in late July. They arrive as bright silver as steelhead, but soon their backs blacken like the night of Arctic winter and their bellies turn as red as an angry sunset. The two-day flyout for about $450 additional is well worth it. Fish the president's pool, so loved by George Bush, or sneak into the little bay behind the lodge and catch char that nobody expects to be there. A ride down to the mouth of the river is a must. You'll see basalt bluffs rounded and smoothed by the ocean, and you'll know then what inspired the Inuit style of stone carving. Accommodations are four-person tents with wooden floors. Hearty meals are served in the main lodge building. The return trip drops you in Kugluktuk (formerly the town of Coppermine) for a chance to buy Inuit crafts.

TROPHY LODGE: Found at the west end of Great Bear Lake. Sited on a sweeping beach where the Smith arm hooks into Ford Bay, the motel-style Trophy Lodge is surrounded by trees and flowers. It's pretty, but trophy fish are the attraction here. Four IGFA records for lake trout, two for grayling and one for char on a fly have been set by anglers staying at Trophy. Water is shallow here, a fly-fisher's dream for big lakers. Trophy also has the best pike fishing on Great Bear. Guests fish two to a boat with Inuit guides, and stay in modern, carpeted rooms with private baths. Food is exemplary. Daily flyouts to the Coppermine for arctic char are also a possibility.

NEILAND BAY: On the lake's south shore, near the site of the original Plummer's lodge. This rustic motel-style lodge on Great Bear Lake is smaller than either of its siblings, but the fishing and food are at least as good. You'll find lakers up to 60 pounds (an unofficial record fish weighing 74 pounds was taken not too long ago). Grayling are also good, both in the lake and tributary rivers. Grayling are in the four-pound range and pike to 20 pounds.

Though Plummer's five lodges are close to the Arctic Circle, temperatures in summer frequently nudge the mid-80s. And while climate is semi-arid in summer, fronts with lots of moisture move through fairly quickly. Bring a thick Polar fleece pullover, a set of long underwear (synthetic fiber) and a hooded Gore-Tex rain jacket. A pair of rubber-bottomed L.L. Bean-style boots will pay dividends, as will a billed cap, a small bottle of bug dope and a soft tackle satchel that you can swing over your shoulder. Prepare for the worst; think layered and travel light.

Athabasca Fishing Lodges

Otherside River, Saskatchewan

Even though these two lodges are on the same side of the river, it isn't the same river. Whatever, the fishing is good.

VITAL STATISTICS:

KEY SPECIES:
Grayling, lake trout, pike, walleye

Tackle:
Casting, fly-fishing, spinning, trolling
Flyouts to Remote Waters: Yes
Major Season:
Mid-June through mid-September
Accommodations:
FRAME AND LOG LODGE WITH CABINS
NUMBER OF CABINS:
OTHERSIDE RIVER: 10 W/CAPACITIES
FOR 2 TO 8
ENGLER LAKE: 5 W/ CAPACITY FOR UP
TO 4 anglers in each
Meals: Hearty family-style fare
Conference Groups: No
Rates:
OTHERSIDE RIVER: $3,095 / 7 days
ENGLER LAKE: $2,395 / 7 days
Guides:
OTHERSIDE RIVER: Included
ENGLER LAKE: Self-guided
Gratuities: Angler's discretion
Preferred Payment:
Cash, check or credit cards
Getting There:
Fly to Edmonton and catch the free
flight north.
Other Activities:
Boating, canoeing/kayaking/rafting,
hiking, swimming

Contact:
Cliff Blackmur
Athabasca Fishing Lodges
PO Box 7800
Saskatoon SK
S7K 4R5, Canada
Ph: 306/653-5490
Fax: 306/653-5525
e-mail:
athabasca@sask.sympatico.ca
Web:
www.athabascalake.com

LAKE ATHABASCA is the largest body of water in Saskatchewan. Its eastern arm narrows a bit then swells enough to be given its own name: Fond du Lac. The country on either side of the lake is barren of all but the scrubbiest of trees. Soil is scant, sandy, and just barely fertile enough to support low bush blueberries and cranberries. (If you fish here in late August, you can stroll through the woods, picking dessert after your shore-lunch of walleye, fried potatoes and beans.) Lakes are darkly stained by tannin and froth like good dark stout in the tumbling rivers that connect them. Athabasca and nearby lakes are famous for lake trout, northern pike, grayling and walleye. For 25 years, Cliff and Stella Blackmur have run Athabasca Fishing Lodges.

OTHERSIDE RIVER LODGE: With 10 suite-style cabins, each with a living room, two bedrooms, private bath, screened porch and daily maid service, the lodge provides a comfortable, functional home base for fishing Fond du Lac, the river or a number of hotspots on the Athabasca's east end. A 32-foot cabin cruiser ferries anglers and guides to fishing boats cached in the bush. Two anglers fish with each guide, normally Dene Indians who have worked with the lodge for many years. Meals of steak, turkey and prime rib are family-style. Here, you'll find lake trout to 50 pounds, pike that approach 30 pounds, walleye and all the grayling you want to catch.

ENGLER LAKE CAMP: More a mini-lodge than a camp — five wooden cabins, hot showers in a central bathhouse, home-cooked meals and 24-hour electricity — Engler Lake is the place for experienced anglers to fish on their own. You'll have a 16-foot aluminum boat, motor and all the gas you need at your disposal. A camp manager provides advice and assistance. Then you're off on your own to explore the lake and the portage to Rious, the next lake up the chain. These waters primarily hold huge pike, ample walleye and grayling.

At both lodges, there's good grayling water within walking distance of the lodge, and anglers have the chance for one free side-trip. Fly out to a lake known for huge lake trout, or go after walleye for your cooler. An overnight trip to Fontaine Lake, 32 miles north of Otherside River where lakers are the mainstay, is also available. Cliff also offers neat canoe trips. Best time to come? If you want a crack at all species, head for late June or early July. Or make your plans for the first week in September. At those times, everything is high in the water column, feeding like crazy.

[C A N A D A   W E S T]

Camp Grayling

S t o n y   R a p i d s ,   S a s k a t c h e w a n

At this friendly and laid-back lodge, pike and grayling never stop, and there's always walleye for lunch.

VITAL STATISTICS:

KEY SPECIES:
Grayling, lake trout, pike, walleye

Tackle:
Casting, fly-fishing, spinning, trolling
Flyouts to Remote Waters: Yes
Major Season:
June through September
Accommodations:
RUSTIC CABINS AROUND A SUNNY GLEN
NUMBER OF CABINS: 8
MAXIMUM NUMBER OF GUESTS: 22
Meals: Family-style
Conference Groups: No
Rates: From $305 / day, double occupancy
Guides: Included
Gratuities: Angler's discretion
Preferred Payment:
Cash, check or credit cards
Getting There:
Fly to Stony Rapids and you'll be met.
Other Activities:
Bird-watching, boating, canoeing/kayaking/rafting, hiking, wildlife photography

Contact:
Margy Michel
Camp Grayling
General Delivery
Stony Rapids SK
S0J 2R0, Canada
Ph: 306/439-2178

Off Season:
111 Gathercole Crescent
Saskatoon SK
S7K 7J3, Canada
Ph: 306/249-2655

HIGH UP near the border of Saskatchewan and the Northwest Territories is a chain of lakes and connecting rivers that are filled with fine pike, lake trout, and walleye. Rivers that feed the lakes, and those that carry downstream flows, are chock full of grayling, more fun than you can imagine on an ultralight or three-weight rod. Camp Grayling, established more than 40 years ago, sits at the outlet of Black Lake, one of the major bodies of water on Fond du Lac, a river that feeds big Lake Athabasca.

After a breakfast that'd founder most of us, you'll climb into vee-hulled fishing boats and beat a path for the cove of the day. There your Dene guide will suggest lures that have proven effective on pike. Buzz baits, spinner baits and the ever popular Five O' Diamonds are the mainstays up here, but hey, throw what you want. Maybe that new lure will provoke a 50-inch monster into a slamming strike. If you arrive early in the season, you'll find lake trout near the surface. Walleye abound in the runs between islands. It's your job to catch enough for lunch each day. Among the reasons for the good fishing at Camp Grayling is its commitment to catch-and-release, and a policy that rotates anglers over productive bays so each has a chance to rest before it's fished again.

But if large lakers is your game, then you have some options. Arrange for a flyout to one of eight smaller lakes where the water warms earlier in the season and lake trout become more active. There's also a nifty overnight package to an outpost camp on Selwyn Lake, just a stone's throw from the Northwest Territories boundary. Fly in early one morning, fish all day, spend the night, fish the next day and return to camp that evening. Selwyn lakers run to 45 pounds and more. You'll be accompanied on this trip by a guide and you'll all pitch in with the cooking chores. With three cabins — one for the guide, one for the guests and another for cooking and eating — this outpost has a lot to offer.

The main camp is extremely comfortable. Eight barn-red cabins with white trim nestle on a rise within walking distance of Black Lake's outflow. The main lodge includes the dining room, a wall of proven lures, and a screened porch that's delightful. Cabins contain private baths with hot showers. Families are enthusiastically welcome here: special discounts are available for parents who bring their children fishing. This is a great place to introduce your kids to the north country angling.

Hatchet Lake Lodge

Elk River, Saskatchewan

World-class pike and lake trout roam Hatchet and nearby lakes, just waiting for your spoon or fly.

VITAL STATISTICS:

KEY SPECIES:
Grayling, lake trout, pike, walleye

Tackle:
Casting, fly-fishing, spinning, trolling
Major Season:
June through mid-September
Accommodations:
MODERN LOG CABINS WITH PRIVATE BATHS
NUMBER OF CABINS: 24
MAXIMUM NUMBER OF GUESTS: 60
Meals: Hearty steaks and chops
Conference Groups: No
Rates: From $2,395 / 4 days / person
Guides: Included
Gratuities: Angler's discretion
Preferred Payment:
Cash, check or credit cards
Getting There:
Fly to Winnipeg and take the charter jet.
Other Activities:
Bird-watching, boating, wildlife photography

Contact:
George Fleming
Hatchet Lake Lodge
PO Box 262
Elk River MN 55330
Ph: 800/661-9183
Fax: 306/922-1575
e-mail:
george@hatchetlake.com
Web:
www.hatchetlake.com

G REASE SNAPPED in the skillet over a fire of driftwood gathered by the Cree guide. Soon he'd slip in the walleye filets which you'd taken on an ultralight half an hour earlier. In another skillet, potatoes and onions were just starting to brown nicely. Time for a cast or two from the granite outcrop that pushed out into the bed of flooded grass on this lake in the northeasternmost corner of Saskatchewan. You picked up your fly rod, checked the chartreuse and yellow frog, and worked out 60 feet of line carefully so your back cast wouldn't grab a stunted spruce.

Standing on the rock made you feel good. The sun warmed your back and a faint breeze kept the mosquitoes at bay. You pushed the line out into a hole in the grass and let the frog land with a plop! And there it sat. You counted to 20, slowly. Then you gave it a twitch and let it rest again. Another pull skittered it across the surface for maybe five feet. Then you paused it again. Just as you thought, there was nobody home, but then a great grey head with a huge white mouth rose with a swirl and consumed the fly. You'll always remember that take. So deliberate, so sure. The rest of the fight was almost anticlimactic; hell, it was work. The fish, a laker you supposed from its color, ran you to backing and, after pulling lunch off the fire, the Cree managed to get you in the boat so you could follow the fish into open water. Eventually, it rolled and you saw it was as big as it felt but you were anxious to get it in. It had been on a long time, now. Too long. You did not want to kill it. It was a grand and noble fish that had lived in this lake for 35, maybe 50 years. It was about your age, you reckoned, as the guide held it gently in the net while you slipped the barbless hook from its jaw. You rested, hands on knees, as the fish's big gill plates pumped steadily. Then the Cree lowered the net from around the fish and it swam gratefully off into the deep tannin-stained water.

Fishing on Hatchet Lake is not always like this. But it can be. You never know. In the main, you'll catch scores of lake trout and pike in the 10- to 30-pound range, and walleye up to five pounds. Spincasters generally use medium-action rods and reels spooled with 10- to 12-pound-test line. Casting reels carry 17- to 20-pound line. Six- to nine-inch steel leaders are essential. Favorite lures include the ever-popular Five O' Diamonds, Johnson's Silver Minnows and no. 3 and 4 Mepps. Fly-fishers will want a nine- or 10-foot rod for an 8-weight, steel leader material and a selection of big white, chartreuse and yellow streamers. Spinning gear works all the time; fly-fishers do better in late June and early September. Grayling play in the little rivers that link one lake to the other. Flyouts to other lakes are available at extra cost.

Located on an island on the northern end of the lake, the three-level main lodge is built of hand-peeled log and has a dining room, bar, game room and conference room, plus a fully-stocked tackleshop. Scattered in the trees nearby are woodsy, comfortable guest cabins of hand-peeled log with private baths for parties of two to four. Meals give new definition to "hearty." Bacon, eggs, steaming Red River Cereal, French toast and pancakes start you off. Dinners include steak, ham, turkey, fresh salads and vegetables, all topped off by a definitely high-cal dessert. And there are seconds on everything, including the fishing.

Walleye filets, potatoes and onion, beans fresh
from the can — these are the important food groups
of a shore lunch in northern Saskatchewan.

Reindeer Lake Trout Camp
Southend, Saskatchewan

You can drive north as far as the road goes in Saskatchewan, or you can fly. Either way, you're headed for first-class fishing.

VITAL STATISTICS:

KEY SPECIES:
Grayling, lake trout, pike, walleye

Tackle:
Casting, fly-fishing, spinning, trolling
Flyouts to Remote Waters: Yes
Major Season:
May through September
Accommodations:
RUSTIC YET FULLY-EQUIPPED LOG CABINS
NUMBER OF ROOMS: 12
MAXIMUM NUMBER OF GUESTS: 40
Meals: Hearty meals of steaks and chops
Conference Groups: Yes
Rates: From $700 / week (outpost); $2,275 / week (main lodge)
Guides: Varies with package
Gratuities: $20 / day
Preferred Payment:
Cash, check or credit cards
Getting There:
Fly from Minneapolis or Denver.
Other Activities:
Big game, bird-watching, boating

Contact:
Ron & Cindi Holmes
Reindeer Lake Trout Camp
Southend SK
S0J 2L0, Canada
Ph: 800/272-6359
Fax: 308/527-4364
e-mail:
reindeer@nctc.net
Web:
www.reindeer.nctc.net

Off Season:
Rt. 1, Box 81
Sargent NE 68874
Ph: 800/272-6359
Fax: 308/527-4364

NORTHEASTERN SASKATCHEWAN is a land of lakes, but Reindeer Lake stands out from all the others. A meteorite slammed into the earth here, and its seven-mile-wide, 700-foot-deep crater is now known as Deep Bay. When the high sun of summer warms other lakes this far south to the point that they can't support lake trout, the depths of Deep Bay provide shelter for these cool-water fish. Ron and Cindi Holmes' Reindeer Lake Trout Camp spreads amongst birches and maples on a cusp of shore, a ten-minute boat ride from Deep Bay.

Lakers, northern pike, walleyes and grayling make up the sporting species here. In comparison to other lakes, the trout and northerns are not huge. Lakers run in the five- to 12-pound range, and pike, six to 10. Don't lose heart; these are average sizes, and much bigger fish are taken from these waters every season. What they lack in size, they make up for in numbers. Pike and trout frequent shallow waters as the season opens in June. That's the best time to nail them on a big streamer. Otherwise, you'll fish weedbeds for pike with big spoons and spinners, and go deep with jigs for trout. Both make cameo appearances near the surface in September before sounding for the winter (a great time to fish *and* hunt bear and moose). Grayling from one to three pounds fall to small spinners and dark dry and wet flies.

While walleyes are caught near the main lodge, the better fishing is found at remote outpost camps where you and your party hole-up for a week of self-guided fishing. The Holmes' have cabins at Harriot (trophy lakers in spring and fall), Kyaska (big northerns) and Johnson (northerns) lakes. At each, you'll find a cabin completely stocked with all the cooking and camping gear you'll need, except sleeping bags and towels. You'll have unlimited use of boats and motors. If you know a little about lake fishing, here's a place to solo at a reasonable rate. If you're new to the game, hire a guide for a day, go to school on his advice, and then do it yourself. Baggage, including food, is limited to 60 pounds per person on outpost trips. Travel light and eat well.

The main lodge features contemporary yet rustic log cabins, each with private bath, refrigerators and decks. In the central log lodge, you'll lounge in front of a wood stove and look out over the lake before dinner, your basic rib-sticking home cooking. Ron offers numerous packages, including some with airfare from Denver or Minneapolis.

[C A N A D A   W E S T]

Selwyn Lake Lodge

S e l w y n   L a k e ,   S a s k a t c h e w a n /   N W T

Wrestle a big old lake trout from one of the north country's premier fishing lakes.

VITAL STATISTICS:

KEY SPECIES:
Grayling, lake trout, pike, walleye

Tackle:
Casting, fly-fishing, spinning, trolling
Major Season:
June through September
Accommodations:
FIRST-CLASS MAIN LODGE AND OUTPOST CAMPS
NUMBER OF ROOMS: 6
MAXIMUM NUMBER OF GUESTS: 22
Meals: Eclectic menu of fish, game, fowl
Conference Groups: Yes
Rates: From $2,395 / 3 days
Guides: Included
Gratuities: $25
Preferred Payment:
Cash, check or credit cards
Getting There:
Fly to Saskatoon and hook up with the lodge staff.
Other Activities:
Big game, wingshooting, bird-watching, boating, hiking, snowmobiling, swimming, wildlife photography

Contact:
Gordon Wallace
Selwyn Lake Lodge
1105-620 Spadina Cres. E
Saskatoon SK
57K 3T5, Canada
Ph: 306/664-3373
Fax: 306/664-3445
e-mail:
selwyn@sk.sympatico.ca
Web:
www.selwynlakelodge.com

A SHORT HOP of less than two hours from Saskatoon, Selwyn Lake Lodge puts anglers in the cat-bird seat when it comes to fishing for lake trout, northern pike, grayling and walleye. Rocky points, reefs, drop-offs, shallow weedy bays, unnamed streams tumbling down from feeder lakes, deep holes — all abound on this 45-mile-long, 18-mile-wide, 135,000-acre lake.

Lake trout typically range in the 20-pound class, although occasional 40- and even 50-pounders are caught each year. Early in the season, you can take lake trout on flies when they are feeding on baitfish near the surface. Floating lines and lines with varying sink rates should be in the kits of lake trout-seeking fly-fishers. Dahlberg Divers, long chartreuse snake flies, and three- to four-inch Clouser-style minnow imitations work well. Crankbaits and spoons carry the first part of the season for anglers who favor spinning gear. Later on, casting tackle comes in handy for trolling or jigging.

Shallows teem with northern pike averaging 20 pounds. Spoons, spinners and buzzbaits provoke strikes from these alligators of the north. Fly-fishers will want a bit of fine steel tippet. Use the same patterns that you brought for lake trout; they'll work just fine. Plan, though, to bring a dozen of each major pattern. Those short, swift little rivers (and some not so little) that feed Selwyn Lake carry stocks of grayling of two pounds or so. Voracious feeders, they'll take virtually any small dark pattern. Along with your other gear, pack an ultralight spinning rig with 2- or 4-pound-test line; or take a 4- or 5-weight fly rod. With luck, you may also tie into a whitefish in the four- to five-pound range.

Selwyn Lake Lodge offers anglers two styles of accommodations. The long, low, wood-sided main lodge sits in the trees on a rise over the lake. Here are a pair of comfortable, two-room suites for four anglers apiece. Each suite enjoys a private bath. Meals, family-style American cuisine with European accents and prepared by a Swiss chef, are served in the sunny country dining room. The main lodge also includes a lounge with complimentary beverages and a tackle shop. Experienced anglers might consider the lodge's outpost camp at the other end of the lake. Two cabins sleep eight anglers who serve as their own cooks and guides. Boats and motors are provided. A camp manager is always on hand to offer advice.

Tincup Wilderness Lodge

Whitehorse, Yukon

When you visit Jose and Larry's Lodge, there's always something cooking besides great fishing.

VITAL STATISTICS:

KEY SPECIES:
Grayling, lake trout, pike

Tackle:
Fly-fishing, spinning, trolling
Flyouts to Remote Waters: Yes
Major Season:
June through mid-September
Accommodations:
LOG CABINS
NUMBER OF CABINS: 4
HANDICAPPED ACCESSIBLE: ALL
MAXIMUM NUMBER OF GUESTS: 8
Meals: Continental country cuisine
Conference Groups: Yes
Rates: From $2,200
Guides: Two days included, then $150 / day
Gratuities: $50 / week
Preferred Payment:
Cash, check or credit cards
Getting There:
Fly to Whitehorse and take the floatplane.
Other Activities:
Big game, bird-watching, boating, hiking, swimming, wildlife photography

Contact:
Larry Nagy
Tincup Wilderness Lodge
PO Box 30049
Whitehorse
Y1A 3M2, Canada
Ph: 604/689-4121
e-mail:
tincup@internorth.com
Web:
www.tincup.yk.ca

A CHOCOLATE MAKER by training, and operator of a wonderful catering service in Whitehorse, the capitol of the Yukon, Jose Janssen is a lady of verve and boundless energy. And she's one hell of a cook. Add that to the fishing, and you've got a winning combination in a locale that's well off the beaten tourist track.

The lodge is located in the lee of the St. Elias Mountain Range at the doorstep of Kluane National Park. Tincup Lake's 25 miles of shore hold ample shallow bays, rock bluffs, drop-offs and stony reefs which provide good structure for lake trout and pike. Lake trout are the main event, and fishing for them is stellar as soon as Tincup becomes free of ice in mid-June. Drawn to warmer waters in shallow bays in search of the first active baitfish, five-pounders are plentiful and behemoths of 40-pounds-plus are not all that infrequent. Early in the season, fly anglers with 8- or 9-weight rods casting big saltwater streamer patterns like Tabory's Sea Rats or Snakes ought to find themselves hooked into trophy lakers. So, too, for hurlers of hardware. Spinners and spoons fished with medium to heavy rods through weedy cover in six to 10 feet of water often produce bragging-size fish.

Bring an ultralight rig, too. Small spinners will seduce grayling in Tincup and lakes and rivers in the Kathleen drainage, reachable by the lodge's deHavilland Beaver. Grayling rise to dries, particularly dark patterns of no. 14 or so, and they'll hit dull or dark-colored weighted nymphs as well. A 5-weight system is about right. The Kathleen also holds rainbows up to 20 inches. In addition to one-day flyouts, Tincup offers overnight adventures to outcamps as well. Guests have use of motorboats and the first two days of guiding are included.

Larry Nagy, a retired geologist, and his brother, Ernie, built the current lodge — four cabins and a main lodge all of log and roofed in red — on the site of one already well-known by international anglers. Jose runs the kitchen — scrumptious Hungarian goulash, Cuban paella, Thai fish soup with homebaked bread and smoked lake trout pate — and offers free cooking lessons with each meal. Guests are always welcome in the kitchen to observe and, better yet, wash their hands and pitch in. One-on-one cooking workshops are also available. Inside the stylish cabins you'll find all the modern conveniences: private baths, ample closets, a wood stove to shake the morning chill, and 24-hour electricity.

CANADA EAST

MANITOBA, NEW BRUNSWICK, NEWFOUNDLAND/LABRADOR, NOVA SCOTIA, ONTARIO, QUEBEC

SHALLOW LAKES brim with pike and walleye where waters are warm. Colder lakes hold lake trout and landlocked salmon, and the rivers that feed them teem with brook trout. The prince of North America's game fish — the Atlantic salmon — is staging a marvelous comeback. Fishing the rivers of Canada's maritimes is at once a step back into the days of cane rods and cedar canoes, and a step forward into the bright future of sport fishing unfettered by commercial netting. To the north in the Ungava region of Quebec and the eastern slopes of Labrador's Torngats, terrain is as barren as it gets, but angling for char, brookies and salmon is hard to beat. However, much of this region's better angling is no more than a two-day drive from the cities of the eastern U.S. Lodges range from plain to fancy. But the fish don't seem to know the difference.

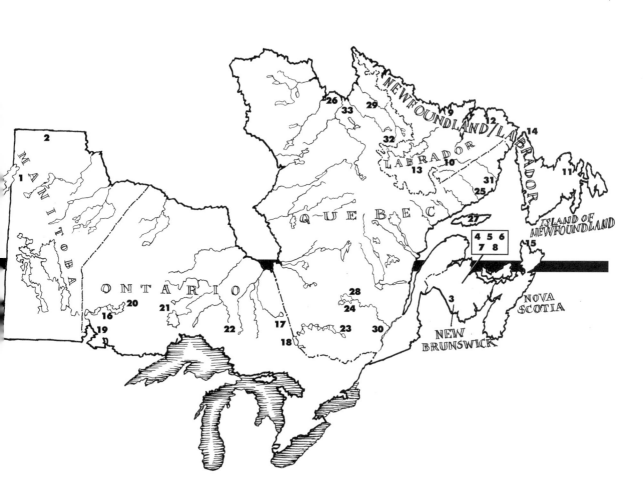

References:

A MASTER'S GUIDE TO
ATLANTIC SALMON FISHING
by Bill Cummings and Lefty Kreh
International Marine/McGraw-Hill
Companies
Customer Service Dept
PO Box 547
Blacklick, OH 43004
800/822-8158

THE ATLANTIC SALMON HANDBOOK:
AN ATLANTIC SALMON
FEDERATION BOOK
by Peter Bodo,
Jonathan Milo (Illustrator)
Linden Publishing (TK)

RIVER JOURNAL: MIRAMICHI RIVER
by Paul Marriner

ONTARIO BLUE-RIBBON
FLY FISHING GUIDE
by Scott Smith
Frank Amato Publications
PO Box 82112
Portland, OR 97282
503/653-8108

BUGGING THE ATLANTIC SALMON
by Michael Brislan
Currents in the Stream
by Wayne Curtis
Home Pool
by Philip Lee

RIVER GUIDES OF THE MIRAMICHI
by Wayne Curtis
Goose Lane Editions
469 King St
Fredericton, NB
Canada E3B 1E5
506/450-4251

Resources:

DEPARTMENT OF NATURAL RESOURCES
Box 22, 200 Saulteaux Crescent
Winnipeg, Manitoba
R3J 3W3, Canada
204/945-6784 or
800/214-6497

TOURISM MANITOBA
21 Forks Market Road
Winnipeg MB
R3C 4T7 Canada
204/945-3777
800/665-0040
web: www.gov.mb.ca/natres

DEPARTMENT OF NATURAL
RESOURCES & ENERGY
FISH & WILDLIFE
Box 6000
Fredericton, New Brunswick
E3B 5HI, Canada
506/453-2440
web: www.gov.nb.ca

INLAND FISH AND WILDLIFE DIVISION
Building 810 - Pleasantville
PO Box 8700
St. John's, Newfoundland
A1B 4J6 Canada
Ph: 709/729-2815

DEPARTMENT OF TOURISM,
CULTURE AND RECREATION
PO Box 8700
St. John's. Newfoundland
A1B 4J6 Canada
709/729-6857
www.gov.nf.ca

DEPARTMENT OF NATURAL RESOURCES
Box 698
Halifax, Nova Scotia
B3J 2T9, Canada
902/424-5935

MINISTRY OF NATURAL RESOURCES
Information Center
900 Bay St.
Toronto, Ontario
M7A 2C1, Canada
416/314-2000
800/667-1940
web: www.mnr.gov.on.ca

FISH & WILDLIFE DIV., DEPT. OF
TECHNOLOGY AND ENVIRONMENT
Box 2000
Charlottetown, PE
C1A 7N8 Canada
902/368-4683
web: www.gov.pe.ca

MINISTERE DE L'ENVIRONMENT
DEPT. OF RECREATION,
FISH AND GAME
Box 88, 675 Boule. Rene-Levesque Est.
Quebec, QC
G1R 4Y1 Canada
800/561-1616
web: www.mef.gouv.qc.ca

TOURISME QUEBEC
1010 Sainte-Catherine Ouest
Room 400
Montreal, QC
H3B 1G2 Canada
800/363-7777
web: www.tourisme.gouv.qc.ca

*Hang your waders on the porch of one of Keith Pond's
antique cabins on the Southwest Miramichi and
travel back to the early days of
angling for the king of game fish, Atlantic salmon.*

Gangler's Lodges

N o r t h   S e a l   R i v e r ,   M a n i t o b a

New wilderness lodges of the finest quality put anglers in bed with trophy pike and lake trout.

VITAL STATISTICS:

KEY SPECIES:
Grayling, lake trout, pike, walleye

Tackle:
Casting, fly-fishing, spinning, trolling
Flyouts to Remote Waters: Yes
Major Season:
June through September
Accommodations:
MODERN CABINS
MAXIMUM NUMBER OF GUESTS:
NORTH SEAL RIVER LODGE: 18
MARIA, BURNIE and
STEVEN'S/NICKLIN: 8 EACH
Meals:
NORTH SEAL RIVER LODGE AND
MARIA: Hearty family-style
BURNIE and STEVEN'S/NICKLIN:
You're the cook
Conference Groups: Yes
Rates:
NORTH SEAL RIVER LODGE:
$2,995 / week
MARIA: $2,295/ week
BURNIE: $2,195 / week
STEVEN'S/NICKLIN: $1,995 / week
Guides: Depends on package
Gratuities: $300 / week
Preferred Payment:
Cash, check or credit cards
Getting There:
Fly to Winnipeg and catch the charter.
Other Activities:
Big game

Contact:
Wayne Gangler
Gangler's Lodges
1568 E. Wedgewood Lane
Hernando FL 34442
Ph: 352/637-2244
Fax: 352/637-2240
Web:
www.ganglers.com

WAYNE GANGLER'S MOVED his base of operations to the North Seal River drainage in northcentral Manitoba. He's always had a foot in that door with his camps on Steven's and Nicklin lakes, and another on nearby Maria. In 1997, he added cabins at Burnie Lake, and the following year, constructed the headquarters lodge on the North Seal River. At each lodge, the fishing and accommodations are slightly different. Airfare from Winnipeg is included.

NORTH SEAL RIVER LODGE: Located on Egenolf Lake, this brand new lodge hosts a maximum of 18 guests in cabins. Trophy pike and lake trout are the name of the game here, though there are plenty of walleye and grayling in the rapids between lakes. Two anglers fish from 18-foot boats captained by a guide. Flyouts to Blackfish, Chatwin, Clifton, Minuhik and No Name Lake are available at additional cost, and new lakes are being added all the time. One flyout is included in the standard package, which includes everything except incidentals and a tip for the guide.

MARIA LAKE: You can still have fine fishing, but save yourself $100 a day at this lodge, on a lake that sandwiches excellent trout holes and grass flats for pike between in- and out-flows where grayling can't be beat. Cabins for two are first class with private baths, with a maximum of eight guests in camp. Meals are provided by a camp manager who also suggests hot spots for your fishing. You, however, captain your own boat. Dinner will wait your return. Guides can be arranged on special request.

STEVEN'S/NICKLIN LAKE: These are the eastern pair of a trio of lakes that includes Dean on the west. Most anglers head for trout holes and jig for big lakers. Two, two-bedroom cabins sleep four. The camp manager will keep your boat in shape, but you'll do your own cooking (the kitchen is fully stocked) and guiding.

BURNIE LAKE: Just east of the North Seal is a spring-fed lake where northern pike really earn the title "Great." Weed beds are abundant, as are sheltered bays. You'll be your own guide and cook (food is provided) but here, cabins are one big room that sleep four and include kitchen facilities. A central bath is a short walk through the woods.

When packing for any of these trips, watch your baggage weight. Fifty-pounds per person is the max. Trips run from Saturday to Saturday, beginning and ending in Winnipeg.

Nueltin Fly-In Lodges

A l o n s a ,   M a n i t o b a

Four main lodges and a dozen outpost camps give anglers the chance to fish waters that see very little pressure.

VITAL STATISTICS:

KEY SPECIES:
Grayling, lake trout, pike

Tackle:
Casting, fly-fishing, spinning, trolling
Flyouts to Remote Waters: Yes
Major Season:
June through August
Accommodations:
TREELINE: INDIVIDUAL CABINS FOR 2
NUELTIN NARROWS: CABINS FOR UP TO 3
WINDY RIVER: FOUR SLEEPING AREAS
KASMERE: 5 HOTEL ROOMS
HANDICAPPED ACCESSIBLE: Some
MAXIMUM NUMBER OF GUESTS: 24
TREELINE: 24
NUELTIN NARROWS: 10
WINDY RIVER: 10
KASMERE: 10
Meals: Top quality camp cuisine
(even if you cook it)
Conference Groups: Yes
Rates:
TREELINE: $3,095 / week
NUELTIN NARROWS: $2,295 / week
WINDY RIVER: $2,295 / week
KASMERE LAKE: $2,295 / week
Guides: Included
Gratuities: $100 - $150;
Angler's discretion
Preferred Payment:
Cash or check
Getting There:
Fly to Winnipeg and ride the charter
aircraft.
Other Activities:
Wildlife photography

Contact:
Shawn Gurke
Nueltin Fly-In Lodges
Box 500
Alonsa MB
RON OAO, Canada
Ph: 800/361-7177
Fax: 204/767-2331
e-mail:
nueltin@mts.net
Web:
www.nueltin.com

SPLIT BY THE PROVINCES of Manitoba and Nunavut, Nueltin Lake is the focal point of a growing network of first-class lodges and comfortable outpost camps on water known for pike, lake trout and grayling. Started by Garry Gurke more than 20 years ago, Nueltin Lodges have earned a reputation for putting anglers on big fish. Why? Garry was one of the first to recognize a simple fact: it takes a long time to grow lunkers up where trees are thin and winters long. He advocated a strict catch-and-release policy and it's paid dividends. Lake trout of more than 50 pounds, northern pike of 30-pounds-plus, and grayling in excess of four pounds are brought to net with uncommon frequency. At all of the lodges, seven-day packages are the norm, but some four-day packages may be available.

TREELINE: Garry's favorite. Staff delivers a pot of hot coffee to guests in 12 cabins scattered on a low ridge with a stunning view of the lake. Nearby, the Thleiwaza River cascades into the lake; it's great for grayling and lake trout. Pike roam the bays. You'll be pampered with excellent meals and guides who really know their stuff.

KASMERE LAKE: A corporate retreat for groups of up to 10. Rooms have all the amenities of first-class hotel rooms. Add near-gourmet cuisine, complimentary bar, phone/fax/copier/overhead projector, and a dining room that becomes a comfortable venue for hashing out corporate strategy, and you have to work hard to remember to fish. But, hey, you owe it to the lakers and pike to go give them a tumble.

NUELTIN NARROWS: Here you can do it yourself or not. It's up to you. Ten guests share three cabins. A new kitchen and dining facility is fully stocked with groceries and gear. If nobody in your group wears a toque with ease, the wife of the camp manager will make sure you don't leave camp without a good meal under your belt. Two guests share each 16-foot Lund and they follow their noses to fine pike and lake trout.

WINDY RIVER: Fish the northern reaches of the lake from four snug cabins hosting up to 10 anglers. The drill here is the same as at Nueltin Narrows, but here, you're almost in the barren lands and the scenery, as well as the fishing, is astounding.

Along with the four lodges, Garry has built a dozen new outpost cabins that each hold up to four anglers and two guides. You'll fly in one morning, fish for two days, dine on chow prepared by the guides (hey, they can really cook), and fly out late the next afternoon.

Rivers of New Brunswick are flush
with new runs of Atlantic salmon.

Chickadee Lodge

Prince William, New Brunswick

The fish that makes drags scream here in the St. John is none other than our old friend the smallmouth.

VITAL STATISTICS:

KEY SPECIES:
Smallmouth

Tackle:
Casting, fly-fishing, spinning
Major Season:
May through October
Accommodations:
WOODEN CABINS
NUMBER OF ROOMS: 5
MAXIMUM NUMBER OF GUESTS: 11
Meals: Hearty family fare
Conference Groups: No
Rates: From $80 / night
Guides: $325 / 2
Gratuities: 10% - 15%
Preferred Payment:
Cash, check or credit cards
Getting There:
Fly to Fredericton and the lodge van will pick you up.
Other Activities:
Big game, wingshooting, boating, canoeing/kayaking/rafting, golf, swimming

Contact:
Vaughan Schriver
Chickadee Lodge
20 Lodge Lane
Prince William NB
E6K 3S9, Canada
Ph: 506/363-2759
Fax: 506/363-2929

RISING WAY TO HELLANDGONE in the forests near Quebec's eastern border with Maine, the St. John flows north until it picks up the waters of the Allagash. Then it begins bending further to the northeast until it reaches Edmondston, New Brunswick. There, it begins to curve to the south. Not far upstream from Fredericton, the river is impounded, becoming the long, narrow Lake Mactaquac, home waters for Chickadee Lodge.

This is smallmouth country in a big way. From May through October, average fish run about three pounds, although four- and five-pounders are netted and released with regularity. Four-pound-test line is enough. The rod should be supple enough to flip-cast light lures into pockets under brush. Fly-fishermen should arm themselves with 5- or 6-weight rigs. The trick, of course, is to challenge the fish with light lines or tippets, but to avoid working them to fatal exhaustion.

Mactaquac fishes well from the middle of May through the June spawn. Then, the water warms and fish go deeper. As fishing in the river loses momentum, action picks up in four lakes worked by Chickadee guests. Lake George is the shallowest of the quartet. It teems with two- to three-pounders, and it's really good throughout the season. Lakes Harvey and Magaguadavic are larger, and they consistently yield fish more than four pounds. Topwater fishing is hot early in the season, then crankbaits and spinnerbaits take over. Little Magaguadavic rounds out the quartet. Vaughan Schriver, who owns Chickadee Lodge, will recommend guides with fully-rigged bassboats for day trips to these lakes, as well as excursions on the St. John. You don't have to have a guide unless you want one.

Chickadee also offers guided float trips on 12 miles of the Meduxnekeag River, which crosses from Maine into New Brunswick south of Bloomfield, and joins the St. John at Woodstock. Ideal for fly-fishing, the river's record is a five-pound 12-ounce bronzeback taken on a streamer. Gentle riffles and clear pools make this an idyllic trip, and as a bonus you may pick up a brown trout or two. Many area rivers also have Atlantic salmon runs, fished with flies only. If you're interested in salmon, get Vaughan to recommend a good guide.

When you see the price, you won't believe it. Chickadee offers lakefront room and board for less than $400 per week. Rooms share baths, and meals are substantial.

Miramichi Inn

R e d   B a n k ,   N e w   B r u n s w i c k

Where salmon roll and grouse flush in the magic of the Little Southwest Miramichi.

VITAL STATISTICS:

KEY SPECIES:
Atlantic salmon

Tackle:
Fly-fishing
Major Season:
April through mid-October
Accommodations:
Log lodge and cabin
Number of Rooms: 9
Handicapped Accessible: 1
Maximum Number of Guests: 14
Meals: Fine regional cuisine
Conference Groups: Yes
Rates: From $295 / day / 2
Guides: Included
Gratuities: 10%
Preferred Payment:
Cash, check or credit cards
Getting There:
Fly to Chatham and ride the lodge van.
Other Activities:
Big game, waterfowling, wingshooting, bird-watching, hiking, wildlife photography

Contact:
André Godin
Miramichi Inn
PO Box 331
Red Bank NB
E9E 2P3, Canada
Ph: 506/836-7452
Fax: 506/836-7805
Web:
www.angelfire.com/biz/miramichiinn

SLOW, IS A WORD USED CHARITABLY to describe late season fishing when the water is low and the sun's been on it for a while. But all is never lost. From high gravel banks in the land of glacial outwash and stubby forest, you can look down into the river and see the fish, olive torpedoes against a khaki riverbed. It is not deep. Angular boulders are scattered on its bottom. In other places, the bed is cobble, and still others, ledges of rock shoot the river down into pools below. It is all first-class salmon water.

In the spring, April and May, kelts ride the river down to the ocean. You can hook into a dozen of these hardy salmon that wintered over in the spawning runs. The summer run of bright salmon shows up first in June, and they keep coming into August. Then, late in the month, the river drops, and runs become more sensitive to rainy spates which draw fresh corps of salmon upriver. The salmon of fall are larger than their summer siblings, but they are tougher to catch. Small flies of single hook, #6s, are the ticket. So, too, are lighter leaders of six-pound-test. You fish light because you have to. When the fishing is slow on bright summer days, climb a bank and spot for your buddy who's standing and casting in the stream. Guide his presentation past the dark shapes lying in the water. If you and he are lucky, you'll dredge your fly past the snout of a bruiser and he'll lunge for it in anger. And then, if you are really, really lucky, the salmon won't toss the hook, snap the leader on a rock, or engage in any number of shenanigans that spell "lost fish."

Built of rustic pine logs, the Miramichi Inn and its adjacent cabin are tucked in the trees on a bench above the Little Southwest Miramichi. Don't confuse this with the Southwest Miramichi River, a river three times the size that points southwest from its mouth in the city of Miramichi. The Little Southwest is smaller water and, to some, more manageable. Meals at the lodge are delectable. And a cadre of loveable Irish setters wander about like well-behaved children

Come the chill of the fall, the setters get anxious. Eau du woodcock and grouse waft on the gentle breeze. The Irish know this, and they know that wise guests have brought along a delightful 20 or 28. Fish salmon when the run is fresh in the pools in the morning. Tote the double behind a setter for birds as the sun slides down into the forest. Afterwards, stoke up on smoked salmon, ceasar salad, strip steak and keylime pie. Then melt toward your room and dream of casts and coverts.

Pond's . . . on the Miramichi

L u d l o w ,   N e w   B r u n s w i c k

From the porch of your brown wood cabin, you can hear splashes of salmon leaping in the river below.

VITAL STATISTICS:

KEY SPECIES:
Atlantic salmom, brookies

Tackle:
Fly-fishing
Major Season:
April through mid-October
Accommodations:
LUXURIOUS MOTEL-STYLE ROOMS OR OLD-TIME CABINS
NUMBER OF ROOMS: 24
HANDICAPPED ACCESSIBLE: 2
MAXIMUM NUMBER OF GUESTS: 60
Meals: Fine regional cuisine
Conference Groups: Yes
Rates: From $420 / day
Guides: Included
Gratuities: $25 (Cdn)
Preferred Payment:
Cash, check or credit cards
Getting There:
Fly to Fredericton and rent a car.
Other Activities:
Wingshooting, bird-watching, canoeing/kayaking/rafting, golf, hiking, snowmobiling, tennis, wildlife photography, leadership courses

Contact:
Keith Pond
Pond's . . . on the Miramichi
91 Porter Cove Road
PO Box 73
Ludlow NB
E9C 2J3, Canada
Ph: 506/369-2612
Fax: 506/369-2293
e-mail:
flyfisher@net.nb.ca
Web:
www.pondsresort.com

Agents:
Orvis endorsed

THE DAY WAS AS GLORIOUS as only a September day on the Miramichi can be. The morning began at the pool in front of the lodge. You and your guide walked across the bridge at Ludlow, and skirted down through the popple, just tinged with gold. Rigging your rod with a bomber, you were convinced to take one on top. Why not? You'd seen them rolling from the front porch of your cabin overlooking the pool. Nobody was on the water yet. A weak front had brought a little rain yesterday, and the charge of fresh water moved salmon up the river. You were there, on this pool that had yielded so many fish to so many other anglers, and you were the first of the day. It was the best shot.

You knew the drill. Cast quarter down from dead across, slow the fly above, and then skate-dance it over likely lies. The 8-weight you held might be a bit light if you nailed one of the bigger fish in the run. But what the heck? You could work this rod all day and never feel tired. That was important. Because if the pool failed to prove out, you'd work on down the river, casting until nightfall if need be. Your first cast crossed the river, landing by the cobbles on the other side of the chute that fed the pool. No takers. A step downstream and you cast again. There was no hurrying this, not for you, not this morning.

They call Atlantic salmon the fish of 1000 casts a sobriquet also applied to steelhead. And fishing for them is a discipline. Each cast, you must believe, will produce a strike. If you don't believe, it will never happen. An hour after your first cast, a mighty swirl engulfed your fly. You're belly tightened and your arms tensed, but there, the fly bobbed free, swinging down with the current. More rolls, different bomber patterns. They were striking short.

The day found you working others among the dozens of Pond's private runs. A grilse took a little after 9:00, and another gave you a good run and then came to bay, just before you broke for lunch. You fished through the afternoon, and in the lethargy that comes when the sun slides by 3:00 p.m., a strike from a huge salmon so startled you that you jerked the fly from its mouth. "Damn" was not the word you used. Dusk found you back on the home pool. Other anglers were back at the lodge dining in the restaurant. You methodically worked the pool, still with the bomber. It was a dry or nothing. And then, near the spot where the fish had rolled on your fly in the morning, came a take. It was not showy, more of a sip. But you knew what it was, and you eased the steel into his jaw, and he took off hell bent for election down past the abutments to the bridge. A crescent moon had risen above the maples by the time your guide tailed the fish — a dandy of 15 pounds or so.

The restaurant and bar were long closed by the time you returned to your cabin. But there you found a bottle of scotch (for that's what they know you prefer), a plate of hors d'oeuvres — fiddleheads and smoked salmon on cocktail rye, spread with cream cheese — in your refrigerator, along with a thermos of hot chowder, a crisp green salad, and rolls wrapped so they'd stay warm. On the morrow, you'd float the river and then try its upstream runs for brookies. That's what you thought as you lit the chunk stove, poured a drink, and waded into the smoked salmon.

[C A N A D A   E A S T]

Upper Oxbow Outdoor Adventures

T r o u t   B r o o k ,   N e w   B r u n s w i c k

For kelts or bright Atlantic salmon, this small lodge offers big service at a fair price.

VITAL STATISTICS:

KEY SPECIES:
Atlantic salmon

Tackle:
Fly-fishing
Major Season:
April through mid-October
Accommodations:
THREE LOG CABINS
NUMBER OF ROOMS: 9
MAXIMUM NUMBER OF GUESTS: 14
Meals: Family-style or self-catered
Conference Groups: Yes
Rates: From $400 / 3 nights, 2 days
Guides: Included
Gratuities: $20
Preferred Payment:
Cash, check or credit cards
Getting There:
Fly to Fredricton and rent a car.
Other Activities:
Waterfowling, wingshooting, bird-watching, boating, canoeing/kayaking/rafting, golf, horseback riding, hiking, swimming, wildlife photography

Contact:
Debbie Norton
Upper Oxbow Outdoor
Adventures
11042 Rt. 430
Trout Brook NB
E9E 1R4, Canada
Ph: 506-622-8834
Fax: 506-622-2027
e-mail:
nortodea@nb.sympatico.ca

A SHORTER SIBLING of the better known and longer Southwest Miramichi, the Little Southwest is a fine stream in its own right. Rising on the flanks of Mount McNair and North Pole Mountain, it flows southeast for about 40 miles before hooking sharply to the northeast to join the larger Southwest Miramichi at Derby Junction. The river continues for a bit, becoming tidal below Red Bank.

About a mile above the tidal section, Upper Oxbow maintains three cabins of log on 40 acres overlooking the river. All contain kitchens. The two larger cabins sleep five and three respectively, and the smallest contains two single beds. You can fish the river in front of the lodge. Its mileage just above the tidal waters puts anglers in good position to intercept the first runs of fresh Atlantic salmon in June and July. Salmon are more plentiful then and your chances of a hookup are better. But if it's larger fish you want, hold out until September. Water levels will be lower, and the angling more difficult, but when that 20-pounder trashes your Black Bear-green butt, you'll be glad you waited. Fishing for summer salmon is generally an affair of wading and endless casting, all for that heart-stopping moment.

The Little Southwest is also known for heavy runs of kelt. These are salmon that traveled upstream to spawn the previous fall, weathered over, and are now heading back down to sea. Atlantic salmon don't feed on their way upstream. But on the way down, it's a different story. Traditionally, the season opens on April 15 and continues through May 15. While the average hookup during spring and fall runs of "bright" salmon is one per day or less, anglers in the spring consistently connect with eight or 10 black salmon each day when the water is not discolored. Kelts range upwards of 30 inches, though most run about 20. The Little Southwest Miramichi is flies-only water. Fishing is generally by boat or canoe, and a guide must accompany nonresident anglers. Sinking or sink-tip lines are used.

Tackle required for bright or kelt salmon is the same: a no. 8 or 9 rod with a reel that has a smooth drag, except that floating lines and smaller flies are the order of the day. Upper Oxbow offers a number of fishing programs — spring trips include a boat and motor; you can cook or eat in the main lodge. The price of kelt trips runs about $350 more a week than trips for bright salmon in summer and fall.

Wade's Fishing Lodge

C a i n s   R i v e r ,   N e w   B r u n s w i c k

Fish from a lodge at the junction of two of the province's finest salmon rivers.

VITAL STATISTICS:

KEY SPECIES:
Atlantic salmon, brookies

Tackle:
Fly-fishing
Major Season:
Mid-April through mid-October
Accommodations:
RUSTIC, YET MODERN LOG CABINS
NUMBER OF ROOMS: 20
HANDICAPPED ACCESSIBLE: SOME
MAXIMUM NUMBER OF GUESTS: 24
Meals: Hearty regional cuisine
Conference Groups: Yes
Rates: From $270 / day / 3
Guides: Included
Gratuities: $15
Preferred Payment:
Cash or check
Getting There:
Fly to Fredericton, Moncton and rent a car.
Other Activities:
Waterfowling, wingshooting, bird-watching, boating, canoeing/kayaking/rafting, golf, hiking, swimming, wildlife photography

Contact:
Willy Bacso
Wade's Fishing Lodge
890 S. Cains Rd
Cains River NB
E9B 1M3, Canada
Ph: 506/843-6416
Fax: 506/843-2334
E-MAIL:
wades@nb.symparico.co

Off Season:
48 Amman Rd
Moncton NB
E1G 2K4 Canada
Ph: 506/384-2229
Fax: 506/858-1996

THE CAINS RIVER gathers its waters from the hilly uplands to the south and east of the fabled Miramichi. The two meet about halfway between Blackville and Upper Blackville, and it is there that Wade's Fishing Lodge is located. At the lodge, the Miramichi is relatively large. Pools are long, open and easily accessed from submerged gravel bars. Wading is not difficult. The Cain is a smaller, tighter stream, but the water is much the same.

No need for long casts on either of these streams; the trick is working each fly thoroughly through each possible lie. At times, it seems that it is more the speed at which a fly passes a salmon, rather than its color, that provokes a strike. Some anglers like to drift their flies toward the lie, slow them as much they can, then zip them past the nose of the fish as if it were a minnow darting for safety. These salmon aren't on the feed, but maybe the memory of a fleeting bait fish will provoke a strike. It's as good a theory as anyone has yet to offer. Take an 8- or 9-weight rod, and load your reel with 150 yards of backing. If you don't have enough flies, don't worry. You can buy all you need at Wade's or W.W. Doak's, an excellent fly-fishing shop in nearby Doaktown.

While the Atlantic salmon season opens on April 15, fish in both rivers then are primarily kelts returning to the sea. You'll get lots of hookups. The water is higher and, usually, you'll be fishing from a boat. In mid-June, the first of the year's bright fish reach these waters and that's when the real fun begins. These are days of piercing blue skies, when the sun on the back of your flannel shirt feels good. Salmon in the first runs are the most aggressive of the year and fight gallantly. Some anglers prefer fall, and feel that's the best time of year to fish the Miramichi. Fish running into the system have fed most of the summer in tidal waters and they've put on weight. Along the banks, the woods have turned gold and scarlet. September and early October are the prime weeks. The fishing can be tough — low water and smaller flies and leaders — but it can be the best you'll ever have.

Wade's main lodge hosts up to 20 guests in five rustic wood cabins set under the trees on a high bank overlooking the river. A mile upstream, Wade's maintains Cains River Camp, a rustic log cabin with a fireplace and screened porch. Cains can accommodate six. Two more outpost camps are downriver. In addition, Wade's runs overnight canoe trips, where everything except a sleeping bag is provided.

[C A N A D A   E A S T]

Wilson's Sporting Camps

M c N a m e e ,   N e w   B r u n s w i c k

How'd you like to catch 10 or 12 Atlantic salmon per day? You can, in the spring, on the Miramichi.

VITAL STATISTICS:

KEY SPECIES:
Atlantic salmon, sea-run brookies

Tackle:
Fly-fishing
Major Season:
April through mid-October
Accommodations:
PRIVATE CABINS
NUMBER OF ROOMS: 11
MAXIMUM NUMBER OF GUESTS: 22
Meals: Substantial, yet healthy, family-style
Conference Groups: Yes
Rates: From $350 / day / 2
Guides: Inlcuded
Gratuities: $30
Preferred Payment:
Cash, check or credit cards
Getting There:
Fly to Fredericton and rent a car.
Other Activities:
Wingshooting, boating, canoeing/kayaking/rafting, golf, hiking, snowmobiling, wildlife photography

Contact:
Keith Wilson
Wilson's Sporting Camps
303 McNamee Rd
McNamee NB
E9C 2G9, Canada
Ph: 506/365-7962
Fax: 506/365-7106
e-mail:
wilsons@nbnet.nb.ca
Web:
www.wilsonscamps.nb.ca

THERE'S A DEBATE THAT RAGES over this, one of New Brunswick's famed Atlantic salmon rivers. Is it really wise to fish for kelts, the so called "black" salmon that winter over in the Miramichi's headwaters? One school argues that such salmon are in poor shape and should not be further stressed by sportfishing as they make their way downriver to the ocean. Others, and many biologists fall into this camp, maintain that these fish are feeding aggressively as they head to the sea. This group believes that spring salmon are in better shape than spawners that enter the system in periods of low and relatively warm water, swim upstream heavily laden with eggs or milt, do not eat, and are caught and played by anglers along the way. As in most such discussions, there's no clear answer.

Except that biologists with the Province of New Brunswick tend to support the notion of a sport fishery from mid-April to mid-May. Fishing is different then. You'll cast flies from boats rather than wade. On an average day, you'll hook a dozen salmon which will average about eight pounds with a length of 30 inches or so. If you want to experience a lot of salmon, here's the place to do it. As the year evolves, sea-run brook trout enter the system and provide glowing sport in late May and June. The nearby Cains River is particularly good then. Summer salmon begin their spawning runs in late June and early July, and the action continues until the middle of October.

A fine old camp with 75 years of history on the Southwest Miramichi, Wilson's owns 16 pools scattered along five miles of the river. Each day, anglers and their guides take to wood and canvas canoes. No outboards here, except in the spring season (mid-April to mid-May) for kelts that are returning to the sea. During the summer and fall runs, guides pole or paddle your canoe to good water, and you'll fish from the canoe or wade the cobbled river bottom, casting to salmon lying in pools, pockets or runs.

Keith Wilson, fourth-generation owner, is revamping the camp. He's decided to take fewer guests, just six rods per week. That means that every day, each angler has almost three private runs to fish. There's nothing pretentious about Wilson's accommodations, but you'll have everything you need. Eight guest cabins are scattered under the trees across the road from the white farmhouse where you'll eat family-style. The cabins have private baths and hooks for waders and rods on their front porches. The farmhouse also has four guest rooms.

Big River Camps

Pasadena, Newfoundland

A pair of lodges up a wonderful Labrador river offer stellar angling for salmon, char, and sea-run trout.

VITAL STATISTICS:

KEY SPECIES:
Arctic char, Atlantic salmon, sea-run brookies

Tackle:
Fly-fishing

Major Season:
July into September

Accommodations:
RUSTIC LODGES OF NATIVE TIMBER
NUMBER OF ROOMS / GUESTS:
BIG RIVER: 8 / 16
GREAT WHITE WAY: 6 / 12
HANDICAPPED ACCESSIBLE: Some

Meals: Well-prepared regional fare

Conference Groups: Yes

Rates: From $3,000 / week

Guides: Available

Gratuities: $100 / week

Preferred Payment:
Cash, check or credit cards

Getting There:
Fly to Goose Bay and catch the free shuttle to the lodge.

Other Activities:
Big game

Contact:
Bob Skinner
Big River Camps
PO Box 250
Pasadena NF
A0L 1K0, Canada
Ph: 709/686-2242
Fax: 709/686-5244
e-mail:
bigriver@nf.sympatico.ca
Web:
www3.nf.sympatico.ca/bigriver

LABRADOR MIGHT AS WELL BE two distinct countries. The southwesternmost lands are high, boggy and filled with scored of lakes. That's brook trout country par excellence, and also fine for lake trout, landlocked salmon and pike. But the northeastern coast of Labrador is very different. It's as bony as the back of your hand. Rivers tumble and crash down from the spine that divides Labrador from Quebec; lakes are long and sinuous. Trees, mostly spruce with some fir mixed in, are huge. Big River is not long or particularly big. But it sees regular runs of Atlantic salmon, sea-run brook trout, and arctic char.

In 1965, Bob Skinner was looking for a place to set up shop. He wanted a river with a sustainable population of trophy fish. Eventually, his travels took him to the mouth of Big River, and there, he found what he sought: a river flowing fast and free. Of native timber, sawed on the spot, Bob constructed a pair of lodges.

BIG RIVER LODGE: This lodge is located high on a bench on the north side of the river at the foot of the first set of rapids that impede the journey of upstream migrating fish. Fish rapids, runs and eddies among the islands in front of the lodge, or boat downstream to Rattling Brook where sea-run brookies and Atlantic salmon pile up. Eight rooms, for a maximum of 16 guests, share five baths.

GREAT WHITE WAY: This is a heck of a hike from Broadway, but at times the river is as crowded with migrating salmon as Manhattan's theatre district is crammed with show-goers. Named for a three-mile run of nearly impassable rapids flowing out of White Bear Lake, this is the newer of the two lodges, constructed in the late 1980s. Most anglers wade when they fish. Your chances are excellent for catching brook trout. Six rooms share two baths.

At both lodges, Atlantic salmon run up to 22 pounds, sea-run trout top six, and arctic char can reach seven. Char are fished here only in the last two weeks of August. If you want to fish for all three species, book your trip in the middle weeks of August. Guests headed this way fly into Goose Bay where they'll more than likely overnight before riding a floatplane to the lodges the next morning. Meals are very good, with dinners of steak, chops and chicken. But beware! At the end of the week, the camp cook goes on strike and its up to guests to prepare dinner. Slip some extra herbs and spices in your luggage and maybe a bottle or two of something red or white.

Cooper's Minipi Camps

H a p p y   V a l l e y ,   L a b r a d o r

At Cooper's, brook trout grow as big as southern largemouths.

VITAL STATISTICS:

KEY SPECIES:
Brookies, pike

Tackle:
Fly-fishing, spinning
Major Season:
June through September
Accommodations:
RUSTIC WOODEN LODGES
NUMBER OF ROOMS: 18
HANDICAPPED ACCESSIBLE: 10
MAXIMUM NUMBER OF GUESTS: 36
Meals: Prime rib, steak, turkey
Conference Groups: Yes
Rates: $3,295 / week, double
occupancy
Guides: Included
Gratuities: Angler's discretion
Preferred Payment:
Cash, check or credit cards
Getting There:
Fly to Goose Bay and take the
air shuttle.
Other Activities:
Bird-watching, wildlife photography

Contact:
Jack E. Cooper
Cooper's Minipi Camps
PO Box 340
Station B
Happy Valley NF
AOP 1E0, Canada
Ph: 709/896-2891
Fax: 709/896-9619
e-mail:
info@minipicamps.com
Web:
www.minipicamps.com

Agents:
Angler Adventures: 860/434-9624

BROOK TROUT ARE A CHAR, a member of the same family as the bull trout of the West and Dolly Varden of Alaska. The farther south in the lower 48 you go, the smaller and more dainty they become. In Maine, a full grown brookie may edge four pounds, with a back blued as dark as a Colt revolver and a belly flaming orange like a rising harvest moon. Down in the southern Appalachians, you'll find native at elevations of 3,000 feet or more. Here, a fine brookie will be no longer than the foot of the angler whose dry fly it inhales.

But in Labrador, the rules are different. Leviathans of eight pounds and more — the size of respectable Alaskan rainbows — prowl waters so deep brown and rich that they take on the look of cowboy coffee. On your first day of fishing these streams, you'll delight in the numbers of three- and four-pounders that slash your streamers and slam drys. We're not talking little flies here, but big ties — mice and muddler minnows and anything else that makes a commotion on the water. On your second and third day in camp, you begin to hunt for behemoths of five pounds or more. And each one you return (as return them you must) whets your appetite for the next. You'll find out just what your six-weight rod can do on these waters. To use less overtires the fish, and threatens their chances of fighting again.

Three-and-a-half decades ago, Lee Wulff learned the secret of these brookies and the fishery that spawns them. It's still true today. Pure water, abundant aquatic insects and crustaceans, and restricted access combine to ensure that the fishery does not decline. Fishing in the Minipi watershed's two lakes, their feeder streams and the Minipi River, is restricted to guests of Cooper's Minipi Camps. The season is open from June through September, and the best brook trout fishing runs through mid-August. Pike are also prevalent; spoons, spinners and dry flies will suffice.

Jack Cooper operates a trio of lodges up here, hence the plural on camps. The largest of the three, Minipi Lodge, has 10 bedrooms and four baths. Its two-story glass prow opens the lodge to the lake and lights the anglers' library in the second-floor loft. Anne Marie Lodge is log and rustic and sleeps half a dozen who share a bath. Ranch-style Minonipi Lodge is a little bigger. Meals are first class. But, afterwards, before you go to sleep, there's something you must do: Fish the twilight caddis hatch and when that is done, should you be angling in September, spend a moment and let your mind wander with the wavering northern lights.

Gander River Outfitters

St. John's, Newfoundland

Take a gander at the number of salmon in this river!

VITAL STATISTICS:

KEY SPECIES:
Atlantic salmon, brookies, sea-run brookies

Tackle:
Fly-fishing, spinning

Major Season:
June through mid-October

Accommodations:
RUSTIC CABINS
NUMBER OF ROOMS: 4
MAXIMUM NUMBER OF GUESTS: 10

Meals: Excellent cuisine of fish and beef

Conference Groups: Yes

Rates: From $285 / day

Guides: Included

Gratuities: Angler's discretion

Preferred Payment:
Cash, check or credit cards

Getting There:
Fly to Gander and you'll be met.

Other Activities:
Big game, wingshooting, bird-watching, boating, canoeing/kayaking/rafting, wildlife photography

Contact:
Terry Cusack
Gander River Outfitters
PO Box 21017
St. John's NF
A1A 5B2, Canada
Ph: 888/725-6663 or
709/753-9163
Fax: 709/753-9169
e-mail:
GanderRiver@GrandRiver.com
Web:
www.GanderRiver.com

EVERY MORNING, salmon stream by your door, running up the 37-mile-long Gander River from the bay by the same name on the northeastern coast of Newfoundland. At the head of the river is a large lake, and above that, a fine network of feeder rivers. The absence of netting near the mouth of the river has resulted in a phenomenal increase in the number of salmon. Slightly more than 7,000 made the run in 1991. Today, estimates range upwards of 30,000, a four-fold increase. More than a fifth of those are adults, says lodge owner Terry Cusack. Odds are each angler will tie into more than one fish per day on the Gander.

Outboard-powered 25-foot freighter canoes, run by the guides, carry anglers to pools where the salmon are. Runs begin in late June, and the best angling falls between mid-July and mid-August. As is the case with some of the other rivers in the Maritimes, bigger but fewer salmon use the river in fall. Fishing then may offer the best chance for joining Gander's 20 Pound Plus Club. And while the focus is primarily on salmon — you can often count upwards of 100 jumping in front of the lodge — don't overlook brook trout in the two- to three-pound range and their sea-run cousins of slightly bigger size.

Fly rods and reels are the tackle of choice at Gander River. Use Terry's gear or bring your own. Plan on taking 6- and 8-weight rods. If you're buying a new salmon rod, consider a 10-foot for an 8, an ideal combination for big open salmon water. Load both reels with at least 100 yards of backing. Why a #6 as a second rod? It may be a little heavy for the big brookies, but once in a while anglers drifting big mouse patterns for brook trout have been surprised by a take from a salmon. Gander River Outfitters supplies licenses, raingear and flotation jackets. If you forget anything, you can borrow or buy what you need at the lodge.

The log lodge is unpretentious but comfortable. It includes two guest rooms, one with a private bath. Guests also stay in two nearby cabins. Meals are straightforward, home-cooked affairs: dijon chicken with rice, baked cod with Hollandaise sauce, roast beef. Gander attracts an increasingly cosmopolitan crowd. You'll find yourself fishing with anglers from as far away as Australia and Africa. Because this lodge is close by the river, seniors and anglers who have difficulty walking will have little trouble fishing here.

Rifflin' Hitch Lodge

C o r n e r   B r o o k ,   L a b r a d o r

Luxury, wilderness and large Atlantic salmon — that's what you'll find at this fine lodge.

VITAL STATISTICS:

KEY SPECIES:
Atlantic salmon

Tackle:
Fly-fishing
Flyouts to Remote Waters: Yes
Major Season:
July through early September
Accommodations:
MODERN LODGE OF RUSTIC NATIVE WOODS
NUMBER OF ROOMS: 7
HANDICAPPED ACCESSIBLE: 1
MAXIMUM NUMBER OF GUESTS: 14
Meals: Cuisine as fine as any
four-star restaurant
Conference Groups: Yes
Rates: From $4,400 / week, double
occupancy
Guides: Included
Gratuities: 5% - 10%
Preferred Payment:
Cash, check or credit cards
Getting There:
Fly to Goose Bay and catch Gudie's
taxi.
Other Activities:
Canoeing/kayaking/rafting, hiking,
wildlife photography, iceberg and
whale watching

Contact:
Gudrid Hutchings
Rifflin' Hitch Lodge
PO Box 594
Corner Brook NF
A2H 6G1 Canada
Ph: 709/634-2000
Fax: 709/634-2009
e-mail:
rifflin@nf.sympatico.ca
Web:
www.rifflinhitch.nf.ca

LABRADOR IS A PLACE of subtle motion. Clouds borne of western winds slide by overhead. The current piles the river against your waders or against the transom of your square-sterned canoe. Pine and spruce bend and sigh as osprey and eagles sail overhead. You cast your Silver Doctor or Undertaker or other fly of your choosing over and across and down. It greets the water and swings in a steady arc, slowed or quickened as you desire, to where salmon lie. You do this, once, twice, ten, a hundred times, and your cast and drift become part of the perpetual motion of this day in this place. Peace suffuses your soul.

Then strikes a salmon, as it surely will. Your heart clutches with failure-fearing anxiety. Will its leaps part the tippet? Will the run strip away all your backing? Will it seek rocks with which to dislodge the impediment in its jaw? A million things can go wrong, and your mind worries about each until your guide tails your salmon. Catching salmon anneals the peace spawned of casts on the Eagle River. You will have it with you always, to draw on when there is no water to fish and none in the future.

Working about 10 private miles of the 125-mile-long Eagle, roughly 23 miles upstream from the mouth, you'll fish with a number of guides during your week-long stay. Owner Gudie Hutchings, an angling pioneer in these parts, believes that knowledge of the river and salmon therein is the most efficient predictor of guest success on Atlantic salmon. By canoe or wading, guides will position you to make the best possible cast. You'll work at a pace that's comfortable for you. And you will catch fish. Fish run from five to 30 pounds. The season opens in July and runs through early September. Be there in mid-July if you can.

Accommodations are first class, period. Each of the seven guest rooms are paneled with native wood and furnished with twin beds with handmade quilts. All have private baths. Meals are utterly delicious from breakfasts that open with fresh juice and eggs benedict made of smoked salmon. Don't be late for dinner of shrimp in a sauce of basil brandy and strip loin like you'd find at Smith & Wolinsky's in Manhattan. Throughout it all is the warm, but not cloying, friendliness of Gudie and her staff. That's why anglers in the know book the same week years and years in advance.

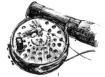

VITAL STATISTICS:

KEY SPECIES:
Brookies, lake trout, land-locked salmon, pike, whitefish

Tackle:
Casting, fly-fishing, spinning
Major Season:
Mid-June through early September
Accommodations:
WOODEN CABINS
NUMBER OF ROOMS / GUESTS:
RIVERKEEP: 4 / 8
KEPIMETS: 2 / 8
Meals: Family-style fish, steak, chicken
Conference Groups: Yes
Rates:
RIVERKEEP: $2,700 / week
KEPIMETS: $2,000 / week
Guides: Included
Gratuities: $300 / week
Preferred Payment:
Cash, check or credit cards
Getting There:
Fly to Wabush and take the floatplane.
Other Activities:
Wildlife photography

Contact:
Matt Libby
Riverkeep Lodge
PO Box 810
Ashland ME 04732
Ph: 207/435-8274
Fax: 207/435-3230
e-mail:
matt@libbycamps.com
Web:
www.libbycamps.com/riverkeep

Agents:
Orvis endorsed

Riverkeep Lodge

A s h l a n d ,   L a b r a d o r

Brookies on drys, landlocked salmon and lake trout on streamers, all in the wilds pioneered by the Libbys of Maine.

THINK HUGE BROOK TROUT and you think Labrador, but this easternmost flank of mainland Canada is also known for lakers and landlocked salmon. How come? Labrador's southwestern section bulges around Smallwood Reservoir, the largest body of water in a rolling highland of lakes and rivers. Rivers rumble from lake to lake providing fast water habitat. Lake trout and landlocked salmon move up into the rivers to feed and spawn, then retreat to the lakes for winter. Lakes also hold excellent pike.

A few years ago, Matt and Ellen Libby added to their angling tradition, established with their Libby Camps in Maine, and opened a pair of lodges in the Atikonak and Kepimets district about 100 air-miles east of Labrador City / Wabush on the border with Quebec.

RIVERKEEP LODGE: Atikonak River. Don't let the sweetly flowing river in front of the rustic green lodge buildings fool you. This is a river of many faces: raging cataracts and deep gorges, back channels and rapids, serene stretches that look for all the world like mill ponds. Stones and mayflies come off in late June. July is the month for caddis. You'll encounter some of both as the season ebbs through August. Brook trout up to eight pounds, salmon up to 10, and lakers in the double digits (best fished early in the season when they're feeding in the rivers) are all here. Chase pike of five to 25 pounds with poppers in the grassy shallows. Guest cabins are comfortable; baths are generally shared; meals are legendary.

KEPIMETS LAKE CAMPS: Kepimets Lake. Matt and partner, Scott MacArthur, opened this camp for up to eight anglers so they could fish a pair of rivers where brook trout and landlocked salmon play. Forget dainty hatch-matching patterns. Here, you'll use the big ugly: a battered inch-and-a-half deer hair mouse on a six-weight rod. Sure, lighter rods can provide more challenge, but they'll over fatigue the fish, which may then expire no matter how carefully you release them. Cabins house guests in a setting that's similar but more spartan than Riverkeep.

For both camps, guest fly to Wabush where Libby's crew takes over. You'll climb into a floatplane for the flight out to the lodge. A word of caution. Mosquitoes can be aggressive here. Bring plenty of good repellant. Rubbing some into a bandana tied around your neck or working it into the fabric of your hat can protect you without getting too much on your skin. Head nets can be used, too.

Tuckamore Wilderness Lodge

M a i n   B r o o k ,   N e w f o u n d l a n d

With puffins, whales and icebergs about, it's tough to remember that you came for salmon, trout and char.

VITAL STATISTICS:

KEY SPECIES:
Arctic char, Atlantic salmon, brookies

Tackle:
Fly-fishing, spinning
Flyouts to Remote Waters: Yes
Major Season:
All year
Accommodations:
A-FRAME CHALET AND CABINS
NUMBER OF ROOMS: 9
HANDICAPPED ACCESSIBLE: 2
MAXIMUM NUMBER OF GUESTS: 18
Meals: Eclectic regional cuisine
Conference Groups: Yes
Rates: From $1,500 (Cdn) / week / 2
Guides: Included
Gratuities: $50 - $100 / week
Preferred Payment:
Cash, check or credit cards
Getting There:
Fly to St. Anthony and you'll be met.
Other Activities:
Big game, bird-watching, canoeing/kayaking/rafting, hiking, skiing, snowmobiling, wildlife photography

Contact:
Barb Genge
Tuckamore Wilderness Lodge
PO Box 100
Main Brook NF
A0K 3N0, Canada
Ph: 888/865-6361
Fax: 709/865-2112
e-mail:
Tuckamore.Lodge@thegone.net
Web:
www.tuckamore-lodge.nf.net

A
FTER DINNER — because sun sets late at this latitude — you might ride over to the coast and watch icebergs drift by like balls of sherbet glowing orange in the last rays of daylight. Puffins with bills of red and yellow will totter down the rocky shore. If luck is with you, a whale or an orca may roll offshore. Calls of loons will tickle your dreams as you sleep in your cabin by Southwest Pond, and your subconscious will replay the day's angling for Atlantic salmon in the river that empties into the bay near the lodge.

The river is the Salmon, and it drains a vast watershed in northern Newfoundland and flows unmolested into Hare Bay south of St. Anthony at the very tip of the island. Main Brook, a tiny town, sits at the mouth of the river. Tuckamore is located a mile out of town. The typical recreational fishing season runs from late June through the first days of September. Hooked-and-released salmon have been averaging four pounds (mostly grilse), but Tuckamore's logs show increasing numbers of six- to eight-pound fish with an occasional 10-pounder. Unlike many other Atlantic salmon fisheries where one hookup per day is considered par, fishermen in this river generally raise several fish and play three or four. Not to be overlooked are brook trout and arctic char. The former are common and run in the two- to three-pound range. Arctic char in this system differ from their cousins in one key aspect. The Salmon River stock does not migrate into saltwater. It may be that the depth of the lakes in the river system provides both enough temperate water, as well as bait fish to retard their urge to move. Best month for fishing for char is the four weeks from mid-September to mid-October. In winter, the lodge offers ice fishing, as well as snowmobiling and cross-country skiing.

Home base for angling and eco sight-seeing is Tuckamore Wilderness Lodge, a large A-frame chalet with four guest rooms and a pine and cedar cottage with five guest rooms. All have private baths, and you'll find a sauna and whirlpool in the chalet. Meals are built around local seafood, and desserts feature fresh blueberries and raspberries. While you're in this neck of the woods, you owe it to yourself to visit the Viking settlement at L'Anse aux Meadows that dates back 1000 years when this was, indeed, a new world.

Big Intervale Fishing Lodge

Margaree Valley, Nova Scotia

This famed old lodge on one of Nova Scotia's premier rivers finds exciting new life under its Swiss owners.

THE MARGAREE RISES on the flanks of mountains at the north end of Cape Breton Island and flows south through the quaint river town of Margaree Valley. At Margaree Forks it turns north, and then west at Belle Cote before entering the Gulf of St. Lawrence at Margaree Harbor. More than 40 salmon pools characterize the river's 20 miles of fishable water. The first run of salmon occurs in early summer, with fish tending to stay in the lower section. Each rainstorm charges the river with fresh cool water and impels the fish to migrate up to the next pool. But it is in September that the Margaree receives its largest run of salmon. The best fishing is for salmon fresh from the sea. They have the greatest propensity to take both dries and wets, and somersault as they strip away your backing. Only fly-fishing is permitted on the Margaree, and regulations prohibit the use of weighted flies lest they be used to snag fish. The river also holds brook, brown and rainbow trout. Guides are available through the lodge for an additional, but quite reasonable, fee.

With .6 miles of frontage on the lower Margaree, Big Intervale is a great spot from which to fish the river. Guests stay in three riverside cabins tucked beneath maples and birch that burn as brilliantly as a bonfire in the chill days of early fall. Each cabin contains two rooms with a pair of double beds and a private bath. A five minute walk takes you to the main lodge, frankly, flamboyant with its gabled octagonal room and oriental window — an admittedly eccentric addition to what was once a fairly straightforward riverfront cabin.

Meals, of course, are astounding, prepared with continental flare from fresh cuts of beef. Fish, too, figure prominently on the menu. Anglers are sent fishing with a lunch bucket packed with thick sandwiches, a boiled egg, fruit, chocolate and hot coffee or tea. In the evening, sit on the spacious front deck, or work up new patterns at the three-station fly-tying bench.

If you sense that this lodge is something special, you're right. Ruth and Herman Schneeberger arrived on the Margaree River in the fall of 1996 at the same time as a run of bright salmon. They fell in love with the clear river, the friendly Nova Scotians, and the gentle valley. It was all so different from Switzerland and the crowds of people there. They soon bought Big Intervale on the Margaree. "Oh, it was a quick decision, yes!" says Ruth, laughing, in her lilting German accent.

Hawk Lake Lodge

K e n o r a ,   O n t a r i o

Anglers from this five-star lodge have 15 lakes at their disposal.

VITAL STATISTICS:

KEY SPECIES:
Lake trout, pike, smallmouth, walleye

Tackle:
Casting, fly-fishing, spinning, trolling
Flyouts to Remote Waters: Yes
Major Season:
May through September
Accommodations:
ELEGANT CABINS AND MAIN LODGE
NUMBER OF ROOMS: 20
MAXIMUM NUMBER OF GUESTS: 24
Meals: Fine dinners and breakfasts to match
Conference Groups: Yes
Rates: From $275 / person / night
Guides: $100
Gratuities: Angler's discretion
Preferred Payment:
Cash, check or credit cards
Getting There:
Fly to Kenora and the lodge van will meet you.
Other Activities:
Bird-watching, boating, canoeing/kayaking/rafting, hiking, swimming, wildlife photography

Contact:
Gary Delton
Hawk Lake Lodge
Box 142
Kenora ON
P9N 3X1, Canada
Ph: 807/227-5208
Fax: 807/226-1228
e-mail:
garry@hawk-lake.com
Web:
www.hawk-lake.com

Off Season:
9 Seventh Ave. North
Hopkins MN 55343
Ph: 612/881-7578
Fax: 612/881-7578

SELDOM, IF EVER, does this outstanding retreat book more than 16 guests. Each feels pampered with personal attention, yet it's not that obtrusive hovering kind found in some operations. Anglers fish two to a boat, and each morning, after they've been fed as much breakfast as they want, they're turned loose to fish any of 15 or so lakes known for quality smallmouth. That's the game in this town, though walleye, pike and lake trout are also caught with regularity. With outboard and electric trolling motors, plenty of gas, a chart of the lake, and bag lunch (breakfast and dinner too, if they want), anglers prowl rocky outcrops, bluffs and boulder-strewn beaches that provide cover for smallmouths in the one- to five-pound range. Fish them with flies, stickbaits or spinners, or bait. Best action is in July and August, when fish hug the shore.

Smallmouths dominate the action here, but northern pike to 25 pounds give them a run for their money. June and September are the months for trophies, and spoons and big spinners produce the most. In May and June, lake trout also fall for hardware; you'll have to jig them up from deep holes later on. Walleyes round out the bill of fare on these lakes, but they are difficult to catch. Jig and minnow, or leech rigs, work reasonably well.

You don't need a guide to fish this lake system, as owners Gary and Sandy Delton have developed a self-guiding program that puts anglers on fish. When you arrive, you'll tour the lakes for orientation. And each night you'll discuss plans for the next day. On any day, angles will be fishing about half of the available lakes, meaning that the others get a rest. And it's highly unusual for you to see more than one other boat during a day's fishing.

The log lodge, one of the few to receive Tourism Ontario's five-star rating, is warm, comfortable and scrupulously maintained. Guests stay in spacious waterfront cabins with decks and private baths. A huge stone fireplace dominates the lodge's great room, where dinners (walleye, prime rib, Cornish hens) are served. Guests have a choice of two entrees, and seconds are not a problem. If the fishing is so good that you don't make it back for dinner, the cook will take pity on you, and dish up something delectable just for you. Among the neatest feature of this lodge is its policy of charging a nightly rate. There's no hard and fast schedule that determines how long you must stay. Vacations here can be as brief or as extensive as you wish.

Kesagami Wilderness Lodge

Lake Kesagami, Ontario

Fat walleye are stealing the limelight at this lodge known for its trophy pike.

VITAL STATISTICS:

KEY SPECIES:
Pike, walleye

Tackle:
Casting, fly-fishing, spinning, trolling

Major Season:
May through August

Accommodations:
Lodge and cabins
Number of Rooms: 17
Maximum Number of Guests: 50

Meals: Family-style home cooking

Conference Groups: Yes

Rates: From $950 / 7 days at Edgar Lake; $1200 at the main lodge

Guides: $125

Gratuities: $25

Preferred Payment:
Cash, check or credit cards

Getting There:
Drive to Cochrane to connect with the air charter to Kesagami.

Other Activities:
Bird-watching, boating, canoeing/kayaking/rafting, hiking, swimming, wildlife photography

Contact:
Charlie McDonald
Kesagami Wilderness Lodge
Cochrane ON
Canada
Ph: 800/253-3474
Fax: 941/643-7312

Web:
www.kesagami.com

Off Season:
371 Airport Rd
Naples FL 34104
Ph: 800/253-3474
Fax: 941/643-7312

IF THIS LAKE WERE within walking distance of even the muddiest of back woods tracks, it would have been fished out years ago. But it's so deeply buried in the wilderness 60 miles south of James Bay, that meat anglers just don't bother. Only those souls committed to catch-and-release make the trek, because they know that the catching will be out of this world. And it is. Days of 100 walleyes up to six pounds and two dozen pike in the neighborhood of 20 pounds each are not uncommon. Only about 600 anglers fish these waters and they return everything they catch — save two walleye of less than 18 inches for lunch. (Everybody loves that shore lunch!) Walleye anglers can pick up fish all day with grub-tipped jigs (no live bait allowed), and fly rodders will do reasonably well with Clousers and sink-tip lines.

Why is Kesagami such a fine walleye fishery? The lake is unusually shallow, averaging seven feet deep with holes to nearly 30. Thus, it warms earlier than other lakes of similar latitude, and that means a longer growing season for everything in the food chain that supports pike and walleye. A strict policy of catch-and-release with single, barbless hooks is enforced. With all this catch-and-release angling, there isn't a better place in the world to perfect techniques you'll use on your home waters.

Though walleye are increasingly popular here, don't count those big pike out. The biggest caught in 1999 was a whopping 54 inches. Surrounded by peat bogs and quaking muskeg, Kesagami is deeply tannin colored. Some say that the dark water gives anglers more cover. Others believe that the tannin somehow adds to the pikes' ferocity. Makes little difference, but the fact is that if you cast a Power Spin or chrome and red Mepps Cyclops over the weedbeds, you'll get thrashing strikes, time after time. You don't have to be a fly-casting champ to reach big fish, but it helps if you've figured out how to knot monofilament and steel leader materials. Generally speaking, the bigger the fly, the bigger the pike.

Ten rooms in the log lodge and the six cabins stretched along the lakefront that can accommodate up to eight are attractive and comfortable, all with private baths. The lodge has a bar, and you can even get in a game of pool. Last year, the lodge opened new facilities at nearby Edgar Lake. Three housekeeping cabins are fully equipped. Just bring your own sleeping bag, towels, food and beverages.

[C A N A D A   E A S T]

Lake Obabika Lodge

R i v e r   V a l l e y ,   O n t a r i o

Here, friends, true luxury and great smallmouth fishing go hand in glove.

VITAL STATISTICS:

KEY SPECIES:
Lake trout, pike, smallmouth

Tackle:
Casting, fly-fishing, spinning, trolling
Flyouts to Remote Waters: Yes
Major Season:
May through September
Accommodations:
Elegant lodge
Number of Rooms: 14
Handicapped Accessible: 2
Maximum Number of Guests: 22
Meals: Gourmet dining
Conference Groups: Yes
Rates: From $730 / 3 nights
Guides: $135
Gratuities: 10%
Preferred Payment:
Cash, check or credit cards
Getting There:
Fly to Sudbury and meet your
pre-arranged transportation.
Other Activities:
Big game, bird-watching, boating,
canoeing/kayaking/rafting, horseback
riding, swimming

Contact:
Peter & Margit Herburger
Lake Obabika Lodge
PO Box 1
River Valley ON
P0H 2C0, Canada
Ph: 705/858-1056
Fax: 705/858-0115
e-mail:
obabika@sympatico.ca
Web:
www.obabika.com

IMAGINE THIS. Instead of roughing it in a pine cabin, your chalet is elegant. Terry robes, thick and warm and soft, hang in the bath. On the windowsill stands a vase of flowers, fresh today. Lace curtains complement the plump down duvet from Austria. Chocolates grace your pillow at night and a pot of rich coffee is delivered to your screened porch well before its reached by the rays of the morning sun, just in case you want to leave all this to go fishing.

If you can bestir yourself, the thing to do on Obabika is catch bronzebacks. The lake is dotted with islands and studded with bays. Points are numerous, as are rock reefs. Habitat is outstanding, but fishing pressure is not. Generally, the small-mouth season runs from July through October, with fishing best in the first three months. The bass tend to be deep, so jigs are the order of the day. Crankbaits can also be effective, as are topwater plugs and fly rod poppers at dawn and dusk. The size of the fish is surprising: Every angler should connect with one or more three-to four-pounders, as well as a bunch in the two-pound range. Bigger fish are more common in late August and September.

Obabika also has healthy populations of northern pike (four to 16 pounds) and lake trout (four to 12 pounds). Pike are good from May through October, and lake trout are best in May, June and September. In addition to Obabika, nearby Upper Bass and Wawiagama lakes hold smallmouths, lake trout and pike. Clearwater Lake, also close by, contains primarily smallmouths and lakers. Speckled trout (brookies) populate Sarah Lake.

The fishing package at Obabika includes use of a 16-foot boat, 25-horse motor, gas and bait. Canoes are also included. Keep one smallie for your shore lunch and release the others.

Back at the lodge, dinner awaits, and what dinners they are. Six-course gourmet dinners served on Wednesday and Saturday nights. On other nights, you'll have to make do with standard four-course affairs. Flowers accent the lodge both inside and out, and boardwalks wind through the trees linking chalets, the lodge, marina and miscellaneous recreational amenities. The lodge is located about halfway between Sudbury and North Bay in the town of River Valley, gate-way to the Lake Obabika region of central Ontario.

Lake of the Woods Houseboats

S i o u x   N a r r o w s ,   O n t a r i o

Anchor your houseboat in a productive cove, untether the canoe, and cast for smallmouth to your heart's content.

VITAL STATISTICS:

KEY SPECIES:
Lake trout, muskie, perch, pike, smallmouth, walleye

Tackle:
Casting, fly-fishing, spinning, trolling

Major Season:
May through October

Accommodations:
HOUSEBOATS
HANDICAPPED ACCESSIBLE: 4
MAXIMUM NUMBER OF GUESTS: FROM 2 TO 12

Meals: Whatever you can cook

Conference Groups: No

Rates: From $1,138 / boat

Guides: N/A

Gratuities:
Angler's discretion

Preferred Payment:
Cash, check or credit cards

Getting There:
Fly to International Falls, MN, and meet a shuttle ($100) arranged by the lodge.

Other Activities:
Big game, waterfowling, wingshooting, bird-watching, boating, hiking, swimming, wildlife photography

Contact:
Noreen Luce
Lake of the Woods
Houseboats
Box 179
Sioux Narrows ON
P0X 1N0, Canada
Ph: 807/226-5462
Fax: 807/226-5157
e-mail:
lowhouseboats@kenora.com
Web:
www.ccco.net/hboats

IT'S KIND OF LIKE DRIVING A 1954 BUICK Roadmaster, this business of piloting a houseboat. Proceeding at a regal pace with only the smallest of bones in her teeth, this queen of the waterways carries your bedroom, kitchen (oops, sorry, galley) and main salon where you'll be domiciled for the next week or so. As you motor along, you'll slip through channels between islands in this huge lake just north of Minnesota. There are 14,000 islands at last count, and the shoals, bouldery beaches and drop-offs associated with each provide unparalleled habitat for smallmouths, walleyes, sauger, northern pike, lake trout, crappies, perch and a few muskie!

You're captain of your own ship, free to go where you want. Each wooded cove looks more promising than the last. What about this one? To the left, the tops of three hemlocks are submerged. That looks like a nice boulder point over there. That high stand of spruce will provide afternoon shade and a break from the westerly wind. Set the anchors. You wisely opted to rent an outboard for the skiff they gave you to tow behind the houseboat. In a minute, you've loaded your tackle and you're fishing.

Though this lake system joining Minnesota and Ontario is huge, fishing is quite good. Use jigs and minnows for walleyes. Throw big spoons for northern pike. Cast crankbaits and spinners, or break out the fly rod and fish streamers, poppers or big nymphs for smallmouths. Minnows take crappies. Trolling can be effective for lake trout and muskies. The nice thing about renting a houseboat is that there's room for all of your tackle: spinning rods, fly rods, casting rods. Bring it all. Depending on the species you seek, and the time of year, you may work the shore, drift over submerged bars or troll. Each houseboat is equipped with a 14-foot Lund and oars. A 10-horse outboard can be rented for $150 per week and it's worth it. Canoes are also available for $65 per week.

Houseboats come in various sizes, from the 40-foot Pioneer for two to four, up to the 54-foot Nomad that sleeps 12. Staff at the marina will check you out on the boat's operation and handling, provide maps and directions to waters that hold your favorite species and will resupply your boat if you want to stay out longer than the standard week. All houseboats have showers, ship-to-shore radios and complete kitchens. All you need to provide are the groceries and any libations. You'll reimburse the marina for gas and oil, typically about $150.

[C A N A D A   E A S T]

VITAL STATISTICS:

KEY SPECIES:
Pike, smallmouth, walleye, whitefish, muskie

Tackle:
Casting, spinning, trolling
Flyouts to Remote Waters: Yes
Major Season:
Mid-May through September
Accommodations:
RUSTIC CABINS
NUMBER OF CABINS: 16
MAXIMUM NUMBER OF GUESTS: 58
Meals: Wonderful dinners whether you cook or they do
Conference Groups: Yes
Rates: From $350 / week
Guides: $100
Gratuities: $15
Preferred Payment:
Cash, check or credit cards
Getting There:
Fly to Dryden and rent a car.
Other Activities:
Waterfowling, wingshooting, bird-watching, canoeing/kayaking/rafting, swimming

Contact:
Rej Roy
Manotak Lodge
Perrault Lake
Perrault Falls ON
POV 2K0, Canada
Ph: 800/541-3431
Fax: 807/529-3190
e-mail:
manotak@moosenet.net
Web:
www.duenorth.net/manotak

Off Season:
Box 7 Site 12 RR#1
Minoemoya ON
POP 1S0, Canada
Ph: 800/541-3431
Fax: 807/529-3190

Manotak Lodge

Perrault Falls, Ontario

A week at one of the finest lodges in Ontario can be yours for not much more than fifty bucks a night!

BUILT BY AN AMERICAN OIL COMPANY to woo customers and reward top brass in the years after the second world war, this lodge has all the trappings of an exclusive resort. Scattered under the trees on a manicured lawn, Manotak's 16 cabins are built of log and are rustic, yet modern with full baths, twin or double beds and kitchens. Here you can get away and still have all the comforts. If you've planned to do your own cooking — something I like to do — you can take a night off and walk over to the main lodge for dinner. Rej Roy, owner and operator, has developed a number of packages that will meet the needs of virtually every guest, from those who just want to hang out to those who are hot about their fishing.

Located about 250 miles north of International Falls, Perrault Lake's 50 miles of shoreline include abundant cover reefs, flooded boulder fields and ledges, and oxygen-rich freshwater tributaries. A navigable stream — meaning you can get a boat through it without undue scrapes and knocks — connects Perrault Lake to Cedar Lake, which has another 67 miles of structure. Both are warm water fisheries producing good walleyes (to 12 pounds), northern pike (four to 20 pounds), smallmouths (averaging three- pounds-plus), muskies (between 20 and 45 pounds), whitefish (to five pounds), and perch. Walleyes hit best in May and June, and again at the end of the season in August and September. Pike are hot in June and July. Smallmouth fish well from July through September, and muskies are at the top of their form from August to September. You'll hook whitefish in September as well, and you can take perch pretty near anytime. Guides are not included in most packages, but are available, and many guests hire them for their knowledge of the lakes and the fish. You can also take flyouts to other lakes.

Lund is the boat of choice at Manotak and they are powered by 20-horse, electric-start Yamahas. You'll be given everything you need: cushions, bait buckets, anchors, paddles and nets. At night, after a full day of fishing, amble over to the main lodge. The packages are as infinite as the imagination of Rej and his angling pals. The kitchen staff will even give you all the tools — skillets, grills, cans of beans, fresh potatoes, onions, cornmeal, shortening, etc. — so you can whip up your own hot shore lunch. Or they'll give you a sack of sandwiches instead. Opt for the latter. Takes time to do a shore lunch when you could be fishing.

Mattice Lake Outfitters

Armstrong, Ontario

*Catch walleyes and big pike in the river
and lake system that feeds Nipigon.*

**VITAL
STATISTICS:**

KEY SPECIES:
Brook trout, pike, walleye

Tackle:
Spinning, trolling
Flyouts to Remote Waters: Yes
Major Season:
May through September
Accommodations:
RUSTIC WOODEN LODGES
NUMBER OF ROOMS:
VARIES FROM 1 TO 4 PER CAMP
MAXIMUM NUMBER OF GUESTS:
FROM 2 TO 16 PER CAMP
Meals: Self-catered
Conference Groups: No
Rates: From $650 / 3 days /
person, double occupancy
Guides: Available
Gratuities: Angler's discretion
Preferred Payment:
Cash, check or credit cards
Getting There:
Fly to Thunder Bay and rent a car.
Other Activities:
Big game, canoeing/kayaking/
rafting, wildlife photography

Contact:
Don & Annette Elliot
Mattice Lake Outfitters
PO Box 157
Armstrong ON
POT 1A0, Canada
Ph: 807/583-2483
Fax: 807/583-2114
e-mail:
mattice@cancom.net
Web:
www.walleye.on.ca

IN THE COUNTRY 200 MILES OR SO north of Thunder Bay, well beyond Lake Nipigon, is the locale of Mattice Lake and the small town of Armstrong to its northeast. This neighborhood contains a wealth of natural lakes and not so small impoundments known for heavy walleye and northern pike. This is the outfitting paradise that Don and Annette Elliot found years ago and, recently, they've doubled the number of lakes and fly-in housekeeping cabins that they offer to parties of anglers who enjoy cooking their own meals. Guides are not normally provided, but can be hired as desired. Every pair of anglers has a boat, motor and all the gas needed to fish for a week. Radios link the outpost camps to the main lodge.

WHITEWATER LAKE: This 25-mile-long lake of 26,000 acres brims with two- to three-pound walleyes, just right for eating, and yields a northern topping 30 pounds at least once a season. Bring a light rig for the walleyes and heavier gear for northerns. The camp is comprised of three, two- to six-person cabins, log sauna, hot showers and a white sandy beach. It's staffed by an attendant.

OGOKI RESERVOIR: This biggest lake has thousands of rocky reefs, shallow weedbeds and deep holes. The camp is located on an island two miles from Eight Flume Falls where the Ogoki River enters the lake. Fast water in the falls area provides an alternative to lake fishing and can be particularly good for walleyes that tend to run between three and four pounds. You'll also find pike, whitefish and sturgeon in Ogoki. Five cabins for two to six anglers are scattered on the island's east and north beaches. Here, too, you'll find a log sauna, hot showers and camp attendant.

SHORT LAKE: Short Lake's walleyes and pike are similar in size and number to those at the lodge on the upper end of Ogoki Reservoir. The lodge here is a single cabin for six to 10 anglers. Groups find privacy and all the amenities that the other sites have, without an attendant.

MOJIKIT LAKE: Linked by the channel to the Ogoki reservoir, Mojikit is similar in size to Whitewater, though the walleyes run in the three- to four-pound range. Also offering solitude without attendant, Mojikit's single cabin provides four to eight anglers with all the comforts of a rustic home, along with an icy freshwater spring for drinking water.

GUERIN LAKE: Located on the Attwood River system, anglers also have access to three other small lakes over short portages where boats and motors are cached for additional fishing. Walleye average two-and-a-half to three pounds; pike are in the teens, and there's some fishing for brookies. A new two-bedroom cabin features running water, shower and solar lighting suitable for groups of four to eight.

BELLSMITH LAKE: A catch-and-release lake where you can eat all you want but can't bring any home, this lake is the site of a new one-bedroom cabin for four with the same facilities as the others.

AUGER LAKE: The northernmost cabin (for two to four) in the system, anglers will find very good walleye of two to three pounds, as well as brookies in the portage in Petawa Creek. Reachable via a short portage, a nearby lake provides additional walleye and pike.

WEESE LAKE: With 4,000 acres and miles and miles of shoreline, this lake supports a four-bedroom cabin for up to 10 guests and provides fine fishing for walleye to three-pounds-plus, northern pike, and brook trout in the Weese River.

Bring your coolers loaded with food on the way in, then use them to pack out filets (prepared in accordance with Ontario and U.S. regulations). Rates include flights from Armstrong to the camps, gas, ice, service flights and housekeeping gear. You'll bring your own sleeping bag (and pack a pillow case which, filled with clothes, makes a suitable pillow) and towels. A two-way radio at each site provides communications with home base.

Spruce Shilling Camp

Shining Tree, Ontario

The fish don't care how much you spend to catch them. That only matters to you.

VITAL STATISTICS:

KEY SPECIES:
Brookies, lake trout, pike, rainbows, smallmouth, splake, walleye

Tackle:
Casting, spinning, trolling
Major Season:
All year
Accommodations:
Eight cabins and one room in the lodge
Number of Rooms: 9
Handicapped Accessible: 1
Maximum Number of Guests: 65
Meals: Self-catered
Conference Groups: No
Rates: From $150 / week / person, double occupancy
Guides: $100
Gratuities: Angler's discretion
Preferred Payment:
Cash, check or credit cards
Getting There:
Fly to Sudbury and rent a car.
Other Activities:
Big game, waterfowling, wingshooting, bird-watching, hiking, snowmobiling, swimming, wildlife photography

Contact:
Gary or Verva Gaebel
Spruce Shilling Camp
Hwy. 560
Shining Tree ON
POM 2X0, Canada
Ph: 705/263-2082
e-mail:
shilling@cancom.net

OK, HERE'S THE DEAL: five species of trout, walleye, smallmouth and pike, and a week in a housekeeping cabin (you bring your own food and your own boat and motor). You'll hole up on Cryderman Lake, a calm one-and-a-half-mile-long and narrow lake not far north of Sudbury. If you need them, owner Verna Gaebel will toss in a boat and motor, upping the price to $300 for a week. How can you lose?

Fishing here is pretty laid-back and not the least sophisticated. Nobody's racin' around with bass boats driven by 200 horse Merc's so loaded with piscatronics that they're awash at the gunwales. Odds are you won't see many Leonard bamboo rods, or fly rods at all, for that matter. Angling is reduced to the essence of the sport — catching fish. You'll fish little lakes, linked by channels or streams, for walleyes, smallmouths, pike and five species of trout. Most anglers use spinning or casting gear. The big draw here is walleyes. It's best in late May and June when fish feed at the mouths of rivers flowing into the lakes. Anchor just down from the tail of the rapids. Cast a jig and minnow up into the fast water and bring it back along bottom. Later in summer, you'll jig for walleyes in 15 to 20 feet of water. Good fish run in the three- to four-pound range. Smallmouth here average better than three pounds and are found along the shore of the main lake and in isolated feeder ponds as well. To fish the ponds, you'll have to portage a canoe a short ways to get in, but once there, you stand a chance of catching the bronzeback of a lifetime on small, jointed crankbaits. Northern pike, not as big as in other lakes but still running in the 15-pound range, are thick. Lake trout in the seven-pound neighborhood can be trolled up in the spring, but really dive deep in summer. These lakes also have populations of rainbows, brookies, Auroras and splake. Trout fishing is limited in summer and is generally better through winter's ice.

Four of the cabins feature two beds, hot showers, electricity, heat, stove, refrigerator and kitchen utensils. The other four cabins (and a room in the main building) are similarly decked out, but lack private showers. A shower house is provided. Licenses and productive lures are available at the camp store. If you plan to come, be sure to stock up on groceries before you leave Sudbury. The shopping beyond is mighty slim.

Air Melançon

S t e .   A n n e   d u   L a c ,   Q u e b e c

Three great lakes and more than 30 cabins make this the one-stop shop for fishing in central Quebec.

VITAL STATISTICS:

KEY SPECIES:
Brookies, lake trout, pike, walleye

Tackle:
Casting, fly-fishing, spinning, trolling
Flyouts to Remote Waters: Yes
Major Season:
May through September
Accommodations:
CABINS WITH RUNNING WATER, KITCHENS
NUMBER OF CABINS: 33
MAXIMUM NUMBER OF GUESTS: 4 TO 8 PER CABIN

Meals: Whatever you can cook
Conference Groups: No
Rates: From $400 / 3 days / person, for four or more
Guides: Available on request
Gratuities: Angler's discretion
Preferred Payment:
Cash or check
Getting There:
Fly to Ottawa or Montreal and rent a car.
Other Activities:
Big game, wildlife photography

Contact:
Francine Melançon Milot
Air Melançon
2 Chemin Tour-du-Lac
Ste. Anne du Lac QC
J0W 1V0, Canada
Ph: 819/586-2220
Fax: 819/586-2388
e-mail:
air-melcancon@ireseau.com
Web:
www.airmelançon.qc.ca

STUDDED WITH LAKES that hold excellent walleye, pike and brook trout (called "speckled trout" by the northwood Quebecois), the countryside below Gouin Reservoir is famed for good fishing. Réal Melançon began exploring lakes in the highlands of central Quebec more than 40 years ago, and he pulled together a fleet of Beavers, Otters and Cessnas to fly anglers to the waters he discovered. Today, his charming daughter, Francine, and son-in-law, Gary Milot, carry on the business, expanding here, improving there, but always with the goal of providing men and women who like to fish with fine service at a fair price.

Air Melançon operates in three areas, Baie du Nord, on the famed Gouin Reservoir; the Sauterelle, a little to the south and east of the camps on Gouin; and the Moselle, further south but a bit west of Sauterelle. Trips to these camps originate from St. Anne du Lac, a little town in the highlands a couple hours' drive north by northwest from Montreal. If you'd rather, Francine will arrange to fly you and your party from Montreal.

In the Moselle territory, between the Gatieau and Coucou rivers, Air Melançon operates 20 chalets on 14 lakes. If you're seeking big lake trout as well as pike and walleye, try Sand Lake in mid-May just after ice-out. A steep climb over "Cardiac Hill" will bring you to a delightful brook trout pond where Milot has stashed a canoe and rowboat. On the other hand, brookies up to two pounds hang out with walleyes and big pike in Natakim Lake, probably the most consistent of the bunch. DuCarny is known for its brookies with some lakers on the side. And Fish Lake may be the best overall for brookies.

The Sauterelle territory covers a trio of lakes in a maze of rugged, wooded hills. On the name-sake lake are three cabins, and on Johnson and Sheila, you'll find one cabin each. Fish the lakes or streams, or hike to nearby ponds with cached boats. Wild brook trout are plentiful from small, gaily colored fish in flowages between ponds, to thick two-pounders dredged up from the lakes.

Gouin Reservoir is Quebec's premiere walleye lake. Baie du Nord is a north/south finger of the lake that intersects the main body, which trends east/west. Here, the Melançons have set up two sets of camps, one on Baie du Nord and the other nearby at Point du Nord. Don't worry. It's not so close that you'll see folks from the other place unless you wish. Ten-fish limits are easy, even for novices. And the chances for big pike are good, too.

Air Melançon's camps are clean frame cabins. More than half have running water and indoor showers. You'll fly-in your own sleeping bags and food (perishables can be purchased at a grocery in Ste. Anne du Lac). All camps have propane refrigerator/freezers and stoves, a wood stove with plenty of firewood and boats (14-foot Lunds) with 6.5- or 8-horse outboards. Several boast solar/battery-powered electric light systems. Guests, usually in parties of four to eight, are flown on the day of their choice. At each camp, you'll find a manager who keeps your tanks topped off and who readily dispenses fishing information. Otherwise, cooks and guides are not really needed. They are, however, available for an additional fee.

Barrage Gouin Hunting & Fishing Lodge

S t - M a r c - C a r r i e r e s ,   Q u e b e c

While the lake may be Quebec's finest for walleye, don't overlook the river.

VITAL STATISTICS:

KEY SPECIES:
Brookies, pike, walleye

Tackle:
Casting, fly-fishing, spinning, trolling
Flyouts to Remote Waters: Yes
Major Season:
Mid-May through mid-September
Accommodations:
CABINS, LODGE ROOMS OR HOUSEBOATS
NUMBER OF ROOMS: 15
MAXIMUM NUMBER OF GUESTS: 82
Meals: Roll your own or enjoy the
chef's triumphs
Conference Groups: No
Rates: From $475 / 5 days,
American Plan
Guides: $60 / day
Gratuities: Angler's discretion
Preferred Payment:
Cash, check or credit cards
Getting There:
Fly to St-Hubert Latuque and catch
the shuttle.
Other Activities:
Big game, bird-watching, boating,
canoeing/kayaking/rafting, hiking,
swimming, wildlife photography

Contact:
Ghislain Beaudoin
Barrage Gouin Hunting &
Fishing Lodge
495 Sauvageau St
St-Marc-Carrieres QC
G0A 4B0 Canada
Ph: 819/666-2332
Fax: 819/666-2332
e-mail:
pourvoirie@barragegouin.qc.ca
Web:
www.barragegouin.qc.ca

Off Season:
Ph: 418/268-8900
Fax: 418/268-8210

WITH MORE PRONGS than the compass has points, Réservoir Gouin is Quebec's third largest lake and its best for walleye. Why? The answer is two-fold. First, the lake bottom is that lovely combination of clear rock and clean sand with depths that range only to 50 feet in the main riverbed. Second, waters teem with baitfish — ciscos, little yellow perch, whitefish and suckers — all providing fodder which walleye love. You don't have to fish deep for walleye here; five to seven feet is very common. The season begins in mid-May and continues non-stop into September. Fluorescent red or chartreuse jigs, tipped with half a nightcrawler, are irresistible to walleye, most of which run in the two- to four-pound range. You'll fish either from freighter canoes or cabin cruisers, which are more comfortable should weather be inclement. (Gouin is 200 miles north of Montreal and well into the Canadian Shield.)

Walleye are the mainstays of this fishery and jigging for them is most productive. But you can play another game here and, to my way of thinking, it's much more fun. Réservoir Gouin was created soon after World War I with the construction of a barrage, or dam, across the Saint Maurice River. Below the dam, the river runs dark as Irish stout, and in its swirling pools, tinged with foam the color of the head of the aforementioned brew, you'll find walleye as well. Cast a green and white Clouser with a seven-weight, or flip a small ultralight crankbait and you're just as apt to catch walleye as you will in the lake. This, however, is not really catch-and-keep water. The river can't regenerate the number of walleye like the reservoir. If you fish this river, you should release, unharmed, everything you catch, or else the river's stock will soon be depleted. A few of the back country ponds hold good brook trout. But, the same rule applies. These gaily painted trout are best released to ensure future populations. Plan a trip in May and combine it with a hunt for black bear. Almost 90 percent of all bear hunters are successful.

Barrage Gouin is located on the left abutment of the dam that created the lake. Ten white cabins ring a long, low lodge that contains five rooms (shared bath). If you're thinking about booking in, ask owner Ghislain Beaudoin about his houseboats that sleep six or more. Cabins contain full kitchens if you're of a mind to do your own cooking, but that might be a mistake. The cooks in the restaurant do things with walleye that are truly exquisite.

If you ask Ghislain Beaudoin, owner of Barrage Gouin Lodge,
he'll tell you that walleye from the Gouin Reservoir
are the sweetest tasting in the world. That's why anglers
make a bee-line for his cabins
and restaurant about 200 miles north of Montreal.

Big Intervale Lodge on Nova Scotia offers classic Swiss
hospitality and excellent angling for salmon and trout.

[C A N A D A   E A S T]

Camp Bonaventure

P a s p e b i a c ,   Q u e b e c

Water as clear and cold as good Russian vodka flows down three rivers, drawing Atlantic salmon beyond belief.

VITAL STATISTICS:

KEY SPECIES:
Atlantic salmon, sea trout

Tackle:
Fly-fishing
Major Season:
June through September
Accommodations:
RUSTIC LODGE
NUMBER OF ROOMS: 6
HANDICAPPED ACCESSIBLE: ALL
MAXIMUM NUMBER OF GUESTS: 12
Meals: Gourmet regional cuisine
Conference Groups: No
Rates: From $3,500 / week
Guides: Included
Gratuities: $40 / day
Preferred Payment:
Cash, check or credit cards
Getting There:
Fly to Bonaventure and you'll be met.
Other Activities:
Waterfowling, wingshooting

Contact:
Glenn LeGrand
Camp Bonaventure
PO Box 1002
Paspebiac QC
G0C 2K0, Canada
Ph: 418/534-3678
Fax: 418/534-2478
e-mail:
campbona@quebectel.com

NEW BRUNSWICK IS AS FINE a destination for Atlantic salmon as you'll find, but across Chaleur Bay rises the massif of the Gaspé Peninsula. The land is isolated, surrounded on three sides by saltwater. Three salmon streams of note — the Bonaventure, Petite Cascapedia and Cascapedia — flow southward from the peninsula's central highlands entering the bay in the vicinity of the town of New Richmond. They are known for their exceptional clarity, and for good runs of salmon that move into the systems in June.

Restricted to fly-fishing only, the clear water makes sight-fishing for salmon a reality. In the main, you and your guide will ride a canoe to water that holds fish. You'll either spot fish from the canoe and cast to them, or you'll go ashore and plan your approach much as if you were hunting. Fish in these rivers tend to run fairly large, between 14 and 18 pounds on average. Still, though, it's not like hammering rainbows in Alaska. One or two good fish per day is not bad. Clear water tends to mean smaller flies — down to #12s, if you can believe that — and finer leaders. The lower the water, the smaller fly and tippet. Here is one of the best places in the world to hook Atlantic salmon on dry flies. As the season wanes, fish become fewer but larger. The salmon season draws to a close during the end of September and the last two weeks can offer some of the finest angling of the year.

Chilled nights also bring woodcock into coverts of newly growing spruce. This is one of those magic places where upland birds and salmon seasons converge for two glorious weeks. Glenn LeGrand, owner of Camp Bonaventure, has a kennel of 25 English pointers and a covey of guides who'd rather bird hunt than eat. For those mixing salmon and upland birds, the day most likely begins with a couple of hours of hunting while water temperatures rise. Midday is spent on the river. And the day concludes with those haunting hours in the alders as dusk settles.

Six bedrooms filled with two anglers during fishing season, but only one each for bird hunting, each have private baths. A 30-foot stone double fireplace warms the main lounge, off of which is the dining room where gourmet meals are the norm. You can reach this lodge by car or plane, but a number of savvy guests catch the sleeper out of Montreal, take supper in the dining car, and awaken to the conductor's knock announcing "next stop Bonaventure" just at dawn.

Diana Lake Lodge

Kuujjuaq, Quebec

Given a couple of days, you can have the best northern Quebec has to offer — fish, ptarmigan and caribou.

VITAL STATISTICS:

KEY SPECIES:
Arctic char, brookies, lake trout

Tackle:
Fly-fishing, spinning
Flyouts to Remote Waters: Yes
Major Season:
Mid-July through September
Accommodations:
TENT CABINS
NUMBER OF ROOMS: 10
Maximum Number of Guests: 16
Meals: Excellent cuisine
Conference Groups: No
Rates: From $3,495 / 6 nights
Guides: Included
Gratuities: $50
Preferred Payment:
Cash or check
Getting There:
Fly to Montreal and meet the First Air flight (included in your fee).
Other Activities:
Big game, waterfowling, wingshooting, bird-watching, boating, canoeing/ kayaking/rafting, hiking, snowmobiling, wildlife photography

Contact:
Joe Stefanski
Diana Lake Lodge
PO Box 1053
Kuujjuaq QC
JOM 1C0, Canada
Web:
www.higharcticadv.com

Off Season:
33 Gibbs Rd
Jaffrey NH 03452
Ph: 800/662-6404
Fax: 603/532-6404

RUNNING 65 MILES from Ungava Bay, Diana Lake and the surrounding real estate offers some of the best hunting and fishing you'll ever imagine. The First Air flight will land you in Kuujjuaq, a moderately large town that was once known as Ft. Chimo and home of the Hudson Bay Co.'s first trading post, which opened in 1830. The flight from Montreal takes about half a day, and, if the weather cooperates, you'll spend another couple hours transferring your gear to a Beaver or Otter for the 40-minute hop west to Joe Stefanski's camp on Diana Lake.

Then the fun begins. If you plan your arrival for late August or early September, you'll have the best of all worlds. Brook trout will hit virtually any pattern, but at the falls south of camp and the seven mile rapids to the north, the most productive lure seems to be a two-inch deer hair mouse. Bring a handful; you'll lose a few. Wise anglers arrive with two six-weight and one eight-weight systems. Rig a big sinking streamer or nymph on one of the sixes and put the mouse or a Muddler on the other. Fishing a sink-tip line is not a bad idea. Your job is to get your fly through the smaller fish down to where the big ones lie. It's not a bad idea to pack a collapsing wading staff in your gear, as well as a landing net. Along with brookies, arctic char of 10 to 12 pounds will move into the fast water downstream from the lodge. They'll hit spinners and spoons more readily than flies. But flies, especially streamers fished deep, will connect. Most lakers are caught by trolling.

If the fishing isn't enough, there are ptarmigan aplenty. They flush fast and wild in front of a good pointer or setter. There's something about the tread of a four-footed creature that makes these birds (the same bird, incidentally, as the red grouse of Scotland) hold and flush like quail, only slower. Pack a 20-gauge and have some fun. Big game is common, too. Nearly a million caribou drift through this region each fall, and muskox are often just over the ridge behind camp. Caribou licenses are relatively inexpensive and the meat is delicious. If you opt for caribou, Joe will load you up in his Cessna 206 and fly you west toward his outpost camp. It's possible to fly out in the morning, and be back with your bull in time to fish before dinner.

Meals at this lodge are first class (bring a couple bottles of good reds and whites to accompany your meals), as is the main lodge itself. Guests sleep in platform tents and share baths.

Jupiter 12

Ile Anticosti, Quebec

Want to catch and keep an Atlantic Salmon? Visit this lodge in June.

VITAL STATISTICS:

KEY SPECIES:
Atlantic salmon, sea-run brookies

Tackle:
Fly-fishing
Major Season:
Mid-June through mid-August
Accommodations:
RUSTIC CABINS
NUMBER OF ROOMS: 7
HANDICAPPED ACCESSIBLE: 2
MAXIMUM NUMBER OF GUESTS: 12
Meals: Fine cuisine
Conference Groups: No
Rates: From $3,950 (Cdn)
Guides: Included
Gratuities: Angler's discretion
Preferred Payment:
Cash, check or credit cards
Getting There:
Fly to Sept Iles and meet the lodge van.
Other Activities:
Big game, hiking, wildlife photography

Contact:
Jupiter 12
CP 139 Port Menier
Ile Anticosti QC
G06 2Y0, Canada
Web:
www.sepaq.com

Off Season:
Giles Dumaresq
801 Chemin St.
Louis Bureau 125
Quebec QC
G1S 1C1 Canada
Ph: 418/890-0863
Fax: 418/682-9944

LYING IN THE MOUTH of the Bay of St. Lawrence, Ile Anticosti is best known for its abundant population of trophy whitetail deer. Yet, in summer, this heavily forested island draws other sports — those armed with fly rods who seek Atlantic salmon.

The Jupiter River that winds south through the wooded uplands is the best of the island's rivers. Unusually clear in comparison to the tannin-colored streams of New Brunswick, the Jupiter River runs with Atlantic salmon from mid-June through mid-August. The season is short and intense. During June, when the run is strongest, anglers may hook a maximum of four salmon per day and are permitted to keep two! Two grilse may also be kept. In July and August, all adult salmon must be released, but two grilse may be kept. Think of it. In many of Canada's Atlantic salmon fisheries, you're lucky to hook one salmon per day and you may only be able to keep one grilse per trip.

Part of the success of the Jupiter River stems from steps that ensure reduced pressure on the fish. While the river is 40 miles long, only eight rods may fish it each week. During the 10-week season, only 80 anglers can fish salmon in the river. Not only do the salmon seldom see flies, but anglers almost never see anyone else. Two anglers and a guide will share a 22-foot cedar canoe. You, your partner and guide will plan the day's float over breakfast. With the canoe loaded on a four-wheel-drive pickup, and lunch and gear stowed in the back, you'll drive upstream to your put-in for the day. The float through low spruce-capped hills and rocky canyons is idyllic and serene. You'll see deer that have made this island a hunter's paradise. And you will see salmon in the bottle-glass green river. You may work pools and runs from the canoe or wade and fish as the water dictates. Bring two rods, an eight for salmon and a six for sea-run trout that frequent the river. Patterns that work well include Black Ghosts, Mickey Finns, Silver Cossebooms, Muddlers, Brown or Blue Bombers, White Wulffs and Stoneflies.

Twelve miles from the river's mouth, Jupiter 12 Lodge is a collection of low and rustic wooden buildings on a rise over the river. Operated by the provincial government, the main lodge accommodates 12 guests in six rooms that share two baths. After fishing, slump into an easy chair in the pine-paneled lounge with a cocktail. Dinner will be accompanied with wine from the lodge's cellar.

L'Aventurier du Gouin

Reservoir Gouin, Quebec

From your modern log lodge on a breezy point, launch your boat and catch walleye until you're utterly fagged.

VITAL STATISTICS:

KEY SPECIES:
Pike, walleye

Tackle:
Casting, spinning
Major Season:
Mid-May through mid-September
Accommodations:
Four rustic camps
Number of Rooms: 2 each
Maximum Number of Guests: 20
Meals: As good as your own cooking
Conference Groups: No
Rates: From $425 / 5 nights
Guides: Optional
Gratuities: Angler's discretion
Preferred Payment:
Cash, check or credit cards
Getting There:
Drive from Montreal
Other Activities:
Bird-watching, boating, hiking, swimming, wildlife photography

Contact:
Francois Beaudoin
L'Aventurier du Gouin
680 Rue Ste-Claire, Suite 102
Quebec QC
G7R 3B8 Canada
Ph: 418/524-9215
Fax: 418/524-9215
e-mail:
laventurier@webnet.qc.ca

HERE'S A PLACE that's as secluded as they come — 200 miles due north of Montreal with the last 30 miles or so comprised of unpaved road the condition of which varies as much as the weather. Easily negotiated by pickups with good shocks and springs (you don't really need four-wheel drive), the road ends at Barrage Gouin. Here a low dam impounds the St. Maurice River creating a reservoir that's known throughout the world for its ample supplies of fat walleye.

At the dam is a comfortable, but not fancy, lodge and store. It's owned by Ghislain Beaudoin, whose family has been fishing this lake for more than a generation. Ghislain used to operate three outpost camps on the reservoir, but he's recently sold them to his nephew, Francois, a young man who's not only a fine walleye guide, but a graduate of a four-year program in hotel management. Service is his middle name.

Over the last couple of years, Francois has diligently upgraded the outpost camps. All contain kitchens with gas refrigerators, solar/battery powered electric, and baths with hot water. All you need to do is bring your own sleeping bag, food and fishing gear. At each camp you'll find three 16-foot vee-hulled boats pushed by 15-horse outboards and an unlimited supply of gasoline. You'll prowl the main arms of Reservoir Gouin, looking for water five to 10 feet deep where walleye hang. Most fish run in the two- to four-pound class, but during your week, you'll catch several in the six-pound-plus range and a few that nudge ten. The lake's record is 16 pounds. You're welcome to experiment with whatever tackle you want, but the most successful anglers use light jig/grub combos sweetened with a bit of worm. It's not difficult to take your limit of 10 fish each and every day you're on the lake. When you finish their filleting, settle back on the porch of your cabin while somebody else wrestles up dinner.

Transportation to and from the outpost camps is by 24-foot cruiser. You can get fancy if you wish and book a flight in via floatplane (from either Barrage Gouin or St-Michel-des-Saints where the hard road ends). You can also trundle your own boat up the road to the dam and launch it there. If you want to benefit from a fish finder and trolling motor, bring your own.

[C A N A D A   E A S T]

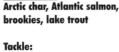

VITAL STATISTICS:

KEY SPECIES:
Arctic char, Atlantic salmon, brookies, lake trout

Tackle:
Fly-fishing, spinning

Major Season:
Mid-June through September

Accommodations:
LOG LODGES OR PLATFORM TENTS
NUMBER OF ROOMS: VARIES PER LOCATION
MAXIMUM NUMBER OF GUESTS: 16 FOR ANY CAMP

Meals: Family-style beef and chicken; self-catered in camps

Conference Groups: Yes

Rates: From $2,995

Guides: Included at Chateauguay and George River Lodge, self guided at others

Gratuities: $200 / week

Preferred Payment:
Cash, check or credit cards

Getting There:
Fly to Schefferville and meet the floatplane.

Other Activities:
Big game, wingshooting, bird-watching, wildlife photography, trekking

Contact:
Jean or Pierre Paquet
Norpaq Adventures
PO Box 66
Cap-Rouge QC
G1Y 3C6, Canada
Ph: 418/877-4650
Fax: 418/877-4652
e-mail:
adventure@norpaq.com
Web:
www.norpaq.com

Norpaq Adventures

Cap - Rouge, Quebec

With six camps on two main lake/river systems, Norpaq can fulfill your sub-Arctic angling dreams.

NORTHERN QUEBEC IS ONE OF THE foremost of North America's angling destinations. Why? It's simple, really. Lots of fish — brook trout, lake trout, Atlantic salmon, arctic char — and relatively few people. Working in partnership with the native Inuit, outfitters are granted exclusive commercial rights to specific regions. You can be reasonably certain that only the guys and gals from your camp will be fishing the water you are. (This is a bit different from most streams in the U.S. where, unless the water is private, anybody can fish it.) Though there are fish in absolute abundance, the season is quite short: June 20 through the end of September. Ice doesn't leave these lakes until late May at the earliest, and most likely it'll be June before it's gone. On the other end of the season, the weather after the first of September gets increasingly dicey. Nobody wants to get snowed into camp.

For more than a dozen years, Pierre Paquet has operated three camps on the George River, a large drainage in eastern Quebec not far from the mountainous border with Labrador. In addition, he has three others over on the Chateauguay River in the central northern part of the province.

GEORGE RIVER LODGE: The mainstay and headquarters for Norpaq, this lodge with seven rooms for up to 16 anglers provides all the creature comforts. Six of the rooms are private cabins, some with private baths. One is in the main lodge. Meals are solid affairs of chicken, steaks and roast beef. Kelt (last year's spawners now returning to the sea) are in the George from mid-June into mid-July. Bright salmon (this year's spawners) show up in August and continue into early September. Brook trout and arctic char (three-pounds-plus), and lake trout up to 15 pounds run from June through August. The best fishing for salmon and brook trout occurs in late August and September. Lakers are strongest in July; char in August. While spin-fishing is permitted in some waters, most of the angling here is by fly rod. You'll need two: an 8- or 9-weight for salmon and a 6-weight for trout and char. Along with the main lodge, Pierre operates housekeeping camps at High Cliff, 30 miles upstream, and Falcon Camp, another 15 miles upriver. At each, you'll bring your own groceries and use 18-foot canoes with 9.9-horse motors to fish for trout, char and salmon. The operation is similar at Falcon Camp, which is 15 more miles upriver. A camp manager serves as a font of general information about fishing.

CHATEAUGUAY RIVER: Here are two fully-guided and staffed camps for up to eight anglers. You'll be quartered in platform tents, share showers and baths, and enjoy excellent meals prepared by the camp chef. Two guests also share a guide. At Loudin Camp, one group spreads out among three platform tents and pitches in on the cooking chores in the central kitchen and lodge. Boats and motors are on hand, and based on the advice of a resident camp manager, you'll head out for the fish. This river and its lake are known for outstanding runs of brook trout and lakers. Early in the season (mid-July), fly-fishing for lake trout in the upper pools of the Chateauguay River is superb. In late August, the lakers turn on again, this time on their spawning beds in Chateauguay Lake.

As well as holding a fine fishery, the northern Quebec tundra sees tremendous migrations of caribou and is thick with ptarmigan. Trophy bulls abound in the massive George River caribou herds. And Paquet, ever flexible, books combination fishing and hunting trips when seasons open in August.

Pourvoire du Lac Blanc

S t e .   A l e x i s   d e s   M o n t s ,   Q u e b e c

Less than two hours from Montreal, this full-service resort dotes on guests who like to eat what they catch.

VITAL STATISTICS:

KEY SPECIES:
Brookies, rainbows, smallmouth

Tackle:
Fly-fishing, spinning
Major Season:
All year
Accommodations:
12 HOUSES AND A LODGE
NUMBER OF ROOMS: 45
HANDICAPPED ACCESSIBLE: SOME
MAXIMUM NUMBER OF GUESTS: 90
Meals: Excellent French
provincial fare
Conference Groups: Yes
Rates: From $95 (Cdn) / night
Guides: $100
Gratuities: Angler's discretion
Preferred Payment:
Cash, check or credit cards
Getting There:
Drive from Montreal or Quebec City.
Other Activities:
Wingshooting, bird-watching, boating, golf, horseback riding, hiking, skiing, snowmobiling, swimming, wildlife photography

Contact:
Gaston Pellerin
Pourvoire du Lac Blanc
1000 Domaine Pellerin
Ste. Alexis des Monts QC
J0K 1V0, Canada
Ph: 819/265-4242
Fax: 819/265-4243
e-mail:
info@pourvoirielacblanc.com
Web:
www.pourvoirielacblanc.com

SOME RECLAMATION PROJECTS are ordered by governments; some are the result of personal initiative. The latter is the case with the 6,000 acres of low rolling hills, small ponds and numerous bogs contained in Pourvoire du Lac Blanc. The father of the owner bought the land and harvested timber, leaving the forest intact around ten ponds. On the verge of the Canadian Shield, the ponds were either gouged out glaciation or kettles, depressions formed by the melting of glacial ice.

The largest of the ten is Lac Blanc, so named, according to legend, for the down of a great white heron felled by a sorcerer's arrow. Some smallmouth bass live in the lake — cast crankbaits among submerged boulders, over the rocky reefs, and in the mouths of shallow, boggy bays. The lake is tranquil, and no outboards are permitted. You'll paddle a canoe or ride a rowboat pushed by a trolling motor. Lac Blanc and the nine other ponds hidden deep in the woods are heavily stocked with brook and rainbow trout of 10- to 12-inches. The trout fall prey to spinners, nymphs and nightcrawlers, the favored bait of most who fish here. This is purely a catch-and-eat fishery. Families come here to catch fresh trout. Everybody fishes — mom, dad, kids, grandma and grandpa, aunts and uncles — and they typically stay for a weekend or a week. A special house has been erected for fish cleaning.

Families cook their catches in the modern kitchen of one of the 12 cottages tastefully sighted on points above Lac Blanc. These are really complete homes, built in traditional style with dormers, three spacious bedrooms, two baths, a large combination living and dining room, and a sunroom with windows on three sides. A porch fronts the lake, and adjacent is an outside fireplace for grilling dinner or for sitting around and talking when the night has a chill. For those who are taking a vacation from cooking, the inn's small dining room with a fireplace looks out across a porch toward the lake. Dinners feature trout: amandine, meuniere, provencale, forestiere or any other way you'd like it prepared. The chef is skilled and the meals are quite good.

There's more to do here besides fish. A five-stand sporting clays course tests shotgunning skills (guns can be rented) and in the fall, you can hunt grouse (wild) or pheasant (stocked). Woods roads provide miles of trails for snowmobiling and cross-country skiing, and as you'd suspect, fishing continues through the ice.

A 30-minute flight from Kuujjuac in northern Quebec takes
you to Joe Stefanski's lodge on Diana Lake where brook
trout, char and lake trout are the order of a summer's day.
Come in late August and add ptarmigan and caribou.

If you come to fish from the Miramichi Inn, consider
mid-October when salmon make their final run and grouse
and woodcock abound in the lovely woods.

[C A N A D A   E A S T]

St. Paul's Salmon Fishing Club

S i l l e r y ,   Q u e b e c

Braided runs of emerald waters on Quebec's easternmost river make fishing for Atlantic salmon the consummate delight.

VITAL STATISTICS:

KEY SPECIES:
Atlantic salmon, sea-run brookies

Tackle:
Spinning

Major Season:
July through mid-September

Accommodations:
LOG LODGE
NUMBER OF ROOMS: 5
MAXIMUM NUMBER OF GUESTS: 10

Meals: Basic roast beef, turkey, salmon and cod

Conference Groups: No

Rates: From $3,000 / week

Guides: Included

Gratuities: Angler's discretion

Preferred Payment:
Cash or check

Getting There:
Fly to Deer Lake, Newfoundland and catch the free floatplane.

Other Activities:
Wildlife photography

Contact:
Jules Goodman
St. Paul's Salmon Fishing Club
PO Box 47096
Sillery QC
G1S 4X1, Canada
Ph: 418/527-4877
Fax: 418/688-4920
e-mail:
sonnygoodman@webtech.net
Web:
www.worldwidefishing.com

IN QUEBEC, FLY-FISHING is the only legal method of taking Atlantic salmon. And at this fine old club, angling for these, the most highly prized trophy in eastern waters, has been refined to a high art. Guides transport anglers in freighter canoes propelled with small outboards. You may cast to difficult lies from the canoe, but more likely you and your guide will beach the canoe on a bit of shingle and work the hole afoot. Seldom fished by others than those staying at select salmon clubs, the St. Paul River is shallow and easily waded for the most part.

Salmon run into the St. Paul in June and by early July have made the 40 miles from the mouth up to club waters. Half a mile above the club, the river braids through a series of small islands interlaced with half-a-dozen small channels. Each channel contains riffles, runs and pools that hold salmon. Fishing here is delightful. You'll see fish in water as green as bottle glass. You'll start at the top of a channel and fish it down, casting to individual fish or over holds where they are lying. The average size of salmon in the waters before the camp ranges from four pounds for grilse to more than 20. Though the club advocates catch-and-release fishing, anglers are allowed to fight three salmon per day and keep four during a week's trip. Salmon of less than 24-1/2 inches are called grilse and must be released immediately and unharmed. The season runs from July through mid-September, when the provincial government closes it down. In the last month of the season, the river fills with sea-run trout, a bonus at this strictly salmon camp.

Rising close to the border with Labrador, the St. Paul passes no settlements of consequence on its run to the Gulf of St. Lawrence. Set on a bench, the club overlooks a wide pool in the river. Behind it rises a hill dark with spruce. Guests fly in to the club in Beaver aircraft from Deer Lake, Newfoundland, or Blanc Sablon, Quebec. During their week's fishing, they stay in one of five rooms (shared baths) in the log lodge. Meals are simple, good and based on roast beef, turkey, salmon, cod and pork. The price includes licenses and air transfer from the commercial airport. Be sure to bring ample spare flies and a backup rod and reel. And don't forget your own libations, if such are important to you.

Ternay Lake Lodge

Kuujjuac, Quebec

Many of the rivers and lakes in this forgotten corner of Quebec have never been fished.

VITAL STATISTICS:

KEY SPECIES:
Brookies, lake trout, land-locked salmon, pike

Tackle:
Fly-fishing, spinning, trolling
Flyouts to Remote Waters: Yes
Major Season:
Early June through early September
Accommodations:
Custom cabins
Number of cabins: 4
Maximum Number of Guests: 12
Meals: Self-catered or American Plan (extra charge)
Conference Groups: No
Rates: From $1,450 / week
Guides: $25
Gratuities: $25
Preferred Payment:
Cash or check
Getting There:
Fly to Wabush, Labrador, and catch the floatplane.
Other Activities:
Bird-watching, hiking, wildlife photography

Contact:
Joe Stefanski
Ternay Lake Lodge
PO Box 1053
Kuujjuac
J0M 1C0, Canada
Web:
www.higharcticadv.com

Off Season:
33 Gibbs Rd.
Jaffrey NH 03452
Ph: 800/662-6404
Fax: 603/532-6404

WELL-KNOWN TO HUNTERS, the upper Caniapiskau River is wild and woolly country. Long ridges are heavily forested with spruce and fir. Rivers are narrow and tortuous, with runs of heavy rapids, long pools with deep and bouldery bottoms, and chutes through cobble that remind you of the land's glacial metamorphosis. At the headwaters of the river is Lake Ternay, as remote and isolated a body of water as you'll find in the eastern half of North America. It holds recordbook landlocked salmon, lake trout, brookies and pike.

The lodge opens in early June and that's one of the two best times for lake trout, landlocked salmon (called Ouananiche in local lingo), and pike. You'll find them in the shallows early in the season. Right after ice-out is the best time. Often you'll be casting your plug or fly and you won't know what took it until you get it close to the boat or shore, if you're wading. You can do both here with equal ease. In late August and early September, the fish go on another feeding binge, and you'll find them high in the water column again. Fish the mouths of the river and smaller streams; work bars and narrows and weedy shallows; there's every kind of water within easy reach of this lodge. It's up to you to take your pick. Most anglers guide themselves, making use of boats and outboards provided for the purpose. If you really want a guide, it'll cost you a couple of $20s — not bad for the local knowledge you'll gain. Flyouts are also available.

Guests here abide in comfortable wooden cabins with showers and flush toilets. You'll bring in your own food and cook for yourselves, unless you make prior arrangements with owner Joe Stefanski. He'll arrange for the grub and a cook to fix it if you wish. You'll fly to Wabush in Labrador from Montreal, and then hook up with one of Joe's floatplanes. In less than a couple hours, you could be fast to a leaping landlocked salmon. Not bad, eh?

[C A N A D A   E A S T]

Ungava Adventures

P o i n t e   C l a i r e ,   Q u e b e c

So benign in appearance yet so wild in temperament, Quebec's sub-Arctic is a marvelous land for salmon, char and trout.

VITAL STATISTICS:

KEY SPECIES:
Arctic char, Atlantic salmon, brookies, lake trout

Tackle:
Fly-fishing, spinning
Flyouts to Remote Waters: Yes
Major Season:
August
Accommodations:
FIXED AND TENT CAMPS
NUMBER OF ROOMS: 12
MAXIMUM NUMBER OF GUESTS: 24
Meals: Solid food like you'd have at home
Conference Groups: Yes
Rates: From $2,495 / week
Guides: Included in most trips
Gratuities: 5% of trip
Preferred Payment:
Cash or check
Getting There:
Fly to Kuujjuaq and meet Sammy's crew.
Other Activities:
Big game, wingshooting, bird-watching, boating, canoeing/kayaking/rafting, hiking, snowmobiling, wildlife photography

Contact:
Sammy Cantafio
Ungava Adventures
46 Ste. Anne St., Suite 3A
Pointe Claire QC
H9S 4P8, Canada
Ph: 514/694-4424
Fax: 514/694-4267

BY THE TIME YOUR FIRST AIR FLIGHT reaches Kuujjuaq just upstream from Ungava Bay, you will have seen the land turn from boreal forest to tundra. Broad strips of vegetation alternate with rock outcrops and tumbles of scree and talus. Here and there stand a few scrubby conifers and maybe some alder. Clumps of willow come up to your thigh. On the flight in, you will have seen mighty rivers — the Caniapiscau, the Mélèzes, and the False — and you know from maps that they ultimately drain into Ungava Bay. Your mind fills with visions of Atlantic salmon, arctic char, brook trout and lake trout. The water is too cold for pike.

Anglers who make the trek up to these wilds are fortunate in the extreme. Fish here have seldom seen lures. While this area certainly lacks the cachet and finesse of the great rivers of the American and Canadian West, you'll play more big fish of harder fighting personality than you will in the land beyond the Rockies. If you must count your catch, carry a clicker in your pocket and flick it each time you hook up. Otherwise, you'll forget to keep score before your first hour is up. That's what catching fish after fish in the three- to 10-pound-plus category does to a person.

In 1954, Sammy Cantafio became the first guide licensed to hunt and fish these Inuit lands. In partnership with the Inuit, he operates three fixed and three mobile camps in the area south of Ungava Bay. Of the three, the camp at Helen's Falls offers the best shot at Atlantic salmon. Runs begin in late July and congregate at the base of the falls, waiting for that primal urge to propel them upstream. Twelve- to 18-pounders are taken consistently, with larger ones up to 25 pounds always a possibility. Located on the east shore of Ungava Bay, Weymouth Inlet Camp specializes in arctic char up to 15 pounds. At Wolf Lake, the camp to the west of Kuujjuaq, lake trout (to 40 pounds), landlocked char and native brook trout will fill your day. All three camps have similar facilities. Eight anglers reside in rustic cabins. A bathhouse provides hot showers and indoor washrooms. Dinners are served in a cabin that offers a panoramic water view of the river. Guided freighter canoes carry you and one or two other anglers to the best fishing water. At these camps, the focus on angling lasts just one month: August. Then you can combine it with hunts for caribou and ptarmigan. What a shame!

Three mobile tent camps (six anglers per week) have been erected at lakes Napier, Lemoyne and Sabrina. Anglers are free to prowl the lakes and rivers that feed them in search of landlocked char, brook trout and lake trout. You'll do your own cooking from groceries that are provided, and guide yourself unless you engage the services of the camp manager. There's no better way to rough it in this wilderness.

And it can get rough. Fronts whip through this country with less than a moment's notice, bringing squalls and plunging temperatures. Gore-Tex and polar fleece are not just preppy conveniences, but an all-important way of life. Occasionally, lousy weather makes flights in and out of the bush a marginal thing. While you may have set aside a pair of weekends and the intervening days, don't be overly surprised, or dismayed, if you're delayed in Kuujjuaq.

CARIBBEAN BASIN

BAHAMAS, BELIZE, COSTA RICA, GUATEMALA, HONDURAS, MEXICO, PANAMA

COME FOR BONES and tarpon. Permit, too, and snook and the blue-water back-breaking reel burners: sail, marlin and tuna. Come for the warm sun on the back of your neck and for the ache in your rod arm as you struggle to keep your tip skyward against the run of whatever free-willed monster that's aiming to strip your spool bare. On flats or the big water, you'll work for your fish. After it's over for the day, there's always a cold beer on the run back to the lodge where bougainvillea blooms. Want to combine romance and angling? This is the venue. Swim in waters of velvet when the moon is full, then stroll back to your cabin, shower, and lie thee down to rest. Many Northerners flock to the Caribbean Basin and adjoining areas to escape winter's chill. But that may not be the best time for fishing in this broad area. April into June and September through November are often the better months for Caribbean angling.

Lodges :

Bahamas

References:

BONEFISH, TARPON, PERMIT
FLY FISHING GUIDE
by Al Raychard

BAJA ON THE FLY
by Nick Curicone

ANGLING BAJA
by Scott Sadil

MEXICO BLUE-RIBBON
FLY FISHING GUIDE
by Ken Hanley
Frank Amato Publications
PO Box 82112
Portland, OR 97282
503/653-8108

Resources:

NOTE:
For the best information on angling
in Caribbean Basin countries, contact
the lodges themselves or reputable
booking agents.

BAHAMAS MINISTRY OF TOURISM
PO Box N3701
Nassau, Bahama
242/322-7500
800/422-4262
www.bahamas.com

BELIZE TOURIST BOARD
83 N. Front St
Belize City, Belize
011-501-27-7213
800/624-0686
www.belize.com

COSTA RICA TOURIST BOARD
PO Box 777-1000
San Juan, Costa Rica
011-506-223-1733

INSTITUTO GUATEMALTECO
DE TURISMO,
78 Avemida 1-17
Zona 4
Cintro Civico
Quatemala City, Guatemala
502/331-1333

HONDURAS INSTITUTE OF TOURISM
PO Box 140458
Coral Gables, FL 33114-0458
800/410-9608
www.hondurasinfo.hn

MEXICO TOURISM OFFICE
405 Park Ave., Suite 1401
New York, NY 10022
212/421-6655
800/446-3942
www.mexico-travel.com

PANAMA:
IPAT
Box 4421
Panama 5
Republic of Panama
507/226-7000
www.pa/turismo

Cape Santa Maria

L o n g   I s l a n d ,   B a h a m a s

Where fine white sand and azure water spells bonefish, tuna, marlin or sailfish, depending on your 'druthers.

VITAL STATISTICS:

KEY SPECIES:
Barracuda, bonefish, dolphin/dorado, grouper, jack crevalle, king mackerel, kingfish, marlin, sailfish, shark, tuna, wahoo

Tackle:
Casting, fly-fishing, spinning

Major Season:
All year

Accommodations:
WHITE VILLAS
NUMBER OF ROOMS: 10
MAXIMUM NUMBER OF GUESTS: 20

Meals: Excellent seafood

Conference Groups: Yes

Rates: From $195 / night

Guides: From $250 / 1/2 day

Gratuities: Angler's discretion

Preferred Payment:
Cash, check or credit cards

Getting There:
Fly to Stella Maris and you will be met.

Other Activities:
Biking, bird-watching, boating, diving, hiking, snorkeling, swimming, wildlife photography

Contact:
Cape Santa Maria
Long Island, Bahamas
Ph: 242/338-5273
Fax: 242/338-6013
e-mail:
obmg@pinc.com
Web:
www.capesantamaria.com

Contact:
Oak Bay Marine Group
1327 Beach Dr.
Victoria BC
V8S 2N4 Canada
Ph: 800/663-7090
Fax: 250/598-1361

LOCATED AT THE VERY NORTH TIP of Long Island in the southern Bahamas, Cape Santa Maria is a haven for snorkeling, diving and sailing. The fishing isn't bad either. Bonefish, generally school fish of three to six pounds, roam miles and miles of flats around the island. Stalk them from a 16-foot skiff pushed-poled by a guide, or wade as you prefer. Fish bait or fly as is your preference. Here, nobody cares but you. If bonefish aren't your bag, charter a cruiser and troll skirts for marlin, kingfish, wahooo, dolphin, tuna or sails. Should light tackle angling be more your style, hook up with a guide and fish the reef for snapper, grouper, jacks, king mackerel or — if you want a slashing fight — barracuda. There is really no bad season to be here; there's always something to catch.

Fishing is just one of the pastimes at Cape Santa Maria. You don't need a rod and reel to enjoy the piscatorial pleasures of this resort. Slip on a mask, and let the velvety saltwater float you over the reef as you watch hundreds of fish of improbably bright color drift in and out of the coral. Scuba gear is available as are lessons for those who want to go deeper. Check out a bike and ride the island's back roads, heading for the 150-foot-high limestone cliffs that Christopher Columbus saw when he passed Long Island in October of 1492. A variety of sailboats can be rented, as can sailboards and windsurfers.

You'll stay in prim white cottages, each with its own veranda, two bedrooms and private baths — all air-conditioned, of course. Bay front gazebos are there for the lounging, out of the sun if that's your wish. At the resort's core is the Beach House, with its open and airy two-story porch and elegant dining room (regional seafoods with conch fritters to die for). Here you'll also find a fitness center, television lounge, library, laundry and gift shop.

Deep Water Cay Club

Deep Water Cay, Bahamas

Mr. Bones rules this roost, one of the oldest and finest clubs in the islands.

VITAL STATISTICS:

KEY SPECIES:
Barracuda, bonefish, jack crevalle, mutton snapper, permit, shark

Tackle:
Casting, fly-fishing, spinning, trolling
Major Season:
All year
Accommodations:
COTTAGES
NUMBER OF ROOMS: 11
MAXIMUM NUMBER OF GUESTS: 22
Meals: Fine Bahamian cuisine
Conference Groups: Yes
Rates: From $1,236 / person, double occupancy
Guides: Included
Gratuities: $30 / day
Preferred Payment:
Cash, check or credit cards
Getting There:
Fly to Ft. Lauderdale / Freeport, Bahamas, and catch the air taxi (about $150 each way).
Other Activities:
Bird-watching, canoeing/kayaking/rafting, swimming, wildlife photography, snorkeling

Contact:
Paul Adams
Deep Water Cay Club
Deep Water Cay, Bahamas
e-mail:
Bahamabone@aol.com
Web:
www.deepwatercay.com

Off Season:
1100 Lee Wagener Blvd.
Suite 352
Ft. Lauderdale FL 33315
Ph: 954/359-0488
Fax: 954/359-9488

MORE THAN 40 YEARS AGO, angling legend A.J. McClane and Gil Drake went wandering through the Bahamas looking for the ideal location for bonefish. They knew about the Florida Keys, and figured that the flats around Grand Bahama Island had to be good too. Their travels took them to a cusp of sandy reef on the southwest side of the main island, known as Deep Water Cay. To the east of Deep Water, channels spread through the southern tail of the big island like fingers of a hand. Through each pass, the tide courses, washing the flats with shrimp on which bonefish feed. Surrounding Deep Water Cay are some 250 square miles of fishable flats. Close to the club, the fish are more finicky; they've seen all the patterns before. But a 20-minute ride in a 16-foot skiff can take you to flats unfished for months. There your chances are better.

Two schools of thought govern one's approach to fishing for bones. Purists stoutly maintain that the most appropriate way to fish for these gray bolts of lubricated lightning is to wade for them, slowly and cautiously, as if you were sneaking up on a grouse that could see you coming. With your feet in the sand (wading shoes are a must), warm water tugging at your khakis, fly rod poised and ready, and your eyes peering for that telling smudge in the water or surface breaking tail, you have entered the fish's environment. And in so doing, you come to know more of the habitat of these elusive fish. And that makes you a better angler.

The other group holds, with equal vigor, that fishing from the casting deck on the bow of a flats boat provides a better vantage point to see what's going on. From the deck, your angle of vision is more acute than when you're wading. And when you see a fish, your elevation enables you to make longer casts from footing much firmer than that in the sandy marl.

You can sort this out — as anglers have been sorting it out for decades — over drinks and hors d' oeuvres, and then continue over a fine dinner and cigar on the screened veranda of the main house. Cottages for guests, all air-conditioned with private baths, are scattered about under the trees. The cottages face west to catch prevailing winds. Were it not for the bones and permit (the club record is better than 46 pounds), it would be tempting to sit on the porch and do nothing.

[C A R I B B E A N   B A S I N]

Moxey's Guesthouse & Bonefishing Club

A n d r o s   I s l a n d ,   B a h a m a s

Fish once with the Bahamian Moxey's
and you're part of the family forever.

VITAL STATISTICS:

KEY SPECIES:
Barracuda, bonefish, jack crevalle, permit, snapper, tarpon

Tackle:
Fly-fishing, spinning
Major Season:
All year
Accommodations:
ISLAND LODGE IN A QUIET TOWN
NUMBER OF ROOMS: 12
MAXIMUM NUMBER OF GUESTS: 14
Meals: Bahamian cuisine
Conference Groups: Yes
Rates: From $1,420 / person, double occupancy
Guides: Included
Gratuities: $40 / day
Preferred Payment:
Cash, check or credit cards
Getting There:
Fly to Mangrove Cay and you'll be met.
Other Activities:
Bird-watching, boating, swimming, wildlife photography

Contact:
Joel Moxey
Moxey's Guesthouse &
Bonefishing Club
Moxey Town
Mangrove Cay
Andros Island, Bahamas
Ph: 242/369.0023
Fax: 242/369.0726
e-mail:
pax@bahamas.net.bs
Web:
www.bahamas.net.bs/clients/moxeys

Off Season:
PO Box CR 55893
New Providence, Bahamas
Ph: 242/362-2186
Fax: 242/369-0726

Agents:
International Anglers:
242/362-2186
World Wide Sportsmen:
305/664-4615
Sight Cast International:
406/585-5598

WHEN IT COMES TO ANDROS, the address belies the facts of the terrain. Andros is not one island, but a series of hammocks where dry land projects above the gentle tides of the Bahamas. The largest island is North Andros and then there's South Andros, and in between a couple of cays, one of which is named Mangrove. How apt. Scores of tidal creeks run through clumps of this stubby tree, the roots of which harbor a vast nursery for baitfish.

Flats grow out from the mangroves and merge with the sea. Tides flush the flats twice daily and with their movement, control feeding habits of pods of bonefish. The trick is knowing where the bones will be feeding given the sun, wind and tide conditions. Unless you were raised on conch chowder and sherry pepper sauce — staples on these islands — bones can be very hard to pattern. Good guides make the fishing better.

At Moxey's, each angler generally fishes solo with a guide. Friends can share if they wish. At their disposal is some 800 square miles of bonefish flats, including the waters once fished by anglers at the old Grassy Creek Lodge. Fish Moxey Creek or Big or Little Loggerhead creeks, or any one of 100 tidal sloughs through the maze of mangroves on these nearly endless flats. Anglers depart the lodge at 7:00 a.m. and fish until 4:30 or 5:00 p.m. If need be, you can boat to distant flats where bones have not been disturbed by other anglers. Your chances of hooking up with eight to 10 fish in the five-pound-plus range are very good. Some anglers tie into 15 to 20 fish per day, and once in a while there's a 10-pounder or better in the bunch. The club record, set in 1983, is 13 pounds.

The most comfortable bonefishing is in October and November, and again in March and April. Despite the heat, summer can provide very good angling too. According to Loundy Moxey, the high sun angle under cloudless skies makes bonefish easier to spot. Obviously lots of sunscreen, long-sleeve shirts, long pants, and hats with long bills are necessities. Yet the ever-present breeze will keep you surprisingly cool. And the months of late spring and early summer are the best for a grand slam: bonefish, tarpon and permit all in one day.

Moxey's is located in a town of the same name and run by its first family. The two-story club with its white stucco and yellow trim is quintessentially islands, and sits only 50 feet from the gentle waters of Middle Bight. As the sun sets, sea breezes ruffle the surrounding palms and wash the day's heat and humidity from the wide front deck that faces the beach across a narrow road. A cool drink tastes good as you watch the sky streak pink and talk about the fishing.

Accommodations are pleasant. Upstairs in the main house are two air-conditioned two-bedroom apartments with private baths. They include sitting rooms that open onto porches. Behind the main lodge is a second building with six guest rooms that share three baths. Meals feature indigenous Bahamian cuisine. Try the minced lobster, peas and rice, steamed grouper or conch. You'll eat on the deck when the nights are velvet, and inside an air-conditioned dining room when they are not.

[C A R I B B E A N   B A S I N]

Peace & Plenty Bonefish Lodge

G e o r g e   T o w n ,   E x u m a

When it comes to angling on Bahamian Flats, the name of the lodge says it all.

VITAL STATISTICS:

KEY SPECIES:
Barracuda, bonefish, dolphin, permit, tarpon, wahoo

Tackle:
Fly-fishing, spinning, trolling
Major Season:
All year
Accommodations:
PEACE & PLENTY: 35 rooms, 70 guests
THE BEACH INN: 16 rooms, 32 guests
THE BONEFISH LODGE: 8 rooms, 16 guests
Meals: Island cuisine with ample fresh fish
Conference Groups: Yes
Rates: From $353 / day, double occupancy
Guides: Included
Gratuities: $40 / day / boat
Preferred Payment:
Cash, check or credit cards
Getting There:
Fly to Exuma and a pre-paid taxi will meet you.
Other Activities:
Boating, diving, kayaking, snorkeling, swimming

Contact:
Magnolia Morley
Peace & Plenty Bonefish Lodge
PO Box 29173
George Town Bahamas, Bahamas
Ph: 242/345-5555
Fax: 242/345.5556
e-mail:
ppbone@bahamas.net.bs
Web:
www.peaceandplenty.com

BONEFISH. Lightning runs that leave your drag smoking and the core of your reel staring you between the eyes. The wariest of fish. Line 'em or plop a Crazy Charlie on their head and they're gone before you can utter the requisite expletive. Anglers who are successful seem to be able to punch an eight-weight into a howling gale. And they must have eyes like radar to see these silver-sided torpedoes against the bright white sandy bottom. Typical schools contain a dozen or more bones of three to six pounds. Permit and larger bonefish operate on the fringe of the flats. Barracuda provide additional excitement.

You don't have to be a Joan Wulff or a Lefty Kreh to connect with bones on Bahama's flats. Distance helps, but precision is more important. If you can consistently toss a line 60 to 70 feet so your fly lands in an area the size of a pie-plate, you'll catch fish. Double hauling — that extra line pull in the midst of your forecast — helps add distance. But don't lose sleep if you haven't mastered it yet. Good guides are essential for all but those fortunate anglers who know the flats and the fish as well as they know their home streams. Over the years, Bob and Karen Hyde, owners of Peace and Plenty, have trained several Bahamians in the arts of fly casting, fly and knot tying, first aid and CPR. These guides are certified and very good. You'll listen to them the way a company commander listens to the first sergeant.

Two anglers fish with each guide in a 16-foot skiff. While the lodge caters to fly-fishers, anglers who fish spinning tackle are also welcome. Bring a pair of rods, generally nine or 10 feet, no. 8 or 9 with weight-forward lines and at least 150 yards of backing. Reels must have good, smooth drag systems. Flies are the usual: Clousers, Crazy Charlies, Gotchas and Puffs in white, orange and pink. Bring a few Merkins and McCrabs for permit.

You'll hang your hat at one of their three lodges: Club Peace & Plenty in George Town, The Beach Inn about a mile west of town on Bonefish Bay, and The Bonefish Lodge ten miles south on a peninsula overlooking the flats. Most dedicated anglers opt for the third. With easy access to fishing (you can stalk the flats right off the beach), this modern wood and glass lodge has everything: a tying bench, video library, air conditioned and eight attractive guest rooms with private baths. Meals are islands in spirit: conch chowder, steamed lobster, broiled grouper and a Bahamian specialty that varies each night.

Belize River Lodge

B e l i z e   C i t y ,   B e l i z e

On then banks of the Old Belize River, this lodge satisfies the mantic and laid-back alike.

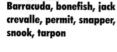

VITAL STATISTICS:

KEY SPECIES:
Barracuda, bonefish, jack crevalle, permit, snapper, snook, tarpon

Tackle:
Casting, fly-fishing, spinning, trolling
Major Season:
All year
Accommodations:
CHARMING CABINS OR MOTOR YACHTS THAT SLEEP FROM 2 TO 6
NUMBER OF ROOMS: 8
HANDICAPPED ACCESSIBLE: 2
MAXIMUM NUMBER OF GUESTS: 16
Meals: Exquisite regional fare
Conference Groups: No
Rates:
LODGE: from $1,949 / 6 nights, 5 days
YACHTS: from $2,693 / 6 nights, 5 days / person, double occupancy
Guides: Included
Gratuities: $30 / day
Preferred Payment:
Cash, check or credit cards
Getting There:
Fly to Belize City and catch the shuttle to the lodge.
Other Activities:
Eco tours, Mayan ruins

Contact:
Marguerite Miles
Belize River Lodge
PO Box 459
Belize City, Belize
Ph: 501-25-2002
Fax: 501-25-2298
e-mail:
bzelodge@btl.net
Web:
www.belizeriverlodge.com

Agents:
Fish About: 408/354-4396
Pan Angling: 312/263-0328
Frontiers: 724/935-1577
Angling Adventures: 860/434-9624

HARD TO SHED THOSE CITY WAYS, isn't it. You've been cooped up in an airplane for a day, and finally made it to the lodge. You briefly note the manicured landscaping, the palms, the flowers, the white boats snugged up to the dock. But man, what you want to do, now, is go fishing. Mike Heusner and Mags (Marguerite) Miles, owners of this lodge, have seen hyper anglers before. As soon as they can, they hook you up with a guide and get you out on the water. They hope you arrive in time for at least some fishing the first day, just so you can get it out of your system. As soon as you do, you'll relax and begin to soak up all the pleasure this fine, old-time Caribbean lodge has to offer.

Some guests choose to stay in Mahogany Lodge and fish for tarpon, snook, bonefish, snapper, jacks or barracuda from Panga skiffs. With a guide, you'll fish the Belize, Sibun and Manatee rivers, Black Creek, and a number of channels and lagoons. You'll work flats, the coast and mangroves using casting, spinning or fly-fishing tackle. Along the way you'll see monkeys, manatees, iguanas and maybe a crocodile. Fishing is as lazy or intense as you want to make it.

That's one way. The other is to book one of three light-tackle cruises. A solo angler or a couple can charter the Permit, a 40-foot Santa Barbara conversion, for five days. You and a captain-cum-guide will consider the weather and the tides, and follow your insights to the kind of fishing you want. The yacht tows a 23-foot skiff that you'll use to work shallow waters. Your schedule is set by the fish, and afterwards, you'll return to the yacht, shower, lounge in the air-conditioned stern cabin and sip something cold as dinner is prepared in the galley.

In addition to the 40-footer, Belize River Lodge operates two larger live-aboard motor yachts: the Blue Yonder, a 52-foot Chris Craft, and the Christina, a 58-foot Hatteras. Normally carrying four guests, these floating lodges will comfortably handle six, and they are ideal for families or groups of serious anglers. As with the Permit, anglers fish from 23-foot skiffs. Angling is best for permit in August; tarpon, February through October; snook, March through October; while bonefish, snapper and barracuda are good all year.

[C A R I B B E A N   B A S I N]

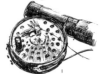

Turneffe Island Lodge

T u r n e f f e   I s l a n d ,   B e l i z e

Want a shot at permit, tarpon and bonefish all in one day? Here you've got a reasonable chance.

VITAL STATISTICS:

KEY SPECIES:
Bonefish, kingfish, permit, snook, tarpon, wahoo

Tackle:
Casting, fly-fishing, spinning, trolling
Major Season:
All year
Accommodations:
TROPICAL CABINS
NUMBER OF ROOMS: 12
MAXIMUM NUMBER OF GUESTS: 24
Meals: Elegant combinations of native seafoods, vegetables and fruit
Conference Groups: Yes
Rates: From $1,560 / 4 days / person, double occupancy
Guides: Included
Gratuities: $25
Preferred Payment:
Cash, check or credit cards
Getting There:
Fly to Belize International and ride the Eagle Ray to the lodge.
Other Activities:
Bird-watching, boating, diving, snorkeling, swimming, wildlife photography

Contact:
Catherine Cochran
Turneffe Island Lodge
PO Box 2974
Gainesville GA 30503
Ph: 800/874-0118
Fax: 770/534-8290
e-mail:
info@turneffelodge.com
Web:
www.turneffelodge.com

JUST AN HOUR'S RIDE by boat from Belize City, Turneffe is an atoll, one of only four in the Western Hemisphere. The eastern side of the atoll is rimmed with 30 miles of wadeable flats. The flats, together with the nearby reef, creates an incredibly rich marine environment.

Baitfish abound, and game species thrive on this abundance. It's not unusual to cast to schools of 50 or more tailing bonefish in the three- to six-pound range, or smaller schools of bones from six to 12 pounds. Permit are becoming plentiful and many anglers who've never fished for them catch their first at Turneffe Island. Tarpon in the 30- to 150-pound range are also prevalent. If you fish in May through September, you'll have a reasonably good shot at a grand slam — all three in a single day. In addition, you'll find barracuda, snook, kings, groupers, wahoo, tuna, snappers and jacks.

Located on a 12-acre island atoll, this lodge doesn't have to rely on long boat rides to put clients over fish. At Turneffe the flats, reef and mangrove cays are in your front yard. You and your guide will sit down in the morning and plan a strategy based on your expectations, capabilities and local conditions. Then it's off in one of the Dolphin skiffs. Most anglers fish fly tackle, but spinning gear is okay too. A dockside tackle shop sells replacements for anything — flies, lures, and other stuff you left at home.

Since 1995, the lodge has undergone extensive renovation. Light and airy guest rooms have two beds, furnishings and air conditioning (optional). Windows open to water views, and all baths are private. The lounge (dinners feature local seafood or steaks) has been expanded and decorated with woods native to Belize. Take a chair on the deck off the bar and let your gaze roam over the Caribbean where Columbus sailed on his last voyage. Along with the fishing, Turneffe Island is a popular destination for divers.

Archie Field's Rio Colorado Lodge

S a n   J o s e ,   C o s t a   R i c a

Snook, tarpon, parrots, monkeys — these are the tropics and this lodge is one of the best in the business.

VITAL STATISTICS:

KEY SPECIES:
Snook, tarpon

Tackle:
Casting, fly-fishing, spinning,
Major Season:
September through June
Accommodations:
TROPICAL LODGE ON STILTS
NUMBER OF ROOMS: 18
HANDICAPPED ACCESSIBLE: SOME
MAXIMUM NUMBER OF GUESTS: 36
Meals: Fresh fish and pork with plenty of local fruits and vegetables
Conference Groups: No
Rates: Packages from $1,367 / 5 days, 6 nights, double occupancy
Guides: Included
Gratuities: $10 - $20 / day
Preferred Payment:
Cash, check or credit cards
Getting There:
Fly to San Jose and take the air taxi to the lodge.
Other Activities:
Bird-watching, boating, ecotours of the rainforest, swimming, wildlife photography

Contact:
Diana Wise
Rio Colorado Lodge
PO Box 5094 1000
San Jose, Costa Rica
Ph: 800/243-9777
Fax: 813/933-3280
e-mail:
tarpon4u@mindspring.com or
tarpon@sol.racsa.co.cm
Web:
www.riocoloradolodge.com

THE DIN CAN BE ALMOST DEAFENING. Monkey's howl from high in the deep green canopy that shades the slow, rainforest river. Bright flashes of yellow, red, blue and brilliant green dash among the trees. Parrots chatter to each other in a language that you and I will never understand. The water is the color of tea with a double dollop of milk in it. Your guide points to where the current swirls behind a handful of mangrove root, reaching deep into the turbid flow. You nod and cast a mirror lure into that bathtub pool eddying downstream of the root. The plug sits for a moment, then you start the retrieve with a jerk. That's when the heavens fall and your line slices upstream, only to surface with a snook of 15 pounds which then dives and races for cover to break you off. The guide has backed the boat into midstream. You're applying what pressure you can. A bead of sweat stings the corner of your eye, but for the next several minutes, you won't have a free hand to wipe it away.

So it goes when you're fishing the Rio Colorado down on the eastern side of Costa Rica. A long, thin sandbar drives the final half-mile or so of the Rio Colorado north to where it finally meets the Caribbean. In some seasons, the mouth of the river almost closes with sand moved along by prevailing currents and tides. Always, the river breaks free. Near the mouth, you'll find snook and tarpon.

Tarpon, those silver-plated leftovers from the age of dinosaurs, are the money fish here. That's what you come to catch; the snook are a bonus. Hook a tarpon and you'll see what I mean. Head shaking, it leaps clear of the water, lands with a crash and bores away with incredible speed. Fighting a tarpon isn't for the faint of heart. You think you've got it whipped, and it thrashes into the air at boatside, so close you can almost count the age rings on its scales. Refreshed, it races away, your drag screams and you thank God that 125 pounds of writhing muscle did not land at your feet. Men have been maimed that way.

Tarpon average 70 to 80 pounds in the Rio Colorado. From January through May, they move upriver to spawn in the jungle backwaters. In fall, you'll find them in the surf off the mouth of the river. There they mix with snook, and trolling or casting can be fabulous for both species. Smaller snook move into the river in

November and December; hookups of 30 fish per day are fairly typical. Most of these fish run about five pounds, but larger ones can be expected. For snook, a medium casting or spinning rig loaded with 8- to 12-pound-test line is ample. An 8-weight fly rod is about right, though you'll want at least a 10 for tarpon.

Founded by Archie Fields, Rio Colorado Lodge has been the standard-bearer on these waters for years. Your room of richly varnished native wood feels cozy yet open, with many windows that catch the breeze from the veranda. All have private baths. Meals are served family-style, and a lounge with billiards and other games provides after-dinner entertainment. The fishing day begins early and runs into late afternoon. You and your partner will fish from 23-foot skiffs, or smaller craft, with a trained guide who most likely grew up in the village, speaks fluent English and knows the river and its fish. Pack carefully for this trip; baggage is limited to 25 pounds between San Jose and the lodge.

El Octal

*Marlin and sailfish roam Costa Rica's west coast,
but there's nothing pacific about them.*

VITAL STATISTICS:

KEY SPECIES:
Dolphin/dorado, jack crevalle, marlin, roosterfish, sailfish, tuna

Tackle:
Fly-fishing, trolling
Major Season:
All year
Accommodations:
HILLSIDE VILLAS
NUMBER OF ROOMS: 71
HANDICAPPED ACCESSIBLE: 12
MAXIMUM NUMBER OF GUESTS: 145
Meals: The freshest fish, fruits and vegetables
Conference Groups: Yes
Rates: From $62 / day
Guides: Included in packages
Gratuities: $25 - $50
Preferred Payment:
Cash, check or credit cards
Getting There:
Fly to David Oliver Int'l and the van will take you to the lodge ($30).
Other Activities:
Bird-watching, golf, horseback riding, hiking, swimming, tennis, wildlife photography

Contact:
Rick Wallace
El Octal
PO Box 1
Playas del Coco
Guanacaste, Costa Rica
Ph: 506/670-0321
Fax: 506/670-0083
e-mail:
elocotal@pop.racsa.co.cr

Agents:
Adventure Sport Fishing:
619/792-8172
Fishing International:
707/539-1320
Pan Angling:
312/263-0328
Rod & Reel Adventures:
209/524-7775

LOCATED IN THE HILLS above the Gulf of Papagayo, this resort is one if the finest where bill-fishing is concerned. The gulf swarms with more than two dozen varieties of sportfish. Combine angling for black marlin in the 300- to 500-pound class in May through July with sailfish of 100-pounds-plus. They reach their peak from May through September. You can also work in yellowfin tuna of up to 200 pounds (the resort record is a 221-pounder taken in January, 1995). If you're after blue marlin, January through March are the hot months; these fish run between 200 and 400 pounds. Forty- to 60-pound roosterfish are taken on live bait all year long. El Octal was one of the first lodges in the world dedicated to reviving and releasing the billfish its anglers boated. It's a commitment that continues today. Sure, some fish are lost and a few brought to dock. But most live to grow bigger and fight another day.

Five boats comprise El Octal's fleet: four 32-foot Sportfishermen and a 43-foot yacht. All boats are powered by twin engines to cut running time to fishing grounds and for peace of mind. Heads and bunks, as well as complete marine electronics, are standard on all boats. Boats also carry a range of trolling rigs loaded with 20- to 80-pound line. Spinning tackle is also available. A limited stock of terminal tackle is maintained at El Octal's marina. Bring what you think you'll reasonably need. If you need more, you can get it there. Fly-fishing for sailfish is a different matter. Best to arrive fully equipped.

El Octal provides a range of fishing packages, from two days on the water to six. Included are room, meals, fishing boat, tackle, ground transfer and airport pick up. Tips, bar bills, and personal expenses are up to you. You'll stay in air-conditioned cottages nestled into the hill above the white sand beach and blue gulf beyond. Each has a private terrace, refrigerator and satellite TV. Three freshwater pools and a Jacuzzi round out amenities. And you'll find a sweeping view of the bay from the resort's hilltop restaurant where dinners feature local fish. If you wish, you can simply book a room and take meals at El Octal's restaurant or at others in the tiny fishing village of Playas del Coco two miles away.

[C A R I B B E A N   B A S I N]

Rain Goddess

S a n   J o s e ,   C o s t a   R i c a

Known for its luxurious houseboat, Blue Wing International is about to open an equally elegant lodge.

VITAL STATISTICS:

KEY SPECIES:
Machaca, mojarra, red snapper, snook, tarpon

Tackle:
Casting, fly-fishing, spinning, trolling
Major Season:
All year
Accommodations:
HOUSEBOAT
NUMBER OF ROOMS: 6
MAXIMUM NUMBER OF GUESTS: 10
Meals: Fish, beef, salads, fine wines
Conference Groups: No
Rates: From $1,750 / 5 days,
3 nights
Guides: Included
Gratuities: $10 / day
Preferred Payment:
Cash, check or credit cards
Getting There:
Fly to San Jose and meet the lodge's driver.
Other Activities:
Bird-watching, boating,
canoeing/kayaking/rafting,
ecotourism, horseback riding, hiking,
swimming, wildlife photography

Contact:
Dr. Alfredo Lopez
Rain Goddess
PO Box 025216
Miami FL 33102
Ph: 011-506-289-8401
Fax: 011-506-289-0009
e-mail:
bluewing@sol.racsa.com.cr
Web:
www.bluwing.com

Off Season:
Apartado 850-
1250 Escazu
San Jose, Costa Rica

Agents:
Pan Angling:
800/533-4353
Quest Global Angling Adventures:
888/891-3474
Costa Rica Outdoors:
011-506-282-6743

FOR YEARS, THE RAIN GODDESS, a very luxurious houseboat, has been ferrying anglers around the brackish waters of Costa Rica's northeast coast. Operating out of Barra Colorado near the mouth of the Rio Colorado, the Rain Goddess may take you up the Rio San Juan, nosing into lakes and rivers that are inaccessible by road, angling for fish that seldom see lures. Or you may cruise to the Gulf, then up the Rio Colorado or into the Totuguero or Parismina. You and your fellow anglers will decide the route based on season, species and your preference.

A pair of 16-foot johnboats and two 23-foot skiffs are towed astern. You'll use the johnboats to fish backwaters for snook, tarpon, rainbow bass and mojarra. The 23-footers come into play in the heavier water at river mouths for big tarpon, and in the Gulf, tuna, jacks, dorado and maybe a sailfish. Blue Wing International, operator of the Rain Goddess, provides guides who know the waters and the fish. You can use their tackle, but it's far better to take your own. Best months for snook are September and December, and February and March are tops for rainbow bass, mojarra and tarpon.

Accommodations aboard the Rain Goddess are above reproach. The salon and staterooms are paneled with deeply polished tropical woods. Upholstered chairs and polished tables — reproductions of fine antiques — grace the salon where guests dine on china and sip wine from crystal. Filet mignon and lobster are on the menu. Staterooms feature queen or double beds. Sixty-five feet long and 18 feet wide, the Rain Goddess has room for a maximum of 12 guests, and it's fully air-conditioned.

In keeping with the classic tradition of the Rain Goddess, Blue Wing plans to open Rio Indio, its new fishing resort and ecotourism center in 2000. Located at the mouth of the San Juan River across the border from Costa Rica in Nicaragua, the complex will contain cottages tucked in the jungle as well as a main lodge with fully-amenitied guest rooms, a first-class restaurant, swimming pool and spa.

Roy's Zancudo Lodge

Golfito, Costa Rica

Customers at this lodge have chalked up 30 world records, more than many places dream about.

VITAL STATISTICS:

KEY SPECIES:
Amberjack, dolphin/dorado, grouper, jack crevalle, marlin, roosterfish, sailfish, snapper, snook, tuna

Tackle:
Casting, fly-fishing, spinning, trolling

Major Season:
All year

Accommodations:
GUEST COTTAGES UNDER THE PALMS
NUMBER OF ROOMS: 12
MAXIMUM NUMBER OF GUESTS: 20

Meals: Seafood and meat entrees

Conference Groups: No

Rates: From $1,450 / 3 days, double occupancy

Guides: Included

Gratuities: $20

Preferred Payment:
Cash, check or credit cards

Getting There:
Fly to San Jose and catch the flight to Golfito, where you'll meet a boat.

Other Activities:
Bird-watching, swimming, wildlife photography

Contact:
Martha Fields
Roy's Zancudo Lodge
5700 Memorial Hwy
Suite 107
Tampa FL 33615
Ph: 800/551-7697
Fax: 813/889-9189
e-mail:
advmk11@juno.com
Web:
www.royszancudo.com

COSTA RICA is a friendly country and a leader in natural resources conservation. From deep rain forests to steep mountains with streams that carry trout (stocked but trout just the same!), this country merits exploring. There's no better place to begin than on the southernmost tip of the country in the little bay village of Golfito.

To the east and south of the bay is Zancudo Beach. Under palms by the beach sit the four cabins and the main house of the lodge. Fishing here is for blue and black marlin (June through September), sailfish (December through May), dorado, yellowfin and big-eye tuna, permit, snook (May through September), wahoo, barracuda, roosterfish, pompano, Sierra mackerel, trevelly, jack crevalle, corvina, amberjack, triple tail, rainbow runner, grouper, and red and yellow snapper. Tackle, of course, depends on the species. The lodge furnishes all you'll need, with the exception of fly-fishing gear. If that's your game, bring your own.

Over the years, Roy's guests have chalked up 30 IGFA world records; 20 are current as of this writing, and three more are pending. You'll fish from 22- to 25-foot center-console boats rigged for the species of your choice. Although some fish may be kept for dinner, most angling here is catch-and-release, so bring a camera.

Depending on the number in your party, you'll have your choice of four suites with bedroom, sitting room with wet bar and refrigerator, and private baths or a private room with a bath. All are air-conditioned. Meals are served family-style, while the menu revolves around local specialties and, of course, fresh fish. Heart healthy and vegetarian diets are no problem. And for relaxing after a day of fighting the big ones, there's a beach-side pool and hot tub.

There's one important caveat for fishing in this region. Air charters that fly from major airports to outlying villages like Golfito are very strict about luggage. You're restricted to 25 pounds. Go light. If yours is a heavy professional model camera with extra lenses, leave it at home and bring a good point and shoot instead. Pack only three changes of clothes — one for traveling and the other two for fishing. Roy's offers free laundry service. Plan to wear lightweight long-sleeved shirts and trousers when fishing, and pack a rain shell along with a water and sun proof hat. Mosquitoes are not usually a problem because of the constant breeze, but a bottle of bug dope won't weigh much and it may be very welcome.

[C A R I B B E A N   B A S I N]

Silver King Lodge

R i o   C o l o r a d o ,   C o s t a   R i c a

So hell-bent on busting your chops, you'll think these tarpon never went to charm school!

VITAL STATISTICS:

KEY SPECIES:
Snook, tarpon, wahoo

Tackle:
Casting, fly-fishing, spinning, trolling
Major Season:
All year
Accommodations:
COTTAGES CONNECTED BY COVERED BOARDWALKS
NUMBER OF ROOMS: 10
MAXIMUM NUMBER OF GUESTS: 20
Meals: Fine regional fare
Conference Groups: No
Rates: From $1,645 / 3 days
Guides: Included
Gratuities: $20 / day
Preferred Payment:
Cash, check or credit cards
Getting There:
Fly to San Jose and meet the shuttle flight.
Other Activities:
Bird-watching, boating, canoeing/kayaking/rafting, hiking, swimming, wildlife photography

Contact:
Shawn Feliciano
Silver King Lodge
PO Box 02516 - 1597
Miami FL 33102
Ph: 800/309-8125
Fax: 011-506-381-0849
e-mail:
slvrkng@sol.racca.co.cr
Web:
www.silverkinglodge.com

Agents:
Adventures: 800/847-3474

YOU GOTTA LOOK AT IT THIS WAY. A tarpon is a kind of lethargic gangster. He'll lie in the shallows sucking down mullet all day long, moving only to where the water is warmer or cooler, or doing whatever it wants. (When you're a 120 pound fish with scales like armor, you can do want you want, when you want.) All goes good for these big thugs, until somebody does something dumb, like sticks a hook in 'em, see? That's when they get attitude. And their attitude isn't friendly. They want to bust something — your rod, your reel, your boat — but mostly what they do is bust your line.

Draining the Barra del Colorado, a wildlife preserve rich with tropical birds and orchids, Rio Colorado teems with fish. Fingers of the river reach back into the mangrove jungle, a nursery for tarpon, snook, guapote and mojarra. When there's been a storm, the Rio Colorado is often murky. You won't sight-cast for tarpon here. Instead, you'll let your fly or lure work down to the bottom. You'll retrieve in short, choppy strips. The rhythm of the retrieve, the gentle rocking of the skiff, and the sun, pleasantly warm on your shoulders, will lull you. That, of course, is when the tarpon throws its first punch. If he catches you sleeping, it could be a knock-out blow. Tarpon here are plentiful. The average fish weighs 70 pounds; the record is a 207-pounder. Heavy casting rods and 12-weight fly rods are required. Best times are February through May, and October.

If tarpon are the heavyweights, snook do the warm-up bouts. Twenty-pounders are average, with the lodge record topping 53 pounds. You'll find them up in the mangroves and also down where the river meets the sea. Use bass tackle, either casting, fly or spinning. For guapote and mojarra, the bass tackle will do, but bring a stock of spinnerbaits and poppers. Guests who book five or more days receive a free offshore trip for wahoo, yellowfin, sails, marlin and dorado. Heavy tackle is provided. Snook fish best from August through December; the other species in spring and fall.

Silver King Lodge earns top marks for its accommodations — spacious, paneled guest rooms with two queen-size beds, high ceilings and private tiled baths. Delicious meals and fine wines fill you up, while a Jacuzzi awaits those with aching muscles. A note of caution: Guests are permitted only 25 pounds of luggage on the flight from San Jose to the lodge.

Posada Del Sol

Guanaja, Bay Islands, Honduras

Be one of only six who fish the Bay Island flats where Columbus stopped before his most important discovery.

VITAL STATISTICS:

KEY SPECIES:
Bonefish, permit

Tackle:
Fly-fishing, spinning
Major Season:
All year
Accommodations:
CHARMING ROOMS IN A MEXICAN-STYLE MANSION
NUMBER OF ROOMS: 24
MAXIMUM NUMBER OF GUESTS: 48
Meals: Exquisite regional cuisine
Conference Groups: No
Rates: From $1,695 / 7 nights
Guides: Included
Gratuities: Angler's discretion
Preferred Payment:
Cash, check or credit cards
Getting There:
Fly to San Pedro Sula and catch the ferry.
Other Activities:
Boating, canoeing/kayaking/rafting, diving, hiking, swimming, tennis

Contact:
Terry Evans
Posada Del Sol
PO Box 877
San Antonio FL 33576
Ph: 800/642-3483
Fax: 352/588-4158
e-mail:
terry@roatan.com
Web:
www.roatan.com

Agents:
Roatan Charter
PO Box 877
San Antonio, FL 33576
352/588-4132

FILLING THE BILL as fine bonefish water are the flats off Guanaja Island, the largest of the Islas de la Bahia, which range from hard sand with grass to marl. Wading is easy. With abundant schools of bones running between two and six pounds, this is a fine place to learn to sight fish. Toss Clousers or Crazy Charlies ahead of those sleek tan shadows or in front of those tailing in the shallows. Look for clouds of sand stirred up by fish rooting along the bottom. Even if your casting is modest, here you should connect with half-a-dozen fish per day. As your casting improves, you'll hook up with more fish. Skilled anglers play 15 or more per day! Permit are plentiful as well, but hookups are not as frequent as they are with the bones. Guides and skiffs are available through the lodge.

As you're fishing these flats, let your mind wander back to the tragic life of Christopher Columbus. In July 1502, during his fourth, final and most disappointing voyage, he anchored his caravels here to take on water and fruit. Columbus was in disgrace. His three prior voyages had failed to find Cathay and the rich lode of gold, jewels and spices demanded by his Spanish masters. He rested near Guanaja, a short time before weighing anchor and making the 30-mile sail to mainland Honduras. There, he encountered the Mayans but no wealth, and he returned to Spain never knowing that his discovery of the Mayans would lead to immense wealth for Spain.

While Posada Del Sol only books six anglers per week to limit impact on the environment, the tile-roofed Spanish-style resort contains 24 guest rooms that front on the ocean, forest or pool. With the coral reef, diving is a big attraction here (there's even a photo lab to process film from underwater cameras). Also popular are walks through the orchid-rich rainforest to a freshwater falls, a favorite spot on this nine-mile long island. Two white sand beaches, a tennis court, and an excellent restaurant round out amenities.

[C A R I B B E A N   B A S I N]

Utila Lodge

U t i l a   I s l a n d ,   H o n d u r a s

Combine flats and offshore fishing with diving on an inexpensive Caribbean vacation.

VITAL STATISTICS:

KEY SPECIES:
Bonefish, marlin, permit, tarpon, wahoo

Tackle:
Casting, fly-fishing, spinning, trolling

Major Season:
All year

Accommodations:
NEW MOTEL-STYLE OCEAN-FRONT ROOMS
NUMBER OF ROOMS: 8
HANDICAPPED ACCESSIBLE: 4
MAXIMUM NUMBER OF GUESTS: 16

Meals: Regional cuisine

Conference Groups: No

Rates: From $1,125 / week

Guides: Included

Gratuities: 10% of package

Preferred Payment:
Cash, check or credit cards

Getting There:
Fly to La Ceiba, or San Pedro Sula and catch the ferry.

Other Activities:
Bird-watching, boating, canoeing/kayaking/rafting, diving, hiking, swimming, wildlife photography

Contact:
Terry Evans
Utila Lodge
Bay Islands, Honduras
Ph: 800/282-8932
Fax: 352-588-4158
e-mail:
utl@roatan.com
Web:
www.roatan.com/utilalodge

T HE COASTS OF BELIZE, Guatemala and Honduras come together in an open "vee" that points east toward Cuba. Islands along the coast rise from a shallow flat and carry some of the best bonefishing in the world. You've heard of many of these, including Turneffe Island off Belize City, and you know the caliber of angling you'll find there.

About 150 miles out along the Honduran coast from the center of the "vee" are the Islas de la Behia. The western most of these is Isla de Utila, and here you'll find excellent flats and offshore angling. To fish here is reasonably inexpensive. On the flats you'll find bonefish in the three- to eight-pound range, permit up to 15 pounds, and tarpon that can top 125 pounds. A seven day package will set you back $1,125. If you want to fish solo, add another $140 to the tab. You'll need to bring your own light tackle or fly-fishing gear. Offshore species include blue and white marlin — which are good all year — and wahoo, best from August through November. Typical marlin run in the 200-pound category. Wahoo can reach 60 pounds. Gather three buddies and you'll each chip in $1,325 for five days fishing and seven nights at the lodge.

The focus at this lodge is diving, and anglers who want to swim with the fishes — an interesting thing to do, by the way — can arrange to combine scuba outings with fishing. You can also mix offshore and flats fishing as you wish. The lodge itself is just three years old. Built on stilts that extend the lodge over the bay, eight air-conditioned guest rooms contain private baths. This place is intimate — only 16 guests at one time — and private rooms are available for an additional $350 per week. You'll enjoy dinners constructed around fresh fish with a distinctly native flavor. This is a naturalist's paradise with caves to explore and profuse tropical flowers, birds and butterflies to enjoy.

Casa Blanca and Playa Blanca

Quintana Roo, Mexico

You might have your best shot at a saltwater grand slam right here.

FEW WATERS IN THE WORLD offer better bonefish than the flats of Ascencion Bay and Espiritu Santo Bay farther down the Mexican coast. Schools of bonefish are large here. You can see them by their shadows or their tails waving above the surface as they root for crabs and shrimp. If you've never fished for bones, this is the place to get your feet wet and your knuckles busted. You'll practice on schoolies of two to six pounds. If you want to hang onto these fish, forget what the fancy angler's tell you, and set up your reel so that you can retrieve line with the hand opposite of the one with which you cast. That way, you won't lose time changing the rod from right hand to left. Not that you'll be in control, but you'll have a better shot at it.

The main event here are big singles of 12 to 15 pounds. You'll stalk them with the same intensity you would a trophy elk or whitetail. Casting to them is like hunting with a single shot. You get only one cast. It's best to get as close as you can. Even more elusive and more skittish when you find them, permit swim these waters in admirable numbers. Once in a while, you'll find yourself in casting range of up to a dozen. And then there are tarpon. While not primarily tarpon grounds, this area does have numbers of fish in the 30- to 50-pound class.

According to angling guru Lefty Kreh, "Casa Blanca offers the very best shot at a 'grand slam' . . . a bonefish, a permit and a tarpon all in one day." That's probably so, but it will take furious dedication on your part. You'll be distracted by the abundance of bones and permit. You may be so busy that you forget about tarpon. If you want to go for the slam, it's best to reserve a trip or two to the tarpon pools when you book.

Take at least two rods (7 weight; 9 weight) and a pair of corrosion-resistant saltwater reels with good drags, loaded with weight-forward saltwater tapers, and at least 100 yards of backing. You can't buy any tackle on the island, though effective patterns and lures (yes, you can fish with spinning or casting tackle) are stocked at the lodge. So are a few loaner rods, in case "you break all your tackle."

Accommodations at Casa Blanca and its sibling Playa Blanca are superlative. The main lodge at Casa Blanca has 10 rooms with tile floors and plenty of windows opening onto shady verandas fronting the Caribbean. The second lodge with five cottages is located 10 miles down the coast at Playa Blanca. Accommodations are similar, and at both locations, dining is exquisite.

[C A R I B B E A N   B A S I N]

Palmas de Cortez, Punta Colorada, & Playa de Sol

B a j a   C a l i f o r n i a   S u r ,   M e x i c o

Three grand hotels at the tip of the Baja offer billfishing beyond belief.

VITAL STATISTICS:

KEY SPECIES:
Dolphin/dorado, marlin, roosterfish, sailfish

Tackle:
Casting, fly-fishing, trolling
Major Season:
All year
Accommodations:
THREE MODERN HOTELS
NUMBER OF ROOMS / GUESTS:
PALMAS DE CORTEZ: 60 / 157
PUNTA COLORADA: 29 / 72
PLAYA DEL SOL: 26 / 64
Meals: Near gourmet, based on seafood, vegetables and fruit
Conference Groups: Yes
Rates: (European plan)
PALMAS DE CORTEZ: From $70
PUNTA COLORADA: From $55
PLAYA DEL SOL: From $60
Boats and Guides:
From $220 for a skiff and guide, to $500 for sport fisherman w/mate
Gratuities: 15% of charter
Preferred Payment:
Cash, check or credit cards
Getting There:
Fly to San Jose del Cabo and rent a car, or take the hotel shuttle for a fee.
Other Activities:
Boating, canoeing/kayaking/rafting, horseback riding, swimming, tennis, snorkeling, diving, jet skis

Contact:
Manager
Hotels Palmas de Cortez,
Punta Colorada, and
Playa de Sol
PO Box 9016
Calabasas CA 91372
Ph: 800/368-4334
Fax: 818/591-1077
e-mail:
bajafishing@pacific.net
Web:
www.bajaresorts.com

LIKE THE PENDANT FOOT of a mollusk, Baja California pokes more than 800 miles south, separating the Pacific from the Gulf of California. Here, from Cabo San Lucas north and east along the coast to La Paz, you'll find some of the finest billfishing waters in North America. The waters of the Gulf of California, like its eastern sibling, the Gulf of Mexico, are gentle. Like so many other areas, the fishery here is dependent on the continued viability of a string of offshore reefs that parallels the coast in spots. Billfish come into the reefs to feed on smaller fish and that's what makes the angling great.

Marlin are available year-round, with striped marlin the main event in January. Blue marlin of 600 pounds make their appearance in April, and are joined by similar-size black marlin in July. The best months to fish these waters are May through October. Along with marlin, you can catch sailfish, tuna, amberjack, roosterfish, jack crevalle, groupers, cabrilla and dorado. This is a big-game fishery: Angling is mostly done from 30-foot cruisers, or center console skiffs or pangas measuring 20 feet or more. Light-tackle anglers will be happy fishing the surf or in the shallows near the reef. Where else could you catch a world-record tuna on two-pound-test line? Sound weird? It's possible.

Three first-class hotels, all served by excellent charter fleets, provide outstanding accommodations. Hotel Playa del Sol is located up the coast from East Cape on Bahia de Las Palmas. The Cerralvo, Pulmo Reef and Los Frailes are within a short boat ride. Just south of East Cape, Hotel Punta Colorado faces the Sea of Cortez. You can see fish on the reef through the windows of your ocean-front room. The southernmost member of the trio is Palmas de Cortez. Mirroring the style of old Mexico, yet thoroughly modern, all three offer light and spacious air-conditioned rooms with private baths, exquisite restaurants featuring regional cuisine, deep shady verandas, sparkling freshwater pools lined with palms and miles of white sand beaches. Snorkel, scuba, sail or just swim. Here you'll find serenity and more than a few fish.

Tropic Star Lodge

Pinas Bay, Panama

Where's the next IGFA record likely to be broken? In Pinas Bay, where light lines are the order of the day.

VITAL STATISTICS:

KEY SPECIES:
Mackerel, marlin, sailfish, tuna

Tackle:
Casting, fly-fishing, trolling
Major Season:
May through September
Accommodations:
TWO LODGES IN LUSH JUNGLE SETTINGS
NUMBER OF ROOMS: 16
HANDICAPPED ACCESSIBLE: SOME
MAXIMUM NUMBER OF GUESTS: 36
Meals: Fine regional cuisine
Conference Groups: Yes
Rates: From $2,070 / week / person, group of four
Guides: Included
Gratuities: Angler's discretion
Preferred Payment:
Cash, check or credit cards
Getting There:
Fly to Panama City and connect with the air charter ($300 additional, round trip).
Other Activities:
Canoeing/kayaking/rafting, swimming

Contact:
Don Crandall
Tropic Star Lodge
635 N. Rio Grande Ave
Orlando FL 32805
Ph: 800/682-3424
Fax: 407/839-3637
e-mail:
tslorl@aol.com
Web:
www.tropicstar.com

PANAMA, if you didn't know it, means "an abundance of fish," and that's indeed the case as Zane Grey discovered when he fished these waters in the 1920s. Grey found that the reef slopes gently from about 20 fathoms to 60, creating an ideal habitat for different kinds of baitfish that attract large numbers and varieties of billfish. Tropic Star Lodge is the place for Pacific grand slams — a combo of black, blue or striped marlin, and sailfish. More than 170 world records have been set here in Pinas Bay, and the lodge holds 40 of them that still stand. In addition, more than 23 Junior Angler World Records have been set here. Families have a big time with big game fish.

Tropic Star is devoted to angling for black marlin, blue marlin, striped marlin, tuna, sailfish and rooster fish. Marlin season runs from December to mid-April, and it's best in January and February. Sails, tuna and roosters pick up in mid-April and run through July, with the better angling for sails in May and the other species in June. In the mouth of the Pinas River and off the rocky islands, you'll find dolphin, rainbow runners, snappers, groupers, amberjacks and mackerel. Though infrequent, tarpon are also taken.

You and your party will fish with a mate and captain on a 31-foot Bertram with tackle and bait provided. While this lodge caters to traditional big-game anglers, fly-fishing is increasingly spoken here, and the lodge offers an excellent chance to hook into blue-water species. Landing them is another matter. If fly-fishing is your preference, bring your own tackle.

Isolated where the mountainous Darien Jungle meets Pinas Bay 150 miles south of Panama City, Panama, Tropic Star may be as remote as any of the lodges in the Alaskan bush, but it knows how to lay on the luxury. Built by Texas oilman Ray Smith in the early 1960s, the lodge and adjacent cabins offer twin beds, private baths with dressing areas, air conditioning and views of the bay. Or you can stay 150 steps up the mountain at El Palacio, Smith's winter retreat with three bedrooms, sunken living room and panoramic view. Before dinner, take a swim in the lushly landscaped pool, then sit down to a five-course supper with complimentary wine.

Because travel to the lodge requires an hour's charter flight from Panama City on a twin Otter or similar aircraft, each guest is permitted only one suitcase, 40 pounds max, a carry-on bag of 15 pounds and one rod tube.

INDEX